Transformed Communication Codes in the Mediated World:

A Contemporary Perspective

Hasan Gürkan
Girona University, Spain

Aybike Serttaş
Istinye University, Turkey

IGI Global
PUBLISHER of TIMELY KNOWLEDGE

A volume in the Advances in Multimedia and Interactive Technologies (AMIT) Book Series

Published in the United States of America by
IGI Global
Information Science Reference (an imprint of IGI Global)
701 E. Chocolate Avenue
Hershey PA, USA 17033
Tel: 717-533-8845
Fax: 717-533-8661
E-mail: cust@igi-global.com
Web site: http://www.igi-global.com

Library of Congress Cataloging-in-Publication Data

Names: Gürkan, Hasan, 1982- editor. | Serttas, Aybike, 1980- editor.
Title: Transformed communication codes in the mediated world : a contemporary perspective / edited by Hasan Gürkan, Aybike Serttas.
Description: Hershey, PA : Information Science Reference, [2024] | Includes bibliographical references and index. | Summary: "This book discusses the challenges and opportunities that the COVID-19 pandemic brings to the communication discipline"-- Provided by publisher.
Identifiers: LCCN 2023050110 (print) | LCCN 2023050111 (ebook) | ISBN 9798369308967 (hardcover) | ISBN 9798369308974 (ebook)
Subjects: LCSH: COVID-19 Pandemic, 2020- , in mass media. | COVID-19 Pandemic, 2020---Influence. | Communication--History--21st century. | Communication and technology--History--21st century.
Classification: LCC P96.C69 T73 2024 (print) | LCC P96.C69 (ebook) | DDC 302.209/052--dc23/eng/20231205
LC record available at https://lccn.loc.gov/2023050110
LC ebook record available at https://lccn.loc.gov/2023050111

This book is published in the IGI Global book series Advances in Multimedia and Interactive Technologies (AMIT) (ISSN: 2327-929X; eISSN: 2327-9303)

British Cataloguing in Publication Data
A Cataloguing in Publication record for this book is available from the British Library.

For electronic access to this publication, please contact: eresources@igi-global.com.

Advances in Multimedia and Interactive Technologies (AMIT) Book Series

Joel J.P.C. Rodrigues
Senac Faculty of Ceará, Fortaleza-CE, Brazil; Instituto de Telecomunicações, Portugal

ISSN:2327-929X
EISSN:2327-9303

Mission

Traditional forms of media communications are continuously being challenged. The emergence of user-friendly web-based applications such as social media and Web 2.0 has expanded into everyday society, providing an interactive structure to media content such as images, audio, video, and text.

The **Advances in Multimedia and Interactive Technologies (AMIT) Book Series** investigates the relationship between multimedia technology and the usability of web applications. This series aims to highlight evolving research on interactive communication systems, tools, applications, and techniques to provide researchers, practitioners, and students of information technology, communication science, media studies, and many more with a comprehensive examination of these multimedia technology trends.

Coverage

- Multimedia Streaming
- Digital Communications
- Mobile Learning
- Web Technologies
- Digital technology
- Digital Images
- Digital Games
- Audio Signals
- Multimedia Technology
- Multimedia Services

IGI Global is currently accepting manuscripts for publication within this series. To submit a proposal for a volume in this series, please contact our Acquisition Editors at Acquisitions@igi-global.com or visit: http://www.igi-global.com/publish/.

The Advances in Multimedia and Interactive Technologies (AMIT) Book Series (ISSN 2327-929X) is published by IGI Global, 701 E. Chocolate Avenue, Hershey, PA 17033-1240, USA, www.igi-global.com. This series is composed of titles available for purchase individually; each title is edited to be contextually exclusive from any other title within the series. For pricing and ordering information please visit http://www.igi-global.com/book-series/advances-multimedia-interactive-technologies/73683. Postmaster: Send all address changes to above address.

Titles in this Series

For a list of additional titles in this series, please visit: www.igi-global.com/book-series/advances-multimedia-interactive-technologies/73683

Examining Multimedia Forensics and Content Integrity
Sumit Kumar Mahana (National Institute of Technology, Kurukshetra, India) Rajesh Kumar Aggarwal (National Institute of Technology, Kurukshetra, India) and Surjit Singh (Thapar Institute of Engineering and Technology, India)
Information Science Reference • copyright 2023 • 301pp • H/C (ISBN: 9781668468647) • US $225.00 (our price)

Handbook of Research on Advanced Practical Approaches to Deepfake Detection and Applications
Ahmed J. Obaid (University of Kufa, Iraq) Ghassan H. Abdul-Majeed (University of Baghdad, Iraq) Adriana Burlea-Schiopoiu (University of Craiova, Romania) and Parul Aggarwal (Jamia Hamdard, India)
Information Science Reference • copyright 2023 • 379pp • H/C (ISBN: 9781668460603) • US $295.00 (our price)

Dynamics of Dialogue, Cultural Development, and Peace in the Metaverse
Swati Chakraborty (GLA University, India)
Information Science Reference • copyright 2023 • 236pp • H/C (ISBN: 9781668459072) • US $240.00 (our price)

Handbook of Research on New Media, Training, and Skill Development for the Modern Workforce
Dominic Mentor (Teachers College, Columbia University, USA)
Business Science Reference • copyright 2022 • 439pp • H/C (ISBN: 9781668439968) • US $295.00 (our price)

Handbook of Research on New Media Applications in Public Relations and Advertising
Elif Esiyok (Atilim University, Turkey)
Information Science Reference • copyright 2021 • 572pp • H/C (ISBN: 9781799832010) • US $295.00 (our price)

Multidisciplinary Perspectives on Narrative Aesthetics in Video Games
Deniz Denizel (Bahcesehir University, Turkey) and Deniz Eyüce Şansal (Bahcesehir University, Turkey)
Information Science Reference • copyright 2021 • 300pp • H/C (ISBN: 9781799851103) • US $195.00 (our price)

Recent Advances in 3D Imaging, Modeling, and Reconstruction
Athanasios Voulodimos (University of West Attica, Athens, Greece) and Anastasios Doulamis (National Technical University of Athens, Athens, Greece)
Information Science Reference • copyright 2020 • 396pp • H/C (ISBN: 9781522552949) • US $215.00 (our price)

Handbook of Research on Recent Developments in Image Processing and Applications
Suresh Kumar Nagarajan (VIT University, India) and R. Mohanasundaram (VIT University, India)
Information Science Reference • copyright 2020 • 1700pp • H/C (ISBN: 9781799802228) • US $565.00 (our price)

IGI Global
PUBLISHER of TIMELY KNOWLEDGE

701 East Chocolate Avenue, Hershey, PA 17033, USA
Tel: 717-533-8845 x100 • Fax: 717-533-8661
E-Mail: cust@igi-global.com • www.igi-global.com

Editorial Advisory Board

Table of Contents

Detailed Table of Contents

This study comparatively examines WHO's utilization of TikTok in health communication during and after the pandemic. Employing content analysis, the research dissects WHO's TikTok account, encompassing engagement, video formats, types, message functions, characters, and emotional elements. Findings highlight WHO's dissemination of instructive and motivational content, predominantly focusing on COVID-19 and other diseases. During the pandemic, WHO educated the public on symptoms and transmission modes while issuing warnings about potential outbreaks. Animated graphics gained prominence, and healthcare professionals conveyed positive messages. Post-pandemic, posting frequency decreased, and content strategies shifted. Optimistic content, increased involvement of public figures, and targeting younger audiences through dance videos characterized this phase.

The chapter presents some of the key communication strategies that can be observed in the expressions of dissent that increased considerably during the pandemic. The dissenting narratives—that is, the texts that speak against dominant institutions and the socio-political consensus by combining elements of conspiracy theories and populism—thrive for two major reasons. First, the narratives voice political sentiments that a significant portion of the population can identify with; they speak against injustices in a way that many would endorse and, simultaneously, include some of the rhetoric of new populist movements on the right. Second, the way dissent is expressed is consistent with the new ways of knowledge acquisition, as the claims are made with the appeal to the individual perspective, fear, and enjoyment. Such conclusions are based on the analysis of the vehement opposition to the World Economic Forum's "The Great Reset" agenda and the pandemic-related conspiracy theories of David Icke.

The COVID-19 pandemic severely affected the film industry in Japan. One of the main problems involved small cinemas in large urban centers. As soon as it became clear that the closure of the cinemas would lead to the collapse of the small ones, many directors and authors immediately mobilised with various initiatives aimed at raising awareness of the risk of this serious loss and urging the government to support them. The temporary closures of small theatres gave way to various alternative solutions, such as online projection channels and the revival of drive-ins, but the most interesting phenomenon is the intensification of film productions by mini-theatre operators themselves. Of the unstoppable Japanese film production of the last few years, some films have centered on stories related to the pandemic and have told of the discomfort during the emergency. This chapter aims to take a snapshot of the situation of Japanese cinema since the beginning of the pandemic, noting some of the main problems and elements of probable continuity in future productions.

Over the past decade, the effects of digitization on Turkey's national and local press have significantly increased. In this study, the authors delve into the specific impact of the COVID-19 pandemic on this ongoing digitization process. The research focuses on two prominent daily newspapers in Turkey: Hürriyet and Yeni Asır. To gain valuable insights, the authors conducted in-depth interviews with 14 media professionals. The study's findings revealed a noteworthy shift in public trust, with social media gaining greater confidence as a news source. Additionally, national and local press have radically transformed their reporting practices, influenced by the growing digital landscape. The study highlights the pandemic's differential impact on various media outlets, underlining the emergence of stale content in the industry. This research sheds light on the dynamic interplay between digitization, the COVID-19 pandemic, and Turkey's national and local press. It offers valuable insights into changing public perceptions, reporting practices, and the diverse effects of the pandemic on media content.

This study aimed to assess whether Spanish hospitals have enhanced their protocols and training for breaking bad news in response to the pandemic. Employing a qualitative approach, the research integrated three tools: in-depth interviews with healthcare professionals, content analysis of medicine curricula from universities in Catalonia and Andalusia, and a literature review of protocols for communicating bad news. The findings revealed a significant increase in the contents and subjects in the communication of bad news within the analyzed curricula due to the pandemic. Additional topics such as technology, emotional management, and humanism were incorporated. While the hospital protocols showed a relatively less pronounced increment, there was evidence of the development of protocols specifically

The objective of this study is to investigate the impact of WhatsApp, an instant messaging application, on various aspects, particularly employee productivity and integration. To accomplish this, the authors formulated five hypotheses centered around the following question: "How does the utilization of instant communication tools influence employee productivity and integration?" To conduct this research, they conducted in-depth interviews with 17 individuals who were working remotely. Subsequently, the data from these interviews were analyzed using a descriptive analysis method. The findings of this research indicate that while instant communication technologies offer convenience in communication, they tend to diminish productivity. This is primarily attributed to their potential disruption of the work-life balance and their perception as informal means of communication.

The COVID-19 virus had a huge impact worldwide and its presence has also implied changes in some advertising campaigns. Given the mobility restrictions and new ways of socializing in times of lockdown, relevant advertisers modified their commercial messages in order to be coherent with the situation lived by most consumers. This research is aimed at understanding the most significant changes in advertising campaigns, mainly on TV, promoted by selected advertisers during COVID-19 lockdown and some months later on. The main hypothesis of this research is that there is a clear relationship between what companies communicate and the circumstances and living experiences of most consumers. Through the qualitative content analysis of selected cases, it can be understood how brands changed their messages to demonstrate their commitment to their consumers; support governmental indications related to health, safety, and mobility recommendations; and, if possible, motivate consumers.

This study examines the hashtag activism of Twitter users who became slacktivists regarding pandemic restrictions and measures in Turkey's first year of the COVID-19 pandemic. From March 2020 to March 2021, 1,464,334 tweets regarding all 13 hashtag activisms, which were the most participated in each month according to the course of the pandemic, were collected using Twitter API and examined with big data analysis. Out of the 13 hashtag activisms with the highest number of tweets analyzed by month, the demand for measures and regulations to be taken to protect against the risks posed by the pandemic came to the forefront in 9, while the demand for lifting or easing the restrictions in 4 of them came to the forefront. Students, detainees and prisoners, and teachers were the actors of the most tweeted hashtag activism. The average mentioned rate of decision makers and authorities in the 13 activisms is 71.52%. As a result, in the first year of the pandemic in Turkey, hashtag activism supporting the implementation of measures and restrictions was more common.

the communication difficulties faced by families during the COVID-19 pandemic and to offer solutions to develop healthy communication dynamics during the stay-at-home period.

Aygül Atay, Independent Researcher, Turkey

This chapter examines the fact-checking content focusing on misinformation and fake news about COVID-19 vaccines, especially in the media, through the example of Doğrula (doğrula.org), an international fact-checking organization (ICFN) approved fact-checking platform. The data were obtained from the website of the relevant platform (www.dogrula.org). Based on the problem that many distortions, fake news, and claims about COVID-19 vaccines are shared through digital media, the study examines Doğrula's evaluations of the posts about COVID-19 vaccines circulated in digital media channels. The descriptive analysis method, one of the qualitative research types, was used in the study. Data were obtained through the document analysis technique. Due to a large amount of data to be analyzed within the scope of the study, it covers a one-year period from 25.02.2021 to 25.02.2022, the date when Doğrula first published content.

Rana Öztürk, İstinye University, Turkey
Simge Esin Orhun, Marmara University, Turkey

Along with the technological advancements in the digitalisation of physical objects and spaces, the COVID-19 pandemic has created an urgent necessity for cultural institutions to display exhibition content online. Exhibition making is a process of knowledge production through an order of display that is integrated into the spatial and architectural context of an exhibition space. The authors believe that virtual tours that are developed by simply creating a replica of the physical exhibition and the virtual display of individual artifacts offer limited spatial experience. They believe that virtual exhibitions as alternatives to physical experience of exhibitions still require a critical reflection in terms of their spatial context, effectiveness, benefits, and limitations. By examining the results of a three-week workshop with communication design students, the chapter discusses the current use of staging and navigation possibilities for displaying digital content. It further highlights the spatial relationality as a key concern for the translation of physical exhibitions into virtual space.

Arzu Kizbaz, Istinye University, Turkey

German philosopher Goethe expressed, "Emotions unite people, while ideas separate them," emphasizing the essential role of emotions in effective communication. The era of the pandemic, which mandated social isolation, underscored the inherent human need for face-to-face interaction. The surge in social media usage post-pandemic and the rapid integration into the digital age have resulted in a decline in face-to-face communication, leading to reduced interaction among individuals. This study seeks to investigate the evolving dynamics of communication in Generation Y, characterized by an increasing social media usage rate, and Generation Z, which is distancing itself from heavy social media usage post-pandemic. Through in-depth interviews, the research will scrutinize how these generations have adjusted their

Preface

SARSCoV-2, more popularly known as COVID-19, has immediately impacted life. While COVID-19 has significantly changed our lives, it has also transformed communication, the workforce, the working environment, and society. Governments and public healthcare institutions worldwide have established homestay rules to combat social distancing and the COVID-19 pandemic (WHO, 2020). Almost every sector (education, media, cinema, commerce, banking, etc.) began to digitalize rapidly with the pandemic (education, media, cinema, commerce, banking, etc.). People spend more time in their homes (Kemp, 2020). In addition, the forms of communication performed in one-to-one interviews have changed as social media and messaging continue to change. Thus, the pandemic has become a part of daily life. However, given that individuals rely on information and communication technologies, it is necessary to consider the impact of the COVID-19 process on communication types and codes. Therefore, this special issue focuses mainly on the effects of COVID-19 on communication practices and usage patterns.

Any healthy relationship has always relied on effective communication. The pandemic has had a significant impact on our daily communication skills. We had to change our way of life and communication due to Covid-19. As a result, we are rethinking our communication strategies and re-evaluating our priorities. The long-term impact of the COVID-19 pandemic brings opportunities and threats (Malecki et al., 2020). On the other hand, as Nic Newman states, it would not be wrong to claim that the main impact of COVID-19 on media is economic (Kunova, 2020). This Special Issue discusses the challenges and opportunities the COVID-19 pandemic brings to the communication discipline. Moreover, how the new communication models shaped by the pandemic will develop in the future is still a matter of debate (Nguyen et al., 2020).

If we think through organizational communication, adults in the COVID-19 pandemic are experiencing high stress and anxiety levels due to significant changes in their day-to-day lives, social structures, and movements. Everything in a pandemic revolves around effective communication, internally among employees, coworkers, or team members and externally among people, communities, and nations. Many people's interactions with one another have changed dramatically due to the COVID-19 pandemic response measures. Interpersonal trust is essential in how we interact with others, and throughout the COVID-19 pandemic, trust has been identified as a critical factor in promoting pro-social and health-aware behavior. Trust is required to induce behavioral change, especially in this time of uncertainty. According to Fell (2020), the impact of the COVID-19 pandemic on the predictability of various aspects of daily life has resulted in a loss of trust in many areas of life, including trust in interpersonal relationships, society, workplaces, governments, and information.

Because public communication frequently emphasizes the death toll of the COVID-19 pandemic, COVID-19 is perceived as a strong mortality cue. As a result, Curşeu et al. (2021) anticipate that the frequency with which COVID-19-related ideas have been used in interpersonal communication will increase the salience of the mortality cues associated with the pandemic, ultimately spurring the state of anxiety and negative emotionality associated with COVID-19 (Curseu et al., 2021).

The proper application of technology will help to facilitate social distance without sacrificing effective oral communication. Furthermore, to navigate the COVID-19 pandemic and any other pandemic that could erupt, we must improve coping mechanisms and skills, making communication with face masks easier. The positive is that many individuals are becoming more skilled at using communication technologies, which might be more useful in the future. Returning to everyday life would most likely take time, but it is also important to note that even without pandemics, what is regular changes over time. Shortly, social and digital media will continue to play a role.

Another issue that the theme of the book evokes is the theory of diffusion of innovations. Everett M. Rogers' theory could help explain how we adapt to the new conditions the pandemic has forced us to experience. Rogers (1995) identified the four main elements of diffusion: innovation, communication channels, time, and social system. Innovation begins with the perception of information and ends with the decision to adopt or reject the innovation. Information passes through five stages when deciding whether to adopt or reject the innovation. This process is an information-seeking and information-processing activity. These five stages in which the individual tries to obtain information that will help reduce the uncertainties about innovation: knowledge, persuasion, decision, application, and verification. In the first stage, the individual learns about innovation and its functions. At the persuasion stage, it evaluates the advantages and disadvantages of innovation for itself and shapes its attitude towards innovation. In the decision stage, the individual obtains additional information about the innovation and decides to accept or reject the innovation. At this stage, the individual is mainly affected by the evaluations of the individuals around him. The fourth stage, implementation, takes place when the decision to adapt to innovation is made. In the final stage, the individual confirms and strengthens the decision to adapt. The greater the individual's perceived advantage of the innovation, the greater the compliance rate. When an innovation is better than the previous one, it is perceived as beneficial (technological, economic, physical (better possibilities) or social (status), etc.) by the target group. As the innovation meets the needs of the individual, the compliance rate increases. Although innovation is seen as a necessity in our example, after a while, different innovations in different media were adopted in a short time with their advantages, and the pre-pandemic conditions were behind.

When all these are evaluated, it is essential to examine the effects of the pandemic, social change, and the transformation of daily rituals, media, and communication actions and products under the umbrella of social sciences.

This book invites appropriate research on the topic from around the world. We are interested in research papers on the effects of this change process on the world of communication. What changes occurred during and after the COVID-19 pandemic for communication research and implementation underlies this number.

The topics of interest included in this book,

- Communication studies during and after the COVID-19 pandemic,
- Changing communication practices and COVID-19,
- COVID-19 across disciplinary borders and its effects on media, film, public relations, and advertising industries,
- COVID-19 and new media,

- The effects of COVID-19 on individuals' communication practices,
- The impacts of COVID-19 on traditional and new media,
- The impacts of COVID-19 on organizational communication

This book has 19 chapters from different countries. All chapters are related to COVID-19 and its influences on media and communication practices. The first chapter written by Zindan Çakıcı and Emre Temiz, titled TikTok Trends to Pandemic Essentials; A Comparative Analysis of World Health Organization's Health Communication Strategies on TikTok examines WHO's utilization of TikTok in health communication during and after the pandemic. Their research dissects WHO's TikTok account, encompassing engagement, video formats, types, message functions, characters, and emotional elements. The second chapter titled Communication Strategies Behind the Expressions of Dissent During the Covid-19 Pandemic by Nemanja Milošević presents some of the key communication strategies that can be observed in the expressions of dissent that increased considerably during the pandemic. The third chapter belongs to Övünç Ege and her article "Anti-Vaccination in the Post-Truth Era: Who Will We Trust?" discusses anti-vaccination in the post-truth era in Turkey. One of the claims in Ege's study is that the reason for insecurity and different information circulation in individuals is that knowledge has become an empty signifier in the post-truth era. Although verification platforms search for the accuracy of information, they cannot keep up with the circulation rate of information pollution. The fourth chapter is a co-written article by Başak Gezmen and Serkan Karatay. Their study titled Digital Data Security Strategies in the Covid-19 Pandemic Period: An Evaluation of Domestic Messaging Applications highlights instant messaging applications, one of the digital communication channels that have increased in importance with the Covid-19 pandemic period, are theoretically discussed in the context of digital data security strategies and evaluated in terms of data security in personal and corporate uses. In the research, the question of how giving a national character to the environments where digital data is produced, hosted, and protected can affect data security, the domestic messaging applications BIP, Dedi, and Havelsan Ileti in Turkey are interpreted in terms of their "national" contributions to digital data security. The fifth chapter belongs to Ceren Saran. Her work titled Mobile News Consumption and News Avoidance: An Overview of User References, Digital Platforms, trust, and Mobile Media Use in Turkey sets out to critically examine the changing positions of users in mobile news consumption against digital platforms, algorithmic selection, and news avoidance. Saran's research aims to find out different types of mobile news reading practices and reasons for news avoidance and to discover divergent positions of readers against digital platforms and mobile applications.

The sixth chapter is written by Maria Roberta Novielli from Venice University. Novielli invites us on a cinematic journey in *The Tsunami of the Pandemic in the Context of Japanese Cinema.* Through the lens of Japanese films, the author reflects on the cultural and artistic responses to the overwhelming impact of the pandemic. The seventh article is a co-written article by Hasan Gürkan and Aslı Güngör-Eral, titled *Media Shaped by Covid-19: How is Media Changing?* It aims to highlight the effects of the COVID-19 pandemic on Turkey's national and local press. While the impact of the COVID-19 pandemic on this digitalization constitutes the main problem of the article, the study reveals that the public is more confident in social media; on the other hand, it shows that the practice of reporting has radically transformed both in national and local media. The eight chapter belongs to Sílvia Espinosa-Mirabet & Mònica Puntí-Brun. Their article on *Medical Protocols to Communicate Bad News to Patients in the Post-Covid Time* aims to review the existing medical protocols to discover if the former protocols have been adapted to the new reality produced by the outbreak of the pandemic. The chapter ninth belongs to Yaren Kalkan-Aluç and Enes Aluç. Their work's title is *Student Opinions on Teaching of Technical Courses Online and Face-To-Face during the Pandemic: Example of Editing Techniques Course*, and the authors examine how university students who switched to online education during the Covid-19 pandemic period process the technical courses they need to take face-to-face with online education. The transition to online education continues during the education period at the end of the pandemic. Despite the change to face-to-face teaching, online courses continue at specific rates in most universities. The tenth chapter takes us away to Portuguese with the title *Navigating Covid-19: How Portuguese Health Authority Managed Social Media*, Branco Di Fátima, Francisco Garcia, Ana Barros, Rita Espanha, Daniel Brandão, and Nuno Martins provide a comprehensive analysis of the strategies employed by Portuguese health authorities in managing the waves of information on social media.

The eleventh chapter written by Aybike Serttaş and Tugay Sarıkaya, titled *The Effects of the Instant Messaging Application WhatsApp on the Efficiency of Employees under Pandemic Conditions* discusses the effects of the instant messaging application WhatsApp usage, which has been observed to increase with the working conditions that have changed with the pandemic process and mainly transformed into a working from home format, on the employees. The twelfth chapter belongs to Jordi Serra Simón. Simón's work *Changes in advertising campaigns in times of COVID-19: Selected cases from Spain* aim to understand the most significant changes in advertising campaigns, mainly on TV, promoted by selected advertisers during the COVID-19 lockdown and some months later. Simon's research focuses on the main changes in advertising campaigns in times of COVID-19 targeted at Spanish consumers to understand to which extent relevant advertisers, independently of their sector, origin, size, or target market, modified their commercial messages to show empathy for their audiences, look updated, but at the same time, keep their brand positioning and highlight their selling proposition and their main characteristics. The thirteenth chapter written by Özlem Çetin-Öztürk and her work *Hashtag Activism Due to the Restrictions and Measures During Covid-19 Pandemic in Turkey* discusses how collective action is framed in hashtag activism due to pandemic restrictions and measures during the first year of the COVID-19 pandemic in turkey, where real-life activism was limited by lockdowns and by the bans on meetings and demonstration marches. The fourteenth chapter authored by Ebru Belkıs Güzeloğlu, Elif Üstündağlı Erten, Asuman Özgür Keysan, Ali Erhan Zalluhoğlu, and Burcu Şentürk. In addition, individuals' distrust of power structures also affects their understanding of information. The intricate web of information-seeking behaviors in the COVID-19 crisis unfolds in *Information Seeking Behaviors in the COVID-19 Crisis in Turkey*. Their exploration spans the types of information sought, sources accessed, and the motivations driving this quest for knowledge. The fifteenth chapter belongs to Miss Mir Kouser Gulzar and she brings us to digital literacy in *Digital Literacy and Health Workers: A Study of Kashmir*. The chapter delves into the intersection of digital literacy and health workers' experiences in the unique context of Kashmir, India.

The chapter sixteen written by Cihan Çakır and Çakır explores *Family Communication and COVID-19 Communication Dynamics During the Stay-at-Home Period*. Through an intimate lens, the author unravels the complexities of family communication dynamics during the challenging stay-at-home period. The chapter seventeen belongs to Aygül Atay and her work *Verification Platforms in Combating Disinformation on Covid-19 Vaccine News:* www.dogrula.org examines the fact-checking content focusing on misinformation and fake news about COVID-19 vaccines, especially in the media, through the example of Doğrula (doğrula.org), an International Fact-Checking Organization (ICFN) approved fact-checking platform. The chapter eighteen belongs to Rana Öztürk and Simge Esin-Orhun titled An Investigation of the Visitor's Spatial Experience in Virtual Exhibitions. The authors discuss that the Covid 19 pandemic has created an urgent necessity for cultural institutions to display exhibition content online. Exhibition making is a process of knowledge production through an order of display that is integrated into the spatial and architectural context of an exhibition space. They believe that virtual exhibitions as alternatives to physical experience of exhibitions still require a critical reflection in terms of their spatial context, effectiveness, benefits and limitations. By examining the results of a 3-week workshop with Communication Design students, their chapter discuss the current use of staging and navigation possibilities for displaying digital content. Arzu Kızbaz is the author of the chapter nineteen with the title Rethinking the Shift in Communication Dynamics Post Pandemic. Her study seeks to investigate the evolving dynamics of communication in Generation Y, characterized by an increasing social media usage rate, and Generation Z, which is distancing itself from heavy social media usage post-pandemic. Through in-depth interviews, Kızbaz's research scrutinizes how these generations have adjusted their communication patterns within the realm of interpersonal communication giving particular attention to aspects such as listening, empathy, feedback, effective speaking & appreciation.

The diverse range of topics covered in this book reflects a comprehensive exploration of the multifaceted impact of the COVID-19 pandemic on communication studies. From the immediate challenges posed by the pandemic to the evolving communication practices, this collection encompasses a broad spectrum of insights. Including interdisciplinary perspectives, spanning media, film, public relations, and advertising industries, adds depth to our understanding of the profound effects felt across various domains. Focusing on new media and examining how individuals and organizations navigate these unprecedented times provides valuable context for scholars, practitioners, and anyone interested in the dynamic intersection of communication and the global health crisis.

The topics covered, ranging from evolving communication practices to the impacts on traditional and new media, showcase the resilience and adaptability of the field in the face of unprecedented challenges. Our exploration of COVID-19 across disciplinary borders emphasizes the interconnectedness of various industries, reinforcing the importance of interdisciplinary approaches in understanding complex phenomena.

As we move forward, let this collection serve as a valuable resource for scholars, students, and professionals seeking to comprehend the profound impact of COVID-19 on communication. May the insights shared within these pages inspire further research, dialogue, and innovative approaches to communication studies in our ever-changing world. Thank you to all who have participated in this collaborative effort, and may the knowledge gained contribute to a more resilient and informed future.

Hasan Gürkan
Girona University, Spain

Aybike Serttaş
Istinye University, Turkey

REFERENCES

Curşeu, P. L., Coman, A. D., Panchenko, A., Fodor, O. C., & Raţiu, L. (2021). Death anxiety, death reflection, and interpersonal communication as predictors of social distance towards people infected with COVID. *Current Psychology (New Brunswick, N.J.)*, 1–14. PMID:33686325

Fell, L. (2020). Trust and COVID-19: Implications for Interpersonal, Workplace, Institutional, and Information-Based Trust. *Digit. Gov.: Res. Pract.*, *2*(1), 1–5.

Kemp, S. (2020, April 24). *Report: Most important data on digital audiences during coronavirus*. Growth Quarters—The Next Web. https://thenextweb.com/growth-quarters/2020/04/24/reportmost-important-data-on-digital-audiences-during-coronavirus/

Kunova, M. (2020). *Digital News Report 2020: COVID-19 accelerates digital shifts in the media industry.* https://www.journalism.co.uk/news/digital-news-report-2020-covid-19-has-accelerated-digital-shifts-in-the-media-industry/s2/a757201/

Malecki, K. C., Keating, J. A., & Safdar, N. (2020). Crisis Communication and Public Perception of COVID-19 Risk in the Era of Social Media. *Clinical Infectious Diseases*, *72*(4), 697–702. doi:10.1093/cid/ciaa758 PMID:32544242

Nguyen, M. H., Gruber, J., Fuchs, J., Marler, W., Hunsaker, A., & Hargittai, E. (2020). Changes in Digital Communication During the COVID-19 Global Pandemic: Implications for Digital Inequality and Future Research. *Social Media + Society*, *6*(3). Advance online publication. doi:10.1177/2056305120948255 PMID:34192039

Rogers, E. M. (1995). *Diffusion of Innovations (4th ed.).* The Free Press.

Taleb, N. N. (2007). *1960-The Black Swan: The Impact of the Highly Improbable*. Random House Trade Paperbacks.

World Health Organization. (2020). *Coronavirus disease (COVID-19) advice for the public*. https://www.who.int/emergencies/ diseases/novel-coronavirus-2019/advice-for-public

Acknowledgment

The idea's genesis for this book dates to June 2021, but since then, it has taken plenty of time for the idea to mature and for the framework to be defined. As it is well known, from the second half of the 19th century onwards, the concept of mass communication began to be mentioned along with mass society. The experience of the interdisciplinary and dynamic field of communication with the COVID-19 pandemic forms the conceptual framework of this book.

This book sets out to explore the questions and navigate the complex terrain of communication in the post-pandemic digital age. It is an exploration into the intricacies of our altered communication codes and an examination of the profound impact of technology on the way we connect, share, and understand each other. From the nuances of digital language to the transformative power of social media movements, each chapter invites the reader on a journey through the multifaceted dimensions of contemporary communication.

We delve into the interplay between technology and human connection, acknowledging the dual nature of this relationship—a source of boundless possibilities and, at times, a precursor of challenges. The book seeks not only to unravel the complexities of our digital communication landscape but also to shed light on the resilience of human communication in the face of unprecedented change.

In the ever-evolving tapestry of human existence, communication is the warp and weft that weaves our stories, binds our societies, and shapes our collective identity. The journey of communication is a perpetual odyssey, marked by the profound impact of technological advancements, societal shifts, and the indomitable spirit of human connection. As we stand at the threshold of a new era, communication dynamics are undergoing a metamorphosis, compelling us to reexamine, redefine, and reimagine the codes that govern our interactions.

The seismic disruptions brought forth by the global pandemic have reshaped the contours of our daily lives and left an indelible mark on the communication landscape. Overnight, our modes of connection shifted from handshakes to virtual embraces, from crowded meeting rooms to the solitude of video calls. The pandemic has forced us to confront the fragility of our traditional communication paradigms and has catalyzed an unprecedented acceleration toward a digital frontier.

"*Graphics don't mean anything to us anymore. We think the world will be a different place!*" We heard these and similar statements a lot with COVID-19, and these statements became the center of our lives. The COVID-19 virus and the pandemic have seriously impacted humanity physically, spiritually, and socially. Pandemics, like natural disasters, cause psychological trauma as they threaten human life and have longer-lasting effects. The uncertainty that started in March 2020 continued until the last months of 2021. During this and the following period, we experienced changes in our daily lives and expectations, which we are still experiencing. From our cleaning to our communication habits, we have undergone a stringent process of evolution. We have seen that we can connect with more people, even if we are physically far away, thanks to access to the internet. In addition, people's priorities have changed; instead of being captive to the excessive consumption imposed by capitalism, everyone now thinks about their basic needs first. As consumption habits change, we expect to see a world where people are more frugal. Perhaps we appreciate simple pleasures more.

On the other hand, people have valued expert opinions and listened to experts, so their importance will be more emphasized. In the space we have been unintentionally given, we have had time to reflect on who we are and what we care about. This can help us discover a better version of ourselves in the long run. We already see the acceleration of digitalization, and people are choosing digital platforms they trust. The issue of trust is something we can face in every field, and the feeling of insecurity we are experiencing now will not quickly disappear. We will continue to feel uneasy when meeting friends and going to public places. However, those who deny this situation and do not take the necessary precautions will continue their lives more comfortably than others.

Although the pandemic is over, it seems like it will be discussed for a long time - like many other black swans1 in history. This event, which changes the code worldwide, has also created a research ground for different disciplines. The effect of code change is an important issue; these codes can be considered from different angles in the field of communication: media products coded by media professionals, codes revealed by the target audience, and content coded according to the characteristics of different channels and their users with other demographic factors. This is how we can break down the post-pandemic situation and examine the pieces according to their characteristics.

Communication and digitalization can be added to the top title of all these. When effects of the pandemic had brought along digitalization applications that we cannot think of: TV series shot in real places with real actors (for example, the Blacklist series) were turned into animation when they were left unfinished due to circumstances and completed with hybrid versions, applications for online doctor appointments became widespread, schools switched to online education, the business world used Zoom offices, etc.

Digitalization emerges as a beacon guiding us into uncharted territories within this transformation's vortex. Once a distant horizon, the digital realm is integral to our communication fabric. Social media, virtual collaboration tools, and online platforms have become the conduits through which our narratives traverse the vast expanse of the internet. As we grapple with the implications of this digital revolution, questions abound. How does the virtual space redefine the boundaries of every kind of communication? What challenges and opportunities does digitalization present for traditional and emerging media?

Different fields that can be examined under the heading of communication, such as official correspondence, official interviews, exams, the concept of the classroom, internal and external communication, and sectoral applications, have become thinkable under the heading of change. Therefore, a wide variety of topics can be included in the topics of this book, from interpersonal communication to mass communication, from marketing communication to educational communication.

As researchers preoccupied with the Media and communication field, we could not remain indifferent to this radical change and decided to prepare this compilation thematic book. My (Hasan Gürkan's) chance to be in Spain after the COVID-19 process allowed us to observe how things progress in geography differently from Turkey and to reach researchers conducting research in the field.

As we embark on this intellectual expedition, let us traverse the crossroads of tradition and innovation, analog and digital, to illuminate the path forward. The following pages are an invitation to ponder, question, and engage with the evolving tapestry of communication in our ever-changing world. We express our gratitude to the chapter authors who have actively contributed to this undertaking, lending their support and significantly expanding the book's breadth. The valuable insights these contributors provided have enhanced the publication's overall scope, and we are sincerely thankful for their collaboration in this endeavor.

Nassim N. Taleb's (2007) phrase, black swan, is a metaphor used to describe events that were not predicted to happen, but that took place and had great effects in many respects. History is full of unprecedented events that no one thought possible. The Black Swan Theory is when something rare and unexpected happens with big consequences. It is almost impossible to predict these events or occurrences and therefore it is also impossible to mitigate their consequences.

ENDNOTE

1 Nassim N. Taleb's (2007) phrase, black swan, is a metaphor used to describe events that were not predicted to happen, but that took place and had great effects in many respects. History is full of unprecedented events that no one thought possible. The Black Swan Theory is when something rare and unexpected happens with big consequences. It is almost impossible to predict these events or occurrences and therefore it is also impossible to mitigate their consequences.

Chapter 1
From TikTok Trends to Pandemic Essentials:
A Comparative Analysis of the World Health Organization's Health Communication Strategies on TikTok

Emre Meriç
İstanbul Bilgi University, Turkey

Zindan Çakıcı
Uskudar University, Turkey

ABSTRACT

This study comparatively examines WHO's utilization of TikTok in health communication during and after the pandemic. Employing content analysis, the research dissects WHO's TikTok account, encompassing engagement, video formats, types, message functions, characters, and emotional elements. Findings highlight WHO's dissemination of instructive and motivational content, predominantly focusing on COVID-19 and other diseases. During the pandemic, WHO educated the public on symptoms and transmission modes while issuing warnings about potential outbreaks. Animated graphics gained prominence, and healthcare professionals conveyed positive messages. Post-pandemic, posting frequency decreased, and content strategies shifted. Optimistic content, increased involvement of public figures, and targeting younger audiences through dance videos characterized this phase.

INTRODUCTION

Health communication is a strategic approach to influence, engage, empower, and provide support to diverse communities concerning health and significant health-related issues (Schiavo, 2013). The evolution of internet technologies has wrought a profound transformation in the domain of health communication, with social media emerging as a pivotal conduit for the widespread dissemination of public health

DOI: 10.4018/979-8-3693-0896-7.ch001

information to a diverse and extensive audience. Health organizations and professionals have harnessed the power of social media to distribute true and reliable health information. (Ventola, 2014; Park et al., 2019; Pianese & Belfiore, 2021; Chen & Wang, 2021). Notably, during the unprecedented coronavirus disease pandemic, social media platforms such as Twitter, Facebook, Instagram, and TikTok played a significant role in disseminating health information, marking a milestone in the history of pandemics (González-Padilla & Tortolero-Blanco, 2020; DePaula et al., 2022). Especially, TikTok has been a new effective medium that provides opportunities to deliver health information to different populations and groups.

TikTok, a mobile video platform characterized by short-form content lasting a maximum of 10 minutes, has become a significant medium for health communication during the pandemic. With availability in over 150 countries, TikTok boasts a user base of over one billion monthly active users and has witnessed over 3 billion downloads (We are Social & Houtsuite, 2023). The notable increase in TikTok downloads can be attributed to the impact of the COVID-19 pandemic. This rapid expansion of TikTok has presented a distinctive opportunity for public health agencies to effectively disseminate COVID-19-related information and educate the population (Li et al., 2021). A considerable portion of TikTok's user base comprises adolescents and young adults, with approximately 50% falling within the age range of 10 to 29 (Roth et al., 2021:2). Consequently, to combat the pandemic effectively, it is imperative that all members of the community, including young individuals, possess an understanding of the gravity of COVID-19 and adhere to appropriate preventive measures. Considering its extensive popularity among young users, TikTok can serve as a viable medium for disseminating health information to this specific demographic (Li et al., 2021).

TikTok provides health organizations with a channel to convey their endeavors, establish a community dedicated to their mission, and secure backing for their undertakings. Additionally, TikTok furnishes a platform for organizations to instruct the general public on diverse health-related issues and mobilize the community to take preemptive actions against an array of health concerns. Extensive research exists regarding the utilization of social media by public health agencies. Nevertheless, research studies tend to generally focus on social media platforms such as Facebook or Twitter (Park et al., 2011; Thackeray et al., 2013; Park et al., 2016; Okay et al., 2020). Despite the abundance of studies exploring the unique features and functionalities of various social media platforms in different domains, there is a scarcity of research investigating the health communication strategies employed by public health agencies specifically on TikTok (Zhu et al., 2019; Basch, Hillyer & Jaime, 2020; Li et al., 2021; Chen et al., 2021; Zhang et al., 2021). These studies also focused on the communication during the pandemic. To our knowledge, no published studies are focusing on health communication strategies after the pandemic and conducting comparative analysis on the content of COVID-19 material on TikTok during the COVID-19 pandemic and after the COVID-19 pandemic.

The primary objective of this study is to comparatively examine the health communication activities carried out by the World Health Organization (WHO) during and after the COVID-19 pandemic. By closely analyzing the communication strategies implemented by the WHO, this research seeks to acquire valuable insights into the efficacy and dynamic nature of health communication in response to the pandemic. Through a comprehensive analysis, this study aims to make a substantial contribution to the existing body of knowledge on health communication practices during times of public health crises, with a specific emphasis on the WHO's engagement across diverse platforms, including TikTok. The outcomes of this study are anticipated to offer significant insights for both public health agencies and researchers, enabling them to enhance future health communication endeavors and effectively disseminate critical information to a global audience.

Health Communication on Social Media

Health communication is a strategy employed to influence, engage, empower, and influence and support different populations or groups about health and significant health issues (Schiavo, 2013, p.9). Health communication prioritizes the audience, aiming to facilitate and support behavior change as well as eliminate health discrepancies. The significance of effective health communication lies in its ability to enhance the comprehension of health threats and provide support to the public in making informed decisions to mitigate risks (Porat et al., 2020, p.2). The selection of credible communication sources, appropriate message presentation, and suitable communication channels play crucial roles in the health communication process to accomplish public health objectives aiming to influence different populations or groups (Kreuter & McClure, 2004, p. 442; WHO, 2017).

The utilization of social media has experienced a swift expansion over the last decade. The total number of users of all major social media platforms has reached 4.76 billion (We are Social & Houtsuite, 2023). Given the substantial degree of adoption, social media have transformed into essential tools for globally distributing messages about health (DePaula et al., 2022). Marshall McLuhan's renowned assertion, "the medium is the message," assumes particular salience within the context of health communication via social media. This assertion underscores the deep-seated influence of the medium itself on how health-related information is not only perceived but also absorbed (McLuhan, 1994, p.11).

There are several uses of social media for health communication by the general public, patients, and health professionals (Moorheed et al., 2013, p.8). Providing health information concerning a variety of ailments (Eysanbach, 2011, Apostolakis et al., 2012; Hanson et al; 2014; Domínguez & Sapiña, 2017; Milley, 2021), providing answers to medical questions (Ventola, 2014) facilitate dialogue between patients to patients, and patients and health professionals (Hawn, 2009; Andersen, Medaglia & Henriksen, 2012; Antheunis et al, 2013), collecting data on patient experiences and opinion (Lupton, 2014; Rastegar-Majarad et al., 2015; Smailhodzic et al, 2016), health intervention (Guttman,2000; Cobb et al., 2010; West et al., 2015) health promotion and health education (Pickle et al., 2002; Kreps, 2009), reducing stigma (Betton et al., 2015; Wang & Liu, 2015; Sampogna et al., 2017; Parrot et al., 2020) providing online consultations (Yeo & Chu, 2017; Lawless et al., 2018; Tang et al., 2018) monitoring of disease pandemics (Mheidly & Fares, 2020; Tsao et al., 2021; Lazebnik et al., 2022) and recruitment of clinical study participants (Khatri et al., 2015; Bull et al., 2015) are seen as significant usage areas of health communication by general public, patients, and health professionals.

Health organizations, both governmental health agencies and non-governmental entities like the World Health Organization, also employ social media platforms as a means of health communication. Health institutions primarily utilize social media for purposes such as infoveillance, the dissemination of health information, countering misinformation, implementing health interventions, and promoting social mobilization (Chen & Wang, 2021, p.4). In particular, health institutions assumed a pivotal role in disseminating pertinent pandemic-related information to diverse targeted populations (Suarez-Lledo et al., 2021, p.2). These organizations endeavored to foster a dialogic mode of communication with the public, aiming to increase public health awareness and facilitate behavioral modifications in response to the pandemic (Al-Dmour et al., 2020, p.12).

Health institutions engaged the public on social media by presenting information about COVID-19 cases, its control, and effective measures during the pandemic. Social media is utilized effectively to update the public about the course of the pandemic (Mheidly & Fares, 2020, p.414). Liu et al. (2021, p.920) conducted research focusing on the Twitter accounts of public health departments and Office of Emergency Management (OEM) entities in Texas. The findings of their analysis prominently indicated that the most frequently utilized terms predominantly centered on strategies related to the prevention and control of the COVID-19 pandemic. Notably, these terms encompassed the promotion and advocacy of preventive measures, such as social distancing, mask-wearing, and COVID-19 testing. An analysis of how Group of Seven (G7) global leaders used Twitter in response to the COVID-19 pandemic indicated that the majority, approximately 82.8%, of their tweets on the subject contained informative content. Additionally, about 9.4% of the tweets served to boost morale, while 6.9% had a political focus (Rufai & Bunce, 2020, p.1). The study of Sutton et al. (2020, p.454) demonstrated that American public health institutions followed communication strategies on their Twitter accounts that emphasized the transfer of information, individual action, and collective action, maintaining motivation and determining social norms in the first 60 days of the pandemic. A similar study by Wang et al. (2021, p.10) found that US health agencies were actively engaged in conveying situational awareness and educating the public on preventive measures about the pandemic on Twitter.

Even if social media serves a beneficial societal function in sharing critical information about the epidemic, it also presents certain obstacles. These could encompass issues such as quality concerns and lack of reliability of health information, dissemination of false or misleading information, adverse health conditions, apprehensions regarding individual privacy, and ethical dilemmas associated with the gathering and sharing of data (Moorheed et al., 2013; Ventola, 2014; González-Padilla & Tortolero-Blanco, 2020). The extensive presence of both veracious and deceptive information has engendered a complex situation where distinguishing between them is a formidable undertaking during the COVID-19 pandemic. The World Health Organization recognizes an excessive amount of misinformation and rumors surrounding COVID-19 as "infodemic" (Pulido et al., 2020).

The proliferation of health misinformation, rumors, and conspiracy theories disseminated with various platforms, including social media, poses a serious problem for public health (Naeem and Bhatti, 2020). Being exposed to an "infodemic" and having extensive knowledge can contribute to psychological disorders, leading to feelings of panic, fear, depression, and fatigue (Mukhtar, 2020, p.514). In addition to this, Nascimento et al. (2022, p. 549) found that misleading and false health-related content during the pandemic influenced the population in several ways such as diminishing patients' inclination towards vaccination, hindering the implementation of disease outbreak containment measures, triggering impediments in accessing essential healthcare services, amplifying, and disseminating discord to exacerbate political crises, raising social fear, panic, stress, and mental disorders. Hence, the existence of governmental agencies and non-governmental entities providing true and reliable information about COVID-19 pandemic carries significant implications for the preservation and sustenance of public health.

From Dance Moves to Health Grooves: WHO on TikTok

In the contemporary digital media ecosystem, a shift in user behavior towards a disinclination to allocate substantial time to long-form video content has exerted a transformative influence on the operational paradigms of various social media platforms. This evolving consumption trend has impelled major platforms such as Facebook, Instagram, and YouTube to pivot towards the creation of shorter video content. Concurrently, it has engendered an environment conducive to the emergence and proliferation of novel, short-video-centric social media platforms. The quintessential manifestation of this evolutionary process is the TikTok application (Uğurhan & Yaşar, 2021, p. 248). The lineage of TikTok can be traced back to the "Musical.ly" application, established in Shanghai, China, in 2014 (Koçer, 2021, p. 1321). Musical.ly swiftly garnered a substantial user base and subsequently underwent acquisition by ByteDance, a Beijing-based artificial intelligence technology enterprise (Da Silva Pereira & Hitotuzi, 2023, p. 23). ByteDance introduced this platform as "Douyin" in the Chinese domestic market in 2016 and as "TikTok" in the international arena in 2018. This strategic move garnered global attention, based on the foundational principle of short-form video sharing (Shengjie, 2021, p. 8). TikTok expeditiously expanded its user demographic, securing its place among the most downloaded applications worldwide within a concise timeframe (Çiçeklioğlu & Ünal, 2021, p. 76).

TikTok, at its core, is a social media application that facilitates users in the creation of concise video content across a multitude of genres or the participation in live-streaming activities (Kobak, 2022, p. 311; Köseoğlu, 2023, p.176). TikTok stands apart from other social media platforms due to its array of distinguishing characteristics. It predominantly finds favor among the Generation Y and Z demographics, offering users two primary formats: the "Following" feed, dedicated to showcasing content from followed users, and the "For You" feed, which employs algorithms to curate content tailored to users' potential interests (Özdemir Çakır, 202, pp. 167-169). TikTok distinguishes itself from other social media platforms by fostering an elevated level of user interaction. In the TikTok milieu, users themselves frequently constitute the subjects or materials of the shared content. Unlike applications such as Facebook, Twitter, or Instagram, which pivot around interpersonal connections, TikTok aligns more closely with the public-facing model akin to YouTube. Notably, TikTok's utilization of hashtags differs substantially from its usage on other social media platforms, predominantly serving as organizational tools for platform-exclusive activities, challenges, pranks, and recurring formats. TikTok augments user creative expression through the incorporation of augmented reality filters, permitting alterations to facial, hair, eye, and bodily attributes, thereby enabling the generation of captivating video content (Widodo, Qur'ani & Putra, 2023, p.947). Furthermore, TikTok empowers users with basic video editing capabilities, including cutting, cropping, and merging functionalities, facilitating users in curating the content and narrative flow of their videos according to their proficiencies and creative inclinations (Kızılkaya, 2022, pp. 234-235).

In the academic realm, TikTok users have been observed to manifest distinct categorizations as delineated by Zhou and Jung (2019), encompassing the Content Consumer Group, the Learner-Creator Group, and the Creator Group. Primarily, the 'Content Consumer Group' predominantly assumes the role of passive spectators in the TikTok milieu. These individuals engage in limited interaction within the platform, primarily encompassing activities such as video consumption, user following, commentary, and video liking. This user cohort primarily gravitates towards the consumption of TikTok's diverse content repertoire while offering minimal contributions to the creative process. Conversely, the 'Learner-Creator Group' employs TikTok as a conduit for learning and content curation objectives. Marked by a proclivity for knowledge acquisition on specific subjects, these users engage in activities such as commentary and video liking while consuming TikTok content. Nevertheless, the incidence of content origination within this demographic remains comparatively infrequent. Lastly, the 'Creator Group' actively employs TikTok as a platform for the expression and dissemination of their creative endeavors. This cohort is characterized by pronounced levels of proactive engagement, encompassing the creation, transformation, and sharing of original content. Additionally, they engage in active following and interaction with fellow creative users. This typology serves to elucidate TikTok users' behaviors in a more granular fashion, accentuating the variances and heterogeneity pertinent to creativity and content production within the TikTok ecosystem (Gül Ünlü, Kuş & Göksu, 2020, p.121).

The TikTok application, which allows users to generate financial gains through live broadcasting, fundamentally operates as a performance space wherein users transmit their quotidian life practices to their audience. TikTok encompasses a wide spectrum of content, featuring moments culled from individuals' daily routines across a diverse array of subjects, ranging from marriage proposals and military send-offs to culinary tutorials, construction-related content, and agricultural production videos. In stark contrast to social media platforms such as Instagram, which predominantly serve as stages for the presentation of idealized selves replete with meticulously curated and stylized content, TikTok primarily functions as a platform where users are inclined to project unscripted facets of their daily lives, thus favoring a more authentic and unvarnished demeanor when facing the camera. TikTok emerges as a milieu where individuals who have historically found themselves marginalized, ostracized, or subjected to derision on platforms like Instagram and Twitter can find a haven for self-expression. In contradistinction to platforms that prominently feature the projection of idealized or aspirational lifestyles, often intertwined with the construction of fictitious identities, TikTok stands as an arena characterized by genuineness, candor, and an unreserved embrace of one's authentic self. Consequently, TikTok's resonance and preference among various user demographics can be attributed to its capacity to provide a distinctive experiential dimension vis-à-vis other social media platforms (Çiçeklioğlu & Ünal, 2021, pp. 79-82).

In recent times, several countries, including Indonesia, Pakistan, Bangladesh, and India, have imposed access restrictions on TikTok due to concerns related to user data privacy violations, national security threats, and the dissemination of inappropriate content (Tam, 2022, pp.186-190). Despite these regulatory measures, the TikTok platform has continued to witness an expanding user base. As of 2023, TikTok has extended its reach to over 160 nations and boasts a user count exceeding 1.1 billion active individuals. TikTok is particularly favored among the demographic aged 16-34, with daily video views surpassing the one billion mark (We Are Social & Meltwater, 2023). A comprehensive examination of the existing literature reveals a multitude of studies that intricately delineate the motivations underpinning TikTok users' engagement (Palupi, Meifilina & Harumike, 2020; Gül Ünlü, Kuş & Göksu, 2020; Kızılkaya, 2022; Hung, 2022; Tam, 2022; Pınarbaşı, 2023; Fan, Luo & Wang, 2023; Feng, Berndt & Ots, 2023). These scholarly endeavors collectively underscore that TikTok users, hailing from diverse social and cultural backgrounds, leverage the platform for a wide spectrum of purposes. These include seeking entertainment, discovering content aligned with their interests, showcasing their creative prowess, pursuing income generation, acquiring novel skills, expanding their knowledge base, refining their fashion sensibilities, fostering interpersonal connections, sharing the endearing qualities of their pets, embarking on virtual voyages to uncharted destinations, and amplifying societal awareness. It is an incontrovertible fact that the TikTok user demographic predominantly consists of the youthful cohort of adolescents and young adults. In recent times, an array of commercial enterprises, institutions, and brands have strategically leveraged TikTok as a direct conduit for engaging with this dynamic and vibrant user base. Utilizing the platform, they disseminate informational content, broadcast public service messages, bolster brand recognition, introduce and promote products, and forge meaningful connections with their target audience (Cervi, Tejedor & Marín-Lladó, 2021; Firmansyah & Junaedi, 2022; Albertazzi & Bonansinga, 2023; Da Silva Pereira & Hitotuzi, 2023; Daud, Listiana & Fauzan, 2023; Fadhli et al., 2023).

In December 2019, the COVID-19 pandemic, which originated in Wuhan, China, was officially declared a global pandemic by the World Health Organization on March 11, 2020. This novel coronavirus disease rapidly disseminated worldwide (Meriç, Çakıcı & Başer, 2022, p. 139). Notably, healthcare institutions seldom utilized TikTok as a communication channel with their target audiences in the pre-COVID-19 era. Before the pandemic, healthcare establishments primarily employed TikTok for purposes encompassing the cultivation of health consciousness, the introduction of diverse therapeutic modalities, dissemination of emergency preparedness guidelines and first-aid instructions to the public, orchestration of public health campaigns, stimulation of interest in healthcare, augmentation of organ donation awareness, provision of wholesome culinary recipes and dietary counsel, underscored the significance of routine health check-ups and diagnostic tests, furnishing information pertaining to family planning, disbursement of guidelines for the judicious utilization of pharmaceuticals, and introduction of novel technologies within the healthcare sector (Zhu et al., 2020; Zhou, You, & Wu, 2021; Zhang, et al., 2021; Bahagia et al., 2022; Rando-Cueto, De las Heras-Pedrosa & Paniagua-Rojano, 2023; Martínez-Sanz, Buitrago & Martín-García, 2023). After the advent of the COVID-19 pandemic, healthcare institutions underwent a paradigm shift in their TikTok utilization. During this period, healthcare establishments primarily harnessed TikTok as a medium for information dissemination to the general populace, expeditious and effective communication during emergencies, instilling awareness, facilitating access to accurate information, elucidating strategies for pandemic mitigation, engagement with the youth demographic, accentuating the imperative of mask-wearing, supporting vaccination campaigns, extending appreciation to healthcare personnel, bolstering morale, proffering insights into social distancing practices, and sharing personal narratives of individuals afflicted by COVID-19. These diverse motivations have collectively propelled healthcare institutions towards active TikTok engagement (Basch, Hillyer & Jaime, 2020; Brennan, 2021; Li, Guan, Hammond & Berrey, 2021; Li, Yan & Wu, 2021; Che, Zhang, & Kim, 2022; Lid Rosenholm, 2022; Van Kampen et al., 2022; Sun et al., 2022; Indira, 2023; Che & Kim, 2023).

The World Health Organization (WHO) stands as a paramount international institution within the realm of global health, with its mission revolving around safeguarding and augmenting the health of the global populace in its entirety. WHO undertakes a multifaceted array of responsibilities, encompassing pandemic containment, orchestration of vaccination campaigns, dissemination of health education and awareness initiatives, collection and meticulous analysis of health-related data, swift and adept interventions in times of crises, and the formulation of policies and guidelines aimed at the enhancement of public health. Following the eruption of the COVID-19 pandemic, WHO adeptly harnessed the potential of popular social media platforms, TikTok among them, as potent instruments to proactively disseminate pertinent information, debunk erroneous assertions, and deliver accurate enlightenment to the public. With a particular focus on TikTok, WHO utilized this platform as a conduit for the dissemination of timely COVID-19 information, elucidation of preventive measures, reaffirmation of vaccine safety, and the propagation of public awareness. Significantly, even after the official cessation of the COVID-19 pandemic, WHO persisted in harnessing TikTok as an active medium for communication. During the post-pandemic era, WHO maintained its pursuit of health-related subject matter, sustained its endeavors in health education, and continued to kindle awareness, while astutely leveraging the communicative prowess of this platform to advocate public health. Notwithstanding, upon meticulous review of extant literature, no in-depth investigations delineating WHO's specific utilization of TikTok during both the pandemic period and the subsequent phase have surfaced. This article endeavors to undertake a comparative examination of the health communication initiatives conducted by the World Health Organization (WHO) on TikTok during and after the COVID-19 pandemic, with the overarching objective of addressing the lacuna present within the extant literature in a meticulously professional and scientific manner.

METHOD

Similar to prior research (Zhu et al., 2019; Basch, Hillyer & Jaime, 2020; Li et al., 2021; Chen et al., 2021; Zhang et al., 2021), this study used a content analysis which is a "*research technique for making replicable and valid inferences from texts to the contexts of their use*" (Krippendorf, 2018, p.24). The objective of employing this approach was to transform the original audio-visual data into a concise and condensed format, while also identifying and presenting the fundamental patterns and themes that emerged from the data. The unit of analysis is post, specifically referring to the short video clips.

In this study, The TikTok account of the World Health Organization (WHO) is examined. To begin, we searched the TikTok platform for the official account of WHO by using its official name and its abbreviation. Although we found the official account of WHO, we also checked the official website of it to see whether any link to its TikTok account was added or not. Then we reviewed all of its videos from 28 February 2020. In total, 315 videos were identified and downloaded on 27 June 2023. Videos were divided in terms of two periods: during the pandemic and post-pandemic. The first video on the WHO TikTok account was shared on 28 February 2020. The period WHO started to share videos on its TikTok account to 5 May 2023 is determined as during the pandemic period. However, the post-pandemic period started on 5 May 2023 after the declaration of WHO chief Tedros Adhanom Ghebreyesus as ending of COVID-19 as a global health emergency. 189 TikTok videos were shared during the pandemic by WHO, and 26 videos were shared by WHO in the post-pandemic era. In total, 315 videos were identified and captured on 27 June 2023.

The coding categories were developed based on previous literature on health communication and organizational communication on social media (Lovejoy and Saxton, 2012; Park, Reber & Chon, 2016; Zhu et al., 2019; Li et al., 2021, Zhang et al., 2021). Corresponding to the research questions, the coding scheme consisted of six parts: (1) engagement, (2) video format, (3) functions, (4) video types, (5) characters (6) emotions.

The first coding frame is engagement. The number of likes, comments, views, saves, and shares of each video were recorded to quantify user engagement. Second, the information including video length, subtitle, spoken language, caption, hashtag, and music about video format is collected (see Table 1). Next, the functions of videos were examined. The functions of videos have been delineated based on the constituent elements that constitute the overarching goal of the video message These functions can be categorized as either about organizational topics or addressing health-related topics. A prior scholarly investigation conducted by Lovejoy and Saxton (2012, p. 342) identified three distinct organizational message functions. The first of these functions is denoted as "organizational information" covering the dissemination of information regarding the activities and undertakings of the organization. The second function, termed "organizational community," involves the facilitation of network establishment, the cultivation of dialogic communication, and the development of communities through the deployment of social media content. Examples of such content include expressions of gratitude and acknowledgment conveyed through videos. The third and final function, herein referred to as "organizational action," is primarily characterized by its central objective of motivating followers to take proactive measures in support of the organization. These measures encompass a spectrum of actions, ranging from financial contributions and product purchases to event attendance, participation in movements, or even the initiation of protest activities. In addition to these three functions determined by Lovejoy and Saxton (2012), two functions related to health knowledge and behavioral change were added to codes originated from the study of Park, Reber, and Chon (2016, p.192). These are called "disease information" and "disease action". There were 7 categories (including other) for disease information topics and eight categories (including "other") for disease action categories (see Table 2).

The fourth coding frame is video types. The video types including acting, animated infographics, oral speech, pictorial slideshow, documentary, TikTok dance, and news were determined by benefitting from previous studies of Zhu et al. (2019) and Li et al. (2021) (see Table 3). In terms of character in videos, each video was coded as one of the following themes, including the general public, health professionals, public figures, WHO members, animated characters, and victims (Zhu et al., 2019) (see Table 4). Lastly, each video was coded in terms of the emotion of the video such as alarm or concern, hope or encouragement, humor, empathy, susceptibility, severity, and no emotion (see Table 5 for details).

All the videos were coded manually. Both authors agreed on the coding frames. To establish a preliminary agreement about coding material, the part of videos was coded together (10%). The rest of them are coded separately. Then, the coded materials were exchanged and checked by the authors. There were no disagreements about coded materials.

Considering the objectives of the research, we identified five research questions listed below:

1) How is the World Health Organization (WHO) utilizing TikTok for health communication, specifically for what purposes are TikTok videos being employed by WHO during and after the pandemic?
2) What types and formats of videos were used by WHO on TikTok?
3) What kinds of characters were featured in WHO's TikTok videos during and after the pandemic?
4) What differences exist in the emotional content of the videos during and after the pandemic?
5) Which type of TikTok video created more engagement with the audience for WHO?

FINDINGS AND DISCUSSIONS

As of 27 June 2023, the 315 COVID-19 videos received a total of 905884 likes, 69867 comments, 487535854 views, 198920 saves, and 387406 shares. During the pandemic, the 289 COVID-19 videos received 9028735 likes, 68112 comments, 478699509 views, 195857 saves, and 384929 shares. In the post-pandemic period, the 26 COVID-19 videos received 30108 likes,1755 comments, 8836345 views, 3063 saves, and 2477 shares.

The videos ranged from 4 to 180 second in length during the pandemic. 81.7% of videos included subtitles, 98.6% used captions in the video, 90.7% had a spoken language, and 87.9% had music. The

Table 1. Video format

	During Pandemic	Post Pandemic
Video Length	4 to 180 s	8 to 168 s
Subtitle	236 Videos (81.7%)	22 Videos (84.6%)
Spoken Language	250 (English) 3 (Arabic) 2 (Spanish) 2 (Portuguese) 1 (Polish) 1 (Ghanaian Local Language) 1 (Dutch) 1 (Japanese) 1 (German) 27 (No Spoken Language)	English (26)
Caption	285 Videos (98.6%)	26 Videos (100%)
Music	254 Videos (87.9%)	20 Videos (76.9%)
Hashtag	276 Videos (95.5)	25 Videos (96.2%)

Table 2. Video message function

	During Pandemic	Post Pandemic
Organization Information	21	5
Organization Community	1	1
Organization Action	1	0
Disease Information	189	9
Disease Action	77	11
Total	289	26

language used in oral messages was predominantly English (86.5%). The majority (95.5%) of videos had at least one hashtag. In the post-pandemic period, the videos ranged from 8 to 168 s in length. 84.6% of videos included subtitles, all of them used captions in the video, all of them had a spoken language, and 76.9% had music. The language used in oral messages was completely English. The majority (96.2%) of videos had at least one hashtag. The analysis showed that the fundamental characteristics of videos, encompassing subtitles, captions, spoken language (entirely in English), and hashtags, persisted consistently across both pandemic and post-pandemic periods. The slight decrease in the presence of music in post-pandemic videos may reflect nuanced shifts in content tone or focus as the pandemic transitioned into a different phase.

As delineated in Table 2, the World Health Organization (WHO) disseminated a total of 289 videos via its TikTok platform during the COVID-19 pandemic. Over this period, 65.4% of the shared videos provided informational content regarding the pandemic, while 26.6% impelled individuals towards undertaking personal measures, seeking vaccination, modifying their lifestyles, or perpetuating health-related behaviors in response to the COVID-19 outbreak. Additionally, 7.3% of the videos directly promulgated the institution and furnished information about the organization's undertakings, with 0.3% dedicated to the establishment of a dialogic communication with the target audience or the cultivation of a follower community, and another 0.3% striving to mobilize individuals for the organization's interests. In the post-pandemic period, a total of 26 videos were disseminated. Among these, 42.3% encouraged individuals to adopt personal precautions, receive vaccinations, adjust their lifestyles, or maintain health behaviors in response to the COVID-19 pandemic, while 34.6% furnished explicit information about the pandemic. Furthermore, 19.2% of the videos served as a direct conduit for institutional endorsement and the communication of information concerning the organization's initiatives, with 3.8% aiming to establish a dialogical discourse with the target demographic or foster a community of followers. No videos were identified to have been disseminated in the post-pandemic phase with the specific intention of motivating followers to act in furtherance of the institution's interests. In summation, it becomes apparent that the World Health Organization actively circulated a profusion of informative videos relating to the pandemic throughout the pandemic era. In the post-pandemic period, while the WHO continued to sustain its presence on TikTok, there was a discernible reduction in the frequency of content dissemination. During this epoch, there was a marked augmentation in content dedicated to the promotion of personal protective measures. The proportion of content focused on the cultivation of dialogic engagement with followers, the nurturing of follower communities, and the mobilization of followers for institutional purposes consistently remained at a low ebb throughout both temporal epochs.

As depicted in Table 2, the World Health Organization (WHO) disseminated a total of 189 videos about disease-related information on their TikTok platform during the COVID-19 pandemic. During this period, 36.5% of the videos provided disease knowledge about COVID-19, encompassing details regarding symptoms, transmission modalities, statistical data, and precautionary measures, 6.3% raised awareness against anti-stigma and misinformation related to COVID-19, 3.2% emphasized health risks of COVID-19, 2.6% addressed social, economic, and political effects of COVID-19, 2.1% presented results of medical research or studies on COVID-19, and 1.1% showed health story of victims. The predominant theme, constituting 48.1% of the videos, fell under the other category encompassing a spectrum of topics, including various diseases such as monkeypox, HIV, sexually transmitted infections, and smallpox, environmental concerns like climate change, and significant health-related observances such as World Vaccination Week, World Clean Air Day, and World Humanitarian Day. Transitioning to the post-pandemic era, WHO disseminated a mere 9 videos. The preeminent theme that endured was disease knowledge about COVID-19, albeit with a marginal reduction to 33.3% in the post-pandemic phase. In contrast, there were no video presentations about the reporting of medical research, the discussion of health-related risks, the addressing of social and economic concerns, endeavors aimed at combatting stigma and misinformation, or the sharing of personal health narratives concerning COVID-19 during the post-pandemic phase. Concomitantly, the other category assumed predominance, accounting for 66.7% of the content, signifying a shift towards encompassing a more extensive array of subjects in the post-pandemic milieu. In general, WHO's video content was principally oriented towards disseminating information and knowledge about COVID-19, alongside a spectrum of other diseases and consequential health-related events during the pandemic. It also undertook the task of addressing health risks, mitigating misinformation, and combating stigmatization. However, in the post-pandemic epoch, there was an observable reduction in content pertaining specifically to COVID-19, coupled with an augmented emphasis on a diversified array of subjects, indicative of the evolving interests and information requirements of the general populace.

The World Health Organization (WHO) disseminated a total of 77 videos about disease-related actions on their TikTok platform throughout the COVID-19 pandemic. 44.2% of the videos were primarily geared towards encouraging individuals to undertake personal precautions, encompassing the utilization of masks, adherence to rigorous hand hygiene practices, and the observance of social distancing measures in the context of COVID-19. Following closely, the second most substantial theme revolved around encouraging individuals to adapt their lifestyle choices and sustain health-promoting behaviors, constituting 33.8% of the video messaging. This category emphasized activities such as physical exercise, recreational walking, adhering to quarantine measures, remaining active, and abstaining from smoking. Additionally, there was a notable emphasis on motivating individuals to partake in vaccination efforts and addressing issues of vaccine equity, contributing to 22.1% of the content. In contrast, during the pandemic era, the "Other" category did not feature in the content dissemination (see Table 2).

Transitioning to the post-pandemic era, a discernible shift in thematic content became apparent. Notably, the emphasis on encouraging personal precautions specific to COVID-19 witnessed a complete cessation, reflecting a realignment of priorities as the pandemic situation improved. Meanwhile, the advocacy for vaccination and equitable access to vaccines persisted but experienced a reduction to 9.1% of the content. Most prominently, the thematic pivot in the post-pandemic period centered on the promotion of lifestyle adjustments and the maintenance of health-conscious behaviors, accounting for a substantial 54.5% of the messaging. This entailed a notable emphasis on advocating for activities such as regular physical exercise, healthy routines, and the avoidance of tobacco consumption. Furthermore,

Table 3. Type of video

	During Pandemic	Post Pandemic
Acting	55	2
Animated Infographic	97	5
Oral Speech	91	12
Pictorial slideshow	12	2
Documentary	16	2
TikTok Dance	13	3
News	5	0
Total	289	26

the "other" category assumed significance in the post-pandemic era, contributing to 36.4% of the content (see Table 2). This observation suggests a broadening of content scope, encompassing subjects extending beyond COVID-19. This diversification potentially mirrors evolving public health priorities and interests, including efforts to reduce tobacco production. Overall, during the pandemic, the principal thematic focus was centered on the promotion of personal precautions, vaccination, and the sustenance of health-conscious behaviors. In the post-pandemic context, the thematic landscape shifted away from COVID-19 precautions, placing a heightened emphasis on the cultivation and maintenance of healthy lifestyles. The emergence of the "Other" category underscored the diversification of content, indicative of evolving public health concerns and interests in a post-pandemic landscape.

As depicted in Table 3, the World Health Organization (WHO) has disseminated various types of videos on its TikTok platform. During the period of the pandemic, 33.6% of the disseminated videos constituted Animated Infographics, 31.5% featured Oral Speech, 19% were characterized by Acting performances, 5.5% comprised Documentary content, 4.5% encompassed TikTok Dance sequences, 4.2% presented Pictorial Slideshows, and a modest 1.7% were News-related. In the post-pandemic epoch, a substantial 46.2% of the released videos were of the Oral Speech variety, whereas 19.2% retained the form of Animated Infographics, 11.5% embraced TikTok Dance segments, and 7.7% each were dedicated to Acting, Documentary, and Pictorial Slideshows. In the broader context, it is discernible that during the pandemic phase, there was a discernible predilection towards the utilization of Animated Infographics and Oral Speech videos as vehicles for informational dissemination. Furthermore, the Acting genre was strategically employed as a means to enhance the appeal of pandemic-related subject matter. In the post-pandemic era, there manifested a shift in the content strategy, with a pronounced emphasis on the Oral Speech format. This strategic pivot is of paramount significance in light of its pivotal role in facilitating the direct transmission of post-pandemic health-related information to the general populace. Animated Infographic videos persisted as an instrument for the visual elucidation of health-related information in the post-pandemic period. The augmented allocation of resources to the TikTok Dance category can be construed as a deliberate endeavor to cater to a youthful demographic. Additionally, it is noteworthy that, except content falling under the purview of the news genre, the other video categories continued to be disseminated, albeit in a somewhat diminished capacity.

As indicated in Table 4, during the pandemic era, TikTok videos exhibited the presence of various spokesperson categories as follows: animation characters in 28.7%, World Health Organization (WHO) members in 23.5%, members of the general public in 22.1%, healthcare professionals in 16.6%, victims

Table 4. Character in video

	During Pandemic	Post Pandemic
General Public	64	2
Health Professionals	48	4
Public Figures	10	5
World Health Organization Members	68	9
Animated Characters	83	4
Victims	16	2
Total	289	26

of the pandemic in 5.5%, and public figures such as artists, journalists, athletes, and politicians in 3.5% of the videos. In the post-pandemic period, TikTok videos featured spokespersons in the following proportions: WHO members at 34.6%, public figures at 19.2%, healthcare professionals at 15.4%, animation characters at 15.4%, members of the general public at 7.7%, and victims of the pandemic in 7.7%. In a comprehensive analysis, during the pandemic period, the World Health Organization prominently employed animated characters in their TikTok videos to render informative messages more captivating. However, this tactic witnessed a discernible decline in utilization during the post-pandemic era. Similarly, during the pandemic, the WHO recurrently featured members of the general public as spokespersons to foster pandemic consciousness using sharing personal narratives and establishing emotional resonance. Nevertheless, this strategy experienced attenuation in the post-pandemic phase. WHO members and healthcare professionals, characterized by their role as credible and authoritative sources, consistently featured as spokespersons in both periods to facilitate the direct and reliable dissemination of information and recommendations. In the post-pandemic context, public figures assumed a more pronounced role as spokespersons, reflecting a strategic shift aimed at engaging the broader societal milieu and extending the reach of health-related messages. Conversely, individuals affected by the pandemic were sparingly integrated as spokespersons in both the pandemic and post-pandemic eras, underscoring their limited involvement in this capacity.

As depicted in Table 5, there are 289 videos during the pandemic examined in terms of emotions. 21.1% of videos evoked alarm or concern, 39.8% of them evoked hope or encouragement, 8,3% of them

Table 5. Video emotion

	During Pandemic	Post Pandemic
Alarm/Concern	61	4
Hope/Encouragement	115	11
Humor	24	0
Empathy	10	1
Susceptibility	11	1
Severity	47	2
No emotion	21	7
Total	289	26

evoked humor, 3.5% of them evoked empathy, 3.8% of them evoked susceptibility, 16.3% of them evoked severity, and 7.3% of them evoked no emotion during the pandemic. The World Health Organization (WHO) disseminated a total of 26 videos in the post-pandemic period. 15.4% of videos evoked alarm or concern, 42.3% of videos evoked hope or encouragement, none of them evoked humor, 3.8% of them evoked empathy, 3.8% of them evoked susceptibility, 7.7% of them evoked severity, and 26.9% of them evoked no emotion in the post-pandemic period. Overall, during the pandemic, there was a mix of emotions expressed, with a predominant focus on hope and encouragement, alarm/concern, and severity. Post-pandemic, hope and encouragement remained high, while alarm/concern decreased. The absence of humor in post-pandemic content suggests a shift in tone. The continued presence of empathy and susceptibility themes indicates a commitment to understanding and vigilance. Additionally, a notable proportion of post-pandemic content adopted a neutral or informational tone. These changes in emotional themes likely reflect the evolving public sentiment and information needs as the pandemic transitioned into a different phase.

When we finally examined the relationship between content type and engagement indicators, the animated infographic received the most likes (3,908,115), with oral speech coming in second (3,224,852). The pictorial slideshow had the fewest likes (9,559). TikTok dance received the fewest comments (443), while animated infographics got the most (23,402). News and pictorial slideshow had the fewest views (1,217,100 and 295,522, respectively), while animated infographics had the most (244,363,166). Animated infographics had the most saves (92,669), while pictorial slideshow had the least (543). animated infographic also had the most forwards (134,415), and pictorial slideshow had the least (79,221).

CONCLUSION

This study conducted a meticulous examination of the communication strategies employed by the World Health Organization on the TikTok platform, encompassing a comprehensive comparative analysis that spanned the pandemic and the subsequent post-pandemic phases. The research findings elucidate the active utilization of the TikTok platform by the World Health Organization (WHO) during the COVID-19 pandemic. Throughout this period, the dissemination of informative content pertaining to the COVID-19 pandemic was a recurrent practice, predominantly manifested through videos of animated infographic and oral speech genres. These videos conveyed crucial guidance on pandemic mitigation strategies and frequently featured a spectrum of emotions, notably concern, hope, and severity. In these video productions, a combination of animated characters and spokespersons representing the World Health Organization was consistently employed. This approach served the dual purpose of conveying the gravity of the COVID-19 pandemic while optimizing content design for enhanced message comprehension by the audience. During the pandemic phase, video content encompassing topics related to COVID-19, misinformation mitigation, and healthy living garnered a noteworthy magnitude of interactions, amounting to millions.

In the post-pandemic era, the World Health Organization (WHO) has been noted to sustain an active presence on TikTok, albeit with a decreased frequency of content dissemination. During this post-pandemic phase, a discernible adjustment in content strategy has been observed. Specifically, there has been a continued emphasis on providing informational content regarding the COVID-19 pandemic, primarily conveyed through videos of the oral speech genre, which elucidate strategies for pandemic mitigation. Notably, in this period, messages have been tailored to resonate more effectively with younger demographics, often being conveyed through dance videos. These videos, characterized by an overarching sense of hope, consistently featured WHO members and healthcare professionals as spokespersons, with the objective of delivering information and guidance directly and authoritatively. In an endeavor to capture the public's attention and disseminate health-related messages to a broader audience during the post-pandemic era, public figures have increasingly been enlisted as spokespersons. It has been observed that video content produced by the World Health Organization in the post-pandemic phase has garnered reduced levels of engagement. This phenomenon can, in part, be attributed to the waning prominence of the COVID-19 pandemic as the primary societal concern, particularly when compared to earlier phases.

Throughout the COVID-19 pandemic and in its aftermath, it can be asserted that the World Health Organization (WHO) displayed a concerted endeavor to establish close contact with individuals, disseminate informative content, and cultivate awareness through its communication strategy on TikTok. Nevertheless, research findings have underscored the imperative for the WHO to formulate a more innovative communication strategy. Notably, it has been ascertained that captions employed in the WHO's videos and the explanations proffered by its spokespersons predominantly adhered to the English language. The organization's expansion of content production into additional languages and the promotion of diversity could serve to extend its reach to a more extensive audience and cultivate a communication strategy that embraces cultural diversity. Moreover, the WHO could enhance its TikTok communication strategy by tailoring content to align with user interests, incorporating elements of originality and entertainment, stimulating user-generated commentary, inquiries, and participation, orchestrating additional hashtag campaigns, and conducting live broadcasts to amplify viewer interaction. These adaptive measures possess the potential to augment the WHO's TikTok communication strategy, rendering it more attuned to user preferences and ultimately more efficacious in disseminating pivotal information and nurturing a heightened sense of global health consciousness.

Prospective investigations necessitate a heightened understanding of TikTok within the domain of health communication. In such scholarly inquiries, a thoroughgoing analysis of user commentary assumes paramount significance in evaluating the impact of content on its viewers. Furthermore, the employment of methodological tools, including surveys and in-depth interviews, may serve to elucidate how TikTok can be harnessed in a more efficacious manner for health-centric campaigns. These research endeavors proffer the potential to empower healthcare institutions to refine their strategies within the realm of social media and, thereby, enhance their substantive contributions to public health.

REFERENCES

Al-Dmour, H., Masa'deh, R., Salman, A., Abuhashesh, M., & Al-Dmour, R. (2020). Influence of social media platforms on public health protection against the COVID-19 pandemic via the mediating effects of public health awareness and behavioral changes: Integrated model. *Journal of Medical Internet Research, 22*(8), e19996. doi:10.2196/19996 PMID:32750004

Albertazzi, D., & Bonansinga, D. (2023). Beyond anger: The populist radical right on TikTok. *Journal of Contemporary European Studies*, 1–17. doi:10.1080/14782804.2022.2163380

Andersen, K. N., Medaglia, R., & Henriksen, H. Z. (2012). Social media in public health care: Impact domain propositions. *Government Information Quarterly, 29*(4), 462–469. doi:10.1016/j.giq.2012.07.004

Antheunis, M. L., Tates, K., & Nieboer, T. E. (2013). Patients' and health professionals' use of social media in health care: Motives, barriers, and expectations. *Patient Education and Counseling*, *92*(3), 426–431. doi:10.1016/j.pec.2013.06.020 PMID:23899831

Apostolakis, I., Koulierakis, G., Berler, A., Chryssanthou, A., & Varlamis, I. (2012). Use of social media by healthcare professionals in Greece: An exploratory study. *International Journal of Electronic Healthcare*, *7*(2), 105–124. doi:10.1504/IJEH.2012.049873 PMID:23079026

Bahagia, B., Wibowo, R., Muniroh, L., Al Wahid, A., Rizkal, R., Noor, Z. M., & Karim, A. (2022). The drawbacks and advantages of TikTok in student amid pandemic COVID-19. *Jurnal Basicedu*, *6*(3), 5302–5310. doi:10.31004/basicedu.v6i3.2459

Basch, C. H., Hillyer, G. C., & Jaime, C. (2020). COVID-19 on TikTok: Harnessing an emerging social media platform to convey important public health messages. *International Journal of Adolescent Medicine and Health*, *34*(5), 367–369. doi:10.1515/ijamh-2020-0111 PMID:32776899

Betton, V., Borschmann, R., Docherty, M., Coleman, S., Brown, M., & Henderson, C. (2015). The role of social media in reducing stigma and discrimination. *The British Journal of Psychiatry*, *206*(6), 443–444. doi:10.1192/bjp.bp.114.152835 PMID:26034176

Borges do Nascimento, I. J., Pizarro, A. B., Almeida, J. M., Azzopardi-Muscat, N., Gonçalves, M. A., Björklund, M., & Novillo-Ortiz, D. (2022). Infodemics and health misinformation: A systematic review of reviews. *Bulletin of the World Health Organization*, *100*(9), 544–561. doi:10.2471/BLT.21.287654 PMID:36062247

Brennan, H. (2021). A qualitative case study on TikTok: The silver lining for brands during the coronavirus pandemic. *Elon Journal of Undergraduate Research in Communications*, *12*(2), 5–12.

Bruns, A., Harrington, S., & Hurcombe, E. (2020). 'Corona? 5G? or both?': The dynamics of COVID-19/5G conspiracy theories on Facebook. *Media International Australia, Incorporating Culture & Policy*, *177*(1), 12–29. doi:10.1177/1329878X20946113

Bull, S. S., Levine, D., Schmiege, S., & Santelli, J. (2013). Recruitment and retention of youth for research using social media: Experiences from the Just/Us study. *Vulnerable Children and Youth Studies*, *8*(2), 171–181. doi:10.1080/17450128.2012.748238

Cervi, L., Tejedor, S., & Marín-Lladó, C. (2021). TikTok and the new language of political communication. *Cultura, Lenguaje y Representación*, 267-287.

Che, S., & Kim, J. H. (2023). Sentiment impact of public health agency communication strategies on TikTok under COVID-19 normalization: Deep learning exploration. *Journal of Public Health (Berlin)*, 1–12. doi:10.100710389-023-01921-5 PMID:37361279

Che, S., Zhang, S., & Kim, J. H. (2022). How public health agencies communicate with the public on TikTok under the normalization of COVID-19: A case of 2022 Shanghai's outbreak. *Frontiers in Public Health*, *10*, 1039405. doi:10.3389/fpubh.2022.1039405 PMID:36505000

Chen, J., & Wang, Y. (2021). Social Media Use for Health Purposes: Systematic Review. *Journal of Medical Internet Research*, *23*(5), 1–16. doi:10.2196/17917 PMID:33978589

Chen, Q., Min, C., Zhang, W., Ma, X., & Evans, R. (2021). Factors driving citizen engagement with government TikTok accounts during the COVID-19 pandemic: Model development and analysis. *Journal of Medical Internet Research, 23*(2), 1–13. doi:10.2196/21463 PMID:33481756

Çiçeklioğlu, A. Ş., & Ünal, R. (2021). Haber üretimi ve dağıtımı bağlamında TikTok uygulaması ne vaat ediyor. *İlef Dergisi,* 69-98.

Cobb, N. K., Graham, A. L., & Abrams, D. B. (2010). Social network structure of a large online community for smoking cessation. *American Journal of Public Health, 100*(7), 1282–1289. doi:10.2105/AJPH.2009.165449 PMID:20466971

Da Silva Pereira, A. A., & Hitotuzi, N. (2023). Enhancing speaking skills and vocabulary in the eal classroom through TikTok: A literature review. *International Journal of English Linguistics, 13*(5), 22–33. doi:10.5539/ijel.v13n5p22

Daud, I., Listiana, E., & Fauzan, R. (2023). Social media marketing activities (SMMAs) as stimulus on purchase intention with customer engagement as mediator on@ avoskinbeauty TikTok's account. Asian *Journal of Economics. Business and Accounting, 23*(4), 35–45.

DePaula, N., Hagen, L., Roytman, S., & Alnahass, D. (2022). Platform Effects on Public Health Communication: A Comparative and National Study of Message Design and Audience Engagement Across Twitter and Facebook. *JMIR Infodemiology, 2*(2), 1–18. doi:10.2196/40198 PMID:36575712

Domínguez, M., & Sapiña, L. (2017). "Others Like Me". An Approach to the Use of the Internet and Social Networks in Adolescents and Young Adults Diagnosed with Cancer. *Journal of Cancer Education, 32*(4), 885–891. doi:10.100713187-016-1055-9 PMID:27251633

Eysenbach, G. (2011). Infodemiology and infoveillance tracking online health information and cyberbehavior for public health. *American Journal of Preventive Medicine, 40*(5, Suppl 2), 154–S158. doi:10.1016/j.amepre.2011.02.006 PMID:21521589

Fadhli, R., Ibrahim, C., Igiriza, M., & Ilmi, B. (2023). How libraries in Indonesia use TikTok: A content analysis of library accounts on the platform. *Artículo de investigación, 36*(96), 27-44.

Fan, X., Luo, J., & Wang, X. (2023). Understanding TikTok usage: Communication strategy of ByteDance based on the background of new media. In *2022 4th International Conference on Literature, Art and Human Development (ICLAHD 2022)* (pp. 226-236). Atlantis Press.

Feng, S., Berndt, A., & Ots, M. (2023). Residents' videographic practices on TikTok (Douyin): Enacting and communicating social sustainability during a COVID-19 lockdown. *Journal of Media Business Studies*, 1–22. doi:10.1080/16522354.2023.2207160

Firmansyah, M. R., & Junaedi, F. (2022). Production management model and distribution of TikTok content as a football information media in@ footballfandom_id account. *Symposium of Literature, Culture, and Communication (SYLECTION), 1*(1), 169-175. 10.12928ylection.v1i1.11327

González-Padilla, D. A., & Tortolero-Blanco, L. (2020). Social media influence in the COVID-19 Pandemic. *International Braz J Urol, 46*(suppl.1), 120–124. doi:10.15901677-5538.ibju.2020.s121 PMID:32550706

Gül Ünlü, D., Kuş, O., & Göksu, O. (2020). Videolarda gerçek hayattaki gibi değilim, rol yapmaktayım: TikTok kullanıcılarının benlik performansları üzerine bir inceleme. *Intermedia International E-journal*, *7*(12), 115–128. doi:10.21645/intermedia.2020.70

Guttman, N. (2000). Public health communication interventions. *Sage (Atlanta, Ga.)*.

Hanson, C. L., West, J., Thackeray, R., Barnes, M. D., & Downey, J. (2014). Understanding and predicting social media use among community health center patients: A cross-sectional survey. *Journal of Medical Internet Research*, *16*(11), 1–11. doi:10.2196/jmir.3373 PMID:25427823

Hawn, C. (2009). Take Two Aspirin And Tweet Me In The Morning: How Twitter, Facebook, And Other Social Media Are Reshaping Health Care. *Health Affairs*, *28*(2), 361–368. doi:10.1377/hlthaff.28.2.361 PMID:19275991

Hung, L. T. (2022). TikTok content in communication strategy: Politics of the 15th general election in Malaysia. *Higher Education and Oriental. Studies*, *2*(6).

Indira, A. (2023). Utilization and rationalization of TikTok application for hospital health promotion during COVID-19 pandemic. *International Journal of Environmental, Sustainability, and Social Science*, *4*(1), 115–124. doi:10.38142/ijesss.v4i1.466

Khatri, C., Chapman, S. J., Glasbey, J., Kelly, M., Nepogodiev, D., Bhangu, A., & Fitzgerald, E.STARSurg Committee. (2015). Social media and internet driven study recruitment: Evaluating a new model for promoting collaborator engagement and participation. *PLoS One*, *10*(3), 1–11. doi:10.1371/journal.pone.0118899 PMID:25775005

Kızılkaya, Z. Z. (2022). Gençlerin TikTok kullanım ve doyumu üzerine nitel bir araştırma. *Anemon Muş Alparslan Üniversitesi Sosyal Bilimler Dergisi*, *10*(1), 231–247. doi:10.18506/anemon.962352

Kobak, K. (2022). # TikTokkapansın hareketi: Twitter'da sosyal ağ analizi. *MANAS Sosyal Araştırmalar Dergisi*, *11*(1), 309–319. doi:10.33206/mjss.935068

Koçer, B. Y. (2021). Dijital etnografi perspektifinden TikTok'ta müziğin kullanımı ve performans pratikleri. *Motif Akademi Halkbilimi Dergisi*, *14*(36), 1317–1332.

Köseoğlu, A. (2023). TikTok'ta mahremiyet algısının dönüşümü. *İNİF E- Dergi*, *8*(1), 172-188.

Kreps, G. L. (2009). Applying Weick's model of organizing to health care and health promotion: Highlighting the central role of health communication. *Patient Education and Counseling*, *74*(3), 347–355. doi:10.1016/j.pec.2008.12.002 PMID:19150591

Kreuter, M. W., & McClure, S. M. (2004). The Role of Culture in Health Communication. *Annual Review of Public Health*, *25*(1), 439–455. doi:10.1146/annurev.publhealth.25.101802.123000 PMID:15015929

Krippendorff, K. (2018). *Content analysis: An introduction to its methodology*. Sage publications.

Lawless, M., Augoustinos, M., & LeCouteur, A. (2018). Dementia on Facebook: Requesting information and advice about dementia risk-prevention on social media. *Discourse, Context & Media*, *25*, 44–51. doi:10.1016/j.dcm.2018.01.011

Lazebnik, T., Bunimovich-Mendrazitsky, S., Ashkenazi, S., Levner, E., & Benis, A. (2022). Early detection and control of the next epidemic wave using health communications: Development of an artificial intelligence-based tool and its validation on COVID-19 data from the US. *International Journal of Environmental Research and Public Health*, *19*(23), 1–17. doi:10.3390/ijerph192316023 PMID:36498096

Li, N., Yan, J., & Wu, F. (2021). Research on the current situation and development strategy of health communication in a short TikTok Video: The "Dingxiang Doctor". *Scientific and Social Research*, *3*(3), 144–149. doi:10.36922sr.v3i3.1170

Li, Y., Guan, M., Hammond, P., & Berrey, L. E. (2021). Communicating COVID-19 information on TikTok: A content analysis of TikTok videos from official accounts featured in the COVID-19 information hub. *Health Education Research*, *36*(3), 261–271. doi:10.1093/her/cyab010 PMID:33667311

Lid Rosenholm, I. (2022). *Health communication on TikTok: A qualitative study of credibility on a humorous platform.* https://www.diva-portal.org/smash/get/diva2:1667733/FULLTEXT01.pdf

Liu, W., Xu, W., & John, B. (2021). Organizational disaster communication ecology: Examining interagency coordination on social media during the onset of the COVID-19 pandemic. *The American Behavioral Scientist*, *65*(7), 914–933. doi:10.1177/0002764221992823

Lovejoy, K., & Saxton, G. D. (2012). Information, community, and action: How nonprofit organizations use social media. *Journal of Computer-Mediated Communication*, *17*(3), 337–353. doi:10.1111/j.1083-6101.2012.01576.x

Lupton, D. (2014). The commodification of patient opinion: The digital patient experience economy in the age of big data. *Sociology of Health & Illness*, *36*(6), 856–869. doi:10.1111/1467-9566.12109 PMID:24443847

Martínez-Sanz, R., Buitrago, Á., & Martín-García, A. (2023). Communication for health through TikTok. Study of influencers in the pharmaceutical field and connection with their audience. *Revista Mediterránea de Comunicación/Mediterranean Journal of Communication*, *14*(1), 83–98.

McLuhan, M. (1994). *Understanding media: The extensions of man.* MIT press.

Meriç, E., Çakıcı, Z., & Başer, B. (2022). Health communication and health information seeking on social media: A study on COVID-19 online support groups on Facebook. In Covid Communication II (pp. 137-160). Klaipeda: SRA Academic Publishing.

Mheidly, N., & Fares, J. (2020). Leveraging media and health communication strategies to overcome the COVID-19 infodemic. *Journal of Public Health Policy*, *41*(4), 410–420. doi:10.105741271-020-00247-w PMID:32826935

Milley, K. M., Chima, S. A., Cummings, K. L., & Emery, J. D. (2021). Look who's talking now: Cancer in primary care on Twitter. An observational study. *BJGP Open*, *5*(1), 1–10. doi:10.3399/bjgpopen20X101134 PMID:33199305

Moorhead, S. A., Hazlett, D. E., Harrison, L., Carroll, J. K., Irwin, A., & Hoving, C. (2013, April 23). A new dimension of health care: Systematic review of the uses, benefits, and limitations of social media for health communication. *Journal of Medical Internet Research, 15*(4), 1–17. doi:10.2196/jmir.1933 PMID:23615206

Mukhtar, S. (2020). Psychological health during the coronavirus disease 2019 pandemic outbreak. *The International Journal of Social Psychiatry, 66*(5), 512–516. doi:10.1177/0020764020925835 PMID:32434402

Naeem, S. B., & Bhatti, R. (2020). The Covid-19 'infodemic': A new front for information professionals. *Health Information &amp. Library Journal, 37*(3), 233–239. doi:10.1111/hir.12311 PMID:32533803

Okay, A., Ašanin Gole, P., & Okay, A. (2021). Turkish and Slovenian health ministries' use of Twitter: A comparative analysis. *Corporate Communications, 26*(1), 176–191. doi:10.1108/CCIJ-01-2020-0019

Özdemir Çakır, H. Ö. (2023). Influencer pazarlamasının satın alma davranışına etkisi: TikTok örneği. *Anasay, 0*(24), 165–183. doi:10.33404/anasay.1249855

Palupi, N. D., Meifilina, A., & Harumike, Y. D. N. (2020). The effect of using TikTok applications on self-confidence levels. *JOSAR, 5*(2), 66–74.

Park, A., Bowling, J., Shaw, G. Jr, Li, C., & Chen, S. (2019). Adopting Social Media for Improving Health: Opportunities and Challenges. *North Carolina Medical Journal, 80*(4), 240–243. doi:10.18043/ncm.80.4.240 PMID:31278188

Park, H., Reber, B. H., & Chon, M. G. (2016). Tweeting as health communication: Health organizations' use of Twitter for health promotion and public engagement. *Journal of Health Communication, 21*(2), 188–198. doi:10.1080/10810730.2015.1058435 PMID:26716546

Park, H., Rodgers, S., & Stemmle, J. (2011). Health organizations' use of Facebook for health advertising and promotion. *Journal of Interactive Advertising, 12*(1), 62–77. doi:10.1080/15252019.2011.10722191

Parrott, S., Billings, A. C., Hakim, S. D., & Gentile, P. (2020). From# endthestigma to# realman: Stigma-challenging social media responses to NBA players' mental health disclosures. *Communication Reports, 33*(3), 148–160. doi:10.1080/08934215.2020.1811365

Pianese, T., & Belfiore, P. (2021). Exploring the Social Networks' Use in the Health-Care Industry: A Multi-Level Analysis. *International Journal of Environmental Research and Public Health, 18*(14), 1–14. doi:10.3390/ijerph18147295 PMID:34299746

Pickle, K., Quinn, S. C., & Brown, J. D. (2002). HIV/AIDS coverage in black newspapers, 1991-1996: Implications for health communication and health education. *Journal of Health Communication, 7*(5), 427–444. doi:10.1080/10810730290001792 PMID:12455762

Pınarbaşı, G. (2023). TikTok'ta bir alt kültür örneği olarak cadılık kültürü ve büyü uygulamaları: Witch-Tok örneği. *Medya ve Kültür, 3*(1), 90–128.

Porat, T., Nyrup, R., Calvo, R. A., Paudyal, P., & Ford, E. (2020). Public Health and Risk Communication During COVID-19—Enhancing Psychological Needs to Promote Sustainable Behavior Change. *Frontiers in Public Health, 8*(573397), 1–15. doi:10.3389/fpubh.2020.573397 PMID:33194973

Pulido, C. M., Villarejo-Carballido, B., Redondo-Sama, G., & Gómez, A. (2020). COVID-19 infodemic: More retweets for science-based information on coronavirus than for false information. *International Sociology*, *35*(4), 377–392. doi:10.1177/0268580920914755

Rando-Cueto, D., de las Heras-Pedrosa, C., & Paniagua-Rojano, F. J. (2023). Health communication strategies via TikTok for the prevention of eating disorders. *Systems*, *11*(6), 274. doi:10.3390ystems11060274

Rastegar-Mojarad, M., Ye, Z., Wall, D., Murali, N., & Lin, S. (2015). Collecting and Analyzing Patient Experiences of Health Care From Social Media. *JMIR Research Protocols*, *4*(3), 1–14. doi:10.2196/resprot.3433 PMID:26137885

Roth, R., Ajithkumar, P., Natarajan, G., Achuthan, K., Moon, P., Zinzow, H., & Madathil, K. C. (2021). A study of adolescents and young adults' TikTok challenge participation in South India. *Human Factors in Healthcare*, *1*, 100005. doi:10.1016/j.hfh.2022.100005

Rufai, S. R., & Bunce, C. (2020). World leaders' usage of Twitter in response to the COVID-19 pandemic: A content analysis. *Journal of Public Health (Oxford, England)*, *42*(3), 510–516. doi:10.1093/pubmed/fdaa049 PMID:32309854

Sampogna, G., Bakolis, I., Evans-Lacko, S., Robinson, E., Thornicroft, G., & Henderson, C. (2017). The impact of social marketing campaigns on reducing mental health stigma: Results from the 2009–2014 Time to Change programme. *European Psychiatry*, *40*, 116–122. doi:10.1016/j.eurpsy.2016.08.008 PMID:27997875

Schiavo, R. (2013). *Health communication: From theory to practice*. John Wiley & Sons.

Shengjie, J. (2021). TikTok analysis. *Journal of Frontiers of Society. Science and Technology*, *1*(1), 8–12.

Smailhodzic, E., Hooijsma, W., Boonstra, A., & Langley, D. J. (2016). Social media use in healthcare: A systematic review of effects on patients and on their relationship with healthcare professionals. *BMC Health Services Research*, *16*(1), 1–14. doi:10.118612913-016-1691-0 PMID:27562728

Suarez-Lledo, V., & Alvarez-Galvez, J. (2021). Prevalence of Health Misinformation on Social Media: Systematic Review. *Journal of Medical Internet Research*, *23*(1), 1–17. doi:10.2196/17187 PMID:33470931

Sun, S., Liu, Z., Zhai, Y., & Wang, F. (2022). COVID-19 vaccines on TikTok: A big-data analysis of entangled discourses. *International Journal of Environmental Research and Public Health*, *19*(20), 13287. doi:10.3390/ijerph192013287 PMID:36293868

Sutton, J., Renshaw, S. L., & Butts, C. T. (2020). The First 60 Days: American Public Health Agencies' Social Media Strategies in the Emerging COVID-19 Pandemic. *Health Security*, *18*(6), 454–460. doi:10.1089/hs.2020.0105 PMID:33047982

Tam, M. S. (2022). Türk TikTokerların içerik paylaşım pratikleri üzerine nicel bir araştırma. *Trt Akademi*, *7*(14), 182–211.

Tang, W., Ren, J., & Zhang, Y. (2018). Enabling trusted and privacy-preserving healthcare services in social media health networks. *IEEE Transactions on Multimedia*, *21*(3), 579–590. doi:10.1109/TMM.2018.2889934

Thackeray, R., Neiger, B. L., Burton, S. H., & Thackeray, C. R. (2013). Analysis of the purpose of state health departments' tweets: Information sharing, engagement, and action. *Journal of Medical Internet Research, 15*(11), 1–10. doi:10.2196/jmir.3002 PMID:24217361

Tsao, S. F., Chen, H., Tisseverasinghe, T., Yang, Y., Li, L., & Butt, Z. A. (2021). What social media told us in the time of COVID-19: A scoping review. *The Lancet. Digital Health*, *3*(3), 175–194. doi:10.1016/S2589-7500(20)30315-0 PMID:33518503

Uğurhan, Y. Z. C., & Yaşar, İ. H. (2021). TikTok'taki reklam ve sponsorlu içeriklerin satın alma niyeti üzerindeki rolü: Sosyo-demografik değişkenler özelinde bir inceleme. *Abant Sosyal Bilimler Dergisi*, *21*(2), 243–269.

Van Kampen, K., Laski, J., Herman, G., & Chan, T. M. (2022). Investigating COVID-19 vaccine communication and misinformation on TikTok: Cross-sectional study. *JMIR Infodemiology*, *2*(2), 1–9. doi:10.2196/38316 PMID:36338548

Ventola C. L. (2014). Social media and health care professionals: benefits, risks, and best practices. *P & T: A Peer-Reviewed Journal for Formulary Management, 39*(7), 491–520.

Wang, W., & Liu, Y. (2015). Communication message cues and opinions about people with depression: An investigation of discussion on Weibo. *Asian Journal of Communication*, *25*(1), 33–47. doi:10.1080/01292986.2014.989238

Wang, Y., Hao, H., & Platt, L. S. (2021). Examining risk and crisis communications of government agencies and stakeholders during early-stages of COVID-19 on Twitter. *Computers in Human Behavior*, *114*(106568), 1–13. doi:10.1016/j.chb.2020.106568 PMID:32982038

We Are Social & Meltwater. (2023). *Digital 2023 global overview report.* https://datareportal.com/reports/digital-2023-global-overview-report

We are Social and Houtsuite. (2023). *The Changing World of Digital in 2023.* https://wearesocial.com/uk/blog/2023/01/the-changing-world-of-digital-in-2023/

West, R., Raw, M., McNeill, A., Stead, L., Aveyard, P., Bitton, J., Stapleton, J., McRobbie, H., Pokhrel, S., Lester-George, A., & Borland, R. (2015). Health-care interventions to promote and assist tobacco cessation: A review of efficacy, effectiveness and affordability for use in national guideline development. *Addiction (Abingdon, England)*, *110*(9), 1388–1403. doi:10.1111/add.12998 PMID:26031929

Widodo, J., Qur'ani, H. B., & Putra, C. R. W. (2023). Abbreviations in the comment column of the Tribunnews account on TikTok. *Journal of Wood Science*, *2*(7), 946–956.

World Health Organization. (2017). *WHO strategic communications framework for effective communication.* https://www.who.int/docs/default-source/documents/communicating-for-health/communication-framework.pdf

Yeo, T. E. D., & Chu, T. H. (2017). Sharing "sex secrets" on Facebook: A content analysis of youth peer communication and advice exchange on social media about sexual health and intimate relations. *Journal of Health Communication*, *22*(9), 753–762. doi:10.1080/10810730.2017.1347217 PMID:28796578

Zhang, W., Mei, J., Song, W., Evans, R., & Xiang, Y. (2021). Why do citizens engage with the TikTok accounts of public hospitals in China? *SAGE Open, 11*(4), 1–11. doi:10.1177/21582440211061568

Zhou, P., You, J., & Wu, W. (2021). Research on health communication strategies of short video on popular medical science. In *2021 3rd International Conference on Economic Management and Cultural Industry (ICEMCI 2021)* (pp. 1060-1063). Atlantis Press. 10.2991/assehr.k.211209.172

Zhou, Q., & Jung, H. (2019). Learning and sharing creative skills with short videos: A case study of user behavior in TikTok and Bilibili. In *Int. Assoc. Soc. Des. Res. Conf* (No. 10, pp. 25-50). Academic Press.

Zhu, C., Xu, X., Zhang, W., Chen, J., & Evans, R. (2020). How health communication via TikTok makes a difference: A content analysis of TikTok accounts run by Chinese provincial health committees. *International Journal of Environmental Research and Public Health, 17*(1), 192. doi:10.3390/ijerph17010192 PMID:31892122

KEY TERMS AND DEFINITIONS

Health Communication: Health communication is a strategic approach aimed at informing the public about health, creating awareness, and taking action on health-related issues.

Organizational Messages on Social Media: Organizational messages on social media aim to provide information about the organization, create a community for the organization, and invite target audiences for action.

Social Media: Social media is an interactive online environment where people can interact and share content with each other on digital platforms.

Social Media Engagement: Social media engagement encompasses a wide range of interactions, including but not limited to liking, commenting on, saving, and sharing content.

Chapter 2
Communication Strategies Behind the Expressions of Dissent During the COVID-19 Pandemic

Nemanja Milošević
University of Deusto, Spain

ABSTRACT

The chapter presents some of the key communication strategies that can be observed in the expressions of dissent that increased considerably during the pandemic. The dissenting narratives—that is, the texts that speak against dominant institutions and the socio-political consensus by combining elements of conspiracy theories and populism—thrive for two major reasons. First, the narratives voice political sentiments that a significant portion of the population can identify with; they speak against injustices in a way that many would endorse and, simultaneously, include some of the rhetoric of new populist movements on the right. Second, the way dissent is expressed is consistent with the new ways of knowledge acquisition, as the claims are made with the appeal to the individual perspective, fear, and enjoyment. Such conclusions are based on the analysis of the vehement opposition to the World Economic Forum's "The Great Reset" agenda and the pandemic-related conspiracy theories of David Icke.

DISSENT IN CONTEXT

As the pandemic caused by the spread of the SARS-CoV-2 virus was reaching its height, the expressions of distrust became a growing concern for those who were trying to provide guidance to citizens and govern through the crisis. Various narratives about the hidden interests, evil intentions, and collusions of elite groups started to spread on the margins of the public sphere—that is, on an unregulated space that is the online media sphere. While some effort has been made to curb their reach, such narratives still continue to exert influence on its highly devoted audience. For the purpose of the current text, the set of claims of such kind will be denominated as "dissenting narratives." This term is used here since it

DOI: 10.4018/979-8-3693-0896-7.ch002

encompasses the ambiguous field that exists at the intersection of conspiracy theories and daily politics (in particular, that of the populist kind). As it will be seen in the later part of the chapter, the dissensus today is not only communicated with references to secret evil plots, and talking about it exclusively through the lens of conspiracy theory misses some of its other key features. In other words, the dissenting narratives, such as those popularized during the pandemic, rely on a pastiche of messages: including accusations of conspiracies, claims from daily politics, references from popular culture, and so on.

For decades, the claims akin to conspiracy theories were becoming integrated into the culture at large. We can observe this in the transition from previous epochs when conspiracy theory had been the tool of extremist groups at the fringes of society to the contemporary highly mediatized society where conspiratorial thinking becomes more widespread. For instance, the document fabricated in 1903 in Russia with the title *Protocols of the Learned Elders of Zion* was reprinted and distributed to advance anti-Semitic causes and incite violence across the West (Bronner, 2003, p. 1). In that context, the conspiracy theory functioned as an elaborate narrative reliant on printing technology that presented a group (the ethnic or religious Other) as an evil force that, in secret, works to aggravate societal ills. However, with the ascendance of the highly mediatized society of late modernity, the conspiracy theory changed in two key ways. First, it moved from extremist fringes into the mainstream culture; conspiracy became the subject of the entertainment industry, the notable examples being the TV series *The X Files* (Carter, 1993) and the bestselling novel *The Da Vinci Code* (Brown, 2003). With that, many started to see a conspiratorial narrative as a useful tool for assigning meaning to complex socio-economic developments through a "cognitive mapping" of a sort (Jameson, 1988). Second, the conspiracy theories now focus largely on internal enemies, instead of primarily depicting the evil Other. This is evident in the popularity of conspiracy theories in the United States that accuse their own government, the Central Intelligence Agency (CIA), the Federal Bureau of Investigation (FBI), or the "Deep State" of controlling society from the shadows and through undemocratic means (e.g., Horwitz, 2021; Webb, 2014; Williams, 2013). In short, as the narratives that detail a conspiracy became ubiquitous in public life—denoting a rise of the "conspiracy culture"(Knight, 2000)—, their field of action became more dispersed, representing the generalized anxiety over the present and future developments in society, politics, and economy.

Simultaneously, the media through which public communication happens has changed as well. The replacement of print as the dominant means of communication by television—which comes out of advances made in photography and telegraphy—has changed the way people evaluate the truthfulness of claims, as Neil Postman (1985) explains. The author points out that the new form of cognition shuns exposition and favors knowledge based on information that is brief, devoid of context, amusing, visual, gratifying, and fragmented in tone. By exposition, the author refers to "a sophisticated ability to think conceptually, deductively and sequentially; a high valuation of reason and order; an abhorrence of contradiction; a large capacity for detachment and objectivity; and a tolerance for delayed response" (Postman, 1985, p. 63). Furthermore, the development of digital media has brought to the fore affect as an important factor. The algorithms structured in a way that maximizes user engagement—and with it, profit—put at the forefront the content that incites strong emotional responses, such as outrage and indignation. As a result, regardless of what is actually happening in reality, online platforms are likely to show the user the most extreme and uncompromising attitudes, claims, and behavior of the perceived adversary (Tufekci, 2017, p. 271). In the context of public communication that is centered on affect and immediate emotional response, it is ever more common for judgments to be formed about the complex socio-political reality by recurring to the "gut instinct, affective response, and 'thin-slicing' (making a snap decision based on a tiny fraction of the evidence)" (Andrejevic, 2013, p. 17). With the pandemic, the above-discussed features of the contemporary public sphere revealed themselves in full light. Political paranoia and the affect-oriented online media, in the context of the health crisis, influenced to a large degree the real-world events and, with that, created the context where dissenting narratives gain prominence.

It is, therefore, of utmost importance to take the dissenting narratives seriously and understand how they explain the world and where their allure lies. This chapter asserts that the expression of dissent today relies on twofold communication strategies: first, the dissenting narratives obtain a high degree of legitimacy for the way they discuss political and socio-economic injustices; and second, dissenting narratives appeal to a new form of cognition that favors individual-oriented epistemology. This will be elaborated on in the rest of the chapter.

The Role of Politics

The way dissenting narratives defend the primacy of their unofficial version of socio-political events is, to a large degree, through the appeal to political sentiments. In that regard, the dissent responds to disillusionment with current political tendencies and the rise of new, anti-establishment fractions. In particular, this strategy can be observed in the way narratives in question explain political grievances that people may feel, whom they see as a political antagonist, and what vision of progress they propose.

The widespread frustration over how politics and the economy are structured comes from the broken promises of liberalism that for decades had defined the collective purpose of Western societies. Having successfully suppressed all other alternatives, the liberal notion of progress of the second half of the 20th century has established high standards of comfort, universal access to luxury goods, and life centered around enjoyment and leisure as ultimate social goals (Lasch, 1991, p. 52). This was particularly relevant for the first years of the Cold War when Western countries made promises of the infinite expansion of middle-class lifestyle and the end of scarcity to counter the threat from the ideological enemy in the East; those promises, which were predicated on the projections of stable high-rates of growth, had to be broken following the oil crisis of 1973 (Bartel, 2022). In the aftermath of the crisis, the governments had to impose some form of financial discipline on large parts of the population, with varying rates of success and with assurances that the sacrifice would get economies back on track; however, the effort never brought the past rates of growth. Moreover, nowadays, Western societies face either stagnation or reversal of once-positive trends concerning the purchasing power and standards of living of ordinary citizens (see Brill et al., 2017; Desilver, 2018; Fuller et al., 2020; Koranyi, 2023). As it became clear that "the lost paradise" would not be regained, the public spirit slipped into despair: nostalgic sentiment started prevailing in politics (expressed in Donald Trump's promise to "Make America Great Again") and young people started to feel less confident that their prospects will be as great as those of their parents (O'Connor, 2021).

The stagnating economy and the prospect of a long and steady decline in the standard of living of the masses are directly related to the frustration expressed in the dissenting narratives. What is more, there is a political deadlock that affects many Western countries: while the dominant socio-economic arrangements prove to be highly unpopular and enjoy low legitimacy, no clear alternative is envisioned by the ruling classes. This state of affairs allows the counter-elites to channel the popular frustration through their media outlets and achieve a sizeable following. Here, the counter-elites refer to the individuals "whose views and goals differ significantly from those of the ruling body of a country and who, by their abilities, by their wealth, and/or by their heritage, occupy positions of influence in a society"

(Sekeris, 2017, p. 152). As this chapter demonstrates, the narratives express dissent that resonates with people by including claims concerning popular grievances and frustrations, those that are responsible for the precarious collective conditions, and the need to return to some form of stability.

The Modes of Public Expression

The second important feature of dissenting narratives (specifically referring to their content and the effect they have on the audience) consists of contemporary modes of public expression—that is, the way claims are made in public and how their legitimacy is defended. As suggested previously, there are three modes of expression that are integral to the dissenting narratives: first is the individual perspective; second, the fear or anxiety; and third, enjoyment. The modes of expression that determine public discussion are largely influenced by the culture of late liberalism, so it is of great importance to examine its key features here and how they come to inform the main premise of the argument defended here.

The ambition of liberalism was not only to provide a subject with the freedom to choose and act independently—as this was already the feature of many pre-liberal societies to a greater or lesser degree—but to free an individual from the obligations to society to allow for the pursuit of the greatest self-interests (Deneen, 2018). Here, liberalism is discussed in the context of political philosophy that determines social and economic relations between people, and not as a concrete political party or fraction (as is the case in some countries). Rather, exactly the opposite is sustained here; the main tenets of liberalism are adopted by all political formations across Western countries, although with different emphasis on the left (i.e., on personal freedoms) and on the right (i.e., on economic freedoms).

As the individual becomes increasingly indifferent to society and history or even starts to perceive it as an arbitrary and despotic imposition, the consciousness that favors gratifications and abhors external constraints imposed by reality gets incentivized (see Lasch, 1979). This attitude originates from the promises made at the height of the capitalist mode of production, which asserted that the old cycles of rise and decline will yield to the system that guarantees infinite expansion (Lasch, 1991, p. 52). Having high expectations of reality—i.e., for it to always conform to one's unending desires—causes discomfort, as reality by definition does not care for what one might want from it and, moreover, imposes limits that go against the expectations of the contemporary subject. The inability for such ambitions to be fulfilled causes the narcissistic injury of the hypersensitive type, the one quite common today, which manifests in:

An antipathy towards claims of evidence and objective knowledge, a tendency to defensively retreat to the politics of identity and victimhood, and to relate to others not in a realistic way but as alternately idealised and denigrated aspects of the self. Such a mindset is characterised both by fundamentalism – states of emotional certainty and concretised thought – and extreme relativism. (Thurston, 2018, p. xv)

As a consequence, the excessive insistence on gratification that is constantly undermined can lead to excessive fear and anxiety expressed towards the external reality. Perceiving objective limitations and other people as obstacles that preclude the fulfillment of one's enjoyment leads to the adoption of a somber outlook on all facets of life: human relationships, society, politics, etc. On top of that, those who govern often send messages that reinforce the negative outlook on social matters. It can be heard frequently that things such as the economy, a human creation, are unresponsive to what humans can collectively do to change it and that citizens can only adapt to the undesirable conditions imposed on them by higher forces (i.e., find a way to sustain the strenuous conditions without too much damage).

This is, for instance, evident in the increasing popularity of the concept of "resilience," which is of the greatest importance for today's mainstream political discourse (see Fusaro, 2022).

Under the above-described circumstances, the public speech tailored to the new form of subjectivity receives a high degree of legitimacy; it justifies its claims by recurring to the authority of the singular point of view (e.g., claims about complex issues are defended with references to someone's experience, opinion, acts, etc.), using fear to describe reality (e.g., hidden interests or agenda for controlling people, the society and economy), and appealing to enjoyment (e.g., amusing language or nostalgic undertones). Both the political elements and the modes of expression, the key features of dissenting narratives, will be elaborated on in the continuation with the references to primary sources.

A NOTE ON METHODOLOGY

The argument presented in the continuation is based on a research project conducted for the sake of obtaining a PhD title[1]. The analysis concerns specifically the Anglo-Saxon cultural sphere and all sources were originally in English language. The research is centered around two case studies that were deemed illustrative of the expressions of vehement dissent during the pandemic. The first study examined the narratives that reject the World Economic Forum's (WEF from now on) "The Great Reset" agenda that proposed changes for the post-pandemic society. The agenda of the Forum in Davos, Switzerland caused a sizeable negative public reaction—as it is seen by some as proof of some sinister hidden plans and collusions—and has served for many as a vehicle to formulate disagreement with the official response to the health crisis. The sources include three electronic publications (Table 1) by influential figures in alternative online media (i.e., members of counter-elites) and the comments posted below YouTube videos (Table 2) of the WEF's channel that talk negatively about "The Great Reset." A total of 1,123 negative comments have been extracted for the analysis from the comment section of two selected YouTube videos (World Economic Forum, 2020a, 2020b) and when quoted in the text, they will be followed by—enclosed in brackets—the name of the author's YouTube account in italics and the date of the comment. The comments were retrieved on January 27, 2021.

The second study is based on the analysis of online media appearances of David Icke, a popular author of conspiracy theories from the United Kingdom. Icke is known since the early 1990s for many of his conspiracies that incorporate New Age elements, highly popular books, and the "Reptilian Thesis," a theory about the infiltration of non-humans into the global orders of power. At the offset of the pandemic, Icke appeared on several podcasts or video streaming platforms where he was interviewed about his ideas concerning the most important events at the moment. His most notable appearances (Table 3)

Table 1. Electronic publications selected for the analysis

Date	Authors	Title
October 2021	Dr. Joseph Mercola Ronnie Cummins	*The Truth About COVID-19: Exposing the Great Reset, Lockdowns, Vaccine Passports, and the New Normal*
January 2022	Glenn Beck Justin Haskins	*The Great Reset: Joe Biden and the Rise of Twenty-First-Century Fascism*
August 2022	Alex Jones	*The Great Reset: And the War for the World*

Table 2. YouTube videos selected for the analysis of comments

Date	Title	URL
03.06.2020.	The Great Reset I Launch session	https://www.youtube.com/watch?v=pfVdMWzKwjc
14.07.2020.	COVID-19: The Great Reset	https://www.youtube.com/watch?v=VHRkkeecg7c

Table 3. Videos selected for the analysis

Date	Platform	Interviewer	Title
18.03.2020.	LondonReal	Brian Rose	"The truth behind the coronavirus pandemic, COVID-19 lockdown & the economic crash"
06.04.2020.	LondonReal	Brian Rose	"The coronavirus conspiracy: How COVID-19 will seize your rights & destroy our economy"
25.11.2020.	InfoWars	Alex Jones	"David Icke exposes The Great Reset with Alex Jones"
02.02.2021.	TCN.Video	Simone Smith	"David Icke – The Awakening World Truth Summit"
06.03.2021.	TCN.Video	Simone Smith	"David Icke – The Awakening Part 2"
21.05.2021.	Oracle Films	N/A	"David Icke Talks To Oracle Films About The Protest Movement"
27.06.2021.	TCN.Video	Simone Smith	"David Icke – Full Interview I The Awakening 3"

were used as a source of the dissenting narrative made by the prominent figure in the area of conspiracist accusations, New Age teachings, and spirituality.

The qualitative analysis of the selected sources was based on iterative coding; that is, the combination of top-down and bottom-up imposition of codes (Bergman, 2010, p. 391). The main premise behind the research served to define two broad categories that all the textual and audio-visual units were placed in: the first concerns the claims of political nature (i.e., selecting claims that express political dissatisfactions, political antagonists, or an idea of progress), and second contains the claims that suggest a mode of expression that contribute to the text's popularity (i.e., references to the individual point of view, claims that incite fear, or appeal to enjoyment). Within these two categories, textual units were grouped according to common themes and the interpretation was conducted by contrasting and comparing them. In the next section, the main findings and conclusions from all studies will be presented, with particular attention given to the features that are common to all of the analyzed sources.

THE POLITICAL ELEMENTS

First, we will discuss here the extent to which the claims of a political nature contribute to their overall appeal and how they communicate the socio-political reality. As explained previously, the dissenting narratives communicate political dissatisfactions, antagonists, and ideas of progress in their specific way and integrate them into the more brazen claims of a conspiratorial nature. The text that follows will be structured according to these three features of dissenting narratives.

Dissatisfactions

Material Conditions

The narratives in question pay special attention to what working people experience regarding their everyday existence and how that experience may contribute to their political frustrations. The members of counter-elites express dissent in a way that makes them appear as a representative of the populace, fully aware of their concerns and the injustices they may suffer.

In that regard, the WEF, its associates, and the elites in general are accused of being the cause of the immiseration of people. For instance, the narratives explain that no one in power cares about "the best interests of Main Street America" (Beck & Haskins, 2022) and that it is their responsibility if there exist problems with "income inequality, human dignity, or degradation of the environment" (Jones, 2022). The mitigation measures employed during the pandemic are seen in the same light: as detrimental to the wellbeing of those who are at the bottom of the economic ladder. So, the lockdowns do not only have a negative effect on people's bodily and mental health, but can provoke a downturn regarding "the economy, poverty, hunger, homelessness, and unemployment," while specifically targeting "low-income groups, minority communities, small businesses, and children" (Cummins, 2021a).

Wealth inequality is talked about in a highly negative tone, with specific emphasis on the propensity of the wealthy to accrue even more resources than they already have. The YouTube comments, for instance, point out that "eight men have as much wealth as half of the world's population (more that [*sic*] 3.5 billion people)" (*Quaalude Charlie*, January 20, 2021) or that "the rich will remain rich and everyone else will have nothing" (*Bee Real*, November 29, 2020). This problem is again related to the pandemic, as it is argued elsewhere: "all covid has done has made rich people richer and poor people poorer and to pay for covid, the poorer but working people will pay through nose for the rest of their days" (*Possle*, December 29, 2020). The fact that people will soon own nothing is another common theme: for the wealthy to keep rising, they, with the help of the anti-pandemic policies, need to keep depriving regular people of what they have to keep them in a state of dependence. The article written by Danish politician Ida Auken (2016) in cooperation with the WEF and titled "Welcome to 2030: I Own Nothing, Have No Privacy and Life Has Never Been Better" is used as proof of such intentions.

David Icke (2020a), on his part, describes this socio-economic dynamic through the concept of the "Hunger Games Society," referring to the one percent of the richest who are helped by the complex police-military state in defending their interest through the destruction of small businesses and middle classes. The pandemic is, Icke claims, fabricated so that the state can implement all those measures with the consent of the people, who are scared into accepting the extraordinary measures:

You covertly create a problem. You use the unquestioning, pathetic mainstream media to tell the public the version of the problem you want them to believe, and you're looking at stage two—the reaction for fear. That's the currency of control, outrage, whatever the problem is. And either demand from the public that something must be done or at least an acceptance from the public that things need to change because of the problem. And at that point, those who created the problem got that reaction openly, and changes in society offer the solutions to the problems they have themselves covertly created… and those changes step by step take us further and further to that Hunger Games Society. (Icke, 2020a)

In short, the tendencies in the economy that cause widespread frustration and concern in the public are successfully integrated into the narratives that express dissent towards the authority in the context of the pandemic. The governing bodies are seen as a direct and close accomplice of the economic elites and the government policies, especially those enacted during the health crisis, are seen primarily as a tool for the further immiseration of the people. Dissenting narratives draw examples from real-life developments and events, as most of the people who consume such narratives indeed experience the downturn in their standard of living and hear everyday reports on the accumulation of wealth among the richest in the world; both tendencies, while being noticeable for a decade, aggravated significantly during the pandemic (see Beer, 2021; Myers, 2021; Neate, 2020; White, 2020). This sentiment further morphs into the type of claims that are to be discussed next, which are those concerning corruption.

Corruption

The matter of high levels of corruption among the political and economic class is another theme that is prominent in dissenting narratives. In that regard, the authors of the texts discuss politics as a field of action that can be disregarded completely, as those who constitute their orders are too "crooked" and "dishonest" to be trusted on any matter. The politicians who want to accumulate power and through backroom deals disregard democratic principles belong to all factions, that is, "on both the left and the right" (Beck & Haskins, 2022). The YouTube users reiterate this notion, as they suggest the "liquidation of 90% corrupt politicians" (*finding nemo*, June 6, 2020) and withdrawal from the electoral process—that is, "just not vote in politics full stop" (*Ollie Mansfield*, December 18, 2020). The whole field of politics is seen as illegitimate and, with that, any policy regarding climate or public health is, by association, to be distrusted. Claims against technocracy represent another variation of this sentiment. The fact that society is not governed by "elected politicians" but by bureaucrats, scientists, experts, engineers, and technocrats is evidence that the decisions are made are in accordance with the principles of the World Government and not the will of the people (Icke, 2020a, 2020b, 2021a). Such accusations are echoed by YouTube users as well, who warn that "global technocrats dilute a citizen's vote" (*Yvonne E.*, December 6, 2020).

These assumptions are further developed by addressing the relationship between the public and private sectors. For instance, public support for environmental and socially conscious enterprises is seen as a transfer of public funds to those who are already privileged and as a government's attempt to tip the scale in favor of large businesses and against the smaller ones. Beck & Haskins (2022) point out that no business, "especially a large multinational corporation," would refuse "free cash" should the government offer it to them. The measures concerning the pandemic are seen in the same light; for instance, Jones (2022) points out that according to the regulations in the United States, you were not allowed to shop "at the mom-and-pop retailers," but you could go to large stores or order things on Amazon. He argues further:

Whether you believe it was part of a plan, or just how things happened during the lockdowns, many small retailers went out of business, leading to record profits among the large retailers, just the sort of people who attend the yearly meetings of the World Economic Forum in Davos, Switzerland. By thinning the ranks of the competitors, the globalists can much more easily pick off the few remaining survivors. (Jones, 2022)

Here as well, the dissenting narratives rely on political and economic circumstances that predate the pandemic to voice the popular discontent and increase the forcefulness of the dissent. The political sentiment of anti-politics and anti-corruption plays a big role; that is, the narratives use the "politically ambivalent complaint" that everybody participating in politics belongs to the same corrupt group, that they are all the same, self-interested politicians, and similar (Hochuli et al., 2021, pp. 77–78). These claims reflect the growing tendencies in Western political systems among citizens to withdraw their interest in politics and lose faith in the corrective force that the governing bodies are supposed to have. This leads to a situation denominated as "ruling the void" by Pete Mair (2006). On top of this, the narratives make references to the fact that contrary to what neoliberalism promised, the governments do not distance themselves from the market, but intervene in favor of big players. The pandemic has not altered any of the existing deficiencies of the system but has only exacerbated the problem, making the dissatisfaction of the part of the public even greater, which is the development reflected in the dissenting narratives.

Globalism

The last kind of dissatisfaction that the narratives consistently underline is that related to the questions of global nature. Narratives in all instances assign negative meaning to all the words that refer to something "global." In that regard, global markets, supranational institutions, or migration are seen as detrimental aspects of contemporary society and the retreat in the nation-state is, therefore, a way forward.

This sentiment is particularly strong among YouTube users. For them, globalism is a project of the wealthy and privileged, who can use it to their own advantage and at the expense of ordinary people. So, the comments argue that globalism is "preached by the super-rich elites" (*dollarhugo37*, August 10, 2020), and that, should One World Government be established, "the 1% elites will thrive" (*Timothy Griess*, July 9, 2020), or that in a world with no nations, there will be "only the Globalists and the slaves" (*Nhiem Tran*, December 21, 2020).

Opposition to globalism is, as can be expected, celebrated. This is the case with Donald Trump, who is seen as one of "the biggest impediments to the globalist agenda," representing the country (i.e., the United States) with "a strong independent streak" (Beck & Haskins, 2022). Defending the independence of states is counterposed to the idea of the World Government—whose existence is taken as a fact by the authors of the dissenting narrative—, which imposes its will on the countries and "dictates to every community on the planet" (Icke, 2021a). As a corrective force and considering that the "international agencies are captured by technocrats and oligarchs," it is imperative that people act and organize in smaller communities (Cummins, 2021c).

The claims in the narratives confirm that "the struggle over borders" (de Wilde et al., 2019) is one of the most defining cleavages of contemporary Western society. In other words, the attitude one has concerning the question of nationalism or cosmopolitanism gets the central position in his or her political identity. This tendency, on the rise for a decade already, can be seen in the campaign for exiting the European Union held in the United Kingdom in 2016 that aimed to deliver sovereignty back to the nation-state; moreover, the type of claims discussed here are reflected in some contemporary populist movements and the increased Euroscepticism (Henley, 2020). By framing the matters of the pandemic and the mitigation measures in the international context, the dissenting narratives intend to discredit the relevant authorities by assigning to them the label of "globalism" and, therefore, adhere to that sentiment the resentment the "losers from globalization" (Guilluy, 2019, p. 51) feel for the international flow of capital and global corporations. Additionally, they are able to present the pandemic-related policies as an imposition from the outside of the national context.

Antagonists

When it comes to those individuals or entities that the narrative single out as obstacles on the road to a better society, the WEF and all actors within the related context receive the most attention. They are all referred to collectively as "elites" who are faulty in their character (greedy, selfish) or pathological sense (narcissists, sociopaths). Other than as "elites," the amalgam of antagonists is described with terms such as "globalists," "ruling class elites," "titans," "bourgeoisie," "transnational businesspeople," the ones in "corporate suites," and similar.

The agent that is the central political antagonist, the Forum in Davos, is scrutinized for the undemocratic character of their "Great Reset" agenda, primarily because they envision changes to the post-pandemic society that have not been subjected to the popular vote. Along those lines, the YouTube comments ask "who voted this people [*sic*] to decide for our lives & our future" (*The Defector*, August 23, 2020) or who chose WEF's members to be "managers of the world" (*Adson de Oliveira*, June 4, 2020). Besides the discourse concerning the "unelected elites," the members of the WEF and the extremely wealthy in general are accused of causing the same problems they want to fix now. For instance, YouTube users accuse the WEF's members of being "hypocrites" for wanting to solve global warming or immiseration that they have contributed to a large degree. Large corporations are seen in the same light: as entities that seek to take over the baton from the governments and rule without limitations. On top of that, a number of comments talk negatively about the wealthy by referring to them as "one percent"—a term popularized during the 2011 protest Occupy Wallstreet protest (Sharlet, 2011; Weinstein, 2011). The comments, for instance, warn the wealthy: "The 99% will hunt you down, that will be the great reset" (*Killer Ice Lollies*, November 19, 2020) Another comment suggests the following: "Let's start with the 1% giving up all their wealth and distribute it amongst the 99%, the we'll see how we want to go ahead. Oh??? The Great Reset isn't meant for the 1%??? What a surprise!!!!" (*shadowrunner101*, December 4, 2020).

Accordingly, those related to the wealthy "globalists" in any way are guilty by association. In the context of the pandemic, the experts are evaluated according to such criteria. For instance, David Icke (2020a, 2020b) questions the World Health Organization (WHO) and its general director Tedros Adhanom for receiving donations from Bill Gates and accuses the organization of being founded by the Rockefellers and Rothschilds. The same author further distrusts The Imperial College London, the home institution of a prominent pro-lockdown epidemiologist Neil Ferguson, because it receives money from the Bill and Melinda Gates Foundation (Icke, 2020b). Those who, on the contrary, speak out and "go rogue" against their institutions and organized science are celebrated as rebels who risk everything to tell the truth to the public. In this case, the prominent figures during the pandemic are, through their links with the wider pool of antagonists, accused of lacking legitimacy; with that, the dissenting narratives aim "to draw a rhetorical boundary between science and some less authoritative residual non-science" according to the clearly established set of attributes (Gieryn, 1999, pp. 4–5), which in this case is the association with "globalist elites."

Ideas of Progress

The dissenting narratives do not shy away from calls to revolutions, popular resistance, or uprisings. The popular authors emphasize the importance of coming together across religious, ethnic, and political lines to fight "back against this darkness" (Jones, 2022) and remove "much of the power that the ruling class has over your life and the lives of your family members" (Beck & Haskins, 2022). This is not only reiterated in the YouTube comments—where people acknowledge that the elites' agenda for change is an attempt to quench the populist uprising—but is even elevated to calls for a more violent revolt, as one user suggests "start building guillotines and start using them on the central bankers" (*Bart Weijs*, September 10, 2020). The YouTube comments repeatedly remind the WEF of the power of the people, explaining that while elites may have money and political power, the citizens have the advantage of being able to come together in very large numbers. The users make the following remarks: "Remember people of the world, there are multi-billions more of us then them" (*P. F.K.*, September 3, 2020); "You are the 1% of the humanity and we are the rest, we won't have the money but we have the heart, the light and the power to move forward without you! You are evils!!!" (*Gladys Morales*, July 13, 2020).

Here, we should underline the role that new digital platforms have in facilitating the shared desire for popular unity and an uprising. The comment section on YouTube allows users to do two things: first, address the author of the video and voice their complaint or satisfaction with what is being said (with the implicit belief that the authors will read the comment), and second, address other users, either confirming or contradicting their opinion. In the comment section of WEF's YouTube videos, the users not only address the Forum in Davos directly with their accusations and serious charges but also use the opportunity to express unity and agreement with other users, suggesting some kind of popular awakening. This tendency, as a consequence, elevates the comment section to a public forum with greater implications. The like-dislike ratio (1,099 upvotes to 4,896 downvotes for the first WEF's video and 4,247 upvotes to 24,793 downvotes for the second) is taken as proof that should "The Great Reset" agenda be presented for democratic scrutiny, it would have little support. For instance, comments claim: "Half as many likes as dislikes and this comment section says it all. How long till they shut down comments as well" (*Ralphjons*, June 18, 2020). Another points out: "You guys are playing a joke right? You can see by the comments left on this and the amount of thumbs down compared to thumbs up, that humanity is not dumb" (*Tristina*, June 23, 2020). With that, the comments also express sentiments of hope and optimism at seeing so many people agreeing with them, which shows that people are finally waking up. See, for reference, the following comments that express such an idea: "These comments give me hope. Not all are asleep!" (*Kello hey*, January 11, 2021); "These comments give me hope, glad to see so many awake people" (*koolruningz*, December 16, 2020); "Amazing and reassuring that so many comments reflect complete distrust in these globalists" (*Bill Annau*, June 13, 2020). In the observed examples, the ability to post comments or leave any kind of feedback on a digital platform such as YouTube gives an impression of political participation (upvotes and downvotes) and mobilization (the feeling of unity with like-minded users).

The plan for what is to come after the insurgency is less ambitious. The narratives express a desire for some kind of normalcy and stability in the socio-economic affairs and everyday life. For instance, the authors discuss some basic elements of quality of life; this includes "meaningful, socially and environmentally responsible work and a decent standard of living for all who are willing to work" or "natural and integrative health practices" (Cummins, 2021c). Other than that, the narratives advocate for the retreat from globalization. The authors assert that people should "work within [their] communities" (Cummins, 2021c) since, before relying on large corporations and organizations, people used to depend on "their neighbors, local businesses, and churches" for economic and social activities (Beck & Haskins, 2022). The YouTube users remind people to "remember the 'outsourcing' they have done that crippled our economy" (*Patty Dillard*, November 26, 2020) and underline the desire to live "in a sovereign nation with it's [*sic*] own government and laws and rights and freedoms" (*Is402831*, June 19, 2020). The dominant idea of progress is not that of some new form of social formation, but a desire to decelerate and pull back into some imaginings of the solidarity and high standard of living of previous decades. Here, the dissenting narratives show a semblance of many populist movements that express a desire for a renewed local identity, changes to immigration laws, and withdrawal from global to nation-state capitalism. For years already, the attitudes towards the question of borders and national sovereignty that separates high-mobile and cosmopolitan professionals from the population with allegiance to local culture became "integrated into left-right semantics" (Strijbis et al., 2019, p. 64) and thus started defining political cleavages across Western states. At the same time, the nostalgic sentiment started pervading the political discourse through promises of reversing history and retreating into some erstwhile form of economic stability and national glory—as expressed in the famous slogan "Make America Great Again" used in the Donald Trump's political campaign. Therefore, while the dissenting narratives express many dissatisfactions with the current system, they do not conceive of some new form of socio-economic relations that would replace the current one; what they actually serve to do is to primarily channel the popular ire and frustration through a narrative that provides "cognitive mapping" (Jameson, 1988) for what people dislike about the system, focusing specifically on the decrease in the standard of living, high levels of corruption, monopolies, increasing inequalities, etc. In other words, the potential of said narratives to act as a political manifesto and incite some kind of a movement is very limited; they serve as a text to be consumed, rather than acted upon.

MODES OF EXPRESSIONS

The dissenting narratives rely on various kinds of discursive tools to make their point and reach the widest possible audience. The dissenting claims are presented and defended in a specific way that reveals new forms of knowledge acquisition that are characteristic of the contemporary media-centered society. The first one that we will discuss here is the reference to the individual as a way of inquiring about reality.

The Importance of the Individual

The dissenting narratives often evoke one's individual experience or perception to defend a claim. This is particularly common to the conspiracy theories in the context of the New Age traditions, such as those defended by David Icke. He discusses the importance of one's perception in shaping his or her own reality, which is under constant threat from the manipulation from above—from the Death Cult that wants to "control the perception and therefore dictate behavior" (Icke, 2021b). It is, according to Icke, important to exercise skepticism to everything that is told to us by the media or those in power, in order to escape "the prison" they want to put us into (Icke, 2020b). On top of that, Icke refers to personal examples that concern his and his children's experience with Covid-19 and early-childhood vaccines to make broad and authoritative claims about those two topics—that is, that he and his son had the COVID-19 virus before it emerged in China and that the fact that his children were not vaccinated did not harm them in any way (Icke, 2020a). These examples imply that even if we take his claims as a matter of fact, they should be enough evidence for a convincing argument on this issue. Such a defense of claim corresponds with the attempts of novels spiritual traditions in the West to integrate the value of individualism and authentic self and defend them from the "alienating institutions" (Aupers & Houtman, 2010, p. 15). This leads to what Liesteb van Zoonen (2012) calls "I-pistemology," a tendency to make claims to truth with reference to personal experiences and observations, in light of the growing distrust towards official knowledge and experts.

The dissenting narratives also depict the world in their specific way through the insistence on individual agency. What is declared as an undesirable development in socio-economic terms is described through someone's personal faults. For instance, the inequality, corruption, or creation of monopolies are explained with references to the personal characteristics of those involved in such acts—e.g., they are greedy, hypocritical, power-hungry, irresponsible, or self-centered—or with references to some personal pathology—narcissism, psychopathology, or sociopathology. YouTube users resort often to this kind of explanation; for instance, one user addresses the WEF with the following words: "You are evil, hypocritical, dishonest, narcissistic, power-hungry demons" (*Lori Gustin*, November 18, 2020). Others assert that "only psychopaths put themselves above others" (*Sir. Burbonburg*, December 16, 2020) and that people "need to remove all the power hungry, soul-less, corrupt and psychotic assholes" (*The Organic Matrix*, June 6, 2020). This attitude towards society implies that should these individuals with their faults be ousted from positions of power and replaced by more noble and virtuous ones, all collective ills would be remedied. In other words, the complex structure is conveniently reduced to impulses and inner passions; it is the reduction of globalized capitalism "into personal sin, into a private psychological propensity" and thus represents the highest form of ideology (Žižek, 2012). In the time in history when society is seen only as a congregation of individuals, the reality is talked about and examined through their individual units that are believed to be the determining factor in how things function on a larger scale. This feature of today's pattern of communication is successfully incorporated into the expressions of dissent.

The Use of Fear

The Conspiracy

As is to be expected, the dissenting narratives integrate claims that are meant to incite fear and anxiety toward the external reality. In doing that, the narratives reinforce the enclosure into the self and suspicion towards everything that is outside of it. Among other things, the authors discussed here incorporate elements of conspiracy theories into their discursive repertoire.

The first element is the construction of the "maleficent authority"—i.e., the group of diverse actors who in a coordinated way act for the benefit of some plan. This can include reference to "a shadowy international network of thousands of virologists, gene engineers, military scientists, and biotech entrepreneurs" (Cummins, 2021b), "a powerful network of global elites" (Cummins, 2021c), or "a conference of powerful people" (Beck & Haskins, 2022). David Icke talks about "The Death Cult" as a network that is "directed by the spider at the center" who pulls the strings and controls everyone and encompasses a number of secret and semi-secret societies (Icke, 2020c). We can only see the outer part of the collusion, those agencies that act coordinately—for instance, in the censorship accorded between the WHO, Facebook, Google, YouTube, and Twitter—, but we do not always see those for whose benefit those entities act. That authority behind authority, "the rider," "the permanent government," "the shadows," is hidden in secret wherefrom it pulls the strings.

The group of actors wants the establish a new socio-political order; that is their primary goal. Across all analyzed texts, this new order is described either as fascism, socialism, totalitarianism, or feudalism. Often, two systems that are mutually incompatible or opposing in their central premises are put together and labeled "the New World Order." For instance, the narratives claim that the elites want to establish the combination of socialism and capitalism; they discuss "a system that combines the worst of communism with the worst of crony capitalism, a marriage made in hell, quite literally" (*Em Graham*, June 9, 2020) and speculate that WEF wants to "promote worldwide communism by blending it with capitalism. kill small businesses, torn apart families and make themselves as 'god'!" (*Federal POST TV*, December 29, 2020). The narratives not only apply these labels inconsistently but also freely; the meaning of these labels is stretched and, eventually, they are evoked in the narratives to denounce any tendency the authors do not appreciate in contemporary capitalism. By externalizing the features of the current system to some distant historical regimes, they discursively remove the responsibility of contemporary capitalism (see Žižek, 1996, p. 96).

Manipulation and Lies

Next, the narratives develop a high degree of skepticism towards all representations. In general, everything that is said or presented in public can be some sort of manipulation of the medium and, in the most extreme cases, the reality itself can be deceitful. This also includes what those in power do. That is, even when the elites do something that may appear beneficial for society, in reality, something else is hidden behind it. For instance, the pandemic-related measures are paving "the way for a surveillance state," the plan to bring people closer to nature serves to "usher in a tech-driven dystopia," and the policies concerning "sustainability, social justice, food justice, climate-smart agriculture, and poverty reduction" are actually used to eliminate "personal liberty" (Mercola, 2021a). The comments on YouTube reiterate this point: "This minority of people is very corrupt and typically hide their true intentions. No altruism exists in the mind of the power hungry [...]" (*Bob*, January 7, 2021). This results in the distrust and direct dismissal of whatever the WEF proposes, as one user explains: "We are not buying what you are selling" (*the Sage & the Butterfly*, June 8, 2020).

David Icke points out the importance of the media in the manipulation. He claims that the popular perception of the pandemic as a highly dangerous event stems from the media that repeats the lie as many times as necessary for it to become truth, which he compares to the tactics employed by the Nazis (Icke, 2021a). Furthermore, the media uses the fear of death, a strong emotion in humans, to direct the behavior of the masses (Icke, 2020c). The manipulation does not only happen through the information but also via the direct connection to the brain; once the human brain gets connected directly to the artificial intelligence—around the year 2030—those who control AI "will be connecting and driving the perceptions of humanity" (Icke, 2020a). To counter the manipulation, people should break out of the deception, and realize that "there is no freakin' virus, and it's a total scam," which should help them stop acquiescing to those in power (Icke, 2020b).

The insistence on the manipulative nature of the representation that the dissenting narrative exhibits points to the importance that reflexivity has for contemporary subjectivity. As Sherry Turkle (1995, p. 18) argues, as technological development progressively allowed the user to acquaint him or herself with the inner workings of the medium—for instance, anyone can now learn how to edit an image—, the skepticism towards what is being presented publicly grew significantly. The awareness that the media representation is manufactured comes with the belief that behind what is visible on the surface there is some real and unquestionable truth that people can uncover with careful examination (Andrejevic, 2013, p. 14). The population that became technologically conscious integrated its skepticism into their daily life, which we here see in its communication practices concerning the expressions of dissensus.

Dangers

Finally, the narratives incorporate many warnings about dangers that are either present already or will appear soon. The first danger appears in the form of toxic substances that come in contact with human biology; this concerns issues like chemical agriculture, genetically modified food, or pharmaceutical medicine and vaccines. This is the issue that Mercola and Cummins (2021) put a particularly strong emphasis on, signaling out big conglomerates—with references to Big Food, Big Pharma, and Big Ag—that are causing widespread harm for profit. The two authors, in their publication, critique "The Great Reset" agenda from the point of view of alternative and non-institutional medicinal practices.

However, much bigger space is given to the projected dangers of technological developments. What is presented to us as benevolent or even useful tools (e.g., technology that helps track Covid-19 infections) are, actually, large threats. If the development of technology continues, the powerful will have means that will allow them total control of populations. That is the danger the authors see in "digital money," the one that is not in physical form, but exists as a number on a computer, that can be seized or manipulated for some purpose; "banks, financial institutions, and governments would be able to track and control nearly every transaction in the world" (Beck & Haskins, 2022) and we will see the creation of the "digital gulag" (Icke, 2020c). The danger of biometrical tracing is another issue that dissenting narratives underline. The authors discuss the creation of the "digital World ID," "Social Credit Score system," or the "global ID system." The digital proof of vaccination widely used during the pandemic is, according to Mercola (Mercola, 2021b), a "cog in this Great Reset plan." The whole thing will end with the direct technological connection between human biology and the financial system (Cummins, 2021c). Another concern over the merging of biology and technology appears in the form of accusations that microchips are placed in liquids that enter human bodies. In that regard, the comments on YouTube make the following claims: "No I don't want a chip, no I don't want my brain mined, no I do not want a vaccine, no I do not want my entire life controlled by AI" (*Mary Vogt*, June 7, 2020)"; "Cutting trees down everywhere making way for 5g.and nano chip. To control us. Corona HOAX is the excuse for all of this" (*Emily Ryder*, June 13, 2020).

The dissenting narratives voice uncertainty felt due to the rapid development of technology and production and its globalized character. Such developments that are phenomenologically foreign to people's everyday experience cause anxiety and are reflected in accusations of deliberate malintent. We can trace such sentiments to previous epochs when new forms of technology brought widespread fear that their introduction would lead to a rapid increase in unemployment (see Spiezia & Vivarelli, 2002, p. 101). However, it is also important to address the context of the increasing surveillance in contemporary Western societies, where the development of new technologies has been indeed used often to develop ways that various entities use to overreach into people's lives (Zuboff, 2019). Accelerated implementation of various digital mechanisms during the pandemic only incites more concerns and those concerns become an integral part of the expressions of dissent.

Enjoyment

The appeal to enjoyment in the narratives comes in two forms: in the attempts to present claims in an entertaining way, and second, to present claims that incite a specific sentiment. First, the authors integrate humor into their political and social commentary; for instance, to emphasize the type of wealthy and greedy personalities that support "The Great Reset" agenda—including the heads of Microsoft and Mastercard—, Beck and Haskins (2022) make a following comment: "I think even the Monopoly guy and Scrooge McDuck threw in their support for the plan, but my research staff is still waiting for confirmation from McDuck's communications director." Furthermore, the two authors say that inconsistencies between what is said and done by those in power concerning climate change are "enough to drive anyone mad—even Swedish teen, apparently," which is an implicit remark directed at the young activist Greta Thunberg. The narratives, furthermore, use numerous references to popular culture, films, and famous novels, especially those that depict a dystopian society. Those references include George Orwell's *Nineteen Eighty-Four* (1949), Aldous Huxley's *Brave New World* (1932), William Golding's *Lord of the Flies* (1954), films *The Hunger Games* (Ross, 2012), *The Matrix* (Wachowski & Wachowski, 1999), *The Giver* (Lowry, 1993), and similar. The leaders of the WEF are compared with the villains from famous film series that follow James Bond and Austen Powers, as well as Dr. Strangelove from the homonymous film (Kubrick, 1964).

Finally, the narratives make claims that incite the sentiment of the "lost paradise," of longing for some previous state of stability and solidarity. This is evident in the depiction of the past decades of the United States, always seen in a better light when compared to how things stand now. For instance, the claim is made that the vision of the forefathers, "who bled on fields, deserts, beaches, and mountains—both at home and in faraway lands—trying to guarantee the continued existence of this grand experiment in human freedom," is now abandoned (Beck & Haskins, 2022). The past is talked about with romantic undertones:

The America we remember, the America of carefree summers, Saturday night trips to movie theaters, warm family holiday gatherings, and mom-and-pop restaurants, has been replaced with a culture driven by suspicion, rampant fear, and ideological and political tribalism and dominated by massive, multinational corporations. (Beck & Haskins, 2022)

Those involved in the production of dissenting narratives for wide consumption are engaged in affective labor, which refers to the increasingly common commercial activity centered around "the production and manipulation of affect" (Hardt, 1999, pp. 97–98); that is, the authors offer the content with a specific objective to incite intense emotions in their audience. Glenn Beck is a television personality known for his performances tailored to be an affective spectacle, providing a "pastiche of reason" and the combination of tearful performances, skepticism, sarcasm, a sense of victimhood, distress, populist identity (i.e., presenting himself as one of the people), and similar (Andrejevic, 2013, pp. 123–129). Dissenting narratives function as a product of popular culture and the entertainment industry, even if they speak in opposition to power. The amusing elements of narrative, additionally, serve as a counterbalance to those claims of a strictly political nature that are more serious in tone.

CONCLUDING REMARKS

As shown here, the diverse nature of communication strategies (Table 4) of dissenting narratives is an essential part of their appeal and popularity. Their power comes from the reference to the current political events and developments, in which unfulfilled expectations of progress lead to disillusionment and social dislocation. The expressions of dissent are not politically neutral. They incorporate claims concerning political dissatisfactions that many would agree upon, including the WEF itself; for instance, "The Great Reset" agenda discusses the need to address issues such as wealth inequality or unemployment (see Schwab & Malleret, 2020). In other instances, the narratives position themselves clearly with the growing right-leaning populist sentiment, through their negative attitude towards all economic and political activities that are international or global in nature and their rejection of politics as such under the accusations of corruption. Such an approach assures that the messages can reach the widest possible audience without alienating too much any of its segments, as it offers something for people with different degrees of political engagement. The unifying factor—and quite uncompromisingly so—in all political claims is, however, the negative stance towards mainstream politics and the centers of power.

Additionally, the dissenting narratives reveal the importance of the changes that took place concerning literacy; that is, how people acquire knowledge and the strategies they use to evaluate the veracity of claims. While the argument presented in this chapter is based on the analysis of a limited scope—that is, of narratives of a very particular nature—, a clear conclusion can be drawn concerning the role of the media and culture in contemporary political communication. Both the development of the audio-visual entertainment industry and digital media have influenced to a large degree how people engage with texts; the importance of subjective position, fear-inducing claims, and the appeal to enjoyment are becoming increasingly important. The amusement and the emotion-stimulating rhetoric, already discussed by Neil Postman (1985) in relation to television, are clearly a key mechanism in the contemporary expressions of dissent. The advancement of digital platforms that facilitate global communication played a significant role in the growing rate of consumption of dissenting narratives. For instance, electronic books through which counter-elites elaborate on their ideas are sold through online global retailers and can bypass the strict policies that physical bookstores might enforce. Additionally, it is noticeable that the ability of users to respond to content directly on digital platforms (e.g., the YouTube comment section) allows for a generation of a sense of community around the feeling of dissatisfaction and dissent. Both the political sentiments with which an important portion of the population identifies and the novel modes of expression related to the evolution of new media have been exerting their influence over previous decades; however, the pandemic has accelerated the development of these two factors, and this, as a consequence, increased popularity of dissenting narratives at a critical moment.

Table 4. The summary of political claims and modes of expressions found in dissenting narratives

Political Claims	
Dissatisfactions	The frustration over the diminished material conditions The corruption and revolving-door practices. The monopolies. Political and economic activities that are global.
Antagonists	"Globalists" and all those dependent on and relate to them.
Ideas of Progress	Resistance that will bring back the past levels of comfort and stability.

REFERENCES

Andrejevic, M. (2013). *Infoglut: How too much information is changing the way we think and know*. Routledge. doi:10.4324/9780203075319

Auken, I. (2016, November 10). Welcome To 2030: I Own Nothing, Have No Privacy And Life Has Never Been Better. *Forbes*. https://www.forbes.com/sites/worldeconomicforum/2016/11/10/shopping-i-cant-really-remember-what-that-is-or-how-differently-well-live-in-2030/

Aupers, S., & Houtman, D. (2010). Religions of Modernity: Relocating the Sacred to the Self and the Digital. In S. Aupers & D. Houtman (Eds.), *Religions of modernity: Relocating the sacred to the self and the digital* (pp. 1–30). Brill. doi:10.1163/ej.9789004184510.i-273

Bartel, F. (2022). *The Triumph of Broken Promises: The End of the Cold War and the Rise of Neoliberalism*. Harvard University Press.

Beck, G., & Haskins, J. (2022). *The great reset: Joe Biden and the rise of 21st century fascism*. Forefront Books; Mercury Ink.

Beer, T. (2021, January 26). Report: American Billionaires Have Added More Than $1 Trillion In Wealth During Pandemic. *Forbes*. https://www.forbes.com/sites/tommybeer/2021/01/26/report-american-billionaires-have-added-more-than-1-trillion-in-wealth-during-pandemic/

Bergman, M. M. (2010). Hermeneutic Content Analysis: Textual and Audiovisual Analyses within a Mixed Methods Framework. In A. Tashakkori & C. Teddlie (Eds.), *SAGE Handbook of Mixed Methods in Social & Behavioral Research* (pp. 379–396). SAGE Publications. doi:10.4135/9781506335193.n16

Brill, M., Holman, C., Morris, C., Raichoudhary, R., & Yosif, N. (2017). Understanding the Labor Productivity and Compensation Gap. *U.S. Bureau of Labor Statistics, 6*(6). https://ecommons.cornell.edu/handle/1813/77533

Bronner, S. E. (2003). *A Rumor about the Jews: Antisemitism, Conspiracy, and the Protocols of Zion*. Oxford University Press.

Brown, D. (2003). *The Da Vinci code*. Doubleday.

Carter, C. (Director). (1993, September 10). *The X Files* [Crime, Drama, Mystery]. Ten Thirteen Productions, 20th Century Fox Television.

Cummins, R. (2021a). Exploiting Fear to Lock Down Freedom. In J. Mercola & R. Cummins (Eds.), *The Truth About COVID-19: Exposing The Great Reset, Lockdowns, Vaccine Passports, and the New Normal*. Chalsea Green Publishing.

Cummins, R. (2021b). How the Pandemic Plans Unfolded. In J. Mercola & R. Cummins (Eds.), *The Truth About COVID-19: Exposing The Great Reset, Lockdowns, Vaccine Passports, and the New Normal*. Chalsea Green Publishing.

Cummins, R. (2021c). Take Back Control. In J. Mercola & R. Cummins (Eds.), *The Truth About COVID-19: Exposing The Great Reset, Lockdowns, Vaccine Passports, and the New Normal*. Chalsea Green Publishing.

de Wilde, P., Koopmans, R., Merkel, W., Strijbis, O., & Zürn, M. (Eds.). (2019). *The Struggle Over Borders: Cosmopolitanism and Communitarianism*. Cambridge University Press. doi:10.1017/9781108652698

Deneen, P. J. (2018). *Why liberalism failed*. Yale University Press. doi:10.12987/yale/9780300223446.001.0001

Desilver, D. (2018, August 7). *For most U.S. workers, real wages have barely budged in decades*. Pew Research Center. https://www.pewresearch.org/short-reads/2018/08/07/for-most-us-workers-real-wages-have-barely-budged-for-decades/

Fuller, G. W., Johnston, A., & Regan, A. (2020). Housing prices and wealth inequality in Western Europe. *West European Politics*, *43*(2), 297–320. doi:10.1080/01402382.2018.1561054

Fusaro, D. (2022). *Odio la resilienza: Contro la mistica della sopportazione*. Rizzoli.

Gieryn, T. F. (1999). *Cultural boundaries of science: Credibility on the line*. University of Chicago Press.

Golding, W. (1954). *Lord of the flies*. Faber and Faber.

Guilluy, C. (2019). *Twilight of the elites: Prosperity, the periphery, and the future of France* (M. DeBevoise, Trans.). Yale University Press.

Hardt, M. (1999). Affective Labor. *Boundary 2*, *26*(2), 89–100.

Henley, J. (2020, March 2). Support for Eurosceptic parties doubles in two decades across EU. *The Guardian*. https://www.theguardian.com/world/2020/mar/02/support-for-eurosceptic-parties-doubles-two-decades-across-eu

Hochuli, A., Hoare, G., & Cunliffe, P. (2021). *The End of the End of History: Politics in the Twenty-First Century*. Zero Books.

Horwitz, R. B. (2021). Trump and the "deep state.". *Policy Studies*, *42*(5–6), 473–490. doi:10.1080/01442872.2021.1953460

Huxley, A. (1932). *Brave New World*. Chatto & Windus.

Icke, D. (2020a, March 18). *The truth behind the coronavirus pandemic, COVID-19 lockdown & the economic crash* (B. Rose, Interviewer) [London Real]. https://freedomplatform.tv/the-truth-behind-the-coronavirus-pandemic-covid-19-lockdown-the-economic-crash-david-icke/

Icke, D. (2020b, April 6). *The coronavirus conspiracy: How COVID-19 will seize your rights & destroy our economy* (B. Rose, Interviewer) [London Real]. https://freedomplatform.tv/the-coronavirus-conspiracy-how-covid-19-will-seize-your-rights-destroy-our-economy-david-icke/

Icke, D. (2020c, November 15). *David Icke Exposes The Great Reset* (A. Jones, Interviewer) [InfoWars]. https://banned.video/watch?id=5fbe601dc77bbc4fc3cbfcd6

Icke, D. (2021a, February 2). *The Awakening World Truth Summit with David Icke* (S. Smith, Interviewer) [TCN.VIdeo]. https://tcn.video/david-icke-the-awakening-world-truth-summit

Icke, D. (2021b, March 6). *The Awakening Part 2 with David Icke* (S. Smith, Interviewer) [TCN.VIdeo]. https://tcn.video/david-icke-the-awakening-part-2

Jameson, F. (1988). Cognitive Mapping. In C. Nelson & L. Grossberg (Eds.), Marxism and the interpretation of culture (pp. 347–360). Macmillan Education.

Jones, A. (2022). *The great reset: And the war for the world.* Skyhorse Publishing.

Knight, P. (2000). *Conspiracy culture: From the Kennedy assassination to The X-files.* Routledge.

Koranyi, B. (2023, March 10). Analysis: Wage catch-up to prolong Europe's inflation battle. *Reuters.* https://www.reuters.com/markets/europe/wage-catch-up-prolong-europes-inflation-battle-2023-03-10/

Kubrick, S. (Director). (1964, January 29). *Dr. Strangelove or: How I Learned to Stop Worrying and Love the Bomb.* Stanley Kubrick Productions.

Lasch, C. (1979). *The culture of narcissism: American life in an age of diminishing expectations.* Norton.

Lasch, C. (1991). *The true and only heaven: Progress and its critics.* W.W. Norton & Company.

Lowry, L. (1993). *The giver.* Listening Library/Random House.

Mair, P. (2006). Ruling the Void. *New Left Review, 42,* 25–51.

Mercola, J. (2021a). Event 201 and the Great Reset. In J. Mercola & R. Cummins (Eds.), *The Truth About COVID-19: Exposing The Great Reset, Lockdowns, Vaccine Passports, and the New Normal.* Chalsea Green Publishing.

Mercola, J. (2021b). Successful Protocols Suppressed. In J. Mercola & R. Cummins (Eds.), *The Truth About COVID-19: Exposing The Great Reset, Lockdowns, Vaccine Passports, and the New Normal.* Chalsea Green Publishing.

Mercola, J., & Cummins, R. (2021). *The Truth About COVID-19: Exposing The Great Reset, Lockdowns, Vaccine Passports, and the New Normal.* Chalsea Green Publishing.

Myers, J. (2021, December 10). These charts show the growing gap between the world's richest and poorest. *World Economic Forum.* https://www.weforum.org/agenda/2021/12/global-income-inequality-gap-report-rich-poor/

Neate, R. (2020, March 11). Super-rich jet off to disaster bunkers amid coronavirus outbreak. *The Guardian.* https://www.theguardian.com/world/2020/mar/11/disease-dodging-worried-wealthy-jet-off-to-disaster-bunkers

O'Connor, S. (2021, April 25). 'We are drowning in insecurity': Young people and life after the pandemic. *Financial Times.* https://www.ft.com/content/77d586cc-4f3f-4701-a104-d09136c93d44

Orwell, G. (1949). *Nineteen Eighty-Four.* Secker & Warburg.

Postman, N. (1985). *Amusing Ourselves to Death: Public Discourse in the Age of Show Business.* Viking Penguin.

Ross, G. (Director). (2012, March 23). *The Hunger Games* [Action, Adventure, Sci-Fi]. Lionsgate, Color Force.

Schwab, K., & Malleret, T. (2020). *The Great Reset.* Forum Publishing.

Sekeris, P. G. (2017). Counter-Elite. In F. M. Moghaddam (Ed.), *The SAGE Encyclopedia of Political Behavior* (Vol. 1–2, pp. 152–153). SAGE Publications. doi:10.4135/9781483391144

Sharlet, J. (2011, November 10). Inside Occupy Wall Street – Rolling Stone. *Rolling Stone*. https://www.rollingstone.com/politics/politics-news/inside-occupy-wall-street-236993/

Spiezia, V., & Vivarelli, M. (2002). Innovation and Employment: A Critical Survey. In N. Greenan, Y. L'Horty, & J. Mairesse (Eds.), *Productivity, Inequality, and the Digital Economy* (pp. 101–125). The MIT Press. doi:10.7551/mitpress/5609.003.0009

Strijbis, O., Teney, C., & Helbling, M. (2019). Why Are Elites More Cosmopolitan than Masses? In M. Zürn, O. Strijbis, P. de Wilde, R. Koopmans, & W. Merkel (Eds.), The Struggle Over Borders: Cosmopolitanism and Communitarianism (pp. 37–64). Cambridge University Press. doi:10.1017/9781108652698.002

Thurston, I. (2018). *Everything is Permitted, Restrictions Still Apply: A Psychoanalytic Perspective on Social Dislocation, Narcissism, and Post Truth*. Routledge. doi:10.4324/9780429432101

Tufekci, Z. (2017). *Twitter and tear gas: The power and fragility of networked protest*. Yale University Press.

Turkle, S. (1995). *Life on the screen: Identity in the age of the Internet*. Simon & Schuster.

van Zoonen, L. (2012). I-Pistemology: Changing truth claims in popular and political culture. *European Journal of Communication*, *27*(1), 56–67. doi:10.1177/0267323112438808

Wachowski, L., & Wachowski, L. (Directors). (1999, June 23). *The Matrix*. Warner Bros., Village Roadshow Pictures, Groucho Film Partnership.

Webb, G. (2014). *Dark alliance: The CIA, the Contras, and the crack cocaine explosion*. Seven Stories Press.

Weinstein, A. (2011, October 7). "We Are the 99 Percent" Creators Revealed. *Mother Jones*. https://www.motherjones.com/politics/2011/10/we-are-the-99-percent-creators/

White, M. C. (2020, December 30). Wall Street minted 56 new billionaires since the pandemic began—But many families are left behind. *NBC News*. https://www.nbcnews.com/business/business-news/wall-street-s-best-year-ever-why-pandemic-has-been-n1252512

Williams, A. M. (2013). Who shot JFK? Here are 6 conspiracy theories. *USA Today*. https://www.usatoday.com/story/news/nation-now/2013/11/21/john-kennedy-conspiracy-theories-assasination/3661891/

World Economic Forum (Director). (2020a, March 6). *The Great Reset | Launch session 3 June 2020* [YouTube]. https://www.youtube.com/watch?v=pfVdMWzKwjc

World Economic Forum (Director). (2020b, July 14). *COVID-19: The Great Reset* [YouTube]. https://www.youtube.com/watch?v=VHRkkeecg7c&t=2133s

Žižek, S. (1996). "I Hear You with My Eyes"; or, The Invisible Master. In R. Salecl & S. Žižek (Eds.), *Gaze and voice as love objects* (pp. 90–128). Duke University Press. doi:10.1215/9780822379447-005

Žižek, S. (2012, April 24). Occupy Wall Street: What is to be done next? *The Guardian*. https://www.theguardian.com/commentisfree/cifamerica/2012/apr/24/occupy-wall-street-what-is-to-be-done-next

Zuboff, S. (2019). *The age of surveillance capitalism: The fight for a human future at the new frontier of power*. Profile Books.

ENDNOTE

1 The research is part of the dissertation "Dissenting Narratives During the COVID-19 Pandemic: Communication Strategies Behind the Expressions of Dissensus, Conspiracy Theories, and Populist Rhetoric" that is to be defended at the University of Deusto (Bilbao, Spain) in January 2024.

Chapter 3
Anti-Vaccination in the Post-Truth Era:
Who Will We Trust?

Övünç Ege
https://orcid.org/0000-0002-2078-9008
Özyeğin University, Turkey

ABSTRACT

Science denialism, or the decline/loss of trust in scientific knowledge, is related to losing the value of truth as a phenomenon, the post-truth era is a period in which truth is devalued and fluid. This study reveals the relationship between this concept, which permeates a wide range of areas from political discourses to daily life practices, and the pandemic, which is a global crisis. It also seeks to reveal how the pandemic reproduces hegemonic relations. This study addresses the relationship between the post-truth era and anti-vaccination and aims to understand how anti-vaccine individuals view COVID-19 vaccines. The study included in-depth interviews with five vaccine opponents. There were found to be recurring themes in the interview data. One of the core ideas of post-truth, science denialism, was used to investigate these issues. The hierarchy between classes, the prominent theme in the data collected from the opponents of vaccination, was analyzed with a critical perspective.

"Reality" is what we take to be true.
Gary Zukav

INTRODUCTION

In the post-truth era, lying is not a concept that is applied from time to time but can be understood as the main feature of the age in which it is lived. In this age, power structures bend the truth to protect their privileged position. This assumption is certainly not new and valid in almost every period. However, with the post-truth, the problematization of this situation has changed. Today, the truth presented by power structures and the perception of truth by people living in this age is fluid. On the other hand, this understanding spreads to daily life activities in a not-long process.

DOI: 10.4018/979-8-3693-0896-7.ch003

The post-truth era does not describe the temporal process after the truth but the emptying of it by giving it a subjective meaning and reflecting the untruth as accurate. In this context, scientific knowledge, seen as truth by proving its objectivity with modernity, has lost its reality in the post-truth era. The circulation of misinformation has increased with the loss of information accuracy and the digitization of the media.

COVID-19, which we encounter in the post-truth era, shows us that we need to rethink the concept of post-truth and its possibilities and risks. The importance of reaching the correct information has been seen with the coronavirus pandemic. Individuals do not unconditionally trust and question the information shared by their ruler structures. This situation has also manifested itself in issues such as anti-vaccination. Because COVID-19, which has become a political discourse over time, has become a tool through which power structures reproduce themselves. Although the pandemic has brought the credibility of power structures into question for a relatively more expansive audience, this position has also enabled the power structure to revise how it legitimizes itself.

The anti-vaccination movement is not limited to the COVID-19 vaccine. "Opposition to vaccines goes as far back as the 18th century" (Hussain et al., 2018). Anti-vaxxer groups have consistently opposed vaccines for different reasons. Early anti-vaccination movements were often motivated by religious restrictions and taboos. Later, various reasons, such as conspiracy theories, the adoption of "scientific" information spread by word of mouth and unproven by individuals, fear, abstaining, and the domination of the body by power structures took their place in the anti-vaccination stance. As with previous anti-vaccine movements, those against the COVID-19 vaccine have different arguments.

One of the claims in this study is that the reason for insecurity and different information circulation in individuals is that knowledge has become an empty signifier in the post-truth era. The verifiability of information has become almost impossible today. Although verification platforms search for the accuracy of information, they cannot keep up with the circulation rate of information pollution. In addition, individuals' distrust of power structures also affects their understanding of information.

"Post-truth was foreshadowed by what has happened to science over the last several decades" (McIntyre, 2018, p. 17). Also, science loses its importance because it is still not seen as objective enough, even in a global problem. Today, scientific knowledge has been turned into political discourse. In other words, scientific knowledge has become an empty signifier. The empty signifier is "a signifier without a signified" (Laclau, 2005, p. 105). In other words, the different meanings attributed to the signifier emptied the signifier itself. This situation has triggered individuals' distrust of scientific expertise in countries that have become implicitly totalitarian due to central forces in different areas such as social, cultural, economic, political, and others.

When the concept of post-truth is considered from a sociopolitical perspective, it is necessary to examine public security and related factors. It is associated with the spread of misinformation, the consequent undermining of public safety, and the fact that post-truth information, while increasing in quantity, is of questionable veracity. The undermining of public security may cause the public to become anxious and fearful. This case can make manipulating the masses easier for the power structure. The concept that enters daily life enables the production, flow, and reproduction of knowledge for the benefit of the ruling class and strengthens its power. At this point, technological developments affect daily life as a result. According to Enes Aluç and others, who explain the concept of post-truth as the substitution of fake information and images for reality, "In a period when technical possibilities and fakes are perceived as so real, the level of media literacy of people is of great importance and constitutes a separate subject of discussion" (Aluç et al., 2022, p. 4).

Media literacy is not a direct way of showing the truth to individuals and audiences. However, it does teach them to filter and analyze the meaning produced by media content and to question its accuracy before accepting it. "Individuals who have been exposed to false information appear to be more reluctant to receive accurate information presented to correct this misinformation, unlike individuals who have no prior negative knowledge about a topic" (Durmuş & Göztaş, 2023, p. 28). However, while the development of artificial intelligence technologies and the rise of deepfake videos may have positive effects in different sectors, they risk negatively affecting daily life, dynamics in the public sphere, and specializations such as politics. As Yasemin Durmuş and Aylin Göztaş point out, deepfake videos can serve humor and entertainment purposes as well as political manipulation, blackmail, or non-consensual pornography (Durmuş & Göztaş, 2023, p. 31). Deepfake videos for political manipulation threaten both public safety and trust in information in the post-truth era, where truth has become fluid. The information must be verified to prevent rapid circulation and detachment from the truth.

The space created by the public security problem, first in the public sphere and then in the private sphere, can pave the way for developing a climate of fear. Fear that spreads to the social sphere also makes the masses vulnerable to manipulation. At this point, power legitimizes its position. Looking at the general situation, the truth that loses meaning and disappears with post-truth creates systems in which power reproduces itself. However, to say that this situation is only under the control of power structures is to look at the issue from a single perspective. As Steve Tesich pointed out in *A Government of Lies*, published in the Nation Journal in January 1992, as a free people, we have freely decided to live in a post-truth world (Tesich, 2021, p. 25).

Considering all these, it is essential to understand the anti-vaccine movement in the pandemic process in the following respects: to understand social demands, to reveal the sociological situation, and to make forward-looking plans.

WHAT IS THE POST-TRUTH? WHAT IS NOT?

To discuss the meaning of the word "post" in the concept of "post-truth", it is vital to understand the concept's purpose, content, reflection on the social field, and perhaps its possible historical and social consequences. For this reason, looking at the underlying meaning of the word "post" and observing the transformation in the word "post-truth" is essential.

"Post" gives a new meaning to the word that preceded it with phrases such as *postmodernity, post-Marxism, postcolonialism, and post-structuralism.* The reason for the problem in the use of the concept is the idea that "post" means just temporality, like the prefix "pre", for example, prehistory. For instance, "post-production" refers to the stage after video material creation and is based on temporality. However, postmodernity does not mean the time after modernity. The same applies to post-Marxism/Marxism, postcolonialism/colonialism, and post-structuralism/structuralism. So, what exactly is a *post*? Or what is it not?

"Post" expresses a temporal difference and adds different meanings. The concept of *post-*, which is thought to define the process after the word it is attached to, is not the successor of the process but describes an entirely different approach. Based on Lee McIntyre and Yalın Alpay's definitions, as Güven Özdoyran expresses through the concept of modernity, the suffix post "refers to the 'trivialization' and discrediting of modernism" (Özdoyran, 2020, p. 141). Post-truth is semantically and temporally in this context beyond being after the truth. The suffix *post*, which has different functions other than trivialization, in this study, refers to the disappearance of the previous concept in the context of post-truth. Özdoyran's definition of *tezahür edemeyen hakikat* (*unmanifestable truth*) (Özdoyran, 2020, p. 141) is a valid and inclusive conceptualization for this study, especially considering the data obtained from participant interviews. There is no space left for truth scientific knowledge in the context of this study to manifest itself in the social sphere. So, the truth cannot manifest. On the other hand, Klaus Benesch says that there is no such thing as post-truth and that we are not during an epistemological crisis in which truth and falsehood have become indistinguishable. He adds that truth claims face more objections and are more challenging to defend (Benesch, 2021, p. 51).

Lee McIntyre begins to explain the concept of post-truth through the politicians who should still embody the political line of the concept. As Mirgün Cabas, who wrote the introduction (*Bana Tatlı Küçük Yalanlar Söyle – Tell Me Sweet Little Lies*) to the Turkish edition of the book (Lee McIntyre's *Post-Truth*), says, the lies of politicians in the post-truth era are not lies they invent when they are stuck. "These are the tools used by a politician to construct a universe for himself and to convince the masses of this universe" (McIntyre, 2022, p. 16). The fact that power structures use the universe built on lies to persuade the masses turns the lie itself into a propaganda tool. "Propaganda is the management of collective attitudes by the manipulation of significant symbols" (Lasswell, 1927, p. 627). This management style differs in different geographies, regions, and others. Various ways to shape collective attitudes and behaviors in the desired direction exist. For example, Herman and Chomsky's book *The Manufacturing of Consent* (2012) mentions that gaining the masses' consent to mobilize them is necessary. Today, the consent of the masses, especially in countries that have completed their modernization and have the status of developed countries, usually does not come through coercion. It reproduces itself through their voluntarily active engagement and does not change the fact that it is forced. According to Byung-Chul Han, the historical period we are in is one in which freedom leads to coercion (Han, 2020, p. 11). However, with the pandemic, everything turned upside down.

The conflict between Giorgio Agamben and Slavoj Zizek at the beginning of COVID-19 is the face of this inversion in the field of theoretical debate. Drawing on the concept of biopolitics inherited from Foucault, Agamben argued that COVID is "a state of exception created by an unjustified emergency". On February 26, 2020, he criticized the measures taken in the face of the coronavirus pandemic in his first article. His main concern was "the growing tendency to use the state of exception as a normal paradigm of governance" and that the decisions taken would restrict freedoms (Agamben, 2020). On the other hand, Zizek explains this situation by saying that "it should not be reduced to the usual paradigm of supervision and control put forward by thinkers like Foucault" (Zizek, 2020). Zizek's concern is that power structures manipulate data and implement measures so the pandemic cannot be contained. The problem with restricting individual freedoms is that this restriction permeates daily life practices and becomes the "new normal". This virus, which is not only a medical but also a social and class problem, shows what kind of society we live in, according to Han. "We live in a survival society that is ultimately based on fear of death" (Han, 2020). Truth is the first casualty of the authoritarian state established in George Orwell's novel *1984*, which McIntrye also references when thinking about the post-truth phenomenon ((McIntyre, 2018, p. 4). This circumstance is the central concern of the Agamben-Zizek debate and the Han's *survival society*.

The post-truth universe built on lies undermines some communities' trust in power structures. As a result, information from the government can be rejected by them. Rejected knowledge can be replaced by untrue, unverified, and unfounded knowledge in the *zeitgeist*. Especially in the post-truth era, the infodemic, which has increased with digitalization, spreads quickly. "An infodemic is too much information including false or misleading information in digital and physical environments during a disease outbreak" (WHO (World Health Organization), n.d.). The increase in the pandemic-era infodemic is probably fuelled by distrust of power structures.

THE RELATIONSHIP BETWEEN POST-TRUTH AND ANTI-VACCINATION

Anti-vaccination and the emergence of anti-vaccination movements are not new. The history of anti-vaccination is almost contemporaneous with the history of vaccination. "Critics of vaccination have taken various positions, including opposition to the smallpox vaccine in England and the United States in the mid to late 1800s" (Misconceptions About Vaccines: History of Anti-Vaccination Movements, 2022). This opposition to vaccination did not emerge out of nowhere and may have different arguments, although it is based on similar themes.

According to Henrik Enroth (2023, p. 182), on the one hand, there is a growing disbelief in science. On the other hand, there is an increasing belief in conspiracy theories or forms and sources of knowledge that have proven unreliable. As Enroth emphasizes, the concept of authority is vital at this point. Authority is always a common theme in the relationship between science, attitudes toward vaccines, and post-truth. In this context, authority, which should be handled in a comprehensively broad context, is generally understood as the authority of science. The authority of science is inaccessible to non-specialists, but it demands respect and acceptance from them. This authority, especially in times of global crisis, requires that individuals voluntarily accept the information it provides. Likewise, "the word 'post-truth' is irreducibly normative" (McIntyre, 2018, p. 6).

The other authority that needs to be addressed in this regard is the authority of the class that possesses scientific knowledge. The conflict between the classes that do not have this authority occurs in the power struggle sphere. The questioning of this authority is the questioning of power structures and, therefore, of the dominant discourse and constitutes the raw material of all critical studies. In other words, the main discussion of this study is a discussion that has been taking place in the field of communication long before the conceptualization of post-truth. The inclusion of post-truth in this discussion specific to COVID-19 shows that scientific knowledge has been re-normativized with the pandemic. The global crisis made some people accept the unquestionable nature of scientific knowledge while others continued to question it. This disagreement, which serves two different paradigms in terms of communication studies, paves the way for theoretical debates that are difficult to navigate in a period when truth has become insignificant.[1]. Because the pandemic and its effects have reopened, most of what has been known so far. All researchers and academics with different definitions and perspectives agree that COVID-19 has brought about a fundamental societal change. "The coronavirus crisis has suspended, shattered, and necessitated the reorganisation of the practices, structures, and routines of everyday life" (Fuchs, 2021, p. 22).

METHODOLOGY AND THE SAMPLING OF THE STUDY

Vaccine hesitancy is mainly related to insufficient information and the resulting insecurity. This study discusses anti-vaccination in the post-truth era, and an in-depth interview, one of the qualitative research methods, was used. The study will conduct in-depth interviews with people who declare themselves anti-vaccine. Through this method, the underlying reason for the behavior of the anti-vaccine individuals interviewed will be more readily understood. The data obtained from the interview will be analyzed with the discourse analysis approach.

In the post-truth era, the meaning of the elements that shape our language is being emptied. This situation affects the social context in which the discourse is located. The social context here can be addressed based on local governments or countries. It even refers to broader geographies with globalization. It is no coincidence that Brexit and Donald Trump's election process are used as examples in post-truth studies. However, this does not only manifest itself in political communication or as a propaganda tool. It can also be associated with issues such as anti-vaccinationism, which is also the subject of this study, or climate change denial and flat earth beliefs. These issues can generally be addressed under the title of science denialism. Issues such as what the denied subject, event, or phenomenon is and why it is denied can be addressed within the post-truth scope or analyzed in more detail with the help of different disciplines. If we define the denial of scientific knowledge and its recurring practice as a *denial culture*, this concept must be analyzed from sociological, psychological, anthropological, historical, and other perspectives.

In this study, the anti-vaccination movement in Turkey is discussed in the context of post-truth. This study was used to find an answer to the question, "Why are individuals insecure about vaccines in the event of a global pandemic?" The data gathered through in-depth interviews with participants was discussed in the context of the post-truth era's loss of meaning.

This research is built on two primary concerns. The research questions to be answered in the study were determined as follows, and the questions asked of the participants were formed in line with these.

RQ1: Are individuals skeptical of vaccine production processes and portray themselves as human subjects?
RQ2: Will the post-truth era affect the arguments of anti-vaccinationists?

Based on these questions, two hypotheses were put forward in the study. (i) Vaccine opponents are skeptical of vaccine production processes and oppose vaccines because they believe they control them. (ii) It is directly related to the fact that in the post-truth era of anti-vaccination, scientific knowledge has become an empty signifier.

Interview questions were prepared in line with the research questions. The data obtained from the collected responses were categorized. Table 1 shows the questions asked of the participants and the intended outcomes.

Table 1. Questions to ask vaccine opponents and intended outcomes

Questions	Intended Outcomes
1. What are the reasons why you identify as anti-vaccine? What do you think about COVID-19 vaccines?	Reasons for anti-vaccination
2. Where did you get information about COVID-19 vaccines? Have you researched the accuracy of this information?	Information verification methods of anti-vaccine
3. Do you share your opposition to the COVID-19 vaccine with others? If yes, how do you share your opinions (face-to-face, social media, etc.)?	Areas for anti-vaccinationists to share their views
4. Have you been vaccinated against COVID-19?	Vaccines as a tool of domination
5. Do you want to add anything about the COVID-19 pandemic and vaccines?	Vaccines as a tool of domination

Table 2. Demographic data of the participation

Participant	Gender	Age	Graduation Degree
P1	Woman	27	Bachelor's degree
P2	Woman	28	Bachelor's degree
P3	Woman	27	Master's degree
P4	Man	28	Bachelor's degree
P5	Woman	31	Bachelor's degree

Participants abstained from the interview. Despite being informed about personal data privacy, some respondents postponed answering. Therefore, the interview was conducted with five people to make representative inferences. To analyze participant responses, each individual was assigned a number (e.g., P1, P2, etc.). Table 2 shows the participants' demographic data, including gender, age, and education level.

Four of the participants were female, and one was male. The age range of the participants was 27-31, and all of them were at least university graduates. All participants are against the COVID-19 vaccine. Nevertheless, they were vaccinated for similar reasons.

FINDINGS AND DISCUSSION

The answers received from the participants after the interview are not about the truth or reality itself. At the same time, the answers and their analysis are not intended to show what is right or wrong. Because "post-truth is not about reality; it is about the way that humans *react* to reality" (McIntyre, 2018, p. 172). The main concern in the findings, discussion, and conclusion sections is to analyze the reaction of vaccine opponents. This analysis inevitably leads us to distrust of authority.

Reasons for Anti-Vaccination

All participants are against the COVID-19 vaccine. P1 said that she did not trust later vaccines, such as the flu vaccine, and included the COVID-19 vaccine in this context. At the same time, P1 does not define herself as strictly anti-vaccine. `I am against vaccines or using medicines unless I have to," she says, emphasizing the importance of immunity. P1, who thinks that vaccines harm immunity, criticizes vaccines by saying, "I do not find it right to impose vaccination requirements on healthy people who can cope with diseases on their own". All participants expressed negative opinions when asked what they thought about COVID-19 vaccines. P3 said the pandemic was fake, and she did not trust the vaccine. All participants except P3 agreed that the vaccine was produced quickly. P3 has not made a statement on this issue. They are particularly distrustful of the testing phase. P2 says, "When I defend this, it is not because of any medical knowledge; it bothers me that even the simplest flu vaccines have processes such as whether there are any side effects, whether the vaccine affects the genetics of the person who receives the vaccine years later, while the covid vaccine is just that we did it". P2 also said, "I think there is some kind of chemical solution to a disease, and it bothered me that there are so many types of vaccines". P4 added that he is opposed to vaccination because of the problems he has observed in people who have been vaccinated.

Table 3. Common themes of anti-vaccination

Argument From Opposition	Number of People
Rapid vaccine release and inadequate testing	4 person (P1, P2, P4, P5)
Being/becoming a device of oppression	3 person (P1, P2, P4)
Lack of protection and bad reactions in vaccinated people	2 person (P2, P4)
Negative impact on immunity	One person (P1)
A single type of vaccine	One person (P2)
Fake pandemic	One person (P3)
Vaccine is a poison.	One person (P3)
Personal reasons	One person (P1)

Participants' arguments against vaccination are categorized and shown in Table 3.

Information Verification Methods of Anti-Vaccine

Participants generally obtained information about vaccines through the media. P1 received information from the news, P2 first from mainstream media, then from articles and columns, and P4 from social media. P3 stated his source of information as "some sources" and did not give any details. P5 did not conduct any research. None of the participants said that they confirmed the information and became anti-vaccine based on their subjective opinions. P1 questioned the accuracy of scientific knowledge not with a critical approach but from an individual position. She came to a personal conclusion by saying, "It was a sufficient result for me that it did not seem right to me". P4, on the other hand, stated that no channel could convince him. In this sense, this anti-vaccination approach is subjective, like P1. The rejection of scientific knowledge due to subjective interpretation is related to the post-truth era. As discussed in The Relationship Between Post-Truth and Anti-Vaccination, scientific knowledge, which is devalued and becomes an empty signifier, is in a position where individuals can reject it without the need for systematic criticism.

Areas for Anti-Vaccinationists to Share Their Views

All participants except P5 share their opposition to vaccination with other people. P1, P3, and P4 shared their views face-to-face, while P2 shared their thoughts both face-to-face and on social media. P1 shared their opinion with people in a close and closed circle, including close friends, family, and relatives. This participant does not share their opinion with people they do not know. What is noteworthy in P2's response is that he states that he shares his views "without hesitation".

For this study, there were difficulties in finding participants before starting to interview anti-vaccinationists. Some of the prospective participants who were contacted wanted to avoid explaining or were hesitant. In this sense, P2's emphasis on "without hesitation" is noteworthy. The pressure on anti-vaccinationists does not only come from political or professional powers but also manifests itself as neighborhood pressure within society.

P3 said he shares his ideas face-to-face and added, "I am even researching how vaccines can get rid of the poison". P3 responded superficially to all questions, but only in this question did she express the view that the vaccine is a poison. The participant who thinks the pandemic is fake and the vaccine is poison is the most conservative among the others.

Vaccine as a Tool of Domination

All anti-vaccine participants have been vaccinated against COVID-19. All of them emphasized that they were forced to get vaccinated. Three of the four (P1, P2, P5) said they were vaccinated to keep their jobs. Contrary to the view of anti-vaccinationists that it threatens public health, P1's opinion on this issue is as follows: "If I didn't have such a job, I probably would have complied with the restrictions and stayed at home and didn't mix with the public and didn't get vaccinated. I chose to travel by private car during the period I was not vaccinated". During the interview, P1 said that COVID was a disease he initially believed in but later became an ideological repression device. However, the fact that there is a willingness to comply with the restrictions voluntarily shows that the discourses of the power structure over public health persuade the individual. Therefore, although the individual's trust in power structures and vaccination is shaken, it can be said that social consciousness exists. The participant also criticized the curfews by saying, "I find it against logic not to be able to go out for a coffee in the evening", even though the distance measure, which all power structures, especially the Ministry of Health, consider within the scope of the rules to be followed, is ignored in public transportation. The participant who thought COVID was a severe process said that the requirements of being human were ignored. Similarly, P2 said, "I would like to state that I was mobbed one-on-one that if we do not get vaccinated, these people will be dismissed from their jobs. Of course, after that, I was forced to do this because shopping malls, state institutions, or any social areas do not accept unvaccinated people".

The participant, vaccinated under the coercion of power structures, later had COVID and thinks the vaccine is therefore not protective. On the contrary, he said that his body showed different reactions after the vaccine, and he started to experience diseases that he had not experienced before and that "unfortunately, I have personally experienced that you cannot even make your own body's decisions in Turkey". The female participant's emphasis on personal decision-making over the body can be interpreted as a direct reference to the domination of masculine power over the female body. Although P4 answered only about vaccines until the last question, at the end of the interview, he said, "There are hundreds of people who died because of this vaccine requirement. I think the pandemic is a planned, controlled population reduction", emphasizing the control and implicit violence of power structures over the masses.

"Science denial can start from either an economic or an ideological agenda" (McIntyre, 2018, p. 21). In light of the answers obtained from this question, it is recommended that future studies investigate the economic reasons for the motivation of vaccine opponents to be vaccinated.

CONCLUSION

Individuals' negative attitudes towards COVID-19 vaccines are based on mistrust of vaccines and the pandemic, thus naturalizing the lie. At the same time, the surveillance practices and practices of conservative authoritarian regimes, which are on the rise globally, are one of the reasons for distrust against the pandemic. As Söyler and Tekindal point out, the wave of autocratization accelerated before the pandemic. "In contrast, 2019 was a 'year of protest' as civil society mobilized to improve democratic standards in 22 countries with authoritarian tendencies" (Söyler & Tekindal, 2021, p. 3835).

Nevertheless, the impact and success of these protests and their relationship to COVID must be questioned. The pandemic has made researchers re-examine individuals' trust in power structures, especially in the social sciences field. The discourses of power structures, the diversity of arguments developed against these discourses, and the connections between the two need to be re-analyzed.

In this study, it is seen that the participants take a critical position against the discourses of power structures. Since social utility is constructed based on class differences, it is unsurprising that individuals see this utility as a hegemonic interference in their personal space and, therefore, reject it. At this point, the critique of anti-vaccinationism can reach two different conclusions. The debate between Agamben and Zizek mentioned above also shows these two aims at its core. One end of the critique concludes that class differences are reproduced under pandemic conditions, and power structures reproduce them to control individuals. On the other side, there is a threat to public health for individual and subjective reasons. However, it is noteworthy that one of the participants agreed to isolate herself from the public sphere because she did not want to be vaccinated. Nevertheless, the *preference* for abstraction also shows that there is a status difference between vaccinated and unvaccinated.

The rapid availability of vaccines and their compulsory use by power structures have increased negative attitudes towards vaccines. Individuals chose not to trust power structures in the face of the sudden pandemic and the sudden solution that was found. However, in line with the data obtained from the interview results, these preferences are not preferences that have been filtered through systematic criticism because of scientific research. Subjective decisions prevail over issues such as the global crisis and public health. The problem here is not that individual interests are prioritized in times of international turmoil but that authorities and power structures are not trusted even in times of crisis.

Participants obtained information about vaccines through digital media. Considering the media's power to influence and manipulate the masses, it is possible to say that the media is not always an adequate and accurate source of information. The ideological position of the media, which changes depending on its ownership structure, affects its content. The inability of mainstream media channels, which convey the discourse of power, to convince individuals in a critical position is related to individuals' distrust of the medium. Social media is a space where different opinions spread rapidly, often without going through a process of approval and confirmation. This space is closed to contradictory views and is aggressive when necessary, and as a result, it accelerates the circulation of misinformation. Misinformation is consumed faster by people who do not have sufficient knowledge on the subject. The information consumed may result in internalization if it is close to the individual's view or violent rejection if it is the opposite view.

Basing attitudes towards a global pandemic and its vaccine on "scientific" information obtained through the media can be dangerous, especially in the post-truth era of fighting the infodemic. One of the problems in the post-truth universe built on lies is the naturalization of the lie. Although power structures that tend to instrumentalize lies in the post-truth era advocate vaccination, individuals' distrust of power and its tool, the media, has directly triggered distrust in vaccination and the pandemic.

According to the document the Turkish Medical Association created, there are ten main arguments against vaccination.[2] (Azap, 2019). As a result of the interviews with anti-vaccine participants, it was observed that there was a parallelism between the claims numbered 3, 8, 9, and 10 and the participant responses. Apart from this, the participants' opposition to vaccination is directly related to the rapid release of the vaccine.

All participants have been vaccinated against COVID-19. However, this was not by choice. Although the participants did not want to be vaccinated in the private sphere, they were vaccinated because they had to participate in public life. The companies the participants worked for required them to be vaccinated.

This coercion is seen as another form of domination by the participants. The employer, as the power structure with a decision-making mechanism in the professional field, has made vaccination compulsory for its employees in line with the views of another power structure, the states. This necessity is related firstly to politics and secondly to economic class. Even though the class that was higher in status could not impose its truth on the class below it, it forced them to exhibit the behavior they wanted.

Contrary to softened concepts such as voluntarism, consent production, and psychopolitics, the pandemic has shown that coercion and coercion of power have not disappeared. Although the coercion does not appear to be physical, it threatens the economic situation of individuals and, indirectly, their physical unity. The dilemma of public health and individual freedom is frequently seen in global health crises such as pandemics. In line with the answers of the participants interviewed in this study, it was observed that this dilemma also fed a negative attitude towards COVID-19 vaccines.

REFERENCES

Agamben, G. (2020, February 27). Covid-19: Gerekçesiz Bir Acil Durumun Yarattığı İstisna Hali. Terrabayt. https://terrabayt.com/dusunce/covid-19-gerekcesiz-bir-acil-durumun-yarattigi-istisna-hali/

Aluç, E., Serttaş, A., Gürkan, H., Sarıkaya, T., & Kalkan Aluç, Y. (2022). Ukrayna-Rusya Savaşı Sırasında Ülkelerin Kullandıkları Deepfake Videoların İncelenmesi. *Uluslararası Medya ve Toplum Sempozyumu Tam Metinler Kitabı*, 1-13.

Azap, A. (2019). *Aşı Karşıtlarının İddiaları ve Bilimin Yanıtları*. Türk Tabipleri Birliği (Turkish Medical Association). https://www.ttb.org.tr/userfiles/files/As%CC%A7%C4%B1%20kars%CC%A7%C4%B1tlar%C4%B1n%C4%B1n%20iddialar%C4%B1%20ve%20gerc%CC%A7ekler.pdf

Benesch, K. (2021). Hakikat ve Hakikat Sonrası İlişkisi Modernizm ve Postmodernizm İlişkisi Midir? *Cógito*, *104*, 49–66.

Durmuş, Y., & Göztaş, A. (2023). *Deepfake: Post-Truth Çağı İnsanlarında Fırsat ve Tehditlere Yönelik Algılar. In Medya ve Kültür Odağında İletişim*. Akademisyen Kitabevi.

Enroth, H. (2023). Crisis of Authority: The Truth of Post-Truth. *International Journal of Politics Culture and Society*, *36*(2), 179–195. [REMOVED HYPERLINK FIELD] doi:10.100710767-021-09415-6 PMID:34703077

Fuchs, C. (2021). *Communicating COVID-19: Everyday Life, Digital Capitalism, and Conspiracy Theories in Pandemic Times*. Emerald Publishing Limited. doi:10.1108/9781801177207

Han, B.-C. (2020, May 24). *Byung-Chul Han: COVID-19 has reduced us to a 'society of survival'*. EURACTIV: https://www.euractiv.com/section/asia-pacific/interview/byung-chul-han-covid-19-has-reduced-us-to-a-society-of-survival/

Han, B.-C. (2020). *Psikopolitika: Neoliberalizm ve Yeni İktidar Teknikleri*. Metis Yayınları.

Herman, E. S., & Chomsky, N. (2012). *Rızanın İmalatı: Kitle Medyasının Ekonomi Politiği*: bgst Yayınları.

Hussain, A., Ali, S., Ahmed, M., & Hussain, S. (2018, July 3). The Anti-vaccination Movement: A Regression in Modern Medicine. *Cureus, 10*(7). Advance online publication. [REMOVED HYPERLINK FIELD] doi:10.7759/cureus.2919 PMID:30186724

Laclau, E. (2005). *On Populist Reason*. Versus.

Lasswell, H. D. (1927, August). The Theory of Political Propaganda. *The American Political Science Review, 21*(3), 627–631. doi:10.2307/1945515

McIntyre, L. (2018). *Post-Truth*. MIT Press. doi:10.7551/mitpress/11483.001.0001

McIntyre, L. (2022). *Post-Truth*. Tellekt.

Misconceptions About Vaccines: History of Anti-Vaccination Movements. (2022, April 20). History of Vaccines: https://historyofvaccines.org/vaccines-101/misconceptions-about-vaccines/history-anti-vaccination-movements

Özdoyran, G. (2020). Post-Truth Çağı, Kuram-Yüklü Gözlem Sorunu ve Yeni Medya: Facebook "Düz Dünya Türkiye" Grubu Örneği. *Egemia Ege Üniversitesi İletişim Fakültesi Medya Ve İletişim Araştırmaları Hakemli E-Dergisi*, (7), 139–169.

Söyler, M., & Tekindal, M. A. (2021). Covid-19 Pandemisi, Siyasi Rejimler ve Liberal Demokrasi. *OPUS International Journal of Society Researches*, 3832-3868. doi:10.26466/opus.885216

Tesich, S. (2021). Yalanlar Rejimi. *Cogito, 104*, 23–28.

WHO. (n.d.). *Infodemic*. WHO (World Healty Organizastion): https://www.who.int/health-topics/infodemic#tab=tab_1

Zizek, S. (2020, March 18). *Gözetlemek Ve Cezalandırmak Mı? Evet, Lütfen!* terrabayt: https://terrabayt.com/dusunce/gozetlemek-ve-cezalandirmak-mi-evet-lutfen/

ENDNOTES

1 It is a fact that the measures taken in the face of COVID-19, a global health crisis, have restricted personal freedoms. Especially nowadays, when the pandemic has lost its impact and political significance, it is seen that Agamben is right in his concern. However, does this justify Agamben's trivialization of the pandemic by likening it to a kind of flu? Zizek's statement that we must trust scientific knowledge is necessary for the global crisis to be overcome quickly and with minimal damage. However, at this point, the fact that people, whose primary goal is to survive, give all authority to the authority in line with this purpose carries the risk of strengthening authoritarian governments in the long run. From this perspective, the rise of nationalism and right-wing populism after COVID-19 is also noteworthy.

2 These arguments are the following:

1. Diseases disappeared before vaccinations, thanks to healthy living conditions and clean food/water supply.
2. When an epidemic occurs, most people who get sick are vaccinated. Vaccines are ineffective.

3. It is better to be sick than vaccinated because vaccines are not as protective as the disease itself.
4. Giving a tiny baby many vaccines (many and varied antigens) can disrupt the immune system and cause many diseases.
5. Breast milk contains substances that protect the baby from infections. Giving breast milk to babies until they are two is sufficient rather than giving many vaccines in the first two years of life.
6. Since vaccine-preventable diseases are disappearing in our country, we do not need to vaccinate our children.
7. Vaccines contain dangerous elements such as mercury and harmful substances such as aluminum as preservatives.
8. Vaccines are not safe, and many vaccines have hazardous side effects.
9. Whether or not to vaccinate is a personal decision. It is nobody's business if I do not vaccinate my child.
10. There are many side effects associated with vaccines, but vaccine companies prevent them from being known.

Chapter 4
Digital Data Security Strategies in the COVID-19 Pandemic Period:
An Evaluation of Domestic Messaging Applications

Serkan Karatay
https://orcid.org/0000-0002-8637-1915
Istanbul Yeni Yüzyıl University, Turkey

Başak Gezmen
Istanbul Medipol University, Turkey

ABSTRACT

It can be said that the COVID-19 pandemic has an important role in the spread of personal and institutional use of digital communication channels. These developments, which further increase the importance of digital data security, can also be evaluated in terms of messaging applications, which is one of the most used digital communication channels. Digital data security, which has become more and more important with the spread of communication technologies, covers not only privacy and security problems arising from personal use, but also privacy and security problems arising from corporate use, which can also have national security characteristics. These problems may include political, economic, and military dimensions. In this study, messaging applications as digital communication channels are discussed in the context of digital data security strategies. The study aims to question the contributions of nationalization in digital communication channels to data security in messaging applications.

DOI: 10.4018/979-8-3693-0896-7.ch004

INTRODUCTION

The spread of digital communication technologies and the realization of many remote activities through digital channels during the Covid-19 pandemic have caused these technologies to penetrate all areas of societies and states. The increasing demand for digital platforms during the COVID-19 period, which also influences the lifestyles of societies, has rendered discussions on data security more meaningful in various dimensions (Nikiforova, 2023: 3). Digital communication technologies, which make all types of communication independent from time and space, have caused the issue of security of communication, coordination and sharing to come to the fore. Within the scope of this subject, which is in the field of digital data security, the risks involved in personal and corporate digital communication, the dimensions of the risks and the measures taken against these risks are discussed. Risks in digital communication, on the other hand, can go beyond the personal level and can be inclusive enough to concern a government agency or government. For this reason, the security of data that emerges during digital communication and which is open to monitoring and collection is important for states as well as individuals.

Data collected without permission from individuals and institutions and which can be used against individuals by being observed; it can be obtained through various intermediaries, from social media applications to Internet cookies, from speech and voice recordings to special applications developed to collect sensitive information. For personal users, this data, which is often used to show them more and effective advertisements, can sometimes turn into problems that seriously threaten people's safety. Digital data security, which can also be a national security feature for state institutions, politicians, military and law enforcement, gains a special importance in this direction and plays an important role in determining the digital policies of states. These policies, including the national dimension of data security, include having a domestic digital infrastructure and following innovations in all technological fields, especially Internet technology, and taking domestic initiatives. Among these policies, which encompass the national dimension of data security, can be counted the possession of a domestic digital infrastructure, the pursuit of innovations in all technological fields, particularly internet technology, and engagement in local initiatives to ensure digital data security without violating individuals' fundamental rights.

The concentration of technological ownership in the hands of certain states within the economic and technological hierarchy of international power has always been a risk factor for other states. This risk factor also applies to Internet technology and applications that have emerged within this technology. Indeed, 21st-century capitalism views data as a kind of raw material and is focused on its extraction and utilization (Srnicek, 2017: 22). Therefore, being dependent on internet technologies implies not only a significant economic opportunity being ceded but also the potential for foreign companies to collect, process, and sell the data of individuals, organizations, law enforcement agencies, and the state. Because being foreign-dependent in Internet technologies means that, besides the transferring an important economic opportunity, all kinds of data of individuals, institutions, law enforcement and the state can be collected, processed and sold by foreign companies. In addition to the collected and processed data, the implementation of necessary sanctions may be disrupted in various ways in the event that some practices contrary to national law occur on the Internet.

These risks and problems have strengthened the idea of nationalization in digital communication technologies. The Republic of Türkiye Digital Transformation Office also hosts and encourages domestic initiatives in the field of telecommunications, especially internet technologies. The office, which is working on ensuring digital data security with national means, also works to produce local solutions to problems that may arise through internet technologies.

Instant messaging applications, which are used by individuals and institutions at the global level, are seen as an important area where digital data security comes to the fore. As a matter of fact, an update to the confidentiality agreement of Whatsapp, one of the most popular instant messaging applications and owned by Facebook, can quickly become a global event. The frequent occurrence of examples of a monopolistic perspective in the field of digital communication creates an important security vulnerability for billions of people and thousands of institutions using these applications. In addition, this also means that almost no local share can be taken from the digital economy that has become global. Therefore, domestic messaging applications and domestic social media initiatives are important both in terms of data security and to have a share in the digital economy.

Within the scope of this study, the use of digital communication channels and digital data security were first examined during the Covid-19 pandemic period. Then, digital data security strategies and nationalization of communication technologies were examined and domestic messaging applications in Türkiye were questioned in terms of data security.

While the association of a globally interconnected field like technology with local security may appear as a dilemma by nature, it serves as a motivator for the development of domestic technologies. The study primarily addresses the nexus between digital data security arising from the convergence of technology and security, the relevance of domestic technologies, the strategies to consider in developing domestic technologies, and the current status of domestic messaging applications within this context. The theoretical framework of the study will involve discussions and assessments of the importance of digital data security, digital data security strategies, domestic messaging applications in Türkiye, and the value they hold in terms of data security.

Digital Communication During the COVID-19 Pandemic in the Context of Digital Data Security

Social restrictions during the Covid-19 pandemic have had an impact on many aspects of life. Considering that communication takes place in all areas of life, it can inevitably be differentiated and changed in a period of social restrictions. As a matter of fact, social restrictions, including working and educational life, have caused every communication to be carried out in a way that can be defined with the phrase "online". Online education, online working, online meeting and online conference are among the most common examples of this. These practices, which were also carried out before the pandemic period, became widespread due to social restrictions and some forms became permanent after the pandemic.

Zoom, Microsoft Teams, Skype, etc., which are used in remote communication activities during the pandemic period and can be used in many ways from personal conversations to community events. In addition to the applications, the group communication features of the instant messaging applications, which were widely used in the pre-pandemic period, were also frequently used. In a period of social restrictions, digital communication environments used from simple interpersonal communication to international meetings have also caused digital data security discussions to come to the fore more.

Digital data, which has become a security issue for individuals, institutions and governments, "Information created and stored in a computer mediated environment that can potentially be transmitted as discrete information signals over the internet, and may be subsequently processed and/or stored for a range of known and unforeseen purposes." (Charles & Magtanong, 2022: 23). "Security, on the other hand, is defined as the protection of a person, object, country or organization against threats of crime or attack" (Cambridge Dictionary). Therefore, digital data security can be defined as the protection of individuals and institutions against various attacks on their data generated via the internet.

Can be considered in the context of the security of social, institutional and personal data in terms of the security of data on the Internet, which is included in the social life, and the emphasis that the security of these data places on the legal order. Data security, defined by Denning as "the science and examination of the methods of protecting data from unauthorized disclosure and modification in computer and communication systems" (Denning, 1982), includes the security of communication over the Internet, and includes unauthorized disclosure, theft or alteration of private correspondence of individuals and institutions. Srnicek (2017) has listed the functions of digital data as follows (2017: 23):

- Providing a competitive advantage by developing algorithms,
- Enabling coordination of workers and external resource utilization,
- Allowing optimization and flexibility in production,
- Making it possible to transform low-profit-margin products into high-profit-margin services,
- Facilitating data analysis as a generative process.

As evident in Srnicek's enumeration, digital data encompasses several economic functions. These functions can pertain to the economic interests of individuals or organizations and extend to a broader scale, such as the national economy. For instance, in applications dependent on digital systems, like the management of a country's energy systems, data security can hold significance on both institutional and regional or national levels. Therefore, digital data ownership plays a crucial role in data security and economic management of data.

The more frequently digital platforms are used, the more data is generated. As digital platforms have become increasingly integrated into various aspects of personal and societal life, and gained more prevalence in routine practices during the COVID-19 pandemic, the data produced on these platforms has multiplied. With the proliferation of data, defined as a digital footprint and consisting of raw data open to assessment, data security has become a personal and national concern, especially considering the various data mining applications that can be pursued for diverse purposes.

Increasingly increasing digital footprints of individuals and institutions make data security a personal and national problem as digital communication forms are strengthened and expanded. In addition to the possibilities offered by digital communication formats, legal problems frequently arise in terms of problems and practices such as digital privacy and digital surveillance that arise in line with data security. Data security, which means that all activities of individuals and institutions on the Internet can be protected; It includes being traceable and visible at any time and anywhere with the diversification of areas where the Internet can be used, recording and accessing every Internet-mediated activity. While every new application added to the internet technology brings the issue of data security to the fore, the security of data on cloud storage stands out as a problem, not only the security of data recorded on physical disks. Diao, Wang et al. as it states, it is possible to say that data security, which is seen as an urgent problem for cloud storage technology, becomes more important as societies, institutions and states integrate into digital environments. (Diao and Wang, 2017).

It can be said that the types of personal data have diversified and spread to the public much more through social media. Users private areas become much more visible through user-generated content and implicitly collected information (Pierson, 2012). These two types of exposure can be addressed as privacy as subject (Pierson, 2012), which includes information flow and meaning making in a social context, and privacy as object (De Wolf and Heyman, 2013), which includes the processing and objectification of large amounts of data. Both types of exposure can be evaluated in terms of data security. Because the security of internet activities, which include the sharing and visits of users, and the security of big data, which is the result of these activities, are economically and legally linked. While the activities covered by privacy as a subject contribute economically to the platforms that enable these activities, big data that occurs in the context of privacy as an object may be of legal, economic and national importance depending on the use of this data. Therefore, the data covering personal and corporate uses and the security of this data can provide various gains in the fields of economy, law and security for the social media platform in question and the country that is subject to the laws of this platform.

These achievements contribute to the value added by the social media platform, which has the status of a company, to the country's economy and prestige, as well as to the realization of surveillance and sanction activities carried out in connection with the national government, which are important in terms of law and security. Because digital technology has become crucial for modern surveillance activities, and the information obtained through surveillance can help the relevant authorities to prevent crimes and attacks, thereby making society safer (Chayko, 2018). The fact that this surveillance can be carried out quickly and efficiently requires cooperation with the relevant social platform and in this direction, the detection of user identity and IP address, content removal, etc. depends on the implementation of actions. Even if the information and actions requested from the relevant social media outlets by governments or law enforcement agencies are based on legitimate grounds in terms of national and international law, they may be blocked by bureaucratic or arbitrary obstacles. In addition, action or access to information may be delayed, and accordingly, it may pave the way for national security vulnerabilities. In addition, information obtained through surveillance provides benefits to national governments to prevent possible crimes and attacks. Surveillance can also cover the personal and corporate uses of other countries, and every communication that takes place via the internet or telecommunication can be listened to, monitored and tracked legally or illegally. This information, once collected, "can be used in a variety of ways by law enforcement, governments, hackers, employers, and companies." (Chayko, 2018: 91). Information that may be important in terms of national security may also include the data of citizens, bureaucrats or institutions of other countries, so it can be considered as a security problem for countries. Indeed, global surveillance and security industry companies are able to conduct global surveillance in the interest of various countries and organizations, spying on almost everyone on the planet with programs such as PRISM and X-Keyscore. (Arık, 2018). Therefore, economically and technologically leading global powers can threaten the national security of many states 'digitally' in line with their own interests. Because the most challenging and extensive uses of digital data security emerge at the intersection of states' military and political security (Milton, 2010). At this intersection, there are internet and digital security companies, the nation states to which these companies are affiliated, and individuals, institutions and countries that can be seen as social, military or political targets. At this point, all kinds of data are open to be recorded and used in line with political and economic interests.

Digital surveillance, which covers both the monitoring of actions that can take place via the Internet and that poses national and social security, and the security of data collected through the Internet, is carried out by companies that have dominated the digital economy and a few countries to which these companies are legally affiliated. Under these circumstances, it can be safely said that digital surveillance puts the security of other countries at risk. This risk and the concentration of the internet as a hierarchical power in the hands of some states also encourage other states to see the internet as a weapon that provides a strategic advantage in national power rivalries (Milton, 2010). This struggle, which can be compared to the legitimate armament in the name of national security, also reveals the importance of nations having their own digital infrastructures and policies. The said infrastructure and policies, along with secure and well-structured information technology, can not only safeguard networks and services but also ensure public welfare, economic stability, and energy systems (Topor, 2023: 98).

Nation-states' goals of indigenizing their digital structuring and policies for both security-related issues and economic reasons bring up various perspectives on the subject. Indeed, "there is a growing policy debate about how government should act in an environment where personal information is widely collected, analyzed and shared as a new form of currency in the digital economy." (Madden and Cortesi, 2012). The policy discussions in question are shaped in the context of the prevention of content that creates violations of national security and law by social media organizations by filtering, the effective cooperation of social media organizations with governments and law enforcement agencies when necessary, and the strict control of these organizations by the state. It is possible to address these policy debates, which deal with internet governance in the context of digital data security, in terms of the political spectrums of internet governance, which Mueller classifies as nationless liberalism, networked nationalism, global manageability and cyber-conservatism (Milton, 2010). While the nationless liberalism perspective emphasizes the necessity of establishing international governance institutions, it similarly advocates control through institutions that transcend global manageability nation-states. While networked nationalism emphasizes that networks and agreements covering networks should be under the control of nation states, cyber-conservatism argues that the internet and its networks should be adapted to the authority of states (Milton, 2010). In the context of these considerations, it can be said that digital data security can be ensured either by the sanctions and actions of international organizations and internet companies, or by nation-state policies. It can be stated that the perspectives of national liberalism and global manageability neglect the dimension of digital data security that is closely related to nation states. Because digital data security is not limited to personal data, it can reach dimensions that can threaten military, institutional and national security. Networked nationalism and cyber-conservatism ideas, on the other hand, have the potential to be an effective perspective against threats to national security, provided that the privacy rights of individuals are reserved. However, 'excessive cybersecurity measures can potentially impose restrictions on citizens' access to information sources and services, as well as on economic, communication, and freedom of movement.' (Topor, 2023: 98). Therefore, actions taken at the national level for digital data security need to be carried out with a delicate balance

It is not possible to talk about the universal validity of digital policies on a global or national scale. The search for direction on this issue continues both on a global and national scale. According to Van Dijk, institutional political powers, which are at the base of the political system, had to renounce some of their powers due to the use of information and communication technologies. (Van Dijk, 2016). This causes the basis of the system in the national government to be bypassed from time to time. The political pursuits of nations and governments about digital security and digital economy, especially data security, can be considered as a move against the waiver and bypassing that Van Dijk expressed. As a matter of fact, these moves include both a precaution against the risks and threats that may come from abroad, as well as the national and political benefits that can be achieved with digital surveillance within the country. Thus, it is seen as a necessity for nations to position themselves as a powerful actor in a global network without borders. In addition, although network technologies have gained an international dimension in a very short time, laws and punishments for crimes committed through networks are mostly national (Van Dijk, 2016). This situation shows how important the success of nation states in their political pursuits about digital security and digital economy is in terms of internet security. In addition, the fact that states have a strong digital infrastructure can enable governments to demonstrate their capabilities, bring institutions together and provide cost-effective solutions to problems (Chayko, 2018). Therefore, producing local priority solutions to the global problems of the global internet is closely related to the digital development of nation states.

It is a popular point of view that the borderless internet network is seen as a destructive force for nations with borders by its very existence. However, nation states are one of the most powerful actors in societies on digital policies. Because, according to Slaughter, the state does not disappear, but is separated into its institutions that are interconnected by networks (Van Dijk, 2016). In this direction, it can be said that states try to adapt to networks within their hierarchical structures and try to strengthen the connections between their structures with networks. Many countries, including Canada, France, Germany, Japan, the United Kingdom, the United States and Türkiye, have national cyber security strategies (Shafqat & Masood, 2016). In addition, a digital transformation office was established in Türkiye in 2018. In line with "emerging technologies, social demands and reform trends in the public sector, digital transformation (e-Government) carried out separately under different institutions; in order to gather studies on cyber security, national technologies, big data and artificial intelligence under one roof" (Digital Transformation Office of The Presidency of Türkiye, 2022) was established under the digital transformation office and effectively brings together all stakeholders in the digitalization process. The office, which has made moves on issues of national and social economic and security importance, such as cyber security and indigenization in digital technology, can also be cited as an example for states to develop effective digital policies and strategies.

Digital Data Security and Cyber Security Strategies

A strategic approach is required in order to ensure and maintain digital data security, which is important for the security of institutions and nations. As a matter of fact, "today, in many countries of the world, the need for a strategic approach is now recognized in order to take national measures against possible cyber attacks." (Güngör, 2015). It can be said that the strategies in question are of priority in the national context, since they have a national security character and political and public character in connection with the institutional structure of the state. As a matter of fact, Luiijf and Besseling also state that digital data security in cyberspace, which is global in nature, is a high priority issue that requires international cooperation. (Luiijf & Besseling, 2013). Ensuring digital data security is carried out through cyber security methods. Therefore, it is possible to say that digital data security falls within the scope of cyber security. As a matter of fact, digital data security is handled directly or indirectly in national cyber security strategies.

The necessity of a strategic approach in data security has emerged largely in line with the interconnection of communication and information systems by internet technologies at both national and international levels and the security sensitivities that emerged after this connection. In addition, there is a need to develop national strategies to provide the digital infrastructure that nations need to be a part of the growing global digital economy. (Teoh and Mahmood, 2017). The strategic elements that form the basis of national information security, which is the determinant and guide of the developed digital policies, are listed as follows (Güngör, 2015):

- Political ownership,
- Institutional structuring,
- Legal infrastructure in the fight against crime,
- Protection of critical information infrastructures,
- Response teams for computer incidents,
- Security of public information systems,
- Public-private sector coordination and cooperation,
- Training, awareness and R&D studies,
- International cooperation.

In addition, the stakeholders of cyber security strategies are government, non-governmental organizations, military, regulatory agencies, infrastructure operators, industry and businesses, research and development organizations, universities and citizens. (Luiijf & Besseling, 2013).

The strategic elements of Güngör's national information security policies and the stakeholders of Luiijf and Besseling's cyber security strategies reveal that the existence of a political will is necessary with the provision of institutional and technical structuring in order for the digital data and information security strategies to be put forward and to function. In addition, the national nature of data and information security strategies, which also have economic counterparts in the context of law enforcement, legal structure, private sector initiatives and public-private sector cooperation, is also important for states to adapt to networks and make domestic technology moves in this direction.

Although it is important to ensure cooperation between the public and private sectors on cyber security, which includes digital data security, the conclusion reached by Carr in his study is that the private sector approaches the issue of cyber security within the framework of cost/benefit (Carr, 2016). Since this is a factor damaging the public quality of cyber security, it increases the responsibility of the public in cyber security studies.

As can be seen in the UK's cybersecurity strategies, national cybersecurity strategies tend to clearly identify sources of risks. These sources often appear as criminals, terrorists or hostile states (Cyber Security Strategy of the United Kingdom, 2009). Cyber crimes were emphasized in Türkiye's cyber security strategy and action plan, and it was emphasized that these crimes could be of an international nature. (Republic of Türkiye Ministry of Transport and Infrastructure, National Cyber Security Strategy and Action Plan, 2020). In the study of Sabillon et al., it is stated that national cyber security strategies have features of crime, intelligence, research and development, law and military. (Sabillon, et al., 2016).

Examining the cyber security strategies of countries, Azmi, Tibben and Win identified nine features in these strategies. (Azmi and Tibben, 2016). These features are:

- Reducing cyber threats,
- Economic security,
- Necessary policy tools,
- Strengthening national resilience,
- National interests,
- Legal duty,
- Protection of state secrets,
- Strengthening diplomacy,
- Raising the image of the country.

The features identified by Azmi, Tibben and Win reveal the protective, constructive and political aspects of digital data security strategies. The characteristics of security strategies, including a nation's security, interests, image, infrastructure and technical adequacy and its ability to produce policies, also illuminate what kind of elements digital policies should have in the local context.

While creating digital data security strategies, a defense purpose is basically pursued. This defense against attacks that may take place in cyber space is defined as "all the measures that must be taken to prevent attacks on information systems, the negative effects that may arise, and to ensure the survival of the systems" (Şahin, 2015). According to the sources of the attacks taken precautions; while hackers, groups, individuals, cybercriminal organizations, businesses and countries, they are personal users, businesses, political formations and public institutions according to their attack targets (Güngör, 2015). The diversity of attack targets shows that digital data security strategies should be in a range from personal users to public institutions.

It is possible to say that cyber attacks against individuals and institutions, which may be in the nature of espionage, sabotage, and terrorism, are "a series of nation-state-related cyber threats that cause nations to feel insecure" (Güngör, 2015). The best response to this threat is to create digital data security strategies that promote national technological competence. The creation, dissemination and up-to-dateness of domestic technologies in a way that minimizes security weaknesses in the digital environment meets the national nature of digital security strategies. In addition, it contributes to the national level in the establishment of various cooperations necessary for security, economic interests and the fight against crime.

The National Cyber Security Strategy and Action Plan, prepared by the Ministry of Transport and Infrastructure of the Republic of Türkiye, also includes various topics on national capacity building, technology security, combating cybercrime, domestic and national technologies, and international cooperation. Among the primary objectives of the plan are the provision of cyber security with domestic and national products and the protection of critical infrastructures with domestic and national security solutions. (Republic of Türkiye Ministry of Transport and Infrastructure, National Cyber Security Strategy and Action Plan, 2020). In addition to the necessity of the technical applications that will provide cyber security to be domestic, the domestic and national applications used in the digital communication environment are seen as an important step in digital data security and cyber security. In this direction, the fact that the applications used for the security of digital communication are also domestic can be seen as a factor that will contribute to national cyber security.

Evaluation of Domestic Messaging Applications in Türkiye in the Context of National Data Security

Although instant messaging applications were one of the communication channels that were frequently used before the pandemic period, they were used more intensely by individuals and institutions due to social restrictions during the pandemic period. Instant messaging applications, which offer opportunities such as video calls and group messages, have allowed many activities to be carried out online. The security of data in digital channels has become even more important as communication and sharing through these applications increases. As a matter of fact, the security agreement update of Whatsapp, which came to the agenda in the first months of 2021, when the pandemic restrictions in Türkiye partially continued, had an echo in the Turkish public. Concerns about the security of data in Whatsapp in society have aroused interest in alternative applications, especially domestic messaging applications. In line with this interest, there has been a trend towards domestic messaging applications such as BIP and Dedi, which already exist but do not attract much attention. Although the reason for the tendency to domestic messaging applications is personal security concerns, it can be said that these applications are also important in terms of national data security. Indeed, Geetha Rani and Chetena (2023) argue that the element of localization is one of the fundamental aspects in digital data security, as the rules governing data can transform when data is transferred to different regions (2023: 412).

In research conducted on messaging applications in Türkiye (Özemir and Nacar, 2020; Öztürk et al., 2021; Gülpınar Demirci and Buluz Kömeçoğlu, 2022), it was found that users who prefer domestic social media platforms do so for reasons such as 'contributing to the national economy, finding cultural affinity, and the use of the Turkish language' (2020: 65). Furthermore, after the enforcement of stringent policies by these applications, some users tend to prefer domestic applications more (2021: 73). The results also suggest that 'social networks need to persuade users that their personal data is protected through new security measures and methods' (2022: 737). While these findings indicate a certain level of inclination and awareness towards local messaging applications, they also highlight that users may not have a high level of awareness regarding the importance of domestic applications in terms of data security.

There are many instant messaging applications developed by Turkish companies and engineers with domestic and national resources. These applications, which are an indication that there is no technical obstacle or inadequacy in providing personal and national data security in a domestic way, contain all the features of foreign messaging applications such as Whatsapp, Telegram and Signal. In addition to these, having the data that needs to be stored in Türkiye can be seen as an advantage in terms of personal, institutional and national data security.

Domestic messaging applications in Türkiye include Laff Messenger, BİP Messenger, Dedi, Chat-In, Havelsan İleti and Kamapp. Although the existence of these applications is an indicator of technical competence, it is very important to keep the applications up-to-date, to disseminate them, and to carry out advertising and marketing activities. As a matter of fact, Wirofon, one of the domestic messaging application initiatives, was shut down, PTT Messenger and Laff applications cannot be accessed through the Play Store, and the social media accounts used for the promotion of the applications are not actively used. Therefore, the research focused on BIP Messenger, Dedi, Kamapp and Havelsan Message applications, which are still actively used.

BİP Messenger

BIP instant messaging application, developed by Turkcell by Turkish engineers, was put into service in 2013. IOS and Android users can benefit from the BIP application, which has received more than 50 million downloads in the Play Store. Messages in BIP, which contains all communication and interaction features found in popular instant messaging applications, are protected by end-to-end encryption and cannot be accessed by third parties. (BIP, Safety).

Messages sent through the application are not stored by the application, are stored on the device. If the user requests that their messages be backed up, they are protected in an encrypted form in the data centers in Türkiye (BİP). In addition to these, BİP, which has features such as application locking, read receipt, last seen and end-to-end encryption control, also offers video conferencing services.

The end-to-end encryption method, which is an important feature for ensuring data security in instant messaging applications, is introduced by BİP as follows:

- "Privacy and security is a requirement for a messaging app, not a feature. That's why BiP has equipped the architecture of the application on "security".
- With end-to-end encryption, your messages and calls are only between you and the person you're communicating with. No one, including BİP, can read your messages or listen to your calls.
- End-to-end encryption secures sent messages with a lock, making the key of this lock private only to the sender and receiver. Since all these encryption and decryption flows occur on the users' devices and each message is encrypted, third parties, including BİP, are prevented from intervening and accessing the message and call content.
- End-to-end encryption is inherent in the application and it is automatically applied to your one-to-one messaging, one-to-one audio and video calls without the need to activate any settings." (BİP, End to end Encryption)

BİP, which also includes an innovative security measure such as verifying the end-to-end encryption method, creates a special security code for each chat, which can be matched with the other party at any time and thus verified. The BİP application also provides corporate services. This service, called a corporate-specific communication platform, can be used for internal communication and sharing. Promising effective data security for corporate use, BİP's prominent features in corporate data security are;

- Providing access only to designated people, thus making the communication group closed to the outside, and securely performing internal communication,
- The communication data on the application as encrypted in the institution's own data centers and thus preventing the dissemination of in-house information and documents to unsafe channels are possible to list.

BİP application can process identity information, contact information, usage information and device information in terms of legal regulations to which it is subject. The processing purposes are to meet requests from authorized institutions and organizations and user requests and complaints. (BİP, Privacy Policy). While the above information that can be stored and processed by BİP is stored only in Türkiye, this stored information can be shared with the competent authorities in order to ensure rights and security. This means that in case of any security or violation of rights, the competent authorities can quickly and effectively access the data they need to reach.

The information security policy of BİP is also important for digital data security. Because constantly changing and developing internet technologies require keeping up-to-date on information and data security applications. It is stated on the Information Security Policy page of the application that the items listed below are the responsibility of the senior management:

- To determine a strategy, focus, target and roadmap in order to ensure information security,
- To ensure and maintain the objectives of confidentiality, integrity and accessibility of information assets and information security,
- To increase the reputation of the company by working to comply with the standards, laws and contracts related to information security,
- To evaluate stakeholder requests regarding information security,

- To analyze security risks and controls in order to systematically manage information security risks, and to support an effective risk management approach in order to reduce or eliminate the identified risks to an acceptable level,
- To determine the authorities and responsibilities for the management of information security risks and the healthy operation of security controls, to allocate the necessary resources,
- To establish the necessary systems to manage information security breaches and taking appropriate measures to prevent their recurrence,
- To carry out continuous maturation and improvement studies for information security. (BİP, Information Security Policy).

In the light of all these, the data security in the BİP application is end-to-end encryption and its verifiable by the user, storage of messages on the device and not by the application, the data to be taken from users is stored only in data centers in Türkiye, and in addition to these, it is possible to say that in corporate use, institutions can store their data in their own data centers. In addition, the fact that BİP is a Türkiye-based application means that an effective communication and cooperation can be quickly established between the law enforcement officers and the service provider when an illegal action is taken through the application.

Dedi and Havelsan İleti

Dedi, which was developed by Turkish engineers through the Information Technologies and Internet Security Association (BTI), which carries out software and hardware development activities in the field of Internet technologies, can be used on Android and IOS operating systems. Dedi uses Signal's open source infrastructure and has an end-to-end encryption method. Since the Signal infrastructure is used, the end-to-end encryption method can also be used in group chats. In the Dedi application, it is stated that the data is not hosted and stored anywhere (Dedi). Dedi, where many types of content such as location, document, photo and audio can be shared, provides access to transactions such as news, market data, translation and cargo tracking with its Services feature.

Since the Dedi application was developed using the infrastructure of the Signal application, it is estimated that it has a similar structure in terms of data security. Because although there are not many technical details about data security on the website of the application, it is stated that no data is stored anywhere in the use of the application. (Dedi).

Another domestic messaging application, Havelsan İleti, has been developed for corporate use only. Developed by Havelsan Inc., an organization of the Turkish Armed Forces Foundation, Havelsan İleti aims to maximize corporate data security. In addition to its end-to-end encryption feature, Havelsan İleti uses the White Box Cryptography Library for the first time in a messaging application in the world, thus preventing the software protection of personal keys and the seizure of keys (Havelsan İleti). It can be said that this feature, which provides additional protection in terms of data security, is the most important feature that makes the application stand out. The application, which can be used on corporate level, Android and IOS operating systems, runs on the institution's own servers, so the data does not go outside the institution and works in a closed network.

Having developed the secure video meeting application Havelsan Diyalog and the secure storage and sharing platform Havelsan Drive besides Havelsan İleti for corporate data security, Havelsan stands out as one of the prominent developers in providing digital data security with domestic facilities.

Chat-In, Laff Messenger, and Kamapp

Developed by Kale Ileri Teknoloji, a local technology company, the Chat-In messaging application was launched in 2020. Chat-In, where no information is stored in databases, has made various updates to the IOS version "in order to prevent the possibility that some developments resulting from the procedures published by the Apple company pose a security risk in secure communication". On the security page of the application, which has reached more than 500 thousand downloads in the Play Store, it is stated that end-to-end encryption method is used, third parties cannot access the contents of the messages and messages are not stored on Chat-In servers. (Chat-In, Security).

Developed by Türk Telekom's research and development company Argela, the Laff application is also an instant messaging application produced with domestic resources. Providing data security with end-to-end encryption method, Laff incorporates the possibilities of many domestic and foreign messaging applications. Laff Messenger, which was launched in 2019, cannot be accessed through the Play Store. The application, which was last updated in 2020, does not have any promotion or advertising activities.

Introducing itself with the slogan of Domestic, National and Reliable, Kamapp messaging application was developed by Turkish engineers and put into use in 2018. The application, which has received more than 10 thousand downloads from the Play Store, emphasizes its development with domestic and national resources. "The entire technical infrastructure of the application (including all user data, system infrastructure) is hosted within the borders of Türkiye." (Kamapp)

The domestic messaging applications in Türkiye, whose information is shared, have no shortage of foreign examples in terms of both their functions and the security methods they use. In addition, hosting the stored user data within the country can be considered important for both the security of the user and the effective and functional management of situations that may have legal consequences. The high number of downloads of BİP Messenger, Dedi Messenger and Chat-In applications, which are actively serving, in the Play Store proves the interest in the applications. The Kamapp application, on the other hand, has less downloads than other active applications. Among these applications, BIP Messenger is an active advertisement on social media platforms, while the social media accounts of Chat-In and Kamapp applications are not actively used while promoting. Dedi Messenger, on the other hand, could not find a social media account used for advertising and promotion.

The fact that instant messaging applications have an important place in personal and corporate communication has made it essential to ensure the confidentiality and security of the established communication. As a matter of fact, Whatsapp, Telegram and Signal, which are the most used instant messaging applications in the world, use various methods to ensure the personal and corporate data security of their users. The most general of these methods, which are also found in domestic messaging applications, is the end-to-end encryption method. This method ensures that the contents of the message are only accessible to the people involved in the message. End-to-end encryption works by securing messages with a private key and only the people involved in the message can access this private key. Theoretically, it prevents access to the password of the speech, including the internet infrastructure and communication service providers.

End-to-end encryption is seen as an effective security method and is widely used. However, the encryption in question is only valid for messages and cannot be seen as a security measure for the account to which the messages are transmitted. Therefore, accounts in the email or messaging application are not protected by end-to-end encryption. In addition, the end-to-end encryption method does not apply to the application-promoted message backup feature, and the backed up messages are transmitted without encryption.

A common data security practice of messaging apps is that messages are stored on the device being used, not on the app's servers. This situation, which can be considered as a general and effective security method, does not apply to user information other than message contents. As a matter of fact, some user information may be stored and used for service development and security reasons. This information includes service information, undelivered messages (encrypted), connections (contacts), status features, usage and registration information, device information, location information, third-party services and cookies (Whatsapp). This information can also be used by companies such as Meta and Apple, which have more than one product, for cross-product compatibility, service experience and advertising purposes.

The use of the collected personal information by companies defined as third parties poses a privacy problem in instant messaging applications as well as in social media applications. The evaluation of users' information for purposes such as marketing, advertising, product and service development can also be interpreted as the commodification of users and disrupts digital data security. In addition, when this data is collected and used by foreign-based companies, it can complicate an effective cooperation on legal issues that may concern law enforcement.

In general, it is seen that instant messaging applications take security measures such as end-to-end encryption and not storing message contents on servers belonging to the service provider. These measures, which are very important to prevent third parties from accessing the contents of personal messages, constitute only one dimension of digital data security. As a matter of fact, third parties can also violate digital data security by logging into users' e-mail or messaging accounts. In addition to this point where security measures can be varied, the use of personal data collected by users by third parties is also based on a consent included in user contracts, which poses a danger to digital data security. This consent can also enable internet companies to generate revenue through various methods such as advertising, marketing, product development and user classification.

As mentioned in the second part of the study, domestic messaging applications BİP, Dedi, Chat-in, Kamapp secure messages with end-to-end encryption method. Developed for corporate use, Havelsan Ileti uses a more advanced security method to protect messaging with the White Box Cryptography Library technique. In addition, all domestic messaging applications store the message contents in the user's phone memory, not on their own servers. Therefore, in terms of message security, it is possible to say that domestic messaging applications do not have any shortcomings compared to foreign messaging applications Whatsapp, Telegram and Signal. In addition to these, personal data collected about users in domestic messaging applications are stored on servers in Türkiye and not taken out of the country, so digital data is stored in a more reliable way. It also makes it possible to establish a fast and effective cooperation with the said platforms in case of privacy violations that may concern law enforcement and have legal consequences.

In addition to personal use, corporate use is also important in questioning messaging applications in terms of digital data security. Because the security of digital data of private or public institutions has a serious economic, political and social importance. Moreover, considering the data on the security of the state, digital data security may also have a national security nature. Indeed, in the Security Guide prepared by the Digital Transformation Office of the Republic of Türkiye in 2020, the issue of instant messaging security is also addressed, and various security measures have been implemented. Among these measures are topics such as the choice of messaging application, transmission medium security, privacy-rated data sharing, multi-device usage, end-to-end encryption, and storage of encryption keys

(Republic of Türkiye Digital Transformation Office, 2020). Regarding the measure related to the choice of messaging application, it is stipulated as follows: 'Privacy-rated data sharing and communication should not be conducted through mobile applications, except for domestically developed mobile applications authorized for coded or encrypted communication under the legislation' (Republic of Türkiye Digital Transformation Office, 2020)

The Internet has the potential to be used as a weapon (Milton, 2010) and this potential can turn into reality from time to time, by eavesdropping on the leaders of countries, or by cyber-attacks on servers where military or political data is stored. In order to prevent these, in addition to making the necessary investments in cyber security, the digital communication infrastructure needs to be localized. The domestic messaging applications discussed in the study can be seen as one of the most important steps in the localization of the digital communication infrastructure. Because these applications, which do not have any disadvantages in terms of message security, have the potential of effective cooperation in order to store the collected personal data within the borders of Türkiye, not to be taken out of the country, and to process legal processes when necessary. In addition, while providing personal, corporate and national advantages in terms of digital data security, it is important for Türkiye to get a share from the ever-growing digital economy.

Although there is enough variety to create an alternative in domestic messaging applications in Türkiye, it is possible to say that the applications in question do not have the quality of a global brand as in the examples of Whatsapp or Telegram. Since applications developed mainly for personal use are not a public initiative, but a private sector initiative, addressing the global market is important in terms of permanence. In addition, being able to serve the domestic market consistently in order to support localization policies in data security is also of a public nature. For this, a strong capital requirement may raise some question marks for the future of domestic messaging applications.

CONCLUSION

Digital communication technologies, which are used in many areas of life, have completely spread to daily life with the social restrictions during the Covid-19 pandemic period. While communication processes covering education, business and personal relations were carried out online through various applications, digital communication channels continued to be used as hybrids even when the pandemic restrictions ended.

Data security, which is one of the biggest problems of digital communication technologies, has come to the fore with the use of these technologies in all areas of life. Digital data, which emerges in a wide range from personal data to corporate data, can also be a matter of national security in terms of military, economic and political aspects. As a matter of fact, the security of data generated in military, economic and political processes that contain digital communication practices in many respects is gaining more and more importance for nations.

Digital data security, which is evaluated within the scope of cyber security strategies prepared by states, aims to protect the data that emerges in communication, organization, management and decision-making practices through digital channels. The protection of this data is of a public nature as it can also become a national security issue. Therefore, states have important duties in the preparation of technical and economic infrastructures related to data security. As a matter of fact, many states have created their own cyber security strategies and are making efforts to implement the strategies determined by various collaborations and initiatives.

Digital data security, which is of a public nature, covers many digital communication channels, including instant messaging applications. Instant messaging applications, which have the most common personal and corporate use among these channels, are now included in personal and group communication practices at all levels. The digital data that emerges in these practices can also be important for the security of individuals, institutions and nations.

Protecting the communication in messaging applications with end-to-end encryption method aims to prevent third parties from accessing these messages and to keep the data only between the parties involved in the communication. However, end-to-end encryption method, which can be seen as a basic security measure, is far from providing a security guarantee on its own, although it is important in terms of data security. This is because encrypting data does not add to security vulnerabilities that may occur in the application account where the data was created or during and after backup operations. In addition, the answers to questions such as how and where the personal data stored by instant messaging applications and shared with third parties are stored, with whom and why they are shared play an important role in the evaluation of these applications in terms of digital data security.

The foreign-centeredness of the most popular messaging applications creates a vulnerability in terms of data security. It can also be seen as a negative situation in terms of access to stored data in situations that may concern law enforcement and the share that can be taken from the returns of the digital economy. Because these popular applications are in the hands of large digital companies such as Meta, Apple and Google, data on people and usage are shared with other applications of the companies and value is created for companies in this direction. In addition, if foreign-based practices are used in a way that creates an element of crime, it can complicate an effective and rapid cooperation regarding access to data that local courts may request from international companies or their representatives. In addition to all these, the oligopolization of rapidly growing technology and digital communication companies, which have an important place in the economies of countries, can also be evaluated negatively in terms of local economic development.

As seen in the study, domestic messaging applications do not differ from foreign ones in terms of digital data security. In addition, the White Box Cryptography Library measure for institutional use is important in terms of storing the data in the country, which can enable legal cooperation to take place effectively and quickly if needed, and being subject to local law. Thus, since domestic practices are far from the logic of global oligopoly, it also provides an advantage in its contribution to the domestic economy. In addition, domestic messaging applications, which are important for the creation of a domestic digital infrastructure and the domestic construction of digital data security within this infrastructure, have a strong potential in ensuring national data security with its political, economic and military dimensions.

Despite the advantages of domestic messaging applications in terms of personal and national security, it can be said that it has not made progress such as becoming a global brand and being the first choice of users, which is very important for private sector initiatives. Starting and maintaining the competition against foreign messaging applications that are automatically installed on almost every smartphone will be possible with an effective and stable advertising and marketing campaign that emphasizes the advantages of domestic messaging applications. It does not seem possible to state that this competition, which is important in terms of digital data security, can be fully realized. As a matter of fact, some of the domestic messaging applications in Türkiye cannot be accessed from the Play Store market, and social media accounts that can be used for advertising and marketing purposes are not actively evaluated. In addition to Havelsan Ileti, which serves corporate customers, BIP, Chat-In, Dedi and Kamapp are active and accessible. Advertising and marketing activities of BIP, developed by Turkcell, are also actively carried out through social media.

It is obvious that domestic messaging applications should be expanded in line with the guidance of the Presidency Digital Transformation Office, which leads the indigenization policies in technology. Although there are no technical difficulties in the creation of applications, it can be said that advertising campaigns should be continued in a stable manner and competition with foreign applications should be maintained actively. In this direction, it is possible to state that the process of indigenization in terms of messaging applications has some shortcomings arising from the creation of competition and promotion in a stable manner rather than being able to develop applications. Aware that the said indigenization will be a precaution against threats that may arise as a result of personal use as well as national security, promotional campaigns should be organized. It is also thought that keeping the applications up-to-date will contribute to the localization moves in technology. It is very important to be aware that the internet, which can be used as an attack tool, is also a defense tool. It is possible to say that in addition to public support, private companies, which are application developers, should make an intense effort in order to spread the domestic technology moves carried out within the scope of national cyber security policies and to create a user base.

In addition to these measures, the development and proliferation of domestic applications, particularly messaging applications and those with video conferencing capabilities, hold significance in terms of data security in remote education and remote work practices. One of the conclusions of this study is the necessity for increased efforts in technical areas of cybersecurity, such as software development and coding, for the enhancement of digital data security on both national and personal levels.

REFERENCES

Arık, E. (2018). *Dijital Mahremiyet*. Literatürk Yayınları.

Azmi, R., Tibben, W., & Win, K. T. (2016). Motives behind Cyber Security Strategy Development: A Literature Review of National Cyber Security Strategy. *Australasian Conference on Information Systems.*

BİP. (2022a). *Information Security Policy.* Retrieved from: https://bip.com/en/information-security-policy/

BİP. (2022b). *Privacy Policy.* Retrieved from: https://bip.com/en/privacy-policy/

BİP. (2022c). *Safety.* Retrieved from: https://bip.com/en/safety/

BİP. (2022d). *Corporate Communication Platform.* Retrieved from: https://bip.com/en/corporate-communication-platform/

BİP. (2022e). *End to End Encryption.* Retrieved from: https://bip.com/en/end-to-end-encryption-bip/

BİP. (2022f). *Help Center.* Retrieved from: https://bip.com/en/help-center/

Carr, M. (2016, January). Public–private partnerships in national cyber-security strategies. *International Affairs*, *92*(1), 43–62. doi:10.1111/1468-2346.12504

Charles, W., & Magtanong, R. (2022). Ethical Benefits and Drawbacks of Digitally Informed Consent. Applied Ethics in a Digital World, 101-123

Chayko, M. (2018). *Süper Bağlantılı* (B. Bayındır, D. Yengin, & T. Bayrak, Trans.). Der Yayınları.

De Wolf, R., Heyman, R., & Pierson, J. (2013). Privacy by Design through social requirements analysis of social network sites from a user perspective. In European Data Protection: Coming of Age. Springer Science+Business Media.

Dedi. (2022). *Anasayfa.* Retrieved from: https://dedi.com.tr/

Denning, D. E. (1982). *Cryptography and Data Security.* Addison-Wesley Publishing Company.

Diao, Z., Wang, Q., Naizheng, S., & Yuhan, Z. (2017). Study on Data Security Policy Based On Cloud Storage. *IEEE 3rd International Conference on Big Data Security on Cloud.* https://ieeexplore.ieee.org/document/7980332

Dictionary, C. (2022). *Security.* Retrieved from: https://dictionary.cambridge.org/dictionary/english/security

Digital Transformation Office of The Presidency of Türkiye. (2022). *About Us.* https://cbddo.gov.tr/hakkimizda/

Geetha Rani, E., & Chetana, D. T. (2023). A Survey of Recent Cloud Computing Data Security and Privacy Disputes and Defending Strategies. In J. C. Bansal, H. Sharma, & A. Chakravorty (Eds.), *Congress on Smart Computing Technologies. CSCT 2022. Smart Innovation, Systems and Technologies* (Vol. 351). Springer. doi:10.1007/978-981-99-2468-4_31

Goel, S. (2020). National Cyber Security Strategy and the Emergence of Strong Digital Borders. *Connections: The Quarterly Journal, 19*(1), 73-86.

Gülpınar Demirci, V., & Buluz Kömeçoğlu, B. (2022). Sosyal Ağlarda Veri Gizliliği: Türkiye'de Whatsapp Gizlilik Sözleşmesine Gösterilen Tepkilerinin Duygu Analizi. *Kafkas Üniversitesi İktisadi ve İdari Bilimler Fakültesi Kaüiibfd, 13*(26).

Güngör, M. (2015). *Ulusal Bilgi Güvenliği: Strateji ve Kurumsal Yapılanma.* Bilgi Toplumu Dairesi Başkanlığı.

Güvenli Haberleşme Uygulaması Dedi. (2022). *Dedi.* Retrieved from: https://btider.org.tr/dedi

Hovendan, D., & Bartlett, C. (2013). The Digital Government. *Strategy+Business.* Retrieved from: https://digitaledition.strategy-business.com/publication/?i=145911&article_id=1308784&view=articleBrowser&ver=html5

İleti, H. (2022). *Havelsan İleti.* Retrieved from: https://www.havelsan.com.tr/en/sectors/information-and-communication/products/security/havelsan-ileti

Kampp. (2022). *Hakkında.* https://www.kamapp.com/hakkinda/

Luiijf, E., Besseling, K., & Graaf, P. D. (2013). Nineteen national cyber security strategies. *Int. J. Critical Infrastructures, 9*(1/2), 3–31. doi:10.1504/IJCIS.2013.051608

Madden, M., Cortesi, S., Gasser, U., Lenhart, A., & Duggan, M. (2012). *Parents, Teens and Online Privacy.* Pew Research Center. Retrieved from: https://www.pewresearch.org/internet/2012/11/20/parents-teens-and-online-privacy/

Milton, M. (2010). *Networks and States*. The MIT Press.

Nikiforova, A. (2023). Data Security as a Top Priority in the Digital World: Preserve Data Value by Being Proactive and Thinking Security First. In A. Visvizi, O. Troisi, & M. Grimaldi (Eds.), *Research and Innovation Forum 2022. RIIFORUM 2022. Springer Proceedings in Complexity*. Springer. doi:10.1007/978-3-031-19560-0_1

Özdemir, K. & Nacar, R. (2020). Yerli ve Milli Sosyal Medyayı Tercih Etme Nedenleri. *Journal of Süleyman Demirel University Institute of Social Sciences, 3*(38), 42-69.

Öztürk, A., Erkan, C., & Erkuş, U. (2021). Türkiye'deki Sosyal Medya Kullanıcılarının Zorlayıcı Politikalar Sonrasındaki Sosyal Medya Kullanımında Alternatif Arayışlar ve Değişimler. *Mediterranean Summit 5th International Social Sciences Congress Book of Full Text*, 60-75.

Pierson, J., (2012). Online Privacy in Social Media: A Conceptual Exploration of Empowerment and Vulnerability. *Digiworld Economic Journal, 88*, 99-120.

Presidency of the Republic of Türkiye Digital Transformation Office. (2020). *Information and Communication Security Guide.* https://cbddo.gov.tr/SharedFolderServer/Genel/File/BG_REHBER.pdf

Republic of Türkiye Ministry of Transport and Infrastructure. (2022). *National Cyber Security Strategy and Action Plan.* Retrieved from: https://hgm.uab.gov.tr/uploads/pages/strateji-eylem-planlari/ulusal-siber-guvenlik-stratejisi-ve-eylem-plani-2020-2023.pdf

Sabillon, R., Cavaller, V., & Cano, J. (2016). National Cyber Security Strategies: Global Trends in Cyberspace. *International Journal of Computer Science and Software Engineering, 5*(5), 67-81. www.IJCSSE.org

Şahin, G. (2015). *Soğuk Savaş Sonrası Değişen Güvenlik Anlayışı Bağlamında Nato* [Phd Thesis]. Trakya Üniversitesi Sosyal Bilimler Enstitüsü, Edirne.

Shafqat, N., & Masood, A. (2016). Comparative Analysis of Various National Cyber Security Strategies. *International Journal of Computer Science and Information Security, 14*(1), 129–136.

Srnicek, N. (2017). *Platform Capitalism.* Polity Press.

Teoh, C. S., & Mahmood, A.K. (2017). National Cyber Security Strategies for Digital Economy. *International Conference on Research and Innovation in Information Systems (ICRIIS).* 10.1109/ICRIIS.2017.8002519

Topor, S. (2023). Values for the Cyber Security Strategy for a National Critical Infrastructure. *Romanian Cyber Security Journal, 5*(1), 97-106. doi:10.54851/v5i1y202309

Van Dijk, J. (2016). *Ağ Toplumu* (Ö. Sakin, Trans.). Epsilon Yayıncılık.

Whatsapp. (2022). *Privacy Policy.* Retrieved from: https://www.whatsapp.com/legal/privacy-policy

Chapter 5
Reasons for News Avoidance on Mobile News Consumption:
An Overview From Turkey

Ceren Saran
https://orcid.org/0000-0003-2444-2455
Uskudar University, Turkey

ABSTRACT

This study examined different news-following practices via mobile phones and questioned the reasons for news avoidance behaviour. In the study where in-depth interviews were conducted with 20 participants, 15 participants remarked that they had news avoidance. Five reasons for news avoidance behaviour have been identified: (1) disappointment, frustration, and stress avoidance; (2) losing curiosity; (3) lack of confidence and distrust of the media industry; (4) reduced quality and poor content of the news; and (5) overstimulation of the user. In the study, which revealed various news follow-up methods, it was seen that the main reason for news avoidance behaviour is the political atmosphere and social despair in Turkey and the world. News avoidance behaviour is both intentional and unintentional and has become a vicious circle that participants cannot escape. The digital platforms shaped by algorithmic selection are the main actors that prepare this outcome for the user who wishes to ignore the social realities despite the many stimuli surrounding daily life.

INTRODUCTION

In parallel with the global trend, mobile media use has expanded in Turkey. Recent research indicates that there has been a steadily increasing acceleration in both mobile news consumption and the rise of digital platforms as a primary news source (Kemp, 2022; Newman et al., 2021, 2022; Yanardağoğlu, 2021). The literature on mobile media use, algorithmic selection, and news consumption through digital platforms has revealed several different user attitudes against news reading (Fletcher & Nielsen, 2018; Ross Arguedas et al., 2022; Thurman et al., 2019; Van Damme et al., 2020). However, during the COVID-19 pandemic, the loss of media trust and news avoidance grew bigger and today became a prominent

DOI: 10.4018/979-8-3693-0896-7.ch005

issue for media and journalism studies (Adekoya & Fasae, 2021; de Bruin et al., 2021; Edgerly, 2022; Ravenelle et al., 2021; Villi et al., 2022).

This study, therefore, set out to critically examine the changing positions of users in mobile news consumption against digital platforms, algorithmic selection, and news avoidance. The research aims to discover different types of mobile news reading practices and reasons for news avoidance and to discover divergent positions of readers against digital platforms and mobile applications. To that end, qualitative explanatory research is designed to determine different news reading approaches in Turkey's post-pandemic period. In-depth interviews were conducted with 20 young adults aged 22-45 who are active digital media users living in Istanbul. The research questions are as follows:

(1) What are the different attitudes towards news consumption on mobile phones?
(2) Are the participants exposed to news or willing to receive news?
(3) According to which factors do the participants trust the news?
(4) Do the participants avoid news on their mobile phones; if yes, what are the reasons?

Background Information: Turkey, Digital Media, and the Rise of Mobile

Freedom House country report (2023) indicates that in Turkey, where the media atmosphere is currently concentrated in capital circles close to the political power, many activities, including digital platforms and internet content, are controlled. As for media pluralism, the indicators of the Media Ownership Monitor (MOM) Turkey project held by Reporters Without Borders (RSF) reveal that while the political pressure on media and news organisations in the country is intense, this situation also affects audience concentration. The Media Audience Concentration indicator is on medium/high level, Cross-media Ownership Concentration, (Political) Control Over Media Outlets and Distribution Networks, (Political) Control Over Media Funding, and (Political) Control Over News Agencies indicators of the project are at the highest level (MOM Turkey, 2023).

The general elections were held in two rounds in May 2023 under unequal conditions. The Supreme Election Council (YSK), court, police, and media are all under the partisan control of President Recep Tayyip Erdoğan and the ruling party Adalet ve Kalkınma Partisi (AKP, Justice and Development Party). In recent years, they have actively employed these institutional mechanisms to subjugate or undermine their opponents, which has limited the opposition's capacity to garner support from voters and win elections in May 2023, when state-run media favoured the AKP in its coverage. The pressure environment increased with the approval of the law in the parliament that would allow individuals to be imprisoned for their social media posts, which could be instrumentalised to silence independent journalists (Freedom House, 2023).

Most Turkish media networks are owned by businesses that depend on public tenders or have close ties to President Erdoğan. Mainstream media reflect government positions and often carry identical headlines. Although independent outlets exist, they face tremendous political pressure and are routinely targeted for prosecution. Media outlets are often censored, fined, or shut down, and journalists are detained regularly. Business elites with close ties to Erdoğan have been accused of bribing journalists and orchestrating negative press against the opposition. (…) The government heavily monitors and censors the Turkish internet, contributing to an atmosphere of self-censorship. (…) The government continues to censor LGBT+ content in the media, including on Netflix (Freedom House, 2023).

Just a few months before the election, the earthquake that affected 11 cities on February 6, 2023, and killed more than 50,000 people was one of the main events that laid the foundations of the state of despair. With the re-election of the party that has been in power for 21 years, which was held in May 2023, a state of mass despair, apathy and alienation dominated the public (Demiralp, 2023; Hansen, 2023; Yetkin, 2023). Under these conditions, alternative media is trying to find a space in the media order dominated by mainstream pro-government media organisations. Independent and alternative media, which have fewer opportunities than the mainstream media under the influence of political power, are trying to gain strength by trying to reach an audience through digital platforms (Kızılkaya & Ütücü, 2021).

According to digital media and internet trends reports, mobile internet usage and traffic have risen worldwide and in Turkey. In early 2023, there were 81.68 million active mobile phone connections in Turkey, 95.4 per cent of the country's total population. By the beginning of 2023, 97,6% of the population were smartphone, and 59% were desktop owners. By the beginning of 2023, YouTube had 57.90 million, Instagram had 48.65 million, Facebook had 32.80 million, TikTok had 29.86 million users, Twitter had 18.55 million, Snapchat had 14.80 million users, and LinkedIn had 13.00 million members in Turkey. Daily time spent using the internet is 7:24 hours, using social media is 2:54 hours, and time spent reading press media (online and physical print is 1:49 hours. The main three reasons for using the internet are finding information (73,2%), keeping up-to-date with news and events (67,6%), and researching how to do things (63,9%). Among devices used to access the internet, mobile phones are at the top with 94,3%, followed by laptops or desktops with 62,3% (57,7% personal devices, and 22,8% work devices). Mobile phones are at the top with 84,92% web traffic share, the highest share of the total traffic (Kemp, 2023).

Mobile News, Algorithmic Selection, and News Avoidance

Mobile news consumption is defined as "a habit of snacking" by Molyneux (2017). A fast and snack-based style of news consumption has dominated in the present digital media environment: regularly checking, snacking, sharing or liking news on social media for a few seconds, unlike reading a printed newspaper once a day (Costera Meijer & Groot Kormelink, 2015; Drok et al., 2018).

A study on news consumption habits of youth in Turkey and the UK revealed that there has been a shift towards consuming news on mobile phones and accessing news on their mobile phones, followed by their laptops (Yanardağoğlu, 2021). The research showed that most participants in Istanbul tend to rely on news aggregators like Bundle or Nabız or social media platforms like Twitter to access news online instead of using news applications. Indicating YouTube stands out in news consumption practices, another finding of the study is that digital media has nearly completely supplanted conventional media as a source of news, and traditional media's formats are challenging for young people to integrate into their daily schedules of job, school, and commuting (Yanardağoğlu, 2021).

A conceptual model for news recommendations on a smartmobile phone was presented in the study by Van Damme et al. (2020), based on mobile accidental news exposure, which illustrates the interaction between editors, algorithms, and peers in making news recommendations. According to the study's findings, a diversity of topics arises from editorial recommendations; audiences are unaware that brand variety results from both algorithmic and peer recommendations. Although they rarely result in topic or viewpoint diversity, peer recommendations are nevertheless valued when they occur (Van Damme et al., 2020).

Figure 1. The incidental news continuum based on user agency plotted the adjusted conceptual model for incidental news on smartphones (Van Damme et al., 2020, p. 59)

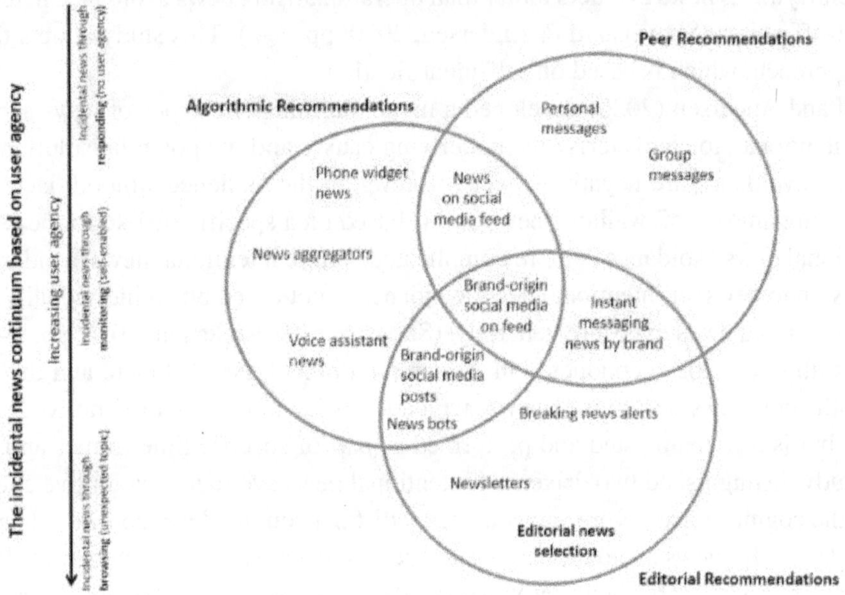

What makes these possible lies at the heart of this system; algorithmic selection, on the other hand, has been a timely problem for digital media and journalism studies for a while. OECD has determined several risk categories of algorithmic selection: Abuse of market power, bias, censorship, manipulation, privacy rights, property rights, and social discrimination (OECD, 2017, p. 44). These categories draw attention to the digital inequalities and the ever-widening gap that occur on digital platforms due to algorithmic selection expressed in the literature with concepts such as filter bubbles (Pariser, 2011), information cocoons and echo chambers (Sunstein, 2007).

The instrumentality of digital platforms is emphasised in the "post-publication gatekeeping" concept by counting them among the actors who determine the fate of news after publication, along with the publics, paraphernalia, and practices (Hermida, 2020). In the news ecosystem formed by the agency of digital platforms and algorithmic selection, readers' news reading practices have been discussed with various concepts existing in the literature. News exposure or exposure to news (Beam & Kosicki, 2014), news finds me (Gil de Zúñiga et al., 2017), incidental or accidental exposure (Park & Kaye, 2020), computational news discovery (Diakopoulos, 2020), distributed discovery (Toff & Nielsen, 2018), automated news discovery (Diakopoulos et al., 2021), 'attraction' to news (Thorson, 2020), automated serendipity (Fletcher & Nielsen, 2018) are among the most prominent ones. The primary consequence of the habitat that is tried to be explained with these concepts is the news avoidance behaviour.

A study on conceptualising and modelling news avoidance (Skovsgaard & Andersen, 2020) identified four approaches to operationalising news avoidance in the literature. The first approach applies cluster analysis or latent class analysis to determine groups based on their news exposure inductively. The second approach classifies news avoiders by applying a relative cut-off point in the amount of news consumption. The first and second approaches both identify people who avoid reading the news according to how much news the ordinary citizen is exposed to. The third approach employs an absolute cut-off point for news avoidance. For instance, they consider news avoiders as those who did not watch any news show or did not use any information channels to get a news overview during the week. A fourth approach depends on people self-identifying as news avoiders rather than operationalising news avoidance in terms of relative or absolute cut-off points (Skovsgaard & Andersen, 2020, pp. 3–4). This study adopts the perspective of the fourth approach, which is based on self-identification.

Skovsgaard and Andersen (2020) developed a model defining two types of news avoidance, intentional and unintentional, to characterise the underlying causes and the potential solutions. Reasons for intentional news avoidance are negative effects of news on the audience's mood, lack of trust in the news, an increasing amount of available news and is based on a specific dislike for news. On the other hand, unintentional news avoidance is more complicated. While intentional news avoidance is based on a specific aversion to news, unintentional news avoidance is not based on an individual's deliberate and active decision to avoid news exposure generally. (Skovsgaard & Andersen, 2020, pp. 5–7).

Research (Villi et al., 2022) conducted in Argentina, Finland, Israel, Japan, and the US and based on 488 in-depth interviews scrutinised news avoidance behaviour is shaped not only by individual characteristics but is also manifested and performed as part of specific time frames and socio-cultural factors. The study distinguished two drivers of intentional news avoidance: cognitive and emotional. It indicated that the cognitive drivers are accentuated by distinct country-level contextual factors, whereas the emotional drivers for news avoidance are shared across diverse national contexts (Villi et al., 2022).

Previous research has established that news avoidance behaviour has become extremely common during the COVID-19 pandemic period (de Bruin et al., 2021; Schäfer et al., 2023; Vandenplas et al., 2021). While a study from Australia (Mannell & Meese, 2022) discussed limiting news as a wellbeing strategy during the COVID-19 lockdown, a recent study conducted in the Netherlands identified five groups of news users who showed various reactions to the COVID-19 pandemic: news avoiders, followers turned avoiders, stable news users, frequent news users and news junkies (Broersma & Swart, 2022). In contrast to news avoidance, another type of news consumption behaviour, a term already existing in the literature, prevailed: doomscrolling. The Merriam-Webster dictionary declared doomscrolling a "word to watch" for a future formal entry in 2020: *"doomscrolling or doomsurfing are new terms referring to the tendency to continue to surf or scroll through bad news, even though that news is saddening, disheartening, or depressing"* (Ytre-Arne & Moe, 2021, p. 1741).

Research: What Do Users Think About Mobile News Consumption and Avoidance?

This chapter aims to understand the different positions of users in mobile news consumption, analyse the changing news consumption practices, and interrogate the reasons for news avoidance. To this end, this study has been designed as qualitative research, and a series of interviews were conducted. News consumption habits were collected from participants formed by a group of young adults (aged 22-45) who live and work in Istanbul, the most crowded city in Turkey with 15 million 907 thousand 951 inhabitants (TÜİK, 2023). The demographics of the participants are listed in Table 1. In this respect, the research questions are as follows:

(1) What are the different attitudes towards news consumption on mobile phones?
(2) Are the participants exposed to news or willing to receive news?
(3) According to which factors do the participants trust the news?

(4) Do the participants avoid news on their mobile phones; if yes, why?

In-depth interviews are the primary data collection method and were conducted face to face. In qualitative research, researchers can conduct different types of interviewing suited to different situations, as Punch (2014) states and the selected type of interview influences the practical aspects of the interview and how the researcher manages the process. Therefore, the semi-structured interview type was applicable. Since this type of interview necessitates the main questions and categories to collect data were prepared, and during the interview, emerging questions and topics were inquired (Berger, 2011).

Accordingly, an interview form has been prepared and used in interviews. The participants were asked to answer questions about their daily news consumption practices and mobile phone use. After collecting data from the participants, the findings were analysed and discussed according to the thematic analysis method, a data reduction and analysis strategy through which qualitative data are segmented, categorised, summarised, and reconstructed to capture the essential concepts (Ayres, 2008). With the aim of answering the research questions, the following questionnaire forms were prepared and asked of the participants:

1. How do you identify yourself politically?
2. What is the preferred channel and method to receive news?
3. How much free time can you spend on the phone in everyday life?
4. Do you read the news during the day? How often? Do you feel the need?
5. In what format do you like to receive news? (Video, image, text, audio, social media post, etc.)
6. How do you read the news on your mobile phone? (Application, digital platform, browser)
7. Do you personalise and customise news applications?
8. Do you trust the news you read or you are exposed to? Based on what factors do you trust? (Source, site, source in the news, image, reference, etc. of your own choosing.)
9. Do you search for news on Google Search?
10. What do you think about the notification? Do you open it or leave it to algorithmic selection?
11. What do you think about the news you are exposed to, brought to you through digital platforms and algorithms?
12. Would you rather have the news selected and recommended by an algorithm or read it with an editor's recommendation?
13. Do you have a different approach to news suggested or sent by an acquaintance?
14. Is there a news-related app within the top-used applications on your mobile phone?
15. Do you think you avoid the news? Are you bored of following the news?
16. Has your media, phone usage, and news following changed due to the pandemic and lockdown?

The participants' professions and demographic characteristics, as well as their political stances and how they define themselves politically, are determinants for them to follow the news and what is happening in the country. Therefore, participants were asked how they defined themselves politically, and it was stated that this data would be used anonymously. During the informal conversation before the interview, two participants stated that they used to be socialists, while one participant gave the impression of being culturally inclined towards political Islam. However, these participants refused to identify themselves politically and are included in Figure 2 in their self-declared ways.

Table 1. Demographics of the participants

	Occupation	Age	Sex	Education	Degree Field
P1	Video editor on a news channel	40	Male	Bachelor	Radio, Television and Cinema
P2	Unemployed (Former newscaster)	37	Female	Bachelor	Journalism
P3	Administrative Affairs Specialist	25	Female	Vocational school	Justice
P4	Landscape Architect	33	Female	Bachelor	Landscape Architecture
P5	Office Intern	23	Female	Vocational school	Laboratory
P6	Laboratory Technician	24	Male	Vocational school	Biomedical
P7	Administrative Affairs Specialist	38	Female	High school	-
P8	Finance Manager	43	Male	Bachelor	Business Administration
P9	Architect	37	Male	Bachelor	Interior Architecture
P10	Architect	33	Female	Master	Architecture
P11	Topographer	28	Male	High school	-
P12	Production Engineer	38	Male	Bachelor	Mechanical Engineering
P13	Industrial Product Designer	33	Male	Bachelor	Industrial Design
P14	Accounting Manager	30	Male	Bachelor	Economics
P15	Architect - Postgraduate student	27	Female	Bachelor	Architecture
P16	Attorney	29	Female	Master	Law
P17	Marketing Specialist	31	Female	Bachelor	Economics
P18	Project Management Director	31	Male	Bachelor	Law
P19	Advisor	29	Male	Bachelor	Informatics
P20	Attorney	31	Male	Bachelor	Law

Figure 2. The answers of the participants to the "How do you define yourself politically?" question

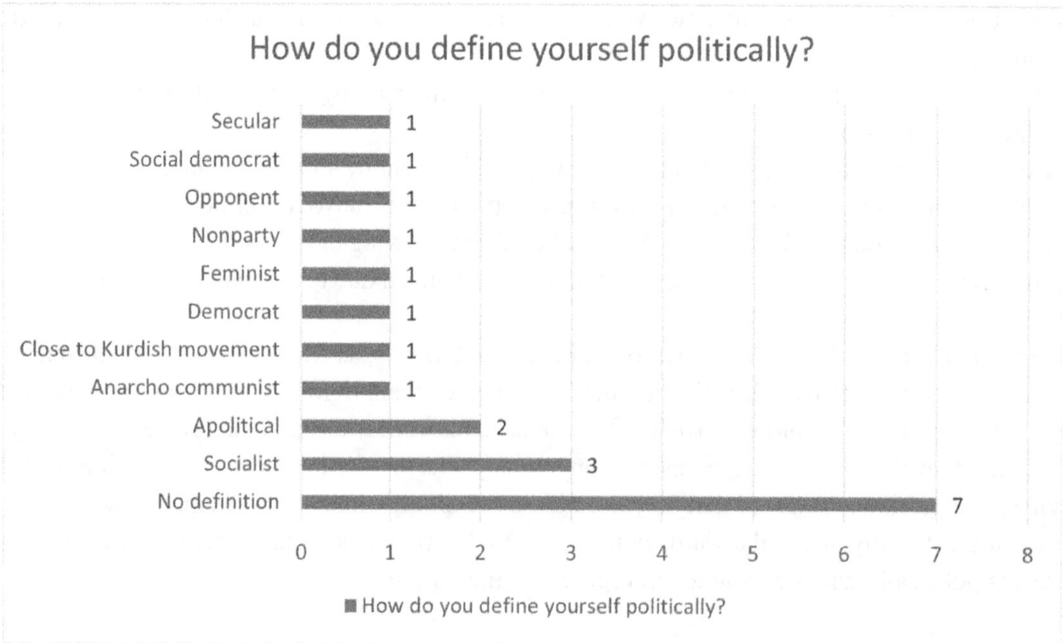

Everyday Life: Mobile Phone and News Consumption

Being able to check current events and spend time on the phone during the day largely depends on the conditions of the participant's occupation. In the daily work tempo, those who work in the office can spend free time on the mobile phone or desktop. However, those who are in the field outside the office do not have the opportunity to do this. As can be seen in Figure 3, people who spend much time on the phone are desk-based office workers. The average screen time is 3 hours and 13 minutes.

The people with the least screen time are parents of young children. Participants with children say that screen time and news consumed within the family environment are related to the time spent with the children. In the sample, there are two mothers with children younger than 4, 1 mother with an adolescent, one father with a 6-month-old baby, and two fathers with children aged between 4-12 years.

One participant, a father of three children, stopped watching the news at home for his children's psychological wellbeing and continued all news and media consumption on his mobile phone. The participant, a production engineer in a workshop, cannot find time to be on the phone all day, so he can only find time in the traffic and the evenings. However, his children asked him not to spend time on his mobile phone, and he had to restrict his screen time. Similarly, two participants restricted using mobile phones to spend time with their children. The mother of a 4-year-old child, who went on leave after having a child and could not return to work because her workplace was closed during this period, says that she feels unhappy and guilty spending too much time on her mobile phone. Her screen time is between 20 minutes to 1 hour:

Figure 3. Daily mobile screen time of the participants in hours

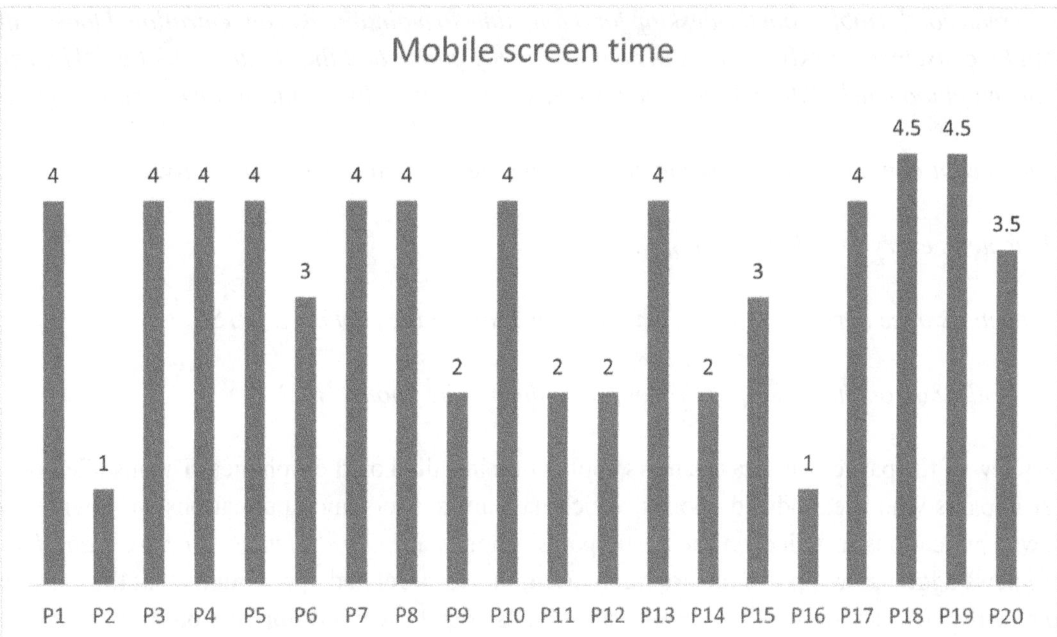

Individually, maximum 1 hour. I look at it for 20 minutes, and after 20 minutes, I feel a huge guilt; then I read a book, take care of the housework, and watch a movie with my husband. As screen time increases, depression increases. At first, I thought the problem was with me. But after I had a child, I studied psychology and experienced major depression, and then I learned that such a thing happens. That's why I act accordingly. (P2)

All participants have Instagram accounts, except one who does not use social media. Except for P8, all have the application installed on their phones and rank first among the most frequently used applications. When they can spend free time on the phone during the day, Instagram is often the first application they access on their mobile phones. Some participants set screen time for Instagram to prevent overuse, "I have screen time for Instagram, 1 hour, it closes automatically, then I log in again" (P3):

There is an idle time warning I set 2 years ago. All applications are locked at midnight. If you pass that time, it will not enter the applications. I usually experience this on Instagram, and I postpone using that application. (P15)

Half of the participants do not feel the need to read news during the day. Some who do not read the news do not because they think they will be informed about a significant development. Ten participants who stated that they need to read news during the day show different news reading practices. While some prefer reading the news on their desktop, others spend a short time looking at it on their phones to be informed about what is happening. Those who generally prefer to read news on their desktop read it customised on the sites, sources, authors and categories they prefer. Purposes of reading news vary from meeting the need for information about a subject to learning to being informed about what is going on:

I want to read comfortably from the desktop for a long time to maintain my concentration. I look at things that can be consumed quickly, such as Instagram, on my phone and that I can look at quickly, without tiring my mind too much. I think I lack knowledge, so I mostly do long, informative readings. (P15)

I used to need it more. I need to read the news during the day, but it decreases daily. (P20)

I read the news every weekday morning. (P17)

I read the news once a month to follow what is happening in the economy. (P18)

I usually follow up on the desktop; I do not prefer the mobile phone. (P13)

Very few of the participants have a news application installed on their phones. The installed ones are the participants who use Android phones, which have more users and applications worldwide. While the news applications installed on the participants' phones are *Gazete Duvar, Birgün*, *Haberler.com*, and the news aggregator app Bundle are rarely used, the news-related applications that the participants use to read the news are shown in Figure 4. Participants do not use many applications or personalise and customise applications. Only two participants customised their news feed on Haberler.com and Bundle according to categories.

Figure 4. News-related applications on mobile phones

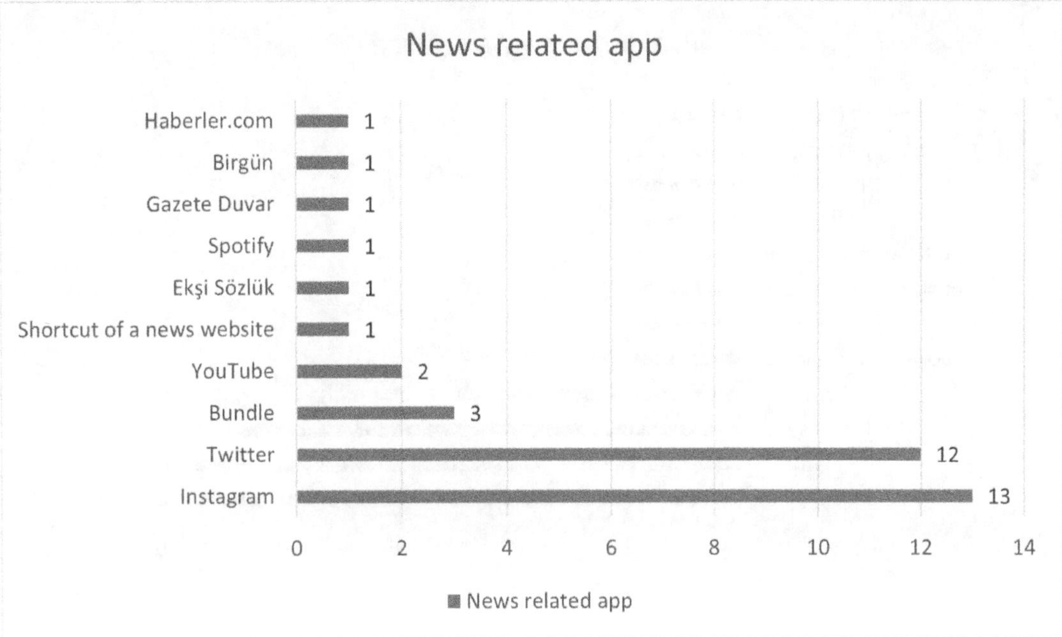

App notifications are turned off on many participants' phones. The participants allowing the pop-up and on-screen notifications are usually the instant messaging apps and Instagram, also including instant messaging option. It has been observed that application notifications often tire, distract and disturb users. While some participants allowed desktop notifications, most participants also turned off desktop notifications.

There are too many notifications. I deleted them. I do not read them. I do not read what is sent. I turned off all notifications, and this time, I turned on some of them because I did not notice work-related things. (P8)

I even turned off all notifications on the desktop because it drives me crazy. I never click on them. Only Instagram, YouTube and WhatsApp notifications are on. (P9)

Mynet was installed, sending too many notifications, so I deleted it. (P3)

Preferred News Source and Format

There are considerable differences in participants' news consumption preferences. Just as the news channels they prefer vary, the news formats they prefer differ. While social media stands out in terms of format and channel, Instagram is at the forefront among social media platforms. While Twitter is a platform that participants use to be informed about current developments, it was observed that some participants deleted their Twitter accounts. Interestingly, interpersonal communication was also among the participants' preferred news channels. Two participants also listed email and newsletters among their preferred ways of news sources. Preferred news sources can be seen at the Figure 5.

Figure 5. Preferred news source

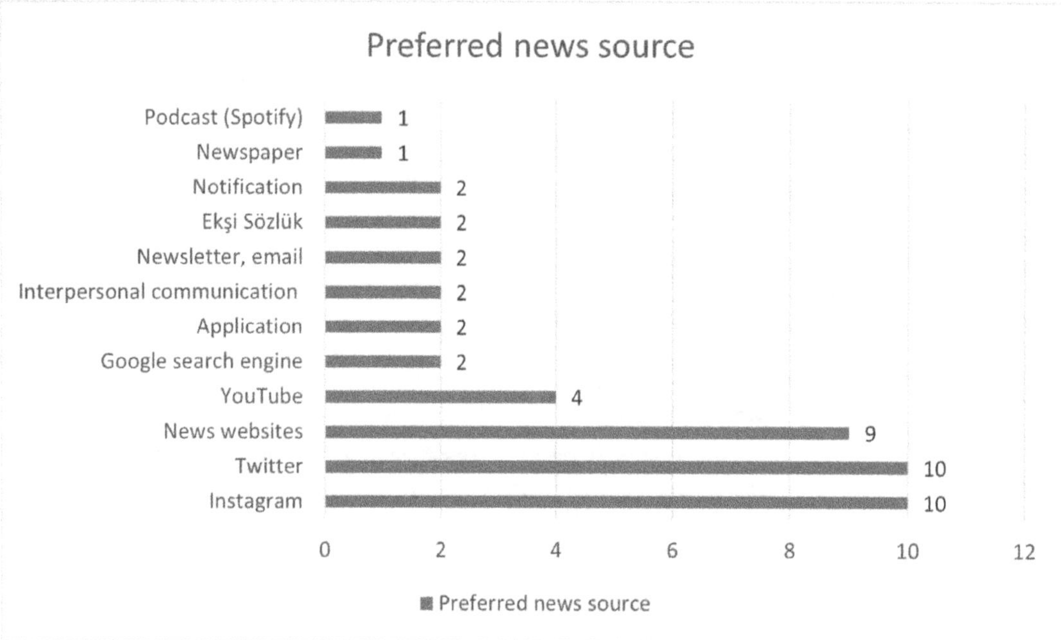

Generally, the preferred format is text, as seen in Figure 6. Seventeen participants stated they prefer news stories as text, seven also opt for video news, and two chose to receive news stories as images, such as Instagram posts. Some participants said they found classic news in text format more preferable because the user is the one who sets the pace. Otherwise, it would be tiresome to pursue the news story. Also, it is a time-consuming activity: "News is already tiring, you can be selective in text news. If there is something I am curious about, I research it myself" (P8).

Figure 6. Preferred news format

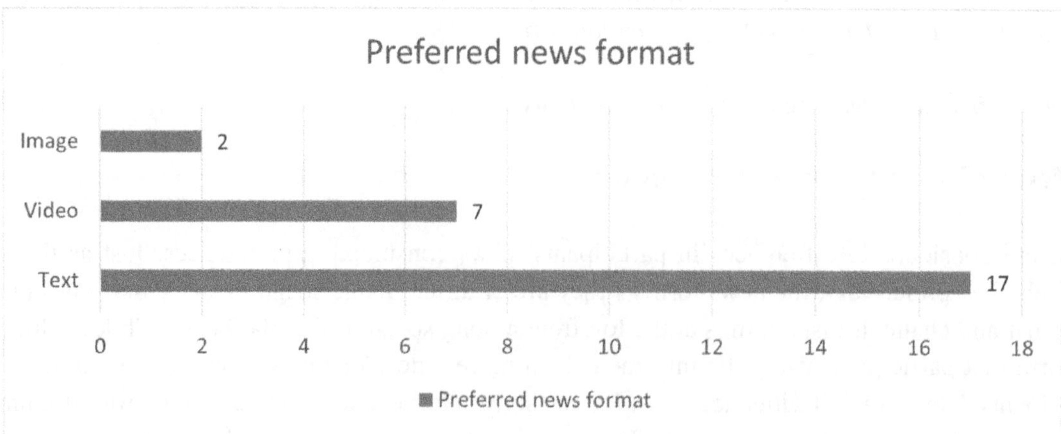

News Websites

About our question on the preferred news source, nine participants replied as news websites: *"I go directly to the website. If there is no news on the website, then I look at Twitter (P1)."* They visit the news websites via the browsers on their mobile phones rather than using news apps.

Social media is preferred because news browsing on the phone is generally about fast and instant developments. Preferring websites in terms of reading news is related to checking different sources, getting the news from different sources, and understanding how different news organisations represent the events.

If I have read the news before, I do not click on it. If we are talking about the same news story, if there is other news about it somewhere else, then I look at this subject. For example, if I encounter a news story about corruption, I look at an expert on this subject, Tolga Şardan on T24 and Timur Soykan on Birgün. If it is something about the government, I look at Murat Yetkin. If it is about foreign news, I look at Transatlantik on Medyascope. Moreover, regarding the Arab world and Russia, I will check out what Fehim Taştekin writes. (P1)

My trust factor varies depending on the content of the news I read and the website of the news. I try to read the same news from more than one source. (P14)

In between, I look at all sides, from left and right. I need to look at all sources. (P11)

In this respect, this preference, which has been found to require more active reader behaviour, requires more time and effort. For these reasons, users often access different websites and read news from their desktop computers during the parts of the day when they have spare time:

For news, I go to the website 'Yazar oku' (Read the authors) from my desktop. I force myself to read lots of people who do not agree with my opinion, but I do this rarely. (P15)

I access sites from my desktop computer to read news from newspapers representing all parties, such as Sabah and Sözcü. (P8)

Among the sites where participants regularly follow the news, there are primarily alternative media organisations websites such as *Birgün, Evrensel, Gazete Duvar, Artı Gerçek, Medyascope, T24, Diken, İleri Haber, Solcu Gazete, Dark Web Haber*. The other websites are mainstream digital-born websites *Haberler.com* and *Sondakika.com*, the website of mainstream TV news channel *Haber Global*, fact-checking platforms *Teyit* and *Doğruluk Payı*, mainstream newspapers such as nationalist opponent *Cumhuriyet* and *Sözcü*, pro-government partisan *Sabah*, and international news organisations such as *BBC News, Voice of America*, and *The Guardian*.

Instagram

Instagram and Twitter were the news sources that received the highest rate among participants. Here, participants either follow the accounts of news organisations directly or do indirect news follow-up by following political accounts, people, or influencers with social aspects:

I do not particularly follow news organisations. Instagram is where I get my news. I follow political people; they also have news content. (P4)

I do not look at any news sites anymore. I only learned from Instagram. If it is a big event, it is already exploding. Everyone shares. I see any news, especially from Onedio (a popular content platform) on Instagram. It immediately delivers the important news on the agenda and appears before me. I see news from phenomenal pages and funny pages. (P7)

I do not look at things that bother me. Few people I follow share news content. For example, many people supported TİP (Workers' Party of Turkey) during the election period, and I unintentionally learned a lot about TİP. When there are critical agendas in the country, such as forest fires and floods, I learn from Instagram. I generally learn from influencers who have a strong social aspect. (P2)

Instagram also acts as a bridge that directs the user to the news source. Some participants said they visited news sites based on posts they came across on Instagram. Thus, a two-step news reading practice is developed; the user goes to the site when seeing the triggering element:

When I see news on Instagram, I go to the source. (P1)

I follow the news as I come across it on social media. (P18)

Instagram is puffery, but at least I'm doing more detailed research with a title emphasis. I see something and look at it in more detail on Google. (P4)

It is like a pop-up. I check the videos of some accounts on YouTube and Instagram to see if their content is new. If the subject interests me, I can go in and take a look. (P10)

Unlike other participants, one participant underlined that Instagram was not a suitable platform for following the news. This participant, who says that he never follows the news here and does not trust the news he sees on this medium, uses Instagram only for certain functional information in several interests in accordance with the visual and personalisation-based character of the platform:

Instagram is a complete garbage dump. You cannot find any reliable news from there. I am just looking for things that will be useful in woodwork, guitars, music, architecture, etc. (P8).

Twitter

Twitter is the most preferred news source, with Instagram among the participants. Participants prefer Twitter to follow current developments or the latest news: "I check Instagram regularly and Twitter whenever something happens" (P15).

Twitter is a digital platform followed by politically engaged audiences and used for social opposition in Turkey. The platform is visited more, significantly, when opposition rises in society and society becomes politicised, such as in elections. In parallel, many participants stated that they did not want to log in to Twitter after the re-election of the AKP, which has been in power since 2002, in the general elections held in the country in May 2023:

I was usually active on Twitter. However, I am not even considering what happens after the election (May 2023). It was my last vote, I will not even go to vote again. (P9)

I left Twitter when Elon Musk bought it. I used to use it a lot before. Especially during the Gezi Park movement in 2013, it became both a communication channel and a news medium for people. It is no longer a news medium, and I do not even want to look at it. (P7)

The fact that there are different news sources on Twitter, as opposed to the conventional media's use of official news sources, was noted by the participants who follow alternative media.

We were following the statements on TV during the pandemic period. I did not trust the official statements; I also looked at Twitter then. We were following on Twitter for real information. (P7)

In addition to providing alternative news sources, Twitter is also followed for allowing different voices to discuss and create a public space. By providing this opportunity, Twitter seems more trustworthy to some participants because it is a medium where many ideas and opinions pit against:

I do not watch the news on TV; I look at Twitter. It is more reliable because everyone comments on the event there. Everyone does it from their point of view to persuade on TV, but on Twitter, there are so many approaches (P3).

YouTube and Spotify

Four participants stated that they prefer receiving news in video format via YouTube. Additionally, one of the participants stated that she likes video news stories and adds news bulletin podcasts from Spotify. However, video news, which consumes more data, may strain users economically. A participant who prefers to watch videos of journalists' analysis rather than reading. However, it depends on the status of his mobile internet package:

To watch video news, I must have enough mobile internet package. Otherwise, I read news in text format. For example, (journalist) Murat Yetkin publishes the text in the video on his website. If I do not have an internet package, I read it from there. But if I have enough mobile internet package, I watch the video on YouTube. (P1)

Some participants pointed out the importance of the reliability and credibility of the news rather than its format: "For me, the thing about news is its reliability, source and provability, not the format" (P18), "The content of the news is important, not the format" (P17). In this context, it is essential for the news to contain video in terms of credibility:

Some text, some video. I want to see evidence since I do not believe what I read. I want to believe what I read by seeing it with my own eyes, so I want to have a video within the news story. (P3)

News stories in video format on social media platforms can attract the attention of users whose interest in the news has decreased: “Sometimes video news catches my attention. If I come across it, I will watch the video in the news for 2 minutes. If it does not work, I will skip it” (P7). Video news can also be exaggerated and repetitive: “Sometimes the video news stories can be very unnecessary. They repeatedly show a 10-second video for 2 minutes” (P6).

It was observed that participants generally preferred to receive news from YouTube and Spotify in video and audio format to follow experts and specific people. While some users were optimistic about the content suggested by the algorithmic selection offered by YouTube, they said they mostly watched new videos of experts and channels in specific fields, such as academics, journalists and economists. Receiving news in the form of videos and podcasts is essential as it allows user to actively use their time when they are busy with another occupation:

I log in to YouTube and listen while doing something else in the house. (P1)

I do not read news on my phone other than briefly browsing social media. I just listen to the podcast on my phone when I am out. There are Spotify podcasts and current news broadcasts that I regularly follow. (P15)

News Apps

News applications are not very commonly used within the sample group. Only two participants used certain news outlets’ applications on their mobile phones. One participant has *Haberler.com*, one participant uses *Gazete Duvar*, and the same participant has *Birgün* on his phone. Three participants have the news aggregator application Bundle on their mobile phones. One of the Bundle users turned off the notifications after the general elections in May 2023, and she sometimes browses the news via the app. One Bundle user customises the app according to her interests. She especially reads science and technology news to be informed and considers the pop-up notifications: “News notifications are on. It sends notifications once an hour. I do not read everything, but I read what interests me” (P5).

The participant who uses the *Haberler.com* application on his mobile phone customises the categories; however, he cannot effectively read the news because he spends time with his kids at home. He says he follows the news via his phone because it is “a medium that he keeps under his control” (P12). He stated that his use of this application came from habit: “News reading preferences stem from people’s habitual behaviour. Since I started from haber.com in the first place, I continued from this website’s application” (P12).

The participant who has *Gazete Duvar* and *Birgün* apps on his phone, which are among Turkey’s most influential alternative media outlets, regularly follows news from these applications and has notifications turned on. He also follows Artı Gerçek, another alternative media outlet. However, it does not have a mobile app and gave up a news outlet’s app:

Since Artı Gerçek does not have an application, I downloaded the page shortcut from the browser to my mobile phone desktop and read it there. I also followed T24 on the app, but they overloaded me with ads, so I removed it. (P1)

A User-Generated Website: Ekşi Sözlük

Two participants stated a user-generated website built on user contribution, Ekşi Sözlük (Sour Dictionary), as the primary news source. One follows Ekşi Sözlük because *"the categories are separated and specified"* (P6). Furthermore, the other participant underlines the polyphony and pluralism of this medium created by organic user comments. The participant, who spends much time on this site, prefers to read news in the evenings on the desktop instead of his mobile phone:

I am reading here to get the whole agenda very quickly, to see what I like, what I do not like, and where I will continue. In the news media, editors and interns write the news. They do not pay attention to spelling or writing of the news. There is unrelated news on different sites about the same subject. Nevertheless, since there are so many opinions in Ekşi Sözlük's entries, you see right and wrong from different angles. You can learn what is and what is not from the news that a cure for cancer has been found. An expert can comment below. Since there are people who know everything specifically, there is specific content and freedom to receive news. (P13)

Back to the Basics: Interpersonal Communication

As a result of distrust and mental exhaustion, two participants stated that they chose to receive news from their interpersonal communication network. Apart from their relations, they follow up on Instagram, and they get to know if there is anything they need to be aware of:

If there is an incident, my mother, to follow it in more detail. She is involved in active politics. So, my main source of news is my mother. (P4)

I get the news by word of mouth or on Instagram. If it is a big event, it is already exploding. Everyone shares. At worst, I become aware of it after a long time, but somehow, I do. (P7)

Searching for News

Although the preferred source of news is not the Google search engine, participants use the Google search for different purposes. The most important of these is searching for the details of the breaking news:

I search for news on Google 1-2 times a week. For example, something like an explosion happened. I wonder what happened; how many people died? I learn details like this and do not read the other things I am not interested in. (P13)

One purpose of Google search is to find something to read: "If there is nothing left to read on the websites that I regularly check, I use Google search to see what is on other sites" (P1). Another aim is to access specific categories or topics; "I am interested in historical events. To research the subject I am curious about, I search randomly by submitting myself to Google" (P11), "If there is a specific topic, I search" (P10). Another purpose of Google search is confirmation and verification:

I do a Google search to confirm the information. For example, in a news article, the interest rate was written twice in the same sentence, with different rates. When I looked on Google, I realised that the correct word for one of them was 'inflation' and that it was written wrong. (P1)

News search is preferred to see how news sites from all poles cover the news and to read news from different sources: "Sabah, Sözcü, etc. I search news on Google to see what they are saying from all sides, from left and right. I do this from a desktop computer, not on a mobile phone" (P8).

The participants also use Google search for general information they are interested in. In this process, they encounter and read news: "Yes, if it is something I am specifically looking for, I use the search engine" (P18), "Google is my everything, I do search. I am a terrible user in this respect. I search for everything on Google, I use Google to find the source I want" (P2).

Several participants pointed out that they "definitely do not search" for news on Google. The reasons behind this are that the Google search algorithm highlights dominant sites, distrust, and exposure to advertising:

No. After searching on Google, the first thing that comes up is news from (mainstream) sites like Sabah, Hürriyet, Milliyet etc. I hate visiting them. It puts the baloney websites at the top. I did not see (alternative sites like) Birgün in the first row. (P8)

If you click on the notification, you are afraid of whether a virus will appear or what kind of site it will be. Trust is all gone. (P7)

I am exposed to too many advertisements to read news. In the end, there is no news at all. (P6)

News Exposure and Trust: Algorithmic or Editorial Selection?

The participants were asked to evaluate their news selection method and "Do you prefer algorithmic or editorial selection?". Their responses can be seen in Figure 7; eleven prefer editorial selection, four prefer algorithmic selection, and four replied as "none". Interestingly, one participant both trusts algorithmic and editorial selection: "I do not have a negative attitude. I am not picky. I read whatever comes my way" (P5).

Participants who preferred the news they read to be editorially selected drew attention to professional competence, balance, the editorial approach of the news institution, the relevance of one's field of interest, digital surveillance and algorithmic manipulation. It was observed that the participants who gave the "editorial" response are aware of the negative consequences that algorithmic selection could create and are active news readers, even if they avoid news:

I would like the news I read to be selected editorially. I do not want it to be how I want it to be. I read it by filtering it anyway. Without editorial intervention, I will think about it thoroughly when I read it. (P1)

The news has passed through the filter of a professional expert, which is a good thing. (P10)

By the editor. I do not like surveillance, being created by algorithms, the digital fingerprint issue, collecting data about you and being presented with the same thing you talked about yesterday. (P2)

Figure 7. Preferred news selection method: "Algorithmic or editorial selection?"

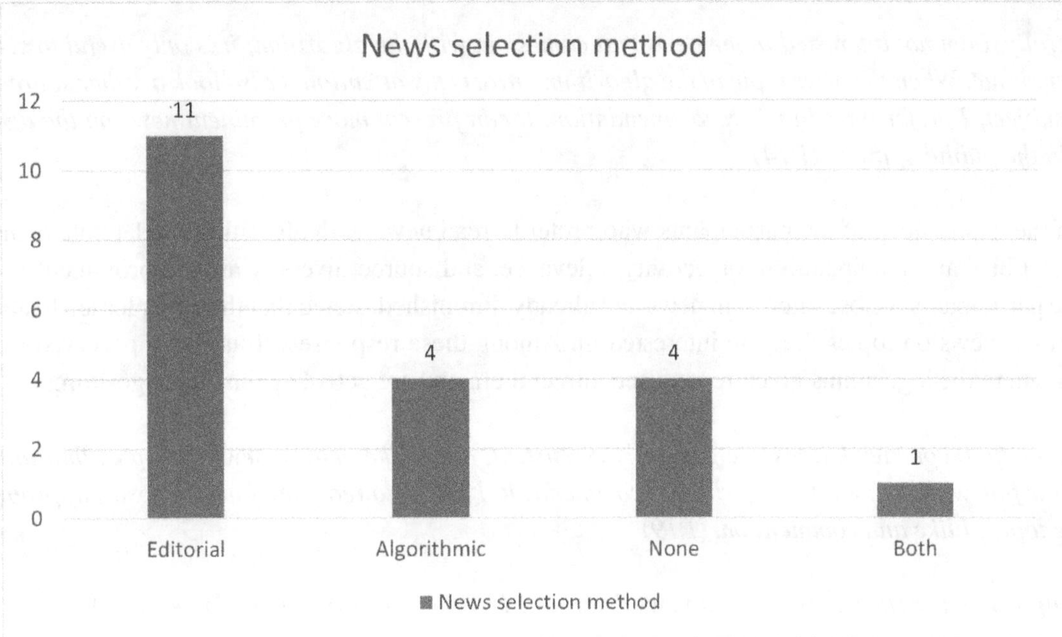

I think algorithmic recommendations push me towards the general populist news trend, and I do not like to be classified. I do not think the algorithm knows me well enough. I prefer to follow at least the suggestions of editors I know. (P18)

I ignore algorithmic suggestions because they bother me. In order not to fall into the trap of algorithms, I even have a single playlist on Spotify, and I throw all other genres into it. (P9)

Criticism of being exposed to news due to algorithmic selection came to the fore in the participants' answers, who stated that they did not trust both algorithmic and editorial selection. The participants replied to our question as "none", underlining that the algorithms disregard the user's will:

I am unhappy about being exposed to news that comes my way through algorithmic selection. I do not want to follow them. Algorithmic or editorial choice does not matter. I prefer to read by choosing myself. (P17)

I want to choose the news I read, and the ones I choose are usually about topics that interest me. (P16)

I do not trust the news I am exposed to; I reject 90% of it. It shows things that are both irrelevant and that I do not want to read. Neither of them inspires confidence. An ordinary person writes the news we read. So it does not make much difference. (P13)

We reject it on Google, but there are suggestions on YouTube too. We watch these like idiots. It makes me angry. (P3)

Editorial selection. But I look at the news on social media according to my interest. (P4)

Generally, I am not interested in the news that comes out with the algorithm; it is only useful to see the current issue. When the news topic in the algorithm attracts my attention, I also look at other sources on that subject. I prefer the editor's recommendation. It can present more prominent news on the agenda and in the public opinion. (P14)

In the expressions of the participants who prefer to read news with algorithmic selection, avoiding editorial bias and manipulation, objectivity, relevance, and source diversity are the prominent issues. These participants, whose interest in news had already diminished, stated that they are pleased to at least encounter news on topics they are interested in. Among these responses, it has been observed that in cases where the algorithms go extreme, users direct them and are active against the algorithms:

Algorithmic recommendations are generally consistent, and I like getting news on topics that interest me. It is fine with me that the algorithm recommends it. I prefer to read news in categories appropriate to the topics I like and comment on. (P19)

The algorithm is better. I think that a news determined by the editor is not objective. (P11)

There is a diversity of sources. Occasionally, when I feel like I am following similar news sources, I try to disrupt the algorithm by following opposing views. I would not say I like news that I think has extremist ideas. They both provide guidance. Ultimately, I prefer the algorithm because sometimes it exaggerates, and you can wake up to the situation and change it. (P20)

Many participants underlined that trust in news is mainly based on the source. At the same time, participants stated that they compared different sources to gain confidence in the news they read or were exposed to:

If I know and trust the source of the news, then yes, I trust the news. Otherwise, no. (P18)

I do not trust the news. I am trying to gain insight by observing the consistency between different sources. (P16)

I establish trust by comparing different sources. (P12)

I trust sources who publish articles that can also comment against the political ideology of the news organisation. (P20)

I look at different news organisations' websites from all different angles. (P8)

Attitudes Against Peer Recommendation

Regarding our question about peer recommendation (Van Damme et al., 2020), more than half of the participants stated the positive impact of being advised by a credible acquaintance. They found a higher

Table 2. Participants' attitudes towards peer selection and personal news recommendations

Do you approach the news recommended by an acquaintance differently or sent, for example, from a WhatsApp group with your inner circle?	
(1) Positive	* Yes, I read them. I am reading this because they would not send it in vain. (P7) * Nobody sends it to me, but I would read it if they did. I approach it differently. Not because it is more reliable, but because that friend has read it and made some sense of it and is wondering what I will think. (P3) * Of course, my attitude changes. (P11)
(2) Optimistic - sender	* It depends on the sender. If my aunt had sent it to me, I do not open it. However, if it was sent from people who think like me or like from ecology groups if the news has passed through a filter, then I click on it. (P10) * I read it when someone I know shares it. Otherwise, I do not. (P17) * I have biases and judgments; they vary depending on the sender. For example, if a friend of mine never sends me news or a friend whose perspective I trust sends it to me, I read it. (P1)
(3) Optimistic - source	* It varies depending on the source and content. (P16) * It does not have a positive effect. If I do not like the source, I will not read it if it is a site I would not read. (P6) * According to the source. Even if you do not trust the source, I read it because I am curious about what they are saying. (P8) * The source of the incoming news is essential, not according to the sender, but according to the source of the news (P18)
(4) Neutral	* If she asks me to post it privately and ask me to read it, I will read it. Nevertheless, I will not read it if it comes up in groups. (P2) * I look at it, but I do not pay too much attention to it. (P8) * I try to read it if I find spare time. (P12) * I open it. It does not make any difference to me. (P20)
(5) Negative	* My mother constantly sends news to the family WhatsApp group, I do not look at them. If I do not enter some news by my own will, I am negative to the news coming from someone else. If it does not particularly interest me, I don't look at it, or I may wait a while and look at it later. (P15) * At first, I approached the news sent to me negatively and looked at the subject myself from other sources. (P14) * Most of the time, I do not trust. Honestly, I do not receive it frequently. (P5) * I will take a look, but it does not affect much in terms of trust and credibility. (P4) *Even if I read it myself, I doubt its accuracy when a person I do not like sends it. (P6) * I do not read. (P9) * If I am interested, I search directly through Ekşi Sözlük. If that is not enough, I search on Google. I usually look at what it is like. I do not read much to avoid being led too much. Mainly, the reason for my attitude is not to be guided. Because both extremes are bad. (P13)

possibility of reading the news. Several different attitudes to this issue have emerged, and some of the interesting answers given are in Table 2:

(1-3) Positive: "I should read it; they did not send it in vain."
(2-1) Optimistic: considering news according to the sender,
(3-2) Optimistic: considering news according to its source,
(4) Neutral: taking a look, but it does not change anything,
(5) Negative: dissatisfaction and distrust against the news sent to him/her.

Reasons for News Avoidance

Fifteen participants answered "yes" to the question, "Do you avoid reading news?" While one participant stated he was picky, another said he was not wholly avoidant: "Rather picky. I get the news I want, not

Figure 8. The answers to the question: "Do you avoid reading the news?"

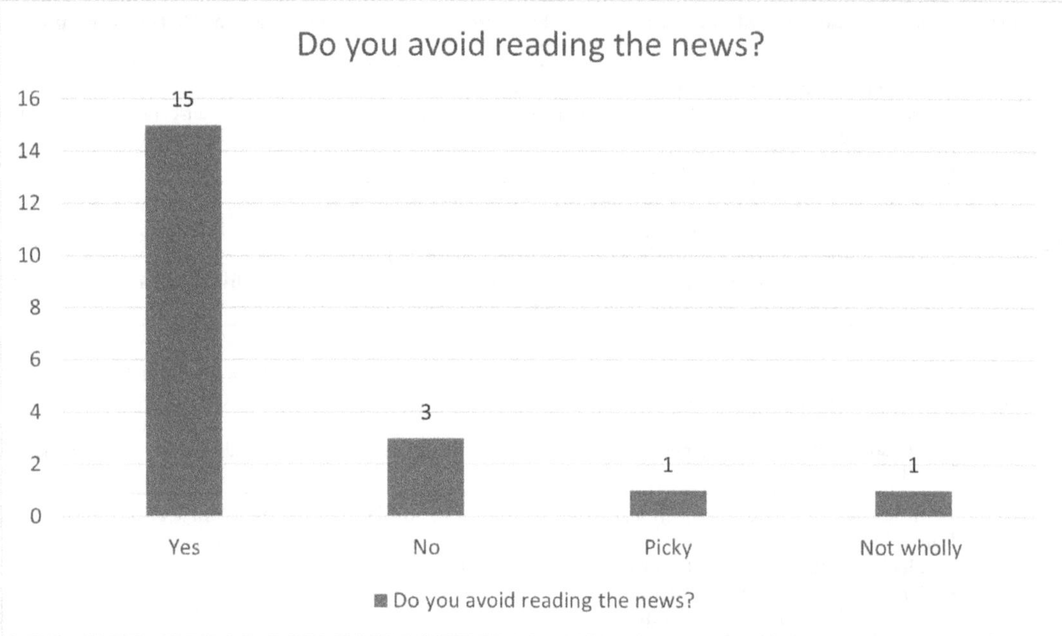

just any" (P13). Three participants do not avoid reading news, but there are some issues that they are uncomfortable with in the current digital news order:

I avoid excessive notifications and topics I am not interested in. (P5)

No, on the contrary, I am chasing the news. But I avoid algorithmic notifications. After the last election, I lost my ability to be sad. I focus on my life. (P6)

The findings obtained from the interviews were compiled, and various categories were determined regarding news avoidance behaviour. These categories, which are not entirely unrelated, sometimes intersect and complement each other. The categories cover the entire process, from the reasons why users deliberately avoid news to the point of losing curiosity and unintentionally losing touch with the environment.

Disappointment, Frustration, and Stress Avoidance

It has been observed that news avoidance behaviour begins with the user's need to avoid the dire realities of life to avoid experiencing negative emotions. While what is ostensibly to be avoided is news, the user is avoiding stress, disappointment, unhappiness, and frustration. While some participants said they did not know why they avoided the news, some realised that their disappointment decreased when they consciously avoided the news and continued this behaviour. One of these turning points was the COVID-19 pandemic:

I spent time with the child during the pandemic; media use was nearly nothing. I have never read news about the pandemic, but I have always been exposed to news about the pandemic on Instagram. At first, I wanted to avoid the news during the pandemic period, and I never wanted to look at that news. Then I quite liked this situation and avoided it completely. (P2)

After the pandemic, my news following practices have decreased. Not because of the pandemic, but because I felt like I was reading the same news over and over again. (P20)

Before the pandemic, I had inner energy, but now I do not. This is a total media impact. (P3)

Another turning point is the May 2023 elections, which were described as a "defeat" by most participants. However, elections are generally known as periods when the political level of the public increases. Participants stated that there was a more hopeless atmosphere after the May elections when the opposition created a serious agenda. After these elections, some participants stopped reading the news, while others even stopped logging into Twitter. Pointing out that community psychology is negatively affected by the news, the participants say that the media industry intentionally focuses on negative news:

I was following the news regularly before the elections, but after the elections, I never followed the news for 4-5 months. Sometimes I did not even look at a single news story for a week. (P10)

I avoid it so as not to become demoralised. The situation of the country is deteriorating. The current situation is like not watching the match because the team is relegated. (P8)

We are depressed as a society. The news is making us even more depressed. I know that I will encounter news that will make me unhappy. (P4)

If something is depressing, like after losing an election, I do not want to be on Twitter. Alternatively, if someone you follow did something stupid, then I do not look. I do not want to look at Twitter when there are organised, planned lynchings on certain issues. I also briefly looked at news sites and applications. I know what I'm running away from. (P1)

I realise I am happier avoiding the news if I read the news during the day, I lose my motivation. So, I prefer to read in the evening. (P3)

When people are exposed to too much news, they lose their temper. People become irritable and demoralised because they have the perception that the only things that can be reported are bad things. (P13)

It is one hundred per cent correct and natural for society to escape from reality. Everyone wants to read what suits their book. (P9)

I used to follow the news, but now everything gets me so depressed. I already have a stressful job. On top of that, why should I put the stress on the country and the world? (P7)

Participants with children are dependent on them in terms of daily life routine and phone use. They also stated that they had to protect their mood for the psychological state of their children:

I do not avoid it completely. There are news that I avoid for the sake of my psychology and the psychology of my children. Children's psychology deteriorated when they saw affairs like earthquakes and murders. They said, 'Dad, do not turn the TV on.' That is why we started watching the news less, and if I need to read it, I try to read it on my mobile phone. This time, there is another pressure from the children, saying 'you read too much'. Because of the children, you have to limit some things. (P12)

Being a mother is already a very stressful occupation. Moreover, I did not want to put any extra stress on myself. For example, when I watch the news about a child, it ruins my day. If normal people forget the news within an hour, I remain under its influence for a few days. Similar situations happen while watching movies. (P2)

Losing Curiosity

This category is related to the previous title. However, it also shows how a situation that develops unintentionally turns into a vicious circle. After a certain point, participants began to involuntarily continue their behaviour of avoiding news. In this respect, although this title is a cause, it can also be considered a consequence. This situation can lead to the person breaking ties with their social environment. Fortunately, some participants are aware of this. However, there is a real sense of despair in the responses of some:

After the Gezi Park movement ended in 2013, I continued reading the news for a while, but frankly, I no longer had faith in any views in this country. That is why I am in the mood for what I can do alone. How can I make money? I feel like I have cut off my connection with the world and the country. I get involved during election times because I have to. Under these conditions, what would happen if I engraved this inflation information in my mind? (P7)

Sometimes I feel apolitical. There are long periods when I never see Erdoğan. I say some things, and they become very trending on Instagram and Twitter, and I say, 'There was a guy called Tayyip right back then.' I was most active in the news before the election but have not looked since then, except for women's news. This does not seem right either, but I do not feel like doing anything. (P15)

I do not want to see the news anymore. I am bored, but I am reading again because I think I need to be aware of the environment. Despite it getting boring, I continue because I do not want to be left unaware. It is a cycle. (P20)

Notifications are on at both the phone and the desktop. Nonstop. But it does not interest me, I do not look at them. (P7)

Lack of Confidence and Distrust in the Media Industry

It has been observed that the country's problematic media and political power relations also affect the participants' trust. The participants are seriously questioning the media organisations that wrote the news, the content, credibility, reliability and accuracy of the news:

I do not trust all of them. The reliability of the author and the news outlet is important. Even if the author of the news is a journalist that I trust, the news can sometimes disturb me, so I can even unfollow the author. News sources, their quality, the author's knowledge, and the fact that covers the event from a different perspective than what everyone else sees. (P1)

There is no freedom of the press anyway. They show us what we want to think, not what we want to hear. That is why I do not want to follow anymore. (P4)

Everyone has a party that they support and defend, and they speak in a way that defends them. It would be okay if they were objective, but they are never. (P3)

Trusting the news requires serious effort to verify it by reading and comparing multiple news sources. In this respect, while active news readership shows its importance, this requires the reader's determination. Therefore, it was observed that the number of participants who showed this determination and stubbornness was relatively low:

For a while now, for about three years, I have been approaching everything I read with hesitation. My research practices are also improving, both with this and the effect of knowing that what we see is not real. Reading a news story will take me an hour to research its background. I will read it, then I will look at another source, then I will not believe it, etc. That keeps me away from reading the news. My distrust, then the development of the research process. Media is in a very different place for me. It is something I cannot break away from and also something I do not trust. (P15)

We are exhausted. I do not trust it 100 per cent, no matter what the source is. But when I look at it in detail, see the title and verify it, you gain trust yourself by researching. (P4)

I do not trust the news I come across. I also do not trust the sources; I trust myself. Kurdish media, alternative media, mainstream media. When I actively read the news, I looked at all of them and came up with something average. (P2)

Reduced Quality and Poor Content of the News

News avoidance behaviour varies mainly depending on the interests and curiosities of the participants. It was observed that this situation resulted from getting used to receiving news in content rather than news format. Participants also criticised the quality and similarity of the news. The fact that digital journalism in the country is based on speed and the struggle of media organisations to stand out and have their content consumed on digital platforms, especially the Google search engine, leads to the production of very similar poor-quality news (Saran Doğan, 2022). This situation affects news readers and alienates them from the news:

The quality of the news is horrible. (P4)

Our news is like honking traffic horns on the way to work. (P9)

A very long paragraph questions asks questions but does not give the news. It drives me crazy. It must give very brief information. Finally, I come to the point that I cannot deal with this, and I say I will hear from someone anyway, and I stop reading. (P7)

There is a headline, but underneath it is something completely different, an unrelated event. (P4)

It varies depending on the category of the news. If it is a topic I am interested in, I am more interested in news that's long and written due to research, rather than news that goes beyond 20 pages and does not provide any content. (P18)

I used to get bored before; I would read the spot and the ending and then quit, but the situation now is unbearable. (P2)

It has been observed that this situation is valid not only for commercially oriented mainstream media organisations but also for alternative media outlets that use populist moves to attract users. A participant who drew attention to this situation thought that it was a tactic adopted to attract the attention of the audience who turned away from the news after the victory of the ruling party in the election in May 2023:

I had this perception, including the news sites I follow. After the election, Gazete Duvar's Instagram news started to become irrelevant, and it seemed like it started to become empty. I think this way: During the election period, news organisations were very political and made propaganda-based news. Nevertheless, after the elections, they started to use more empty content, perhaps to keep the audience. They choose this way to gather followers and increase the number of clicks with clickbait news. (P10)

Overstimulation of the User

Overstimulation is another reason to create news avoidance. Two main factors generate this consequence: algorithmic selection and notifications. Excessive notifications can tire the users and create apathy against news and current affairs. Suppose she sees a notification about a subject she is not interested in. In that case, she will not click on the notification, and her distance from the application or topic sending the notification will increase:

I block all ads and notifications on both my phone and computer. It bothers me that something about that issue comes against my will. If I were available, I could continue to follow the news, and all notifications are turned off on the phone. (P10)

Algorithmic selection and notifications are practical elements that drive users away from those sites and applications. Several participants said they had previously deleted news apps on their phones because they sent too many notifications:

I was using an app called Nabız (Pulse). It bothered me because I received so many notifications and finally deleted the app. I wanted to be informed about everything; I was in such a period. Right now, I do not read the notifications; I just press the cross button. I am getting annoyed. However, for example, the recommendation system works on YouTube. I agree with it, but I do not like it in the news. (P15)

CONCLUSION

This study, conducted within a society that fell into mass apathy and despair after the February 2023 earthquake and the May 2023 elections, focused on dissociating the reasons for news avoidance behaviour. Most participants (15 of 20) have news avoidance behaviour that they have started intentionally or unintentionally or found themselves in. They are determined to be intentionally avoiding the news. This act of avoidance, which started deliberately, became unintentional and a vicious circle.

As a significant outcome of the research, five categories were identified for the reasons that led to news avoidance behaviour in participants: (1) Disappointment, frustration and stress avoidance, (2) losing curiosity, (3) lack of confidence and distrust to the media industry, (4) reduced quality and poor content of the news, and (5) overstimulation of the user. While daily life pace, physical conditions resulting from working and business life, and economic and family situations determine news reading practices, they also shape news avoidance behaviour.

The most advanced and active participants in terms of news reading practices were P1, who works as a video editor on a news channel; P10, who is a field and project architect working in a boutique architecture firm; P15, who is an architect and postgraduate student, and P20, a lawyer who works in his own office. Each participant has clearly defined themselves politically, and in news avoidance condition, one stated that she took a precise stance. The news reading practices informed by P1 are those he exhibits in his private sphere outside his business life. Of course, being in contact with news throughout the day contributes to his perspective and understanding of industry dynamics. However, he is not the only person in the sample with a news media and communication background.

The approaches of P1, a video editor in a newsroom, and P2, a former newscaster, to reading and following news differed significantly. Being educated in media and communications and working or working in a job within the news and news media did not bring these two participants together with the same attitude. P1 stated in every statement that these news reading practices were not due to work but to his curiosity and were specific to him. His job at his workplace is editing the news videos in line with the prepared news texts and creating the video news package. He does not follow the news, and even though he is in the newsroom all day, surrounded by the news, he continues to read the news in his free time. Nevertheless, P1 stated that he also developed news avoidance behaviour. Still, despite his behaviour of avoiding news, he is among the most active news readers. As we understand from these examples, people's news avoidance behaviours cannot be compared with each other but can only be evaluated within their context and personal history.

Two participants who said they did not avoid reading news preferred not to define themselves politically, and one stated that he was a social democrat. Two of these participants, whose ages are still very young, 23 and 24, stated that they were not politically engaged and were not overly affected by the country's political situation. The participants who showed the most apparent news avoidance behaviour were those who defined themselves as socialists, democrats, close to the Kurdish movement, feminists, anarcho-communists and opponents. These participants include people who used to identify as socialists but no longer identify as such and who openly describe themselves as more politically engaged.

Almost all participants, especially the ones we just remarked, stated they intentionally adopted news avoidance behaviour. At the same time, a participant who clearly expressed himself politically said he did not know why he was avoiding the news. Another participant remarked that this behaviour started during the pandemic and continued because he realised that he felt better in this way. The primary triggers of news avoidance behaviour are the political atmosphere, political agenda, apathy and hopelessness in the country, which also determine the quality, content and agenda of the country's news organisations. Half of the participants said they stopped reading the news after the election. As a result of the interviews, it was understood that the participants were not essentially avoiding the news but the country's political realities. It is understood that this, arising from political reasons, is also the result of the vicious circle that has formed.

Another primary outcome of the research is the significant awareness and reaction to the algorithmic selection of most participants. Digital platforms, whose contents are shaped by algorithmic selection, can recommend different resources and contents to users and offer suggestions in line with preferences by processing user data. Therefore, these algorithms can make it extremely easy for a user who avoids news to continue this behaviour by suggesting content she can consume. Hence, the social consequences of news avoidance behaviour will strengthen due to the action of digital platforms and algorithmic selection. One of the participants (P15), while exemplifying how successful the action of avoiding the news was, said, "Sometimes it makes you forget that there is a person called Recep Tayyip Erdoğan". As can be seen from this example, digital platforms, which are news distributors due to algorithmic selection, personalise content so effectively that they do not show the user the most represented and most visible political figure in the country's mainstream media organisations.

It has been observed that users have very different attitudes towards reading news and following current events on their mobile phones. Participants were asked about their attitudes about receiving the news with algorithmic selection or editorial selection, and eleven of them preferred editorial news selection. This does not mean that users who prefer editorial selection are not exposed to news compiled via algorithmic selection. These participants stated that they prefer editorial choice as an attitude and preference. In some studies in the literature (Van Damme et al., 2020), it has been observed that there are different positions in terms of attitudes towards peer recommendations and news sent by personal acquaintances, the effect of which has been questioned. Five different attitudes were determined on this issue: positive, optimistic, neutral and negative, and it was observed that the participants took very different positions.

Users preferred news aggregator apps like Bundle and social media platforms instead of news outlets' apps. Similar to the findings of Yanardağoğlu's (2021) study, Twitter comes to the forefront with an addition: Instagram. This study revealed that Instagram is crucial in everyday life practices and news following processes. In future studies, it is recommended to question in detail how Instagram meditates news consumption practices and examine the trends that are effective on social media platforms from time to time. Considering the platform trends, TikTok, which has been on the rise in recent years, is expected to stand out and display originality in this field as well.

REFERENCES

Adekoya, C. O., & Fasae, J. K. (2021). Social media and the spread of COVID-19 infodemic. *Global Knowledge. Memory and Communication*, *71*(3), 105–120. doi:10.1108/GKMC-11-2020-0165

Ayres, L. (2008). Thematic Coding and Analysis. In L. M. Given (Ed.), *The SAGE Encyclopedia of Qualitative Research Methods* (pp. 867–868). SAGE Publications.

Beam, M. A., & Kosicki, G. M. (2014). Personalised News Portals: Filtering Systems and Increased News Exposure. *Journalism & Mass Communication Quarterly*, *91*(1), 59–77. doi:10.1177/1077699013514411

Berger, A. A. (2011). *Media and Communication Research Methods: An Introduction to Qualitative and Quantitative Approaches* (2nd ed.). SAGE.

Broersma, M., & Swart, J. (2022). Do Novel Routines Stick After the Pandemic? The Formation of News Habits During COVID-19. *Journalism Studies*, *23*(5–6), 551–568. doi:10.1080/1461670X.2021.1932561

Costera Meijer, I., & Groot Kormelink, T. (2015). Checking, Sharing, Clicking and Linking. *Digital Journalism (Abingdon, England)*, *3*(5), 664–679. doi:10.1080/21670811.2014.937149

de Bruin, K., de Haan, Y., Vliegenthart, R., Kruikemeier, S., & Boukes, M. (2021). News Avoidance during the Covid-19 Crisis: Understanding Information Overload. *Digital Journalism (Abingdon, England)*, *9*(9), 1286–1302. doi:10.1080/21670811.2021.1957967

Demiralp, S. (2023, October 28). Siyasete ilgi serbest düşüşte: Seçmen yeni liderini mi arıyor? *Yetkin Report*. https://yetkinreport.com/2023/10/28/siyasete-ilgi-serbest-dususte-secmen-yeni-liderini-mi-ariyor/

Diakopoulos, N. (2020). Computational News Discovery: Towards Design Considerations for Editorial Orientation Algorithms in Journalism. *Digital Journalism (Abingdon, England)*, *8*(7), 945–967. doi:10.1080/21670811.2020.1736946

Diakopoulos, N., Trielli, D., & Lee, G. (2021). Towards Understanding and Supporting Journalistic Practices Using Semi-Automated News Discovery Tools. *Proceedings of the ACM on Human-Computer Interaction*, *5*(CSCW2), 406:1-406:30. 10.1145/3479550

Drok, N., Hermans, L., & Kats, K. (2018). Decoding youth DNA: The relationship between social engagement and news interest, news media use and news preferences of Dutch millennials. *Journalism*, *19*(5), 699–717. doi:10.1177/1464884917703469

Edgerly, S. (2022). The head and heart of news avoidance: How attitudes about the news media relate to levels of news consumption. *Journalism*, *23*(9), 1828–1845. doi:10.1177/14648849211012922

Fletcher, R., & Nielsen, R. K. (2018). Automated Serendipity. *Digital Journalism (Abingdon, England)*, *6*(8), 976–989. doi:10.1080/21670811.2018.1502045

Freedom House. (2023, November). *Turkey: Freedom in the World 2023 Country Report*. Freedom House. https://freedomhouse.org/country/turkey/freedom-world/2023

Gil de Zúñiga, H., Weeks, B., & Ardèvol-Abreu, A. (2017). Effects of the News-Finds-Me Perception in Communication: Social Media Use Implications for News Seeking and Learning About Politics. *Journal of Computer-Mediated Communication*, *22*(3), 105–123. doi:10.1111/jcc4.12185

Hansen, S. (2023, May 30). The Turkish Elections Swung from Hope to Despair. *The New Yorker*. https://www.newyorker.com/news/dispatch/the-turkish-elections-swung-from-hope-to-despair

Hermida, A. (2020). Post-Publication Gatekeeping: The Interplay of Publics, Platforms, Paraphernalia, and Practices in the Circulation of News. *Journalism & Mass Communication Quarterly*, *97*(2), 469–491. doi:10.1177/1077699020911882

Kemp, S. (2022). *The Global State of Digital 2022: Global Overview Report*. We are Social & Hootsuite. https://hootsuite.widen.net/s/gqprmtzq6g/digital-2022-global-overview-report

Kemp, S. (2023). *Digital 2023: Global Overview Report*. https://datareportal.com/reports/digital-2023-global-overview-report

Kızılkaya, E., & Ütücü, B. (2021). *IPI Turkey Digital Media Report: 'The New Mainstream' Is Rising (And It Seeks Support) – Free Turkey Journalists*. International Press Institute (IPI). https://freeturkeyjournalists.ipi.media/wp-content/uploads/2021/03/ENG-IPI-Turkey-Digital-Media-Report-01032021-finaI-.pdf

Mannell, K., & Meese, J. (2022). From Doom-Scrolling to News Avoidance: Limiting News as a Well-being Strategy During COVID Lockdown. *Journalism Studies*, *23*(3), 302–319. doi:10.1080/1461670X.2021.2021105

Molyneux, L. (2017). Mobile news consumption: A habit of snacking. *Digital Journalism (Abingdon, England)*, *6*(5), 634–650. doi:10.1080/21670811.2017.1334567

Newman, N., Fletcher, R., Robertson, C. T., Eddy, K., & Nielsen, N. Rasmus Kleis, (2022). *Digital News Report 2022*. Reuters Institute for the Study of Journalism. https://reutersinstitute.politics.ox.ac.uk/digital-news-report/2022

Newman, N., Fletcher, R., Schulz, A., Andı, S., Robertson, C. T., & Nielsen, N. Rasmus Kleis, (2021). *Digital News Report 2021*. Reuters Institute for the Study of Journalism. https://reutersinstitute.politics.ox.ac.uk/sites/default/files/2021-06/Digital_News_Report_2021_FINAL.pdf

OECD. (2017). *Algorithms and Collusion: Competition Policy in the Digital Age*. Organisation for Economic Co-operation and Development (OECD). https://www.oecd.org/daf/competition/Algorithms-and-colllusion-competition-policy-in-the-digital-age.pdf

Pariser, E. (2011). *The filter bubble: What the Internet is hiding from you*. Penguin Press.

Park, C. S., & Kaye, B. K. (2020). What's This? Incidental Exposure to News on Social Media, News-Finds-Me Perception, News Efficacy, and News Consumption. *Mass Communication & Society*, *23*(2), 157–180. doi:10.1080/15205436.2019.1702216

Punch, K. F. (2014). *Introduction to Social Research: Qualitative & Quantitative Approaches* (3rd ed.). SAGE Publications.

Ravenelle, A. J., Newell, A., & Kowalski, K. C. (2021). "The Looming, Crazy Stalker Coronavirus": Fear Mongering, Fake News, and the Diffusion of Distrust. *Socius: Sociological Research for a Dynamic World*, *7*. doi:10.1177/23780231211024776

Ross Arguedas, A., Badrinathan, S., Mont'Alverne, C., Toff, B., Fletcher, R., & Nielsen, R. K. (2022). *Snap Judgements: How Audiences Who Lack Trust in News Navigate Information on Digital Platforms.* Reuters Institute for the Study of Journalism. https://reutersinstitute.politics.ox.ac.uk/snap-judgements-how-audiences-who-lack-trust-news-navigate-information-digital-platforms

Saran Doğan, C. (2022). *Enformasyonel Kapitalizm, Veri ve Gazetecilik: Türkiye'de Dijital Kullanıcı Verilerinin Haber Sitelerinde Kullanımı* [Doktora, Galatasaray Üniversitesi Sosyal Bilimler Enstitüsü Radyo Televizyon ve Sinema Ana Bilim Dalı]. https://tez.yok.gov.tr/UlusalTezMerkezi/TezGoster?key=RsTBl6RWK25OBMIKtIgYYQ_31Z86aiZ936ELp8_3wpf7-ty-ATi5xUB9VXnip5BD

Schäfer, S., Aaldering, L., & Lecheler, S. (2023). "Give Me a Break!" Prevalence and Predictors of Intentional News Avoidance During the COVID-19 Pandemic. *Mass Communication & Society*, *26*(4), 671–694. doi:10.1080/15205436.2022.2125406

Skovsgaard, M., & Andersen, K. (2020). Conceptualizing News Avoidance: Towards a Shared Understanding of Different Causes and Potential Solutions. *Journalism Studies*, *21*(4), 459–476. doi:10.1080/1461670X.2019.1686410

Sunstein, C. R. (2007). *Republic.com 2.0.* Princeton University Press.

Thorson, K. (2020). Attracting the news: Algorithms, platforms, and reframing incidental exposure. *Journalism*, *21*(8), 1067–1082. doi:10.1177/1464884920915352

Thurman, N., Moeller, J., Helberger, N., & Trilling, D. (2019). My Friends, Editors, Algorithms, and I. Digital Journalism, 7(4), 447–469. doi:10.1080/21670811.2018.1493936

Toff, B., & Nielsen, R. K. (2018). "I Just Google It": Folk Theories of Distributed Discovery. *Journal of Communication*, *68*(3), 636–657. doi:10.1093/joc/jqy009

TÜİK. (2023, February 6). *Adrese Dayalı Nüfus Kayıt Sistemi Sonuçları, 2022.* Turkish Statistical Institute (TÜİK). https://data.tuik.gov.tr/Bulten/Index?p=49685

Turkey, M. O. M. (2023). *Media Ownership Monitor (MOM) Turkey Project.* Reporters without Borders (RSF) & IPS Communication Foundation. https://turkey.mom-gmr.org/en/

Van Damme, K., Martens, M., Leuven, S. V., Abeele, M. V., & Marez, L. D. (2020). Mapping the Mobile DNA of News. Understanding Incidental and Serendipitous Mobile News Consumption. *Digital Journalism (Abingdon, England)*, *8*(1), 49–68. doi:10.1080/21670811.2019.1655461

Vandenplas, R., Truyens, P., Vis, S., & Picone, I. (2021). Tuning Out the News. A Cross-Media Perspective on News Avoidance Practices of Young News Users in Flanders During the COVID-19 Pandemic. *Journalism Studies*, *22*(16), 2197–2217. doi:10.1080/1461670X.2021.1990788

Villi, M., Aharoni, T., Tenenboim-Weinblatt, K., Boczkowski, P. J., Hayashi, K., Mitchelstein, E., Tanaka, A., & Kligler-Vilenchik, N. (2022). Taking a Break from News: A Five-nation Study of News Avoidance in the Digital Era. *Digital Journalism (Abingdon, England)*, *10*(1), 148–164. doi:10.1080/21670811.2021.1904266

Yanardağoğlu, E. (2021). 'Just the way my generation reads the news': News consumption habits of youth in Turkey and the UK. *Global Media and Communication*, *17*(2), 149–166. doi:10.1177/1742766520979729

Yetkin, M. (2023, November 7). Turkish main opposition elects new leader: What 'change' can he bring? *Yetkin Report*. https://yetkinreport.com/en/2023/11/07/turkish-main-opposition-elects-new-leader-what-change-can-he-bring/

Ytre-Arne, B., & Moe, H. (2021). Doomscrolling, Monitoring and Avoiding: News Use in COVID-19 Pandemic Lockdown. *Journalism Studies*, *22*(13), 1739–1755. doi:10.1080/1461670X.2021.1952475

Chapter 6
The Tsunami of the Pandemic in the Context of Japanese Cinema

Maria Roberta Novielli
Ca' Foscari University of Venice, Italy

ABSTRACT

The COVID-19 pandemic severely affected the film industry in Japan. One of the main problems involved small cinemas in large urban centers. As soon as it became clear that the closure of the cinemas would lead to the collapse of the small ones, many directors and authors immediately mobilised with various initiatives aimed at raising awareness of the risk of this serious loss and urging the government to support them. The temporary closures of small theatres gave way to various alternative solutions, such as online projection channels and the revival of drive-ins, but the most interesting phenomenon is the intensification of film productions by mini-theatre operators themselves. Of the unstoppable Japanese film production of the last few years, some films have centered on stories related to the pandemic and have told of the discomfort during the emergency. This chapter aims to take a snapshot of the situation of Japanese cinema since the beginning of the pandemic, noting some of the main problems and elements of probable continuity in future productions.

INTRODUCTION

The Covid-19 pandemic severely affected the film industry in Japan, leading to both negative and positive consequences. The emergency immediately forced authors and producers to find useful alternatives on several fronts to return to previous modes. One of the main problems, as we shall see, involved small cinemas (so-called mini-theaters) in large urban centers. Between February and March 2020, restrictions imposed on cultural events intensified in Japan, culminating in April in an approximately two-month lockdown on public screenings, without, however, a clear government support plan. Fortunately, the lockdown and temporary closures of small theaters gave way to various alternative solutions, such as online screening channels and the revival of drive-ins. However, the most interesting phenomenon was the intensification of film productions, many of which were initiated by the mini-theater operators themselves, including various experimental operations — facilitated, for example, by the more wide-

DOI: 10.4018/979-8-3693-0896-7.ch006

spread use of new digital technologies — undertaken to protect auteur cinema. These initiatives were complemented by a range of mobilizations among film industry players to ensure production continuity for national works, particularly in the form of successful fundraising or public awareness campaigns.

In the unstoppable Japanese film production of the very last few years — with an average of 600 productions per year — a portion of films have centered on events specifically related to the pandemic, depicting the country's new sociological context. Moreover, in the midst of the emergency there have been almost unprecedented box-office successes, and overall the Japanese the film market has recovered at a faster pace than in the West, demonstrating that cinema remains one of the most vibrant arts in the archipelago.

The Effects of the Pandemic on Small Cinemas

Japan was among the first countries to register cases of Covid-19 as early as in January 2020. The state of emergency and the associated lockdown, initially applied only in some prefectures, was finally extended to the entire archipelago from April 16 of the same year. For about two months, movie theaters and film sets were of course closed as well. In many cases, this choice caused extremely negative fallout for the film industry; in others, it stimulated the emergence of interesting alternatives.

Mini-theaters (small art houses used for the distribution of non-commercial films and extensively present in major urban centers throughout the country) suffered a particularly heavy toll. Established in the 1980s, based on models formed in the previous two decades —the most famous example being the Art Theater Guild, known by its acronym ATG[1] — these small theaters allowed the viewing of newly released independent films, and organized retrospectives about little-known Western and native authors as well as frequent talks with the authors themselves. They opened the door to a broader and more multicultural world than the one offered by the mainstream theaters of large distribution circuits, soon stimulating a diversified and in many cases auteur production[2]. However, these circuits went through several ups and downs over the years. An initial reduction in audiences had already occurred with the rise of the home video market, followed by that of digital technologies, multiplex cinemas, and video-on-demand[3]. The pandemic emergency dealt the final blow, as the government failed to respond with supportive actions, leaving operators at the mercy of an uncertain future and forcing them to look for alternative solutions that led to the proliferation of drive-ins and online screening channels. Among the latter, an interesting example is the "Temporary Cinema" experimented by director Sōda Kazuhiro with distributor Tofoo Films in the very early days of the lockdown: a circuit of about 40 mini-theaters and film distributors made available, through a streaming portal, some of the Japanese and Western films already scheduled for screening in the months of the crisis. As indicated by the name, the project was born as an interim solution in the hope of a return to physical viewing after the lockdown, and the cost of tickets for online viewing did not differ from the one normally charged in theaters[4].

Fortunately, the actions of many private individuals, especially filmmakers and actors, contributed some form of aid to the partial survival of theaters. In particular, two campaigns launched since the beginning of the lockdown tried to curb the collapse of these venues. The first was the petition "Save the Cinema", launched among others by director Koreeda Hirokazu and actor Arata Iura, which collected over 90,000 signatures asking the government to support mini-theaters. The second was the crowdfunding effort "Mini-Theater Aid", sponsored among others by filmmakers Fukada Kōji and Hamaguchi Ryūsuke, and with the support of various video messages recorded by actors and filmmakers, which raised more than 330 million yen. Part of these funds was then donated to small theater operators, who in turn came up with additional solutions to revitalize their businesses: for example Sugawara Kazuhiro, operator of the Iris Cinema in Hakodate (Hokkaido), used some of the funds for the production of independent films, including Saitō Hisashi's *The Sound of Grass* (*Kusa no hibiki*, 2021), and to finance Jack & Betty Cinema in Yokohama (beginning with *Somebody's Flowers - Dareka no hana*, 2021 by Okuda Yusuke) and a fledgling circuit of three historic theaters — Eurospace in Tokyo, Nagoya Cinematheque in Nagoya, and Ciné Noveau in Osaka[5].

In 2023, an important initiative was finally added by the government-run Japan Foundation[6]: its annual program of free, online international screenings of Japanese films included a special feature on mini-theaters, telling their story, introducing some of the major venues, and defining the "mission" of each.

The Return to Theatrical Screenings

In Japan and around the world, the impact of Covid-19 on theatrical screenings was obviously not limited to economic damage or the drastic reduction of available "art-house films". What was missing the most, in fact, was the possibility of enjoying the film together — a collective experience that can shape the subjectivity of viewers in their encounters with other individuals. The idea is well emphasized by scholar S. Brent Plate (2020, p. 203):

Cinema is a georeligious aesthetic. Since its mytho-historical origins in the 1890s, cinema has traversed the world, nestling into the nooks and crannies of big cities and rural villages alike. From the cafes of Paris to the Nigerian New Wave, from Mexico's first and second Golden Ages to Bollywood's star system, cinema has transformed most everything it has come into contact with. Gender, sex, age, race, language, ethnicity, religion, sexuality, nationality, body image and ability, and history itself have all been remade through the apparatus of filmmaking, distribution, and reception. Cinema is never neutral, never just an "escape," and never less so than when it is connected to religious life and tradition.

In the specific case of Japan, however, this strong sense of collective experience could partly be preserved thanks to a particular form of film viewing that had emerged a few years before the pandemic: the so-called "supported screenings" (*oen joei*, sometimes called *chiaringu joei* from the English "cheering screening"), a phenomenon that exploded with the animated film *King of Prism by Pretty Rhythm* (2016) by Hishida Masakazu, but with precedents such as Jim Sharman's *The Rocky Horror Picture Show* (1973) and many Indian films in the "masala" genre. During screenings, viewers are allowed to use their cell phones, for example, to tweet what is happening in the theater. They also sing along to the soundtrack, dub the voices of the characters, comment the viewing among themselves, and possibly cosplay. The involvement is total and the performance within the performance heightens the excitement, to the point that many viewers return several times to repeat the experience. Although *oen joei* most often involves the screening of animated films, this practice was also extended to live and action films such as Kubo Shigeaki's *High&Low The Movie* (2016[7]) and *Teiichi: Battle of Supreme High* (*Teiichi no kuni*, 2017, based on a manga by Furuya Usamaru) by Nagai Akira.

With the pandemic emergency, restrictions were obviously imposed on this practice. In particular, viewers were asked to stop talking in the theater and to communicate only by waving bright flashlights, making sounds with various devices or by clapping, or even through a cell phone app designed for the occasion. Examples include the screening of the film *Rambo: Last Blood* (2019, by Adrian Grünberg) released in 2020 at the Toho Cinemas theater in Ikebukuro, in the heart of Tokyo: comments uploaded on the app were even projected onto the screen at the same time as the film was being shown. This strategy not only made it possible to continue the practice of *oen joei*, but even intensified the sense

Figure 1. Number of films released

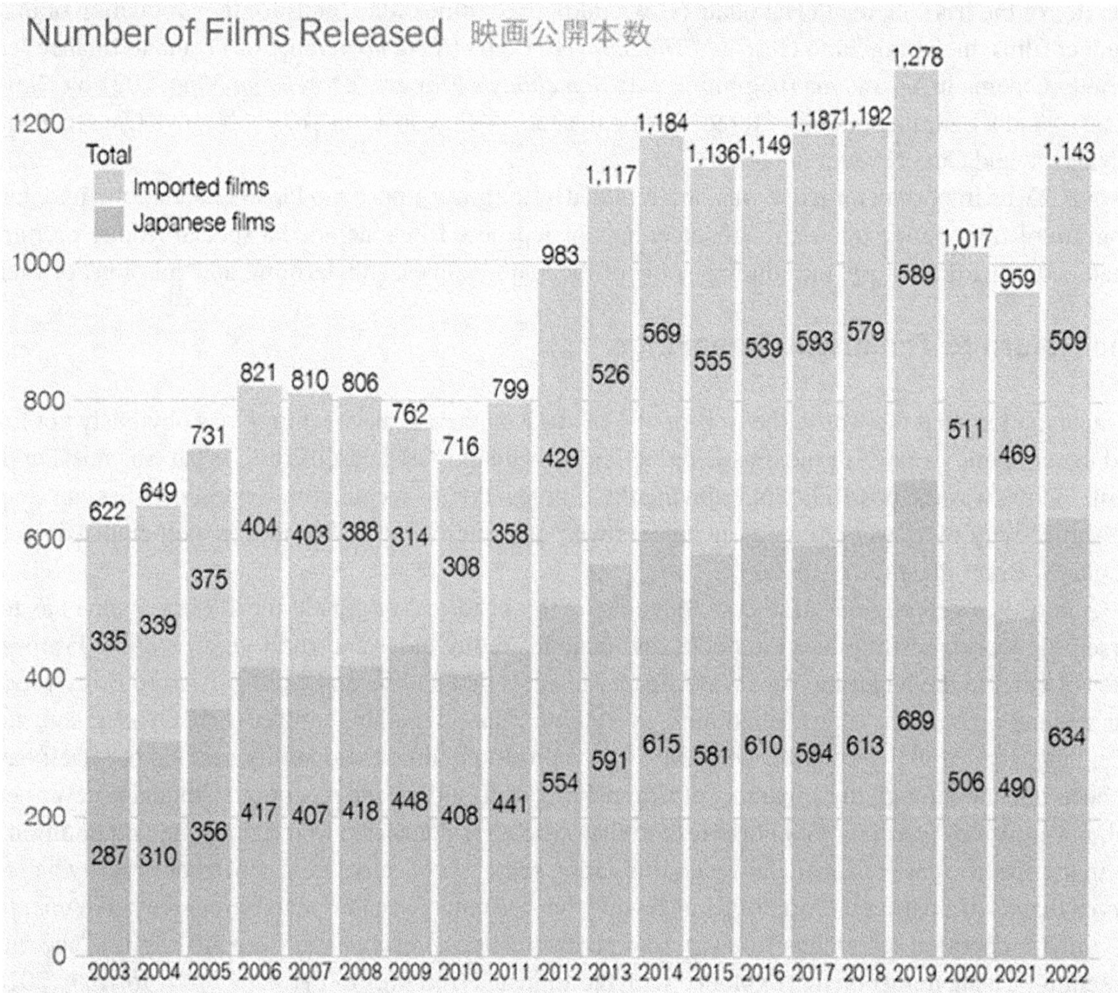

Figure 2. Cinema admissions

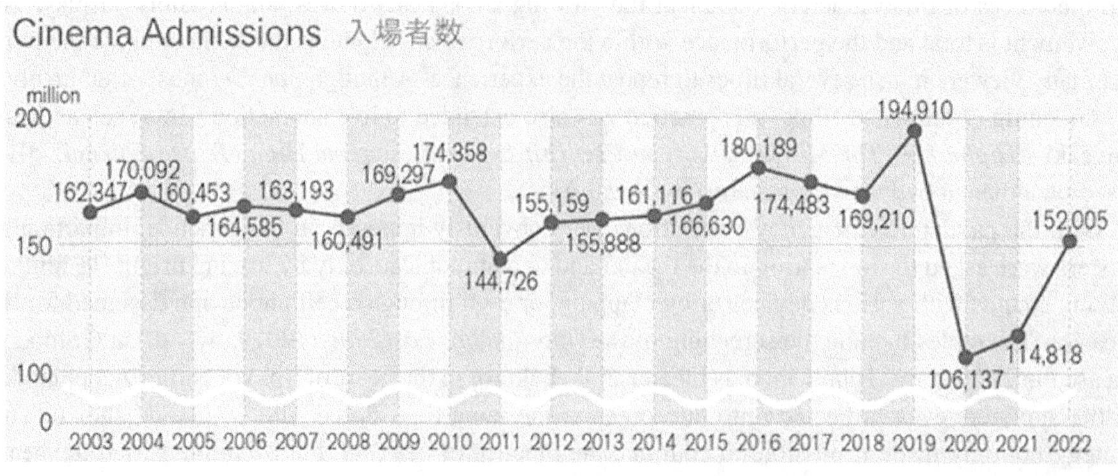

Figure 3. Box office receipts

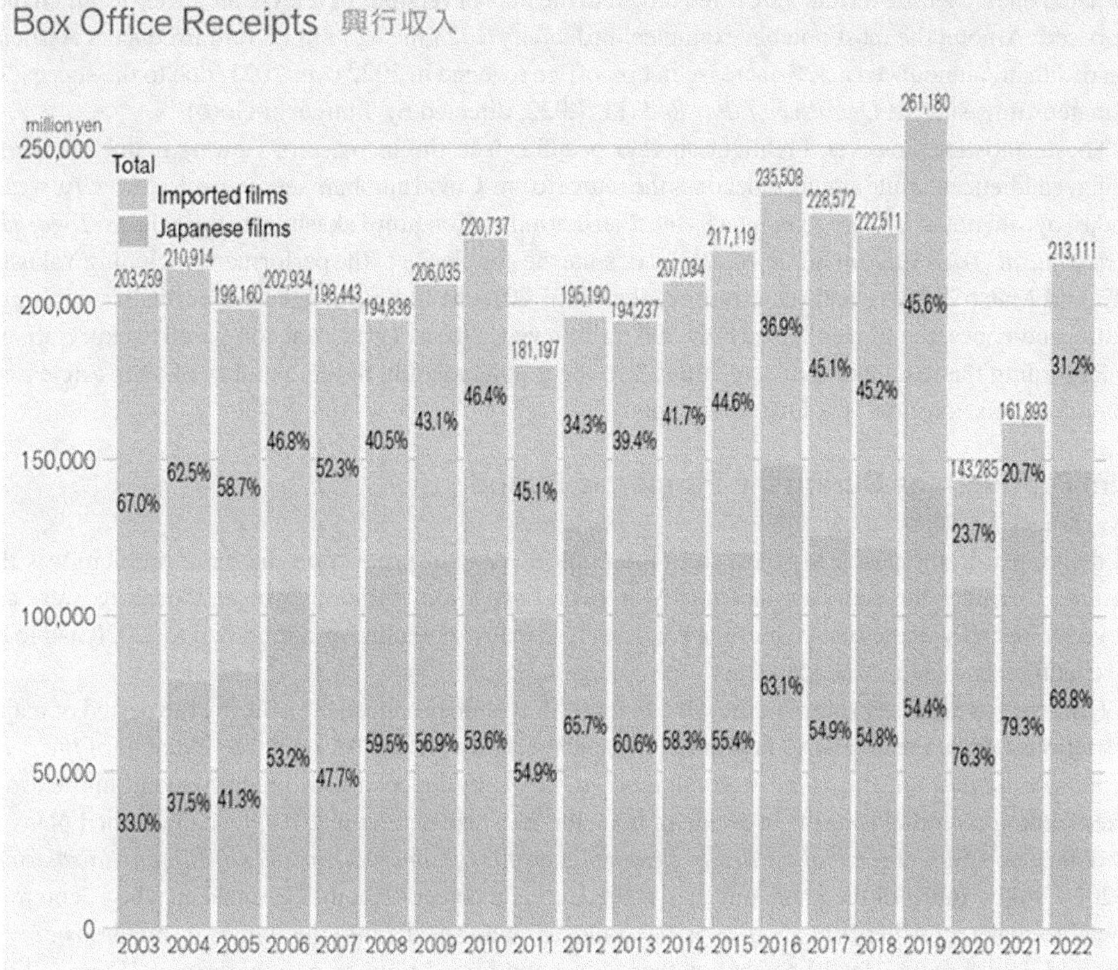

of belonging to a community of admirers of the same cultural product — a feeling born in the theaters and then protracted for days through social media, with obvious benefits for the promotion of the film.

Unfortunately, despite its positive effects, the ploy failed to prevent defections. The rapid multiplication of online channels dedicated to both live and animated films, coupled with forced lockdown periods, induced many users to permanently lock themselves into the dimension of home viewing, and in many cases to become addicted very quickly. This factor also contributed to exacerbating pre-existing social problems, such as the so-called *hikikomori*[8] — a pathology whose numbers have soared because of the pandemic. What is more, the drastic reduction in film productions, again due to the lockdown and to restrictions on the use of film locations, led to a tragic chain of suicides in the ranks of famous actors[9].

However, 2022 saw a partial reversal of the trend. The number of theaters increased by about 50[10] over the previous year. The number of moviegoers and distributed films also grew exponentially[11]. The upswing should also be ascribed to the relaxation of the restrictive measures imposed by Covid-19 and to a general increase in the technological equipment of theaters, ranging from "augmented audio" facilities to 3D and 4D projections that include moving seats, vaporized scents and other effects such as wind simulations. Another important contributor was the growing success of certain films, particularly animated ones[12], whose fortunes are often linked to the manga versions or television series on which they are based. Among the most notable examples, in January 2023 the Motion Picture Producers Association of Japan[13] announced a 32% increase in box office revenue in 2022 over 2021, due to the success of animated films such as *One Piece Film: Red* (id., 2022, directed by Taniguchi Gorō)[14].

These statistics, however, highlight another peculiar fact: the increase in viewers mainly concerns younger audiences, while among older ones the return to pre-Covid numbers seems much slower. As writer Inada Toyoshi notes[15], a case in point was the distribution of Koizumi Takashi's historical film *Toge: The Last Samurai* (*Tōge Saigo no samurai*, 2022): despite the popularity of the performers, including Yakusho Kōji and Matsu Takako, and the costumes that until 2019 would have appealed particularly to more mature audiences, the film collected only 500 million yen, a derisory amount compared to expectations.

Regarding the resumption of screenings, see the graphs relating to the Number of Films Released, Cinema Admissions and Box Office Receipts[16]:

Film Productions During the Pandemic Period

As mentioned in the past few pages, from the point of view of production the main problem was the inability to gather the crews on location. Moreover, only a limited number of new projects were approved, especially in the first year of the pandemic, as many screenings programmed for 2020 had to be re-scheduled and then suspended due to the emergency.

However, as necessity sharpens the wits, several films were produced even during the period of major restrictions. An interesting case in point is the unexpectedly successful sequel to *One cut of the dead* (*Kamera o tomeru na!*, lit. *Don't stop the camera*, 2017) by independent director Ueda Shin'ichirō[17]. After filming an initial spin-off of about an hour for the small screen in 2019, Ueda launched plans to shoot the short film *One cut of the dead - Remote Operation* (*Kamera o tomeru na! Rimoto daisakusen*) in 2020, in the midst of the pandemic crisis: the film is a comedy about a filmmaker who is commissioned to make a thriller film about a "serial attacker" who sneaks into the homes of hundreds of victims and tickles them. Unable to get together on set and forced to interact only through Zoom, all the actors (many of whom had also performed in the first film) were asked to film themselves on their cell phones in various comic situations, including "botched" effects due to their inability to get good shots. In addition, Ueda issued a call for participations on social networks, asking people to interpret the role of victims. The response, amounting to as many as 300 amateur videos, further underscored the urgent need for aggregation and for getting back together, especially through cinema.

Another interesting experiment in remote production is the short film *From Beyond* (*Kanata yori*, 2020) by Takahashi Hiroshi — a director best known in the West as the screenwriter of Nakata Hideo's famous film series *The Ring*. In this case, three actors interact through computers positioned in front of one another, and their faces are joined by some projections on the wall behind one of the three, as well as mutual reflections from the monitors. With a predominantly theatrical imprinting, Takahashi reworks and mixes famous literary works on the theme of specters[18] — an obvious metaphor for the pandemic and the condition of individuals finding themselves alone in the face of something unknown and terrifying. The dialogues among the three characters are seemingly unconnected, and one of the actors even leaves the room only to return. For the director, the entire performance also becomes a means of reiterating how only images — the essence of cinema itself — can still manage to unite individuals by transcending physical space.

With the first relaxation of restrictions, other interesting production experiments were conducted, including the feature film *Divoc-12* (id., 2021), a project launched during the openings of early 2020 by Sony Pictures Entertainment and coordinated by filmmakers Mishima Yukiko, Fujii Michiito and Ueda Shin'ichirō. Composed of 12 short films by as many filmmakers, including the coordinators themselves and three young people recruited through a "call for participation", the film's intent is to propose a new idea of cinema and at the same time to allow filmmakers —especially younger ones — film workers, and actors to remain active despite the limitations of the period. The title *Divoc* ("Covid" spelled backwards) becomes a symbol of the desire to overturn the current difficult situation but also stands for "Diversity, Innovation, Value, Originality, Creativity" — the themes addressed by each of the 12 shorts. In the short *Ode to Joy*, about "diversity", Mishima Yukiko invites the audience to overcome all barriers and to share what the world is experiencing: with a focus on social anxiety, she tells the story of an elderly woman of little means who lives on her own. One day, she accepts a dubious job from a young stranger met on a beach — a symbol of human frailty in the face of unpredictable risk and of the need to hope in a better future.

In addition to the originality of its content, *Divoc-12* also became an ideal platform for new technical experimentation. In the short film *Yumemi's Half Life* (*Yumemi no hansei*), Ueda Shin'ichirō tells the story of a young woman who, during a theatrical film screening, approaches a boy who dreams of becoming a filmmaker. She begins to tell him about her own life through images that are reminiscent of other films, beginning with black-and-white silent films and ending with color films, with a constant variation of shooting locations. The new technique of virtual production with Crystal led screens was used instead of the usual chromakey, reproducing in the studio entire landscapes that do not exist in reality[19], as the tightening of the restrictions had limited the use of many locations and movements between different places.

Between Apocalypse and Desire for Reconstruction

We have all personally witnessed how a virus of the magnitude of Covid-19 can subvert many dynamics of social living, to the point of partially altering the cultural scene of a country. The phenomenon is best summarized by scholar Márió Z. Nemes (2023, p. 122), who describes its devastating impact as follows:

The virus, as a complex of organic components, demonstrates the presence of a structure that in itself is subversive of humanism. It is a liminal agent, situated between life and death, the organic and the inorganic, transgressing the borderlines between these categories, as an almost living dead entity. . . . The subversive potential of the virus is enhanced by the way it disarranges and invades the imaginary unity of the individual human body. Culture as a whole can become infected by nonhuman agents. Virality, after all, is also a metaphor from 1990s cyberculture.

As for Japan, a country with decades-long exposure to cyberculture, much has been written about its conception of the apocalypse as compared to the one prevalent in the West. One reason for this difference, as many scholars have pointed out, is to be found in its particular perception of historical and temporal development. Whereas time is seen by Westerners as a linear flow, in parts of Asia it follows a predominantly circular course, especially in light of the Buddhist conception of *mappō*, a term for the third and final period of history, marked by a degeneration of moral laws[20]. By virtue of circularity, destruction can be followed by rebirth and reconstruction — an idea that has helped many Japanese people overcome various natural disasters such as earthquakes.

The "post-apocalyptic" season is not always connoted in Japanese culture as entirely negative, and its death-related meaning often romantically elevates the ideal of subsequent rebirth, as in the case of the literary theme of the double suicide of lovers —linked to the hope that their souls may rest on the same lotus flower in the afterlife. In other cases, however, the scenario is as dramatic as it could be: for example, survivors of the Hiroshima and Nagasaki atomic bombings (called *hibakusha*) are often represented as facing continuing apocalypse on Earth due to the consequences of radiation. Furthermore, quoting the words of John Whittier Treat (1995):

The people of two cities were, and some still are, forced to live in a compromised state of both life and death at the same time; that fate is a consequence of having barely survived a deliberate and methodical human plan to eliminate them. (p. 8)

An analogous vision of destruction and death is also present in the film production about the great earthquake that followed the Tōhoku tsunami of March 11, 2011, and the Fukushima nuclear disaster. Many films have approached the aftermath of the catastrophe with an emphasis on individual drama, sometimes depicting how the tragedy sneaks even into the relationships between family members in the grip of a widespread sense of uncertainty, suffering from the symptoms of a "sickness" brought about by the event itself[21].

Similarly, viruses are often portrayed not only as agents of pain but also as a discriminating factor between those who came into contact with them and those who did not. An emblematic case, in some ways grimly prophetic of the recent Covid-19 pandemic, is Irie Yū's disaster film *The Sun* (*Taiyō*, 2016): a virus has divided humanity into two groups — those who have been infected and survived, now equipped with antibodies but in danger if exposed to sunlight, and those who have never been infected and are therefore discriminated against by the former and forced to live with few means. Interestingly, however, only few films made after 2020 overtly deal with the pandemic, while most prefer a more veiled reference to the resulting conditions of loneliness and isolation, using metaphors to describe the social disorientation to which any catastrophe of this magnitude exposes individuals.

Among the few films that directly refer to the pandemic is the recent anthology film by Nakamura Mayu *She is Me, I am Her* (*Watashi no naka no kanojo*, 2022), consisting of four episodes centered on women of different ages and social backgrounds[22] — all played by actress Nahana —each a victim of social disconnect. The main message of the film is that mending the effects of social distancing is always difficult, but possible.

Takahashi Banmei makes a harsher point with the film *No Place to Go* (*Yoake made basu tei de*, lit. *At the Bus Stop Until Dawn*, 2022), inspired by a tragic crime story that took place in 2020: a woman working part-time at a yakitori restaurant in Tokyo loses her job and home due to the pandemic, until one night she is killed by a man who smashes her skull with a sack full of stones while she sleeps on a bench at a bus stop. Although her double state of physical and psychological degradation is here closely linked to the pandemic contingency, which has led to the closure of several restaurants and bars and therefore to many job losses, it also makes the point that society itself can no longer offer valid alternatives to those who live alone, untethered from a solid family context.

In analyzing what catastrophes — including the Covid-19 pandemic — represent for human beings, Valerio Nitrato Izzo [2023, pp. 253-254] distinguishes three types of effects. First, they give visibility to what was previously invisible (a virus), making us aware of the consequences and of the real risk they entail, as well as of the necessity to protect ourselves. The second effect specifically refers to technological disasters such as the Fukushima incident, showing us that even extensively tested technologies that seem completely safe can in fact hide a flaw. The third, based on an anthropological model, reveals the ongoing separation between humans and nature, particularly in the West, or the end of a world shaped by human beings, as nature suddenly seems to rebel and take over.

In this regard, Alice Cati (2021) rightly notes:

Among the effects of forced isolation due to the pandemic, one has particularly struck the collective imagination: the revenge of Nature on man. In fact, within numerous social and media discourses, the anguish over the void that initially dominated the public space in the months of the first lockdown has gradually transformed into the search for an otherness, capable of redefining the boundaries of existence starting from a foundation that unifies the phenomenal reality of the human and the non-human. Numerous amateur videos have circulated online, on social media and on TV to demonstrate the re-appropriation of living spaces by animals that live hidden in large cities . . . , showing themselves for once free to cross without danger and interferences within the confines of daily living in contact with man and his means of transport and communication. . . . Through these images, a rhetoric modeled on the idealization of the natural is somehow reaffirmed, where however a strong nostalgic tension towards a previous state to which one would like to return prevails. Thus, the relationship with nature in the pandemic era emerges as a real effect of meaning aimed at contrasting the euphoric values of an original sacred and harmonious vision of our planet with the "dysphoric present reality." (pp. 79-80)

Once the initial shock was overcome, Japanese cinema also proposed an increasing number of films set in nature or that enhance in various ways its salvific value. Yoneyama Shoko [2020], for example, suggests considering the epistemological work of the two animators Miyazaki Hayao and Shinkai Makoto, who always place nature and spirituality at the center of their narratives. In the case of live cinema, the most recent film by award-winning director Hamaguchi Ryūsuke, *Evil Does Not Exist* (*Aku wa sonzai shinai*, 2023, Silver Lion at the Venice Film Festival) is emblematic of the need to reconsider one's existence in natural contexts and no longer in strictly urban ones. In this film, the community of the small village of Mizubiki seems to have sealed a pact of mutual respect with nature. The protagonist Takumi, a widowed man living with his young daughter, follows a rigorous daily ritual: he always cuts the same amount of wood at the same pace, draws water from a stream for himself and the other inhabitants, and so on. However, this peaceful cohabitation is disturbed when a non-local company decides to build a tourist center in the area. This intrusive alteration of the ecosystem evokes the social damage caused by the virus. The arrival of two company managers alters a precious balance and the colors grow darker, until the protagonist's daughter disappears and is symbolically swallowed up, together with her father, by a now painful nature.

CONCLUSION

As we enter, in many ways, into a new era, we find our interest increasingly shifting to environmental issues and to an unprecedented reevaluation of our own fragility. In the case of Japan, the need to rediscover authentic values such as communion with nature is perhaps even more accentuated, given the historical memory of past tragedies — in particular the double nuclear bombing of Hiroshima and Nagasaki, the Tokyo subway sarin attack of 1995[23] and the Fukushima disaster of 2011.

Due among other factors to the insular nature of the country, the long closure of national borders has also created a fracture in the internationalization practices of recent decades. One of them was the government campaign "Cool Japan": launched during the mandates of prime ministers Koizumi Jun'ichirō and Abe Shinzō, it aimed to culturally and politically enhance the media industry, for instance through a "film fund" to co-finance film productions, incentivize film commissions and for the distribution of Japanese media on international markets[24]. More generally, the government put in place various policies to promote Japanese culture, tourism and other economic areas on a global level. However, only in recent months did production and distribution start running according to the directives of the campaign.

In conclusion, one can say that the pandemic caused a tsunami in Japanese cinema not only in terms of human lives, but also by highlighting a range of social, economic and political fragilities. Cinema, as always, has found a way to portray every nuance of this development, sometimes through a merciless gaze and in other cases by giving viewers a glimpse of hope that there may be better, happier times ahead.

REFERENCES

Cai, Q., Okada, A., Jeong, B. G., & Kim, S-J. (2021). Civil Society Responses to the COVID-19 Pandemic. *China Review*, *21*(1), 107–138.

Cati, A. (2021). Piccole finestre sul nonumano — Immagini per l'educazione ambientale nell'era della pandemia. In T. Lancioni & F. Villa (Eds.), *Visual Cultural Studies 2* (pp. 77–96). Mimesis Edizioni.

Chakrabarty, D. (2020). An Era of Pandemics? What is Global and What is Planetary About COVID-19. *Critical Inquiry*. https://critinq.wordpress.com/2020/10/16/an-era-of-pandemics-what-is-global-and-what-is-planetary-about-covid-19/

Hisamitsu, A. (2005). Intellectual Property Strategy in Japan. *International Journal of Intellectual Property — Law, Economy, and Management*, *1*, 5–12. https://ipaj.org/english_journal/pdf/Intellectual_Property_Strategy.pdf

Izzo, N. (2023). Valerio, "Pandemic, humanities and the legal imagination of the disaster". In C. F. Stychin (Ed.), *Law, Humanities and the COVID Crisis*. University of London Press.

Nemes, M. Z. (2023). Going Viral. *Hungarian Journal of English and American Studies*, *29*(1), 121–142.

Novielli, M. R. (2022). *Storia del cinema giapponese nel nuovo millennio*. Marsilio.

Plate, S. B. (2020). Cinema: The Georeligious Aesthetic. *CrossCurrents*, *70*(3), 203–205.

Poulton, M. C. (2023). Realism, the Real, and Mediated Reality: Hirata Oriza and Beyond. In J. Nakamura & K. Saltzman-Li (Eds.), *Realisms in East Asian Performance* (pp. 160–174). University of Michigan Press.

Rivadossi, S. (2023). Estetica del vuoto in Mori Mariko — Un uso strategico del discorso sullo Zen. In L'estetica del vuoto — Suoni, silenzi, vuoti, pieni, presenze, assenze. Edizioni Ca' Foscari. doi:10.30687/978-88-6969-701-2/010

Treat, J. W. (1995). *Writing Ground Zero: Japanese Literature and the Atomic Bomb*. The University of Chicago Press.

Yoneyama, S. (2020). Rethinking Human-Nature Relationships in the Time of Coronavirus: Postmodern Animism in Films by Miyazaki Hayao & Shinkai Makoto. *The Asia-Pacific Journal, 18*(16). https://apjjf.org/2020/16/Yoneyama.html

ENDNOTES

1 Initially founded in 1962 with the intention of distributing foreign and Japanese art films in a group of theaters, ATG later engaged in financially supporting the production of auteur films to be presented in its own circuit. Another important example is the project "Équipe du Cinéma", launched in 1974 to present art-house films that were unlikely to be distributed in major theaters, including the masterpieces of the French New Wave.

2 An exemplary case is that of Eurospace, a mini-theater of only eighty-five seats opened in 1982 by Horikoshi Kenzō in Shibuya, in the heart of Tokyo and subsequently expanded with the addition of a screen in 1994. Specialized in Western and indigenous art-house films, Eurospace gradually began to contribute to various films productions, not only local but also by filmmakers such as Aki Kaurismaki and Abbas Kiarostami. In 1997 Horikoshi opened the Eiga Bigakkō filmmaking school, and since 2005 he has become one of the main proponents of founding the filmmaking course at Tokyo University of the Arts (Tōkyō Geijutsu Daigaku). To date, Eurospace has produced more than twenty films, including Kurosawa Kiyoshi's *Barren illusion* (*Ōinaru gen'ei*, 1999), Shimizu Takashi's *Marebito* (id., 2004), and the award-winning *Tokyo Tower – Mom and Me, and Sometimes Dad* (*Tōkyō Tawā - Okan to boku to tokidoki oton*, 2007) by Matsuoka Jōji.

3 Among the major casualties, Cine Vivant had to close in 1999, Cine Saison in 2011, and Ginza Theater Cinema in 2013. All of them were once true "cult" venues for independent cinema.

4 Among the many titles, one can mention Sōda's film *Zero* (*Seishin 0*), which was scheduled for release in small theaters. In this as in other cases, there was an incentive to purchase the ticket for online viewing directly from the mini-theater site, so as to recover part of the expenses. The program, no longer running today thanks to the end of restrictions, can be found on the initiative's website: http://www.temporary-cinema.jp/

5 Here is another noteworthy initiative: eleven filmmakers linked to Kobe's Motomachi Eigakan and led by Oda Kaori made the collective film *Let's Go to the Movies Today?* (*Kyō, eigakan ni ikanai*?, 2021). An interesting interweaving of in-person and online distribution, film production, small-screen presentations, meetings with filmmakers, and many other events dedicated to art-house film connoisseurs. The project is still active thanks to the incessant work of Tsuboi Atsushi, director of the mini-theater Cinema Skhole (founded in Nagoya by Wakamatsu Kōji in 1983). This evolution is still in full swing and underscores the need to protect authorial cinema, and at the same time gives hope for its imminent revival through innovative circuits.

6 The Japan Foundation (in Japanese Kokusai Kōryū Kikin) is a government agency under the management of the Ministry of Foreign Affairs, devoted to the dissemination of Japanese culture around the world. Since the beginning of the pandemic, it has been organizing an annual, free, and internationally distributed "online festival" to showcase some of the country's latest film releases.

7 Based on the television series *High&Low: The Story of S.W.O.R.D.*, released by Nippon TV between 2015 and 2016.

8 *Hikikomori* are people who pathologically self-seclude at home, refusing contact with the outside world except through the computer. It has been estimated that after Covid the number of *hikikomori* has reached the record figure of 1,500,000 individuals. Source: https://www.theguardian.com/world/2023/apr/03/japan-says-15-million-people-living-as-recluses-after-covid. *The Guardian,* April 3, 2023.

9 By 2020, various actors of the big and small screen had committed suicide, including Kimura Hana, Miura Haruma, Ashina Sei, Takeuchi Yūko, Kubodera Akira and even the eighty-year-old Fukiji Takashi.

10 Source: https://www.ntttp-db.com/

11 The cumulative exit rate in September 2022 was 88% of the pre-Covid level, recording a steady recovery. Japanese films were 96%, foreign films 77%, and Japanese anime 119%, exceeding pre-Covid levels.

12 Some animated films were highly successful even during the first year of the pandemic, as in the case of *Demon Slayer: Mugen Train* (*Kimetsu no yaiba - Mugen resshahen*, 2020) by Sotozaki Haruo: distributed starting in October of the same year, it recorded over three million spectators in theaters in the first weekend of release.

13 The MPPAJ is the association of the four major production and distribution companies in the country, namely Shōchiku, Tōhō, Tōei and Kadokawa Corporation. It was created with the aim of increasing the number of productions, exports and participations in international festivals.

14 The film earned $206.7 million internationally, making it the fifth highest-grossing Japanese film worldwide.
Statistics provided by Unijapan at the link https://www.unijapan.org/english/overview/statistics.html

15 Source: https://www.sbbit.jp/article/cont1/106807

16 All graphs are available at the link https://gem-standard.com/columns/635 October 28, 2022

17 Shot on a very low budget and with the support of crowdfunding, this collaboration project with the Enbu Seminar film school in Tokyo tells in a comic and parodic key the story of a down-at-heel film crew involved in shooting a horror film about zombies and attacked by "real" zombies during the process. It is an experimental work in many ways, especially for the creation of an elaborate, 37-minute long sequence and for the use of different types of shots to differentiate the linguistic levels of the "film within the film". The film was unambitiously released in a mini-theater for just six days and intended to be viewed by a group of spectators directly invited by the director and his staff. Selected in 2018 by the Far East Film Festival in Udine, it won the audience award and obtained a number of positive reviews, followed by numerous awards at various festivals. Thanks to its popularity, it was initially shown in three theaters in Tokyo and immediately afterwards distributed by Asmik Ace in 200 different cinemas, earning an exorbitant amount that was calculated to be around 1000 times the initial budget.

18 *Hamlet* and *Macbeth* by William Shakespeare, *Spectres de Marx* by Jacques Derrida and *On the Knocking at the Gate in Macbeth* by Thomas De Quincey.

19 Unlike chromakey, which requires the actor to act in front of a blue or green backdrop while the digitized background image is added only later, with this system the scene that the director or actor

is shooting is instantly projected onto screens, thus combining computer graphics (CG) with live action acting without elaborate post-production and with a much more natural performance effect.

20 Many Asian countries share the cosmic vision according to which Buddha's death was followed by three ages, the last of which is called the "degeneration of laws".

21 A still current social consequence of the disaster is the discrimination against women who have been exposed to radiation, "incriminated" if pregnant of carrying a sick offspring. Moreover, gender discrimination leads to the belief that women "complain about the damage caused by radiation only out of female hysteria".
See https://mainichi.jp/english/articles/20210310/p2a/00m/0na/030000c

22 In the first episode, three characters talk about their dead friend Sayoko, an emerging actress involved in a scandal. The conversation becomes an opportunity to open up about the inconveniences of the pandemic. In the second story, a woman invites a delivery man to eat with her, establishing an increasingly deeper relationship with him. The third is dedicated to a woman who prostitutes herself and who meets an older homeless woman. They discover that they both used to dream of becoming actresses, but their dream was broken by the pandemic. The last episode tells the story of a blind woman who receives a visit from a young telephone scammer: by caressing his face, however, the woman manages to change his attitude.

23 On March 20, 1995, five members of the Aum Shinrikyō sect, founded and managed by Japanese Asahara Shōko, deposited five bags containing sarin-type nerve gas in several key locations of subway stations in central Tokyo. This sudden attack, responsible for twelve deaths and thousands of poisoned people, brought to light a number of previously obscured issues and spread panic across the country. The use of a chemical weapon was tragically reminiscent of the nuclear explosions of Hiroshima and Nagasaki in 1945, and therefore of the possible "distorted" applications of science. What is more, the attack did not come from outside but from an indigenous sect that already had 9,000 members in Japan and approximately 40,000 scattered around the world. This exposed an ongoing fracture in the Japanese social system, hitherto considered by its inhabitants as being among the healthiest in the world. The Aum Shinrikyō sect, which over time had extended its activities to extortion and murder, based its doctrine on a mix of religions and philosophies, some of which were foreign to Japanese culture (for example, Asahara defined himself as the Christ), bringing into the spotlight the messy mix of influences of recent decades, despite Japan's apparent ethnic and cultural homogeneity.

24 See Arai Hisamitsu, "Intellectual Property Strategy in Japan", in *International Journal of Intellectual Property – Law, Economy, and Management,* Vol. 1, 2005, pp. 5-12, available at the link https://ipaj.org/english_journal/pdf/Intellectual_Property_Strategy.pdf

Chapter 7
Media Shaped by COVID-19:
How Is Media Changing?

Hasan Gürkan
https://orcid.org/0000-0002-3805-9951
Girona University, Spain & Istinye University, Turkey

Aslı Güngör-Eral
Balıkesir University, Turkey

ABSTRACT

Over the past decade, the effects of digitization on Turkey's national and local press have significantly increased. In this study, the authors delve into the specific impact of the COVID-19 pandemic on this ongoing digitization process. The research focuses on two prominent daily newspapers in Turkey: Hürriyet and Yeni Asır. To gain valuable insights, the authors conducted in-depth interviews with 14 media professionals. The study's findings revealed a noteworthy shift in public trust, with social media gaining greater confidence as a news source. Additionally, national and local press have radically transformed their reporting practices, influenced by the growing digital landscape. The study highlights the pandemic's differential impact on various media outlets, underlining the emergence of stale content in the industry. This research sheds light on the dynamic interplay between digitization, the COVID-19 pandemic, and Turkey's national and local press. It offers valuable insights into changing public perceptions, reporting practices, and the diverse effects of the pandemic on media content.

INTRODUCTION

Since the turn of the century, the digitization of content, the rise of social media, and the acceleration in mobile consumption have compelled media companies to adapt their content, monetization strategies, and news production. The Covid-19 pandemic, most recently, has brought about a transformative impact on the media industry, presenting both crises and opportunities. Social distancing measures have increased home media consumption as individuals turn to news providers for timely and reliable information during the crisis.

DOI: 10.4018/979-8-3693-0896-7.ch007

This pandemic has highlighted the essential role of news organizations in keeping people informed during complex and uncertain times (Nielsen et al., 2020). Numerous critical studies by Hess & Waller (2020), Richards (2014), Zelizer (2015, 2019), and Alpert and Hagy (2020) have shed light on the significant contribution of professional journalists in this endeavor. Journalists have been crucial in holding governments accountable and explaining their crisis responses, though some attempts to mislead the public about journalists and their work have also been observed.

Despite the pandemic's global effects becoming apparent, many local and national media organizations now face the risk of closure. These media entities, which have been severely impacted during this global crisis, represent the core of the news industry. Furthermore, long-established local newspapers have experienced a decline in advertising revenue (Meade, 2020; Hess & Waller, 2020).

Focusing on the effects of the Covid-19 pandemic, this study examines how local and national media organizations in Turkey have undergone a transformation and explores its implications on traditional journalism practices. The study aims to provide a fresh perspective on the future of Turkey's local and national media organizations. Within this study, *Hürriyet*[1], a national and mass market newspaper with the highest circulation, and *Yeni Asır*[2], the oldest and most influential local media newspaper, are included in the analysis. Consequently, while analyzing the critical need for local and national journalism in Turkey amidst the Covid-19 pandemic, the study also offers valuable suggestions for the way forward.

MAIN FOCUS OF THE CHAPTER

The study focuses on the impact of the Covid-19 pandemic on journalism in the context of the Internet, new communication environments, and the influence of social media on journalistic practices. Moreover, this study delves into the evolution of media organizations in Turkey during the Covid-19 pandemic, focusing on its effects on national and local media.

Issues, Controversies, Problems

Specific research questions were considered:

RQ1: How has the traditional media transitioned to digital, especially with the Covid-19 outbreak?

RQ2: How has this process affected the local and national media industries regarding traditional journalism practices?

Table 1 presents the questions asked during the interviews:

Table 1. Questions to the journalists

Sex
1. How long have you been working for this media organization?
2. How does the pandemic transform news organizations?
3. How do news organizations perceive this pandemic?
4. In what ways do you think the pandemic has directly or indirectly impacted male and female professionals working in the media industry?
5. Can you evaluate the effects of this process on the construction of news?

The study is organized into the following subjects:

i. Distance journalism[3]
ii. Low-quality journalism
iii. The changing future of media
iv. The pandemic's impact on male and female media professionals

To collect data from journalists, the study conducted in-depth interviews with 14 professionals working in national and local media organizations. In-depth interviews, a qualitative research method, were conducted following a systematic data collection process (Boyce et al., 2006; Gürkan, 2019; Ruiz-Cabrera & Gürkan, 2023; Gürkan et al., 2023). Seven media professionals from Hürriyet and seven from Yeni Asır participated in the interviews, which took place from 12th May 2022 to 17th June 2022. The interviews were semi-structured, with open-ended questions tailored to each journalist and their organization. The aim was to prompt the journalists to provide detailed insights into their experiences, roles, and the events they witnessed during the Covid-19 pandemic. All interviewees had at least ten years of journalistic experience, and the gender distribution (female/male ratio) was considered in the study's analysis and conclusions.

National and Local Media

Journalism in Turkey has a rich and longstanding tradition, accompanied by public service broadcasting (Dursun, 2004; Adaklı, 2006; Gezmen et al., 2015). As technology continues to evolve, these rapid developments and changes in various aspects of life are also reflected in the media.

As far back as the 1960s, McLuhan predicted that technological advancements would turn the world into a global village. Today, with electronic breakthroughs and the prevalence of the internet, this prophecy has become a reality. The boundaries between people have blurred, and information can be accessed within seconds. The speed of electronic communication has allowed a constant influx of data into the human mind (McLuhan, 1962: 31; 1967: 63).

While the global village brings people closer together, local importance has remained partially. Media plays a vital role in preserving local values and passing them on to future generations, influencing the regional perspective on global issues. Local media outlets provide information about their immediate environment to the local public while reporting on significant national developments. Topics covered by local media include media developments, election periods, and district, provincial, and regional events (Büyükbaykal, 2012).

The local media facilitates the communication of community problems, helping individuals connect with the places they live in and fostering a sense of belonging to a larger city or region. Most provinces or districts have local radio stations, newspapers, or internet news sites. Additionally, local media plays a crucial role in agenda-setting. Hester and Gibson (2007) found that the agenda-setting of national and local media differs. In cases where an issue is national and local, local media significantly influences agenda-setting.

Despite the decline in readership and circulation of print media due to technological advancements and the demand for more visual and instantaneous communication, the circulation of local newspapers has persisted. However, the advent of technology has also led local media to find its place on internet sites. As Gaile (2013) pointed out, local media nurtures common values and culture, promoting a strong sense of local identity and fostering internal unity within the local community.

Media and Digitalism

As media increasingly adopts a digital identity, it has been shaped by the constant development of advanced and affordable digital devices (Storsul et al., 2007; Appelgren, 2004; Makarova et al., 2019). However, the landscape becomes more complex with the competition from social media, video streaming services, and smartphone apps, all vying for our attention. Media companies are in a constant battle for consumers' attention, producing content every second to capture their interest (Nielson, 2021). Furthermore, the Covid-19 pandemic has accelerated the transformation of the media landscape (Perez-Escoda et al., 2020; Agostino et al., 2021; Wade et al., 2020; Tunez-Lopez et al., 2020).

Digital journalism has rapidly evolved over the years, reshaping the media landscape in Turkey and worldwide. Before the pandemic, Turkey's digital journalism landscape was characterized by a complex interplay of economic, political, and technological factors. There are essential factors to explain digital journalism in Turkey. One of them is economic factors. Turkish media organizations witnessed a shift toward digital platforms as readers increasingly consumed news online. This transition posed challenges to traditional print media but offered revenue opportunities through digital advertising. Despite digitalization, many media outlets struggled with financial sustainability. The advertising market faced disruptions, impacting the revenue streams of both legacy and digital-born media. Moreover, another critical factor is politics. Pre-pandemic Turkey experienced constraints on media freedom, with journalists facing intimidation, censorship, and legal actions. This environment influenced the editorial stance of news outlets. Besides this, the government implemented internet censorship measures, affecting the digital news landscape. Access to specific websites and social media platforms was periodically restricted, impacting news dissemination. Another vital factor is technology. Social media platforms have become essential for news distribution and citizen journalism. News outlets leveraged these platforms to reach wider audiences, although concerns about misinformation also arose. Turkish media invested in digital innovation, including mobile apps and multimedia storytelling. Emerging technologies like virtual and augmented reality began playing a role in immersive journalism. Before the pandemic, Turkey's digital journalism landscape was marked by the digital transformation of media organizations, concerns over media freedom, the prominence of social media in news dissemination, and digital innovation. Understanding this context is essential for comprehending the challenges and opportunities faced by Turkish journalism as it navigates an evolving media environment (Özgül & Veneti, 2022; Çiftçi and Ayhan, 2023).

During the pandemic, people turned to local and national media to stay informed about regional developments. Simultaneously, remote work became a norm during the pandemic, leading institutions, including the media, to adapt to new technologies and seek talented employees capable of using these technologies effectively. Consequently, whether the digital transformation will decrease the need for media professionals arises.

The social sustainability of printed newspapers is being discussed amidst the decline in income and readership of printed newspapers with the rise of digital media (O'Sullivan et al., 2018; Yao, 2020; Shearer, 2020). Recent years have seen rapid changes in technological advancements, profoundly affecting the media sector, particularly print media. National and local media practices have undergone daily changes, experiencing a significant transformation, especially in the last decade (Dylko et al., 2012; Nielson et al., 2016). Boyer (2013) emphasizes that in the USA and Europe, news focused on public interest and public issues before 1980 but has since transformed into a neoliberal model, viewing the reader or viewer as an individual consumer rather than a public citizen. Nielson et al. (2016) highlight that traditional media's function has become less critical with digitalization, making the development of new digital business models crucial as current sources of income decline. This study focuses on examining the effects of the Covid-19 pandemic on the ongoing digitalization process in the media industry.

Moreover, the contemporary digital media environment is shaped by several key actors, with digital platforms and AI algorithms playing pivotal roles. These actors have brought about significant consequences for journalism, reshaping how news is produced, distributed, and consumed (Mihelj & Jimenez-Martines, 2020; Gaenssle & Budzinski, 2021).

Digital platforms, such as social media networks (e.g., Facebook, Twitter), search engines (e.g., Google), and content-sharing platforms (e.g., YouTube), have become dominant players in the media landscape. They serve as intermediaries between news organizations and their audiences, influencing the flow of information in several ways. Digital platforms control the distribution of news content. Their algorithms determine what content appears on users' feeds, impacting the visibility and reach of news articles. This gatekeeping power has implications for media diversity and the potential for echo chambers. Platforms have disrupted traditional revenue models for journalism. While they provide advertising opportunities, they also absorb a significant share of digital ad revenue, affecting the financial sustainability of news outlets. Platforms enable user-generated content and citizen journalism, allowing anyone to participate in news production. However, this democratization comes with challenges related to the authenticity and credibility of information (Nechushtai, 2018; Presual & Sierra, 2019; Meese & Hurcombe, 2021).

On the other hand, Artificial intelligence (AI) algorithms have gained prominence in journalism, primarily in content recommendation and personalization. These algorithms analyze user data to tailor news content, but their consequences are multifaceted. AI algorithms curate news feeds based on individual user preferences, creating filter bubbles where users are exposed to information that aligns with their existing beliefs. This can limit exposure to diverse viewpoints. AI algorithms are used to identify and combat fake news and misinformation. While they have the potential to enhance fact-checking and content verification, their accuracy remains a concern. AI-powered bots and algorithms are employed in newsrooms for tasks like data analysis and content generation. While automation improves efficiency, it also raises questions about the future of journalism jobs (Gentzkow, 2018).

Besides this, the interplay between digital platforms and AI algorithms has both positive and negative consequences for journalism. Digital platforms offer unparalleled reach and engagement opportunities for news organizations, enabling them to connect with global audiences. However, the algorithms that govern content distribution can amplify sensational or divisive content. The dominance of platforms in the digital advertising landscape poses revenue challenges for journalism. News outlets must compete for a share of the ad revenue generated on these platforms. AI algorithms can help improve information quality by identifying misinformation, but they need to be foolproof. Striking a balance between automation and human oversight is essential. The digital environment requires media literacy skills for users to critically navigate the influx of information. News organizations and educational institutions play a role in promoting media literacy (Lim, 2017; Gran et al., 2021).

Digital platforms and AI algorithms are central to the contemporary media landscape. While they offer new opportunities for journalism, they also present challenges related to content distribution, revenue models, and information quality. Navigating this complex terrain requires ongoing adaptation and ethical considerations by news organizations and digital platform providers.

FINDINGS AND DISCUSSION

The study employs descriptive statistics to categorize and analyze the characteristics of the participants. Table 2 provides an overview of the number of participants from each of the two newspapers, the gender distribution (number of men and women media professionals), and the number of years of professional experience for each participant.

In the study, there were seven female participants from the two institutions, with three from *Hürriyet* and four from *Yeni Asır*. Additionally, there were seven male participants, four from *Hürriyet* and three from *Yeni Asır*.

Figure 1 shows the distribution of journalists participating in this study according to *Hürriyet* and *Yeni Asır*. An equal proportion of journalists from both media institutions participated in the study.

Figure 2 shows the distribution rate of the participants by gender. An equal number of female and male journalists participated in the study. This contributes to the objectivity of the comments, especially on the issue of the Covid-19 and gender impact.

Figure 3 shows the percentage of total working time for each participant in the study. A minimum of ten years work experience was required for participants to be accepted to the study. The majority of the participating journalists had worked for at least 10 years, followed by 15 to 20 years.

Figures 4 and 5 display the years participants have worked, categorized by gender. Among the female journalists, those at the local newspaper Yeni Asır have more working years than those at the national newspaper *Hürriyet* (Figure 4). This observation suggests that circulation in the national media is faster than in the local media. Similarly, male journalists at *Yeni Asır* have more working years than at *Hürriyet*

Table 2. Participant ratios of surveyed daily newspapers

Daily Newspaper	The Number of Participants	Female Participant	Female Participant Working Year	Male Participant	Male Participant Working Year
Hürriyet	7	3	10-10-18	4	10-11-12-15
Yeni Asır	7	4	10-16-17-18	3	20-22-30

Figure 1. The percentage of participants from the surveyed newspapers

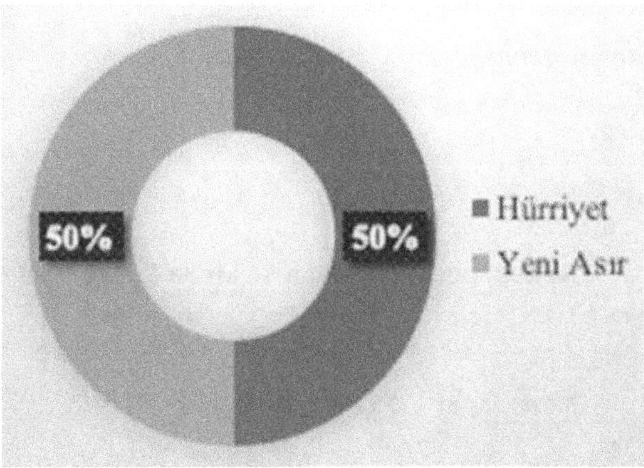

Figure 2. The percentage of participants concerning sex

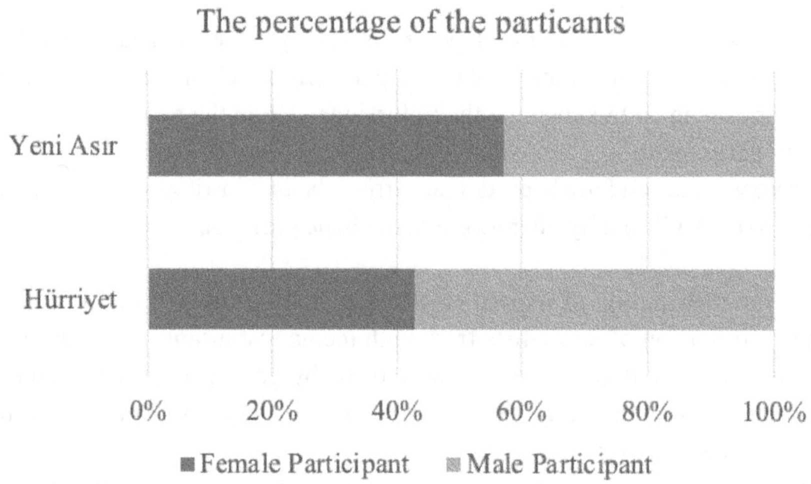

Figure 3. Histogram of the participants' work year

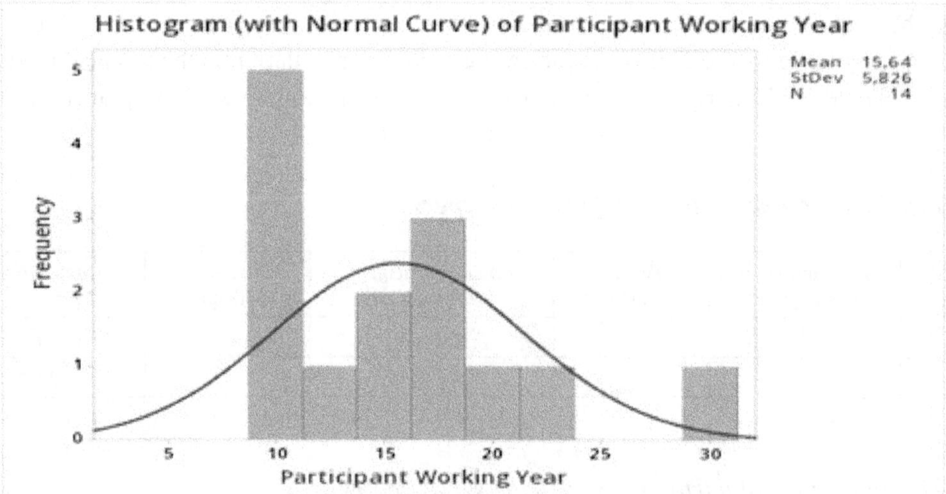

Figure 4. Female journalists' working years

Results for Gender = 1

Statistics

Variable	Newspaper	N	N*	Mean	SE Mean	StDev	Minimum	Q1	Median
Participant Working Year	1	3	0	12,67	2,67	4,62	10,00	10,00	10,00
	2	4	0	15,25	1,80	3,59	10,00	11,50	16,50

Variable	Newspaper	Q3	Maximum
Participant Working Year	1	18,00	18,00
	2	17,75	18,00

Figure 5. Male journalists' working years

Results for Gender = 2

Statistics

Variable	Newspaper	N	N*	Mean	SE Mean	StDev	Minimum	Q1	Median
Participant Working Year	1	4	0	12,00	1,08	2,16	10,00	10,25	11,50
	2	3	0	24,00	3,06	5,29	20,00	20,00	22,00

Variable	Newspaper	Q3	Maximum
Participant Working Year	1	14,25	15,00
	2	30,00	30,00

(Figure 5). This trend is consistent for both female and male journalists. Additionally, it is worth noting that in the study, the interviewees from *Hürriyet* are identified as "H1, H2, H3..." while those from *Yeni Asır* are identified as "YA1, YA2, YA3...".

Distance Journalism

Unfavorable economic conditions and advances in digital technology have brought significant changes to journalism, and the recent impact of Covid-19 has further shaped journalists' professional ideologies and labor. Lievrouw and Livingstone (2002) argue that digitalization has entered all sectors, including 20th-century journalism, revolutionizing how news is presented, and journalists operate within newsrooms. Deuze (2001) emphasizes newsrooms as sites of constant journalistic experimentation, as media organizations continuously push the technological boundaries of news production.

The study participants affirm that the journalism profession is rapidly undergoing digitization. H1 highlights how the pandemic has made people more active on social media, and video content has gained importance in journalism. Audiences now connect with news sources digitally, demanding entertaining and easily accessible content that makes staying at home more enjoyable. H2 echoes this sentiment, noting that news organizations have almost entirely shifted to digital platforms with the influence of Covid-19. The reader's demand for digital content has expanded beyond mere text to include social media and video formats, prompting news organizations to extend their presence in these spaces. For many journalists, the decline in hard-copy newspaper sales, observed before the pandemic, accelerated further during Covid-19. H3 and H4 point out that news organizations face a growing responsibility in the digital media segment, continuously updating news in response to the increased time people spend on digital channels due to lockdowns and curfews. The demand for continuous breaking news has led to lighter content formats. H5 and H6 emphasize that news production and access to news sources have undergone complete digitalization, leading to remote working schemes and shrinking office spaces. H7 commends news organizations for rapidly adopting work-from-home systems from the initial days of the pandemic.

Regarding developments in local media, YA1 predicts that the future will be characterized by distance, much like distance education or health journalism. The reporting process has become remote, relying on digital means. YA2 and YA4 draw attention to magazine pages featuring social media celebrities and increasing news consumption via smartphones. However, they also express concerns about potential decreases in news quality and quantity and the potential negative impact on employees' moral responsibility. YA3 and YA6 observe that people increasingly turn to the internet for news. At the same time, YA5 notes that working from home has made accessing news sources more challenging, mainly due to various restrictions across the country. YA7 highlights the importance of social media as a resource but also mentions the increased reliance on it during the pandemic by authorities and news outlets alike. The constant news stream has led to heightened scrutiny, with journalists continuously monitoring information pollution and news production's fast-paced digitalization.

Overall, the Covid-19 pandemic has acted as a catalyst for the digital transformation of the journalism industry, affecting news production, working practices, and audience consumption patterns.

Furthermore, historically, news distribution proceeded in one direction, from publisher to audience. However, recent advancements in communication technologies have transformed media production and consumption patterns. The rise of social media, blogs, and smartphones has significantly impacted the process. Over the last decade, journalists have delivered content directly to the public on social media. While some critics argue that this new process may have adverse effects, the study participants highlight that readership increasingly turns to social media for news. H1 and H5 point out that social media has become an integral part of our daily lives, with increased time spent on these platforms during the Covid-19 pandemic. People now rely on social media for various activities, including obtaining information, continuing education, business interactions, entertainment, communication, shopping, and virtual meetings. As a result, their news consumption habits have also shifted toward social media channels. H3 and H7 echo similar sentiments, emphasizing how social media has bridged the social distance between individuals during the pandemic.

On the other hand, H2 notes that people have become more skeptical of news during this period, as readers can create and edit news content on social media platforms. H4 and H6 highlight that younger generations, particularly, have gravitated towards social media for news consumption, accelerating this trend with the Covid-19 pandemic.

The journalists from *Yeni Asır* also share their observations. YA1 and YA3 point out that the internet and social media have been gaining prominence in the news media landscape, especially with the Covid-19 pandemic further accelerating this shift. YA4 and YA7 stress the importance of transparency in journalism and the development of internet-based media, providing readers with direct access to news sources through social media and blogs.

In conclusion, the Covid-19 pandemic has accelerated the digitalization of the media industry and significantly impacted news production and consumption patterns. Social media and digital news platforms have become the preferred choices for accessing news content, reflecting the changing preferences and habits of the audience.

Low-Quality Journalism

Economic, social, and technological changes have significantly shaped the journalism landscape, especially over the last 15 years. The Covid-19 pandemic has further accelerated the transformation of journalistic practices. As news content is produced across multiple platforms, different standards emerge for different media, leading to increased workload and fewer resources. Traditional "national/local" media organizations transitioning online have seen a general decline in the quality of produced content (Singer, 2010: 91).

H1 highlights the increased misinformation during the pandemic, particularly in health news, and emphasizes the importance of careful filtering to prevent the spread of fake content. H2 discusses the challenges of miscommunication in the sector, which negatively affects content quality. On the other hand, H3 points out the positive impact of technology, such as conducting Instagram broadcasts with government officials, which has contributed to the news-building process. H4 provides a different perspective, stating that the pandemic had no significant negative or positive effects on the digital side of the news-writing process, as they were already accustomed to using tools like phones and emails to reach news sources. However, H5 and H6 draw attention to the significant changes in the news-writing processes, particularly in video news. They note that many exclusive interviews have shifted to online video interviews using platforms like Zoom and Cisco Webex, accelerating the video creation process. This shift from traditional in-person interviews has resulted in a perception that less effort is given to the audience.

Turning to the *Yeni Asır* participants, YA1 mentions the growing reliance on social media as a news source, prompting journalists to make live broadcasts from platforms like Instagram. However, they also emphasize that journalism maintains its seriousness and introduces innovations, such as breaking news and foreign news coverage. YA2 and YA3 discuss the changes in news production and content due to the pandemic. Contacting news sources has become more time-consuming, affecting the efficiency and quality of news content. Similarly, YA4 and YA6 point out that the attenuated process reduces activities that involve large groups, like face-to-face shooting, leading to a decline in content quality. YA5 adds that the need for distance and speed in the news production process can be troublesome, leaving little time for critical thinking. YA7 highlights the mechanization of the news production process and the emotional toll on news reporters, who may become alienated from their content due to the increased focus on death and disease during the pandemic.

The Changing Future of Media

Picard (2010) asserts that the news industry, which plays a vital role in fostering social cohesion and democratic governance, is rapidly creating and disseminating news and information. Communication technologies and social changes primarily drive the transformation in the industry at both local and global levels. The Covid-19 outbreak directly impacts media organizations and news production processes, significantly influencing the future of media.

H1 acknowledges that the pandemic is temporary but foresees lasting changes in news organizations: "*Many aspects of news organizations have changed during the pandemic. Remote work has become the norm, and it may become permanent. This pandemic could lead to lasting alterations in the working arrangements of news organizations.*" H3 and H7 echo a similar sentiment, emphasizing that news organizations have embraced remote work, which has not negatively affected productivity. Tools like Zoom, which have become prevalent during the pandemic, have made remote work more accessible, resulting in news being produced from homes. Technological advancements are also playing a significant role in shaping the future of journalism. H2 and H5 highlight the long-term effects of the changes brought about by the pandemic. They mention that the shift to remote work has not slowed down their pace of work, but it has transformed their working spaces from traditional offices to their homes. This trend is expected to continue, but it might present challenges regarding reporting on last-minute developments. H4 and H6 also indicate that remote work has become a new reality, facilitated by video interviews and digital tools that allow journalists to reach news sources from home. They believe that reporting from home will define the future of journalism, and news organizations will continue to function effectively in this setup.

Regarding Yeni Asır journalists, their comments can be summarized as follows: YA2 and YA5 emphasize that digitalization has permeated all media institutions, with meetings and news dissemination primarily occurring online. This shift suggests a move toward the future's digital landscape. YA1 and YA7 point out the acceleration of the pandemic's impact on digital media, highlighting the significance of social media in disseminating information. They raise concerns about spreading misinformation through various channels and question the future need for journalists in such a context. YA3 observes that the pandemic has influenced media content and production and brought about transformations in education. YA4 notes that news organizations worldwide have swiftly adapted to remote work and redefined digital fields, making journalism an entirely digital profession. YA6 believes traditional journalism was already evolving before the pandemic, but the crisis has expedited the process. News centers are now operating through digital platforms, resulting in cost savings for institutions, and remote work might continue even after the pandemic.

Based on the participants' statements, it is evident that newsrooms will continue to evolve, considering various operational elements, regardless of pre-existing structures and physical office layouts. The process will no longer be the same, and new strategies will be developed to navigate the future landscape.

The Pandemic's Impact on Male and Female Media Professionals

Evaluating gender in the context of the media reveals three problem areas:

- the employment of women and men in the media sector
- the portrayal of women and men in media products
- the positioning of women and men as target audiences

It is evident that the traditionally male-dominated media sector has been transforming how it views male and female professionals. The Covid-19 pandemic has heightened the burden on women media professionals in Turkey's national and local media organizations.

Reports like "*The Economic and social impact of COVID-19 on Women and Men: Rapid gender assessment of COVID-19 Implications in Turkey*" and "*The Impact of COVID-19 on Gender Equality, 2020*" demonstrate how the pandemic affected men and women. H1 highlights that the pandemic has particularly adverse effects on women media workers: "*During the pandemic period, many institutions shifted to remote work, resulting in women managing household responsibilities while working from home. This placed an extra burden on women, especially those with families.*" H5 states that the boundaries between home and workplace have entirely disappeared, negatively impacting both male and female media workers: "*Both mothers and fathers now work from home, and they have to allocate time for their children attending online education. This has led to increased fatigue and psychological strain.*" H2 and H6 note that the pandemic's effects are not solely gender-specific, as it affects everyone. While it offers some advantages, such as working from the comfort of one's home, it can also make people monotonous and overwhelmed.

H3 states that the pandemic created significant difficulties for women media workers who are married and have children, mainly as family members were constantly together at home. H4 and H7 add that the exchange of news ideas has been minimized during the pandemic, hindering both male and female media workers' ability to produce high-quality work and adding to their workload. In families with children, the workload of male and female employees increased, but women faced additional responsibilities, especially concerning their children. Thus, the pandemic has disproportionately burdened women media workers.

Regarding the *Yeni Asır* participants, YA1, YA4, and YA7 comments share a similar sentiment. They acknowledge that the pandemic has negatively affected all sectors and genders. The shift to remote work has disrupted the dynamics of the media sector, hindering personal connections and interactions that were once essential in the industry. YA2 adds that working from home has had positive and negative impacts, making daily tasks more challenging for those living alone while possibly offering some advantages for women who previously faced difficulties with night shifts. YA3 emphasizes that the pandemic and its accompanying restrictions have affected almost everyone worldwide, with girls and young women being among the most severely affected due to existing inequalities and threatening conditions. YA5 predicts that women will face immediate threats from the pandemic and suffer the long-term consequences the most. YA6 notes that the pandemic has accelerated digitization and the adoption of home offices, potentially leading to a positive effect on the distribution of tasks between women and men, as fathers' increased presence at home may foster a more flexible approach to balancing work and childcare.

It is crucial to recognize that women and men have not been equally affected by this crisis, further exacerbating pre-existing gender inequalities. The pandemic has highlighted the need to address gender disparities in the media industry and other sectors, promoting a more equitable and inclusive future.

CONCLUSION

This study focuses on the impact of technological and economic changes and the effects of the Covid-19 pandemic on journalistic monetization practices and labor patterns. In the past, news workers have organized journalism around normative values and ideology. However, with the increasing digitization of the media industry and the shift towards digital platforms by readers, news managers are now seeking ways to reduce costs, particularly given the decreased impact of national and local newspapers during the pandemic.

The study sampled two daily newspapers in Turkey, *Hürriyet* and *Yeni Asır*. Interviews with journalists from both media organizations revealed that traditional journalism production practices, such as accessing and discovering news, reaching news sources, collecting facts and stories, and writing, have been digitized in response to the Covid-19 pandemic. The pandemic has accelerated breaking news, interactions on social media, and digitized news distribution and presentation, resulting in a radical transformation of newspapers.

As the news production process has evolved and news is now more widely distributed on digital platforms, the media sector has gained momentum, similar to the education sector. Readers' interest in social media has increased significantly, leading to a decline in the quality of news texts produced and distributed through digital platforms. Additionally, the workload of women media professionals has increased, mainly due to the pandemic's impact on their work and family responsibilities.

The study highlights how the media industry has adapted to technological and economic changes and how the Covid-19 pandemic has further accelerated the digitization of news production and distribution.

However, it also sheds light on the challenges news organizations face, including reduced quality of news texts and increased workload for women media professionals.

REFERENCES

Adaklı, G. (2006). *Türkiye'de Medya Endüstrisi*. Ütopya Yayınları.

Agostino, D., Arnaboldi, M., & Diz-Lema, M. (2021). New development: COVİD-19 as an accelerator of digital transformation in public service delivery. *Public Money & Management*, *41*(1), 69–72. doi:10.1080/09540962.2020.1764206

Alon, T., Doepke, M., Olmstead-Rumsey, J., & Tertilt, M. (2020). *The Impact of Covid-19 on Gender Equality*. National Bureau of Economic Research. doi:10.3386/w26947

Alpert, L. I., & Hagey, K. (2020). Coronavirus Is Giving Readers Plenty of News. But Local Outlets Are Still Teetering. *Wall Street Journal*. Retrieved from https://www.wsj.com/articles/news-outlets-win-audiences-yet-lose-revenue-during-coronavirus-crisis-11584708390?mod=searchresults&ns=prod/accounts-wsj

Appelgren, E. (2004). *Convergence and divergence in media: different perspectives*. ICCC 8th International Conference on Electronic Publishing, Brasilia, Brazil.

Boyce, C. N. P. (2006). *Conducting In-Depth Interviews: A Guide for Designing and Conducting In-Depth-Interviews for Evaluation Input*. Watertown: Pathfinder International.

Boyer, D. (2013). *The Life Informatic: Newsmaking in the Digital Era*. Cornell University Press.

Büyükbaykal, G. N. (2012). Türkiye'de yerel basının işlevi ve önemi. *İstanbul Üniversitesi İletişim Fakültesi Dergisi*, *0*(23), 83-88.

Ceron, A. (2015). Internet, news, and political trust: The difference between social media and online media outlets. *Journal of Computer-Mediated Communication*, *20*(5), 487–503. doi:10.1111/jcc4.12129

Çiftçi, M. E., Ayhan, B. (2023). 'The first to report wins': The McDonaldization of digital journalism in Turkey. *Journal of Applied Journalism & Media Studies*. doi:10.1386/ajms_00100_1

Deuze, M. (2005). What is journalism? Professional identity and ideology of journalists reconsidered. *Journalism*, *6*(4), 442–464. doi:10.1177/1464884905056815

Deuze, M. (2008). Understanding journalism as newswork: How it changes and how it remains the same. *Westminster Papers in Communication and Culture*, *5*(2), 4–23. doi:10.16997/wpcc.61

Dursun, Ç. (2004). Haber, Hakikat ve İktidar İlişkisi. Elips kitap.

Dylko, I., & McCluskey, M. (2012). Media Effects in an Era of Rapid Technological Transformation: A Case of User-Generated Content and Political Participation. *Communication Theory*, *22*(3), 250–278. doi:10.1111/j.1468-2885.2012.01409.x

Gaenssle, S., & Budzinski, O. (2021). Stars in social media: New light through old windows? *Journal of Media Business Studies, 18*(2), 79–105. doi:10.1080/16522354.2020.1738694

Gaile, S. M. (2013). The role and functions of social media in modern society. Is social media worthwile for local media? *Journalısm Research, Science Journal Communication Information, 0*(6), 43–62.

Gentzkow, M. (2018). *Media and Artificial Intelligence*. Standford University. Accessed Date: 20.09.2023: http://web.stanford.edu/~gentzkow/research/ai_and_media.pdf

Gezmen, B., & Gürkan, H. (2016). *Haber Uygulamaları*. Artes Yayınları.

Gran, A., Booth, P., & Bucher, T. (2021). To be or not to be algorithm aware: A question of a new digital divide? *Information Communication and Society, 24*(12), 1779–1796. doi:10.1080/1369118X.2020.1736124

Gürkan, H. (2019). The Experiences of Women Professionals in the Film Industry in Turkey: A Gender-Based Study. *Acta Univ. Sapientiae. Film and Media Studies, 16*, 205–219.

Gürkan, H., Serttaş, A., & Sarıkaya, T. (2023). The virtual mask: The dark underbelly of digital anonymity and gender identity construction in Turkey. *Journal of Arab and Muslim Media Research*. doi:10.1386/jammr_00068_1

Hess, K., & Waller, L. (2020). Charting the media innovations landscape for rural and regional newspapers. *Australian Journalism Review, 42*(1), 59–74. doi:10.1386/ajr_00019_1

Hester, J. B., & Gibson, R. (2007). The agenda-setting function of national versus local media: A time-series analysis for the issue of same-sex marriage. *Mass Communication & Society, 10*(3), 299–317. doi:10.1080/15205430701407272

Kalaylıoğlu, Y., Öztürk, A. M., & Eker, G. B. (2020). *The economic and social impact of COVİD-19 on women and men: Rapid gender assessment of COVİD-19 implications in Turkey. United Nations Entity for Gender Equality and the Empowerment of Women*. UN Women.

Kunova, M. (2020). *Digital News Report 2020: Covid-19 accelerates digital shifts in the media industry*. https://www.journalism.co.uk/news/digital-news-report-2020-Covid-19-has-accelerated-digital-shifts-in-the-media-industry/s2/a757201/

Lee, C. (2015). The double-edged sword: The effects of journalists^ social media activities on audience perceptions of journalists and their news products. *Journal of Computer-Mediated Communication, 20*(3), 312–329. doi:10.1111/jcc4.12113

Lee, S. K., Lindsey, N. J., & Kim, K. S. (2017). The effects of news consumption via social media and news information overload on perceptions of journalistic norms and practices. *Computers in Human Behavior, 75*, C. doi:10.1016/j.chb.2017.05.007

Lievrouw, L., & Livingstone, S. (2002). *Handbook of new media: Social shaping and consequences of ICTs*. Sage.

Lim, M. (2017). Freedom to hate: Social media, algorithmic enclaves, and the rise of tribal nationalism in Indonesia. *Critical Asian Studies, 49*(3), 411–427. doi:10.1080/14672715.2017.1341188

Makarova, E. L., & Makarova, E. A. (2019). The functional model of using visualization and digitalization for media literacy development in media education process. *Slovak Republic Media Education.*, *59*(4), 547–556.

Mcluhan, M. (1962). *Gutenberg Galaxy: The making of typographic man.* Retrieved December 2, 2021, from http://www.ocopy.net/wp-content/uploads/2017/10/mcluhan-marshall_the-gutenberg-galaxy-the-making-of-typographic-man.pdf

Mcluhan, M. (1967). *The medium is the massage: An inventory of effects.* Retrieved December 5, 2021, from https://designopendata.files.wordpress.com/2014/05/themediumisthe massage_marsh allmcluhan_quentinfiore.pdf

Meade, A. (2020). *More than 150 Australian newsrooms shut since January 2019 as Covid-19 deepens media crisis.* Available at: https://www.theguardian.com/media/2020/may/18/more-than-150-australian-news-rooms-shut-since-january-2019-as-Covid-19-deepens-media-crisis

Meese, J., & Hurcombe, E. (2021). Facebook, news media and platform dependency: The institutional impacts of news distribution on social platforms. *New Media & Society*, *23*(8), 2367–2384. doi:10.1177/1461444820926472

Mihelj, S., & Jmenez-Martinez, C. (2020). Digital nationalism: Understanding the role of digital media in the rise of 'new' nationalism. *Nations and Nationalism*, *27*(2), 331–346. doi:10.1111/nana.12685

Nechushtai, E. (2018). Could digital platforms capture the media through infrastructure? *Journalism*, *19*(8), 1043–1058. doi:10.1177/1464884917725163

Nielsen, R. K., Kalogeropoulos, A., & Fletcher, R. (2020). *Most in the UK Say News Media have Helped them Respond to COVİD-19, But a Third Say News Coverage has Made the Crisis Worse.* Reuters Institute for the Study of Journalism.

Nielson, R. K. (2012). *Ten Years that Shook the Media World Big Questions and Big Trends in International Media Developments.* The Reuters Institute for the Study of Journalism.

Nielson, R. K., A. Cornia, A. Kalogeropoulos. (2016). *Challenges and opportunities for news media and journalism in an increasingly digital, mobile, and social media environment.* Council of Europe report DGI: 18.

O'Sullivan, J., & Fortunati, L. (2018). Situating the social sustainability of print media in a world of digital alternatives. *Telematics and Informatics*, 37.

Özgül, B. A., & Veneti, A. (2022). The Different Organizational Structures of Alternative Media: Through the Perspective of Alternative Media Journalists in Turkey and Greece. *Digital Journalism (Abingdon, England)*, *10*(8), 1302–1321. doi:10.1080/21670811.2021.1943482

Perez-Escoda, A., & Jimenes-Narros, C. (2020). Social Networks' Engagement During the COVİD-19 Pandemic in Spain: Health Media vs. Healthcare Professionals. *International Journal of Environmental Research and Public Health*, *17*(14), 5261. doi:10.3390/ijerph17145261 PMID:32708231

Picard, R. G. (2010). The Future of the News Industry. In J. Curran (Ed.), *Media and Society* (pp. 365–379). Bloomsbury Academic.

Presuel, R., & Sierra, J. (2019). Algorithms and the News: Social Media Platforms as News Publishers and Distributors. *Revista De Comunicación, 18*(2), 261–285. doi:10.26441/RC18.2-2019-A13

Richards, I. (2014). Differences over difference: Journalism beyond the metropolis. *Australian Journalism Review, 36*(1), 5–14. doi:10.1386/ajr.41.1.5_1

Ruiz-Cabrera, S., & Gürkan, H. (2023). Effects of Turkish cultural products on its foreign policy toward Africa: Turkish TV series as an example of soft power in Kenya, Mozambique, and Senegal. *El Profesional de la Información, 32*(2), 1–16. doi:10.3145/epi.2023.mar.26

Shearer, E. (2020). *Local news is playing an important role for Americans during COVİD-19 outbreak.* https://www.pewresearch.org/fact-tank/2020/07/02/local-news-is-playing-an-important-role-for-americans-during-Covid-19-outbreak/

Singer, J. B. (2010). Quality control: Perceived effects of user-generated content on newsroom norms, values, and routines. *Journalism Practice, 4*(2), 127–142. doi:10.1080/17512780903391979

Storsul, T., & Dagny, S. (2007). *Ambivalence Towards Convergence: Digitalization and Media Change.* Nordicom, University of Gothenburg.

Túñez-López, M., Vaz-Álvarez, M., & Fieiras-Ceide, C. (2020). Covid-19 and public service media: Impact of the pandemic on public television in Europe. *Professional de la Infarmacion., 29*(5), 1–16.

Wade, M., & Shan, J. (2020). New development: COVİD-19 as an accelerator of digital transformation in public service delivery. *MIS Quarterly Executive, 19*(3), 213–220. doi:10.17705/2msqe.00034

Yao, H. (2020). The more exposure to media information about COVİD-19, the more distressed you will feel. *Brain, Behavior, and Immunity, 87*, 167–169. doi:10.1016/j.bbi.2020.05.031 PMID:32413557

Zelizer, B. (2015). Terms of choice: Uncertainty, journalism, and crisis. *Journal of Communication, 65*(5), 888–908. doi:10.1111/jcom.12157

Zelizer, B. (2019). Why journalism is about more than digital technology. *Digital Journalism (Abingdon, England), 7*(3), 343–350. doi:10.1080/21670811.2019.1571932

KEY TERMS AND DEFINITIONS

Distance Journalism: "Distance journalism" is a term that is not widely recognized in the field of journalism or media studies. It is not a commonly used or established term in the industry or academic literature. Therefore, there is no specific definition or widely accepted meaning associated with "distance journalism." However, based on the term itself, one might infer that "distance journalism" could refer to journalism or news reporting conducted remotely or from a distance, often utilizing digital communication technologies.

Local Media: "Local media" refers to media outlets and communication channels that operate at the community, city, or regional level within a specific geographical area. These media organizations serve the interests of a particular local community or region and focus on covering news, events, and issues relevant to that area. Local media can take various forms, including newspapers, radio stations, television channels, online news sites, and community publications.

National Media: The term "national media" refers to the media outlets and communication channels that operate within the boundaries of a specific nation or country. These media organizations, which can include newspapers, television channels, radio stations, websites, and other forms of communication, primarily serve the population of the nation where they are based.

ENDNOTES

1 Hürriyet is a prestigious Turkish newspaper, established in 1948 and currently owned by the Demirören Group. It holds a prominent position in the media landscape and is widely recognized for its contributions. As of January 2017, Hürriyet boasted the highest circulation figures among newspapers in Turkey, with approximately 334,000 copies in distribution. Notably, the publication maintains a dominant presence, presenting a balanced outlook encompassing liberal and conservative perspectives.

2 Yeni Asır, with the motto "Turkey's oldest newspaper," holds a distinguished legacy as the country's oldest newspaper, founded in 1948. In line with technological advancements, the newspaper expanded its reach online in December 1998, catering to a broader audience through digital platforms. Subsequently, on March 1, 2017, it made its mark in the national press, solidifying its position as a significant player in the Turkish media landscape. While having a rich history, Yeni Asır has adapted to the modern era, serving as a prominent local newspaper.

3 Based on the term, "distance journalism" can be a concept or practice where journalists report on events, news, or stories from afar, relying on various remote tools and technologies to gather information and communicate with sources. This involves conducting interviews via video conferencing, utilizing social media and online sources for research, and relying on digital communication to file stories to their news organizations.

Chapter 8
Has the COVID-19 Pandemic Changed Communication Training at the Medical Faculties in Spain?

Mònica Puntí-Brun
https://orcid.org/0000-0001-7101-1151
University of Girona, Spain

Sílvia Espinosa-Mirabet
https://orcid.org/0000-0002-8304-5882
University of Girona, Spain

ABSTRACT

This study aimed to assess whether Spanish hospitals have enhanced their protocols and training for breaking bad news in response to the pandemic. Employing a qualitative approach, the research integrated three tools: in-depth interviews with healthcare professionals, content analysis of medicine curricula from universities in Catalonia and Andalusia, and a literature review of protocols for communicating bad news. The findings revealed a significant increase in the contents and subjects in the communication of bad news within the analyzed curricula due to the pandemic. Additional topics such as technology, emotional management, and humanism were incorporated. While the hospital protocols showed a relatively less pronounced increment, there was evidence of the development of protocols specifically focused on communicating bad news via phone or video calls. In conclusion, the COVID-19 pandemic has brought about changes in the training of doctors, leading to an enriched curriculum despite a more modest increase in hospital protocols.

DOI: 10.4018/979-8-3693-0896-7.ch008

INTRODUCTION

The coronavirus has generated new social and economic scenarios that must be explained based on a very complex health crisis. In the field of health, the pandemic has generated new routines for communicating bad news and accompanying the most serious patients. How should difficult diagnoses be communicated when isolation is imposed? During the pandemic, the media showed shocking scenarios in which families said goodbye to a loved one isolated in the ICU, thanks to the personal initiative of a doctor who provided them with a mobile phone. The medical protocols did not contemplate a situation like the COVID pandemic, and the training of the doctors suffered from this fact.

The Hospital Universitario 12 de Octubre (2020) from Madrid has been the first to publish its protocol to guide the communication of bad news by telephone during the pandemic. With the end of the crisis, we realized that the number of medical protocols has increased substantially in Spanish hospitals. It seems appropriate to study how health centers have updated their protocols for communicating bad news to patients. Therefore, the main objective of this work is to check if Spanish medical centers have increased and/or changed their protocols to communicate bad news because of the pandemic.

To study this issue, the existing medical protocols in Spain that regulate the communicative relationships between doctors and patients have been reviewed. Thus, both a review of the scientific literature and the medical institutions themselves have been used to check whether there are more protocols than before the pandemic and whether the new protocols include different communication scenarios, based on what has been learned due to the SARS-CoV-2 pandemic.

The harshness of the virus has caused, according to the data of *Laboratorio de Psicología del Trabajo y Estudios de la Seguridad* de la Universidad Complutense de Madrid published in ABC journal, in Madrid "three out of four health workers suffer from anxiety, 40 per cent are emotionally exhausted, and 53 per cent, just over half, suffer from post-traumatic stress" (Medialdea, 2020). The fear of infecting himself or infecting their family is the reason that explained the emotional situation suffered by the health sector. But in addition, medical professionals suffered from not having sufficient preparation to be able to communicate bad news and this is also a great source of stress, and it is not a new point. The pandemic unveiled the essential need for training in managing emotions within a high-risk, crisis-driven healthcare communication process. While the literature on health and communication addresses this studied topic, as referenced in the theoretical framework of this work, the truth remains that the emotional management of healthcare professionals during a real pandemic highlighted significant deficiencies in Spain.

Twenty years ago in Spain, as the family medicine doctors from Navarra, Ayarra and Lizarraga (2001), affirmed, the training of doctors in communication skills was almost nil: "Giving bad news generates anxiety and insecurity, and may even cause more pain than necessary when reporting" (Ayarra & Lizarraga, 2001: 55). It is a long-term trend: "We are not prepared for this situation, nobody tells us how and that is why we must be prepared by people specialized in the subject" (Sánchez et al., 2014: 23). Currently, the situation regarding the training of doctors in how to give bad news is still a cause for concern, since it is a skill that is not worked on sufficiently in the medical degrees, but even so, doctors are expected to acquire it (León-Amenero & Huarcaya-Victoria, 2019).

For all the above and to solve this issue, the research aims to review the existing medical protocols to discover if the former protocols have been adapted to the new reality produced by the outbreak of the pandemic.

Bad Medical News, Well Communicated, Is Less Bad

There is no agreed procedure for communicating bad news. Each professional has developed their strategies based on experience" (Bascuñán et al., 2007: 51). In a study by Flores-Funes et al. (2018), it is concluded that there is still insufficient training for the communication of bad news, and this continues to be a cause for concern. It appears to be a subject that is not extensively covered in medical faculties; however, despite this, it is expected that doctors acquire the necessary competencies.

A series of skills are required, which will be developed throughout our growth as individuals and professionals and will be rooted in empathy and a continuous desire to adhere to the well-known principles of bioethics, especially beneficence. However, often in the teaching of Medicine, we overlook the concept of death symbolically and technically, resulting in avoidance and failure to inform our patients and their families about death or loss. (León-Amenero & Huarcaya-Victoria, 2019: 87)

Breaking bad news in medicine is a discipline that, in some faculties, falls under the umbrella of bioethics. In line with Gómez-Sancho (2016), it can be affirmed that in medicine, bad news is considered information communicated to a patient about their health condition that negatively affects or modifies their well-being and/or life choices. According to Solano et al. (2022: 268), if the communication of bad news is understood as an "occasion for care", it is deduced that it is not only about conveying information or communicating but also about "accompanying", especially emotions (fear, guilt, anger, sadness, etc.). This perspective is a commitment to humanize the process of communicating bad news.

In the classical conception, the basic clinical competencies of doctors did not include communication skills, as Moore et al. (2012: 359) explain, "most doctors considered communication to be an innate skill, inherent to the professional, not something that could be learned, and therefore, did not require teaching". Hence, the same authors recommended developing teaching in small groups and basing it on innovative methodologies "that allow structured observation of interviews". They also advocated for educating residents and clinical doctors and "attaining professional levels in relational competence" (Moore et al., 2012: 364).

Over time, the perception of communication training has changed (Almanza, 2003: 174): "There is a well-defined interest in driving specific efforts to expand the curriculum of Medicine and related disciplines to include diverse topics related to doctor-patient communication and especially the communication of bad news". Nevertheless, in Spain, according to Borrell-Carrió et al. (2012), "communication . . . has not been recognized in the study plans . . . until very recently with the development of the Bologna Plan" (Quoted by Ferreira, et al., 2015: 401).

Practicing doctors support this thesis: "We are not prepared for that situation, no one tells us how, and that is why specialists in the field should prepare us" (Aranda, et al., 2014: 23). Furthermore, not all patients are the same, and therefore, they don't respond to a bad diagnosis in the same way, so the training that doctors should receive should be comprehensive. The bad news has an objective component and a subjective one (which depends on the patient): "Therefore, patients respond to bad news influenced largely by the psychosocial context in which they live. It is not surprising, then, that bad news is received differently by each person" (Rodríguez-Salvador, 2010: 1).

Medical students, on the other hand, do not consider themselves sufficiently prepared in their undergraduate studies to face the communication of bad news. A study by Mayo et al. (2020) confirms this with an online questionnaire to 120 sixth-year medical students. Despite almost all of them having witnessed some situation of this kind during their internships or rotations (90.8%) and nearly half acknowledging having received training in the communication of bad news (67.5%), only half considered themselves prepared for these types of situations (Mayo et al., 2020).

Written Protocols to Guide Bad News Communication

Although it is true that there is medical literature on how to proceed to communicate bad news, it is also clear that much of this literature collects and is based on three medical protocols from the 1990s: Buckman (1992), Benett and Alison (1996) and Rabow and McPhee (1999). These authors lay the foundations on how to approach, in phases (before, during and after), a communication situation as complex as giving a terminal or very complicated prognosis to a patient. In summary, these three old protocols agree on the need to properly prepare for the meeting with patients and families, which also means that the doctor must know how to deal with their emotions.

The medical protocols that guide on how to deliver bad news to physicians who must deal with it are written documents, widely used, sometimes published by hospitals and sometimes not visible. However, they are tools that doctors, especially younger ones (residents), greatly appreciate. As stated in an interview for this work by Dr. Candela Álvarez Vázquez, a medical resident in medical oncology at the Catalan Hospital in Mataró (personal communication, September 17, 2023): 'Each patient is unique, although we follow some standard advice (active listening, ensuring there are no barriers between us, etc.)".

Robert Buckman (1992) wrote SPIKES, an acronym representing the strategy to follow when breaking bad news: Setting up the interview (S), assessing the patient's Perception (P), obtaining the patient's Invitation (I), giving Knowledge and information to the patient (K), addressing the patient's Emotions with Empathic responses (E) and Strategy and Summary (S) (Baile et al., 2000; Buckman, 2005). This author already published an article in 1984 about the difficulty of breaking bad news and some of the fears that doctors had in that situation: fear of being blamed, fear of the unknown and untaught, fear of unleashing a reaction, fear of expressing emotion, fear of not knowing all the answers and personal fear of illness and death (Buckman, 1984).

The SPIKES protocol follows six steps and is based on the premise that bad news is best received when it is a planned event (Gordillo Navas, Trujillo Martínez & Filizzola Bermúdez, 2020). They emphasize the importance of delivering bad news in clinical practice and the inadequate training of healthcare professionals in this skill; therefore, they propose a reflection on the use of simulated scenarios for professional training. Some of the current protocols are based on the SPIKES strategy, which is one of the most widespread and commonly used within the healthcare field. Other authors have adapted it and even complemented it with the EMPATHY protocol, created by Jankowska in 2014, an acronym for Emotions, Meeting, Patient's perspective, Adequate language, Truth, and Hope and Yes for patient empowerment (Witt & Jankowska, 2018).

A second protocol is the Bennett and Alison's (1996), which is based on the following steps preparation for the interview, beginning the interview, clarifying the patient's story, and coping strategy, breaking the news, handling the responses, identifying other concerns, discussing prognosis, and closing the interview (Bennett & Alison, 1996). On the other hand, Rabow and McPhee (1999) created the ABCDE protocol: Advance preparation (A), Build a therapeutic environment/relationship (B), Communicate well (C), Deal with patient and family reaction (D) and Encourage and validate emotions (E) (Rabow & McPhee, 1999).

Other classic protocols are those by Edlich and Kubler-Ross (1992) and Kaye (1996) cited by Álvarez Aparicio (2020). Kaye outlines the ten steps to follow when breaking bad news: 1. Preparation; 2.

What does the patient know?; 3. Is more information wanted?; 4. Give a warning shot; 5. Allow denial; 6. Explain (if requested); 7. Listen to concerns; 8. Encourage venting of feelings; 9. Summary an plan; and 10. Offer availability (Kaye, 2023). The classic models can be simplified into the four phases of emergency protocols (Taylor, 2007; Belli, 2020): 1. Preparation; 2. Delivering the news; 3. Managing emotions; and 4. Planning the next steps (Álvarez Aparicio, 2020). In another article (Ebn Ahmady et al., 2014), the protocols are reviewed and simplified into three steps: Preparation (When), Delivering (What) and Arrangement (How).

Villagran et al. (2010) devised their COMFORT protocol to precisely facilitate the communication of bad news to patients, after identifying the deficiencies in American medical students, even after receiving training based on Buckman (1992). The authors proposed working on seven competencies to make the communication process more empathetic. These competencies define the English acronym: communication, orientation, mindfulness, family, ongoing, reiterative messages, and team. In a study on the effects of a communication skills training program for oncologists based on patient preferences, Fujimori et al. (2014) used the SHARE protocol: S, setting up a supportive environment for the interview; H, considering how to deliver the bad news; A, discussing additional information that patients would like to know; and RE, providing reassurance and addressing patient's emotions with empathic response.

In recent times, a renewed interest is observed in reviewing the paradigms that advise healthcare professionals on how to approach communicating a poor diagnosis. Rebello et al. (2017) have developed a protocol for nursing staff known as P-A-C-I-E-N-T-E. This represents another adaptation of Buckman (1992) in a Brazilian healthcare context. The acronym corresponds to the words in English: P, prepare; A, assess how much the patient knows and how much they want to know; C, invite the patient to the truth; I, inform; E, control emotions; N, do not abandon the patient; and finally, T and E, outline a strategy.

In Spain, the Bioethical Care Committee (CBA) of the Department of Health in Castellón and the General University Hospital of Castellón recommends that its healthcare professionals confront the communication of a fearsome diagnosis, understanding that communication is an "essential therapeutic tool of the doctor-patient relationship that contributes to respecting autonomy and promotes the patient's participation in their own care" (CBA, 2019: 2). The idea of communication as a therapeutic tool is an interesting perspective for crisis communication.

Despite some attempts to update these guideline documents, Vicente's thorough review (2020) of public medical protocols used to communicate bad news concludes that most of the new texts do not differ essentially from the older ones: "no significant difference is observed, nor any completely contradictory recommendation, which either indicates that all the previously written protocols already encompassed many essential measures that are still valid in our culture, or that the more recent protocols still have gaps" (Vicente, 2020: 23). One notable change is that doctors now have the option to recommend external support professionals to patients or their family members, and they can also collaborate with fellow healthcare professionals when communicating bad news.

During the pandemic, Hospital 12 de Octubre in Madrid (2020) created a protocol that recognizes the telephone as an effective communication tool and recommends how to use it. In this sense, a study by Álvarez Aparicio (2020) reviews telephone communication of bad news in the healthcare setting during the COVID-19 pandemic. The author acknowledges that remote communication should be used in exceptional situations, as it reduces the likelihood of effective communication by losing the non-verbal component. Additionally, she states that "well-performed communication can be therapeutic in itself" (Álvarez Aparicio, 2020: 233) as it provides benefits for the transmitter (reducing, for example, the onset of burnout syndrome) and for the receiver (facilitating acceptance and adaptation to the situation).

Previous research has explored the communication of bad news by phone (Taylor, 2007) and has developed protocols or recommendations specifically related to the COVID-19 pandemic (Belli, 2020; Espasandín-Duarte et al., 2020; GIZ, 2020). In this regard, some of the protocols and recommendations that emerged during the pandemic will be analyzed, especially those published subsequently (Junta de Castilla y León & Sacyl, 2020; Instituto Nacional de Gestión Sanitaria, 2021; Sobczak, 2022; SECIP, 2023). Some of these protocols or recommendations are more oriented towards telephone or remote communication of bad news, while others are related to specific areas such as palliative care or communication in the pediatric ICU.

Breaking Bad News

The fear of communicating a bad diagnosis incorrectly is a widespread concern among healthcare professionals. Villa (2007), Gómez-Sancho (2016), and Alves (2003) state that the fear of causing pain, the fear of being guilty, and the fear of death, among other factors, are difficult elements to reconcile. Among all, the most significant is legal fear, as a significant portion of negligence claims are caused by poor doctor-patient communication (Gómez-Sancho, 2016: 52).

For Buckman (1992), one of the fathers of the communication of bad news, this process can alter the prospects of patients concerning their illness. García-Díaz (2006) considers that the communication of bad news lasts for some time after receiving the information. It is a subjective phenomenon and each patient experiences it differently. Núñez et al. (2006) add that any negative information about the state of health is bad news, but different levels of severity or types of reactions can be differentiated depending on each person, their values, or their type of life.

The most cited medical protocols on this matter highlight certain elements to prepare for a consultation where breaking bad news is required. They emphasize two critical moments: when the physician prepares for the meeting and when handling their own emotions during that meeting. Thus, there is a prior need before conveying a poor diagnosis, which also means the physician must be adept at managing their emotions.

Amid the Covid-19 pandemic, the protocol at Hospital 12 de Octubre in Madrid promptly incorporated keys to assist healthcare personnel with their emotions. The hospital protocols explained what should be done via telephone to ensure that emotions are not overwhelming when communicating bad news, as conveying understanding, support, and especially identifying the emotions evoked is more challenging in a telephonic conversation:

The effort of the person conveying the news will have to be greater, always trying to convey listening to cues and inquiring about sensations and feelings. There are few guidelines regarding how to respond to emotional reactions, but a positive aspect is that the psychological and social needs of those being spoken to are considered. (Vicente, 2020: 24)

The purpose of explaining how to act in a communicative context to explain a pandemic to the population is a subject of Public Relations study, especially in the subject of crisis communication. Adapting Coombs (2015), a crisis is an unforeseen event that negatively affects organizations. There is a vast theoretical corpus since Fink (1986) compared the phases of a crisis with those of a disease. Within this area, we also find the communication of bad news in health. This recommends to doctors how they should deal with a delicate situation with their patients.

The chronology on how this type of news should be communicated shows that it has gone from a situation in which a paternalistic model of medical communication dominated (Gómez, 2016), in which the doctor decided what to explain, to the current situation in which maximum transparency guides the process. Patients are the ones who decide what they want and what they do not want to know about their disease (Rodríguez-Salvador, 2010) and rely on their family.

Due to its complexity and its novelty, the coronavirus was explained based on the guidelines that, in Spain, the government set through the Ministry of Health. But according to Costa-Sánchez and López-García (2020), the management was incorrect because the previous references were not considered: "There is a disregard for the guidelines and recommendations extracted from the analysis of communication in previous public health crises (...) the applied spokesperson formula is contrary to crisis communication recommendations" (Costa-Sánchez & López-García, 2020: 10).

Non-verbal communication is emphasized as a crucial aspect of training in this communicative situation, sometimes even more important than verbal communication (Rodríguez-Sanz et al., 2011). For this author, when the verbal and non-verbal messages are contradictory or exclusive, the non-verbal should prevail. There is a considerable amount of medical-academic literature recommending control over the verbal and non-verbal communication tandem when delivering a bad diagnosis.

Practicing physicians consider empathy as the most crucial element for breaking bad news. However, unlike students, professional experience shows that "there is no standard behavior pattern to do it well; rather, different approaches need to be considered" (Espinosa-Mirabet & Puntí-Brun, 2021: 502-503). One of these approaches involves accompanying patients and their families and adapting to their needs.

For medical students, mastering emotions when communicating a difficult diagnosis is a crucial deeply concerning element, as seen as aligned with the perception of novice doctors (Espinosa-Mirabet & Puntí-Brun, 2021). In both scenarios, opinions gathered by the authors in a previous work pointed to the experience as a crucial element in handling the situation. Students interviewed to gather their perception of their university preparation for breaking bad news found that the most important aspects they learned in their university education, in descending order, were to act with empathy, to listen, and to perceive the patient's emotional state. However, only half of the participants felt adequately prepared to convey difficult news. Future doctors were hopeful for their future and collectively expressed that clinical practice would equip them with the necessary knowledge:

It begins when you have contact with patients and convey difficult news. The guidance we receive on how to do it is fundamental, and evidently, I feel much more prepared than before receiving the training, but it is in the actual field where we get to know ourselves and learn to handle these situations. (Espinosa-Mirabet & Puntí-Brun, 2021: 504)

METHODOLOGY

The main objective of this research is to ascertain if Spanish hospitals have enhanced their protocols and training for delivering bad news because of the pandemic. The secondary objectives are as follows:

- Examine the training on breaking bad news provided in the medical faculties of Catalonia and Andalusia before and after the pandemic.

- Understand professionals' perception of the training they have received and determine if it was sufficient for practical application in their daily routines.

This is a qualitative study that has drawn upon three analytical tools: a literature review of protocols for breaking bad news, in-depth interviews with healthcare professionals representing different territorial realities, and content analysis of the curriculum of Medicine programs at universities in Catalonia and Andalusia that offer this degree. These two autonomous communities were selected as they have the largest populations in Spain. According to the INE (2022), Andalusia has a population of 8,500,187 inhabitants, while Catalonia has 7,792,611 inhabitants.

Firstly, a review of existing literature was conducted, searching for publications on medical protocols or related guidelines. Bascuñán (2013) considers these protocols useful in structuring communication effectively, describing the steps to follow in breaking bad news. The search was conducted through the social sciences database Scopus. The initial hypothesis was that if there were many published medical protocols, it was possibly because the deficiencies in the university education of doctors were recognized and needed to be supported subsequently within healthcare centers, or because there was a strong emphasis on ongoing training for medical professionals. In any case, understanding the state of the art allowed us to focus the interviews and questionnaires.

To search for existing protocols from the pandemic to the present day, searches were conducted on the websites of the top 10 public hospitals with the highest reputation according to the Health Reputation Monitor (Merco, 2022). The hospitals are: Hospital Universitario La Paz (Madrid), Hospital Clínic (Barcelona), Hospital Gregorio Marañón (Madrid), Hospital Universitario 12 de Octubre (Madrid), Hospital Vall d'Hebron (Barcelona), Hospital Universitario y Politécnico La Fe (Valencia), Hospital Universitario Ramón y Cajal (Madrid), Hospital Universitario Virgen del Rocío (Seville), Hospital Universitario Fundación Jiménez Díaz (Madrid), and Hospital Clínico San Carlos (Madrid). A total of 122 different pages were visited, and more than 110 documents in PDF format were reviewed.

In-depth interviews were considered essential for the research. Fourteen professionals representing various healthcare areas in Catalonia, both public and private, of different ages and from diverse territorial realities (major cities, metropolitan areas, and/or rural areas) residing in the 4 Catalan provinces were interviewed, but from diverse backgrounds in line with the geographic diversity of Spain. They included doctors, psychologists, or nursing staff, all unfortunately experts in delivering bad news. The aim was to understand their perception of the training received at university and to obtain an overview of the inequalities that might exist among their different contexts. Hence, an unstructured and lengthy interview format was chosen to allow the interviewees to express themselves freely, following the approach of Varguillas and Ribot de Flores (2007). Data were recorded and collected using various channels: face-to-face interviews or phone calls for interviews conducted after the pandemic, and phone calls, video calls with Skype and Zoom, email, and even WhatsApp audio messages to gather units of analysis during the pandemic.

Finally, content analysis was used to review the teaching plans of the medical faculties in the autonomous communities of Catalonia and Andalusia. Krippendorff's model (1980) was followed. A codebook was developed to determine the searches that would be carried out to identify subjects related to communication, their types, credits assigned, and the profile of the teachers delivering them, whether in public, subsidized, or private institutions. To achieve this, over 360 different pages from institutional websites and PDF documents of teaching guides were traced.

Table 1. Catalan and Andalusian universities and medicine curricula

Catalonia	Andalusia
UAB	UCA
UB	UCO
UdG	UGR
UdL	UMA
UPF	US
URV	
UViC	
UIC	

Source: Own elaboration

The universe of the studied universities offering Medicine (See Table 1) comprises 8 Catalan universities and 5 Andalusian ones. The Catalan universities are: Universitat Autònoma de Barcelona (UAB), Universitat de Barcelona (UB), Universitat de Girona (UdG), Universitat de Lleida (UdL), Universitat Pompeu Fabra (UPF), Universitat Rovira i Virgili (URV), the subsidized Universitat de Vic (UVic), and the only private institution, Universitat Internacional de Catalunya (UIC). The universities in Andalusia are: Universidad de Cádiz (UCA), Universidad de Córdoba (UCO), Universidad de Granada (UGR), Universidad de Málaga (UMA), and Universidad de Sevilla (US).

RESULTS

In the year 2020, content analysis of the 8 Catalan universities that teach Medicine demonstrated that most of the centers (87.5%) had one or more (two) subjects related to communication, directly or indirectly, but the most common (62.5%) was to offer only one subject in the communicative field. The private university UIC was the only one that did not offer communication-related subjects. On the other hand, in the 5 Andalusian universities, there was a similar scenario, as the content related to communication was minimal. Out of the 5 Andalusian universities, 4 offered only one subject in this area, and one, the University of Cádiz (UC), had no content in communication (Romero, 2022).

The situation of communication-related content in the Medicine curricula has changed substantially after the pandemic. The content analysis conducted in 2023 shows that all Medicine curricula in Catalan and Andalusian universities have communication-related content in several of their subjects. Catalan universities with more subjects in this area are UAB and UB, while the one with the fewest is UPF (see Figure 1). The average number of subjects dedicated to communication training is 6.5. As for the Andalusian universities, there is some dispersion. While at least one subject is offered, as is the case with UC, US offers 5, the maximum number. The rest of the faculties offer 2, 3, or 4 subjects (see Figure 2).

Typically, these are subjects that, in a general sense, explain the principles of communication, encompassing aspects of both verbal and non-verbal communication, as well as focusing on the doctor-patient relationship and how to conduct a clinical interview. No evidence was found in the curricula from 2020 and 2021 that linked communication to the enabling technologies or the development of cross-cutting competencies in media and information literacy (Wilson, 2012; Gutiérrez and Tyner, 2012). There were

Figure 1. Number of subjects with communication content in the Medicine curricula of Catalan universities in 2020 and 2023 (Own elaboration)

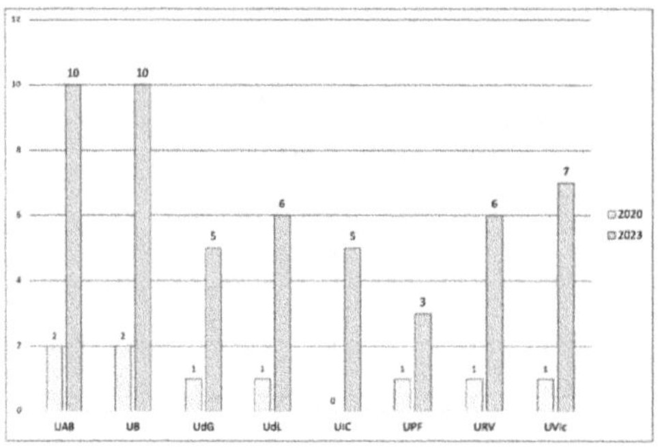

Figure 2. Number of subjects with communication content in the Medicine curricula of Andalusian universities in 2020 and 2023 (Own elaboration)

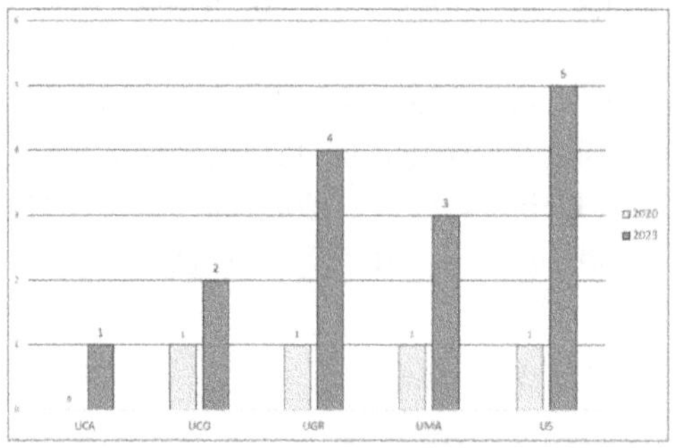

no mentions of phones, computers, tablets, nor were there subjects revolving around "media training"—elements that the COVID-19 pandemic has brought to the forefront, and which have been detected in the 2023 curricula.

The communication-related contents detected during the pandemic were prioritized based on their presence in the curricula. As can be seen, these contents were approached from both a communicative and psychological, ethical, or bioethical perspective (see Figure 3). The figure shows that managing bad news was not the focus of the contents; rather, it ranked fourth, and there was an emphasis on starting with a more general training to later delve deeper into the doctor-patient relationship.

Looking at the syllabi taught in the medical faculties of Catalonia and Andalusia in the post-COVID period, it can be observed that most of the communication content taught during the pandemic has been retained. Nevertheless, the number of communication-related topics in the subjects has increased, as well as their level of definition. The new topics found in the content analysis are related to the use of technologies, emotional management, humanism, and the profession (see Figure 3).

Comparing the content before and after the pandemic, a new category emerges: technology. During and after the lockdown, technology has been relevant for medical communication and the doctor-patient and doctor-family relationships. The content in the remaining categories is becoming increasingly specific and detailed. Moreover, the subjects' topics are described in more detail, and adjectives are used to define communication more precisely (interpersonal, social, effective, non-face-to-face, etc.). It is no longer a communication that is so general or focused solely on doctor-patient communication. The only two categories that remain with similar content are medical psychology and legal aspects, issues that probably have not changed their approach.

The inclusion of communication content in Medicine curricula is recent, so not all practicing doctors have received it yet. Dr. Álvarez Vázquez (personal communication, September 17, 2023), a 5th-year medical oncology resident at Mataró Hospital, confirms this in the interview because she did not receive training at university on breaking bad news. She adds that during her residency, she had "a single one-week workshop that combined theory and practice", and she personally enrolled in some communication courses outside the hospital. On the other hand, Dr. Laura Puntí, an oncologist at the same hospital and interviewed for this research, did receive training in this area: "At university, we used the Problem-Based Learning (PBL) method, so we had some theory on communication and even conducted some practice simulations" (Puntí, personal communication, September 17, 2023). She also took some voluntary courses during her residency and emphasized the training received from attending physicians, with advice and their example during visits.

Deficiencies in healthcare professionals' training were already reported before the pandemic, and these issues have become even more pronounced now. 78.5% of the interviewees have not received any training on breaking bad news during their university education. "The university practically provides no training on these topics [...]. It's a deficiency that has already been identified. As for our hospital, we provide the training primarily when you are already a healthcare specialist or a resident in a specialty, so you are already linked to a department", explains Dr. Guila (personal communication, April 1, 2020).

The perception of having received insufficient training aligns with the opinion of the former director of the Pere Mata Institute in Reus (Tarragona). For this retired psychiatrist, things are changing. In the 1960s when he studied Medicine, communication with patients was not a subject of study. Now, he acknowledges that workshops based on simulation, where actors play the role of patients, are offered at the Faculty of Medicine of the URV (Tarragona). For him, medical protocols are not significant, although they are indeed known.

The data from 2020 and 2021 showed that the oldest universities in Catalonia, UB and UAB, offered a greater number of communication-related subjects. In this regard, it was found that 44.4% of the offerings were mandatory subjects, meaning they were in line with the specific competencies of the degree and had to be taken by all students, typically in the 2nd year of the program (77.8%). Only at UAB were optional communication subjects offered. Looking at the data for Andalusia, it was confirmed that all subjects were mandatory (except for UC in Cádiz) and were also taken in the 2nd year (except at UMA, where they were taken in the 1st year). The offerings were limited to semester-long subjects in both Catalonia (66.7%) and Andalusia (100%), with an average of approximately 6 credits.

The data from 2023 reflect that almost half of the subjects are mandatory: 48.08% for Catalan universities and 46.67% for Andalusian universities (see Figure 4 and 5). Moreover, the majority continue to be taught in the 2nd year in Andalusian universities (40%) and in Catalan universities (30.77%), although with a lower percentage since the subjects are more evenly distributed across the years, and in some cases, students can choose in which year to take them (especially for the optional ones). Over 73% of the subjects are semester-long, both in Catalan and Andalusian universities, with an average of approximately 5 credits.

The assessment system in the years 2020 and 2021 varied significantly, although all faculties agreed on assessment through theoretical exams. At UdG, the Medicine degree is based on Problem-Based Learning (PBL), making its assessment substantially different, and UPF combines exams and seminars

Figure 3. Communication contents in medical faculties of Catalonia and Andalusia during and after the pandemic (Own elaboration)

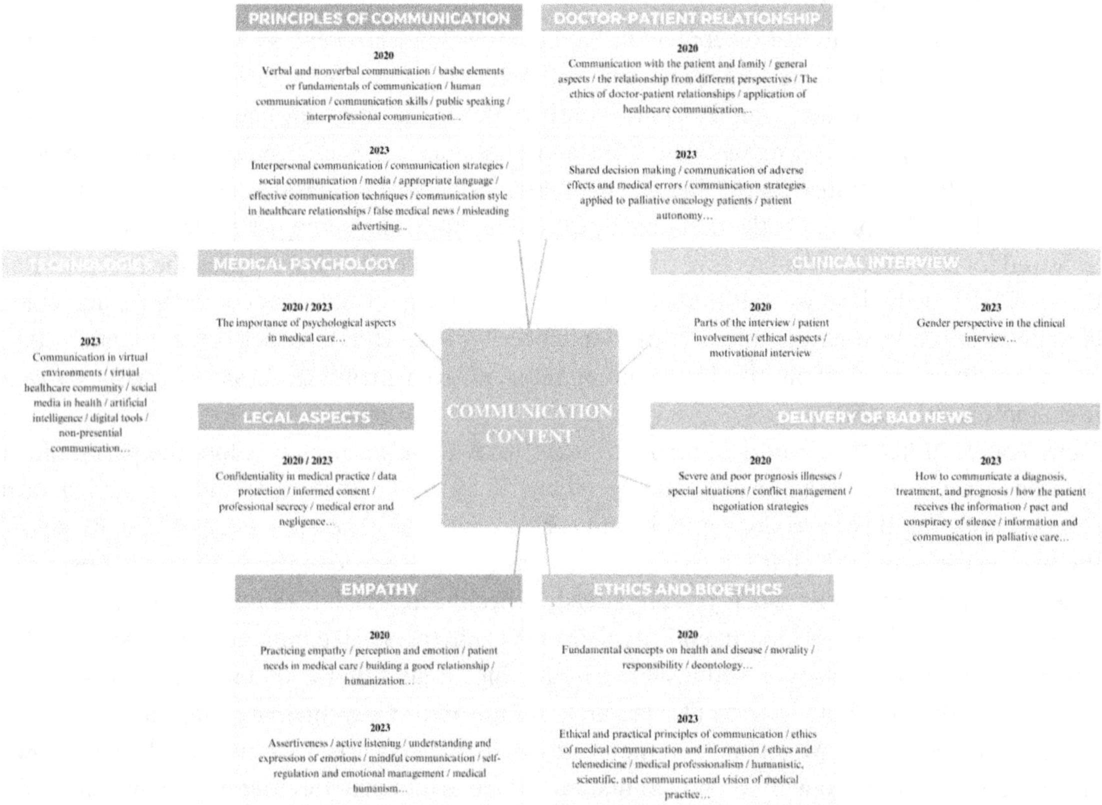

(proprietary methodology) for evaluation. In 2023, there continues to be disparity in assessment systems, although the use of theoretical exams remains common. For example, in the universities of Andalusia, the weight of the theoretical part, commonly assessed through an exam, is present in 12 out of 15 analyzed subjects (80%), with weights ranging from 30% to 80%. In Catalonia, looking at 30 out of 52 subjects (57.69%), the weights range from 20% to 100%.

Nevertheless, in general, a wide variety of different assessment methods have been introduced. On one hand, classroom practices, fieldwork, role-playing, and simulation are used in 25% of Catalan universities and 20% of Andalusian universities. On the other hand, written assignments, reports, or portfolios are utilized in 48% of Catalan universities and 26% of Andalusian universities. Finally, assessment systems through oral presentations, participation, attendance, and PBL sessions are included in 32% of Catalan universities and 26% of Andalusian universities. As mentioned, there is disparity in the assessment systems and a great diversity with the inclusion of methods such as seminars, clinical practices, case studies, tutoring, self-assessment, OSCE exams, practical activities, among many others.

The extensive medical literature on how to communicate bad news is not heavily based on many protocols. Searching Scopus over a period of 20 years (1999-2020), 29 publications on the topic were detected, directly related to the keyword "comunicar malas noticias" in Spanish or "breaking bad news" in English, or the expressions "protocolo médico" or "healthcare protocol". Most of the texts focus on

Figure 4. Types of subjects with communication content in the Medicine curricula of Catalan universities in 2020 and 2023 (Own elaboration)

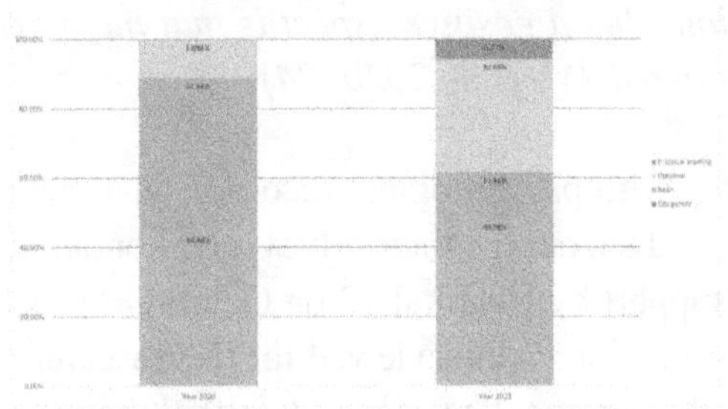

Figure 5. Types of subjects with communication content in the Medicine curricula of Andalusian universities in 2020 and 2023 (Own elaboration)

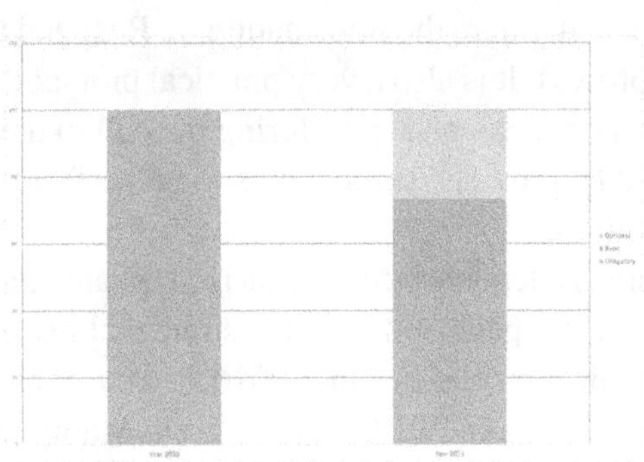

how to train novice doctors to enhance their skills in this regard. Many starts from the recommendations of classic protocols. Workshops using role-play methods are recommended to enhance competency in dealing with patients with poor prognoses (Back et al., 2010; Greenberg et al., 1999), as well as the use of videos depicting various situations of breaking bad news and the debriefing[1] as a suitable method for this training (Flores-Funes et al., 2018). Even the most recent ones avoid relating the communication of bad news to new information technologies or digital competencies (Gavilan et al., 2017). Although that trend is changing after the pandemic, as will be seen with the analysis of recent protocols for communicating bad news.

After the pandemic, only 4 hospitals in Spain publish their medical protocols. It is just one additional protocol compared to before Covid-19 (Vicente, 2020). The novelty comes from the Department of Health of the Junta de Castilla y León and Sacyl, Regional Health Management. The oldest protocol detected in Spain remains relatively new. It is from Hospital Sant Joan de Déu (2016), a reference pediatric center in Barcelona. Another belongs to the General University Hospital of Castellón in collaboration with the provincial Health Department (CBA, 2019). Their protocol focuses on 6 steps, revisiting the classics. Finally, a protocol born during the pandemic is revealed (Vicente, 2020), signed by the Hospital 12 de Octubre in Madrid. It is the first directive that includes the isolation variant and the phone as a mechanism to communicate and connect family members separated from their hospitalized loved ones.

In a phone communication, it's more challenging to convey understanding, support, and identify emotions. The effort of the one delivering the news will need to be greater, consistently trying to show signs of listening and asking about sensations and feelings. There are few guidelines included regarding how to respond to emotional reactions, but a positive aspect is that the psychological and social needs of those being spoken to are considered. (Vicente, 2020: 24)

It is a very practical protocol with psychological recommendations for doctors. It advises them to drink water, take deep breaths, and encourage themselves after conducting phone communication with family members. The prompt support by Hospital 12 de Octubre for its healthcare staff contrasts with the perception held by active professionals interviewed for this research.

In the review for this research, a protocol has been identified that adapts the proposal from Hospital 12 de Octubre regarding phone communication and the protocol by Baile and Buckman (Junta de Castilla y León & Sacyl, 2020). It is a six-step protocol with very similar recommendations to those mentioned. The six steps are: 1. Prepare for the interview; 2. Find out what the family member knows; 3. Assess what the family member wants to know; 4. Share the information; 5. Respond to the patient's feelings; and 6. Planning and follow-up of the process. It is also a very practical protocol as it provides example phrases on how to start the call, questions that can be asked during the call to the patient's family member, and relevant information that should be provided (procedures to be performed, patient's treatment, or next time of contact), among other things.

In the studied hospitals, there is a tendency to emphasize humanization plans. In five out of the ten analyzed hospitals, a document or webpage outlining the strategic lines of such plans was found. In the Community of Madrid, the humanization plan began in 2016, and the public hospitals that have developed it with their own documents are La Paz in 2018, and Gregorio Marañón and Ramon y Cajal in 2022. On the other hand, at the Vall d'Hebron Hospital in Barcelona, documents on humanization plans have been available since 2018, just like at the Virgen del Rocío Hospital in Seville.

As mentioned, only one of the studied hospitals has a protocol for delivering bad news, mainly focused on telephone communication. This is Hospital 12 de Octubre. The rest of the hospitals, including this one, mention the communication of bad news in documents such as: teaching or training guides, supervision protocols, and resident guides; hospital reports or bulletins with courses or workshops on this topic for continuous education and updating, for residents or nursing; or white papers, for instance, on palliative care, among others. The only hospitals for which no such open-access documents were found are Vall d'Hebron Hospital in Barcelona and La Fe University and Polytechnic Hospital in Valencia. While not the primary objective of this study, which centers on the analysis of protocols for breaking bad news, an increase in documents related to mental health has also been noted.

In addition to protocols related to Spanish hospitals, protocols such as the one by Belli (2020) and recommendation guidelines like Espasandin et al.'s (2020; 2021) for telephone communication have also emerged in academic literature. More specifically, a protocol has been developed for breaking bad news through phone or video calls, known as CONNECT (Sobczak, 2022): Context (C), Organization (O), Near and Niceties (NN), Emotions (E), Counseling (C) and Taking care (T). On the other hand, in the healthcare field, technical guidelines have been found for remote psychosocial support with guidelines for breaking bad news (GIZ, 2020). Finally, in specific publications, there are updated recommendations for breaking bad news, as is the case with *Cuidados paliativos, Guía para atención primaria* (Ministerio de Sanidad, 2021) or *el Protocolo de herramientas de comunicación en UCI pediátrica* (SECIP, 2023).

Table 2. Comparison of two protocols for breaking bad news via phone or video call

Recommendations for Breaking Bad News by Phone (Belli, 2020)	CONNECT Protocol (Sobczak, 2022)
First phase Clearly identify oneself and explain the purpose of the call. Ensure that the receiver is not in any potentially dangerous situation. **Second phase** Speak clearly, stay calm, and maintain an empathetic and warm tone of voice. Avoid technical terms. Plan the conversation in advance and find a quiet moment to prevent interruptions. **Third phase** Anticipate that the purpose of the call is to deliver bad news. Respond to the interlocutor's questions directly and carefully. Honesty and compassion. Empathy and respect for the interlocutor's reaction times. **Fourth phase** Address concerns, outline the next steps, and record the interaction in the medical record or the designated system for it.	**C – Context** Verify medical records and plan what to say and how to say it. **O – Organization** Ensure privacy and test the connection. **NN – Near and Niceties** Introduce yourself and ask the other party to make appropriate arrangements (connection, conversation setting, privacy, etc.). **E – Emotions** Avoid medical jargon, be tactful and careful, be empathetic and compassionate, use questions and refer to facts. **C- Counseling** Make sure the message has been understood and agree on further proceedings. **T – Taking care** Make sure whether there is additional support, summarize key findings and provide your contact details.

Source: Own elaboration based on Belli (2020) and Sobczak (2022).

Below, we analyze and summarize the protocols by Belli (2020) and Sobczak (2022). As can be seen, the recommendations in both protocols are similar (see Table 2). Prior to the call, one should prepare the information and plan how to deliver the bad news. Subsequently, establish communication, identify oneself, and ensure the interlocutor can take the call. In both protocols, there are recommendations concerning tone of voice and using simple language to enhance information comprehension. Finally, they emphasize the importance of addressing the interlocutor's questions and providing closure to the call. The decalogue of recommendations by Espasandín-Duarte et al. (2020; 2021) generally follows the same guidelines as these two protocols. It emphasizes the recommendation to take a narrative approach during communication, meaning to describe the situation "with short and concise phrases, avoiding hesitation and asking if the transmitted information was understood", while avoiding irrelevant details or extending the explanation (Espasandín-Duarte et al., 2021: 63).

Regarding specific publications on how to deliver bad news, it is observed that classic protocols, especially the SPIKES strategy (SECIP, 2023; Ministry of Health, 2021), are explained and adapted to the pediatric ICU and palliative care settings, respectively. Additionally, in the one by the Spanish Society and Foundation of Pediatric Intensive Care (2023), the NURSE protocol (name, understand, respect, support, and explore) is added, an acronym for key steps to express empathy. This concept, empathy, is reiterated in practically all protocols for breaking bad news that have been used, and as seen, it has also been utilized to create the EMPATHY protocol. In the technical guide for remote psychosocial support (GIZ, 2020), there is a section providing guidelines for breaking bad news. These guidelines align with the recommendations and protocols mentioned earlier.

All interviewed subjects are familiar with Buckman protocol (1992), but only 17% of the sample claims to use it as a guide. For active physicians, experience is much more effective, as each patient and their situation are unique. Only the pediatric Oncohematologist at Vall d'Hebron acknowledges that their medical center recommends relying on protocols, although they are not adapted to the pandemic emergency. On the other hand, Dr. Puntí (personal communication, September 17, 2023) explains that in her hospital, they do not have an established protocol, but they are introducing a form with different items for proper communication and acknowledges that there are guides to assist professionals that are applied intrinsically. For her, experience is important "when breaking bad news since it allows you to develop more empathy, but paternalism should be avoided in order to make the best decisions and not let it affect your personal life".

Practicing doctors consider empathy to be the most crucial element in delivering a difficult diagnosis. Nevertheless, they believe that professional experience demonstrates "there's no one-size-fits-all approach to do it well; it's more about different approaches" (Brugués, personal communication, April 9, 2020). One of these approaches is providing support to patients and their families: "Each situation has its own peculiarities, and one must adapt to the patient, the environment, and their health condition" (Fina, personal communication, April 9, 2020). The level of empathy also depends on the number of patients assigned to the doctor, as it influences the relationship established between them. The rural doctor from the Pallars Sobirà ABS knows this well: "Not only do we have more time for each patient, but the doctor-patient relationship transforms into a doctor-neighbor relationship [...]. We all know each other well. We shop at the same places, go to the same spots [...]. I can deliver the diagnosis at their home" (Bretcha, personal communication, April 15, 2020).

For the oncology specialist at Khuab Institute, it is important to promote hope:

When you have the information about the reality, you explain it in the least harsh way possible, without figures, without numbers... but by making all the options available to the patients and their families. So, whenever you give news with negative connotations, you try to bring hope alongside it. Even in moments when you provide information about a terminal condition, hope, that is to say, 'we are here and we will accompany you, we will be by your side', must exist. (Vidal, personal communication, March 23, 2020)

In summary, according to Dr. Puntí (personal communication, September 17, 2023), the main techniques for breaking bad news are active listening, empathy, silence to allow time to process the information, and time for the patient's and the physician's questions. According to this oncologist, the pandemic has further developed the empathetic side of professionals and has highlighted the importance of allowing the patient to be accompanied during the consultation or hospitalization. Dr. Álvarez Vázquez (personal communication, September 17, 2023) agrees that the pandemic has brought out more feelings and empathy, but it has not increased training on how to deliver bad news. The lack of time for professionals means that training in communication and breaking bad news is put on the back burner compared to the increasing knowledge about diseases, studies on new drugs, and treatments. However, as this study has shown, this fact has been compensated for by the increase in communication training in the Medicine curriculum.

DISCUSSION AND CONCLUSIONS

In 2020, the Catalan universities with the most tradition, UAB and UB, offered the most subjects in the field of communication (2), while in the newer medical faculties, increasing the offering in communication skills was not considered important. Even one of the universities, UIC, had no dedicated communication subjects, although some seminars on this topic were held. UdG was the last Catalan university offering the Medicine program and had only one mandatory communication subject. Therefore, Borrell-Carrió's idea (2012) that with the Bologna Plan, this training would change, seemed not to have been established

(Cited by Ferreira et al., 2015). A similar situation was observed in Andalusia (with only one mandatory communication skills subject or none in the case of the University of Cádiz).

With the pandemic, the situation regarding the offering of communicative content in the curriculum of the Medicine Degree in Catalan and Andalusian universities changed substantially. Currently, the Catalan universities with the most subjects in this field are UAB and UB with 10, while the Andalusian university with the most is US with 5. All the universities studied have increased the number of subjects with communication content. It seems reasonable to say that universities are responding to the demand from active professionals who identified a lack of communication training. Additionally, training in technologies and emotional management has been added to the syllabus, two needs that have become evident after the pandemic.

The coronavirus has shown the need to develop medical protocols that regulate the use of new technologies or social networks, in states of pandemic and isolation. Given the situation and in line with learning from this crisis, it would be recommended that professional protocols are developed to provide such sensitive information from new channels.

The COVID-19 pandemic has highlighted the importance of knowing how to communicate bad news to family members and patients during isolation. Smartphones and tablets have been instruments that have aided and facilitated these tasks. Their use has been a result of necessity and isolation, as well as the experience, expertise, and initiative of healthcare personnel, but it has not been a specific medical instruction or a recommended guideline for those facing death every day and in proportions they had not previously experienced. As this research has shown, few protocols emerged during the pandemic for breaking bad news through these devices. Only the 12 de Octubre Hospital in Madrid was able, amid the crisis, to publish guidelines to combat communication gaps with patients, reduce stress among healthcare staff, and include the phone as an appropriate channel for breaking bad diagnoses. Others adapted existing protocols (Junta de Castilla y León & Sacyl, 2020).

Spanish hospitals were unable, during the pandemic, to develop or create protocols for breaking bad news, especially using the telephone or video call. In 2023, there are still three hospitals with protocols for breaking bad news remotely (Hospital San Joan de Déu, 2016; CBA, 2019; Hospital 12 de Octubre, 2020). In this research, the adapted protocol from the Junta de Castilla y León was found, and in the review of the top ten public hospitals with the best reputation in Spain (Merco, 2022), no protocol was found, except for the one from the Hospital 12 de Octubre. It is worth mentioning that in practically all the analyzed hospitals, documents were found mentioning training for delivering bad news, especially in teaching or resident supervision guides, as well as in annual reports listing courses and workshops on this subject.

In academic literature, some protocols focused on delivering bad news through telephone and/or video calls have emerged both during the pandemic (Belli, 2020) and subsequently (Sobczak, 2022). Both protocols have been analyzed in this chapter (see Table 2). On the other hand, in technical literature, publications have also been found adapting existing protocols such as SPIKES or NURSE to specific areas such as palliative care (Ministry of Health, 2021) or pediatric ICU (SECIP 2023).

Effectively communicating a poor prognosis is a task that is part of the medical profession, but until now, it hadn't come to the forefront of public opinion so strongly. The coronavirus has shifted this traditional and nearly one-sided communication towards a new, more public and technological scenario. The reality of daily practice has pushed for new dynamics in the doctor-patient and doctor-media relationships, possibly leading to a change in the curriculum of medical faculties in Catalonia and Andalusia.

Now, a change in healthcare facilities is also necessary to enhance education and existing protocols regarding the communication of bad news and the use of technologies for this purpose. While there is still a gap in this aspect, it has been observed that some hospitals already have initiatives that could align with this direction, such as humanization or mental health plans. Searching for these types of plans was not the objective of this study, but it is a possible line of investigation for the future, as hospital centers have new initiatives in this direction. It will be a learning process to address a need generated by the pandemic.

ACKNOWLEDGMENT/SUPPORT

This text has been made possible thanks to the collaboration of the graduates in Advertising and Public Relations from the University of Girona, Maria Salvatella, Andrea Chaves, Laura Vicente, and Andrea Romero.

REFERENCES

Abarca, A., Alpízar, F., Sibaja, G., & Rojas, C. (2013). *Técnicas cualitativas de investigación*. UCR.

Almanza, J. de J. (2003). La comunicación de las malas noticias en la práctica médica. *Neurologia, Neurocirugia, Psiquiatria, 36*(4), 165–176. https://bit.ly/3ynZdhL

Álvarez Aparicio, A. I. (2020). Comunicación de malas noticias en el ámbito sanitario en tiempos de COVID-19. La comunicación telefónica. *Revista de Comunicación y Salud, 10*(2), 211–248. doi:10.35669/rcys.2020.10(2).211-248

Alves, A. E. (2003, May-June). ¿Cómo comunicar malas noticias a nuestros pacientes y no morir en el intento? *Revista Argentina de Cardiología, 71*(3). https://bit.ly/3f3bDEj

Aranda, C. I., Cedillo, R., del Campo, M. G., Omelas, R. O., & Góngora, J. (2014, September-October). Factores que influyen y dificultan la comunicación de malas noticias en el personal de salud. *Acta Universitaria, 24*(5), 20–26. doi:10.15174.au.2014.600

Ayarra, M., & Lizarraga, S. (2001). Malas noticias y apoyo emocional. *Anales del Sistema Sanitario de Navarra, 24*(Suplemento 2), 55–63.

Back, A. L., Arnold, R. M., Tulsky, J. A., Baile, W. F., & Edwards, K. (2010, June). Could I add something? Teaching communication by intervening in real time during a clinical encounter. *Academic Medicine, 85*(6), 1048–1051. doi:10.1097/ACM.0b013e3181dbac6f PMID:20505408

Baile, W. F., Buckman, R., Lenzi, R., Glober, G., Beale, E. A., & Kudelka, A. P. (2000). SPIKES—a six-step protocol for delivering bad news: Application to the patient with cancer. *The Oncologist, 5*(4), 302–311. doi:10.1634/theoncologist.5-4-302 PMID:10964998

Bascuñán, M.L. (2013). Comunicación de "malas noticias" en salud. *Revista Médica Clínica Las Condes, 24*(4), 685-693. doi:10.1016/S0716-8640(13)70208-6

Bascuñán, M. L., Roizblatt, A., & Roizblatt, D. (2007). Comunicación de malas noticias en medicina: Un estudio exploratorio. *Revista de Medicina de la Universidad de Navarra, 52*(2), 28–31. https://bit.ly/3f8vvpD PMID:17886712

Belli, L. F. (2020). Recomendaciones para la comunicación de malas noticias por teléfono durante la pandemia por SARS-CoV-2. *Revista Panamericana de Salud Pública, 44*, 1–6. Advance online publication. doi:10.26633/RPSP.2020.69 PMID:32523607

Bennett, M., & Alison, D. (1996). Discussing the diagnosis and prognosis with cancer patients. *Postgraduate Medical Journal, 72*(843), 25–29. doi:10.1136/pgmj.72.843.25 PMID:8746281

Bernardo, Y., & Brunet, N. (2010). Comunicación de malas noticias. *Cuadernos de crisis y emergencias, 9*(2), 48-58. https://bit.ly/3f9YTeO

Buckman, R. (1984). Breaking bad news: why is it still so difficult? British Medical Journal, 288(6430), 1597-1599. doi:10.1136/bmj.288.6430.1597

Buckman, R. (1992). How to break bad news. A guide for health care professionals (J. Hopkins, Ed.). Academic Press.

Buckman, R. A. (2005). Breaking bad news: The SPIKES strategy. *Community Oncology, 2*(2), 138–142. doi:10.1016/S1548-5315(11)70867-1

CBA. (Ed.). (2019). *Recomendaciones para la comunicación de malas noticias*. Documento CBA nº 16. Comité Bioética Asistencial (CBA), Generalitat Valenciana y Departamento de Salud de Castelló. https://bit.ly/3oze2cX

Coombs, T. (2015). *Ongoing Crisis Communication: Planning, Managing, and Responding*. Sage publications.

Costa-Sánchez, C., & López-García, X. (2020). Comunicación y crisis del coronavirus en España. Primeras lecciones. *El Profesional de la Información, 29*(3). Advance online publication. doi:10.3145/epi.2020.may.04

Ebn Ahmady, A., Seyedzadeh Sabounchi, S., Mirmohammadsadeghi, H., & Rezaei, A. (2014). A suitable model for breaking bad news: Review of recommendations. *The Journal of Medical Research*, 1–15. doi:10.5171/2014.776618

Espinosa-Mirabet, S., & Puntí-Brun, M. (2021). Revisión de la formación en habilidades comunicativas en los planes de estudio de Medicina de Cataluña. In *Cuestiones transversales en la innovación de la docencia y la investigación de las ciencias sociales y jurídicas: especial referencia al impacto del covid-19, las nuevas tecnologías y metodologías, las perspectivas de género y la diversidad* (pp. 487–509). Dykinson.

Ferreira, G., Fernández-Antón, T., Baleriola, J., & Aleida, R. (2015). Competencia en comunicación en el currículo del estudiante de Medicina de España (1990-2014): De la Atención Primaria al Plan Bolonia. Un estudio descriptivo. *Atencion Primaria, 47*(7), 399–410. doi:10.1016/j.aprim.2014.09.007 PMID:25435473

Fink, S. (1986). *Crisis Management: Planning for the Inevitable*. American Management Association.

Flores-Funes, D., Aguilar-Jiménez, J., Lirón-Ruiz, R. J., & Aguayo-Albasini, J. L. (2020). ¿Comunicamos correctamente las malas noticias en medicina? Resultados de un taller de formación basado en videos y debriefing. *Educación Médica*, *21*(2), 118–122. doi:10.1016/j.edumed.2018.07.005

Fujimori, M., Shirai, Y., Asai, M., Kubota, K., Katsumata, N., & Uchitomi, Y. (2014). Effect of communication skills training program for oncologists based on patient preferences for communication when receiving bad news: A randomized controlled trial. *Journal of Clinical Oncology*, *32*(20), 2166–2172. doi:10.1200/JCO.2013.51.2756 PMID:24912901

García-Díaz, D. (2006). Comunicando malas noticias en Medicina: Recomendaciones para hacer de la necesitad virtud. *Medicina Intensiva*, *30*(9), 452–459. doi:10.1016/S0210-5691(06)74569-7 PMID:17194403

Gavilan, D., Martinez-Navarro, G., & Fernández-Lores, S. (2017). Universitarios y redes sociales informativas: Escépticos totales, moderadores duales o pro-digitales. *Comunicar. Revista Científica de Educomunicación*, *25*(53), 61–70. doi:10.3916/C53-2017-06

GIZ. (2020). *Guía técnica orientadora para el acompañamiento psicosocial remoto. Deutsche Gesellschaft für, Internationale Zusammenarbeit (GIZ)* GmbH.

Gómez-Sancho, M. (2016). Cómo dar las malas noticias en medicina (3a ed.). Plataforma Editorial.

Gordillo Navas, G. C., Trujillo Martínez, J. D., & Filizzola Bermúdez, J. D. (2020). Estrategia de simulación para aplicar el protocolo SPIKES en la comunicación de malas noticias. *Universitas Medica*, *61*(3). Advance online publication. doi:10.11144/Javeriana.umed61-3.spik

Greenberg, L. W., Ochsenschlager, D., O'Donnell, R., Mastruserio, J., & Cohen, G. J. (1999, June). Communication bad news: A pedriatric department's evalua-tion of a simulated intervention. *Pediatrics*, *103*(6), 1210–1217. doi:10.1542/peds.103.6.1210 PMID:10353931

Guillén-López, O. B., & Olascoaga-Mesía, S. C. (2017). Habilidad de los médicos residentes para comunicar malas noticias. *Revista de la Sociedad Peruana de Medicina Interna*, *30*(2), 77–81. doi:10.36393pmi.v30i2.65

Gutiérrez, A., & Tyner, K. (2012). Educación para los medios, alfabetización mediática y competencia digital. *Comunicar. Revista Científica de Educomunicación*, *XIX*(38), 31–39. doi:10.3916/C38-2012-02-03

Hospital 12 de Octubre. (2020). *Protocolo para la comunicación telefónica de malas noticias a familiares de pacientes con coronavirus en situación de últimos días*. Equipo de soporte a cuidados paliativos del H.U. 12 de octubre. https://tinyurl.com/ys52785c

Hospital Sant Joan de Déu. (2016). *La primera noticia. Claves para el profesional*. https://bit.ly/2QIAKCU

Junta de Castilla y León & Sacyl. (2020). Protocolo para profesionales sanitarios para la comunicación telefónica de malas noticias a familiares de pacientes con coronavirus en situación de cuidados de últimos días. In *Protocolo integral de actuación ante situaciones específicas de gravedad, últimos días y fallecimiento en la crisis COVID-19*. DG de Planificación y Asistencia Sanitaria y la DG de Sistemas, calidad y Prestación farmacéutica de la GRS. https://tinyurl.com/2cpj534h

Kaye, P. (2023). *Breaking Bad News: a ten step approach*. Scion Publishing Ltd.

Krippendorf, K. (1980). *Content Analysis: An Introduction to its Methodology*. Sage Publication.

León-Amenero, D., & Huarcaya-Victoria, J. (2019). El duelo y cómo dar malas noticias en medicina. *Anales de la Facultad de Medicina. Universidad Nacional Mayor de San Marcos*, *80*(1), 80–91. doi:10.15381/anales.v80i1.15471

Medialdea, S. (2020). *La mitad de los sanitarios sufren estrés postraumático y un 40% están emocionalmente agotados*. ABC. 19 mayo 2020. https://bit.ly/3u5BUWu

Merco. (2022). *Monitor de Reputación Sanitaria – Hospitales*. https://tinyurl.com/ytnnhwbw

Ministerio de Sanidad. (2021). *Cuidados paliativos. Guía para Atención Primaria*. Instituto Nacional de Gestión Sanitaria, Ministerio de Sanidad. https://tinyurl.com/twkaywkd

Moore, P., Gómez, G., & Kurt, S. (2012). Comunicación médico-paciente: Una de las competencias básicas pero diferente. *Atencion Primaria*, *44*(6), 358–365. doi:10.1016/j.aprim.2011.07.008 PMID:22079197

Mora-Rodríguez, A., & Melero-López, I. (2021). Seguimiento informativo y percepción del riesgo ante la Covid-19 en España. *Comunicar, Revista Cien-tífica de Educomunicación*, *29*(66), 71–81. doi:10.3916/C66-2021-06

Núñez, S., Marco, T., Burillo-Putze, G., & Ojeda, J. (2006). Procedimientos y habilidades para la comunicación de las malas noticias en urgencias. *Medicina Clínica*, *127*(15), 580–583. doi:10.1157/13094002 PMID:17145016

Rabow, M., & Mcphee, S. J. (1999). Beyond breaking bad news: How to help patients who suffer. *The Western Journal of Medicine*, *171*(4), 260–263. https://bit.ly/3yo06qB PMID:10578682

Rebello, C., Marchetti, M. A., Lemonica, L., & Moreira, G. A. (2017). The P-A-C-I-E-N-T-E Protocol: An instrument for breaking bad news adapted to the Brazilian medical Reality. *Revista da Associação Médica Brasileira*, *63*(1), 43–49. doi:10.1590/1806-9282.63.01.43 PMID:28225878

Riquelme, A., Martín, M., & Ortigosa, J. M. (2011). ¿Cómo dar malas noticias? Adaptación de La comunicación con el enfermo y el manejo de información. In *Manual de atención psicosocial*. Instituto Monsa de Ediciones. https://bit.ly/2QxBQRI

Rodríguez-Salvador, J. J. (2010). *Comunicación clínica: cómo dar malas noticias*. https://bit.ly/3f8xWrS

Rodríguez-Sanz, J., Kurtz, C., & Álvarez-Ude, F. (2011). Aspectos clave de la comunicación no verbal en la consulta. *FMC: Formación Médica Continua-da en Atención Primaria, 18*(7), 401-409. https://bit.ly/2SZ8b4M

Romero, A. (2022). La capacitat de comunicar males notícies. Com ensenyen les universitats d'Andalusia a comunicar males notícies als estudiants de Medicina. Unpublished Final Degree Project of Advertising and Public Relations, University of Girona.

Sánchez, C. I. A., Zaragoza, R. C., del Campo Acosta, M. G., Segovia, R. O. O., & Ortega, J. G. (2014). Factores que influyen y dificultan la comunicación de malas noticias en el personal de salud. *Acta Universitaria*, *24*(5), 20–26. https://www.redalyc.org/pdf/416/41632450003.pdf

Sobczak, K. (2022). The "CONNECT" Protocol: Delivering bad news by phone or video call. *International Journal of General Medicine*, *15*, 3567–3572. doi:10.2147/IJGM.S358723 PMID:35392027

Solana López, I., Juez Martel, I., Martínez Moreno, E., de Zea Luque, C., Martín Fernández de Soignie, A. M., Sánchez Baños, N., & Guerra Martínez, J. A. (2022). Humanización en la comunicación de malas noticias en el paciente oncológico y paliativo. *Oncología (Ecuador)*, *32*(3), 266–272. Advance online publication. doi:10.33821/639

Szyld, D., F Arriaga, A., & León-Castelao, E. (2021). El debriefing clínico, retos y oportunidades en el ámbito asistencial; aprendizaje en la reflexión colectiva para mejorar los sistemas sanitarios y la colaboración interprofesional. *Simulación Clínica*, *3*(2), 69–73. doi:10.35366/101430

Taylor, E. (2007). How best to communicate bad news over the telephone. *End of Life Care, 1*(1), 30-37. https://tinyurl.com/tmc4fb55

Varguillas, C., & Ribot de Flores, S. (2007). Implicaciones conceptuales y metodológicas en la aplicación de la entrevista en profundidad. *Laurus: revista de educación*, *13*(23), 249-262. https://bit.ly/3oQt7Hj

Vicente, L. (2020). *La comunicación de males notícies en l'àmbit de la salut. Investigació sobre la comunicación de les males notícies en medicina, la seva evolució i l'adaptació a les necessitats especials en situación de COVID-19.* https://bit.ly/3oyL1hs

Villa, B. (2007). Recomendaciones sobre cómo comunicar malas noticias. *Nure investigación*, (31). https://bit.ly/33Z6erh

Villagran, M., Goldsmith, B., Witenberg-Liles, E., & Baldwin, P. (2010). Creating COMFORT: A Communication-based model for Breaking Bad News. Communication Education. Issue 3. *Communication Education*, *59*(3), 220–234. doi:10.1080/03634521003624031

Wilson, C. (2012). Alfabetización mediática e informacional: Proyecciones didácticas. *Comunicar. Revista Científica de Educomunicación*, *20*(39), 15–24. doi:10.3916/C39-2012-02-01

Witt, M. M., & Jankowska, K. A. (2018). Breaking bad news in genetic counseling—Problems and communication tools. *Journal of Applied Genetics*, *59*(4), 449–452. doi:10.100713353-018-0469-y PMID:30255485

ENDNOTE

1 A clinical debriefing is a structured conversation among multiple individuals aimed at analyzing performance with the goal of improving or maintaining future performance (Szyld, Arriaga & León-Castelao, 2021).

Chapter 9
Student Opinions on the Processing of Applied Courses Online and Face-to-Face During the Pandemic Period and Editing Techniques:
Course Example

Yaren Kalkan Aluç
İstinye Üniversitesi, Turkey

Enes Aluç
İstinye Üniversitesi, Turkey

ABSTRACT

This study focuses on the impact of the COVID-19 pandemic on university students' completion of applied courses through the transition to online education. It explores the persistent presence of online education even as universities gradually return to face-to-face instruction. The study employs in-depth interviews to elicit participants' perspectives on the experience of taking practical courses in both online and face-to-face formats. The research encompasses (1) the transition to online education, (2) a comparative analysis of online and face-to-face courses, (3) the extraction and analysis of shared and contrasting viewpoints from student interviews, and (4) strategies for enhancing online education. The investigation provides valuable insights into the evolving landscape of higher education, emphasizing the enduring significance of online learning in a post-pandemic world.

DOI: 10.4018/979-8-3693-0896-7.ch009

INTRODUCTION

Throughout the world, the Covid-19 pandemic necessitated the rapid implementation of emergency distance education, as highlighted by Bozkurt (2020). This global crisis compelled both teachers and students at primary, secondary, and high schools to convene via television channels and internet-based platforms. Universities, in their pursuit to address this challenge, made efforts to navigate the uncharted waters through the establishment of their own distance education centers, often referred to as UZEM. However, this transition was marred by various disruptions arising from the country's internet infrastructure limitations and the unpreparedness of educational institutions. These issues manifested in the incomplete setup of distance education systems, the time required for students and educators to acclimate to the new online learning environment, and connectivity issues.

While online education had been explored in theory and select common courses for years, these common courses primarily encompassed foundational subjects applicable to various departments, such as Ataturk's Principles and Revolutions, Turkish Literature, and Basic English. The roots of web-based education in Turkey trace back to a state university in 1997. By the academic year 2000-2001, a notable transition to Internet Supported Education had been achieved, and in 2002-2003, YÖK (Council of Higher Education) made a pivotal decision to initiate distance education associate degree programs in Turkey (Kırık, M.A., 2014).

This study embarks on an exploration of how applied courses are taught in both online and traditional face-to-face settings, focusing on the strengths and weaknesses of online education in applied courses, as well as the impact of face-to-face applied courses on students' perceptions. Specifically, the research targets students who have undertaken a fiction course at the university, examining their experiences with both online and face-to-face instruction through in-depth interviews. Ten students, aged 18-25, enrolled in this course will be interviewed, delving into their encounters with online and face-to-face fiction classes.

In addition, the study delves into the 2020-2021 online editing techniques course at Istinye University, conducted during the academic year 2021-2022. The research aims to contribute to the existing literature by shedding light on the potential advancements in practical courses achievable through online education, offering valuable insights and direction for future developments in this area.

Effects of COVID-19 Pandemic on Education

The Covid-19 virus, originating in Wuhan, China in late 2019 and early 2020, swiftly spread across the globe, leading the World Health Organization (WHO) to declare it a 'pandemic' in March 2020. This onset of the pandemic prompted nations worldwide to institute new measures, particularly in the realm of education. Initially, concerns centered on the rapid transmission of the virus among students and educators, particularly within schools, leading to the suspension of in-person education to mitigate its spread (Angoletto and Queiroz, 2020). Consequently, both administrative and academic staff in public and private educational institutions, alongside students, commenced a period of remote work. However, as the number of Covid-19 cases continued to surge, it became evident that the pandemic would not abate swiftly. Hence, various alternative methods were explored, leading to the widespread adoption of online education on a global scale (Abdalla, 2020; Lau, Yang & Dasgupta, 2020; Zhong, 2020). This transition to online education was not without its challenges, as many nations were ill-prepared for the sudden shift, resulting in negative repercussions for educational systems. Additionally, some regions encountered obstacles related to internet accessibility, while exorbitant data costs impeded access and opportunities in others (Balcı, A., 2020). In the case of Turkey, a rapid transition to online courses was executed within the distance education system in response to the crisis.

Online Education

Demiray and İşman (2003) have identified five historical phases of online and distance education. These phases encompass the pre-literacy period, which featured correspondence education utilizing printed materials sent via mail. Subsequent phases involved the utilization of radio and television as teaching tools, the introduction of two-way communication between students and teachers, and the evolution towards modern distance education methods. In its contemporary form, distance education entails the use of the internet to deliver lessons, allowing students and instructors to engage from different locations and at varying times. This mode of education relies on active technology integration to enhance the learning experience (Valentine, D., 2002).

In the present era, technological advancements have facilitated seamless two-way communication between students and teachers. With just a computer and internet connection, instructors can enrich their lessons with slides, videos, relevant visuals, and scanned books. The field of distance education has seen significant growth through the development of web-based learning environments, content creation, and increased use of live virtual classrooms (Yenal, A. Ç., 2009).

In Turkey, the Ministry of National Education introduced the Education Information Network (EBA) for primary, secondary, and high schools, marking the country's initial foray into online education. Simultaneously, universities swiftly established Distance Education Centers (UZEM) to continue their courses seamlessly. Within this system, universities adopt various approaches; some employ online synchronous methods, wherein students and instructors engage in live sessions via live broadcasts, video conferencing tools, or institutional platforms. These synchronous lessons demand students to be present at specific times, fostering direct interaction.

On the other hand, offline asynchronous methods are used, offering flexibility in terms of when students access course materials. However, self-discipline becomes crucial in this format, as students must manage their own schedules to avoid losing track of lessons and engagement. Ensuring uninterrupted educational activities is a key goal of distance education, particularly in unforeseen circumstances (Can, 2020; Kaçan and Gelen, 2020; Karakuş and Yanpar Yelken, 2020).

The Covid-19 pandemic has catalyzed the worldwide digitization of education. This transformation has had a profound impact on primary and secondary education, as well as universities, especially in faculties of communication where applied courses are prominent. As a result, students have undergone substantial changes in their experiences with both theoretical and applied courses, particularly in fields like radio, television, cinema, advertising, photography, graphics, and graphic animation. Applied courses such as camera operation, 3D animation, and editing have all been significantly influenced by this shift towards online education.

Advantages and Disadvantages of Online Education

The transition to distance education has prompted each educational institution to establish its own online learning system. However, this shift is part of a broader worldwide transformation in education, which has persisted even beyond the pandemic. The convergence of students and educators from diverse locations through the use of internet and computers, as essential tools, has brought about both advantages and disadvantages.

Speaking of the advantages of online education, institutions benefit from reduced education costs, while students enjoy increased flexibility without the constraints of a fixed classroom. Individualized learning is fostered, allowing students to explore diverse fields online. The need for specific time and physical space is eliminated, and experts can be seamlessly integrated into the educational process. Students in distance education are encouraged to enhance their learning skills, and they have the autonomy to plan and oversee their own learning process (Duman, S. N., 2020). In this context, students studying at their own pace save valuable time. As per the findings of Chan, So, Wong, Lee, and Tiwari (2007), distance education contributes to reducing anxiety levels and demonstrates the effectiveness of distance communication methods in enhancing knowledge dissemination, which can span the globe via the internet.

On the other hand, considering the disadvantages of online education, students face challenges during the adaptation process, moving from the familiar in-person education to an entirely different system. It results in isolation, social disconnection, and barriers for students with special needs. Insufficient technological infrastructure in some homes further hinders students' ability to effectively follow lessons. Additional drawbacks include difficulties in maintaining motivation, limited interaction, the potential for an isolated and antisocial lifestyle, issues in receiving timely feedback, and overreliance on technology and tools (DePaepe, Zhu, and Depryck, 2018; Gewin, 2020; Horspol and Lange, 2012; Lei and Gupta, 2010; Venter, 2003; Zuhairi, Wahyono, and Suratinah, 2006). Moreover, students may easily become distracted during online lessons, particularly if their cameras are off. In such cases, teachers might continue the lesson without noticing, leading to disengagement. Thus, active and conscious participation in the lesson is crucial. This issue is particularly pronounced in skill-oriented courses, where students may struggle to keep pace and encounter comprehension difficulties in applied subjects, as highlighted in this study.

Online Processing of Applied Courses

Amid the Covid-19 pandemic, a significant shift towards the adoption of distance education was witnessed, encompassing both theoretical and applied courses. The theoretical subjects had already found a place within the distance education framework, but the inclusion of practical courses presented unique challenges for both students and educators. While it's feasible to incorporate theoretical coursework into distance education, applied courses posed distinctive challenges (Sahu, 2020; Wang et al., 2020). It's evident that students encountered difficulties, especially in workshops, studios, laboratories, and computer-based courses within the distance education model (Kahraman, 2020). Various factors contributed to these challenges, including students quickly returning home from dormitories, internet connectivity issues, shared access to a single computer for online learning, location-specific internet problems, occasional technical glitches in the distance education systems, and the psychological strain stemming from the Covid-19 pandemic, which sometimes manifested as anxiety.

For students, participating in applied courses online can prove daunting. Those enrolled in technical courses, for instance, might hesitate to ask questions in an online environment, fearing they won't get a turn or that there won't be enough time for individualized attention. Additionally, effective engagement in video-based applied courses necessitates students possessing the requisite equipment, such as a camera for hands-on experience in lessons or a computer with the necessary software for editing courses. Interaction within online applied courses can also become a hurdle, given the variance in socio-economic resources among students.

Despite the challenges, applied courses also present unique advantages. Students enrolled in courses like editing techniques can leverage their own equipment to enhance learning by rewatching course materials repeatedly. Similarly, photography course students equipped with cameras and video applications can gain quicker mastery of subjects by experiencing them firsthand in their own environments. The asynchronous nature of online learning allows for increased flexibility, benefiting students who are juggling work and studies, enabling them to watch lessons at their own convenience after work. The assessment of the pros and cons of online education in applied courses largely hinges on an individual's work schedule, personal preferences, and available resources.

METHOD AND SAMPLING OF THE STUDY

This study explores the perceptions of students regarding the delivery of applied courses, both online and face-to-face, in the context of the Covid-19 pandemic. The sudden inclusion of practical courses, alongside theoretical ones, within the distance education system, a global norm until the pandemic's disruption, has uncovered various challenges. The research focuses on contrasting the experiences of students in applied online courses with those of their peers in traditional face-to-face courses.

Numerous resources, including articles, books, and papers, have examined online and distance education in Turkey. These investigations are particularly prevalent in faculties like Architecture, Visual Arts, Engineering, Medicine, and Communication, where applied courses are central. In this study, a specific emphasis is placed on the Editing Techniques course, delving into the experiences of students within the realm of an applied course.

The study involves a comparative analysis of the Istinye University's online Editing Techniques course for the academic year 2020-2021 and the face-to-face Editing Techniques course for the academic year 2021-2022, both of which are integral to the research. To obtain detailed insights and tangible information, in-depth interviews were conducted with ten students between the ages of 18-25 who had enrolled in the Editing Techniques course, addressing their experiences with both online and face-to-face instruction. The study aims to answer critical questions and gain valuable perspectives from these students regarding their encounters with the course in both educational formats.

Stages of Research:

i. Investigating the methods employed in online education for delivering applied courses.
ii. Conducting in-depth interviews with students enrolled in the Editing Techniques course, assessing their experiences in both online and face-to-face settings.

Table 1. Questions to ask students

1. Was the online editing course productive for you? Please Explain
2. What are the strengths and weaknesses of online and face-to-face editing courses? For example, what materials are used, body language, communication with the student, and eye contact?
3. With Covid-19, applied courses were also digitized, even in academic fields. So which one would you prefer as a student? Why?
4. In online lessons, has it been possible to get ahead of face-to-face classes while communicating with your friends and teachers during the lecture?

iii. Analyzing the interview findings to identify shared and distinctive perspectives.
iv. Drawing conclusions to inform the evolution of applied courses within the realm of online education.

The research employed an in-depth interview approach as the primary analysis method. In-depth interviewing entails conducting in-depth, individual interviews with a limited number of participants to gain insight and analyze their perspectives on a specific subject (Boyce et al., 2006; Gürkan, 2019). Open-ended questions were posed to ten students who had completed the Editing Techniques course in both online and face-to-face formats at İstinye University. This approach enabled the comparison of responses and facilitated the subsequent analysis of these comparisons. For the purpose of anonymity, participants are denoted as E1, E2, E3, and so forth.

The research focuses on the online delivery of applied courses and delves into the students' discussions of its advantages and disadvantages. The findings section of the study entails an analysis of the responses provided by the students during the in-depth interviews.

FINDINGS AND DISCUSSION

This study leveraged the in-depth interview research technique to assess the effectiveness of teaching applied courses to students during the Covid-19 pandemic. The distinct disparities between the in-depth interview approach and the applied Editing Techniques course in the pandemic and the same course conducted in a face-to-face setting have come to light.

The interviews uncovered the following key areas of discussion:

- The implementation of the distance education system in applied courses.
- The contrasting aspects between online education and traditional face-to-face instruction.
- Identifying the limitations of applied courses within online education.
- Proposing recommendations for the improvement of online applied courses.
-

How the Online Editing Techniques Course is Taught

The Editing Techniques course, a practical subject, swiftly transitioned to online education in response to the Covid-19 pandemic. The course content primarily delves into the theoretical underpinnings of editing while preparing students for practical applications. In subsequent weeks, the instructor shared their screen during class sessions to elucidate and demonstrate the stages of fiction construction. Students were familiarized with video editing, music incorporation, and generic creation in the software, with the expectation that they would follow the instructor's lead step by step. However, certain challenges arose during this process. E2 expressed their difficulties:

Our teacher concurrently covered both the theoretical and practical aspects of editing. Nevertheless, there were instances when demonstrating certain aspects online, instead of showcasing them physically, proved challenging for both the teacher and us. In the Editing Techniques course, I gained a better understanding of the theoretical aspect of editing rather than hands-on application.

E3 found the online Editing Techniques course to be less effective:

It proved to be an exceedingly unproductive course for me. My limited computer capabilities hindered my progress in the editing program course. Furthermore, struggling with inadequate internet connections while attempting to view the teacher's videos concurrently posed significant challenges. The most crucial aspect of the editing course was obtaining immediate answers to our queries, which proved impossible due to the congestion and internet issues. Consequently, this course was far from being a success.

E7 commented on the insufficiency of technical equipment for the online Editing Techniques course:

The course did not offer any benefits to me. I could have learned more by exploring tutorials on YouTube. To be honest, it felt pointless and unnecessary because I lacked a computer at home suitable for editing. Acquiring such a computer was cost-prohibitive for me.

E4 emphasized the lack of hands-on experience in the online Editing Techniques course:

While the course was practical, it felt predominantly theoretical to me. I failed to engage with it, as I found it challenging to grasp the concepts without practical application. We consistently viewed videos and discussed the 'what' and 'where' aspects, but I, as a student, struggled to understand without applying it myself. My participation was limited to observing the lessons.

The students, accustomed to hands-on practical courses within laboratory settings equipped with the requisite tools, encountered distinct challenges when transitioning to online education. The presented insights highlight the students' experiences and underscore that both students and teachers faced significant unpreparedness during the rapid transition to the online system.

Student and Teacher Communication in the Online Editing Techniques Course

Effective communication between students and instructors is a pivotal factor in the success of courses conducted within the distance education system. The absence of camera utilization by students during online classes can pose a disadvantage for instructors. Conversely, the comfort of students learning in their own environments, without the necessity of physical presence, can lead to disengagement from the lessons over time. Body language represents a critical component of communication; however, online courses limit its effectiveness for both students and instructors. E1 remarked:

Communication was more straightforward in face-to-face education. We could readily seek guidance and assistance from instructors while performing tasks under their supervision. The same ease of interaction was not replicated in online education. Occasionally, I hesitated to ask questions, and at other times, an influx of questions from other students left me with insufficient time. I do not favor exclusively online communication with instructors because it feels inadequate. Communicating via text messages or emails restricts the clarity of my queries.

E2 addressed the issue of adaptation during the online Editing Techniques course:

Throughout the online course, most instructors strived to maintain interaction. Nevertheless, it never replicated the sense of engagement present in face-to-face courses. During online lessons, once instructors commenced the session and shared their screen, they appeared as miniature icons in the corner. It was as if they were reduced to mere screens and audio, resulting in the loss of eye contact. Consequently, I often disengaged from the lesson unless something particularly captured my interest. As a result, I frequently exited the session without posing any questions.

E4 highlighted the importance of communication skills in the online Editing Techniques course:

Being physically present in a classroom surrounded by peers bolsters my communication and enables me to acclimate to the subject matter. In a face-to-face class, I can communicate more effectively with the instructor, as I can promptly ask questions. This dynamic differs significantly from online lessons. In these, the instructor provides explanations, and unless you document your questions, they may be forgotten. Furthermore, any discussion that arises during online classes can shift in different directions before you express your opinion. Consequently, I find it challenging to remain focused during class.

E8 accentuated the limited use of body language for online and face-to-face classes:

The most significant advantage of online courses lies in post-class accessibility, which allows students to revisit the content. Nonetheless, this convenience can backfire, as it may extend the learning process due to students' awareness that they can access the course at their leisure. In face-to-face education, classes are generally better attended, as the interactive environment often makes learning more enjoyable. This enhances class participation and imparts a firmer foundation for learning.

E7 discussed the issue of distraction during online Editing Techniques courses:

I become easily distracted in online classes. The absence of eye contact with the instructor and the inability to gauge my level of interest during class hinders my concentration. The monotony of online classes and the impression that I am being observed when turning on the camera dissuade me from utilizing this feature.

E9 tackled the subject of communication skills within the online Editing Techniques course:

Online courses are notably deficient in terms of student-teacher communication. Given the limitations of body language, troubleshooting issues proves challenging. Whether you cannot locate the instructor or you write messages that go unnoticed, the limitations of online interaction become apparent. During the lesson, the instructor may overlook messages, as they are preoccupied with delivering content. My experience of the online Fiction course left me unsatisfied.

Student feedback underscores that communication during the online Editing Techniques course was weaker compared to in-person instruction. Students often found themselves in the background of online lessons, while the virtual setting diminished the impact of eye contact, body language, and materials on the learning experience. Notably, the limitations associated with body language, eye contact, and general communication had significant repercussions on the students' overall learning experience.

Differences Between Online and Face-to-Face Editing Techniques Course

Incorporating applied courses into the distance education system proved to be more challenging than delivering theoretical courses. The abrupt transition of courses, originally designed for a laboratory environment equipped with essential tools, to the online sphere presented substantial difficulties for both instructors and students. The participating students shared their perspectives on the variances between online and face-to-face Editing Techniques courses. E1 emphasized:

In face-to-face courses, I could receive one-on-one assistance by directly consulting the instructor whenever I encountered difficulties with the software. This was unfeasible in the online course. Additionally, when I attended classes on campus, I could socialize with friends and experience the sense of studying in a university environment. However, during online classes, I would simply wake up at home and sit in front of the computer, which was far from an ideal situation for me, both psychologically and academically.

E2 elaborated on the limitations of online Editing Techniques courses:

In an online class, you watch the instructor deliver the content because most of my friends and I lack computers that allow us to listen to the lesson, run the program, and emulate the instructor's actions simultaneously. My equipment inadequacies restricted my participation, relegating me to the role of a passive observer. Even if I had access to a computer, keeping pace with the instructor proved daunting. The online Fiction course did not shine in this regard.

E10 highlighted the role of equipment and organization for online and face-to-face Editing Techniques courses:

Each student must address their internet connection, home environment, and other factors independently in the context of online education. However, this self-organization is not always possible. The classroom environment, by contrast, offers equal and interactive learning opportunities. The same applies to computers; it appears that the computers available at our homes often lack the necessary software for editing. Classroom settings offer a superior experience.

E9 echoed the constraints associated with equipment for the online Editing Techniques course:

When you possess a computer suitable for the editing program at home, you can pause the online lesson and review the instructor's actions. However, this was not the case for me and my friends. Our academic experience was far smoother when we utilized the school's computers in face-to-face lessons. We could readily interact with the instructor and address any queries.

E8 explored the dynamics of self-discipline for online and face-to-face Editing Techniques courses:

One of the primary advantages of online courses is the ability to access content post-class, which is beneficial. Nevertheless, this convenience can also become a drawback, as the absence of scheduled class times may prolong the learning process. In face-to-face education, the class typically garners full participation, owing to the interactive and enjoyable atmosphere. If students possess a genuine interest in the subject, they rarely miss classes, and learning is established on a solid foundation.

E7 delineated the positive and negative facets of online and face-to-face Editing Techniques courses:

The strength of online courses lies in the capacity to review content. You can revisit any challenging portions you did not grasp. However, beyond this advantage, online editing courses offer no further merits. Hands-on application is crucial, and online courses do not facilitate it. These courses must be conducted in person, in a laboratory environment. The sole advantage is the ability to revisit the content.

According to the participants' feedback, the preference for face-to-face education stemmed from the opportunities it offered for more direct interactions with the instructor. Online learning lacked these extensive interactions, leading students to favor in-person classes. Students voiced their preference for face-to-face courses, which allowed for a more social experience. Challenges related to equipment and accessibility further contributed to the divergence in student preferences. Students noted that classroom settings provided equal access to the necessary tools and materials.

Students' Perspective on Online Applied Courses

The final segment of the study delves into the students' perspectives on online applied courses. This aspect is highlighted since the students participating in the study experienced the Editing Techniques course in both face-to-face and online formats, with the majority expressing a distinct preference for face-to-face classes. The insights shared by students regarding online applied courses contribute to the comprehensive understanding of the subject. E3 expressed her views on online practical courses:

Online courses foster a sense of detachment from the educational institution. This situation is exacerbated when applied courses are conducted online, leading to a significant drop in the number of students who fully grasp the lesson. I struggle to maintain focus during online lessons. Communication with the instructor is hindered. Connectivity issues, sound disruptions, and difficulty understanding the instructor's responses are recurring problems. I do not feel as if I am part of the class during online sessions.

E5 affirmed that online education cannot surpass traditional face-to-face learning for online applied courses:

Online classes have never matched, nor can they surpass, the effectiveness of face-to-face lessons. My preference is unequivocally for face-to-face education, whether the subject is theoretical or practical. Face-to-face instruction excels in terms of body language, communication, eye contact, and the use of materials. These elements are significantly more potent in face-to-face education. Consequently, my perception of the subject matter is far sharper. Over time, I tend to drift away from the online course and struggle to grasp its content.

E6 emphasized the holistic role of universities and the significance of physical presence for applied courses:

A university experience extends beyond coursework. At a broader level, the transition of universities to the online realm presents significant issues. For many individuals, the university experience represents the culmination of their journey into adulthood and professional life. If students lack essential social skills and fail to develop interpersonal communication, it could result in a deficit for their generation. Online versions of applied courses do not yield any tangible benefits, based on my personal experiences.

E7 pointed out the socialization aspect of online practical courses:

In my view, communication in online classes consistently falls short. Authenticity diminishes. At times, I merely ran the online course in the background, and any assignments from the instructor were postponed for post-class discussions. Online education not only impacts the quality of instruction but also hinders communication. Despite studying alongside peers for a year, there were classmates with whom I had no interaction. This absence of connection is disconcerting. I firmly believe in the indispensability of face-to-face education. Online education represents a loss for us, particularly in a department such as Cinema.

E10 highlighted the challenge of adaptation during online practical courses:

Online classes do not capture the essence of studying. My focus wanes, and it feels more like watching an educational video rather than engaging in university-level study. Particularly in the case of practical courses, my computer is inadequate for participating effectively, prompting me to ultimately abandon the course. I long to experience the university spirit, which online education fails to provide. Socializing with friends becomes an impossible feat. How can one build meaningful connections from a distance? Over time, I become disengaged and perceive the experience as isolating.

Student perspectives on online applied courses underscore the difficulties related to financial constraints, communication challenges, and a diminished sense of belonging to the university community. Moreover, universities are more than mere classrooms; they represent a space for holistic development and socialization. In the online setting, the absence of physical interaction precludes this essential aspect of the university experience.

CONCLUSION

The Covid-19 pandemic, which has instigated profound global changes, has significantly reshaped the education sector, necessitating a swift transition to distance education. This transformation encompasses all courses, including practical ones that are traditionally conducted in a physical setting with specialized equipment. Given the inherent challenges in migrating applied courses to the online realm, this study undertakes in-depth interviews with students who have experienced both online and face-to-face sessions of an applied course, namely editing techniques. The research aims to investigate how applied courses are delivered in the online context, assess student perceptions, and explore their preferences between online and face-to-face learning.

Several common issues related to online applied courses have surfaced among the students, which are highlighted in the following sections:

- Communication difficulties
- Challenges in grasping course content and susceptibility to distractions
- Limited opportunities for social interaction
- Shortages of essential materials (computers, internet access, etc.)
- Disruptions in the teacher-student relationship
- An absence of a sense of belonging

The study offers valuable insights into the challenges faced within the online education system for applied courses. It underscores the significance of conducting further research to enhance and refine online applied courses and devise solutions for the identified issues. Additionally, it is important to recognize that different results may emerge from studies involving students across varying age groups and educational levels. The findings are based on analyses of students from a specific university within a particular age range, and these results may differ in other contexts.

To address the concerns raised by students, it is crucial to improve communication within online courses. Drawing from the outcomes of the in-depth interviews, initiatives that foster a sense of belonging and online socialization should be considered. Moreover, the lack of access to essential materials, which affects students disparately, should be tackled through temporary solutions, such as providing equipment from schools.

It is essential to avoid making sweeping negative judgments about online education based on these challenges, as they largely stem from the sudden onset of the Covid-19 pandemic and the unpreparedness for the shift to distance learning. Online education, particularly for theoretical courses, presents a viable solution for reducing overcrowding and reaching a broader student demographic. This educational model also offers potential for further development and enhancement in the context of applied courses.

REFERENCES

Abdalla, J. (2020). *US universities switch to online courses due to coronavirus*. https://www.aljazeera.com/news/2020/03/universities-switch-online-courses-due-coronavirus200310202804023.html

Angoletto, R., & Queiroz, V. C. (2020). COVID-19 and the challenges in education. *The Centro de Estudos Sociedade e Tecnologia*, *5*, 2.

Balcı, A. (2020). The Effects of Pandemics on Education, with a Focus on COVID-19. *International Journal of Leadership Studies. Theory into Practice*, *3*(3), 75–85.

Başar, M., Arslan, S., Günsel, E., & Akpınar, M. (2019). Öğretmen adaylarının uzaktan eğitim algısı. *Journal of Multidisciplinary Studies in Education*, *3*(2), 14–22.

Bıyıklı, C., & Özgür, A. O. (2021). Teachers solution suggestions for the problems experienced in the synchronous distance education process during the Covid – 19 pandemic. *Journal of Open Education Applications and Research*, *7*(1), 110–147.

Boyce, C., & Neale, P. (2006). *Conducting In-Depth Interviews: A Guide for Designing and Conducting In-Depth-Interviews for Evaluation Input*. Watertown: Pathfinder International.

Bozkurt, A. (2020). Koronavirüs (Covid-19) Pandemi süreci ve pandemi sonrası dünyada eğitime yönelik değerlendirmeler: Yeni normal ve yeni eğitim paradigması. *Açıköğretim Uygulamaları ve Araştırmaları Dergisi*, *6*(3), 112–142.

Bozkurt, A., & Sharma, R. C. (2020). Emergency remote teaching in a time of global crisis due to CoronaVirus pandemic. *Asian Journal of Distance Education*, *15*(1), i–vi. doi:10.5281/zenodo.3778083

Can, E. (2020). Korona virüs (Covid-19) pandemisi ve pedagojik yansımaları: Türkiye'de açık ve uzaktan eğitim uygulamaları. *Journal of Open Education Applications and Research*, *6*(2), 11–53.

de Paepe, L., Zhu, C., & DePryck, K. (2018). Drop-out, retention, satisfaction and attainment of online learners of Dutch in adult education. *International Journal on E-Learning*, *17*(3), 303–323.

Demiray, U., & Ve İşman, A. (2003). *History of distance education. Online Distance Book*. Tojet.

Doğan, A., & Paydar, S. (2019). Öğretmen adaylarının açık ve uzaktan öğrenme ortamlarına yönelik görüşleri. *Educational Technology*, *1*(2), 154–162.

Duman, S. N. (2020). Salgın döneminde gerçekleştirilen uzatktan eğitim sürecinin değerlendirimesi. *Milli Eğitim C.*, *49*(1), 95–112. doi:10.37669/milliegitim.768887

Eken, Ö., Tosun, N., & Eken, D. T. (2020). Urgent and compulsory move to distance education upon covid-19: A general evaluation. *The Journal of National Education*, *49*(1), 113–128.

Erfidan, A. (2019). *Derslerin uzaktan eğitim yoluyla verilmesiyle ilgili öğretim elemanı ve öğrenci görüşleri: Balıkesir Üniversitesi örneği*. Balıkesir Üniversitesi, Fen Bilimleri Enstitüsü.

Gewin, V. (2020). COVID-19 bekletilirken öğretimi çevrimiçi taşımak için beş ipucu. *Doga*, *580*, 295–296.

Gürkan, H. (2019). The Experiences of Women Professionals in the Film Industry in Turkey: A Gender Based Study. *Acta Universitatis Sapientia-Film and Media Studies Journal*, *16*(1), 205–219. doi:10.2478/ausfm-2019-0011

Horspool, A., & Lange, C. (2012). Applying the scholarship of teaching and learning: Student perceptions, behaviours and success online and face-to-face. *Assessment & Evaluation in Higher Education*, *37*(1), 73–88. doi:10.1080/02602938.2010.496532

Kahraman, M., E., (2020). COVID-19 Salgınının Uygulamalı Derslere Etkisi ve Bu Derslerin Uzaktan Eğitimle Yürütülmesi: Temel Tasarım Dersi Örneği. *İMÜ Sanat Tasarım ve Mimarlık Fakültesi Dergisi*, *6*(1), 44-56.

Kırık, M. A. (2014). Uzaktan eğitimin tarihsel gelişimi ve Türkiye'deki durumu. *Marmara University Journal of Communication*, (21), 84.

Lau, J., Yang, B., & Dasgupta, R. (2020). Will the coronavirus make online education go viral. *Times Higher Education*. https://www.timeshighereducation.com/features/will-coronavirus-make-online-educationgo-viral

Lei, S. A., & Gupta, R. K. (2010). College Distance Education Courses: Evaluating Benefits and Costs from Institutional. *Faculty and Students' Perspectives. Education, 130*(4), 616-631.

Miles, M. B., & Huberman, A. M. (1994). Qualitative data analysis: An expanded sourcebook. *Sage (Atlanta, Ga.)*.

Özdoğan, A. Ç., & Berkant, H. G. (2020). Covıd-19 pandemi dönemindeki uzaktan eğitime ilişkin paydaş görüşlerinin incelenmesi. *Milli Eğitim Dergisi*, *49*(1), 13–43. doi:10.37669/milliegitim.788118

Sahu, P. (2020). Closure of universities due to coronavirus disease 2019 (COVID-19): Impact on education and mental health of students and academic staff. *Cureus*, *2019*(4), 4–9. doi:10.7759/cureus.7541 PMID:32377489

Valentine, D. (2002). Distance learning: Promise, problems, and possibilities. *Online Journal of Distance Learning Administration*, *5*(3).

Venter, K. (2003). Coping with isolation: The role of culture in adult distance learners' use of surrogates. *Open Learning*, *18*(3), 271–287. doi:10.1080/0268051032000131035

Wang, C., Cheng, Z., Yue, X.-G., & McAleer, M. (2020). Risk Management of COVID-19 by universities in China. *Journal of Risk and Financial Management*, *13*(2), 36. doi:10.3390/jrfm13020036

Yenal, A. Ç. (2009). *Uzaktan Eğitim*. Yayınlanmış Yüksek Lisans Tezi, Yeditepe Üniversitesi Sosyal Bilimler Enstitüsü.

Zhong, R. (2020). *The Coronavirus exposes education's digital divide*. https://www.nytimes.com/2020/03/17/technology/china-schools-coronavirus.html

Zuhairi, A., Wahyono, E., & Suratinah, S. (2006). The historical context, current development, and future challenges of distance education in Indonesia. *Quarterly Review of Distance Education*, *7*(1), 95–101.

Chapter 10
Navigating COVID–19:
How the Portuguese Health Authority Managed Social Media

Branco Di Fátima
University of Beira Interior, Portugal

Francisco Garcia
https://orcid.org/0000-0002-9195-6627
ISCTE, University Institute of Lisbon, Portugal

Ana Barros
Portuguese Society of Pneumology, Portugal

Rita Espanha
ISCTE, University Institute of Lisbon, Portugal

Daniel Brandão
https://orcid.org/0000-0001-6331-0354
University of Minho, Portugal

Nuno Martins
https://orcid.org/0000-0002-5228-5453
Research Institute for Design, Media, and Culture, Polytechnic of Cavado and Ave, Portugal

ABSTRACT

This chapter examines the activities of the official Instagram and Facebook pages of the Directorate-General for Health (DGS) in Portugal during the most critical period of the COVID-19 pandemic in the country. Data were collected using social media APIs via CrowdTangle, resulting in 1,841 public posts spanning from March 2, 2020 to December 27, 2020. This period covered the onset of the pandemic and the launch of the national vaccination program. Social media platforms played a crucial role during the COVID-19 pandemic. The key findings reveal Facebook had twice as many posts (n = 120) compared to Instagram (n = 64). April saw the highest post volume on Facebook (13.4%), while June was the most active month on Instagram (14.3%). Images were the dominant content format on both platforms, with 70.7% on Instagram and 80.5% on Facebook. Facebook experienced significant growth (497.0%) over 10 months while Instagram's growth was more modest (207.0%).

DOI: 10.4018/979-8-3693-0896-7.ch010

INTRODUCTION

During the Covid-19 pandemic, governments and health authorities worldwide confronted the singular challenge of effectively conveying the health risks associated with a lethal menace. This juncture undeniably marked a pivotal moment in modern human history, with its repercussions continuing to reverberate. Social media platforms assumed a pivotal role in the dissemination of information to the public, encompassing guidance on protective measures against the virus and utilitarian data pertaining to the national pandemic status. Furthermore, they wielded substantial influence over citizens' risk perceptions and satisfaction levels, all the while facilitating the swift exchange of information between experts and the general people.

This chapter delves into the initiatives undertaken by Portugal's Directorate-General for Health (DGS) in disseminating health-related information, especially on prominent social media platforms such as Facebook and Instagram, amidst the peak of the Covid-19 crisis. The extraction of data was automated through the utilization of the Application Programming Interface (API) provided by these social media platforms, with support from CrowdTangle. These messages were subsequently archived in CSV files and subjected to comprehensive analysis via the Voyant Tools software.

The sample has 1,841 public posts, covering a ten-month period from March 2, 2020, to December 27, 2020. These messages are distributed across two social media platforms: Instagram (n = 642) and Facebook (n = 1,199). This specific timeframe coincided with the most tumultuous phase of the pandemic within the country, encapsulating both the onset of the first reported Covid-19 case and the launch of the national vaccination program. By adopting this method approach, this research was able to yield valuable insights into the communication strategies employed by the DGS and the characteristics of their social media audiences.

Health Information on Social Media

Since the beginning of the pandemic, governments and health authorities on a global scale have dealt with a unique situation requiring effective communication on health risks. Similarly, to its counterparts, the Portuguese government and health authorities were forced to rapidly implement and develop the existing communication channels.

The present analysis will consider the main entity responsible for communicating health matters/information to the Portuguese population through social media (Facebook and Instagram), more specifically it is focused on the action of DGS during the Covid-19 crisis. Not only is this entity considered to be on the frontline against the pandemic, but because it is also a relevant source of guidance and clarification for citizens about their potential health issues and fears.

To contextualize, the first cases of Covid-19 infection were confirmed in Portugal on the 2nd of march, 2020, and the first death was registered on the 16th of the same month, roughly two weeks later. Henceforth, both the Directorate General of Health (DGS) and the National Authority of Medicines and Health Products, I.P. (INFARMED), applied a series of health measures, norms, and orientations for the management of the pandemic kick off. On 27th of December 2020, the first set of vaccines against Covid-19 (Comirnaty®; BioNTech Manufacturing GmbH/Pfizer) was authorized and administered by the Portuguese Government firstly at Centro Hospital Universitário de São João (Oporto), thus marking the beginning of the vaccination task force on a national scale.

Gonçalves et al. (2021) argue that there are to opposite positions concerning the Portuguese Government's communication during the Covid-19 pandemic: on one hand, there are those who consider that this communication was conveyed accordingly with the right timings and that it was trustworthy. On the other hand, even people who are categorised as "more critical" about the Government's communication are prone to trust the authorities, and non-governmental entities such as the DGS.

Moreover, the authors add that the Portuguese people revealed higher trust levels towards medical experts and other prestigious health field personalities, namely, medical doctors, epidemiologists, or the director of the WHO. These sources are considered to be more reliable when compared to media outlets and government authorities, not only on a national, but also on a regional level.

In retrospection, the Covid-19 pandemic created a synergy between scientific experts (more specifically, those who worked in the health sector) and journalism/media outlets. Be that as it may, decision-makers often contributed to the state of entropy by not communicating decisions properly, namely, through the adoption of different strategies, imposing severe lockdowns, and other restrictive measures, that made the pandemic harder to manage – mostly due to the lack of technological knowledge and the cooperation/coordination gap between the government, stakeholders, health authorities and field experts.

About the Portuguese context, Lopes et al. (2021) explain that the prime minister, António Costa, played a leading role in the news texts about Covid-19, consistently outranking the president of the Portuguese Republic, Marcelo Rebelo de Sousa, in what concerns media visibility. Although, when it comes to communicating major decisions that alter the social dynamics, the authors reiterate that the prime minister took on this endeavour himself, thus excluding other prominent figures from the mediatic stage.

Hence, Espanha (2020a) alerts about the fact that the Portuguese health authorities tend to have a generic and disperse approach, and somehow ineffective in conveying health messages to the public. Also, that daily press conferences, have progressively lost their traction, become more and more inconstant, reckless, and political agenda driven.

The author contends that throughout the pandemic, the way the Portuguese Government worked alongside with the news media to distribute health information wasn't always as effective as it was expected to be by the authorities. Mostly because such information doesn't always reach every segment of the population equally, and because, frequently, it doesn't satiate people's needs.

Espanha (2020b) states that health communication and information technology go hand in hand, and are crucial for the provision of healthcare, to public health, and to the way society understands health. These processes are part of the types and contexts in which health professionals and audiences look for, comprehend, and utilize health information, therefore significantly impacting their decision-making and actions concerning health.

Lastly, the author underlines the importance of envisioning and achieving a more autonomous relationship between a society and its healthcare system, namely, a situation where citizens can find and use both information and knowledge in their favour, but also interact with other citizens (specialists, or not) and produce information based in experience. In this context, it is through and because of media that citizens establish and acquire experience in the health field.

In fact, Sørensen et al. (2021) states that the way health literacy is being approached nowadays, even though it has a clear focus on organizational and individual change, is not sufficient. The authors point out that health literacy challenges are somewhat complex and often characterize the structural mismatch between engaged institutions, their context of action/work, and the needs they intend to facilitate.

More importantly, in the authors' perspective, to build a better equipped systems it is mandatory to give recognition to the untapped potential of elements such as health literacy, as an asset to overcome potential failures in the systems. What's more, the authors strongly affirm that a reenforced health literacy system capacity prevents system failure by guaranteeing a stronger link between the organizations, the context where they provide their services, and the needs they meet by addressing and enhancing the capacity of the workforce, organizational structures, data governance, financial resources, partnerships, leadership, technology, and innovation as well as people-centred services and environments based on user engagement.

Sepulveda & Espanha (2022) explain that online social media strategies have progressively been adopted by state-owned agencies as a form of public communication, and such is the case of the Portuguese National Health Service (NHS) official Instagram page. The authors explain that, through this platform, during the Covid-19 pandemic, the NHS has had a prolific activity through the publication of visually appealing health messages, namely, these could either be informative, focused on awareness-raising, or prevention-related.

Moreover, the followers of this page have shown to be inclined to interact more with content related to commemorative and/or symbolic dates, institutional publications, and healthcare themes. The authors also refer that, on one hand, the number of publications increased significantly in the years 2020 and 2021 (primarily having doubled its numbers and then quadrupled them on the second year), and, on the other hand, that the interaction with publications had a large increment both in 2020 and in 2021.

In this context, Kim et al. (2023) suggest that Digital Health Literacy (DHL) is a unique concept and competency within the changing social and economic contexts, stating that it's necessary that individuals explore health-related information through the use of digital technologies. The authors strongly advise that, in order to nurture Digital Health Literacy, governmental entities must invest in educational programs for adult populations and for preparing healthcare professionals and the general workforce to have the ability to critically use electronic health information proficiently, especially during pandemics such as the Covid-19.

In accordance, Malecki et al. (2021) consider social media to have an elementary role in the act of informing audiences during periods of crisis and emergencies. On one hand, the authors underline that, more than ever, social media has influenced the audiences' levels of risk perception and sense of dissatisfaction, and, on the other hand, that social media allow that both specialists and audiences can rapidly share information with many of their acquaintances – from the authors' perspective, the latter might also be considered both a blessing and a barrier for the creation and implementation of effective health risk communication strategies.

Nutbeam (2021) states that the advent of digital media has enabled unprecedented access to health information, but simultaneously brought along new challenges and opportunities. Therefore, the author stresses that digital health literacy skills such as managing the volume of information and assessing its quality and reliability are becoming more relevant than ever. In the author's perspective it is not only a matter of understanding the opportunities and challenges, but it is also a chance to reshape the role of health education in exposing the social determinants of health, advocating for policy change, and supporting the development of communities.

During the pandemic, both DGS and the Portuguese Government attained a high level of media coverage, with emphasis on the joint daily press conferences, broadcasted live and simultaneously by the main media and online media. These press conferences usually involved a high figure of the Portuguese Government (Minister of Health or Secretary of State) and the Director of the DGS.

According to Silva et al. (2022), during the first wave of the pandemic, DGS used its Twitter page to publish small and merely informative messages. Whereas throughout this period the entity has shown great improvement by developing and adapting new communication strategies, presenting more detailed content, namely, asserting its brand image on social media.

Moreover, DGS social media was a privileged communication channel for disseminating information about Covid-19. Hence, DGS presents itself as an entity endowed with administrative autonomy and which ensures that the information coming from the World Health Organization (WHO) reaches the Portuguese public, having been progressively, yet gradually, active on Facebook, the social media where the DGS amounts the largest number of followers, approximately 830,000 (eight times more than Twitter, 11 times more than Instagram and 55 times more than YouTube).

Retrospectively, on one hand, the public health crisis resulting from the Covid-19 pandemic presented a set of new challenges to the Portuguese society, as well as on a global scale. On the other hand, health systems were forced to respond quickly and promptly to the doubts, fears, and questions of the populations regarding the progression of the disease caused by the coronavirus.

Due to the increase of confirmed cases and the beginning of the forced confinement process, the Portuguese health authorities started to use social media as one of their main means of communication. Hence, Cheng & Espanha (2021) explain that it is through social media that audiences increasingly obtain, generate and exchange information about health and, particularly, about Covid-19.

In the case of the Directorate-General for Health (DGS), although it assumed a high level of media coverage in the traditional media (television, radio), through daily press conferences broadcasted live, the present study concluded that the entity invested strongly in communicating through its official social media pages.

Moreover, in this context, the relevance of health literacy and the need to increase its levels in the Portuguese society is emphasised, particularly in the segments of the population that have lower literacy indexes, according to reports (for example: ILS-PT, 2016) and more recent studies (for example: Arriaga et al., 2022) on literacy in Portuguese society. In addition, social media platforms are becoming essential tools to give both emotional support and provide social welfare to people. Hence, the outreach of these health messages conveyed through social media depend on elements such as their tone and content (Bowles, Larreguy, & Liu, 2020; Manganello, 2020).

Constant exposure to media messages shapes the way audiences perceive social reality, more specifically, the amount of time spent consuming media messages influence how one might align their world views with the portrayals of reality made by the media outlets. During the Covid-19 pandemic, social media played a crucial role in the act of communicating and informing the broader public about health developments such as the creation of vaccines against Covid-19. Notwithstanding its positive effect on people's health knowledge, social media was also partly responsible for the infodemic that accentuated vaccine hesitancy through the circulation of conspiracy theories, misleading facts, and rumours.

Xin et al. (2022) argue that regular exposure to positive information on social media about vaccine efficacy and safety is related to increased Covid-19 vaccination intention, and that higher net exposure to negative information was associated with decreased vaccination intention. Moreover, the authors underline that media literacy helped to contradicting the effects of the potential exposure to negative information, and simultaneously strengthened the effect of positive information on individuals.

About the positive impact that social media can have on people's lives, Wu et al. (2020) believe that social media platforms can work as a new channel to improve health outcomes. The authors refer that patients' communication with medical doctors on social media can produce positive effects, namely, through interactions such as: following, favouring, and responding to doctors' posts, and recommending doctors to others – such acts are considered by the authors to be associated with patients' health outcomes including e-Health literacy and healthy behaviours. Finally, the authors suggest that leveraging information technology to promote health outcomes is becoming an extremely beneficial tool for both health providers and health policymakers.

Xue & Taylor (2022) state that individuals produce and distribute health information on social media in real-time, with a certain degree of anonymity and, more importantly, without information gatekeepers, therefore, vaccine rumours on social media can endanger public health significantly.

It is relevant to stress that this study revealed that:

1) Rumours with anecdotal statistics were perceived by certain individuals as more relevant than rumours with anecdotes;
2) Evidence types tend to affect perceived persuasiveness and the intentions to seek information and share indirectly through perceived relevance – thus revealing a preference for statistical evidence beyond objective statistics to contexts in which information veracity is low;
3) Anecdotal statistics are more likely to be shared by individuals when vaccine rumours are pro-attitudinal, namely, when pro-vaccine individuals read pro-vaccine rumours;
4) Null effects were more prevalent when vaccine rumours were counter-attitudinal and when anti-vaccine participants read anti-vaccine rumours.

Finally, the authors reiterate that a clear negative relationship is established between objective vaccine knowledge and perceived relevance and intentions to share and seek information. Therefore, health communication professionals play an important role in the monitoring of viral information, especially that which involves anecdotal statistics, in order to stop it from reaching larger audiences.

Contrarily, Schub et al. (2022) argue that the launch of vaccination campaigns through social media can be very effective with audiences, since they require minimal equipment (e.g., smartphone or laptop computer) and minimal technological expertise, which allow content to be viewed, amplified, and engaged with, both on a national and international level. Moreover, the authors underline that even during times of political division and growing misinformation, controversial topics can be addressed in a non-judgemental and celebratory tone, envisioning a relationship based in trust and authenticity with individuals and communities that feel hesitant towards vaccination.

In this case, Schub et al. (2022) state that storytelling driven campaigns can help promote single-event behaviour change, more specifically, a vaccine uptake, through influencing, shaping, and changing people's attitudes – transportation and identification are elements that allow narrative storytelling to influence and facilitate behaviour change, especially when the conveyed message is culturally relevant to the audience.

Storytelling can also play a vital role in countering hate speech that proliferates on social media and is exacerbated by misinformation during significant social crises, such as a pandemic (Fan, Yu, & Gilliland, 2023; Bek, 2023). One example of this is the hatred directed towards scientists and doctors, which has been observed in numerous countries. In this context, the main objective would be to reshape the community values that are voiced online, as they can infiltrate the offline world and potentially impede trust in vaccination.

Similarly, the study conducted by Chesser et al. (2020) confirmed the importance of increased public health information through trusted information channels and sources. What's more, the study revealed that in populations, such as university students, the belief that public health experts versus government entities will create solutions to the Covid-19 pandemic could become a widespread belief in communities and could affect future communication strategies and messaging.

The authors stress that communities, not only, must continue reinforcing where their members can consume reliable health information, but also supporting and/or reaching out to local news media with public health messages aimed at increasing Covid-19 knowledge and disease prevention strategies. Lastly, this study shows that most respondents have said that they can prevent being infected, therefore the authors recommend that additional content about signs, symptoms, and prevention strategies for Covid-19 should perpetually be shared through community social media accounts and new partners.

Choukou et al. (2022) identified three types of needs related to Covid-19 in vulnerable populations: informational, transformational, and adaptive. Firstly, the informational need was characterized as a need to increase public awareness of health literacy in different disease conditions. Despite being widely available, health-related information is not always accessible to everyone, particularly to vulnerable populations. Secondly, the transformational needs which included increasing digital knowledge and skills required to use any digital health literacy enabling e-service, decreasing health literacy barriers, and increasing technology acceptance among specific target groups. Lastly, the adaptive needs which were reflected in the methods of delivering healthcare amid the pandemic situation, including relevant adjustments supported by digital means.

Furthermore, Abonizio et al. (2023) state that the use of chatbot technologies can help to resolve a wide variety of citizens' doubts about subjects such as Covid-19 and acting as a cost-effective tool against fake news and misinformation related to Covid-19. The authors present the case of CoronaAI chatbot in Brazil, through which users could access and search for valuable and updated information about Covid-19, including checking the veracity of potential fake news about the spread of cases, symptoms, death counts, protocols, tests, among other themes.

This investigation also revealed that users' behaviour towards the chatbot changed accordingly with the increasing death toll and the growing need for information applicable to self-care. Additionally, users showed that the constant updating of the chatbot technology might have contributed to the broader public health through the enhancement and provision of general information on the pandemic and clarification of potential doubts about Covid-19. In conclusion, the authors state that the maintenance and constant updating of a machine learning tool made available on a widely used platform such as WhatsApp can potentially generate public health benefits to its users.

Regarding YouTube, for example, Gentile et al. (2023) point out that this platform is the second most popular social media in the world. After criticism regarding the quality control during the pandemic, YouTube incorporated banners on its videos with the purpose of directing viewers to official health/Covid-19 information providers. Even though YouTube has implemented policies to combat misinformation related to Covid-19, the authors argue that there is a significant variation concerning the quality and reliability of the videos available on the platform. Also, that viewers should have caution when consuming content produced by non-medical users, especially those that originate from non-scientific sources such as Internet media and news agencies. More importantly, the authors argue that public health institutions and professionals should take advantage of popular social media platforms such as Facebook and Instagram to stimulate and promote accurate and reliable information about different health topics, such as vaccination.

DATA AND METHODS

This research analyzes the communication strategy employed by the Directorate-General for Health (DGS), as well as the practices of the users, on its official Instagram and Facebook pages in the context of the pandemic in Portugal. The methodology employed is rooted in a quantitative framework for knowledge production, utilizing social network analysis (SNA). This approach allows us to work with social data that reveals the practices of organisations and users on these platforms, and not just a representation of their online behaviour.

Facebook and Instagram were chosen for several strategic reasons. Firstly, when excluding instant messaging and open video platforms, these two social media platforms are the most widely used among the Portuguese population and have a significant influence on information consumption (OberCom, 2023). Furthermore, these platforms allowed us to observe how the communication team of the Directorate-General of Health (DGS) operated on a platform with prior experience (Facebook) and how they adapted to a new media system during the pandemic (Instagram). Finally, these platforms attract diverse audiences across the country, enabling us to analyze their online behavior using official data – it is not possible on other social media. Facebook is primarily used by older individuals, while Instagram is predominantly popular among the younger demographic. Through this methodological approach, the research has provided valuable insights into the communication strategies employed by the DGS and the characteristics of a broader social media audience.

The data extraction process was automated using the Instagram and Facebook Graph API, following the parameters established by CrowdTangle, a tool developed by Meta company. This tool was precisely configured within the Search and Intelligence analysis modules. The extracted data encompasses a broad spectrum of information, including DGS publications, posting dates, message URL addresses, page and post IDs, as well as the quantity and nature of user interactions (such as likes, shares, and comments), and more. By employing this approach, this research gained valuable insights into the communication practices of DGS and the characteristics of their audiences on social media.

The sample consists of 1,841 public posts, particularly those accessible to the entire community following the pages. This time frame includes publications made over a period of ten months, starting from March 2, 2020 (the date of Portugal's first confirmed Covid-19 case) and ending on December 27, 2020 (the star of the national vaccination program). These messages, comprising 642 from Instagram and 1,199 from Facebook, have been saved in CSV files and subsequently analyzed using the open-source software Voyant Tools.

Given the nature of this work, several ethical issues are being addressed. The data has been collected and processed in an aggregated format, following the guidelines of the *General Data Protection Regulation* (2016/679) currently enforced within the European Union. These databases are securely stored in a protected Google Drive folder, with access restricted solely to the individuals responsible for this research. If necessary, this dataset can undergo an irreversible anonymization process to ensure the safeguarding of sensitive or personal information.

MAIN RESULTS

The Directorate-General for Health (DGS) published a total of 1,841 public posts on its official Instagram (n = 642) and Facebook (n = 1,199) pages between March 2 and December 27, 2020. This time frame

Table 1. Post formats on Instagram and Facebook (n = 1,841)

	Instagram (n = 642)		Facebook (n = 1,199)	
	n =	%	n =	%
Image	454	70.7	966	80.5
Video	47	7.3	186	15.5
Album	141	22.0	-	-
Link	-	-	42	3.5
Status	-	-	5	0.4
TOTAL	642	100.0	1,199	100.0

Source: CrowdTangle

encapsulates the most critical period of the Covid-19 pandemic in Portugal, spanning from the confirmation of the first case in the country to the beginning of the national vaccination program. In terms of frequency per month, Facebook exhibited twice the number of publications (n = 120) compared to Instagram (n = 64), underscoring the platform's significance in the country. In fact, Facebook remains the platform boasting the highest number of registered Portuguese users.

April witnessed the highest volume of posts on Facebook (13.4% of its total sample), while June emerged as the most active month on Instagram (14.3%). Table 1 presents the distribution of all posts based on DGS's preferred format (image, video, link, album, etc). The data reveals that, as a general trend, one particular category tends to encompass the highest volume of content. Several factors can contribute to this phenomenon, including the proficiency of the teams responsible for platform management and the importance attributed to the audience.

According to data from DGS, the image emerges as the most widely shared content format on both Instagram (70.7%) and Facebook (80.5%). This official data implies that identical images may have been posted on both platforms indiscriminately. An illustrative example is the table that presents the total count of individuals affected by, recovered from, and succumbed to Covid-19 in the country. This message conveys the following on both platforms: "The situation report for today, October 24th, is now accessible and can be viewed in its entirety at [link to DGS website]". The prevalence of such graphic content may suggest a dearth of diversity in storytelling from the DGS communications office across these platforms, without recognizing the diverse sociodemographic characteristics of their audiences.

Table 1 highlights the significance of audiovisual in health risk communication in Portugal. Videos hold the second place in content preferences on Facebook (5.5%). However, on Instagram, albums (photos, videos) take the lead with a substantial 22.0%. These dynamic visual elements encompass a wide range, including lives, content from YouTube, and videos created directly on the platform. Conversely, links (3.5%) and status updates (0.4%) have a comparatively lesser impact. On Instagram, video represents 7.3% of the total, also indicating a slightly smaller influence.

This combination of messages – including photos, videos, albums, links, and more – may have contributed to the increase in the audience during the initial months of the pandemic in Portugal. Facebook recorded a 497.0% growth over ten months, going from 110,972 followers in March to 662,699 in December, 2020. Instagram had a smaller growth of 207.0%, increasing from 5,906 to 18,143 followers – it is important to highlight that the DGS account on the platform only presents data from end of April and, naturally, it underwent a hard process of gaining followers.

Figure 1. Post on Instagram and Facebook over time (n = 1,841) (CrowdTangle)

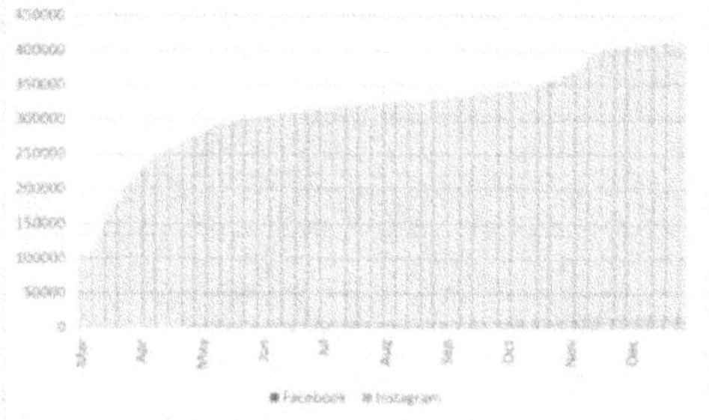

In any case, these social media platforms have emerged as crucial hubs for disseminating official pandemic-related information within the country. They also serve as a virtual gathering place for the Portuguese community, whether individuals seek utilitarian information or a sense of belonging to a larger collective. Nonetheless, while this data underscores the significance of online posts and the sense of connection during this profound crisis, certain moments hold greater importance and wield more significant impact from the users' standpoint.

Figure 1 shows the peaks in follower growth across DGS platforms during the ten-month period under examination. The Facebook page shows the most significant cumulative growth over time, as depicted by the prominent blue lines, in contrast to Instagram (where the orange lines are nearly imperceptible). This trend raises the need for further research, as several factors may have influenced or reinforced this phenomenon. One plausible explanation is the potential interest of an older demographic in seeking information on social media platforms, particularly given the older user profile associated with Facebook. On the other hand, it's worth considering that the delayed establishment of the DGS's Instagram page might have contributed to these results – while the page did not experience significant growth during its initial stages.

Despite the consistent growth in pages activity and DGS's ability to maintain its follower base throughout the 43-week duration of this study, there was a gradual decline in the average rate of acquiring new followers over time. The most significant surge in Facebook followers occurred during the week of March 8 to 14, with an impressive increase of 43,772 followers. In contrast, Instagram experienced its peak week of follower growth from November 8 to 14, resulting in a gain of 1,400 followers. As the initial surge of interest in pandemic-related content diminished, coinciding with the launch of the national vaccine program, it appears that overall engagement with this topic on social media has also dwindled. Alternatively, it can be noted that DGS pages began to attract a substantially smaller audience of new followers.

As the months went by, a "new normal" would be established in the country and around the world. However, events on the ground influenced behavior on social media, emphasizing the emotional impact of the high number of virus-related deaths. DGS social media received just over 3.6 million interactions during the ten months of this study. Facebook is responsible for the vast majority of this online activity (98.3%) compared to Instagram (1.7%). Again, the results may be associated with both the sociodemocratic characteristics of the audience and the entity's own activities on the platforms.

On Instagram, the most common practice among users is to leave a like on a post (98.7%), far surpassing comments (1.3%). On Facebook, the most prevalent practice is also to leave a like (53.8%), fol-

Figure 2. Engagement rate on Instagram and Facebook (n = 3.6 million) (CrowdTangle)

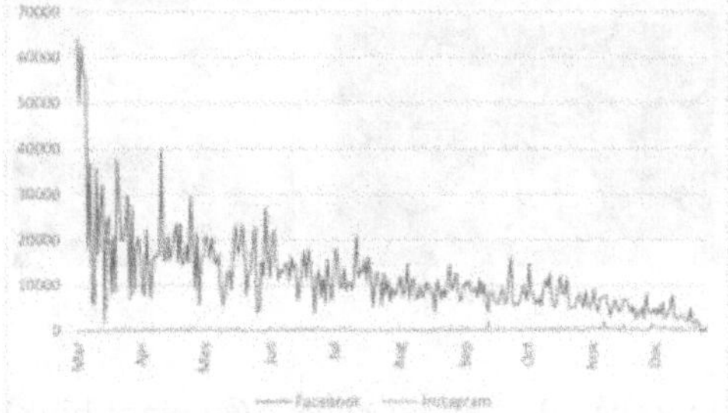

lowed by sharing (25.0%) and commenting (9.1%) a post. Because of the uniqueness of the event under research, users also express their emotions. On the page, reactions such as Sad (6.2%), Care (2.4%), and Love (2.0%) also reflect the country's state of mind, the fear of the unknown, and the impact of high mortality rates in Portugal.

The overall engagement rate, as determined by the reactions (such as likes, shares, comments, loves, etc.) from page followers in response to posts, exhibited consistent patterns over time. Nevertheless, occasional spikes in interaction were observed on both social media platforms. Figure 2 illustrates that the average engagement rate on Facebook remained at 0.59% throughout the months under consideration. The most significant peak occurred on November 16th, registering 644,005 interactions, constituting 3.3% of the total follower count at that specific time. In contrast, Instagram displayed an average monthly engagement rate that was twice as high, reaching 1.42%. The largest peak on Instagram was documented on September 12th, with 2,179 interactions, representing a substantial 10.5% of the total follower base.

This phenomenon on social media can be influenced by a variety of factors, including the platform's algorithms, whether the post is organic or sponsored, and even the significance of events associated with Covid-19 at the time. On the surface, one could argue that older audiences tend to engage more with the page (see the engagement rates and Facebook audience). However, there is still a lack of data to support this conclusion, and future research could explore this relationship with a focus on different age groups.

In any case, it is true that the direct actions taken by the DGS communications office may not have a very significant influence on some of these factors. For instance, the platform's algorithm determines the size of the audience, unless the publication is sponsored. This highlights the importance of planning health risk communication activities during times of crisis. A crucial first step is accurately defining the type of content.

DGS used twice as many unique words on Facebook (n = 46,650) as compared to Instagram (n = 24,256). This observation suggests the complexity of the discourse and the greater number of sub-themes associated with the main topic. Despite these differences, the expression "take care" stands out as the most frequently used on both social media, indicating a certain discursive pattern on the platforms: Facebook (n = 861) and Instagram (n = 697). This pattern is further reinforced by the consistent use of hashtags such as *#DGS*, *#UmConselhodaDGS*, or *#EstamosOn*. Figure 3 illustrates which publications have generated the highest levels of public engagement on each social media as part of an effort to construct a narrative of events in Portugal.

The Instagram post with the most interactions was created at 18:07 p.m. on September 12, 2020 (image on the left). The post is a video in which a Portuguese YouTuber explains how to protect oneself

Figure 3. DGS posts with the most interactions on social media (CrowdTangle)

against the virus. Accompanied by the ad, the text says: "@wuant highlights the main precautions we should take with COVID-19. It adheres to the recommendations of the DGS. Take care of yourself, take care of EVERYONE!". This content received 31,588 views, 2,073 interactions, and its performance is 16.5% higher than that of previous posts on the DGS page.

On the other hand, the Facebook post with the highest number of interactions was posted at 11:40 a.m. on December 27, 2020 (image on the right). This post is associated with the launch of the national vaccination program, marking the immunization of the first patient. It is accompanied by two photographs capturing that moment, and the text emphasizes: "Today is a day of hope!". The content received 55,763 interactions, representing a performance that is 150.3% higher than that of previous posts on this page.

While catering to distinct audiences, both publications address methods of safeguarding against the virus, encompassing personal care and the vaccination program. Consequently, the followers of the DGS on various social media platforms have acknowledged the significance of the content for the entire community. The elevated engagement rates, each within its unique context, indicate that irrespective of the format, whether it be a photo or video, it should harmonize with the collective consciousness rooted in the current moment.

CONCLUSION

The Covid-19 pandemic has altered how health information is conveyed and perceived by individuals. Digital platforms have emerged as the preferential channels for legal authorities and institutions to disseminate health information regarding the pandemic. The work presented in this chapter highlights this reality based on DGS's social media activity during the critical period of the Covid-19 pandemic in Portugal.

DGS's social media strategy appears to have been well-thought-out, considering the social media presence of this entity, platform preference, monthly activity peaks, content format strategy, and audience engagement. These findings reflect the importance of effective communication and adaptability during a public health crisis and highlight the role of social media in disseminating crucial information to the public.

Firstly, there was the growth of the DGS's social media presence during the initial months of the Covid-19 pandemic in Portugal, which reflects the importance of dynamic and diverse content in attracting and retaining followers on platforms like Facebook and Instagram. These platforms served as vital channels for official information dissemination and community engagement during a profound crisis. However, it is essential for organizations to remain responsive to the evolving needs and concerns of their audience, particularly during critical moments, to ensure the continued effectiveness of their social media communication strategy. Facebook cumulative growth in followers was more prominent than Instagram's during the pandemic, and several factors may have contributed to this phenomenon, including demographic differences, the timing of platform establishment, and potentially varying content strategies. Further research is needed to understand these dynamics comprehensively and inform future social media communication strategies for public health organizations during crises.

The results presented also emphasize the evolving dynamics of social media engagement during the Covid-19 pandemic. Initial peaks in follower acquisition and high levels of interaction were followed by a gradual decline as the pandemic escalated and the public's interests and priorities shifted. The emotional impact of the pandemic, combined with platform-specific audience characteristics and content strategies, played a significant role in shaping the engagement patterns observed on DGS's social media platforms.

The content formats that were used in both platforms, Facebook and Instagram, especially the heavy reliance on images, indicate a specific communication strategy during the Covid-19 pandemic. While this approach simplifies complex information and engages audiences effectively, it may also result in a lack of diversity in storytelling across platforms. To better cater to the diverse sociodemographic characteristics of their audiences, DGS may consider tailoring content to the specific preferences of Instagram and Facebook users while maintaining a balance between visual and text-based communication.

Successful health risk communication on social media during times of crisis requires a nuanced understanding of various factors that influence engagement. While some factors may be beyond the control of communication offices, such as platform algorithms, careful content planning and understanding audience demographics can help maximize the impact of communication efforts. Additionally, further research into how different age groups interact with health-related content can provide valuable insights for tailored communication strategies.

The use of unique words, key expressions, and hashtags on DGS's Facebook and Instagram pages reflects a deliberate effort to communicate effectively during the Covid-19 pandemic. While Facebook's discourse appears more extensive, both platforms share common discursive patterns, emphasizing the message of taking care and using consistent hashtags. Analyzing the publications that generated high levels of public engagement provides insights into the audience's interests and priorities, aiding in constructing a coherent narrative of events in Portugal during this critical period.

The success of these Instagram and Facebook posts in terms of engagement highlights the importance of providing timely, relevant, and diverse content formats to cater to different audiences and address evolving concerns during a public health crisis. These posts effectively harmonized with the collective consciousness of the moment, resonating strongly with the followers of DGS on different social media platforms.

Successful health communication on social media during times of crisis requires a nuanced understanding of various factors that influence engagement. While some factors may be beyond the control of communication offices, such as platform algorithms, careful content planning and understanding audience demographics can help maximize the impact of communication efforts. Additionally, further research into how different age groups interact with health-related content can provide valuable insights for tailored communication strategies.

While it is not the objective of this research and entails a substantial qualitative analysis effort, future studies should emphasize the thematization of posts on Facebook and Instagram. Additionally, future research should apply this same approach to other social media platforms within the context of the pandemic, such as X or TikTok. In the Portuguese context, it is important to analyze other health institutions in addition to the DGS. The new research could yield valuable insights into the effectiveness of health communication on social media during public health crises and help develop strategies for future emergencies.

ACKNOWLEDGMENT

This research was funded by the Foundation for Science and Technology (FCT) with reference 2022.06008. PTDC.

REFERENCES

Abonizio, H. Q., Barbon, A. P. A. C., Rodrigues, R., Santos, M., Martínez-Vizcaíno, V., Mesas, A. E., & Junior, S. B. (2023). How people interact with a chatbot against disinformation and fake news in Covid-19 in Brazil: The CoronaAI case. *International Journal of Medical Informatics*, *177*, 105134. Advance online publication. doi:10.1016/j.ijmedinf.2023.105134 PMID:37369153

Arriaga, M., Francisco, R., Nogueira, P., Oliveira, J., Silva, C., Câmara, G., Sørensen, K., Dietscher, C., & Costa, A. (2022). Health Literacy in Portugal: Results of the Health Literacy Population Survey Project 2019-2021. *International Journal of Environmental Research and Public Health*, *19*(4225), 4225. Advance online publication. doi:10.3390/ijerph19074225 PMID:35409905

Bek, M. G. (2023). Disseminating and resisting online hate speech in Turkey. In B. Di Fátima (Ed.), *Hate speech on social media: A global approach* (pp. 121–141). LabCom Books.

Bowles, J., Larreguy, H., & Liu, S. (2020). Countering misinformation via WhatsApp: Preliminary evidence from the COVID-19 pandemic in Zimbabwe. *PLoS One*, *15*(10), e0240005. Advance online publication. doi:10.1371/journal.pone.0240005 PMID:33052967

Cheng, C., & Espanha, R. (2021). Revisão Crítica: Uma Abordagem aos Estudos Sobre o Uso dos Media Sociais Durante a Pandemia Covid-19. *Comunicação & Sociedade*, *40*, 149–167. doi:10.17231/comsoc.40(2021).3174

Chesser, A., Ham, A. D., & Woods, N. K. (2020). Assessment of Covid-19 Knowledge Among University Students: Implications for Future Risk Communication Strategies. *Health Education & Behavior*, *47*(4), 540–543. doi:10.1177/1090198120931420 PMID:32460566

Choukou, M., Sanchez-Ramirez, D., Pol, M., Uddin, M., Monnin, C., & Syed-Abdul, S. (2022). Covid-19 infodemic and digital health literacy in vulnerable populations: A scoping review. *Digital Health*, *8*, 1–13. doi:10.1177/20552076221076927 PMID:35223076

Espanha, R. (2020a). A Literacia em Saúde e a Comunicação de Risco em Saúde. *Comunicação Pública*, *15*(29), 1–13. doi:10.4000/cp.11303

Espanha, R. (2020b). O valor da comunicação em gestão pública um exemplo aplicado à área da saúde pública. In J. Toledo (Ed.), *Comunicação estratégica e orientada: a visão de 21 renomados autores em 5 países* (pp. 337–363). Rede Integrada.

Fan, L., Yu, H., & Gilliland, A. J. (2023). Aggravated anti-Asian hate since Covid-19 and the #stopasianhate movement: Connection, disjointness, and challenges. In B. Di Fátima (Ed.), *Hate speech on social media: A global approach* (pp. 35–74). LabCom Books.

Gentile, L., Bertuccio, P., Ancona, A., Cucchi, A., Dallagiacoma, G., Godoy, M. A., Signorelli, C., & Odone, A. (2023). Can YouTube be trusted as a source of quality and reliable information on Covid-19 vaccination in Italy? *Acta Biomedica*. Advance online publication. doi:10.23750/abm.v94is3.14558 PMID:37695176

Gonçalves, G., Piñeiro-Naval, V., & Toniolo, B. P. (2021). Who Do the Portuguese Trust? Government Communication Management in the Covid-19 Pandemic. Comunicação e sociedade, 40, 169-187. doi:10.17231/comsoc.40(2021).3251

Kim, J., Livingstone, M. A., Jin, B., Watts, M., & Hwang, J. (2023). Fundamentals of Digital Health Literacy: A Scoping Review of Identifying Core Competencies to Use in Practice. *Adult Learning*, *0*(0). Advance online publication. doi:10.1177/10451595231178298

Lopes, F., Araújo, R., & Magalhães, O. (2021). Covid-19: A Pandemic Managed by Official Sources Through Political Communication. *Comunicação e Sociedade*, *40*, 17–32. doi:10.17231/comsoc.40(2021).3520

Malecki, K. M. C., Keating, J. A., & Safdar, N. (2021). Crisis Communication and Public Perception of COVID-19 Risk in the Era of Social Media. *Clinical Infectious Diseases*, *72*(4), 697–702. doi:10.1093/cid/ciaa758 PMID:32544242

Manganello, J., Bleakley, A., & Schumacher, P. (2020). Pandemics and PSAs: Rapidly Changing Information in a New Media Landscape. *Health Communication*, *35*(14), 1711–1714. doi:10.1080/10410236.2020.1839192 PMID:33106041

Nutbeam, D. (2021). From health education to digital health literacy – building on the past to shape the future. *Global Health Promotion*, *28*(4), 51–55. doi:10.1177/17579759211044079 PMID:34719292

OberCom. (2023). *Retrato digital de Portugal: caracterização e tendências de utilização das redes sociais - 2015 a 2023*. OberCom – Observatório da Comunicação. https://obercom.pt/retrato-digital-de-portugal-caracterizacao-e-tendencias-de-utilizacao-das-redes-sociais-2015-a-2023/

Schub, T., Swan-Potras, L., & Rabin, K. (2022). Big Shots: A Social Media Campaign to Honor Local Heroes who Promote Covid-19 Vaccine Literacy and Increase Vaccine Acceptance. *The American Behavioral Scientist*, *0*(0), 1–8. doi:10.1177/00027642221138272

Sepulveda, R., & Espanha, R. (2022). Online social media and public health institutions: An analysis of the Portuguese National Health Service on Instagram. *Cadernos de Saúde Societal*, *3*, 63–73.

Silva, M., Machete, A., Gonçalves, A., Teixeira, A., Alves, B., & Silva, C. (2022). Estratégias Comunicacionais da Direção-Geral da Saúde – estudo das Publicações no Twitter Sobre a COVID-19. *Revista Comunicando*, *11*(1), 2–19.

Sørensen, K., Levin-Zamir, D., Duong, T. V., Okan, O., Brasil, V. V., & Nutbeam, D. (2021). Building health literacy system capacity: A framework for health literate systems. *Health Promotion International*, *36*(S1), 13–23. doi:10.1093/heapro/daab153 PMID:34897445

Wu, T., He, Z., & Zhang, D. (2020). Impact of Communicating With Doctors Via Social Media on Consumers' E-Health Literacy and Healthy Behaviors in China. *The Journal of Health Care Organization. Inquiry*, *57*, 1–7. doi:10.1177/0046958020971188 PMID:33238788

Xin, M., Luo, S., Wang, S., Zhao, J., Zhang, G., Li, L., Li, L., & Lau, J. T. (2022). The Roles of Information Valence, Media Literacy and Perceived Information Quality on the Association Between Frequent Social Media Exposure and COVID-19 Vaccination Intention. *American Journal of Health Promotion*, *37*(2), 189–199. doi:10.1177/08901171221121292 PMID:35972385

Xue, H., & Taylor, L. (2022). When do people believe, check, and share health rumors on social media? Effects of evidence type, health literacy, and health knowledge. *Journal of Health Psychology*, *28*(7), 607–619. doi:10.1177/13591053221125992 PMID:36168751

Chapter 11
The Effects of the Instant Messaging Application WhatsApp on the Efficiency of Employees Under Pandemic Conditions

Aybike Serttaş
İstinye University, Turkey

Tugay Sarıkaya
İstinye University, Turkey

ABSTRACT

The objective of this study is to investigate the impact of WhatsApp, an instant messaging application, on various aspects, particularly employee productivity and integration. To accomplish this, the authors formulated five hypotheses centered around the following question: "How does the utilization of instant communication tools influence employee productivity and integration?" To conduct this research, they conducted in-depth interviews with 17 individuals who were working remotely. Subsequently, the data from these interviews were analyzed using a descriptive analysis method. The findings of this research indicate that while instant communication technologies offer convenience in communication, they tend to diminish productivity. This is primarily attributed to their potential disruption of the work-life balance and their perception as informal means of communication.

INTRODUCTION

With the advancement of communication technologies, significant changes are underway on both individual and societal levels. Various interpersonal networks, including private, professional, and educational spheres, have experienced profound transformations. The decoupling of communication from temporal

DOI: 10.4018/979-8-3693-0896-7.ch011

and spatial constraints, coupled with the proliferation of versatile communication tools, has altered the dynamics of numerous routine activities. Notably, the outbreak of the COVID-19 pandemic forced many individuals to work remotely, leading to a heightened reliance on internet-based communication applications.

Numerous studies have recently explored the impact of instant messaging programs within organizations on employee productivity and cohesion. In a study conducted by Rajendran et al. (2019), it was observed that using instant communication applications in work environments correlated with improved communication quality and overall task performance. Other research endeavors have delved into the delicate equilibrium between using instant messaging applications and work-life balance. While promoting constant communication, these applications also blur the boundaries between professional and personal domains (Adisa et al., 2017). Wang et al. (2016) found that employees using instant messaging applications often struggle to maintain this balance, potentially resulting in increased workloads (Lee et al., 2020, pp. 1-2).

Conversely, deficient communication within the workplace fosters a more authoritarian atmosphere. It fosters detrimental relationships among employees (Kholisoh and Sulastri, 2017: 21). Numerous studies have unveiled those inundating employees with excessive messages and transmitting surplus information beyond necessity yields adverse consequences (Ellwart et al., 2015; Memmi, 2014). Excessive communication with employees and the accelerated information flow can escalate uncertainty among staff members (Cho et al., 2019: 1746).

The research questions and hypotheses stem from the considerations mentioned above. This study seeks to provoke a discourse on the efficacy of instant messaging programs in internal communication. Consequently, five beliefs have been delineated.

H1: Using instant messaging programs within the organization fosters positive employee integration.
H2: Instant messaging programs employed in the corporate setting enhance workplace efficiency.
H3: The usage of instant messaging programs contributes to democratization in the workplace.
H4: Excessive utilization of messaging programs for business purposes within the workplace diminishes managers' perceived prestige in the employees' eyes.
H5: Prolonged use of instant messaging programs within the organization adversely impacts employees' work-life balance.

Building upon these deliberations and assessments, this article aims to illuminate the impact of employing instant messaging applications within organizational activities on university staff. To delve into this matter, we conducted in-depth interviews with 17 individuals occupying diverse roles within several foundation universities in Istanbul. These interviews were analyzed using a descriptive approach, and the findings were examined through critical concepts, including productivity, democratization, compatibility, and the dissolution of the boundaries between professional and personal life.

ORGANIZATIONAL COMMUNICATION

Communication stands as the paramount element that molds an organization's identity. It is the quintessence of effective management, encompassing planning, organization, coordination, direction, and control. Daily planning loses its efficacy without a robust communication framework, rendering attaining organizational goals and objectives an elusive pursuit. As elucidated by Stephen and Ayaga (2014), communication emerges as a pivotal factor in job satisfaction, asserting, "Regardless of the workload, effective communication reigns supreme in an employee's role within modern organizations." This underscores the significance of fostering an effective communication structure within an organization, which, as highlighted by Monika (2013), fosters and exerts influence on the most precious resource of any company – its people. A robust communication culture empowers employees while delineating their roles and responsibilities, creating a fertile ground for the continuous recognition of talents and achievements.

The acknowledgment of the pivotal role of communication in the management process owes a substantial debt to the pioneering work of Chester Barnard (cited in 1938, Rajhans 2009). Barnard contended that communication is the very "heart" of the management process. The 1940s ushered in the human relations movement, significantly contributing to the notion that organizational communication should adopt a two-way trajectory. During this era, a heightened emphasis on employees' attitudes and satisfaction emerged, fostering research into employee participation in decision-making, the dynamics of two-stage communication flows, and the nuances of upward and downward communication channels (Rajhans, 2009, pp. 145-146).

The concept of "communication control" was initially introduced by Odiorne in 1954 (as cited in Rajhans, 2009) to describe the process employed in assessing the accuracy of subordinates' perceptions regarding communication within management. Within the business realm, motivation serves as a primary guiding force for individuals. Work motivation, in particular, acts as the driving energy propelling employees toward attaining an organization's goals. The satisfaction derived from internal communication is crucial in all organizations and is influenced by the quality and consistency of communication processes. Consequently, job satisfaction assumes a pivotal role in shaping employee behavior.

The foundational model elucidating the communication process traces its origins to Shannon and Weaver in 1949. Shannon conceptualized communication as a mechanical system, and this model effectively clarifies why even the simplest communication forms can be misinterpreted. As signals are transmitted through various media, the intricacies of communication grow, raising the potential for distortion.

Within an organization, individuals typically possess a wealth of experience employing various communication methods. Messages flow vertically, traversing different levels of the hierarchy, and circulate horizontally among peers occupying the same organizational level. As Hall (1987) underscored, the greater an organization's emphasis on people and ideas, the more central communication becomes to its functioning. Furthermore, Hall (1987) posits that the linchpin of the communication process within organizations lies in guaranteeing that pertinent information reaches the appropriate individuals at the right juncture.

Communication is a pivotal common denominator in pursuing organizational objectives (Mamuli et al., 2013, p. 258). Various approaches offer insights into the multifaceted functions of corporate communication. The first perspective categorizes these functions into four key management areas: the control of employee behavior, motivation of personnel, development of interpersonal relationships, and decision-making (Spaho, 2012, p. 111). A second approach outlines five organizational communication functions: adaptation, direction, motivation, influence, meaning creation, problem-solving, decision-making, conflict management, negotiation, and bargaining (Spaho, 2012, p. 111). Moreover, every organization should facilitate communication in multiple directions: downward communication, upward communication, horizontal communication, and cross-communication.

The effectiveness of downward communication hinges on the scope of control, as the span of power relates to the number of individuals reporting to a senior manager and engaged in planning, organizing, and managerial functions. This is encapsulated in the Six Ms of Management: tools, people, money, methods, machines, and the market (Sari & Martinus, 2016: 78). In an empirical study concerning employee motivation factors mentioned in this article, motivation is delineated as a process that organizes the selection among various forms of voluntary activities, a process governed by the employee (Sari & Martinus, 2016: 79). Thus, the factors influencing motivation in organizations are tangible motivators. Beyond non-verbal communication, direct interpersonal interactions with employees and leaders substantially shape work motivation. A leader's interpersonal communication skills can motivate employees to excel in their assigned tasks (Sari & Martinus, 2016, p. 80).

Rajhans' study, conducted in 2009, delivers valuable insights into the impact of organizational communication on employee motivation and performance (2009: 147). The study's findings underscore the pivotal role of open and transparent communication in fostering and fortifying relationships that can propel employees toward peak productivity.

Mamuli et al.'s research in 2013 reveals that the success of universities primarily hinges on their teaching and research endeavors rather than their administrative management. Nevertheless, effective governance can create the conditions necessary for teaching and research to flourish, just as poor management can undermine these core functions. An essential characteristic of prosperous universities lies in the speed of communication among the various university entities. High academic performance doesn't emerge from isolated processes but is an intricate activity network that converges to produce a robust educational product. In the competitive intercollegiate landscape, even the most minor actions, like filling a staff vacancy or allocating specific resources, hold strategic significance for a department and, consequently, the long-term performance of the university (Mamuli et al., 2013, p. 260).

The study by Oteyza, Balmoria, and Sabularse, conducted in 2018 (88-89), delves into a fundamental question: What is the communication effectiveness of selected staff members at the Polytechnic University of the Philippines? In this research, the scholars employ the Input-Process-Output model. This model comprises three components: Input, representing the information and resources within a system; Process, encapsulating the actions and processes that employ the collected data and resources; and Output, representing the outcomes derived from the processed information and resources.

Using Practices of the Instant Messaging Program WhatsApp

WhatsApp, initially founded by Jan Koum and Brian Acton in 2009 as an iPhone app, made headlines in February 2014 when Facebook acquired it for a staggering $19 billion (Akintola et al., 2019: 3). The data generated by users has been a subject of frequent scrutiny, with communication scientists often raising concerns about its use, ownership, and the sale of user data to advertisers (Fuchs, 2016). However, it's important to note that WhatsApp's political economy is not this article's central focus.

Research studies, such as those by Bhratt and Arshad (2016), have delved into why young people are drawn to WhatsApp. These studies have found that a significant motivator for WhatsApp usage, at 72%, is its ability to facilitate effective communication. Numerous other studies, including those by Ahad et al. (2014), Bouhnik et al. (2014), Church and Oliveira (2013), O'Hara et al. (2014), Yeboah and Ewur (2014), and Mols and Pridmore (2020), have explored the effects and advantages of using WhatsApp.

For example, a study conducted in Spain involving 140 participants aged 20-60 revealed that the most prevalent reason for using WhatsApp is its cost-effectiveness and user-friendly interface (Ahad et al., 2014). A similar outcome was observed in a different study conducted by Soliman and Salem (2014), which included 450 participants aged 18-55 in Riyadh. Participants in this study emphasized that they preferred WhatsApp due to its affordability and ease of use.

Interestingly, a qualitative study involving individuals aged 17-49 in England yielded different results. It highlighted that WhatsApp effectively extends real-life routines into the virtual sphere, reinforcing social connections, a sense of belonging, and feelings of security, ultimately strengthening social ties. Yeboah and Ewur (2014) also noted positive and negative effects in their study, demonstrating that communication tools like WhatsApp can adversely impact language structure and concentration.

Furthermore, a study by Devi and Tevera (2014) indicated that applications like WhatsApp and Facebook are not solely used for personal relationships but also serve for academic communication and information sharing. Survey results involving 169 students showed that 26% frequently use social media applications like WhatsApp and Facebook to search for information, 40% utilize these platforms for professional support, and 58% for information sharing with others.

Kassim et al. (2020) conducted semi-structured interviews with 105 human resources and management employees. According to the data obtained from the participants, using WhatsApp in business life allows doing more work with less effort. One of the essential results of the research is that WhatsApp has replaced the more traditionally accepted e-mail (Kassim et al., 2020). The study contributes to making sense of the work this paper has put forward in the context of the importance of WhatsApp and organizational communication. The interview questions, which will be mentioned in the method part, are formed depending on these issues and the hypotheses mentioned in the introduction.

METHOD AND SAMPLING

In the context of this research, we conducted in-depth interviews with 17 individuals holding administrative and academic responsibilities within foundation universities in Istanbul, each of whom is actively engaged in multiple WhatsApp groups. The data thus collected was subjected to analysis using the descriptive analysis method. During these interviews, participants were presented with four key questions.

1) Does the presence of WhatsApp affect your work and daily life balance?
2) What do you think of using WhatsApp to establish groups for business?
3) What does the distribution of hierarchical relationships mean to you in WhatsApp? How does it feel to use WhatsApp to write to someone more competent than you?
4) Do you actively send messages and convey your opinions on various topics in organization messaging groups?

As outlined by Walcott in 1994, descriptive analysis entails the straightforward transmission of acquired data to the reader. This method requires establishing a predefined framework and subsequently interpreting qualitative data within the confines of this framework. In the context of this research, hypotheses were initially formulated. Aligned with these hypotheses and the research's overarching objectives, the questions above were posed to the participants. The responses collected have been presented to the reader within a specific framework. The hypotheses were rigorously examined through the analysis results, and their implications are expounded upon in the conclusion section.

RESULTS

The 17 participants interviewed within the study represent a diverse age range from 24 to 72 years. Each participant has been assigned a unique identifier, denoted by the letter "K" followed by a specific number. These individuals occupy roles as administrative staff and managers within various units of foundation universities. Notably, all participants are actively involved in multiple WhatsApp groups related to their professional responsibilities.

Regarding the query, "Does the presence of WhatsApp impact your work-life balance?" one participant conveyed a positive perspective:

K6

The existence of WhatsApp does not affect my daily and business life practices. On the contrary, I prefer to use WhatsApp in my private life plans and business organizations.

One participant underlined that WhatsApp is a practical application, but if he still had a choice, he would not want to include this application in business life.

K11

The presence of WhatsApp positively affects the balance of work and daily life in terms of increasing my workflow in my working relations and negatively affects the unnecessary amount of daily sharing. I wish my workflow would have been slower if I hadn't been so overwhelmed by posts. My rate of wasting time is high. I am unhappy

Other participants emphasized that the intensive use of WhatsApp in business life has a nature that is distracting and goes beyond the limit of formal relations.

K1

Not only the use of WhatsApp but other social media tools; I can say that sometimes they hinder me from the things I need to focus on.

K2

It can affect. While focusing on another job, an urgent message about work or daily life via WhatsApp can cause you to change your focus and disrupt your previous job occasionally.

K3

Affecting. Messaging, which can be performed at any time of the day, disrupts the balance. Entering our lives by facilitating social group communication, WA has gradually become an in-house communication tool. While it facilitates business communication with its instant feature, it has also become a pressure tool on employees. While it is considered reasonable to reply to an email on the same day or the next day, returning WA messages within minutes is necessary. This puts a new responsibility on the employees, such as the constant follow-up of WA messages.

K4

It affects. The presence of WhatsApp is one of the reasons why I think about work from the moment I wake up in the morning until I fall asleep at night.

K5

Using any communication tool other than Mail, especially tools/applications used for personal communication, affects the work-daily life balance as it makes the employee constantly accessible.

This situation causes the concepts of working hours and out-of-hours to disappear. I do not find it favorable.

K7

Yes. In a wrong way. If I need to concentrate, I leave the phone in the other room. So, I only hear the calls.

K8

It is imposing; it causes my business life to occupy much space in my daily life, which means an endless amount of work. Even if you take the time for daily life, you have a direct transition to business life with an incoming message. It affects both your quality-of-life balance and those around you. In the beginning, I was looking positive to make things healthier and more instant, but now I start to worry that each newly formed group will take more time, and unfortunately, it does.

K9

Yes, it does. When WhatsApp was first used, it was a digital supporter of social life or a platform for sharing social life with our friends. However, over time, especially with the COVID-19 pandemic process, WhatsApp has almost become a platform where workflows and job responsibilities related to our professional lives are shared. This has become such that one can now realize that even our most sincere friends are communicating through "business." In our daily lives, there are almost no "moments' that are special to us and belong to us; it makes one feel more like every moment belongs to our business. Of course, the job is a responsibility to be done; however, being bombarded with work over WhatsApp gives us the feeling that the concept of private life has almost disappeared, and we live as more mechanized individuals.

K10

Yes, it affects it significantly because, with the existence of WhatsApp, accessibility is expected at any time, especially during the pandemic. Situations solved by mail in the standard period are expected by instant access via WhatsApp outside of business hours in this period. This situation affects the balance of work and daily life.

K12

It makes me more accessible; when the employer uses it, the distinction between work hours and the time I devote to myself is blurred. They spread our working hours to almost all of our lives, especially during the pandemic, when we work remotely. Unfortunately, there are no more evenings or weekends.

K17

The existence of WhatsApp serves for the rapid transmission and planning of the works through the application. However, the effect it has on daily life is not very optimistic. The reason is that the managers pass the work quickly to the subordinates through the application and wait for an answer, disregarding the working hours. There is a negative effect of the concept of working hours to become ambiguous. Establishing business groups on WhatsApp affects the work-life balance and causes managers to be constantly included in the private life sphere. In this sense, I prefer business communications to be by mail.

Perceptions regarding the use of WhatsApp for creating business groups tend to be split into two general categories. For some participants, employing the application for work increases their stress levels. While many participants acknowledge the application's speed and practicality, there is a recurring theme of negative psychological impacts, heightened stress levels, and the proliferation of information overload among common grievances.

K1

Although it is thought to allow practical and rapid communication, its misuse by some people in the workplace negatively affects me mentally.

K4

Although using WhatsApp by establishing groups for work speeds up communication between employees, this situation creates a stress factor as it requires being online at all hours of the day. For this reason, I think corporate email addresses should be used for workplace communication.

K7

I prefer not to use it unless necessary. The groups that are banned from answering, written by the group managers, are relatively better. Otherwise, there is information pollution, and essential issues get out. In addition, messages are received day and night, regardless of the weekend or holiday. In this case, I must always look at the phone in order not to miss possible urgent things, and this is very tiring. Another problem is that, let us say you wrote something to the group or someone; then you wonder if they saw the message, did not see it, or if they see it but maybe did not look at it in depth. Didn't they care? You are left with a thousand kinds of unnecessary thoughts. Most of the time, it does not turn out how you think. I have never overcome myself when we worked face to face. On WhatsApp, on the other hand, you are together with all levels of our superiors. For the reasons I explained above, I prefer not to write. I feel the need to pay attention to everything else. Whatever comes to mind, also hold the uppercase and lowercase letters. Should I joke or not? Should I put an emoji or not? In short, I do not feel free in WhatsApp groups where my superiors and people who are not sincere are participants.

K8

It makes you feel nervous; this puts pressure on you to write more in control. On the other hand, sometimes, when dealing with another job, you must immediately reply to the instant message. You need to check if you have paid attention to the hierarchy later, but you are left worried because the message has been delivered, and the double blue click appears.

K12

Being so accessible bothers me. While chatting with my friends, I also look at WhatsApp in the evening; there are always messages about work. I often feel compelled to respond because they see me online. For example, some people write at night; I often wonder if it matters. Usually, it doesn't matter. I think it has been abused a lot. If you write to someone at midnight, this must be something important.

A subset of employees believes that utilizing the application for business purposes expedites workflow and enhances overall productivity. Nonetheless, they advocate for some limitations on this use, with a notable emphasis on delineating boundaries related to working hours.

K2

I find it necessary and valuable if it is not used beyond its intended purpose and purpose. Suppose it is used within reasonable hours, of course.

K6

I find the use of WhatsApp to establish groups for business much more effective and valuable than the mail system.

K10

I think it is very suitable for business groups to know the boundaries of the subject and people. I see that it is generally beneficial to get faster results during business hours.

One participant adopts a middle-ground perspective on the matter. While acknowledging discomfort with the incorporation of formal relationships within an otherwise informal platform like WhatsApp, the participant also recognizes that the novel professional experiences encountered through the application have the potential to bring about positive personal growth and transformation.

K11

In a way, it destroyed the formal workflow tradition and reduced bureaucratic seriousness in business relations. Before my retirement, when I was the manager at another university, I was among those who rejected the student's suggestion of communication via WhatsApp, saying that it would be correct to communicate with the student through official channels. Today, I overcame this fear, which sped up communication. Since it can be legally certified, I think there will be no legal problem. It saves time, and I think it is practical. Contrary to what I have said, I am not experiencing any internal difficulties while writing to my superiors. I come from a bureaucratic family. I do not find it serious, and I am suffering from it. However, we must get used to this different feeling when we are mutual and see that it accelerates the flow of things. I also enjoy receiving immediate feedback on a request from my subordinates. So, I see that I have changed over time. This gives me a feeling of being intellectually younger.

Another participant articulates a sense of unease regarding the limitation of communication when it is tailored to mimic face-to-face interaction rather than the unique features of the digital medium itself. This participant underscores the substantial impact of body language in in-person interactions and asserts that the array of digital communication tools available cannot fully compensate for the absence of body language cues.

K16

It is a fact that, according to many people, individuals can be more comfortable in the relationships established with writing during traditional or digital communication. For this reason, textual fiction can be created more comfortably and self-confident in contact with senior people in the groups within the said communication medium. However, a problem may also arise as follows: it may reveal the inability of individuals to express themselves fully (independent from gestures, hand and arm movements). Sometimes, emojis also cannot fix the issue in question.

The distribution of hierarchical relationships within WhatsApp and the use of the platform to message authorized individuals represent another point of contention among participants. Many participants are reluctant to choose WhatsApp for communication with their superiors, and if compelled to use it, they express discomfort with this arrangement. Notably, the responses reveal a precise categorization: email is typically regarded as a formal communication tool, while WhatsApp is seen as informal.

K1

I do not prefer WhatsApp when communicating with more authorized people than me, as I think it is a more informal tool.

K2

Naturally, it differs from your conversations with your friends in your daily life; it creates the necessity of speaking more formally and paying attention to style. It takes extra seriousness and care.

K3

WhatsApp is not an official messaging platform. Therefore, the topic of style turns into a problem. Mail style and WhatsApp style are not the same. Adjusting the style in vertical relationships is always difficult for everyone. There may be messages that we find strange.

K5

I write more carefully when writing to someone more competent than me, but this is not the case for everyone. My general observation is that online communication tools also disrupt this hierarchical order. Students can write to us no matter the time and see it as usual.

K7

I do not write much if there are not sincere in the group. An environment is prone to misunderstanding. You may offend or upset the other party, or you may not be able to fully express yourself, even if you do not want to. I observe that exceptionally long messages are not read from the questions already asked. Of course, the short ones are not read, either. I think giving opinions is either face-to-face or over the phone, not in 2-3 words. WhatsApp only works for yes-no.

K10

Being in WhatsApp groups established by senior executives is a situation that makes people more worried. Reaching someone more competent than me on WhatsApp does not seem right because I find it more appropriate to e-mail a senior manager or someone more senior than me on their phone.

K13

If I take a pragmatist approach, it helps solve problems instantly. (Especially during the pandemic period) However, regarding professionalism, using WhatsApp this way does not seem professional. Maybe because it is an app we use for daily conversation, the program's image makes me think that way. I think every application has a unique language. For example, when we say Twitter, the image of an application used for a political purpose comes to mind. In contrast, when we say Instagram, we think of an application used for entertainment. I think this situation also applies to WhatsApp. Its use for work is unsuitable for professionalism (compared to my intended use before the pandemic).

K15

I think the use of WhatsApp weakens hierarchical relationships. Regardless of the hour, the messages that come to me via WhatsApp cause me to be disrespectful and nervous.

K17

Communicating with more authorized people via WhatsApp makes me nervous. Using an application that I use more freely in private life, in business correspondence, and when communicating with people who are my hierarchical superiors makes me feel uncomfortable. If I have a choice, I am conducting my correspondence via email.

However, a segment of the participants discern no fundamental distinction between WhatsApp, face-to-face communication, or email. This group asserts that as long as the established norms governing subordinate-superior relationships are maintained, the specific medium employed becomes inconsequential. According to these participants, the hierarchy should not be interpreted about different communication channels, and consistent communication codes should be applied across all forms of interaction. They view the emergence of new communication channels as a reflection of the evolving conditions in the business world.

K4

There is no significant difference between WhatsApp's distribution of hierarchical relationships and existing hierarchical relationships. I do not see much difference between writing to someone more authorized than me on WhatsApp and emailing those people.

K6

If the hierarchical style in the mail system is maintained, I do not feel any discomfort or discomfort in this regard.

K9

The situation is not that different from face-to-face communication. Just as there is an extra strain and seriousness when communicating face-to-face if the person is hierarchically higher than us, WhatsApp does not change this. Sometimes, when I write to a sincere friend via WhatsApp, I wonder whether I am writing to the right person or writing to my manager or supervisor repeatedly. This, of course, is quite uncomfortable and irritating.

K16

I do not think WhatsApp creates incompatibility regarding daily usage practices and job responsibilities. Since professional responsibilities are also a part of daily life, I think it is important to take psychological precautions in using such communication platforms, which is why it does not affect my daily routine negatively.

K12

At first, I did not write unless necessary; I was afraid of disturbing it because WhatsApp was a private area in my mind. However, I saw they were unafraid, so I started writing without hesitation. Nevertheless, this relationship developed not with everyone but with the people I worked with. Everyone has a different attitude about hierarchical relationships; not everyone is authorized to establish one; some behave more friendly, and we talk to them more comfortably. People's attitudes are also practical.

In contrast, another participant contends that email accentuates hierarchical divisions and fosters a sense of distance between parties during the communication process. This participant believes that leveraging WhatsApp for organizational communication proves advantageous, as it is perceived as a means to bridge such divides.

K14

The way to communicate with someone hierarchically superior via mail was usually by adding to cc. This usually caused communication with the main interlocutor through intermediaries. In other words, a specialist transmits to the director, and the manager transmits your requests and complaints to the deputy general secretary or the general secretary. Alternatively, you will indicate that you have fulfilled the given task by adding the upper authorities to the CC, or you can put your friend working in the institution in a difficult situation in this way. I do not find the communication process via email sincere. I find the communication process through WhatsApp more sincere, and I think it is more open to interaction. I can instantly reach an authorized person on WhatsApp without an intermediary. I find this process more sincere than the mail.

Furthermore, based on statements from the participants regarding the research topic, many individuals primarily engage with smaller groups within the organization. Although they are not typically very active, they do feel compelled to contribute to these groups when they encounter important, incomplete, or corrective situations or when they need to relay urgent information. Several participants who assume a moderator role within these groups, often managers, continue to perform functions reminiscent of the traditional management approach within the WhatsApp context.

For some participants, the catalyst for engaging in active discussions via messages within organizational groups stems from processes that reflect a heightened sense of loyalty, commitment to the institution, and a strong responsibility toward their work. In this context, it is deemed crucial to share opinions actively. Most participants use text messages in these organizational group settings for more personalized gestures, such as offering congratulations or expressing good wishes on occasions like birthdays, engagements, weddings, etc. However, they typically refrain from commenting on other matters or issues within these settings.

Regarding communication with students, faculty members appear to leverage WhatsApp as a tool for motivating students in their coursework. They express that this approach is a positive strategy for bridging their generational gap.

On the flip side, some participants believe that sending official correspondence via WhatsApp diminishes the message's perceived importance and the level of respect accorded to the recipients of the message.

CONCLUSION AND EVALUATION

The primary role of organizational communication is to foster relationship building. Effective relationship building lays the cornerstone for resilient crisis management and equips parties to navigate organizational changes. It contributes to enhancing employee morale and bolsters the pursuit of the organization's strategic objectives. Furthermore, consistent communication, particularly with younger employees, can catalyze unlocking employee creativity. It is worth noting that at the core of every organizational process lies human behavior and the interactions between individuals. In hierarchical systems, managers act as vital links in the communication chain, directing the flow of communication and imposing certain constraints. Management decisions and directives typically flow from higher echelons to lower levels within the organization, while responses and reports travel in the opposite direction, from lower-level managers upward.

The advent of the pandemic compelled many university employees to experience remote working for the first time, necessitating a swift adaptation of communication models within universities to a new system. During this transition, WhatsApp and similar chat applications emerged as powerful tools for maintaining current operations, sustaining employee motivation, and preventing declines in productivity.

Despite the undeniable advantages of digital networks, it is imperative to reevaluate the balance between personal life and work. The pervasive accessibility of employees at all times and locations in the digital age may lead to an unhealthy expectation of constant availability. Recognizing the potential impact on employees' social lives due to their perpetual accessibility through instant communication applications is paramount.

The hypothesis "H5: Prolonged use of instant messaging programs within the organization adversely impacts the work-life balance of employees," initially posited in this study, has been substantiated. Fifteen of the participants explicitly noted that the work-life balance was disrupted. However, our other hypothesis, "H2: Instant messaging programs employed in the corporate setting enhance workplace efficiency," yielded mixed results. While some participants observed enhanced work efficiency, others reported a less efficient work environment. Furthermore, it has been evident from the results that this outcome is interrelated with H5.

Contrary to "H3: The usage of instant messaging programs contributes to democratization in the workplace," the hypothesis was incorrect. Many participants expressed reluctance to engage with administrators in these networks, with managers often taking on coordination and leadership roles. Most participants also characterized WhatsApp as an informal communication platform. This has substantiated "H4: Excessive utilization of messaging programs for business purposes within the workplace diminishes the perceived prestige of managers in the eyes of employees." Participants generally consider WhatsApp messaging as a factor that diminishes the perceived dignity of managers. Sufficient data could not be gathered to confirm or refute the hypothesis "H1: The utilization of instant messaging programs within the organization fosters positive employee integration." However, many participants are reluctant to contribute to large WhatsApp groups with administrators, except for sending congratulatory messages, which might indirectly suggest that WhatsApp may not be very effective in promoting integration. Nevertheless, this does not categorically imply its inefficacy.

Furthermore, it is essential to recognize that digital networks and emerging communication possibilities allow individuals to select their workspaces and working hours. Instead of adopting a rigidly binary view of their impact as beneficial or detrimental, the individual nuances and contextual variations within such studies should be acknowledged as meaningful.

Fundamentally, WhatsApp, a digital instant messaging program, can be viewed as an extension of physical space rather than a distinct alternative. It is no longer necessary to perceive digital communication networks as separate from reality; a shift has occurred wherein physical presence and work processes must be integrated with the digital sphere. The COVID-19 pandemic has underscored this shift. The key lies in comprehending how these changes and adaptations affect people's lives rather than assessing new communication tools solely in terms of their advantages or drawbacks.

REFERENCES

Adisa, T. A., Gbadamosi, G., & Osabutey, E. L. (2017). What happened to the border? The role of mobile information technology devices on employees' work-life balance. *Personnel Review*, *46*(8), 1651–1671. doi:10.1108/PR-08-2016-0222

Ahad, A. D., & Lim, S. M. A. (2014). Convenience or nuisance? The 'WhatsApp' dilemma. *Procedia: Social and Behavioral Sciences*, *155*, 189–196. doi:10.1016/j.sbspro.2014.10.278

Akintola, M., Bello, M. B., & Daramola, D. S. (2016). Usage of WhatsApp as a social media platform among undergraduates in Kwara State. *Nigerian Journal of Educational Technology*, *1*(1), 1–14.

Bhatt, M. A., & Arshad, M. (2016). Impact of WhatsApp on youth: A sociological study. *Social Sciences*, *4*(2), 2016.

Bouhnik, D., Deshen, M., & Gan, R. (2014). WhatsApp goes to school: Mobile instant messaging between teachers and students. *Journal of Information Technology Education*, *13*(1), 217–231. doi:10.28945/2051

Campbell, D. T., & Stanley, J. C. (1963). *Experimental and Quasi-Experimental Designs for Research*. Houghton Mifflin.

Cho, J., Lee, H. E., & Kim, H. (2019). Effects of communication-oriented overload in mobile instant messaging on role stressors, burnout, and turnover intention in the workplace. *International Journal of Communication, 13*, 21.

Church, K., & De Oliveira, R. (2013, August). What is up with WhatsApp? Comparing mobile instant messaging behaviors with traditional SMS. In *Proceedings of the 15th International Conference on Human-Computer Interaction with Mobile Devices and Services* (pp. 352-361). 10.1145/2493190.2493225

Devi, T. S., & Rivera, S. (2014). Use of Social Networking Site in the University of Swaziland by the Health Science Student: A Case Study. *Journal of International Management, 1*(1), 17–24.

Dugguh, S. I., & Dennis, A. (2014). Job satisfaction theories: Traceability to employee performance in organizations. *IOSR Journal of Business and Management, 16*(5), 11–18. doi:10.9790/487X-16511118

Ellwart, T., Happ, C., Gurtner, A., & Rack, O. (2015). Managing information overload in virtual teams: Effects of a structured online team adaptation on cognition and performance. *European Journal of Work and Organizational Psychology, 24*(5), 812–826. doi:10.1080/1359432X.2014.1000873

Fuchs, C. (2017). Social Media: A Critical Introduction. *Sage (Atlanta, Ga.).*

Glass, G. V., & Hopkins, K. D. (1984). *Statistical Methods in Education and Psychology*. Prentice Hall.

Hall, R. H. (1987). *Organizations: Structures, Processes & Outcomes*. Prentice-Hall International Inc.

Kassim, N. H., Mohamed Noor, N., Ali, J. K., Saleh, J., Dealwis, C., & Nurhisham, M. A. (2020). Sustaining job performance through technology acceptance with the usage of WhatsApp mobile application. *International Journal of Service Management and Sustainability, 5*(1), 1–26.

Kholisoh, N., & Sulastri, R. (2017). New Media Technology in Developing Effective Organizational Internal Communication. *Humaniora, 8*(1), 21–29. doi:10.21512/humaniora.v8i1.3693

Lee, C. S., Ker, E. S., Ng, C. H., Ye, J., & Watson-Manheim, M. B. (2020). Effects of mobile instant messaging applications in the workplace. *Proceedings of the Association for Information Science and Technology, 57*(1), e354. doi:10.1002/pra2.354

Mamuli, L., Mutsotso, S., & Namasaka, D. (2013). The influence of communication channels on management practices in Kenyan public universities. *International Journal of Academic Research in Progressive Education and Development, 2*(1), 257–267.

Memmi, D. (2014). Information overload and virtual institutions. *AI & Society, 29*(1), 75–83. doi:10.100700146-012-0428-9

Mols, A., & Pridmore, J. (2020). Always available via WhatsApp: Mapping everyday boundary work practices and privacy negotiations. *Mobile Media & Communication.*

Monika, P. (2013). *Communication in Employees' Motivation and Remuneration System*. Academic Press.

O'Hara, K. P., Massimi, M., Harper, R., Rubens, S., & Morris, J. (2014, February). Everyday dwelling with WhatsApp. In *Proceedings of the 17th ACM Conference on Computer Supported Cooperative Work & Social Computing* (pp. 1131–1143). ACM.

Oteyza, A. M., Balmoria, B. E., & Sabularse, M. (2018). Effectiveness of Oral and Written Communication of University Employees. *Asia Pacific Journal of Multidisciplinary Research*, *6*(1), 88–95.

Rajendran, J. A., Baharin, H., & Kamal, F. M. (2019, November). I understand Instant Messaging in the Workplace. In *International Visual Informatics Conference* (pp. 640-652). Springer.

Rajhans, K. (2012). Effective organizational communication: A key to employee motivation and performance. *Interscience Management Review*, *2*(2), 81–85.

Ramadanty, S., & Martinus, H. (2016). Organizational communication: Communication and motivation in the workplace. *Humaniora*, *7*(1), 77–86. doi:10.21512/humaniora.v7i1.3490

Shannon, C. E., & Weaver, W. (1949). *The Mathematical Theory of Communication*. University of Illinois Press.

Soliman, D. A., & Salem, M. S. (2014). Investigating intention to use mobile instant messenger: The influence of sociability, self-expressiveness, and enjoyment. *The Journal of American Academy of Business, Cambridge*, *19*(2), 286–293.

Spaho, K. (2012). Organizational communication process. *Ekonomski Vjesnik*, *25*, 318–318.

Wang, C. C., Yang, Y. Y. H., & Tseng, C. Y. (2016, June). Always on Duty? The Positive and Negative Effects of Using Mobile Social Networking Tools for Work. *PACIS*, 270.

Wolcott, H. F. (1994). Transforming Qualitative Data: Description, Analysis, and Interpretation. *Sage (Atlanta, Ga.)*.

Yeboah, J., & Ewur, G. D. (2014). The impact of WhatsApp messenger usage on students' performance in Tertiary Institutions in Ghana. *Journal of Education and Practice*, *5*(6), 157–164.

Chapter 12
Changes in Advertising Campaigns in Times of COVID-19:
Selected Cases From Spain

Jordi Serra Simon
University of Girona, Spain

ABSTRACT

The COVID-19 virus had a huge impact worldwide and its presence has also implied changes in some advertising campaigns. Given the mobility restrictions and new ways of socializing in times of lockdown, relevant advertisers modified their commercial messages in order to be coherent with the situation lived by most consumers. This research is aimed at understanding the most significant changes in advertising campaigns, mainly on TV, promoted by selected advertisers during COVID-19 lockdown and some months later on. The main hypothesis of this research is that there is a clear relationship between what companies communicate and the circumstances and living experiences of most consumers. Through the qualitative content analysis of selected cases, it can be understood how brands changed their messages to demonstrate their commitment to their consumers; support governmental indications related to health, safety, and mobility recommendations; and, if possible, motivate consumers.

INTRODUCTION

The COVID-19 involved a lockdown in most countries of the world. In the case of Spain, there were several mobility restrictions from March 2020 which considerably altered the patterns of consumption and mobility of citizens (Gobierno de España, 2020) and also the media consumption (Blanco-Herrero, D.; Gallardo-Camacho, J.; Arcila-Calderón, C., 2021; Cadena Ser, 2020). Although this situation was unexpected by most people, society had to assume new restrictions and regulations related to mobility, consumption habits, lifestyle and social behavior. In that sense, advertising, which can be considered a partially reflection of society (Grau-Rebollo, J., 2021; Eguizábal, R., 2011), partially evolved and new

DOI: 10.4018/979-8-3693-0896-7.ch012

messages related to this unusual situation emerged. This research analyses qualitatively seven cases of spots from different companies and sectors with the aim to understand which were the points in common between the commercial messages of these organizations and, independently of the product or service provided or sold, how companies linked their product or service with the situation of the lockdown in order to show empathy, amiability and respect for their consumers.

However, "prior to the coronavirus crisis, the advertising industry grew in all its aspects, both in the above the line and below the line media. Specifically, in 2018 the turnover in the Advertising and Market Research sector was above the annual average of the general index of the Services Sector and what represented an increase of 3.1% compared to the previous year according to data from the Observatory of Advertising in Spain" (de Castro Pérez, Irene, 2021: 15).

Spanish Advertising TV Campaigns in Times of COVID-19

The aim of this research is to identify up to which extent the advertising campaigns promoted by companies from different sectors adapted their advertising campaigns during the months of lockdown of COVID-19 pandemic. In fact, this research focuses on the main changes in advertising campaigns in times of COVID-19 targeted at Spanish consumers to understand how relevant advertisers, independently of their sector, origin, size or target market, changed their commercial messages in order to show empathy for their audiences, look updated, but at the same time, highlight the company' selling proposition and its main features.

In that sense, the evolution of advertising messages during the lockdown periods and how companies adapted their messages in order to remain relevant, maintain their purpose and be coherent with governmental indications. At the same time, through this analysis, new insights, previously not used in advertising campaigns, have been spot.

In the context of the pandemic, consumption habits and trends changed massively due to the situation of confinements and restrictions decreed by the government, in such a way that television and digital media consumption skyrocketed during the months of lockdown. Digital newspapers received almost 50% more page views and increased their traffic by 100%. Moreover, digital audiences of online radio grew by 112% and live online television obtained up to 93% unique users. Television also became the main source of entertainment and information (Montaña Blasco, M.; Ollé Castellà, C. and Lavilla Raso, M, 2020).

This context allows the understanding of the role of the media in an emergency situation. In addition to this, considering the notable increases in audiences, it makes sense for companies to create advertising campaigns that include the situation related to lockdown. In the Spanish case, as pandemic advanced, the media consumption carried out to stay informed mainly consolidated 3 sources of information, which were television, official statements and online press (Montaña Blasco, M. ; Ollé Castellà, C. and Lavilla Raso, M, 2020).

Considering the types of products that were advertised on television during the time of confinement, the category Other goods and services stands out as the category with the greatest presence of advertisements (26.9%), Food (25.0%), Health (16. 1%) Leisure and culture (14.8%) (Blanco-Herrero, D., Arcila-Calderón, C. and Gallardo-Camacho, J., 2022).

As commented by Blanco-Herrero, D., Arcila-Calderón, C. and Gallardo-Camacho, J., (2022), health was one of the topics that had the most prominence during confinement, while aspects such as Leisure and culture, Transportation or Restaurants and hotels, categories especially affected by lockdown reduced their proportion of ads.

The COVID-19 and Its Impact on Health Perception

The COVID-19 lockdown implied high rates of negative mental health disorders that affected the general population (Rossi R, Socci V, Talevi D *et al.,* 2020). However, the situation caused by the COVID-19 has not affected all the population in the same way. In fact, this situation has generated more emotional stress in women than men. As for the impact of the effects of COVID-19 from ages, young people aged 18-34 feel more frustrated (53%) and those over 55 show a little more hope (27%) and confidence (11%) (Pérez, Pablo & Lobato, María, 2021). According to the standards promoted by the World Health Organization (2022) in order to avoid the expansion of COVID-19 people should avoid spaces that are closed, crowded or involve close contact. Moreover, people are encouraged to meet people outside because outdoor gatherings are considered safer than indoor ones, especially if indoor spaces are small and without outdoor air coming in. In any case, people are motivated to wear masks and if possible open windows in order to increase the natural ventilation of rooms. As will be mentioned later on, these are recommendations that tend to appear in ads launched in times of COVID-19.

The advertisements during the home confinement dropped in Spain in March 2020 and it replicated the consumption patterns of that moment. In fact, those sectors that were able to continue their activity maintained their advertising activity. Notwithstanding, those sectors whose activity was paralyzed to a greater extent also reduced the number of ads. This occurred in a context of high television consumption, but a decline in general consumption and investment in advertising (Blanco-Herrero, D., Arcila-Calderón, C. and Gallardo-Camacho, J., 2022).

The Consumer in Times of COVID-19

According to Chow & Stanford (2021) consumers have changed their attitude towards local businesses and tend to show more respect to protect local shops. In that sense, brands try to create a deeper connection with their consumers. This is the reason why they create messages to engage with consumers through emotional and messages. According to European Commission (2021) 42% of Europeans considered delaying a major purchase during Covid-19. These trends explain the need to show empathy with the fears, concerns and situations experienced by citizens and create advertising messages that show a coherent connection between the lived context, the economic situation and the role that brands play in people's lives.

The Consumer Confidence in Times of COVID-19 (Evolution)

Consumer confidence has been affected during the Covid pandemic. According to the data obtained, in the month of January 2020, a few months before the pandemic, this indicator had 87.2 points out of 100. However, during the month of March 2020, the date on which the Covid pandemic broke out in Spain, this indicator was at 63.3 points and 49.9 points in the following month. In fact, April 2020 and October 2020 were the months with lower consumer confidence. The months between July and October 2020 this figure was very close to 50 out of 100. Actually, a significant comeback related to consumer confidence is not identified until January 2021, almost a year after the start of the Covid pandemic in Spain (CIS, 2020, 2021, 2022). These data can help understand to what extent society felt affected and conditioned by the evolution of the health situation in Spain.

The Media Consumption in Spain in Times of COVID-19

The amount of consumption during the lockdown implied a historical register of TV consumption in Spain. An average of 347 minutes was spent watching television per person per day, which implies 97 minutes more than last year. In that period of time, 33,6 million of Spaniards watched the television daily, which represents 74.2% of the population (Cadena Ser, 2020). Particularly, in April 2020 the average viewer watched TV more than 5 hours per day, this amount of time is more than one hour larger than the same period of the previous year. Regarding the profile of viewers, in April 2020 people older than 64 years old used to watch almost 7 hours and a half hours of TV daily. The average amount of time that women spent watching TV in Spain in April 2020 was 5 hours and 16 minutes (Cadena Ser, 2020).

Brand Positioning Through Advertising

Advertising makes it possible to generate expectations and present the use of a product or service. Advertising wants to condition the behavior of its viewers, as well as generate, reinforce or modify feelings and emotions (Puig, 2011).

In other words, advertising aims to link the products it promotes with meanings that can generate interest and be relevant to the consumer. Therefore, advertising can be understood as a series of messages loaded with symbolism and created to condition people's consumption decisions (Serra Simón, 2021).

In this sense, McCracken (2005) maintains that consumers can see in advertisements symbolic resources and concrete visions of an "ideal self" and that they consume the advertised goods and services to resemble them in some way. Therefore, it can be understood that advertising aims to convey meanings and generate associations of concepts in order to link brands, and the products that are marketed through these brands, with ideals that promote differentiation and increase the desire to consume these items (Corrigan, 2010).

Considering the advertising message and its role in the transmission of meanings for brands and products, we can understand that the brand is a promise of satisfaction from a company to the consumer, although it is not a written contract, consumers expect a quality based on their experience with the brand. The emotional components towards a brand can condition the choice of the brand (Casanoves, 2017). For this reason, advertising often uses emotions to enhance the desired brand positioning.

In fact, for McCracken (2005), brands can be understood as a series of aggregations of meanings. In other words, brands are made up of several components (Ollé and Riu, 2009) and what the consumer ends up perceiving is the sum of all the parts or contact points that make them up. When the consumer perceives that the result of this set of interactions is favorable, satisfaction is given, and if appropriate and there is a possibility, loyalty towards a brand is enhanced (Serra Simón, 2021).

All in all, brands facilitate the purchase process as they allow an association to be established between the brand and a certain level of quality and performance. This makes it possible to make people understand that consuming a product of a certain brand implies reducing risks, satisfying their consumption need and reinforcing their concept of consumer (Ollé and Riu, 2009; Bauman, 2007).

Advertising Investment in Times of COVID-19: TV

Television played a prominent role as a source of information, ahead of the rest of the media. This data seems to contradict previous studies that stated that television had lost its young audience in favor of

Table 1. Comparison of advertising investment (in millions €) between period of time Jan-Sept 2019 and Jan-Sept 2020

TV Channels	Jan-Sept. 2019	Jan-Sept. 2020	% Evol.	Jan-Sept. 2019	Jan-Sept. 2020
Total TV	**1.412,2**	**1.067,6**	**-24,4%**	**100,0**	**100,0**
Total TV. National (open channel)	1.274,4	953,1	-25,2%	90,2	89,3
Total TV. autonomic	61,4	49,2	-19,8%	4,3	4,6
Total TV. Payment channels	74,7	64,0	-14,3%	5,3	6,0
Total TV local	1,7	1,3	-22,7%	0,1	0,1

Source: Rivas (2020). Adapted from InfoAdex

digital media (Montaña Blasco, M.; Ollé Castellà, C. and Lavilla Raso, M, 2020). The growth of the television audience during confinement, also prolonged to a lesser extent over the following weeks, translated into an increase in advertising consumption. However, there was a decrease in the number of advertisements issued (Blanco-Herrero, D., Arcila-Calderón, C. and Gallardo-Camacho, J., 2022).

However, as Rivas (2020) suggests, "the coronavirus pandemic has caused a considerable drop in advertising spending. Ad spends are down 9% on average across Europe, with Germany and France falling by 7% and 12% respectively. Three of this year quarters are expected to have a greater impact that the financial crisis in 2008" (World Economic Forum, 2020). In Spain, there is a significant drop in advertising spending in TV in Spain. In fact, this investment drops -22.2% in the first nine months of 2020.

As Jiménez-Sánchez, Álvaro, Margalina, V.-M., & Vayas-Ruiz, E. (2021, p.30) suggest, COVID-19 has had an impact on both marketing and advertising across industries and countries. Particularly, there has been a drop in marketing and ad spending.

Nevertheless, In March 2020 in Spain, in comparison the previous month, public institutions increased their investment in digital advertising (6.2%). Also did the alimentation sector (2.8%) and the energy (2.2%) sector. On the contrary, the sectors of automotive (6.7%), beauty, hygiene and cosmetics (2,9%) and big distribution (2.6%) suffered the highest drop in the investment of digital advertising (International Advertising Bureau, 2020b, p.8).

The Transformation of Advertising Messages in Times of COVID-19

Considering that brands advertise in order to raise awareness, increase sales and build loyalty, brands try to use media appropriate to reach each objective. As for global brands, tend to run multiple campaigns, including values-based marketing to build association with consumers' identities. (World Economic Forum, 2020),

According to the World Federation of Advertisers (2020), the COVID-19 implied that most marketers (81%) from major multinationals deferred planned campaigns as a result of the crisis. Specifically, 34% initiated short one- to two-month delays; 28% held off for a full quarter and 13% waited for six months before bringing campaigns back to market. Nevertheless, 79% of advertisers expressed that opted for creating new messages that responded directly to the huge impact of the crisis on the people using their products and services. As for the role of brands in time of COVID-19, Jiménez-Sánchez, Álvaro, Margalina, V.-M., & Vayas-Ruiz, E. (2021, p.39), suggest that the main messages promoted by brands have consisted in enhancing the idea of cohesion and solidarity, for instance, using the global hashtag #StayHome, as well as, "generating a positive message, beyond selling their products or brand image"; "express their gratitude to professionals and citizens"; "under the context of a new normality, being aware of having overcome the crisis and . . . products are promoted in relation to the de-escalation phases."

As it will be explained later on, these strategic messages cohabit in order to make ads more memorable and perhaps more persuasive. Therefore, the context of COVID-19 must not be ignored, inasmuch as communications and advertisements obviating the pandemic context generate some kind of strangeness between viewers (Pérez, Pablo & Lobato, María, 2021). According to the authors, this is the reason why advertisers, through their commercials, raise the prospect that there is a better future, although there is a price to pay to get there. In that sense, keeping a brand promise that there will be a tomorrow and a clear possibility of betterment is something that awakens sympathy between viewers In order to raise the increase the liking of viewers, brands should release messages with subtle "calls to action" that do not urge consumers what to do right now, but to invite or suggest to buy in a near future. In fact, brands become more relevant and acquire more liking when, through advertising, they empathize with the viewers by presenting a situation, related to COVID-19, which may result quite familiar to the viewers. Moreover, transmitting the idea that the challenges and harsh situations can be faced more easily if people cooperate is another aspect to be taken into consideration. Likewise, brands should focus more on pull marketing than in push marketing (Pérez, Pablo & Lobato, María, 2021, p.46).

The authors affirm that brands should provide content and inspiration about the consumption of certain categories once the situation improves. This measure is aimed at increasing the desire of consuming a product or service. A solution to achieve this goal is proposing long-term proposals, which can be adjustable to the needs of each consumer. This solution can be provided by measures such as fragment payments, monthly installments, among others (Pérez, Pablo & Lobato, María, 2021, p.47).

As for the emotions and feelings in advertising, the creation of emotional messages in the ads is created with the aim of improving the connection with the audiences and, if possible, generate the buying intention (Grau-Rebollo, 2021).

According to Segarra (2020) "The crisis has made us see the frivolity of many things we do, or what we did two weeks ago, which now seems almost fictitious to us. What this situation allows is to rethink the basics, what I have come to contribute to society as a brand or company. Obviously, I want to make money and progress, but it has to come as a result of something you contribute to society, even if it is a cheaper, easier to consume or beautiful product. I have the feeling that in recent years or decades, which have been very financial, this has been forgotten in pursuit of growth, short-termism, a very shareholder economy, before thinking about what I offer to the market. In the end, the market is a place where we give what we think we can offer to people and we get something in return, money, fame or prestige.. (…) In an increasingly virtual and fragmented world, brands are essential, if I didn't believe it, I wouldn't work on this. In the end we choose based on emotional affinities, desires, and that is caused and generated by brands. That ability that we have to love some more than others, and that in the end has to do with the emotional, is achieved by working on branding. On the other hand, the brand is still the product, how it is explained, how the company acts, those things that we do and communicate build perceptions, and that is the brand. Even if you don't work on it, someone does, everyone has an idea of you, and that is your brand."

- **Research and questions/hypotheses**
  The main hypothesis of this research is that most advertisers included, totally or partially, the context of COVID-19, in order to become more empathetic and respectful with consumers.
  Adapting the message to the new context involves creating new ads in order to keep brands relevant and coherent given the situation of mobility restrictions and social distancing.
  Therefore, through a content analysis of different ads shown in Spanish TV Channels, we will try to identify the main features of these messages:
  -Which is the purpose of the ad?
  -How does it include the context of Covid-19?
  -Which is the main feeling each brand wants to transmit?
  -Is there a relationship of feelings in each sector analyzed?
- **Methods**
  The methods used in this research encompass qualitative content in order to identify key aspects and insights of the creation of these audiovisual spots, and at the same time, understand the value proposition of the brand and its relationship with the core message presented.

KEY FINDINGS: MAIN INNOVATIONS IMPLEMENTED IN ADVERTISING IN TIMES OF COVID-19

Cupra (2021) CUPRA x Ansu Fati: Our Wish for 2021

In that case the brand creates this ad to link, first of all, this brand with the successful soccer player Ansu Fati, which has achieved relevant goals in 2020, even that this year has been harsh for most families, businesses, the cultural sector and a huge part of the society.

For this reason, the brand is trying to provide a positive message of hope thorough this sentence: "We're not going back to normal. We're going Forward", which in fact, can be understood as a positive message both for the brand, the soccer player and the society as a whole. In this sense, the brand on the one hand tries to explain how the team's talent evolves, and how they are facing challenges in difficult times. This explanation aims to encourage fans of the sports club, encourage the concept of self-improvement and the ability to improve thanks to adversity. This comparison, then, aims to amplify the meanings of the brand through unfavorable situations.

Evo Banco (2021) Anuncio: Hipoteca Inteligente EVO Banco

The main insight of this ad is related to the acquisition of new habits, such as having to turn most kinds of socialization, related to work meetings and hobbies, into video calls and online meetings. Due to COVID-19 most people, in order to keep working or keep participating in their hobbies, had to show part of their homes during videoconferences.

The places most shown during these conversations or online activities were living rooms and kitchens. In this specific case, the insights used focus on forced digitalization, mainly in work circumstances. This brand decides to explain a new situation, generated by the pandemic, and relate it to the solutions that can be purchased through the financial products that the company sells.

Table 2. List of ads selected related to COVID-19

Advertiser	Type of Product / Service	Advertising Campaign	Brand Goal	Feeling Related to the Ad
CUPRA	Car Company	"CUPRA x Ansu Fati. Our wish for 2021"	-Enhance partnership between FCB and CUPRA -Promote the brand CUPRA	Positive, encouragement, future positive
Evo Banco	Bank company	"Anuncio - Hipoteca Inteligente EVO Banco"	-Sell mortgage services through insights	Positive, encouragement, future positive
Lay's	Food Company: snacks	"El aperitivo estuvo y estará. Campaña verano 2020"	-Sell the product and positive lifestlye	Positive, encouragement, future positive, the relevance of social interactions
Mahou	Beverage Company: beer	"Ahora más que nunca, Juntos para Siempre I Mahou"	-Show commitment with the bars	Positive, encouragement, future positive
McDonald's	Food Company: fast food	"Es hora de volver a encontrarnos"	-Sell the product and enhance the relevance of socializing	Positive, encouragement, future positive
Mútua Madrileña	Insurance company	"Anuncio 1 Grupo Mutua Madrileña Navidad 2020"	-Sell the service in a friendly way	Positive, change of priorities due to COVID-19.
Schweppes	Beverage Company: tonic water	"Schweppes: Imperfectamente perfecta"	-Sell the product and positive lifestlye	Positive, encouragement, future positive

Source: own elaboration

The brand, a banking company, uses this insight to explain up to which extent people judge the others by their homes, and how unconsciously people tend to compare to each other.

Therefore, in an apparently comical tone, the brand intends to relate social reputation with economic status, indicated by the qualities or characteristics of the home. All in all, this insight is used to sell mortgages, considering that "if your house is better, your social reputation will increase".

Lay's ESP (2020) "El Aperitivo Estuvo y Estará: Campaña Verano 2020."

In that particular case, the brand suggests its role as a product related to socialization, leisure and related to human contact between people who live close to each other. Although there are some restrictions related to human contact (World Health Organization, 2022), the brand tries to explain that the product is related to social gatherings, and even if they are not possible in the same way as they used to be, the brand tries to reinforce the idea that casual meetings with friends are relative are more fun with that snack. This campaign reflects new habits that emerged in some cases during covid-19. It is about a closer relationship with neighbors, despite the restrictions and limitations of social distancing (El Periódico, 2020).

Thus, the brand is based on feelings of proximity, security, sympathy, solidarity and respect towards other people, while at the same time highlighting the concept of a healthy snack and the relevance of quality social interaction. In the context of the pandemic and confinement, loneliness has been one of the main aspects that has affected people the most. All in all, the brand aims to become involved as an agent capable of helping people and neighbors to socialize in a safe and domestic way.

Mahou (2020) Ahora Más Que Nunca, Juntos Para Siempre | Mahou

The main insight of this ad is explaining the harsh situation caused by the lockdown of the bars and restaurants in Spain. This is the reason why the first part of the ad appears in black and white and with a nostalgic tune. As for the second part, it encourages, when possible, people to meet, go to restaurants and enjoy live as they used to do. All in all, this message tries to achieve a double goal, first of all, avoid the closing of restaurants in Spain, which are a relevant part of the economy (Antena 3, 2017); In fact, it should be explained that "Spain is the country with the most bars and restaurants per person in the world: one for every 175 inhabitants, according to the National Institute of Statistics (INE)" (El Mundo, 2020); and secondly, show the commitment of the brand with the places in which its products are sold and consumed. Considering this fact, we can understand how the brand intends to value a part of the country's heritage and the "bar culture". At the same time, it aims to encourage restaurateurs and consumers to maintain the habits of consuming in bars.

It can be understood that this piece brings together feelings such as nostalgia, drive and motivation to persevere and support local businesses.

Consequently, the brand, through this message of collective encouragement, also aims to reinforce its brand presence and encourage different audiences to have a predisposition to consume the brand's products.

McDonald's (2020) Es Hora De Volver a Encontrarnos

This ad, which is quite nostalgic and sentimental, uses a call of a daughter to her father. In that case, the daughter leaves a message to her father's answering machine to explain him how much she loves him, although previously she had not said it as often as she wanted to, and that she and her daughter, a little girl, are coming to visit him. Perhaps someone else will come with them too, but it is not directly mentioned.

In her monologue, she emphasizes that the granddaughter has been told, supposedly by her and her partner, and not to hug him, in order to follow the safety instructions in times of COVID promoted by the World Health Organization.

Although in that ad it does not appear directly any person at any time, the characters: the daughter, who is the speaker, the little girl and the father, are supposed to meet near the house, in a McDonald's restaurant.

The relevance of the advertising message is based on different factors. Firstly, the tonality of the advertising piece. At the beginning, the dim light of the house conveys the concept of loneliness, sadness, emptiness and even mourning. These are concepts linked to the collective imagination of the pandemic and its consequences on the most vulnerable groups, especially the elderly and people in nursing homes.

However, the advertisement proposes a twist, focused on optimism, which is communicated through contact between the elderly person and the figure of the granddaughter. The concept of hope is communicated in the advertising piece through the light appearance of the yellow chromatic tone, representative of the food brand. Thus, we see how the ad uses the storytelling to approach the brand to the consumers. To do so the ad is based on an emotive story related to familiar relationships and the difficulty to interact during the pandemic.

Mútua Madrileña (2020) Anuncio 1 Grupo Mutua Madrileña Navidad 2020

This advertisement can be understood as an example of the genre "slices of life". Specifically, it is formed by moments or situations are shown that are apparently catastrophic for the people who are experiencing them. All situations refer to carelessness, damage to property, defects, expensive repairs... These are problems that in principle imply a complication in people's lives, or a high cost due to material damage. However, the protagonists of the different pieces, instead of getting frustrated, angry or showing anger at the situation they experienced, begin to laugh and put all these problems into perspective.

The core message of this ad is created to explain that the service provided by the company is very reliable for all its customers. Therefore, given the difficulties caused by the COVID-19, its consumers do not need to worry about "details" such as damages caused to their properties, such as cars and houses, because this company is there to assist them.

In this context, the brand, through this advertising campaign, is indirectly taking advantage of the concept of pandemic and inconveniences related to confinement and restrictions on mobility and freedoms of the collective imagination to relativize the damage to material products since, considering the tragic moments and social distancing that have been experienced, repairs and damages have a solution.

Through this audiovisual piece, the brand aims to show sympathy in the different cases and reinforce the idea that its function is to ensure that the company's clients can live without fear of domestic catastrophes and repairs since the mission of the insurance company It is to protect clients and ensure that they can live without worries or complications.

Schweppes España (2021) "Schweppes: Imperfectamente Perfecta"

This ad clearly shows the situation of lockdown and tries to promote the product as a way of socializing, even if virtually. Moreover, it can be understood as a reminder of the role of brand and it is trying to motivate its viewers of going to bars with friends and relatives when possible. At the same time, it ads contains relevant insights related to the pandemic, such as the moment of clapping hands at the balconies as homage to health workers, which in Spain happened every day, at 8:00 p.m during some months.

We can understand that drinks and soft drinks are usually social products, that is, they are largely consumed in the company of other people or in informal or meeting situations. Considering this fact, we see how the brand intends to maintain its role as a social drink, despite mobility restrictions. Thus, the advertiser chooses to incorporate the product in new contexts, such as virtual meetings, and contexts in which the product is linked to a social encounter, whether in person or online format.

This way of advertising serves to maintain brand positioning, remember the product and imply that the brand is still valid despite the changes in routines caused by Covid-19.

Ads Beyond COVID-19 Lockdown and Its References to This Period of Time

Once the lockdown situation was over, some of the advertisers in the food and beverage sectors chose to, indirectly, refer to some moments of those weeks. The purpose of these indirect mentions was to highlight different aspects related to learning from Covid. Some of the aspects to comment on could be learning about the use of technology, the relevance of social meetings, family interactions and, above all, linking these learnings from society with the product or the brand's value proposition.

One of the examples to comment on would be the advertising campaign of the company Casa Tarradellas. This company, which is dedicated to the production of pizzas, *fuet*, and pastry dough, through its ads links themes related to family, tradition, close and quality family relationships and the concept of homemade, healthy and, depending on the ad, informal contexts.

Through the protagonists of the piece it can be seen how two people from different generations interact, apparently to maintain contact, through electronic devices in a fairly fluid way (Casa Tarradellas, 2020). Although the concept of lockdown is not directly mentioned in this piece, it can be understood that the pretext of lockdown is used to justify the interaction of a grandfather and his granddaughter through screens. This fact is a clear reference that, some people, especially senior people, had to learn digital skills to be connected with their relatives due to mobility restrictions.

Thus, from this case, we can explain that most ads aim to be a kind of idealized reflection of society and aim to transmit values that are beneficial for the brand, the product and the desired positioning of the brand. In this specific case, this message contains an extra layer of meaning, as it values the product, enhances the relationships between relatives from different generations and also explains in an indirect way that the lockdown involved a process of learning for some consumers.

MAIN CONCLUSIONS

Advertising provides insights and images representative of an exceptional period who most people did not to expect to live at any time. These commercial messages have captured the essence of temporary restrictions and can be used to witness some new habits adopted by society due to lockdown caused by COVID-19 (Grau-Rebollo, J., 2021).

Considering this, the selected spots of these brands tend to use include a layer feelings in the messages in order to link the feelings associated to these messages to the consumption of a product, service or the overall brand (Batey, 2013). Therefore, it can be understood that brands have found ways to readjust their communication in order to become coherent, relevant and plausible in a quite uncertain context (Pérez, Pablo & Lobato, María, 2021; Blanco-Herrero, D.; Gallardo-Camacho, J.; Arcila-Calderón, C., 2021).

Given a context in which consumers have to face lots of restrictions related to patterns of mobility, consumption and limitations that have affected people wellbeing, brands want to demonstrate their commitment with their customers and express solidarity, respect, empathy and consciousness. In that sense, most selected brands tend to highlight its features, its role in the life of consumers and how its consumption can help people live a life as good as possible in a context that is not very favorable for citizens.

Considering these cases, regardless of whether they are sectors related to the automotive, food or motorsports, the selected speakers aim to arouse interest and sympathy with the audiences and maintain popularity. This change in advertising communication is the result of an unexpected situation. However, the rapid reaction of brands and their discourse contributes to generating an updated brand positioning, in line with the needs, fears, concerns of consumers and with the situations or insights they are experiencing during these times.

All in all, COVID-19 has had tangible effects in advertising campaigns because companies have adapted their commercial communication to show empathy, respect and coherence with the rules encouraged by government and global health organizations (World Economic Forum, 2020). Hence, these cases are examples of commercial messages created due to COVID-19 and, at the same time, aligned with the communication goals of each selected brand.

The communicative approach of the campaigns must be carried out with respect and coherence for each brand. However, it can be understood that brands opted for selecting key moments in people's lives during the months of lockdown to generate new speeches and stories, adapted to the context and created with the desire to connect with audiences. Thus, we see how engagement is a relevant part for brands since these messages are created with the clear goal of creating connections with users and awaken their emotions that induce them to prefer one brand over another.

Although each brand analyzed communicates messages in its own way, common guidelines are identified in relation to the brand. Firstly, each brand maintains the aesthetics of its ads in a way similar to the ads before confinement. This allows the messages to be coherent, both in terms of aesthetics and also in terms of the meanings they want to transmit.

The main values that are transferred to the recipients are the ability to face challenges, perseverance and courage, through consumption, to overcome the situation. In addition to this, audiovisual pieces include aspects that allow the brand to be easily recognized, be it the logo, corporate colors and pre-defined contexts of use.

Thus, the feelings that brands transmit respond to the objective of positioning the brand, generating sales in the short or medium term and, at the same time, encouraging the population to follow the measures decreed by the government and authorities.

Regarding the common point of the brands analyzed is, broadly speaking, optimism and the perspective that the situation will improve if people behave in a way that is respectful and consistent with the instructions. In fact, this expectation of improvement in the situation invites enthusiasm and the belief that the confinement situation can be overcome. Thus, we can affirm that through the analysis of the selected cases we can have a qualitative idea of the messages that companies from different sectors have transmitted to their audiences.

In reference to the possible avenues of study to be taken into consideration, it would be interesting to qualitatively analyze advertising pieces from similar sectors in other territorial areas. This would allow us to identify similarities, insights related to confinement and transversal messages in the different sectors.

REFERENCES

Antena 3. (2017). *España es el país con más bares del mundo con más de 250.000 establecimientos.* https://www.antena3.com/noticias/economia/espana-es-el-pais-con-mas-bares-del-mundo_201710235 9ee45720cf2fc58bffee31a.html

Banco, E. (2021). *Anuncio - Hipoteca Inteligente EVO Banco.* https://www.youtube.com/watch?v=Sxzdg5pD7ec

Batey, M. (2013). El significado de la marca. Cómo y porqué ponemos sentido a productos y servicios. Granica.

Bauman, Z. (2007). *Vida de consumo.* Fondo de Cultura Económica.

Blanco-Herrero, D., Arcila-Calderón, C., & Gallardo-Camacho, J. (2022). Efectos del confinamiento y la pandemia en los anuncios emitidos en las dos principales cadenas de televisión privadas en España. *Palabra Clave (La Plata), 25*(1), e2512.

Blanco-Herrero, D., Gallardo-Camacho, J., & Arcila-Calderón, C. (2021). Health Advertising during the Lockdown: A Comparative Analysis of Commercial TV in Spain. *Int. J. Environ. Res. Public Health, 18*, 1054. doi:10.3390/ijerph18031054

Boix, C. J. (2017). Fundamentos del Branding. Claves para construir una marca poderosa. Barcelona: Editorial Profit.

Chow, M., & Stanford, K. (2021). *Cuatro tendencias de la era COVID-19 que tendrán un impacto duradero en los productos y las experiencias de consumo*. Available at: https://www.thinkwithgoogle.com/intl/es-es/futuro-del-marketing/transformacion-digital/covid-19-tendencias-1-ano/

CIS. (2020). *Índice de confianza del consumidor. Mes de diciembre evolución de resultados Estudio nº 3304 Diciembre 2020*. https://www.cis.es/cis/export/sites/default/-Archivos/ICC/2020/ICC_12-20_3304.pdf

CIS. (2021). *Índice de confianza del consumidor. Mes de diciembre evolución de resultados Estudio nº 3345 Diciembre 2021*. https://www.cis.es/cis/export/sites/default/-Archivos/ICC/2021/ICC_12-21_3345.pdf

CIS. (2022). *Índice de confianza del consumidor. Mes de abril evolución de resultados Estudio nº 3361 Abril 2022*. https://www.cis.es/cis/export/sites/default/-Archivos/ICC/2022/ICC_04-22_3361.pdf

Corrigan, P. (2010). *The Sociology of Consumption*. SAGE Publication.

de Castro Pérez, I. (2021). *Impacto del covid-19 en la industria publicitaria española*. https://repositorio.comillas.edu/xmlui/bitstream/handle/11531/46556/TFG%20-%20De%20Castro%20Perez%2C%20Irene.pdf?sequence=3

Eguizábal, R. (2011). Teoría de la Publicidad (3rd ed.). Cátedra.

España, S. (2021). *Schweppes: Imperfectamente perfecta*. https://www.youtube.com/watch?v=xPUB5zdr1Xw

European Commission. (2021). *Factsheet on key consumer data 2020*. Accessed online 20 March 2023 at: https://commission.europa.eu/system/files/2021-03/120321_key_consumer_data_factsheet_en.pdf

Gobierno de España. (2022). *Crisis sanitaria COVID-19: Normativa e información útil*. Available at: https://administracion.gob.es/pag_Home/atencionCiudadana/Crisis-sanitaria-COVID-19.html

Grau-Rebollo, J. (2021). Confinement narratives: TV advertising during the coronavirus outbreak in Spain. *Perifèria, revista de recerca i formació en antropologia, 26*(1), 7-28. doi:10.5565/rev/periferia.822

International Advertising Bureau. (2020b). *Monthly Flash de Inversión y Audiencia en Medios Digitales IAB-PwC. Seguimiento mensual Febrero – Marzo*. International Advertising Bureau - Spain. Available at: https://iabspain.es/estudio/flash-mensual-de-inversion-y-audiencias-en-medios-digitales-febrero-marzo-2020/

Juran Institute. (1994). *Gestión de la Calidad. Mejora de la calidad en los servicios*. AENOR.

Lay's, E. S. P. (2020). *El aperitivo estuvo y estará. Campaña verano 2020*. Available at: https://www.youtube.com/watch?v=q0pICV_9bHo

Madrileña, M. (2020). *Anuncio 1 Grupo Mutua Madrileña Navidad 2020 (06/12/2020)*. Available at: https://www.youtube.com/watch?v=18PbhF8K9Sg

Mahou, T. V. (2020). *Ahora más que nunca, Juntos para Siempre | Mahou*. Available at: https://www.youtube.com/watch?v=o3DjRl1fBYY

McCracken, G. (2005). *Culture and consumption II. Markets, meaning, and Brand Management*. Indiana University Press.

McDonald's. (2020). *"Es hora de volver a encontrarnos", la nueva campaña de #McDonald's*. Available at: https://www.youtube.com/watch?v=mAxAlwv0PmA

Montaña Blasco, M., Ollé Castellà, C., & Lavilla Raso, M. (2020). Impacto de la pandemia de Covid-19 en el consumo de medios en España. *Revista Latina de Comunicación Social, 78*, 155-167. https://www.doi.org/10.4185/RLCS-2020-14

Mundo, E. (2020). *España, el país con más bares y restaurantes del mundo, pide convertirlos en Patrimonio de la Humanidad*. Accessed 20 March 2023: https://www.elmundo.es/viajes/espana/2020/06/19/5eeb49defdddffe66b8b4587.html

Oficial, C. U. P. R. A. (2021). *CUPRA x Ansu Fati. Our wish for 2021*. Available at: https://www.youtube.com/watch?v=jtjj_3Yo8Qs

Ollé, R., & Riu, D. (2009). El nuevo Brand Management. Cómo plantar marcas para hacer crecer negocios. *Gestion*.

Perceptions, A. (2020). *Coronavirus Effect on Advertising Report*. Available at: https://www.advertiserperceptions.com/wp-content/uploads/2020/03/03.25.2020-Coronavirus-Effect-on-Advertising-WEBINAR-PDF-1.pdf

Pérez, P., & Lobato, M. (2021). *Un nuevo año, ¿un nuevo comienzo?* Google. Available at: https://www.thinkwithgoogle.com/intl/es-es/insights/descubriendo-al-nuevo-consumidor-nuevo-comienzo/

Periódico, E. (2020). *Cultura de cuarentena: Begoña Alberdi, la soprano que cada noche regala ópera a sus vecinos*. Accessed 20 March 2023 at: https://www.elperiodico.com/es/ocio-y-cultura/20200317/cultura-cuarentena-begona-alberdi-soprano-regala-opera-vecinos-sant-antoni-7892439

Puig, N. (2011). *Emocions i publicitat. El lligam emocional entre l'emissor i el receptor de la publicitat*. Tesi doctoral. Accessed 20 March 2023 at: https://www.tesisenred.net/handle/10803/31846

Rivas, C. (2020). *La Inversión Publicitaria cae un -22,2% en los nueve primeros meses de 2020. Infoadex*. Available at: https://www.infoadex.es/home/inversion-publicitaria-cae-22-septiembre-2020/

Rossi, R., Socci, V., Talevi, D., Mensi, S., Niolu, C., Pacitti, F., Di Marco, A., Rossi, A., Siracusano, A., & Di Lorenzo, G. (2020). COVID-19 Pandemic and Lockdown Measures Impact on Mental Health Among the General Population in Italy. *Frontiers in Psychiatry, 11*, 790. doi:10.3389/fpsyt.2020.00790 PMID:32848952

Segarra, T. (2020). *Ahora mismo hay que hacer lo más posible y decir lo menos possible.* Accessed 23 March: https://www.modaes.com/back-stage/toni-segarra-ahora-mismo-hay-que-hacer-lo-mas-posible-y-decir-lo-menos-posible

Ser, C. (2020). *El Confinamiento Lleva a Récord Histórico el Consumo de Televisión: 5 Horas al Día por Persona.* Available at: https://bit.ly/3VfU6dZ

Simón, S. J. (2021). *Disseny d'un model d'anàlisi per a la qualitat percebuda: productes, destinacions i serveis.* Doctoral Thesis. Accessed 20 March 2023 at: https://www.tdx.cat/handle/10803/673754#page=1

Tarradellas, C. (2020). *Sigamos haciendo las cosas buenas que hemos aprendido - Espetec Casa Tarradellas.* https://www.youtube.com/watch?v=9CGAObU1lZY

World Economic Forum. (2020). *This is how COVID-19 is affecting the advertising industry.* Available at: https://www.weforum.org/agenda/2020/06/coronavirus-advertising-marketing-covid19-pandemic-business/

World Federation of Advertisers. (2020). *Eighty Percent of Multinationals Deferring Campaigns But the Same Number Are Creating New Content in Response to the COVID-19 Crisis.* World Federation of Advertisers - WFA. Available at: https://wfanet.org/knowledge/item/2020/04/07/Eighty-percent-of-multinationals-deferring-campaigns-but-the-same-number-are-creating-new-content-in-response-to-the-Covid19-crisis

World Health Organization. (2022). *Coronavirus disease (COVID19) advice for the public.* Available at: https://www.who.int/emergencies/diseases/novel-coronavirus-2019/advice-for-public

Chapter 13
Hashtag Activism Due to Restrictions and Measures During the COVID-19 Pandemic in Turkey

Özlem Çetin Öztürk
https://orcid.org/0000-0002-4155-3352
Istanbul Gelisim University, Turkey

ABSTRACT

This study examines the hashtag activism of Twitter users who became slacktivists regarding pandemic restrictions and measures in Turkey's first year of the COVID-19 pandemic. From March 2020 to March 2021, 1,464,334 tweets regarding all 13 hashtag activisms, which were the most participated in each month according to the course of the pandemic, were collected using Twitter API and examined with big data analysis. Out of the 13 hashtag activisms with the highest number of tweets analyzed by month, the demand for measures and regulations to be taken to protect against the risks posed by the pandemic came to the forefront in 9, while the demand for lifting or easing the restrictions in 4 of them came to the forefront. Students, detainees and prisoners, and teachers were the actors of the most tweeted hashtag activism. The average mentioned rate of decision makers and authorities in the 13 activisms is 71.52%. As a result, in the first year of the pandemic in Turkey, hashtag activism supporting the implementation of measures and restrictions was more common.

INTRODUCTION

The efforts of social movements to use the media, to be present in the media, and to create their own media is, of course, not a new phenomenon. From Vladimir I. Lenin (1992) attributed a revolutionary role to the socialist press in the struggle of the proletariat to ensure solidarity, organization, and class consciousness, to the Zapatistas' use of the Internet to build alternative networks of resistance against neoliberal policies around the world (Burbach, 2001; Castells, 2008). Social movements have positioned

DOI: 10.4018/979-8-3693-0896-7.ch013

the media as one of the strategic tools of their struggle for organizing, forming public opinion, expressing their opinions, and solidarity, despite the different nature of the means of communication and the mechanisms of repression and censorship.

However, it is an irrefutable reality that digital media, and social media in particular, have differentiated and diversified the action repertoires of social movements. According to Bonilla and Rosa (2015), Twitter has a different significance among the forms of digital activism used to express forms of action mediated by digital communication technologies: Twitter's "multivocality and dialogicality" nature distinguishes it from other digital tools used by social movements to disseminate and amplify their struggles, as it makes it possible to see different perspectives and feel individual reactions at the same time (p.7). The use of hashtags has supported Twitter's use as a 'multivocal and dialogical' activist tool. The transformation of the hash (#) into an activist tool as a marking and indexing system on digital platforms in the form of tags is defined as hashtag activism.

While hashtags can become a means of making a global impact on activism, the power of hashtags in terms of their impact on the real world is a matter of debate. This debate is shaped on the one hand by the possibilities that hashtag activism provides for real-life forms of social dissent (Shirky, 2008, 2011; Soriano, 2013; Zulli, 2020) and on the other by the claim that its role in achieving concrete political results for real political gains does not go beyond slacktivism (Morozov, 2009, 2011; Christensen, 2011; Halupka, 2014; Glenn, 2015).

Although this study inevitably questions these debates in a conceptual context, it seeks to emphasize the importance of the collective narrative structure and themes that emerge with hashtag activism, rather than focusing on the impact of activism that is collectively manifested through the use of hashtags on political decision-making mechanisms in terms of achieving concrete political gains. This study evaluates hashtag activism in the context of the collective production of political discourse and how this collective narrative structure also includes a guiding character in how collective action is framed.

In this context, the study aims to reveal how Twitter users who had to become slacktivists in the first year of the COVID-19 pandemic, when real activism was restricted by imposing bans on demonstrations and mass marches in Turkey, framed collective actions in their hashtag activism practices regarding the measures and restrictions imposed. In line with this purpose, the hashtag activism on Twitter regarding the restrictions and measures imposed due to the COVID-19 pandemic in the one-year period between March 11, 2020, and March 11, 2021, when the COVID-19 case was seen, is examined using big data text analysis technique. The main problem of the study is shaped to explain whether hashtag activism against pandemic measures and restriction policies supports these policies and which issues come to the fore.

HASHTAG USAGE

The first use of hashtags in the digital environment actually began in 1988 in Internet Relay Chat (IRC), long before Twitter, first to mark channels and then to group videos, images, and topics (Chu, 2017, p. 390). One example of the widespread use of hashtags in IRC occurred during the Iraqi invasion of Kuwait in the Gulf War, when the Internet remained the only source of news due to a week-long radio and TV broadcast blackout (Salazar, 2017, p. 23). In fact, this can be regarded as an early example of the hashtag's later spread and current use on Twitter, reflecting the origins of creating a common narrative by sharing and following news on a certain topic. Therefore, the hashtag offered usage experiences similar to current usage, albeit much more limited, in IRC before Twitter.

The hashtag feature on Twitter was created in 2007 by Chris Messina, a former Google programmer, as free software designed as an unmoderated forum function to allow users to interact with each other on a specific topic and to allow the free circulation of ideas (Couts, 2015). Messina responds to a question about the hashtag being a free software product as follows: "*I've been asked, "Why didn't you patent it?" and it's because I saw it as a way of shaping thoughts, and it's important that thought remains free. That idea would be imperiled or hindered had I tried to assert some kind of ownership over it.*" (Stephens, 2018, p.46). The first hashtag on Twitter was also created by Messina: "*how do you feel about using # (pound) for groups?. As in #barcamp [msg]?*" (Stephens, 2018, p.44). The use of the hashtag to encourage participation and discussion on a particular topic, as Messina intended, occurred on October 22, 2007, when several users tweeted under the hashtag #sandiegofire to report on the events during the San Diego fires in California. Soon, many other users began to follow the #sandiegofire hashtag for important updates. In this way, the hashtag was used to reach a large and immediate audience to share and follow up-to-date information on a particular topic (Sharf, 2013; Bruns & Burgess, 2011, p.3).

HASHTAG ACTIVISM

The use of hashtags on Twitter has become widespread over time, both through its incorporation into users' habits and through its inclusion as a cross-reference to search and trending topic features in Twitter's system architecture (Bruns & Burgess, 2011). Since 2007, the hashtag's ability to unite followers over a specific topic has been used both as a part of popular culture for commenting on TV shows, etc. for entertainment purposes and for the use of jargon, caps, and memes generated within the platform itself, and for social responsibility, awareness, and solidarity campaigns to coordinate in emergencies and directly achieve political goals (Bruns & Burgess, 2011, pp. 3-5).

The hashtag was first discussed as a form of activism by Eric Augenbraun in The Guardian newspaper in 2011 for the Occupy Wall Street movements as "*the birth of a new form of technology-based social movement*" (Augenbraun, 2011). The conceptualization of hashtag as a form of activism can be defined in the simplest terms as a type of collective action in which several users share political and social arguments that they put forward in a pre-planned time frame or spontaneously with a single hashtag or similar hashtags.

Tombleson and Wolf (2017) defined hashtag activism as the act of fighting or supporting a struggle, using hashtags as the primary channel to raise awareness about an issue and promote discussion through social media (p.15). Hence, their emphasis is on the hashtag as a means of raising and participating in the debate. Ofori-Parku and Moscato (2018) define hashtag activism as the use of hashtags to draw attention to social issues and mobilize communities into action. Using the #BlackLivesMatter protests as an example, they emphasize that hashtags can be political slogans and political slogans can be hashtags. They, therefore characterize hashtag activism as 'hashtag-related activism' (p. 2482). By equating the transformation of slogans into hashtags with the transformation of hashtags into slogans, hashtag-related activism may make it more difficult to conceptually position hashtag activism; however, what should be considered here is its relationship with real-life forms of social opposition.

Anastasia Kavada acknowledges that in terms of real-life impact, online tools have had considerable speed and success in bringing information to a wider audience, stimulating and mobilizing them for collective action. However, she argues that they do not provide the sustainability that collective action requires. According to Kavada, because online activist tools create loose and flexible structures, people can quickly leave the collective action they joined with a single click. Therefore, the stability and continuity that would ensure the success of collective action cannot be guaranteed by online tools (Kavada, 2010, pp.113-118). That is also the case when we consider the ephemeral nature of Twitter and hashtags.

LIMITS AND POSSIBILITIES

Whether or not hashtag activism is related to traditional forms of collective action, its impact on the real world, and its role in achieving concrete political outcomes is open to debate. In the article mentioned above, Augenbraun (2011) used the term hashtag activism for the first time, and at the same time, he also laid out the axis of debate in the literature on digital activism: "*While such technologies can be extremely useful tools, they do not represent alternatives to the exhausting, age-old work of meeting people where they are, hearing their concerns, reaching common ground, building trust and convincing them that it is in their interests to act politically to change their circumstances*" (para.11). Criticisms of all forms of digital activism, including the emphases in Augenbraun's critique, are often couched in terms such as armchair activism, click activism, clicktivism and slacktivism. Scholz (2010) argues that these concepts of the value of social media for activism are "*a kind of liberal catharsis during lunch break that gives participants the impression that they have done something about the issues when, in fact, their online action had no offline effect at all*" (p. 27). Among these concepts, slacktivism, whose use is more widely accepted in the literature, emphasizes the misconception that atomized individuals satisfy themselves in terms of their public existence with the hashtag they share while sipping their coffee in the comfort of their homes and that they are engaged in meaningful action.

Slacktivism or Collective Action

Henrik S. Christensen (2011) notes that the concept of online activism as a pejorative originally had a positive connotation when it was used by Fred Clark and Dwight Ozard in 1995 to characterize the activities of young people to influence society on an individual scale. Over time, however, it has come to refer disparagingly to activities that are easily carried out without political commitment and without the effort to achieve a political goal. The concept is explained around the argument that digital activism has no impact on real life and that these actions are futile and naïve (Lee & Hsieh, 2013). Slacktivism is used to describe low-risk, low-cost, online activism through social media whose goal is to raise awareness, produce change, or satisfy the activist (Rotman, et al. 2011, p. 3), and is more often used as a parallel to traditional activism to bring about social change. Around the concept of slacktivism, forms of online activism are treated as low-effort, low-risk political endeavors that are far from achieving tangible gains. The emphasis on slacktivism reveals an approach to hashtags and online activism that claims that they promote laziness "*where people become satisfied by merely posting from the comfort of their rooms*" (Offori-Parku & Moscato, 2018, p.2483).

Evengy Morozov (2009), who believes that forms of online activism cannot create real political transformation and that political transformations are possible only through reform movements with political institutions and long-standing engaged efforts, considers slacktivism to be an appropriate term to describe feel-good online activism with zero political or social impact (para.1). Morozov's (2009; 2011) emphasis on slacktivism is based on the fact that online activism is entirely dysfunctional in terms of its real-life impact as it cannot elicit engaged political participation in terms of collective action.

Malcolm Gladwell (2010), one of the stronger proponents of this claim, explains why "revolution will not be tweeted" arguing that although social media increases participation in terms of collective action, it destroys commitment to action, which is a crucial element of collective action's success. According to Gladwell, social media is effective in increasing participation by reducing the level of motivation required to engage in real-life collective action. Because by building 'weak ties', social media platforms do not offer a space for activism where real political outcomes can be achieved for participants who are detached from the real risks and sacrifices involved in real action (Gladwell, 2010). In other words, he sees social media as a space for superficial efforts by those who cannot make sacrifices for real change. He finds social media dysfunctional in terms of activism, with his argument centered around the activist's sense of belonging to the struggle and the risks and sacrifices they take for collective action to achieve concrete political results.

From a more reasonable perspective, Christensen (2011) argues that online activism cannot have an impact on real-life politics and that "*Internet activities are at worst harmless fun (or an annoyance, but nonetheless harmless) without any effect on real-life politics. At best, they may help raise awareness about political issues and even mobilize citizens to take other forms of action outside the virtual world*", but adds that political participation is much more than slacktivism (Conclusion section, para.11). Jackson et al. (2020) argued that hashtag activists, vilified as slacktivists, 'can create social change'. They claim that hashtags can influence political decision-making, so criticizing hashtag activism for being "*considered less valid than direct action and is mistakenly regarded as in competition with it*" is disputable (p. xxxii). Drawing on examples of hashtags such as #BlackLivesMatter and #MeToo, they argue that it has had a far-reaching impact, bringing debates about identity politics, inequality, violence, and civil rights from the periphery to the center and even to the presidential agenda in the US.

While its role in achieving tangible political gains is open to debate, treating digital activism in general and hashtag activism in particular as completely dysfunctional tools of collective action means ignoring the potential of collective effort in advance. Therefore, it is necessary to consider that Christensen's best-case scenario can have an impact that cannot be underestimated. Digital platforms, which enable collective actions to reach the masses, can be tactically used according to the purpose of the collective action, such as raising the agenda, raising awareness, solidarity, and organizing. In this context, Shaw points to existing literature that downplays the political potential of digital activist communities that only emerge online, noting that most research on social movement actors' use of digital media focuses on the logistical organization of protests, arguing that online discourse is a mode of activism that can set off sociopolitical change with or without the aid of offline collective action (cited in Clark, 2016, p.4). Thus, following Shaw, hashtag activism should not be seen as an alternative to engaged social movements, but as a means of generating online political discourse that can support the success of real collective action.

Bennett and Segerberg (2012) emphasize that hashtag networks reveal a collectively constructed narrative structure. According to them, collective action occurs when personal frames of action or "easily personalized ideas" are connected through digital networks (pp. 743-744). They conceptualize this type of collective action as "connective action". Connective action is understood as a type of activism that emerges within communication networks rather than organizational structures. Bennett and Segeberg's theory of connective action emphasizes the mechanisms by which tweets, despite their brevity, can become building blocks for thematically connected narratives, collectively constructed through hashtag networks (Clark, 2016, p.5).

Yang (2016), who considers hashtag activism as "*discursive protest on social media united through a hashtagged word, phrase, or sentence*" as a field where political discourse is formed, draws attention to the differences in the narrative structures of social media platforms (p.13). Digital forms of activism create online protest activity by publishing longer narratives that can be widely disseminated, but the voices involved are more limited than in hashtag activism. Hashtag activism facilitates users to search, connect, and interact through the hashtag and share stories about it, creating a narrative structure with a beginning and an end that is co-created by everyone who posts with the hashtag. According to Yang, the narrative structure that emerges in hashtag activism expresses objections, demands, and protests aimed at immediate action, often challenging narratives in mainstream media. With hashtags, textual signals and rhetorical devices are also used to guide followers' comprehension of how symbolic action is framed, thereby encouraging them to participate. People participate in the action by reading, retweeting, commenting on others' tweets, or sending their tweets with the same hashtag. It allows people to interact with each other and collectively create a larger narrative (pp.14-15). Therefore, following Yang, it can be argued that hashtag activism is more vocal, pluralistic, and interactive than other forms of digital activism and that a collective narrative structure emerges that can encourage more engagement in action. A narrative structure co-produced by many people also guides how collective action is framed.

Today, we are no longer expected to see an example of activism that does not use social media platforms such as Twitter (Gurak, 2014; Uçkan, 2012). According to the usage practices of hashtags; (a) hashtag activism for supporting offline actions (coordination of activism forms in real life, organizing, gaining supporters for them, and using them for purposes such as creating public opinion, providing informational flow, calling for actions), (b) hashtag activism that continues and ends entirely on the social media platform, and (c) hashtag activism that initiates offline actions that start using hashtags and spill out onto the streets. However, the common point of all these usage practices includes the collective narrative structure created. Hashtag activism involves "at best" the collective production of political discourse, and this collective narrative structure also has a guiding character in terms of how collective action is framed.

SAMPLING OF THE STUDY AND METHOD

With the COVID-19 pandemic, a period in which various restrictions and measures were taken all over the world, activists were necessarily led to use forms of activism criticized as slacktivism under pandemic conditions. Because pandemic measures restricted traditional forms of collective action in many parts of the world, hashtag campaigns were organized on social media. In 2020, #COVID19 ranked first, and #StayHome ranked third among the most shared hashtags on Twitter worldwide (McGraw, 2020). In Turkey, in the same year, #Survivor2020 ranked first, #evdekal ranked fifth, and #covid19 ranked eighth as the most used hashtags. In parallel with the course of the fight against the pandemic and the start of controlled normalization processes, pandemic-related hashtags decreased significantly worldwide and also in Turkey in 2021 and could not be included in the ranking of the most used hashtags.[i] It is possible to assume that 2021 is expected to see a decrease in pandemic-related posts on Twitter as normalization processes are initiated and the measures and restrictions taken become a part of daily life.[ii]

On the other hand, since Twitter has come to the forefront as an activist social media platform since the beginning of the pandemic and since Twitter is the social media platform most actively used by the Minister of Health Fahrettin Koca in Turkey, discussions and demands regarding the pandemic process have been intensively put forward on this platform.

The study focuses on hashtag activism on Twitter during the one-year period between March 11, 2020, when the first case was observed in Turkey, and March 11, 2021. The aim is to understand how hashtag activism regarding pandemic management was shaped and which demands came to the fore during this one-year period. Accordingly, the study aims to answer the following questions about hashtag activism on Twitter in the first year of the pandemic:

- What are the most common demands regarding measures and restrictions according to the course of the pandemic?
- Are there more hashtag campaigns in favor of or against restrictions during the pandemic?
- Which organizations/individuals have been targeted by hashtag campaigns during the pandemic?
- What social demands and objections do the collective narrative structure regarding the restrictions that emerged through hashtag activism include?
- Through which contexts, such as collective narrative, number of participants, continuity, topicality, importance of secondary hashtags, etc., do the analyzed hashtags foreground the discussion of hashtag activism?

Data Collection and Analysis

In order to find answers to the research questions, hashtag activism on Twitter regarding the restrictions and measures implemented due to the COVID-19 pandemic in the one-year period between March 11, 2020, when the COVID-19 case was seen and March 11, 2021, was examined using the big data text analysis. Big data text analysis involves the process of transforming unstructured data into structured information (Hurwitz et al., 2013, p.155). A significant portion of the unstructured content that an organization collect is in textual form, ranging from emails to web pages and social media. (Chen et al., 2012, 1775). Big data text analysis is the method used to explain what this unstructured textual data means in relation to certain predetermined conditions or purposes. Defined as "*the process of extracting implicit knowledge from unstructured textual data*", big data text analysis is "*used for text classification, clustering and association*" in order to "*automatically understand and extract meaningful information from text data*" (Ahmed & Navla, 2021, pp. 325-326).

Since the main problematic of the study is shaped to explain whether the hashtag activism carried out against pandemic measures and restriction policies supports these policies and what issues come to the fore, in order to take into account the course of the pandemic, the one-year period should be analyzed on a monthly basis to determine the activism with the most hashtags shared each month regarding COVID-19 restrictions and measures, what their goals are, and at what points the narrative of support or opposition to restrictions is established.

The study used raw data from the History of Trending Topics on Twitter Project[iii] database, which contains daily trending topics. As part of the project, trending topics are stored in the database every 10 minutes in Turkey and worldwide. For our study, a total of 366 days of trending topic data between March 11, 2020, and March 11, 2021, were extracted from this database which stored separately for each day. The first step in the analysis was to classify the data by month using MS Excel and then determine the most tweeted hashtags related to pandemic restrictions and measures for each month. Thus, a dataset was created by dividing the 1-year period between March 11, 2020, and March 11, 2021, into months, and a total of 13 different hashtags divided into months were identified. At the same time, different spellings of the relevant hashtag were determined to be used as queries in the next step.

In the second step, the Mozdeh Big Data Analysis program was used to gather the tweets of the hashtags. In the general-use version of this program, Twitter provides data for a maximum of the last 7 days, while the Academic Research API[iv] provided by Twitter provides data for a maximum of ten million tweets per month in the desired date range. The Academic Research API Token obtained from Twitter was generated into the program and the tweets were obtained as raw data by using the most shared hashtags that we predetermined limited to the start and end dates of each month as a query. The raw data was generated with the number of records set to 100,000 as the average of the data. When creating the raw data, not only the exact copy of the most shared hashtag but also different spellings were considered and included in the study by searching with queries.

A total of 1,464,334 tweets were collected under 13 hashtags. Again, through Mozdeh, the 10 most used words, the 10 secondary hashtags used with the query hashtags, the 10 most mentioned accounts, and the 10 most retweeted tweets were determined. The relationship between primary hashtags and secondary hashtags reveals the scope of the activism; the most retweeted tweet reveals the purpose of the activism; the most mentioned accounts and the most retweeted tweet reveal who the activism is targeting and/or expecting support from. The tables created for each month show the number of uses of the 10 most used words and the ratio of the 10 most used words to the total number of uses; the number of uses of the 10 most used secondary hashtags and the ratio of the 10 most used secondary hashtags to the total number of uses; the number of tagging of the 10 most mentioned users and the ratio of these 10 users to the total number of tagging. In this way, a quantitative framework is presented on how collective action is framed in the examples of hashtag activism that emerged in a process that had to be slacktivist.

FINDINGS AND DISCUSSIONS

Moving Individual Stories Into a Collective Narrative: Prisoners' Demands

In March 2020, the first month of the pandemic in Turkey, the most tweeted hashtag related to the pandemic was #MeclisTahliyeDesin, (*Eng.* #ParliamentShouldSayYestoRelease) with a total of 1,663,606 tweets, expressing the demand for the rapid release of detainees and prisoners due to the pandemic during the period when the Execution Law was expected to be brought to parliament. In the study, 138,603 tweets covering the date range of 30/03/2020- 31/03/2020 were collected and analyzed using the queries *#MeclisTahliyeDesin #MeclisTahliyeDesin #meclistahliyedesin.* As seen in Table 1 for March 2020, the most commonly used words were used to emphasize support, help and demand for the purpose of activism. In secondary hashtags, hashtags that could be related to the demand in the hashtag "#MeclisTahliyeDesin" were used by 51.67% in total, while hashtags in Twitter trends that are not related to the issue raised in the activism were used by 48.33%; secondary hashtags that are related to the primary hashtag and secondary hashtags that are not related to the primary hashtag are used at similar rates and there is no significant difference between them. The most mentioned account in the analyzed tweets was Abdelhamid Gül, the then Minister of Justice, to whom the request was directly addressed; however, apart from official institutions and parliamentary accounts, 3 individual accounts accounted for 25.5% of the total mention used. Decision-making mechanisms or accounts that are expected to be able to influence them were used by 74.5%; thus, with a significant difference, it was determined that in this activism, names that can contribute to the solution of the problem were mentioned (see. Table 1). Retweeted 5215 times during the hashtag activism, HDP MP Ömer Faruk Gergellioğlu's message of

Table 1. Analysis of most used words, most used secondary hashtags, and most mentioned users to related #MeclisTahliyeDesin hashtag in March 2020

Most Used Words	*Count*	*Ratio*	Most Used Secondary Hashtags	*Count*	*Ratio*	Most Mentioned User	*Count*	*Ratio*
tahliye	4119	19,00%	#meclis	1050	34,17%	@abdulhamitgul	2624	20,72%
lütfen	2688	12,40%	#zırnıkyok	583	18,97%	@vyagmuru	1876	14,81%
allah	2413	11,13%	#bizbizeyeteriz	558	18,16%	@adalet_bakanlik	1826	14,42%
zaman	2231	10,29%	#vaka10827	300	9,76%	@rterdogan	1202	9,49%
takip	1777	8,20%	#mügeanlıözürdile	134	4,36%	@tbmmgenelkurulu	1090	8,61%
destek	1735	8,00%	#ıban	113	3,68%	@tbmmresmi	1089	8,60%
güzel	1726	7,96%	#covıd19	100	3,25%	@gergerliogluof	963	7,60%
adalet	1714	7,91%	#iban	97	3,16%	@profelvanaktas	685	5,41%
masum	1654	7,63%	#covid_19	69	2,25%	@multecili	673	5,31%
yeter	1625	7,49%	#parliamentshouldsetfree	69	2,25%	@meral_aksener	638	5,04%

support, *"I say it most effectively!! Parliament ShouldEvacuate All MPs should do what the nation has been eagerly reflecting on social media in recent days. All MPs should take our mothers, fathers and children out of this stress and reunite them with their loved ones"*[1] was the most retweeted tweet. The tweet directly reflects the activists' demands.

In April 2020, the most tweeted hashtag related to pandemic measures and practices was "KomisyonAyırmaYaşat" (*Eng.* Commission, don't separate and keep alive), which expressed the demand to the Justice Commission, which will convene on April 3, 2020, on the same topic as the hashtag activism in the previous month, to implement pandemic-related releases of prisoners and detainees without discrimination of crimes. On April 3 and 4, 2020, the hashtag appeared in Twitter trends and was used 1,380,433 times during April. In the study, 109,371 tweets were collected between 03/04/2020-30/04/2020 using the queries *Komisyon AyırmaYaşat komisyon ayırmayaşat #KomisyonAyirmaYasat #komisyonayirmayasat*. As seen in Table 2 reflecting April 2020, the 10 most used words reflect that the purpose of activism is shaped around the expectation of justice in the decision to be taken. In the secondary hashtags used, the total rate of hashtags that can be associated with the issue addressed in hashtag activism was found to be 48.04%, while the rate of off-topic hashtags was 51.97% and there was no significant difference between them. It was found that the top 10 most tagged users in the analyzed tweets were all members of the TBMM Justice Commission (See Table 2). Hence, the hashtag activism in question is an attempt to convey their voices to members of decision-making mechanisms directly. The top 5 most retweeted tweets were from accounts that were closed in response to Turkey's official request to Twitter. The tweet *"My husband has been in quarantine for a week because she came to see Ahmed, he says I have 1 more week. he is in a cell alone. İt is very small, he says GOD HELP ALL those who have been in the cell for years. hear our voice now commissioooooonnn Commission don't separate and keep alive"*[2] was retweeted 3765 times and became the sixth most retweeted tweet. Therefore, there is a transformation of the individual narrative into a collective voice.

At the beginning of the pandemic when the curfew was imposed, in both hashtag activism, prisoners and detainees in prison and their relatives have carried the narrative reflecting their common feelings and expectations to the hashtag in order to make their voices heard directly to decision-making institutions

Table 2. Analysis of most used words, most used secondary hashtags, and most mentioned users related to "KomisyonAyırmaYaşat" Hashtag in April 2020

Most Used Words	Count	Ratio	Most Used Secondary Hashtags	Count	Ratio	Most Mentioned User	Count	Ratio
adalet	4002	15,56	#komisyon	496	22,67	@yilmaztunc	3783	11,95%
allah	3124	12,15	#helinbölek	474	21,66	@avsabriozturk	3653	11,54%
lütfen	3070	11,94	#20yaş	279	12,75	@avabdullahguler	3354	10,60%
daha	3045	11,84	#vaka20921	238	10,88	@ramazancan0071	3281	10,37%
insan	2993	11,64	#duysesimi	154	7,04	@gulaysamanci42	3112	9,83%
sayın	2418	9,40	#coronavirus	146	6,67	@abdulkadirozl	3104	9,81%
masum	1837	7,14	#devamke	136	6,22	@matillakaya	2925	9,24%
tahliye	1825	7,10	#covıd19	103	4,71	@avyusufbaser	2907	9,19%
rabbim	1783	6,93	#turkey	94	4,30	@belginuygur10	2816	8,90%
karar	1622	6,31	#askeriöğrencilermasumdur	68	3,11	@emine_gozgec16	2713	8,57%

and authorities and to draw attention to the risk posed by the pandemic in prison with this hashtag. It is seen that individual stories have become part of the collective narrative. On the other hand, there is an effort to address decision-making institutions directly.

Aiming to Stay in Twitter Trends: Students' Demands

In May 2020, when the New Normal Plan was announced, high school students shared a total of 1,740,507 tweets within the "#ykstarihinedokunma"(*Eng.* #Don'tchangeYKSdate) hashtag activism they started on May 1 following the statements of the then Minister of National Education Ziya Selçuk, following the allegations that the YKS (*Eng.* Higher Education Institutions Examination) would be moved from July 25-26, 2020, when it was previously postponed due to the pandemic, to June 27-28, 2020. In the study, 127,925 tweets were collected and analyzed between 01-31/05/2020 using the queries *#ykstarihinedokunma #ykstarihimedokunma*. When Table 3 is analyzed, the most used words reflect the effort to make their voices heard and intensify hashtag activism by staying in Twitter trends. Therefore, with the most used words, it is not the purpose of hashtag activism but the effort to popularize hashtag activism that stands out. The call for support for hashtag activism has taken a back seat to the demands of a collective narrative in activism. Secondary hashtag use was found to be 85.28% directly related to hashtag activism. 92.41% of the accounts mentioned in the tweets are official institutions and officials that will have a direct impact on the decision in question (See Table 3). CHP Ankara MP Yıldırım Kaya's tweet *"Students don't want to take the exam with fear of death, exacerbated exam stress and masks. Why is this so hard to understand that? #ExamattheEndofJuly"*[3], which includes his support for activist students and identification of their problems, was retweeted 1126 times and was the most retweeted tweet during the hashtag activism.

In June 2020, when restrictions such as curfews were largely lifted, the allegations of May became reality after ÖSYM (*Eng. Student Selection and Placement Center*) announced that the exams would be held in June. As a continuation of the hashtag activism in May, students who will take the YKS exam shared a total of 1,908,528 tweets throughout the month to make their voices heard with the hashtag

Table 3. Analysis of most used words, most used secondary hashtags, and most mentioned users related to #ykstarihinedokunma Hashtag in May 2020

Most Used Words	Count	Ratio	Most Used Secondary Hashtags	Count	Ratio	Most Mentioned User	Count	Ratio
ne	5575	13,84	#yks25temmuzdakalsin	3033	25,05%	@rterdogan	8980	33,41%
daha	5441	13,50	#yks2020	2923	24,14%	@ziyaselcuk	5033	18,73%
olsun	5138	12,75	#trumpyksyiertele	1120	9,25%	@yekta_sarac	5011	18,64%
biz	4964	12,32	#ykstarihinidegistirme	1053	8,70%	@osymbaskanligi	2098	7,81%
sesimizi	3631	9,01	#ykstemmuzsonu	1006	8,31%	@drfahrettinkoca	1879	6,99%
tweet	3599	8,93	#avmler	747	6,17%	@halis_aygun	1354	5,04%
milyon	3372	8,37	#ykserteleviruсuyayma	597	4,93%	@haluklevent	795	2,96%
hadi	2907	7,21	#ykstakiplesiyor	593	4,90%	@fatihportakal	747	2,78%
duyun	2870	7,12	#millihesaplaryanyana	528	4,36%	@novavetus	500	1,86%
destek	2799	6,95	#survivor2020	510	4,21%	@tcmeb	480	1,79%

"#TurkishStudentLivesMatter", which entered Twitter trends on June 15 and 16, 2020, demanding that the exams be held in July as previously announced. Within the study, 110,855 tweets were collected and analyzed between 15-30/06/2020. As seen in Table 4, the most frequently used words in both Turkish and English, indicate the expectations for help and their interaction with each other regarding the postponement of the exam. All of the secondary hashtags used are directly related to hashtag activism. Of the most mentioned accounts, 57.58% were official decision-making institutions and officials, 16.57% were international media, and 16.02% were official accounts of the World Health Organization (See Table 4). Therefore, unlike in May, the hashtags used in English and those tagged were international accounts and students carried out hashtag activism in an effort to make their voices heard by the world public. Retweeted 4489 times, Memleket Party Chairman Muharrem Ince, who expressed the arguments

Table 4. Analysis of most used words, most used secondary hashtags, and most mentioned users related to #TurkishStudentLivesMatter hashtag in June 2020

Most Used Words	Count	Ratio	Most Used Secondary Hashtags	Count	Ratio	Most Mentioned User	Count	Ratio
sınav	5501	14,94%	#yks2020	4233	33,38%	@drfahrettinkoca	2992	28,41%
we	4765	12,94%	#ösym	2360	18,61%	@who	1687	16,02%
arkadaşlar	4551	12,36%	#ykslgs2incidalgademek	1497	11,80%	@rterdogan	1409	13,38%
exam	3596	9,77%	#osym	1401	11,05%	@ziyaselcuk	1219	11,58%
yks	3369	9,15%	#yksvelgsyehayır	844	6,65%	@bbcworld	738	7,01%
tag	3329	9,04%	#lgs2020	513	4,04%	@drserdarsavas	623	5,92%
help	2982	8,10%	#ykslgsriskiniduyur	470	3,71%	@abc	530	5,03%
our	2935	7,97%	#ykstakiplesiyor	468	3,69%	@foxnews	477	4,53%
biz	2901	7,88%	#ykslgs2ncidalgademek	466	3,67%	@osymbaskanligi	443	4,21%
students	2881	7,83%	#ösym2020	431	3,40	@guclukalmisra	412	3,91%

and demand of hashtag activism by supporting students, said, "*2.5 million students will take YKS, use public transportation, families will wait in front of schools. Don't take risks, don't play with the future of our children. Postpone the exam. #TurkishStudentLivesMatter*"[4] was the most tweeted tweet.

In both of these hashtag activisms, students who will take the YKS exam emphasized the importance of staying in Twitter Trends and expanding the campaign, and in the first case, they tried to attract the attention of the national and in the second case, the international public. Therefore, the collective narrative is constructed to provide supporters for their demands.

The Importance of the Number of Participants in Hashtag Activism

Between July 1 and 9, 2020, it was found that the students of the AÖF (Open Education Faculty) shared 138,709 tweets within the hashtag activism #yazokuluistiyoruz (*Eng.* #wewantsummerschool), demanding that the summer school, which was abolished due to the pandemic, be opened with distance education. In the study, a total of 92,968 tweets were collected and analyzed. When Table 5 is examined, it is seen that the emphasis on students' loss of rights and victimization is at the forefront in both the most used words and the most used secondary hashtags, and accordingly, accounts that are seen as the source of victimization and/or the solution to the problem are mentioned. All of the secondary hashtags are hashtags used in activism; 92.49% of the mentioned accounts are accounts of decision-makers and officials (See Table 5). The tweet "*#wewantsummerschool Bravo to you, Kütahya MP Ali Fazıl Kasap!" STUDENTS WANT SUMMER SCHOOL!*"[5] shared with the video of CHP Kütahya MP Ali Fazıl Kasap's parliamentary speech in support of summer school demands was the most retweeted tweet with 365 retweets.

With the hashtag campaign, students succeeded in bringing their voices to the parliament and ensured the opening of the summer school. On July 8, 2020, Anadolu University and then Atatürk University Open Education Faculties shared the information that the summer school would be opened and the hashtag activism was successful. What is noteworthy here is that the #TurkishStudentsLiveMatter hashtag activism, which managed to stay in Twitter trends for a long time and shared nearly 2 million tweets in the previous month, failed to fulfill the demands, while the #yazokuluistiyoruz hashtag activism fulfilled

Table 5. Analysis of most used words, most used secondary hashtags, and most mentioned users related to #yazokuluistiyoruz hashtag in July 2020

Most Used Words	*Count*	*Ratio*	**Most Used Secondary Hashtags**	*Count*	*Ratio*	**Most Mentioned User**	*Count*	*Ratio*
mağdur	7430	17,34%	#ataaofyazokuluistiyor	5916	24,73%	@proffuaterdal	16376	26,02%
lütfen	5418	12,64%	#aöfyazokuluhakkımız	4244	17,74%	@anadolu_univ	13932	22,13%
sesimizi	4864	11,35%	#yazokulumadokunma	2518	10,53%	@atauni_rektor	10172	16,16%
hakkımızı	3986	9,30%	#yazokuluhakkımız	2294	9,59%	@yekta_sarac	6696	10,64%
ders	3912	9,13%	#ataaofyazokuluistiyoruz	1944	8,13%	@rterdogan	5754	9,14%
akademik	3870	9,03%	#yazokulumuver	1720	7,19%	@atauni1957	3042	4,83%
hakkımız	3522	8,22%	#rektörününinsafınakaldik	1328	5,55%	@yuksekogretimk	2248	3,57%
mezun	3448	8,05%	#birmilyonöğrencikıyımı	1326	5,54%	@aofortak	1712	2,72%
duyun	3298	7,70%	#anadoluüniyazokuluaç	1320	5,52%	@online_aof	1532	2,43%
sayın	3108	7,25%	#yazokulu	1310	5,48	@deliliriseverim	1484	2,36%

the demands despite sharing only 138,709 tweets. Therefore, the need to discuss hashtag activism in the context of its impact on decision-making and its functionality reappears. On the other hand, this raises the question of whether it might be more important to be in Twitter Trends than to share fewer tweets.

Hashtag Activism as a Means of Communicating Demands to the Institution They Work For

In August 2020, when the number of daily COVID-19-related deaths started to increase again, contrary to the decrease in the previous month, teachers who opposed the face-to-face teacher seminars of the MEB (Ministry of National Education) Vocational Work Program tried to make their voices heard by sharing a total of 221,922 tweets on the hashtag #ÖgretmenEgitimiOnline (*Eng.* #TeacherTrainingOnline), which they started on August 20, 2020, demanding that the seminars be held online. In the study, 96,329 tweets were collected and analyzed with the queries *#oegretmeneğitimionline #ögretmenegitimionline #teacheregitimionline #ogretmenegitimionline #ÖgretmenEgitimimiOnline #ÖgretmenEgitimimiOnline #OgretmenEgitimimiOnline* between 20-29/08/2020. As seen in Table 6, the most frequently used words show the teachers' efforts to make their voices heard to the Minister of National Education to organize the seminar online due to the increase in cases. In the most mentioned accounts, 68.65% of the acounts were tagged directly with the relevant ministry, minister, and relevant unit manager to reach the decision-making mechanism. All of the most used secondary hashtags directly reflect the demands and arguments put forward in hashtag activism (See Table 6). The tweet *"Education Expert said Teachers' Seminar should be ONLINE! #TeacherTrainingOnline"*[6], which was shared 541 times along with the video of Education Expert Nihat Şener's statement on HaberTürk TV that teacher training should be done remotely and emphasized the rightness of hashtag activism, was found to be the most retweeted tweet.

Hashtag activism was used as a means of reaching the Ministry of National Education directly and a professional group's demand for online work to take measures was expressed. Therefore, the situation in question here seems to be directly related to communicating an apparent demand. This situation

Table 6. Analysis of most used words, most used secondary hashtags, and most mentioned users related to #ÖgretmenEgitimiOnline hashtag in August 2020

Most Used Words	*Count*	*Ratio*	Most Used Secondary Hashtags	*Count*	*Ratio*	Most Mentioned User	*Count*	*Ratio*
online	17385	24,04%	#ikinciildışıyapılsın	1348	15,67%	@ziyaselcuk	24415	38,89%
olmalı	8564	11,84%	#sağlıkiçinonlineseminer	1112	12,92%	@tcmeb	9303	14,82%
seminer	7878	10,89%	#semineruzaktanolsun	1083	12,59%	@adnanboyaci	7598	12,10%
olsun	7876	10,89%	#24ağustostaonline	856	9,95%	@drfahrettinkoca	5973	9,51%
seminerler	6581	9,10%	#ziyahocamkulakveroeğretmene	812	9,44%	@ogretmenlersyfs	5233	8,34%
vaka	5671	7,84%	#semineruzakegitimyakin	796	9,25%	@evrim1881	3068	4,89%
öğretmen	5431	7,51%	#sağlıkicinonlineseminer	760	8,83%	@omerinan06	2042	3,25%
eğitim	4800	6,64%	#semineronlineolsun	671	7,80%	@safran1958	1780	2,84%
sayın	4223	5,84%	#sağlıkiçinonline	663	7,70%	@zlem88753330	1695	2,70%
bakanım	3915	5,41%	#ikinciildısıyapılsın	504	5,86	@yildirimkaya40	1676	2,67%

can be considered to reflect the effort to overcome the lack of communication within the organization through hashtag activism.

Updating Hashtags in Activism

Although the upward trend in the number of cases continued in September 2020, it was found that as the start date of the universities approached, students tweeted a total of 357,061 tweets using the hashtag #HibritevetOnlineHayır (*Eng.* #HybridYesOnlineNo), which they started on September 6, 2020 to announce their demand for hybrid education instead of online education. Of these tweets, 121,324 shared between 06-30/09/2020 using the queries *#HibritevetOnlineHayır #HibritEvetOnlineHayır #HibritevetOnlinehayır #hibritevetonlinehayır* were collected and analyzed. Table 7 shows that the most used words reflect the desire for hybrid education and directly the purpose of activism. All of the most used secondary hashtags also reflect students' demand for hybrid education instead of online education. 75.06% of the most mentioned accounts belong to official institutions and officials (See Table 7). Educational scientist and mentor Emrah Adaklı's tweet to support for students; "*O rectors! O faculty members! If I don't burn, if you don't burn, who will shed light on these young people with their fire? Who will shed light on our future? Dry wood needs fire. I invite you to burn... #HybridYesOnlineNo*"[7] was shared 253 times, making it the most shared retweet during this hashtag activism.

In October 2020, as the upward trend in the number of cases continued to accelerate, as in the previous month, university students continued their demand for hybrid education and sent 245,496 tweets to the Presidential Cabinet with the hashtag #kabinedenhibritevet (*Eng.* #cabinethybridyes). Within the study, 90,885 tweets were collected and analyzed with the queries *#kabinedenhibritevet #KabinedenHibritEvet #kabinedenHibritEvet #kabinedenhibriteevet* between 04- 25/10/2020. Table 8 shows that the most used words are similar to those used in the previous month's activism and reflect the students' demand for hybrid education; unlike the previous month, the most used secondary hashtags are irrelevant or opposite to the primary hashtag, with 20.11% of the hashtags reflecting the demand for online education, while the remaining 79.89% are not related to the hashtag activism. Secondary hashtags are therefore not

Table 7. Analysis of most used words, most used secondary hashtags, and most mentioned users related to #HibritevetOnlineHayır hashtag in September 2020

Most Used Words	Count	Ratio	Most Used Secondary Hashtags	Count	Ratio	Most Mentioned User	Count	Ratio
eğitim	12722	22,70%	#onlineegitimistemiyoruz	3425	21,56%	@yekta_sarac	12635	40,81%
online	8469	15,11%	#ünileriyöketme	3092	19,46%	@drfahrettinkoca	4397	14,20%
hibrit	6155	10,98%	#hibriteğitimistiyoruz	2768	17,42%	@rterdogan	4246	13,71%
uzaktan	4743	8,46%	#onlineegitimegitimdegildir	1926	12,12%	@moneyistime3	2032	6,56%
artık	4599	8,21%	#5ekimdeyüzyüze	1399	8,81%	@emrahadaklı	1876	6,06%
istiyoruz	4151	7,41%	#hibrityoksaoyyok	1242	7,82%	@selinozrn	1372	4,43%
biz	4090	7,30%	#atauniyeisteyengelsin	548	3,45%	@aycaabuluut	1352	4,37%
arkadaşlar	4015	7,16%	#saühibritistiyor	536	3,37%	@edaelk14	1088	3,51%
lütfen	3631	6,48%	#onlineeğitiminharcıolmaz	480	3,02%	@ziyaselcuk	1043	3,37%
açın	3467	6,19%	#uenileriyoeketme	471	2,96%	@pauedutr	919	2,97%

Table 8. Analysis of most used words, most used secondary hashtags, and most mentioned users related to #kabinedenhibritevet hashtag in October 2020

Most Used Words	*Count*	*Ratio*	Most Used Secondary Hashtags	*Count*	*Ratio*	Most Mentioned User	*Count*	*Ratio*
eğitim	10207	19,45%	#zorlamayıngideceksiniz	422	16,22%	@yekta_sarac	3579	21,06%
hibrit	7567	14,42%	#nusret	351	13,49%	@rterdogan	3233	19,02%
artık	6366	12,13%	#ünileronlinedevam	328	12,61%	@mevaye2	2420	14,24%
online	6238	11,88%	#iyihaber	270	10,38%	@ılginctwitist	1347	7,92%
arkadaşlar	5310	10,12%	#medenikanun	264	10,15%	@kurtbey2626	1183	6,96%
yarın	4930	9,39%	#besiktasinmacivar	231	8,88%	@polyannaaa_	1182	6,95%
ben	3170	6,04%	#uenileronlinedevam	195	7,50%	@drfahrettinkoca	1154	6,79%
sadece	2972	5,66%	#azerbaijanarmy	195	7,50%	@kendisinekiral	1012	5,95%
bizi	2970	5,66%	#pazar	192	7,38%	@adetahelga	957	5,63%
istiyoruz	2757	5,25%	#alanya	153	5,88%	@alsedef1	931	5,48%

related to the primary hashtag. Secondary hashtags show that it is possible for a hashtag campaign that has made it to the Twitter trending list to be shared with unrelated or opposing content just to increase visibility. Of the mentioned accounts, 46.87% are decision-makers (See Table 8). The most retweeted post directly expresses the demand of the hashtag activism: "*If necessary, only education should be discussed in the Cabinet and necessary measures should be taken to provide face-to-face classes in all education. Not a single student should be left without the opportunity to get the education they deserve and want. An individual is the whole society. #cabinethybridyes*"[8].

Although the goal of hashtag activism was the same in both months, the secondary hashtags used in October were less related to activism and were intended to increase visibility. However, instead of putting forward their demands with the same hashtag, the students tried to make their voices heard in October with a different hashtag, updated directly to the cabinet that would take the decision. This situation indicates that two hashtag activisms with a common goal are articulated with each other and the same demand is brought to the agenda again with another hashtag updated in accordance with the conjuncture, rather than the continuity of the same hashtag.

Professional Reputation and Demand for Precautions

Following the decision to continue face-to-face preschool education, on November 21, 2020, preschool teachers reacted to this decision and shared a total of 214,270 tweets with the hashtag #OkulÖncesiAşıyıMıBuldu (*Eng.* #HasPreschoolInventedtheVaccine). Within the study, 99,621 of these tweets were collected and analyzed with the queries *#OkuloencesiAsıyıMıBuldu #OkulÖncesiAşıyıMıBuldu #okulöncesiaşıyımıbuldu #OkulOncesiAsiyiMiBuldu #okuloencesiasıyımıbuldu #okuloncesiasiyimibuldu.* As seen in Table 9, the most frequently used words emphasize preschool teachers' critics to this decision, which was not taken for other levels of education; also expressed both in the primary hashtag with the question and in the secondary hashtags with the emphasis that they are not "babysitter" and that their lives are also important. All secondary hashtags were found to be related to the primary hashtag and 72.84% of the most mentioned accounts belonged to official institutions and officials (See Table 9). The most retweeted

Table 9. Analysis of most used words, most used secondary hashtags, and most mentioned users related to #OkulÖncesiAşıyıMıBuldu hashtag in November 2020

Most Used Words	Count	Ratio	Most Used Secondary Hashtags	Count	Ratio	Most Mentioned User	Count	Ratio
okul	26851	23,03%	#okuloencesioegretmenibakicidegildir	1325	14,89%	@ziyaselcuk	23637	40,04%
öncesi	21613	9,51%	#okuloncesiogretmenibakicidegildir	945	9,33%	@tcmeb	13135	22,25%
eğitim	8919	8,44%	#bakıcıdeğiloeğretmeniz	592	9,33%	@drfahrettinkoca	4106	6,95%
öğretmenleri	7920	7,24%	#okuloncesidecandir	592	8,15%	@talipgeylan06	3799	6,43%
biz	6798	4,86%	#ziyahocamokulöncesinesesver	517	8,10%	@cerenhocam	2886	4,89%
okula	4559	4,78%	#ziyahocamokuloncesinesesver	514	7,75%	@yetkinberkin	2526	4,28%
çalışan	4482	4,59%	#ziyaögretmenimsesver	492	7,64%	@hilal12984984	2438	4,13%
yüz	4310	4,56%	#okuloencesidecandır	485	7,00%	@naimunver	2202	3,73%
yüze	4281	4,37%	#ziyahocamokuloencesinesesver	444	6,95%	@ ogretmenlersyfs	2187	3,70%
okulöncesi	4098	23,03%	#ziyaöğretmenimsesver	441	14,89%	@tuncay_morkoc	2123	3,60%

tweet was posted by Assistant Professor Dr. Naim Ünver's tweet *"2020 Preschool ÖABT [Teacher Field Knowledge Test] Question That's it. That's the tweet.!!!*#HasPreschoolInventedtheVaccine*"*[9], including the visual of a Public Personnel Selection Examination Teaching Field Knowledge Test question that stated one of the purposes of preschool education is not to provide child care of working mothers.

It seems that a collective narrative has emerged by associating a common reproach and anger related to the professional reputation of preschool teachers with the risk posed by the pandemic. However, unlike the teacher demand in August 2020, a clear demand to the Ministry of National Education itself is associated with professional reputation, directly targeting the Ministry of National Education, as well as an effort to strengthen their professional reputation in public opinion.

A Hashtag That Calls Directly to the Decision-Maker

In December 2020, when cases and deaths began to increase at an alarming rate, students demanding that high school exams not be held shared a total of 2,689,760 tweets on December 23, 2020 using the hashtag #mebartıkduybizi (*Eng.* #mebhearusnow). Within the study, 114,396 tweets were collected and analyzed between 23-31/12/2020 using the queries *#mebartikduybizi #MebArtikDuyBizi #mebartikduybizi #Mebartikduybizi #MEBARTIKDUYBIZI #Mebartikduybizi #MEBARTIKDUYBIZI.* Table 10 shows that the most used words do not reflect the demand put forward in hashtag activism; however, the call for participants to comment on posts in order to keep the hashtag in Twitter Trends for longer is reflected in the most used words. All of the most used secondary hashtags directly reflect the demands and reactions of the activism in question. Of the most mentioned accounts 87.89% are decision-maker official institutions and officials who will ensure that the students' demand is realized (See Table 10). The most retweeted tweet was an anchor and journalist Ece Üner's tweet *"#mebhearusnow:)"*[10], which was shared 2109 times.

Table 10. Analysis of most used words, most used secondary hashtags, and most mentioned users related to #mebartıkduybizi hashtag in December 2020

Most Used Words	*Count*	*Ratio*	Most Used Secondary Hashtags	*Count*	*Ratio*	Most Mentioned User	*Count*	*Ratio*
yorum	17604	20,37%	#ziyaselcukistifa	23312	68,11%	@ziyaselcuk	14576	53,33%
yorumu	9472	10,96%	#sinavlariptalolsun	3701	10,81%	@tcmeb	4911	17,97%
sadece	9115	10,54%	#ziyaselcuk	1366	3,99%	@drfahrettinkoca	3609	13,20%
bilgi	8650	10,01%	#sinavagitmiyorum	1126	3,29%	@rterdogan	927	3,39%
mizah	7718	8,93%	#sinavlariptaledilsin	1007	2,94%	@foxhaber	794	2,91%
yorumum	7474	8,65%	#ziyaselcukgoermezdengelme	812	2,37%	@eceuner12	786	2,88%
yapistirin	6917	8,00%	#kulakverbizemeb	795	2,32%	@osman0zgr	606	2,22%
trendlerden	6682	7,73%	#mebartikbiziduy	756	2,21%	@mutsuzm09	403	1,47%
sebebi	6591	7,62%	#ziyaselcukduybizi	745	2,18%	@ronicivank1	381	1,39%
yorumdur	6219	7,19%	#mebduyartikbizi	609	1,78%	@solcugazete	339	1,24%

Using Hashtags for Visibility Out of Activism

In January 2021, with the announcement of the first vaccination program and the possibility of a solution to the pandemic, university students expressed their demand for the start of face-to-face education in the second semester on January 21, 2021, with the hashtag #bahardakampüslere (*Eng.* #tocampusesin-spring). In order to analyze the hashtag activism in which 143,845 tweets were shared in total, 94,433 tweets were collected with the queries *#bahardakampüslere #BahardaKampüslere #bahardakampueslere #bahardakampuslere #Bahardakampuslere #BahardaKampuslere.* As seen in Table 11, the most used words reflect the purpose of hashtag activism. However, none of the most used secondary hashtags reflect the content of the hashtag activism in question. Of the most mentioned accounts, 47.09% include the account of the decision-making mechanisms to which the demand raised in the activism is directed (See Table 11). On the other hand, the most retweeted tweet contains a topic completely independent of the content of the activism being discussed: Uyghur activist Kuzzat Altay's tweet *"Release the Uyghur Turks detained in the foreigners branch. #BahardaKampueslere"*[11] has been shared 843 times.

What is noteworthy here is the use of a hashtag in the list of Twitter trends on another activism issue. On the other hand, in the specific case of this activism, secondary hashtags to get into Twitter trends have nothing to do with building the collective narrative structure of activism. Therefore, it is crucial to recognize that secondary hashtags do not always have a direct link to activism and to keep in mind that a hashtag that is in trending topics is only used to enter trending topics.

Sustainability of Hashtag Activism

The hashtag #TurkishStudentsLivesMatter, which was used to protest the postponement of the YKS exam in June 2020, was again used by high school students, this time to protest the decision to hold high school exams face-to-face. A total of 8,35,8045 tweets were shared as part of the activism launched on February 24, 2021, and the hashtag entered the list of worldwide Twitter Trends. Within the scope of the study, 129,821 tweets were collected and analyzed using *#TurkishStudentsLivesMatter #TurkishStu-*

Table 11. Analysis of most used words, most used secondary hashtags, and most mentioned users related to #bahardakampüslere hashtag in January 2021

Most Used Words	*Count*	*Ratio*	Most Used Secondary Hashtags	*Count*	*Ratio*	Most Mentioned User	*Count*	*Ratio*
eğitim	10749	21,91%	#fbvkys	1981	18,23%	@emrahadaklı	7695	24,32%
artık	8045	16,40%	#enyalancichpli	1762	16,21%	@yekta_sarac	7659	24,21%
üniversite	7862	16,02%	#sondakika	1602	14,74%	@rterdogan	3017	9,54%
yüz	3913	7,97%	#covid_19	1467	13,50%	@drfahrettinkoca	2771	8,76%
üniversiteler	3713	7,57%	#yeterartık60binnerede	919	8,46%	@kuzzat_altay	2226	7,04%
online	3147	6,41%	#ailebakanlığındaşok	860	7,91%	@hibritt03	1889	5,97%
oteller	2961	6,03%	#sikkim	618	5,69%	@kurtbey2626	1743	5,51%
yüze	2919	5,95%	#maraşlı	582	5,36%	@zkusagiplatform	1637	5,17%
virüs	2901	5,91%	#öğrenciaffı	555	5,11%	@unibilgihat	1556	4,92%
bahar	2858	5,82%	#uygurlu	522	4,80%	@tcbestepe	1448	4,58%

dentsLivesMatters #turkishstudentslivesmatter #turkishstudentslivesmatters #TurkishStudentLivesMatter #turkishstudentlivesmatter queries. When Table 12 is analyzed, it is seen that both the purpose of activism and support for the hashtag come to the forefront in the most used words. In the secondary hashtags, the purpose of the activism and the demands are seen in 66.48% of the hashtags; remarkably, the hashtags started by the students in Egypt with the same demand constitute 33.52% of the hashtags. The fact that the hashtag #egyptianstudentslivesmatter ranked first among the secondary hashtags is reminiscent of Castells' (2012) viral effect of 'networked social movements'. When the mentioned accounts are analyzed, it is noteworthy that only 27.33% of them are accounts of decision-making mechanisms, and the first ranked account is a Twitter phenomenon with a rate of 32.45%, which is more mentioned than the sum of these mechanisms (See Table 12). Retweeted 7656 times, Onedio social content platform's

Table 12. Analysis of most used words, most used secondary hashtags, and most mentioned users related to #TurkishStudentsLivesMatter hashtag in February 2021

Most Used Words	*Count*	*Ratio*	Most Used Secondary Hashtags	*Count*	*Ratio*	Most Mentioned User	*Count*	*Ratio*
iptal	16695	20,09%	#egyptianstudentslivesmatter	7293	30,71%	@muhendisyenn	4399	32,45%
ziya	12246	14,73%	#ziyaselcuk	4594	19,35%	@ziyaselcuk	2462	18,16%
bilim	8959	10,78%	#sorumlusukimolacak	3763	15,85%	@mertayazata	1319	9,73%
selçuk	7475	8,99%	#ertelemedegilıptalistiyoruz	2737	11,53%	@solcugazete	1184	8,73%
kurulu	7342	8,83%	#justiceforturkishstudents	1306	5,50%	@aybukenizzzz	1020	7,52%
tweet	6776	8,15%	#ertelemedeğiliptalistiyoruz	1289	5,43%	@euronews_tr	771	5,69%
sınav	6578	7,91%	#ertlemedeğiliptalistiyoruz	974	4,10%	@tcmeb	684	5,05%
arkadaşlar	5840	7,03%	تومتحب_بالطلا_لكوجرا_سيراي#	668	2,81%	@onediocom	673	4,96%
destek	5763	6,93%	#yaiptalyaistifa	609	2,56%	@drfahrettinkoca	559	4,12%
tag	5436	6,54%	#ziyaselcukistifa	513	2,16%	@who	486	3,58%

Table 13. Analysis of most used words, most used secondary hashtags, and most mentioned users related to #öğrencilerölmekistemiyor hashtag in March 2021

Most Used Words	Count	Ratio	Most Used Secondary Hashtags	Count	Ratio	Most Mentioned User	Count	Ratio
iptal	11301	16,57%	#ziyaselcukistifa	5053	46,77%	@ziyaselcuk	9617	55,95
ziya	9600	14,08%	#iptalkararınıbekliyoruz	1211	11,21%	@tcmeb	2656	15,45
sınav	6781	9,94%	#kadinasiddetehayir	814	7,53%	@drfahrettinkoca	1773	10,31
ne	6395	9,38%	#ziyaselcukladevam	673	6,23%	@rterdogan	935	5,44%
açıklama	6156	9,03%	#riskvarsabizleryokuz	637	5,90%	@ekrem_imamoglu	600	3,49%
var	5988	8,78%	#sonsaniyeiptal	506	4,68%	@muhendisyenn	538	3,13%
artık	5939	8,71%	#ziyaselçukladevam	494	4,57%	@suleymansoylu	294	1,71%
kadar	5751	8,43%	#ziyaselcuk	478	4,42%	@dinckadir43	259	1,51%
arkadaşlar	5190	7,61%	#ibrahimzaraptutuklansın	472	4,37%	@osman_tirasci	259	1,51%
yarın	5099	7,48%	#yönetemediniz	465	4,30%	@akpusmaz	259	1,51%

tweet, *"Students Reacted to Face-to-Face Exams: Nearly 1.5 Million Tweets Were Sent on the Hashtag #TurkishStudentsLivesMatter!"*[12] was the most retweeted post.

In March 2021, when the Gradual Normalization period started, students expressed their demand for the cancellation of face-to-face exams as a continuation of the previous month, this time using the hashtag #öğrencilerölmekistemiyor (*Eng.* #studentsdon'twanttodie), which they started on July 7, 2021. Of the 3,133,923 tweets shared during the hashtag activism, 137,803 tweets shared between 07-11/03/2021 were collected and analyzed using the queries *#öğrencilerölmekistemiyor #ogrencilerolmekistemiyor.* As seen in Table 13, the most used words reflect the demand and expectation of hashtag activism, while the most used secondary hashtags are all related to the primary hashtag. With a significant difference, 87.15% of the most tagged accounts are official institutions and officials in decision-making positions on the issue (See Table 13). CHP Ankara MP Yıldırım Kaya's tweet addressed to the Minister of National Education and mentioned a large number of press and press members, which was retweeted 3409 times, *"Ziya Hocam, students are waiting for an explanation from you. Tomorrow is March 8, you must stop face-to-face exams. Everywhere is red! #öğrencilerölmekistemiyor @tcmeb @ziyaselcuk @FOXhaber @selcukktepeli @KucukkayaIsmail @OzlemGurses @halktvcomtr @krtkulturtv @elifdsenturk @tele-1comtr @cem_tv"*[13] was the most tweeted post.

The desire of the students to be taken into account by directly expressing their concerns in the face of death through the hashtag comes to the fore. On the other hand, there is a commonality in the secondary hashtags #ziyaselcukistifa, and #ziyaselcuk in both February and March activism of students with the same goal. This case reflects the common structure and continuity of demands and anger in the context of secondary hashtags in hashtag activism.

CONCLUSION

In the first year of the COVID-19 pandemic in Turkey, Twitter hashtag campaigns regarding restrictions and measures included both concerns about the course of the pandemic and the measures taken to address these concerns, as well as the lifting of restrictions. Of the 13 hashtag activisms with the highest number of tweets analyzed by months in the study, the demand for measures and regulations to be taken to protect against the risks posed by the pandemic stands out in 9 of them, while the demand for lifting or easing the restrictions in 4 of them comes to the forefront. Twitter users in Turkey used hashtag activism 69.23% to call for implementing restrictions and necessary regulations. During the first year of the pandemic, hashtag campaigns supporting restrictions were supported by more Twitter users. The most tweeted hashtag activism actors in the first year of the pandemic were students, detainees and prisoners (and their relatives), and teachers. Among the 13 activisms, 4 directly carried the decision-making authorities to the hashtag, while 9 of them carried the demands to the hashtag; while the mentioning rate of decision-making institutions and officials in 3 of them is below 50%, they are among the most tagged ones in 10 of them. The average mentioning rate of decision-making institutions and authorities in the total of 13 activisms is 71.52%.

In the analyzed hashtag activism examples; (1) in the formation of the collective narrative, all common concerns, anger, and demands were expressed towards official institutions and representatives, (2) all examples of activism demanded that decision-making institutions and administrators take the desired decisions (3) the actors of activism represent only three segments of society (those in prison, teachers and students) (4) hashtag activism is directed at only two decision-making institutions, the Ministry of Education regarding education and the Ministry of Justice regarding execution practices (5) efforts to stay on Twitter Trends and engage in order to get the decisions demanded are at the forefront of student activism.

In the first year of the pandemic, when the ways of social opposition were confined to social media due to restrictions and being a slacktivist was a must, hashtag activism was used as a means of communicating demands directly to decision-making institutions. Twitter users used the hashtags to express the decisions they wanted to see taken and to call for pandemic-related measures to be taken or relaxed. Since the pandemic has created a process in which all other forms of activism in the repertoire of social action, except digital tools, have disappeared in terms of voicing political and social demands, these demands appear as spaces where these demands can find a place for themselves, whether they have an impact on decision-making mechanisms or not. In the period analyzed for Turkey, the absence of a real public sphere where people could make their voices heard and form a collective narrative and the fact that social media filled the absence of this real sphere makes it necessary to rethink slacktivism.

Moreover, the use of secondary hashtags to increase engagement unrelated to hashtag activism, as demonstrated by the most tweeted hashtag #BahardaKampueslere in January 2021, brings up a discussion that the purpose of a trending topic may be overshadowed, which will be continued in different studies focusing on this issue. On the other hand, it is imperative to keep in mind that the discussion of hashtag activism in terms of its impact on decision-making mechanisms and concrete gains (as the examples of #TurkishStudentsLivesMatter and #yazokuluistiyoruz hashtag activism show) may change conjuncturally depending on the countries and demands. Therefore, the policies in a country and the conditions under which they are implemented or not implemented, whether decision-making mechanisms take into account the demands of the people, in other words, how the democratic demand boundaries of a country are drawn in real life and how they follow a similar course on the digital media, seems will continue to be the subject of studies discussing the relationship between democracy and digital activism.

REFERENCES

Ahmed, S. J., & Navle, V. (2021). Text and Sentimental Analysis on Big Data. *International Journal of Scientific Research in Computer Science, Engineering and Information Technology, 7*(2), 324-334. doi:10.32628/CSEIT217269

Augenbraun, E. (2011). Occupy Wall Street and the limits of spontaneous street protest. *The Guardian.* Retrieved from: https://www.theguardian.com/commentisfree/cifamerica/2011/sep/29/occupy-wall-street-protest

Bennett, W. L., & Segerberg, A. (2012). The logic of connective action: Digital media and the personalization of contentious politics. *Information Communication and Society, 15*(5), 1–240. doi:10.1080/1369118X.2012.670661

Bonilla, Y., & Rosa, J. (2015). #Ferguson: Digital protest, hashtag ethnography, and the racial politics of social media in the United States. *American Ethnologist, 1*(42), 4–17. doi:10.1111/amet.12112

Bruns, A., & Burgess, J. E. (2011). The use of Twitter hashtags in the formation of ad hoc publics. *Proceedings of the 6th European Consortium for Political Research (ECPR) General Conference.*

Burbach, R. (2001). *Globalization and Postmodern Politics: From Zapatistas to Hightech Robber Barons*. Pluto Press.

Castells, M. (2008). *Enformasyon Çağı: Ekonomi, Toplum ve Kültür: Ağ toplumunun Yükselişi, Kılıç, E. (Çev.), 2. Baskı*. İstanbul Bilgi Üniversitesi Yayınları.

Castells, M. (2012). *İsyan ve Umut Ağları: İnternet Çağında Toplumsal Hareketler, Kılıç, E. (Çev)*. Koç Üniversitesi Yayınları.

Chen, H., Chiang, R. H., & Storey, V. C. (2012). Business Intelligence and Analytics: From Big Data to Big Impact. *Management Information Systems Quarterly, 36*(4), 1165–1188. doi:10.2307/41703503

Christensen, H. S. (2011). Political activities on the Internet: Slacktivism or political participation by other means? *First Monday*. Advance online publication. doi:10.5210/fm.v16i2.3336

Chu, D. (2017). #CautionBusinesses: Using Competitors' Hashtags Could Possibly Lead to Trademark Infringement, Catholic University. *The Journal of Law and Technology, 25*(2), 387–413. https://scholarship.law.edu/jlt/vol25/iss2/8

Clark, R. (2016). "Hope in a hashtag": The discursive activism of# WhyIStayed. *Feminist Media Studies, 16*(5), 788–804. doi:10.1080/14680777.2016.1138235

Couts, A. (2015, January 18). The new era of hashtag activism. *The Kernel.* Retrieved from https://kernelmag. dailydot.com/issue-sections/features-issue-sections/11390/hashtag-activism-real/

Gladwell, M. (2010, October 4). Small change: Why the revolution will not be tweeted. *The New Yorker.* Retrieved from https://www.newyorker.com/magazine/2010/10/04/small-change-malcolm-gladwell

Glenn, C. L. (2015). Activism or 'slacktivism?': Digital media and organizing for social change. *Communication Teacher, 29*(2), 81–85. doi:10.1080/17404622.2014.1003310

Gurak, J. L. (2014). Trust and Internet Activism: From Email to Social Networks. In Cyberactivism on The Participatory Web. Routledge.

Halupka, M. (2014). Clicktivism: A systematic heuristic. *Policy and Internet*, *6*(2), 115–132. doi:10.1002/1944-2866.POI355

Hurwitz, J., Nugent, A., Halper, F., & Kaufman, M. (2013). *Big Data for Dummies. John Wiley & Sons.*

Kavada, A. (2010). Activism Transforms Digital: The Social Movement Perspective. In Digital Activism Decoded: The New Mechanics of Change. IDebate Press.

Lee, Y. H., & Hsieh, G. (2013). Does slacktivism hurt activism? the effects of moral balancing and consistency in online activism. *Proceedings of the SIGCHI Conference on Human Factors in Computing Systems*, 811-820. 10.1145/2470654.2470770

Lenin, V. İ. (1992). *Ne Yapmalı? Hareketimizin Canalıcı Sorunları, Erdost, M. (Çev.), 4. Baskı.* Sol Yayınları.

McGraw, T. (2020). *Spending 2020 Together on Twitter.* Available at: https://blog.twitter.com/en_us/topics/insights/2020/spending-2020-together-on-twitter

Morozov, E. (2009). The Brave New World of Slacktivism. *Foreign Policy*. https://foreignpolicy.com/2009/05/19/the-brave-new-world-of-slacktivism/

Morozov, E. (2011). *The Net Delusion: The Dark Side of Internet Freedom.* Perseus Books Public Affaires.

Ofori-Parku, S., & Moscato, D. (2018). Hashtag Activism as a Form of Political Action: A Qualitative Analysis of the #BringBackOurGirls Campaign in Nigerian, UK, and U.S. Press. *International Journal of Communication*, *12*, 23. https://ijoc.org/index.php/ijoc/article/view/8068

Rotman, D. (2011) From Slacktivism To Activism: Participatory Culture In The Age Of Social Media. In *ACM CHI 2011: Conference on Human Factors In Computing Systems*. ACM Press. 10.1145/1979742.1979543

Salazar, E. (2017). Hashtags 2.0 - An Annotated History of the Hashtag and a Window to its Future. *Icono 14, 15*(2), 16-54. 10.7195/ri14

Scholz, T. (2010). Infrastructure: Its Transformations and Effect on Digital Activism. In Digital Activism Decoded: The New Mechanics of Change. IDebate Press.

Sharf, S. (2013, Novembre 7). The Secret Behind Twitter's IPO: How The Hashtag Became A Worldwide Phenomenon. *Forbes*. Retrieved from: https://www.forbes.com/sites/samanthasharf/2013/11/07/the-secret-behind-twitters-ipo-how-the-hashtag-became-a-worldwide-phenomenon/?sh=7a5813a4fd4d

Shirky, C. (2011). The political power of social media: Technology, the public sphere, and political change. *Foreign Affairs*, *90*(1), 28–41.

Soriano, M. R. T. (2013). Internet as a Driver of Political Change: Cyber-pessimists and Cyber-optimists. *Revista del Instituto Español de Estudios Estratégicos*, *1*, 332–352.

Stephens, E. (2018). #Creator The man behind the hashtag. *Brunswick Review, 15*, 44-46. Available at: https://www.brunswickgroup.com/media/4309/br15_44-46_hashtag_v10_cw.pdf

Tombleson, B., & Wolf, K. (2017). Rethinking the circuit of culture: How participatory culture has transformed cross-cultural communication. *Public Relations Review, 43*(1), 14-25. doi:10.1016/j.pubrev.2016.10.017

Uçkan, Ö. (2012). "Dijital Aktivizm" mi, "Aktivizm" mi? *Yeşil Gazete*. https://yesilgazete.org/blog/2012/06/01/dijital-aktivizm-mi-aktivizm-mi-ozgur-uckan/

Yang, G. (2016). Narrative agency in hashtag activism: The case of #BlackLivesMatter. *Media and Communication, 4*(4), 13–17. doi:10.17645/mac.v4i4.692

Zulli, D. (2020). Evaluating hashtag activism: Examining the theoretical challenges and opportunities of# BlackLivesMatter. *Participations, 17*(1), 197–215.

ENDNOTES

1 The original tweet in Turkish: "*En etkili bir şekilde söylüyorum! Meclis TahliyeDesin Tüm milletvekilleri, milletin son günlerde sosyal medyaya büyük bir hevesle yansıttığı isteği yapmalıdır. Canla başla tüm vekiller annelerimizi, babalarımızı, çocuklarımızı bu stresten çıkarmalı ve sevdiklerine kavuşturmalı*" (@gergerliogluof, 30/03/2020).

2 The original tweet in Turkish: "*Eşim bir haftadır Ahmedi görmeye geldiği için karantinada,1 haftam daha var diyor. tek başına hücrede. cok küçük, Yıllardır hücrede olanların ALLAH YARDIMCISI OLSUN. diyor Artik duy sesimizi komisyoooonnn Komisyon AyırmaYaşat*" (03/04/20209).

3 The original tweet in Turkish: "*Öğrenciler ölüm korkusuyla, katmerlenen sınav stresiyle ve maskeyle sınava girmek istemiyor. Bunu anlamak neden bu kadar zor? #SınavTemmuzSonu*" (@yildirimkaya40, 11/05/2020).

4 The original tweet in Turkish: "2*.5 milyon öğrenci YKS'ye girecek, toplu ulaşım kullanacak, aileler okul önlerinde bekleyecek. Risk almayın, çocuklarımızın geleceği ile oynamayın. Sınavı erteleyin. #TurkishStudentLivesMatter*" (@vekilince, 15/06/2020).

5 The original tweet in Turkish: "*#yazokuluistiyoruz Helal olsun sana Kütahya Milletvekili Ali Fazıl Kasap! ÖĞRENCİLER YAZ OKULU İSTİYOR!*" (05/07/2020).

6 The original tweet in Turkish: "*Eğitim Uzmanı Öğretmenlerin Semineri ONLİNE olmalı dedi! #ÖgretmenEgitimiOnline*" (@ogretmenlersyfs, 21/08/2020).

7 The original tweet in Turkish: "*Ey rektörler! Ey öğretim üyeleri! Ben yanmazsam, Sen yanmazsan Kim bu gençlere ateşi ile ışık saçacak? Kim ışık tutacak yarınlarımıza? Kuru odunun ateşe ihtiyacı var. Sizi yanmaya davet ediyorum... #HibritevetOnlinehayır*" (@EMRAHADAKLI, 06/09/2020).

8 The original tweet in Turkish: "*Kabinede gerekirse sadece eğitim konuşulmalı ve tüm eğitim öğretimde yüz yüze ders imkanı sağlanması için gerekli tedbir kararları alınmalı. İmkanı olmayan tek bir öğrenci bile kalmadan eğitimini hak ettiği ve istediği şekilde almalı. Bir birey tüm toplumdur. #kabinedenhibritevet*" (04/10/2020).

9 The original tweet in Turkish: "*2020 Okul Öncesi ÖABT Sorusu Twit bu kadar!!! #OkulÖncesiAşıyıMıBuldu?*" (@Naimunver, 21/11/2020).

10 The original tweet in Turkish: *"#mebartıkduybizi:)"* (@eceuner12spiker, 24/12/2020).

11 The original tweet in Turkish: "*Yabancılar şubesinde tutuklu Uygur Türkleri serbest bırakılsın. #BahardaKampueslere*" (@Kuzzat_Altay, 25/01/2021).

12 The original tweet in Turkish: "*Öğrenciler Yüz Yüze Sınavlara Tepkili: #TurkishStudentsLivesMatter Etiketinde 1,5 Milyona Yakın Tweet Atıldı!*" (@onediocom, 24/02/2021).

13 The original tweet in Turkish: "*Ziya Hocam, öğrenciler sizden açıklama bekliyor. Yarın 8 Mart, yüz yüze sınavlara dur demelisiniz. Her yer kırmızı! #öğrencilerölmekistemiyor @tcmeb @ziyaselcuk @FOXhaber @selcukktepeli @KucukkayaIsmail @OzlemGurses @halktvcomtr @krtkulturtv @ elifdsenturk @tele1comtr @cem_tv*" (@yildirimkaya40, 07/03/2021). [i] See: 2021 #OnlyOnTwitter, https://blog.twitter.com/en_us/topics/insights/2021/2021--onlyontwitter [ii] The gradual normalization period in Turkey was initiated with the circular of the Ministry of Interior dated May 16, 2021. See: https://www.icisleri.gov.tr/kademeli-normallesme-tedbirleri-genelgesi https://www.icisleri.gov.tr/81-il-valiligine-kademeli-normallesme-tedbirleri-genelgesi-gonderildi [iii] History of Trending Topics on Twitter (TT-History) was a project that keeps history of trending topics on Twitter. The trends were collected every 10 minutes and indexed only by date for Turkey and worldwide since July 2013. The project ended in the summer of 2021. The data used in this study was provided on March 14, 2021. See: https://github.com/ilhan-mstf/tt-history and also https://web.archive.org/web/20210531051107/http://tt-history.appspot.com/ [iv] Twitter decided to end free access to its API in February and introduced paid tiers on March 30. As a result, the Academic Research API is no longer available for free access. For this study, the academic level of the Twitter API was approved in March 2021.

Chapter 14
Information-Seeking Behaviors in the COVID-19 Crisis in Turkey:
What Types of Information, From Which Sources, and With What Motivations?

Ebru Belkıs Güzeloğlu
Faculty of Communication, Ege University, İzmir, Turkey

Ali Erhan Zalluhoğlu
Faculty of Economics and Administrative Sciences, Ege University, İzmir, Turkey

Elif Üstündağlı Erten
https://orcid.org/0000-0001-5111-927X
Faculty of Economics and Administrative Sciences, Ege University, İzmir, Turkey

Burcu Şentürk
Faculty of Economics and Administrative Sciences, Ege University, İzmir, Turkey

Asuman Özgür Keysan
Department of Political Science and Public Administration, Atılım University, Ankara, Turkey

ABSTRACT

In this study, information-seeking behavior during the initial quarantine period of the COVID-19 pandemic in Turkey is examined, and predictors of information-seeking are analyzed through the synthesis of Information Repertoire and Protection Motivation Theory approaches. Based on data collected from 2283 participants representing Turkey, the study reveals the changing impact of the need based on information types, information sources, and protection motivation components according to the channels through which information is sought. The results demonstrate that, in addition to the importance of the information need, perceived severity, response efficacy, and perceived susceptibility motivate information seeking. Furthermore, perceptions of the competence of the social environment motivate information seeking, highlighting the role of social context in information seeking. The results underline the need for policies to strengthen the effectiveness of official actors providing information in line with search dynamics in disaster communication and to design messages that are sensitive to social context.

DOI: 10.4018/979-8-3693-0896-7.ch014

INTRODUCTION

The COVID-19 crisis was a worldwide phenomenon that deeply affected social, economic, and cultural life, as well as healthcare. Everyone faced challenges from their own perspective. This process, which we returned to in post-pandemic restructuring, clearly revealed the pandemic policies and consequences that interrupted daily life and social interactions during the acute crisis period. On the other hand, the window of opportunity that emerged pointed to opportunities for reform and restructuring, drawing lessons from public and government experience in the post-crisis period (Munir et al., 2004). This opportunity differed from the short-term opportunities pointed out by some studies, where entrenched behaviors may change but require rapid responses (Hou et al., 2020; Zhang, 2021). In other words, it created an opportunity to rectify flawed practices so that possible disasters can be overcome with the least damage in the future, and a resilient society can be established.

That's why different areas of responses to this crisis are still being debated to explore unnoticed connections. Disaster communication of individuals in the crisis period, where pandemic restrictions and measures are most strictly implemented, has been one of the key issues discussed in the context of missed opportunity windows and gaps. Some researchers have warned of short-term windows of opportunity during the crisis. For example, a study that identified two missed windows of opportunity for early control of the COVID-19 outbreak indicated that delayed disclosure of information by the government and failure to correct misinformation in a timely manner kept public awareness and perception of severity low (Hou et al., 2020). They referred to the importance of governments improving problematic disaster communication practices, as well as supporting individuals' cognitive processes through communication in a way that encourages participation in measures. On the other hand, the fact that the affected people were not limited to a certain segment of society, and that social communication and support that could buffer the stress created by the pandemic restrictions were paradoxically interrupted when it was most needed (An et al., 2023), made the COVID-19 crisis different from previous experiences. All these indicators highlight the importance of disaster communication and providing disaster information to the broader community.

Indeed, in disasters, information plays a critical role in coping during and after the crisis. Providing information is an important part of disaster responses (Sommerfeldt, 2015). The COVID-19 pandemic, as a crisis that interrupts face-to-face communication processes due to both health risks and public restrictions, has made the role of personal communication networks in disaster communication critical. Due to the nature of the crisis, when providing disaster information, it is necessary to consider the guiding effects of the channels and sources through which information is sought and the cognitive dynamics of threat and coping that may influence information-seeking behavior.

While disseminating information, utilizing effective sources and channels tailored to the preferences of target groups for information retrieval enables broader outreach and the exclusion of inefficient channels (Lai and Tang, 2021). Therefore, within the realm of disaster communication, there is a growing interest in elucidating the functioning of the selection and utilization mechanism within the personal information environment where information is gathered. The theoretical framework, founded on information repertoire and curation, posits that individuals select a subset from the array of channels accessible to them in their pursuit of information (Reagan, 1996). They are also subject to the influences of the channels and active participants within these channels in this informational milieu (Thorson and Wells, 2016). 'Curating' entails the selection, organization, and management of information sources within one's repertoire (Marchionini, 1995). The repertoire that individuals curate in relation to information-seeking during disasters encompasses the mechanism of choosing and utilizing the complete array of sources and channels at their disposal (Sommerfeldt, 2015). Studies employing this approach within the sphere of disaster communication and its adaptation to a broader media environment corroborate the correlation between channel curation and the gathering and dissemination of information (Sommerfeldt, 2015; Lai and Tang, 2015; 2018; 2021).

Various elements comprising the information repertoire, including forms of information and sources, influence the processes of information collection (Liu et al., 2015; Austin, Liu & Jin, 2012; Jin et al., 2014). Individuals possessing a well-organized knowledge repertoire are more inclined to engage in effective information-seeking behavior, as they have access to a diverse array of sources and channels enabling them to explore various perspectives and types of information (Sommerfeldt, 2015). Furthermore, configurations involving sources and channels, along with the richness or limitations of the repertoire employed for information consumption in a crisis, can guide behavioral responses in diverse manners (Kim, 2016; Lai and Tang, 2021; Zhao et al., 2022; Kim et al., 2022). The tendency of those affected by a disaster to seek information for survival and coping links the development of the curation mechanism to information-seeking behavior. However, alongside the existing gap concerning information behaviors in health emergencies, there is a necessity for more insights into how information behaviors will be shaped within a new information environment that individuals may not be accustomed to, such as during the COVID-19 crisis (Pan et al., 2020). Many studies have delved into the curation mechanism and information-seeking processes operative in the context of COVID-19 (Kim et al., 2020; Soroya et al., 2021; Zhao et al., 2022; Elsner et al., 2022).

On the other hand, information seeking is influenced by a range of factors including individual preferences, situational context, and information needs (Gibson, 2016). Risk perception, alongside information needs, constitutes direct determinants of the intention to search for information (Huurne & Gutteling, 2008). Possessing a diverse array of information sources enables individuals to compile comprehensive and reliable information, which is crucial for making well-informed decisions (Kostagiolas et al., 2018). However, in a health crisis like the COVID-19 pandemic, where knowledge about pandemic processes is marked by high uncertainty and contradictions (Zhao et al., 2022), the cognitive assessment of the health threat may also influence information seeking in conjunction with the structure of this repertoire. Evidence from the field of risk communication suggests that this cognitive assessment, anticipated by the widely employed Protection Motivation Theory of health behavior, might influence information seeking (Neuwirth, 1995; Neuwirth et al., 2000; Williams and Joinson, 2020; Li et al., 2023). Nevertheless, there are limited studies examining the relationship of these components with information seeking in the COVID-19 crisis. The impacts of the sources or channels from which information is sought on perceived risk, severity, and response effectiveness (Shen et al., 2022; Muturi, 2022), as well as their role in shaping health behaviors (Muturi, 2022; Wang et al., 2021; Maykrantz et al., 2021), are more frequently discussed. However, if factors like response effectiveness and self-efficacy are linked to information avoidance (Sultana et al., 2023), they may also promote more information seeking. Research findings indicate that the scarcity of information during the pandemic is also associated with a heightened demand for more information and increased search intention (Diers-Lawson et al., 2021).

In this study, we synthesize the information repertoire with the PMT approach to examine the effects of the need for various types of information and information sources, along with the PMT components, on information seeking. In this regard, utilizing data from a nationally representative sample in Turkey between August 2020 and September 2020, we concentrate on analyzing information-seeking behavior during the initial COVID-19 quarantine period, characterized by the strictest enforcement of pandemic measures and prevailing high uncertainty among the public. We posit that the information inadequacy gap highlights unforeseen risks in the early stages of the pandemic, underscoring the role of cognitive assessment of the health threat in information seeking. Additionally, we aim to contribute the information-seeking literature by placing emphasis on the early stages of crises, an area that has received limited attention in research (Jin and Spence, 2021).

Information Repertoire in Seeking: Channels, Needs for Information, Sources

Information-seeking behavior emerged after World War II and is regarded as a personal initiative motivated by recognized information requirements. Different research disciplines have produced arguments that explain the divergent search behavior of various subgroups, as well as general patterns (Hemminger et al., 2007). The definition of information seeking behavior may vary between texts and is influenced by various factors (Lalazaryan and Zare-Farashbandi, 2014). From the perspective of media theories, the information repertoire, as an orchestration that often encompasses the type of information, information sources, and channels, shapes the dissemination mechanism as well as the process of information gathering.

Information Channels

Crises, due to the uncertain environment they create, are difficult to manage and often necessitate a substantial amount of information for decision-makers (Van Asselt et al., 2001; Matthes, 2006; Casero-Ripollés, 2020). Given the challenge of swiftly navigating the emerging crisis environment, establishing effective risk and crisis communication with the target audience should be considered a fundamental strategy during such times (Glik, 2007). Within this context, channel preferences that facilitate access to information for effective communication with target audiences emerge as one of the critical elements.

In health communication, policymakers primarily prefer traditional channels such as TV and radio for conveying information, but during the H1N1 emergency in 2009, individuals seeking information about the pandemic increasingly favored internet-based channels (Jones and Salathé, 2009; Chew and Eysenbach, 2010). Traditional and digital communication channels are frequently used in tandem, resulting in media convergence (Kopecka-Piech, 2011; Latzer, 2013). The diversity of communication channels enables information to be disseminated with varying features of interest across different channels, allowing individuals to integrate digital and traditional channels based on their preferences (Li and Zheng, 2022; Zhao et al., 2022). During crisis periods, individuals employing a variety of channels to access information have also given rise to the concept of 'social TV,' wherein individuals share their experiences through digital communication channels, creating interaction in the one-way communication process typical of traditional channels (Krämer et al., 2015; Guo, 2020). While traditional communication channels often facilitate one-way information flow, individuals effectively utilized Social TV during the pandemic by disseminating or interpreting the information they obtained from traditional media through digital platforms (Guo, 2020; Casero-Ripollés, 2020; Kim et al., 2021).

While the opportunities for utilizing multiple channels are pivotal for crisis management due to their capacity to facilitate rapid and precise dissemination of accurate information, information pollution stemming from the propagation of uncertain and false news can also detrimentally impact crisis communication. Especially in severe crisis situations threatening public health, the judicious selection of communication channels can mitigate infodemics, forestall the onset of chaos, and contribute to a reduction in infections (Ataguba, 2020). According to Matthes (2006), the uncertainty induced by crises augments channel usage but also emerges as a significant factor in heightening individuals' skepticism towards the media. In crisis communication scenarios, it is observed that trust issues and information pollution frequently steer individuals toward channels that align with their specific needs or endorse their beliefs (Aqili and Nejad, 2016).

It can be asserted that the role of social media in crisis communication has been progressively expanding owing to the recent surge in social media usage. The information dissemination facilitated by social media channels within the health communication process has also become a frequently scrutinized concern. Information pollution occurs frequently, particularly on social media platforms, attributable to the ease of content production and dissemination (Chew and Eysenbach, 2010). For instance, research conducted during the 'Zika epidemic' in Brazil in 2015 indicated that the majority of infodemics stemmed from social media interactions (Bode and Vraga, 2018).

Channels also predict individuals' disaster preparedness behaviors (Liu et al., 2019). Addressing the significance of information form and its source, the findings demonstrate that channels (such as traditional media, social media, word of mouth, etc.) and sources (including third parties, organizations, etc.) anticipate responses to crisis communication (Liu et al., 2011; 2015). It is also observed that the channels through which disaster information is obtained may exert a greater influence on information seeking than information sharing (Liu et al., 2015).

Information forms and sources for seeking more information influence media choice (Austin et al, 2012; Lai and Tang, 2021). During the COVID-19 pandemic, the landscape of information channels became more diverse. Intercultural research indicates that some groups turned to traditional media outlets, such as television and newspapers, seeking authoritative guidance from established sources. Others embraced digital platforms and social media, driven by the immediacy and interconnectedness they offered, even though these sources could also disseminate misinformation (Sun et al., 2021).

The Internet has gained significant importance as an information platform, but traditional information channels like radio and TV remain crucial during disasters (Armstrong et al., 2021; Maduz et al., 2019). Social media is the preferred choice for immediate disaster updates (Armstrong et al., 2021; Imran et al., 2013). Situational information is primarily disseminated through official channels on social media (Alajmi and Khalil, 2022). However, another study pointed out that during a crisis on social media, most of the information comes from the public and that this source is utilized to a limited extent by official sources (Jin and Spence, 2021).

Information seeking is mostly driven by channels, thus, the seeking behavior was evaluated by how often which channel is followed (Sommerfeldt, 2015; Liu et al. 2015). Therefore, information seeking, which constitutes the dependent variable of this study, is characterized by channels and the frequency of turning to these sources for information. Assessing the effectiveness of the channels through which information is sought and comprehending which channel performs optimally in specific scenarios will enhance effective disaster management.

The Need for Various Types of Information

People generally possess both active and passive needs during times of disaster. Active information needs encompass current status, disaster information, and warnings, while passive needs include current status updates, evacuation instructions, and other disaster informations (Rahmi et al., 2019). Information commonly sought during a disaster comprises explanations of the event, government responses, available sources, updates on shelters and evacuations, medical assistance, and measures for home protection. Wukich (2016) delineates the essential information categories necessary in times of disaster. These categories play a crucial role in directing response efforts. During emergency response operations, protective action messages offer citizens invaluable guidance, instructing them on how to minimize their immediate exposure to risk. These messages are characterized by their clarity, specificity, and inclusion of unambiguous directives, concrete timelines, and thorough hazard descriptions.

In addition, situational information plays a crucial role during emergencies (Alajmi and Khalil, 2022). This encompasses vital updates such as weather conditions, the status of debris removal, and information about damage assessments and casualties, ensuring that the public is kept informed during difficult times (Armstrong et al., 2021; Wukich, 2016). Information on coping strategies, including tips for managing stress and anxiety during a crisis and available help and support services, such as emergency hotlines and relief organizations, is also essential during the disaster period (Yates and Partridge, 2015).

In the dynamics that drive people to seek information in connection with the information repertoire, certain factors related to information types need to be taken into account. The first aspect is determining what information was sought in the early stages of the crisis. The information insufficiency gap, a pivotal concept in models like RISP and PRISM, plays a crucial role in increasing the likelihood of individuals seeking information about risks and systematically processing information (Dunwoody and Griffin, 2015; Kahlor, 2010). This gap becomes quite evident in the initial phases of the crisis.

Some additional information may be necessary in the early stages of health crises. According to Reynolds and Seeger (2005), public health emergencies demand the identification of specific risks stemming from the occurrence of particular diseases or environmental factors. This may encompass guidelines elucidating the event and associated risks (for example, symptoms, treatments, and methods to avoid exposure), information that is unfamiliar to the public, and necessitated lifestyle adjustments. This phase may entail public health authorities furnishing precise advice and directives on how to avert or mitigate harm, what symptoms may indicate concern, and where to seek treatment.

In the initial stages of the COVID-19 crisis, there was an expression of needs, an attempt to resolve uncertainties surrounding the crisis in detail, an assessment of government responses, and a desire to acquire information about mortality (Jin and Spence, 2021; Ebrahim et al., 2020; Lund and Ma, 2022; Diers-Lawson et al., 2021). Alongside accounts of resilience, there is an interest in understanding losses, damages, current developments, interventions by official institutions, as well as medical and evacuation support, and strategies for assisting during the crisis phase (Jin and Spence, 2021). Throughout the COVID-19 period, individuals show less concern for their own risk and are more preoccupied with the well-being of their family members (Chisty et al., 2021). Consequently, any information pertaining to the welfare of the close circle remains pertinent in the initial stage.

Secondly, within the disaster literature, it is posited that information needs may vary contingent upon the frequency and predictability of an event, be it frequently occurring or unforeseen and abrupt in nature (Gowan et al., 2014; Sagun et al., 2009). Within the theoretical framework of risk information seeking, information inadequacy pertains to the disparity between the available information and the requisite information (Dunwoody and Griffin, 2015; Kahlor, 2010). Nevertheless, the primacy of the need for information might surpass the gap in information inadequacy when it comes to seeking behavior (Zhou, 2021). The significance of information needs in the context of information seeking has long garnered empirical support (Ward and Hansen, 1993; Gibson, 2016; Huurne and Gutteling, 2008). The insufficiency of information during a pandemic fosters an increased demand for information and an intention to search, thus underscoring the necessity for additional information (Diers-Lawson et al., 2021). We therefore hypothesize that the need for various types of information is associated with information seeking (H1).

Information Sources

Sources constitute one of the most pivotal factors in crisis and risk communication. Within the domain of disaster communication, preferences for sources stand out as predictors of individuals' preparedness behaviors (Liu et al., 2019). Within the sphere of an actor or institution, source preferences refer to the choice of information sources individuals select in their pursuit of knowledge acquisition. Many studies have been conducted so far showing that information forms and sources affect information seeking behavior (Liu et al. 2015; Austin, Liu & Jin, 2012; Lachlan et al, 2021).

Furthermore, in accordance with the Communication Ecology perspective, which underpins the civic participation envisioned in disaster communication through its theoretical framework, individuals possess sources at different levels, whether micro or macro, and engage with them in any crisis (Ball-Rokeach et al., 2001; Kim and Ball-Rokeach, 2006). From a perspective that accounts for the influence of social norms in horizontal communication, it is posited that having a greater diversity or quantity of sources will positively impact the experience of accessing information and timely coping (Spialek and Houston, 2018; Zaremohzzabieh et al., 2021). In vertical communication, where an official spokesperson, an expert, or non-governmental sources may be involved in the dissemination of information, the element of trust is of great importance (Liu and Mehta, 2021).

Previous research on crisis-related information dissemination during disasters indicates that individuals initially acquire knowledge about disasters from family, friends, or small community circles, and subsequently seek additional information from various channels. Communication and interaction with affected family members and neighbors serve as prominent sources of information, constituting essential components for effective emergency management (Rahmi et al., 2019; Ryan, 2018). A study investigating central roles within disaster networks revealed that while traditional media retained significance in certain networks, others were predominantly influenced by prominent private individuals (Steinberg et al., 2016). Regarding information sources, individuals' reception and utilization of information are shaped by sender characteristics, the availability of visual content, their social connections, and cognitive capacities (Ryan, 2018). Furthermore, individuals who are more open to social influence and perceive others as possessing greater knowledge may exhibit an augmented need for risk-related information provided by their social environment (Huurne and Gutteling, 2008).

During the COVID-19 pandemic, the landscape of information sources has evolved into a more diverse and dynamic domain. Research that associates information sources with preventive behavior underscores the significance of uniform messages emanating from government officials, health authorities, and media platforms, and their pivotal role in promoting precautionary adherence. Empirical evidence from diverse countries has indicated that the multitude of information sources available to individuals may exhibit variability (Sun et al., 2021). In light of this, we posit that information sources have the potential influence information seeking behavior (H2).

Protection Motivation

According to Protection Motivation Theory (Rogers, 1985; Prentice-Dunn & Rogers, 1986), individuals are inclined to undertake preventive action when they perceive a threat as severe, believe themselves to be vulnerable to this threat, and are confident that the preventive actions are effective and within their capability to execute. It is posited that, in order for action to ensue, there must be high levels of perceived response efficacy and self-efficacy, coupled with a recognition of the severity and vulnerability inherent in the situation, all constituting crucial components of the model. Heightened perceptions of threat severity and vulnerability further prompt individuals to pay increased attention to messages delineating protective measures (Cummings et al., 2021). To accurately evaluate threats and the availability of coping mechanisms, individuals will require current and pertinent information (Li et al., 2023).

Individual Context

Due to the connection between protection motivation and information seeking, some studies have integrated PMT components to elucidate the mechanism of information seeking. A seminal study discovered that information concerning the severity of consequences triggers a search for further details about a hazard, and that information regarding vulnerability, severity, and response effectiveness collectively contribute to the formation of an intention for preventive actions (Neuwirth, 1995). Another research has demonstrated that hazard severity, perceived likelihood of threat, and response effectiveness directly influence behavioral intention, and that the impact of message elements is accentuated under heightened perceptions of these factors (Neuwirth et al., 2000). In a more recent study, heightened perceived threat severity, self-efficacy, and response efficacy were linked with elevated intentions, whereas increased perceived vulnerability was associated with diminished intentions (Williams and Joinson, 2020). In certain studies, vulnerability and previous disaster experiences also play a role in the information-seeking process (Alajmi and Khalil, 2022; Armstrong et al., 2021). Li and colleagues (2023) observed that in abnormal temperature situations related to climate disasters, individuals seek information about the threat, but do not actively seek information about preventive actions.

While the impacts of PMT components on preventive behavior have been extensively investigated in the broader COVID-19 literature (Rad et al., 2021; Bashirian et al., 2020; Al-Rasheed, 2020; Prasetyo et al., 2020), there is little information regarding the connection to information seeking. Findings indicating that factors such as response effectiveness and coping self-efficacy affect information avoidance (Sultana et al., 2023) imply that these factors may also foster increased information seeking. Consequently, we posit that perceived severity (H3), perceived sustainability (H4), response efficacy (H5), and perceived self-efficacy (H6) exert an influence on information seeking.

Social Context

The core variables of PMT suggest that protection motivation primarily centers on the individual's self-assessment. However, in fact, this evaluation is not independent of the social context in which the individual is located. Neuwirth et al. (2000) contend that individuals' sense of responsiveness and perceptions of competence towards collective action should also be considered. Similarly, from the perspective of Social Cognitive Theory, there is an emphasis on self-efficacy, a key concept of the theory, expanding within a collective context, where individuals are anticipated to collectively hold beliefs about their capacity to achieve shared objectives (Bandura, 2000). Since threats like the pandemic hinge on the competence of others, individuals might exhibit hesitancy in aligning their actions with their own self-efficacy beliefs, especially in the face of imposed restrictions (González-Castro et al., 2021).

Furthermore, Westcott et al. (2017) posit that individuals assess the threat or their ability to cope with a disaster by considering the potential challenges and supports from those they hold dear. This perspective extends the PMT framework by incorporating the influence of social context. The heightened concern of individuals for others, rather than themselves, observed during the COVID-19 period (Chisty et al., 2021), may serve as an indicator to underscore the importance of factoring in the social environment when evaluating threats and coping strategies in the pandemic. Given that the perceived competency of one's immediate social circle can assume precedence within the framework of collective efficacy (Smith et al., 2007), the group's efficacy may mold endeavors towards seeking information. Additionally, if collective endeavors falter or vulnerabilities increase due to challenges, this will impact the resilience of the group (Arnaud and Schminke, 2012). Hence, we propose that perceived efficacy for the social environment (H7) and perceived susceptibility of the social environment (H8) also exert an influence on information-seeking behavior.

THE SAMPLING OF THE STUDY AND METHOD

Sample

This study was designed by drawing on data on information seeking from a more comprehensive and phased study that linked individual profiles with preventive behavior in close environment ecology during the COVID-19 crisis. Data for this study were collected by a national research company through computer-assisted telephone interviewing (CATI) from August 2020 to September 2020. The sample consisted of 2,283 participants residing in 12 provinces at the NUTS-1 level, aiming to represent the population of Turkey with a 95% confidence level and a margin of error of ±2.0. To enhance the diversity and increase the reliability of the sample, data were collected from urban, town, and village areas, encompassing individuals within the age range of 18-80 years. Participation in the study was voluntary, and ethical approval was obtained from the Ege University Scientific Research and Publication Ethics Board (Approval No: EGEBAYEK20-616).

Materials and Methods

A comprehensive list of various types of information, as well as diverse sources and channels specifically pertinent to COVID-19, was compiled, drawing on prior literature (see Sommerfeldt, 2015; Lai and Tang, 2015; 2018). Participants were queried about the specific types of information and sources they sought, and the channels they employed during the pandemic for their information search. Responses were recorded on a 3-point scale ranging from 1 (Not at all) to 3 (Extremely). The total score of participants' perceived information needs represented the aggregate requirement for different types of information. Information-seeking behavior was delineated by the channels participants utilized for their information search. In line with the assumptions that information repertoire elements together with protection motivation components predict information seeking, channel preferences representing information seeking are utilized instead of clusters forming the repertoire. These channels were included in the analysis as the independent variable of this study.

Four main factors were considered for the threat and coping assessment based on the Protection Motivation Model (Cummings et al, 2013). Participants were asked to describe their perception of protection motivation as motivating information seeking. Perceived severity (5 items), perceived susceptibility (4 items), response efficacy (5 items) and perceived self-efficacy (5 items) were assessed using a 5-point scale ranging from 1 (I completely disagree) to 5 (I completely agree). The items for the PMT component were adapted from previous studies (Clark et al., 2020; Karadağ et al., 2020).

For group efficacy, we adopted the approach of individuals assessing the capacity of their group as a whole (Bandura, 2000). Participants were asked to consider their close social environment and rate and their likelihood of avoiding contracting COVID-19 (perceived efficacy for social circle) and the vulnerability of contracting COVID-19 for them (perceived susceptibility for social circle) using a 5-point scale ranging from 1 (Very low) to 5 (Very high).

Descriptive statistics and principal component analysis were conducted to characterize the information gathering patterns. To identify predictive factors for channel preferences, multivariate linear regression analysis was performed. To avoid issues of multicollinearity, correlation values above 0.80 and standard errors were examined (Tabachnick and Fidell, 1996). All analyses were conducted using SPSS ver. 22 software.

FINDINGS AND DISCUSSION

Based on the sample proportion outlined in Table 1, half of the study population, averaging 37 years of age, comprised women and married individuals. The sample exhibited a generally high level of interest in various types of information, with the highest priority given to updates on vaccines and treatment methods (M = 2.52, SD = .79). As anticipated, there existed a demand for information concerning available treatments, prevention measures, as well as statistics on case rates. This aligns with the observations of Rahmi et al. (2019), who noted that people's information-seeking behaviors alter during a disaster, driven by their paramount concern for safeguarding their health and well-being. Similar findings were presented in the study by Le et al. (2020), which highlighted the need for up-to-date information regarding the spread of the disease, associated risks, and early-stage symptoms in the initial phase of the pandemic. Concerning social life, the primary interest lay in pandemic-related restrictions. Information pertaining to travel restrictions and regulations was rated as less critical (M = 2.19, SD = .91)

The primary sources in the participants' information-seeking processes during the pandemic were officials from the Ministry of Health and members of the Pandemic Scientific Board (Table 1). This board, established in Turkey a few months prior to the declaration of the COVID-19 virus as a pandemic in March 2020 (WHO, 2020), comprised expert scientists who provided recommendations that guided the implementation of measures and treatment protocols in managing the pandemic nationwide (Milliyet, 2020). Additionally, the Board assumed the role of spokespersons, disseminating decisions and current developments to the public through various traditional and social media platforms (Hürriyet, 2020). Our findings demonstrate that these roles established officials and recognized individuals as trusted sources of information (see. Demirbilek et al., 2020). A study encompassing multiple countries noted that a similar role was also taken on by members of scientific committees from other nations, although they encountered challenges in gaining recognition as public figures and in directly communicating with the public (Colman, 2021). Given the nature of the disaster, officials from the central government also played a predominant role in managing the COVID-19 crisis (Yavetz et al., 2020). However, the lower rating assigned to local government entities and non-governmental organizations in information retrieval

Table 1. Proportion of the sample

Demographic Characteristics (n=2283)	N	%		*Types of Information Sought (1-3)*	Mean	SD	α
Gender				Scientific information about the COVID-19 virus	2.37	.85	.934
Men	1142	50		COVID-19 treatment procedure	2.45	.84	.937
Woman	1141	50		Prevention methods	2.44	.86	.934
Marital status				Care and risks during quarantine	2.36	.89	.931
Single	1006	44.1		Scientific developments on vaccines and treatments	2.52	.79	.931
Married	1277	55.9		Case rates from the region	2.44	.84	.929
	Mean	SD		Case rates from the country	2.45	.84	.933
Age (18-80)	37.74	14.48		Case rates from other countries	2.34	.87	.929
				Pandemic restrictions and bans	2.44	.85	.932
Protection Motivation components (1-5)	Mean	SD	α	Regulations for workplaces and institutions	2.36	.87	.935
Perceived severity	4.20	.69	.807	Social life regulations	2.25	.90	.929
Perceived susceptibility	2.64	.87	.682	Domestic and international travel regulations	2.19	.91	.931
Response efficacy	4.32	.59	.807	Coping stories	2.22	.90	.932
Perceived self-efficacy	4.30	.65	.853	*Information sources (1-3)*			
Competence of social environment (1-5)				Presidential officials	2.21	.92	.861
Perceived susceptibility of social circle	3.34	.86	.807	Ministry of Health officials	2.59	.76	.872
Perceived efficacy of social circle	3.51	.89	.745	Other ministry officials (Internal Affairs, Transport, etc.)	1.91	.93	.862
Channels to seek information (1-3)				Local administrators and officials	1.62	.86	.863
National/local print media	1.86	.91	.859	Members of the National Pandemic Science Board	2.39	.87	.861
National/local audiovisual media	2.54	.77	.865	Provincial and district health institution officials	2.04	.94	.864
International mass media	2.10	.92	.856	Doctors and healthcare professionals	2.26	.90	.865
Scientific publications	1.69	.88	.857	Turkish scientists	2.29	.91	.864
Pandemic-specific accounts	2.02	.92	.849	Media actors (journalist, columnist, etc)	2.07	.91	.863
Followed accounts	2.13	.91	.847	Representatives of NGOs	1.47	.78	.864
Science websites and accounts	2.12	.93	.850	Other social actors (Teacher, imam etc)	1.66	.87	.865
Health institutions websites and accounts	2.28	.90	.850	Business and professional environment	1.74	.88	.869
Social media hashtags	1.65	.87	.850	Family and friends	2.06	.90	.872
Mainstream and alternative media accounts	2.06	.93	.852	Neighbors and acquaintances	1.85	.88	.868
Social groups & channels (WhatsApp, telegram etc.)	1.84	.91	.852	Leaders and officials of other countries	1.72	.88	.861
Other groups & channels (WhatsApp, telegram etc.)	1.85	.92	.852	International organizations (WHO, ILO, etc.)	2.25	.90	.860
Search engines	1.96	.91	.851	Foreign scientists	1.92	.92	.862

contradicted results that underscore the primary and active role of local governments and initiatives in disaster management (Malla et al, 2020; Bergström, 2016).

In line with previous findings, traditional mainstream media and official digital channels related to pandemic management were identified as the most frequently used sources for information seeking (Diers-Lawson et al., 2021). Social media searches conducted through hashtags demonstrated the lowest average score (M = 1.65, SD = 0.87). This contradicts the use of hashtags as effective communication channels for disseminating data sources and raising awareness through disaster warning systems (Murzintcev and Cheng, 2017; Grasso and Crisci, 2016), which are also favored by individuals affected by disasters (Thomson et al., 2012). Reasons such as the ineffective operation of this interaction system as an information channel in the first period of the pandemic crisis (Lachlan et al., 2016) or information search habits (Sommerfeldt, 2015) may explain the low use of hashtags.

Based on the findings regarding PMT variables, participants expressed a strong perception of the severity of the health threat and their own vulnerability to it. However, they reported even higher levels of perceived effectiveness of protective measures and self-efficacy in influencing their coping appraisal (Table 1). At this point, we should remember PMT's claim that activity based on high threat and coping appraisals are necessary for the motivation of behavior (Rogers, 1985). Conversely, participants perceived the social environment as being more susceptible and less competent when compared to their own self-assessment.

Principal Component Analysis (PCA), a method within factor analysis, was employed to scrutinize the item list concerning information needs. The Kaiser-Meyer-Olkin (KMO) test yielded a value of 0.950, and the results of the Bartlett Test of Sphericity indicated a significant outcome (X^2= 19477.57, p=.00), affirming the appropriateness of the data for analysis. PCA with varimax rotation based on variance maximization was applied to 13 information types prepared to reveal the dimensions of the information need. The analysis revealed that a single dimension accounted for 57.54% of the total variance (Table 2).

The results of the PCA conducted on the items pertaining to information sources are presented in Table 3. The Kaiser-Meyer-Olkin (KMO) test yielded a value of 0.880, and the results of the Bartlett Test of Sphericity indicated a significant outcome (X^2= 13311.56, p=.00), affirming the suitability of the data for analysis. According to the analysis, the 17 items related to information sources were categorized

Table 2. Results of factor analysis (PCA) for the information needs

Factor Items	Component
	Types of Information Sought
COVID-19 treatment procedure	0.864
Prevention methods	0.840
Pandemic restrictions and bans	0.813
Care and risks during quarantine	0.799
Case rates from the country	0.794
Regulations for workplaces and institutions	0.793
Case rates from other countries	0.765
Social life regulations	0.754
Case rates from the region	0.749
Domestic and international travel regulations	0.711
Scientific developments on vaccines and treatments	0.687
Coping stories	0.670
Scientific information about the COVID-19 virus	0.600

The extraction was based on a Principal Component Anaysis (PCA) with Kaiser normalization (Varimax rotation). Data was adequate for factor solution (KMO = 0.950; Bartlett's Test of Sphericity: Appr. chi-square = 19477.57 df=78, p<0.001). The total variance explained by the components was 57.54%.

Table 3. Results of factor analysis (PCA) for the information sources

Factor Items	Component				
	Pandemic Authorities	Foreign Authorities	Social Environment	National Authorities	Local Authorities
Ministry of Health officials	**0.737**	0.136	0.063	0.324	-0.044
Turkish scientists	**0.697**	0.281	-0.057	0.067	0.172
Members of the National Pandemic Science Board	**0.629**	0.328	-0.044	0.406	0.035
Doctors and healthcare professionals	**0.612**	0.113	0.249	-0.111	0.293
Provincial and district health institution officials	**0.559**	0.019	0.029	0.261	0.399
Foreign scientists	0.267	**0.820**	0.003	0.075	0.153
Leaders and officials of other countries	0.031	**0.754**	0.148	0.217	0.272
International organizations (WHO, ILO, etc.)	0.397	**0.677**	0.083	0.197	0.045
Family and friends	-0.015	0.065	**0.840**	0.037	0.030
Neighbors and acquaintances	0.037	0.027	**0.807**	0.107	0.152
Business and professional environment	0.070	0.087	**0.730**	0.062	0.132
Other ministry officials (Internal Affairs, Transport, etc.)	0.099	0.183	0.077	**0.814**	0.213
Presidential officials	0.271	0.138	0.063	**0.802**	0.070
Media actors (journalist, columnist, etc)	0.138	0.413	0.203	**0.439**	0.124
Representatives of NGOs	0.110	0.217	0.082	0.091	**0.781**
Local administrators and officials	0.116	0.108	0.127	0.234	**0.767**
Other social actors (Teacher, imam etc)	0.234	0.146	0.349	-0.019	**0.500**

The extraction was based on a Principal Component Anaysis (PCA) with Kaiser normalization (Varimax rotation). Data was adequate for factor solution (KMO = 0.880; Bartlett's Test of Sphericity: Appr. chi-square = 13311.56 df=136, p<0.001). The total variance explained by the components was 64.17%. The variances explained by the components were 14.88%, 13.14%, 12.86%, 11.90% and 11.37% respectively.

into five dimensions. The pattern matrix, reflecting the five-component structure, exhibited no instances of cross-loading, signifying that each principal component was distinctly identified. These components accounted for 64.17% of the total variance.

PCA delineated five components of information sources (Table 3). These were classified as pandemic authorities, national authorities, foreign authorities, local authorities, and the social environment. Pandemic authorities encompassed the actors directly responsible for pandemic management and assumed a public information dissemination role. National authorities were characterized by actors primarily concerned with social life arrangements during the pandemic, and who issued guidance in this regard. Foreign authorities consisted of providers of information pertaining to the global pandemic situation and international developments. Local authorities encompassed the local government, social organizations, and civil actors from the community. Lastly, the social environment encompassed individuals' primary and immediate social circles from which they sought information.

Table 4 presents the outcomes of the PCA conducted on the items pertaining to the channels through which information was sought. The data demonstrated sufficient suitability for PCA analysis, as indicated

Table 4. Results of factor analysis (PCA) for the channels for information seeking

Factor Items	Component		
	Digital Channels	**Personalized Channels**	**Traditional Channels**
Pandemic-specific accounts	**0.772**	0.220	0.022
Followed accounts	**0.765**	0.236	0.087
Science websites and accounts	**0.764**	0.053	0.190
Health institutions websites and accounts	**0.670**	0.210	0.173
Social media hashtags	**0.557**	0.390	0.069
Mainstream and alternative media accounts	**0.512**	0.094	0.450
Social groups & channels (WhatsApp, Telegram etc.)	0.179	**0.879**	0.120
Other groups & channels (WhatsApp, Telegram etc.)	0.175	**0.872**	0.123
Search engines	0.368	**0.530**	0.226
National/local print media	0.106	0.113	**0.754**
National/local audiovisual media	-0.102	0.248	**0.651**
International mass media	0.297	0.085	**0.648**
Scientific publications	0.448	-0.073	**0.495**

The extraction was based on a Principal Component Anaysis (PCA) with Kaiser normalization (Varimax rotation). Data was adequate for factor solution (KMO = 0.863; Bartlett's Test of Sphericity: Appr. chi-square = 10270.88 df=78, p<0.001). The total variance explained by the components was 57.89%. The variances explained by the components were 25.34%, 17.02%, 15.53% respectively.

Table 5. Correlations between variables

Variables	1	2	3	4	5	6	7	8	9	10	11	12	13	14
Traditional channels	-													
Digital channels	.477**	-												
Personalized channels	.371**	.529**	-											
Information need	.380**	.366**	.326**	-										
Foreign authorities	.421**	.386**	.282**	.427**	-									
National authorities	.383**	.318**	.276**	.357**	.517**	-								
Pandemic authorities	.396**	.336**	.194**	.386**	.551**	.506**	-							
Local authorities	.321**	.290**	.271**	.316**	.421**	.391**	.479**	-						
Social environment	.150**	.334**	.387**	.297**	.210**	.233**	.157**	.355**	-					
Perceived severity	.260**	.147**	.075**	.181**	.109**	.075**	.117**	.059**	.0,86**	-				
Perceived susceptibility	.031	.083**	-.009	.098**	.045*	.026	.081**	-.019	-.033	.146**	-			
Response efficacy	.233**	.102**	.079**	.135**	.090**	.092**	.130**	.017	.036	.462**	.049*	-		
Perceived self-efficacy	.118**	.082**	.084**	.155**	.093**	.080**	.111**	.024	.002	.408**	.022	.647**	-	
Perceived susceptibility of SC	.120**	.174**	.124**	.148**	.107**	.117**	.096**	.052*	.072**	.219**	.244**	.143**	.079**	-
Perceived efficacy of SC	.143**	.112**	.073**	.091**	.103**	.089**	.150**	.011	-.024	.121**	-.031	.244**	.253**	.39

**p<0.01, *p<0.05

by the results of the Kaiser-Meyer-Olkin (KMO) test (0.863) and the significant outcome of the Bartlett Test of Sphericity ($X^2 = 10270.88$, $p = .00$). According to the analysis, the 13 items related to channels were classified into three dimensions. The three-component structure in the pattern matrix also exhibited no instances of cross-loading, signifying that each principal component was distinctly delineated. These components accounted for 57.89% of the total variance.

The correlation matrix in Table 5 indicates that the variables were generally correlated with each other at low to moderate levels, and in a positive direction. All explanatory variables demonstrated a significant association with information seeking. Nonetheless, it was observed that perceived susceptibility was not correlated with information seeking in traditional channels ($r = .031$, $p > 0.05$) and personalized channels ($r = -.009$, $p > 0.05$).

In the next stage, a series of regression analyses were conducted with predictor variables. The applied multivariate regression analysis is summarized in Table 6, showing the outcomes of the best models that elucidate the predictors of information seeking through different channels. The R^2 values of these models range from 0.22 to 0.29, indicating that the explanatory variables predicted information seeking through various channels within this range. These findings underscore the significance of our explanatory variables in understanding information seeking, while also alluding to the existence of additional variables that predict information seeking, albeit outside the scope of this study.

The results remained consistent even after controlling for demographic variables. These findings indicate that the utilization of information search channels in this study exhibited no significant variation based on factors such as age, gender, and marital status. However, it is worth noting that prior research has explored the impact of various demographic characteristics. For instance, Rahmi et al. (2019) identified that gender and age exert influence on the choice of different media channels. According to their findings, women were more inclined to utilize television and the internet to fulfill emotional needs. Moreover, in the context of the pandemic, older individuals were required to adapt their media consumption habits in comparison to younger and middle-aged individuals. Nevertheless, some faced challenges in making this adjustment (Pan et al., 2020).

For information seeking in traditional channels; information need, information sources other than the social environment, perceived severity, response efficacy and perceived efficacy of the social environment were significant. Information need ($\beta = 0.16$) and foreign authorities ($\beta = 0.16$) were the strongest predictors of information seeking in these channels. These were followed by national authorities ($\beta = 0.14$) and pandemic authorities ($\beta = 0.11$). For information seeking in digital channels; information needs, information sources other than national and local authorities, and perceived efficacy and susceptibility for the social environment were significant. Surprisingly, social environment ($\beta = 0.22$) came first in digital channels. For information seeking in personalized channels, information need ($\beta = 0.16$), national and pandemic authorities ($\beta = 0.09$), and perceived susceptibility ($\beta = 0.05$) were significant. Additionally, perceived susceptibility and perceived efficacy for the social environment ($\beta = 0.07$, $\beta = 0.05$) were found to be significant. Therefore, H1 was supported for all channels, while H6 was rejected. H2, H3, H4, H5, H7 and H8 were supported taking into account the differentiation across channels.

The need for information emerged as a predictor of information seeking across all channels. While some early models of information seeking, albeit originating from outside the disaster literature, illustrate a causal relationship between information-carrying channels and information seeking (Case, 2005), the driving forces behind seeking also encompass selecting information channels based on needs and opting for familiar sources and channel types. The higher coefficient of the need for information in digital and personalized channels may be attributed to these motivating factors. In fact, according to some results,

Table 6. LR analysis results of information seeking predicted by protection motivation components, info needs, and sources

	Traditional Channels			Digital Channels			Personalized Channels		
	B	SE B	β	B	SE B	β	B	SE B	β
Information need	**.150**	**.020**	**.162*** **	**.146**	**.021**	**.142*** **	**.189**	**.026**	**.162*** **
Information sources									
Foreign authorities	**.132**	**.018**	**.165*** **	**.147**	**.021**	**.166*** **	**.094**	**.025**	**.093*** **
National authorities	**.122**	**.016**	**.148*** **	.038	.020	.042	**.097**	**.024**	**.093*** **
Pandemic authorities	**.107**	**.023**	**.113*** **	**.122**	**.026**	**.117*** **	**-.069**	**.031**	**-.057* **
Local authorities	**.092**	**.016**	**.110*** **	.014	.023	.014	.046	.027	.039
Social environment	.034	.018	.039	**.205**	**.018**	**.223*** **	**.060**	**.027**	**.051* **
PMT components									
Perceived severity	**.042**	**.020**	**.045* **	.023	.020	.023	-.029	.024	-.026
Perceived susceptibility	-.012	.013	-.018	.026	.014	.034	**-.037**	**.017**	**-.042* **
Response efficacy	**.060**	**.025**	**.059* **	.011	.028	.010	.019	.033	.015
Perceived self-efficacy	-.009	.022	-.009	.004	.024	.004	.039	.029	.034
Competence of social environment									
Perceived susceptibility of social circle	.024	.013	.034	**.070**	**.015**	**.090*** **	**.063**	**.017**	**.071*** **
Perceived efficacy of social circle	**.047**	**.012**	**.071*** **	**.040**	**.014**	**.054** **	**.046**	**.016**	**.054** **
F	81.151			75.188			56.187		
Adj R^2	.297			.281			.225		

***p<0.001, **p<0.01, *p<0.05

rapidly developing situations have increased the demands for additional channels, such as social networks (Chan et. al, 2020). Moreover, findings that individuals heavily contribute to the dissemination of messages from official authorities (Chen et. al., 2020; Chan et. al, 2020) indicate that digital channels may also have become an environment in which official messages are sought and received. Additionally, as posited by Neuwirth et al. (2000), the type of information that individuals desire or reject serves to more accurately delineate their position in the motivational process of self-protection. The type of information that is deemed more essential may signify which information has greater potential to motivate the individual.

The coefficients for sources were close to each other in traditional channels. One reason for this is likely to be the ability of traditional media to represent various actors as a source of news. On digital channels, pandemic authorities and the social environment assumed greater prominence. Contrary to findings showing the activity of government authorities in digital channels (Yavetz et al., 2020), our findings showed that these actors are more prominent in traditional media. On the other hand, it is not surprising that foreign authorities are sought after as a source on channels. Authorities such as the World Health Organization have played an active role throughout the pandemic, offering counsel and directives to nations in their efforts to combat the outbreak. The guidelines recommended by this organization have essentially guided the overarching pandemic response strategies of countries. However, a cross-country comparative study discovered that the World Health Organization ranked as one of the most crucial sources of information for participants from Vietnam, while it was deemed an unimportant source for participants from Korea (Diers-Lawson et al., 2021).

The role of the social environment as an information source is important. The prominence of the social environment, particularly in digital channels, over other sources aligns with previous findings. Çağlar (2021) similarly discovered that family members, social circles, and famous figures wielded influence over the behavioral decisions of participants who preferred and trusted in digital channels. According to Geçer et al. (2022), women obtained information more from their friends and family and social media than men. Findings from various countries also indicate that a substantial portion of the information reaching individuals originates from sources within their immediate social circles, often through platforms like social media and messaging applications such as WhatsApp (Ahmed, 2020; Yavetz et al., 2022). Moreover, the social environment played a pivotal role in the selection of information sources (Skarpa and Garoufallou, 2021). In contrast, the results of Blasco et al. (2020) ranked family and close circles as the least utilized sources of disaster-related information.

Perceived severity and response efficacy were found to predict information seeking in traditional channels, while perceived susceptibility was a predictor of information seeking in personalized channels. These findings suggest a connection between threat and coping appraisals with messages conveyed through traditional media, and between threat appraisal and messages received through personalized channels. However, it is a surprising result that the basic components of PMT are not generally related to information seeking. On the other hand, a study explains the results, which are consistent with our findings, that information seeking is only slightly affected by PMT variables, as a result of the widespread collectivist cultural tendency in the country (Alhemimah, 2023). In societies such as Turkey, where close social ties and collectivist values are dominant, tendencies such as group belonging, cooperative behavior and coping together increase to avoid uncertainty in times of crisis (Hofstede, 2001 & 2011). This characteristic may also underlie the linkage between threat and coping appraisals with social interactions. It's worth noting that people's perception of risk is influenced by the information they are given; and there is a strong relationship between information-seeking behavior and risk perception which is also influenced by cultural traditions (Chisty et al. 2021; Maduz et al. 2019).

Indeed, perceived efficacy and vulnerability for the social environment serve as predictors of information seeking in digital and personalized channels. The theoretical proposition that collectivists tend to be more motivated by altruism and a desire to strengthen social ties (Finkelstein, 2010) supports the significance of perceptions of others in the context of information seeking. While previous studies have not extensively utilized these variables to elucidate information seeking behavior, one study has implicated online actions and convergence in community resilience as a mechanism in the orchestration of information behavior. This mechanism encompasses seeking the support of others to overcome various information challenges while in isolation (Pan et al., 2020). Hence, extending information support to vulnerable groups in closer social circles can be viewed as an indication that information seeking is influenced by the presence and impact of others. These findings are in alignment with the argument put forth by Westcott et al. (2017), which asserts that individuals assess the threat and coping strategies of a disaster by considering the potential challenges and support from those they care about. This call to expand Protection Motivation Theory (PMT) based on the social context is consistent with our results.

This study exhibits both strengths and certain limitations. Firstly, it is essential to acknowledge that this study operates within a theoretical framework that synthesizes the information repertoire and protection motivation approaches to information seeking. In addition, the use of quantitative design in the research design limits the explanation of information seeking behavior to the explanatory power of certain variables based on the theoretical framework of this research. Hence, it is imperative to recognize the potential of alternative theoretical frameworks and methodologies in elucidating information seeking behaviors. Secondly, even as individuals engage in information seeking, they continue to assess risk (Neuwirth et al., 2000). This implies that changes in people's perceptions, which shape their assessment of threat and coping, may influence their information seeking behavior, contingent on various developments throughout the pandemic. Future research endeavors could enhance our findings by scrutinizing PMT parameters across different levels of information-seeking behavior. Thirdly, the utilization of a cross-sectional research design poses challenges in establishing causal inferences. Finally, in light of prior findings that individual-collective orientations may be linked to media preferences or processes of seeking risk information (Sheldon et al., 2017; Aliperti & Cruz, 2019), research designs that incorporate cultural tendencies can be considered.

CONCLUSION AND RECOMMENDATIONS

This study offers a framework for elucidating the impact of components within the information repertoire on information-seeking behavior, with a specific focus on the Turkish context. Our findings underscore the diverse array of information needs and the pivotal role played by information sources in the process of information seeking. This underscores the significance of communication strategies that prioritize information requirements and available sources, especially in crisis scenarios like pandemics. Furthermore, our results highlight that digital and personalized channels, in addition to traditional media, serve as critical touchpoints for those affected by disasters in their quest for information. Given the likelihood that social communication has shifted towards these channels due to restrictions, it is crucial to recognize that the prominence of the social environment in these platforms may facilitate the dissemination of misinformation. Additionally, when taken in conjunction with evidence suggesting a decline in trust towards information provided by traditional channels and an increase in trust towards social media during emergencies (McDermid et al., 2023), this highlights the importance for policymakers to enhance digital content by securing support from more reliable sources, such as healthcare professionals.

This study identified the role of cognitive assessment factors on information seeking. This role, however, was comparatively less significant when contrasted with information needs and sources. The influence of perceived severity and response efficacy appears to be primarily associated with messages disseminated by official authorities through traditional channels, underscoring the criticality of individual compliance with precautionary measures in combatting the pandemic. Moreover, individuals seem to actively seek messages that address their vulnerability to risks within other social groups. In addition, this study introduces a social contextual perspective, suggesting that perceptions of others' competence can also factor into information-seeking behavior. The prominence of perceptions regarding the efficacy and susceptibility of the social environment in information seeking presents an argument to policymakers that individuals seek information while considering the competency of their immediate circle. This underscores the importance of providing comprehensive information on various vulnerabilities, taking into account the social circles individuals interact with. We recommend that future research further examine these findings through research designs that center on the role of social context in information seeking.

The dynamic nature of information-seeking behavior highlights the importance of alternative perspectives, such as the strategic role of narrative or experiences that drive audience engagement. For example, the role of experiences in the development of different repertoires can emerge through the use of developing instrumental technologies such as social media and platform journalism (Peters et al., 2022). Additionally, particular perspectives, such as the impact of political dynamics (ideological homogeneity or heterogeneity), can transform repertoire configurations. This transformation includes the monitoring of opposing views (Juzefovičs and Vihalemm, 2020) and the reproduction of strategic narratives due to media restrictions imposed by political authorities (Szostek, 2018), thereby expanding the boundaries of information search. Moreover, it is possible to see the existence of information search typologies specific to certain diseases in the field of health (Wahl and Grimm, 2016). The practice of individual interviews, focus group discussions, and in-depth analysis of various qualitative designs offer advantages in exploring individual differences, emerging trends, and underlying mechanisms. Future research should enhance our understanding of qualitative decision-making and alternative perspectives by employing qualitative designs that have been underutilized in the field of disaster management.

ACKNOWLEDGMENT

This study uses data from a larger-scale, multistage, and comprehensive research project. The project was funded by the Scientific and Technological Research Council of Turkey (TUBITAK) ARDEB 1001 Programme, COVID-19 and Community Special Call 2020 (Project No 120K653). The authors would also like to thank the project's fellows for their support and experts from various fields for their suggestions on preliminary data.

REFERENCES

Ahmed, S. T. (2020). Managing news overload (MNO): The COVID-19infodemic. *Information (Basel), 11*(8), 375. doi:10.3390/info11080375

Al-Rasheed, M. (2020). Protective behavior against COVID-19 among the public in Kuwait: An examination of the protection motivation theory, trust in government, and sociodemographic factors. *Social Work in Public Health, 35*(7), 546–556. doi:10.1080/19371918.2020.1806171 PMID:32970542

Alajmi, B. M., & Khalil, O. (2022). The extent of and motivation for disaster information seeking behavior via social networking sites. *Journal of Electronic Resources Librarianship, 34*(3), 219–244. doi:10.1080/1941126X.2022.2099026

Alhemimah, A. (2023). How COVID-19 impacts travel-health information seeking and tourists' travel intentions: A protection motivation theory-based model. *Journal of Destination Marketing & Management, 27*, 100757. doi:10.1016/j.jdmm.2022.100757

Aliperti, G., & Cruz, A. M. (2019). Investigating tourists' risk information processing. *Annals of Tourism Research, 79*, 102803. doi:10.1016/j.annals.2019.102803

An, S., Schulz, P. J., & Kang, H. (2023). Perceived COVID-19 susceptibility and preventive behaviors: Moderating effects of social support in Italy and South Korea. *BMC Public Health, 23*(1), 1–11. PMID:36624437

Aqili, V. D., & Nejad, V. M. (2016). A study on news anchors' meta-language and non-verbal factors and their impact on audiences. *The International Journal of Social Sciences (Islamabad)*, *6*(1), 1–9.

Armstrong, C. L., Cain, J. A., & Hou, J. (2021). Ready for disaster: Information seeking, media influence, and disaster preparation for severe weather outbreaks. *Atlantic Journal of Communication*, *29*(3), 121–135. doi:10.1080/15456870.2020.1731512

Arnaud, A., & Schminke, M. (2012). The ethical climate and context of organizations: A comprehensive model. *Organization Science*, *23*(6), 1767–1780. doi:10.1287/orsc.1110.0698

Ataguba, J. E. (2020). COVID-19 Pandemic, a war to be won: Understanding its economic implications for Africa. *Applied Health Economics and Health Policy*, *18*(3), 325–328. doi:10.100740258-020-00580-x PMID:32249362

Austin, L., Liu Fisher, B., & Jin, Y. (2012). How audiences seek out crisis information: Exploring the social-mediated crisis communication model. *Journal of Applied Communication Research*, *40*(2), 188–207. doi:10.1080/00909882.2012.654498

Ball-Rokeach, S. J., Kim, Y. C., & Matei, S. (2001). Storytelling neighborhood: Paths to belonging in diverse urban environments. *Communication Research*, *28*(4), 392–428. doi:10.1177/009365001028004003

Bandura, A. (2000). Exercise of human agency through collective efficacy. *Current Directions in Psychological Science*, *9*(3), 75–78. doi:10.1111/1467-8721.00064

Bashirian, S., Jenabi, E., Khazaei, S., Barati, M., Karimi-Shahanjarini, A., Zareian, S., Rezapur-Shahkolai, F., & Moeini, B. (2020). Factors associated with preventive behaviours of covid-19 among hospital staff in iran in 2020: An application of the protection motivation theory. *The Journal of Hospital Infection*, *105*(3), 430–433. doi:10.1016/j.jhin.2020.04.035 PMID:32360337

Bergström, J., Uhr, C., & Frykmer, T. (2016). A complexity framework for studying disaster response management. *Journal of Contingencies and Crisis Management*, *24*(3), 124–135. doi:10.1111/1468-5973.12113

Blasco, M. M., Castellà, C. O., & Raso, M. L. (2020). Impact of the Covid-19 pandemic on media consumption in Spain. *Revista Latina de Comunicación Social*, (78), 155–167. doi:10.4185/RLCS-2020-1472

Bode, L., & Vraga, E. K. (2018). See something, say something: Correction of global health misinformation on social media. *Health Communication*, *33*(9), 1131–1140. doi:10.1080/10410236.2017.1331312 PMID:28622038

Çağlar, G. (2021). COVİD-19 pandemisinde bilgi edinme kaynakları, medya kullanım alışkanlıkları ve aşıya yönelik tutumlar. *Akdeniz Üniversitesi İletişim Fakültesi Dergisi*, (36), 178–202.

Case, D. O. (2005). Principle of least effort. In K. E. Fisher, S. Erdelez, & L. E. F. McKenchnie (Eds.), *Theories of Information Behavior* (pp. 289–292). American Society for Information Science and Technology by Information Today.

Casero-Ripollés, A. (2020). Impact of Covid-19 on the media system. Communicative and democratic consequences of news consumption during the outbreak. *El Profesional de la Información*, *29*(2), 1–11. doi:10.3145/epi.2020.mar.23

Chan, A. K. M., Nickson, C. P., Rudolph, J. W., Lee, A., & Joynt, G. M. (2020). Social media for rapid knowledge dissemination: Early experience from the COVID-19 pandemic. *Anaesthesia*, *75*(12), 1579–1582. doi:10.1111/anae.15057 PMID:32227594

Chen, Q., Min, C., Zhang, W., Wang, G., Ma, X., & Evans, R. (2020). Unpacking the black box: How to promote citizen engagement through government social media during the COVID-19 crisis. *Computers in Human Behavior*, *10*, 106380. doi:10.1016/j.chb.2020.106380 PMID:32292239

Chew, C., & Eysenbach, G. (2010). Pandemics in the age of Twitter: Content analysis of Tweets during the 2009 H1N1 Outbreak. *PLoS One*, *5*(11), 271–275. doi:10.1371/journal.pone.0014118 PMID:21124761

Chisty, M. A., Islam, M. A., Munia, A. T., Rahman, M. M., Rahman, N. N., & Mohima, M. (2021). Risk perception and information-seeking behavior during emergency: An exploratory study on COVID-19 pandemic in Bangladesh. *International Journal of Disaster Risk Reduction*, *65*, 102580. doi:10.1016/j.ijdrr.2021.102580 PMID:34540577

Clark, C., Davila, A., Regis, M., & Kraus, S. (2020). Predictors of COVID-19 voluntary compliance behaviors: An international investigation. *Global Transitions*, *2*, 76–82. doi:10.1016/j.glt.2020.06.003 PMID:32835202

Colman, E., Wanat, M., Goossens, H., Tonkin-Crine, S., & Anthierens, S. (2021). Following the science? Views from scientists on government advisory boards during the COVID-19 pandemic: A qualitative interview study in five European countries. *BMJ Global Health*, *6*(9), e006928. doi:10.1136/bmjgh-2021-006928 PMID:34580072

Cummings, C. L., Rosenthal, S., & Kong, W. Y. (2021). Secondary risk theory: Validation of a novel model of protection motivation. *Risk Analysis*, *41*(1), 204–220. doi:10.1111/risa.13573 PMID:32790201

Demirbilek, Y., Pehlivantürk, G., Özgüler, Z. Ö., & Meşe, E. A. (2020). COVID-19 outbreak control, example of Ministry of Health of Turkey. *Turkish Journal of Medical Sciences*, *50*(9), 489–494. doi:10.3906ag-2004-187 PMID:32304192

Diers-Lawson, A., Johnson, S., Clayton, T., Kimoto, R., Tran, B. X., Nguyen, L. H., & Park, K. (2021). Pandemic communication: Information seeking, evaluation, and self-protective behaviors in Vietnam and the Republic of Korea. *Frontiers in Communication*, *6*, 731979. doi:10.3389/fcomm.2021.731979

Dunwoody, S., & Griffin, R. J. (2015). Risk information seeking and processing model. In H. Cho, T. Reimer, & K. A. McComas (Eds.), *SAGE Handbook of Risk Communication* (pp. 102–116). Sage Publications. doi:10.4135/9781483387918.n14

Ebrahim, A. H., Saif, Z. Q., Buheji, M., AlBasri, N., Al-Husaini, F. A., & Jahrami, H. (2020). COVID-19 information-seeking behavior and anxiety symptoms among parents. *OSP Journal of Health Care and Medicine*, *1*(1), 1–9.

Elsner, J. N., Sadler, T. D., Zangori, L., Friedrichsen, P. J., & Ke, L. (2022). Student interest, concerns, and information-seeking behaviors related to COVID-19. *Disciplinary and Interdisciplinary Science Education Research*, *4*(1), 1–11. doi:10.118643031-022-00053-2 PMID:37520636

Finkelstein, M. A. (2010). Individualism/collectivism: Implications for the volunteer process. *Social Behavior and Personality*, *38*(4), 445–452. doi:10.2224bp.2010.38.4.445

Geçer, E., Yıldırım, M., & Akgül, Ö. (2022). Sources of information in times of health crisis: Evidence from Turkey during COVID-19. *Journal of Public Health (Berlin)*, *30*(5), 1113–1119. doi:10.100710389-020-01393-x PMID:33072495

Gibson, A. N. (2016). Building a progressive-situational model of post-diagnosis information seeking for parents of individuals with down syndrome. *Global Qualitative Nursing Research*, *3*. doi:10.1177/2333393616680967 PMID:28462351

Glik, D. C. (2007). Risk communication for public health emergencies. *Annual Review of Public Health*, *28*(1), 33–54. doi:10.1146/annurev.publhealth.28.021406.144123 PMID:17222081

González-Castro, J. L., Ubillos-Landa, S., Puente-Martínez, A., & Gracia-Leiva, M. (2021). Perceived vulnerability and severity predict adherence to COVID-19 protection measures: The mediating role of instrumental coping. *Frontiers in Psychology*, *12*, 674032. doi:10.3389/fpsyg.2021.674032 PMID:34295285

Gowan, M. E., Kirk, R. C., & Sloan, J. A. (2014). Building resiliency: A cross-sectional study examining relationships among health-related quality of life, well-being, and disaster preparedness. *Health and Quality of Life Outcomes*, *12*(1), 85. doi:10.1186/1477-7525-12-85 PMID:24909780

Grasso, V., & Crisci, A. (2016). Codified hashtags for weather warning on Twitter: An Italian case study. *PLoS Currents*, 8. doi:10.1371/currents.dis.967e71514ecb92402eca3bdc9b789529 PMID:27500010

Guo, M. (2020). Second screening: Measuring second screen user behavior in a social television viewing environment. *International Journal on Media Management*, *22*(2), 97–116. doi:10.1080/14241277.2020.1803326

Hemminger, B. M., Lu, D., Vaughan, K. T. L., & Adams, S. J. (2007). Information seeking behavior of academic scientists. *Journal of the American Society for Information Science and Technology*, *58*(14), 2205–2225. doi:10.1002/asi.20686

Hofstede, G. (2001). *Culture's consequences: Comparing values, behaviors, institutions and organizations across nations*. Sage Publishing.

Hofstede, G. (2011). Dimensionalizing cultures: The Hofstede model in context. *Online Readings in Psychology and Culture*, *2*(1), 8. doi:10.9707/2307-0919.1014

HouZ.DuF.JiangH.ZhouX.LinL. (2020). Assessment of public attention, risk perception, emotional and behavioural responses to the COVID-19 outbreak: social media surveillance in China. medRxiv 2020.03.14.20035956.

Hürriyet. (2020). *Koronaya karşı 26 dev savaşçı*. Access at https://www.hurriyet.com.tr/gundem/koronaya-karsi-26-dev-savasci-41478997

Huurne, E. T., & Gutteling, J. (2008). Information needs and risk perception as predictors of risk information seeking. *Journal of Risk Research*, *11*(7), 847–862. doi:10.1080/13669870701875750

Imran, M., Elbassuoni, S., Castillo, C., Diaz, F., & Meier, P. (2013). Extracting information nuggets from disaster-Related messages in social media. *Iscram, 201*(3), 791–801.

Jin, X., & Spence, P. R. (2021). Understanding crisis communication on social media with CERC: Topic model analysis of tweets about Hurricane Maria. *Journal of Risk Research, 24*(10), 1266–1287. doi:10.1080/13669877.2020.1848901

Jin, Y., Liu, B. F., & Austin, L. L. (2014). Examining the role of social media in effective crisis management: The effects of crisis origin, information form, and source on publics' crisis responses. *Communication Research, 41*(1), 74–94. doi:10.1177/0093650211423918

Jones, J. H., & Salathé, M. (2009). Early assessment of anxiety and behavioral response to novel swine-origin influenza A (H1N1). *PLoS One, 4*(12), e8032. doi:10.1371/journal.pone.0008032 PMID:19997505

Juzefovičs, J., & Vihalemm, T. (2020). Keeping channels open or screening out? The digital practices of Baltic Russian-speakers during the Russia-Ukraine conflict. *Russian Journal of Communication, 12*(3), 262–283. doi:10.1080/19409419.2020.1851454

Kahlor, L. (2010). PRISM: A planned risk information seeking model. *Health Communication, 25*(4), 345–356. doi:10.1080/10410231003775172 PMID:20512716

Karadağ, F., Aslan, S., Budakoglu, I., Kucukkarapinar, M., Yay, A., & Ucar, O. (2020). *Turkey COVID-19 Snapshot Monitoring (COSMO Turkey): Monitoring knowledge, risk perceptions, preventive behaviours, and public trust in the current coronavirus outbreak in Turkey*. PsychArchives.

Kim, H. K., Ahn, J., Atkinson, L., & Kahlor, L. A. (2020). Effects of COVID-19 misinformation on information seeking, avoidance, and processing: A Multicountry comparative study. *Science Communication, 42*(5), 586–615. doi:10.1177/1075547020959670

Kim, J., Merrill, K. Jr, Collins, C., & Yang, H. (2021). Social TV viewing during the COVID-19 lockdown: The mediating role of social presence. *Technology in Society, 67*, 97–116. doi:10.1016/j.techsoc.2021.101733 PMID:34538985

Kim, S., Austin, L., Liu, B. F., & Jin, Y. (2022). Exploring differences in crisis literacy and efficacy on behavioral responses during infectious disease outbreaks. *Public Relations Review, 48*(3), 1–13. doi:10.1016/j.pubrev.2022.102204

Kim, S. J. (2016). A repertoire approach to cross-platform media use behavior. *New Media & Society, 18*(3), 353–372. doi:10.1177/1461444814543162

Kim, Y. C., & Ball-Rokeach, S. J. (2006). Civic engagement from a communication infrastructure perspective. *Communication Theory, 16*(2), 173–197. doi:10.1111/j.1468-2885.2006.00267.x

Kopecka-Piech, K. (2011). Media convergence concepts. *Mediaeval Studies, 46*(3), 1–19.

Kostagiolas, P. A., Kourouthanassis, P. E., Martzoukou, K., Korfiatis, N., & Niakas, D. (2018). Information seeking behavioural paths of physicians for diabetes mellitus care: A qualitative comparative analysis of information needs, sources, and barriers. *Health Systems (Basingstoke, England), 7*(1), 13–28. doi:10.1080/20476965.2017.1390050 PMID:31214336

Krämer, N. C., Winter, S., Benninghoff, B., & Gallus, C. (2015). How "social" is Social TV? The influence of social motives and expected outcomes on the usage of Social TV applications. *Computers in Human Behavior, 51*, 255–262. doi:10.1016/j.chb.2015.05.005

Lachlan, K. A., Hutter, E., Gilbert, C., & Spence, P. R. (2021). From what I've heard, this is bad: An examination of Americans' source preferences and information seeking during the COVID-19 pandemic. *Progress in Disaster Science, 9*, 100145. doi:10.1016/j.pdisas.2021.100145

Lachlan, K. A., Spence, P. R., Lin, X., Najarian, K., & Del Greco, M. (2016). Social media and crisis management: CERC, search strategies, and Twitter content. *Computers in Human Behavior, 54*, 647–652. doi:10.1016/j.chb.2015.05.027

Lai, C., & Tang, T. (2021). Disaster communication behaviors in the U.S. and China: Which channels do you use and with whom? *Journal of Applied Communication Research, 49*(2), 207–227. doi:10.1080/00909882.2021.1900588

Lai, C. H., & Tang, T. (2015). Understanding local news consumption and community participation via the lens of information repertoires and media multiplexity. *Mass Communication & Society, 18*(3), 325–349. doi:10.1080/15205436.2014.995768

Lai, C. H., & Tang, T. (2018). From information behaviors to disaster preparedness: Navigating individuals' general and disaster curation in US, China, and Australia. *Computers in Human Behavior, 88*, 37–46. doi:10.1016/j.chb.2018.06.023

Lalazaryan, A., & Zare-Farashbandi, F. (2014). A review of models and theories of health information seeking behavior. *International Journal of Health System and Disaster Management, 2*(4), 193. doi:10.4103/2347-9019.144371

Latzer, M. (2013). Media convergence. Handbook on the digital creative economy, SSRN *Electronic Journal*. 123-133.

Le, H. T., Nguyen, D. N., Beydoun, A. S., Le, X. T. T., Nguyen, T. T., Pham, Q. T., Ta, N. T. K., Nguyen, Q. T., Nguyen, A. N., Hoang, M. T., Vu, L. G., Tran, B. X., Latkin, C. A., Ho, C. S. H., & Ho, R. C. M. (2020). Demand for health information on COVID-19 among Vietnamese. *International Journal of Environmental Research and Public Health, 17*(12), 4377–4389. doi:10.3390/ijerph17124377 PMID:32570819

Li, J., Qin, P., Quan, Y., & Tan-Soo, J. S. (2023). Using Protection Motivation Theory to examine information-seeking behaviors on climate change. *Global Environmental Change, 81*, 102698. doi:10.1016/j.gloenvcha.2023.102698

Li, J., & Zheng, H. (2022). Online information seeking and disease prevention intent during COVID-19 outbreak. *Journalism & Mass Communication Quarterly, 99*(1), 69–88. doi:10.1177/1077699020961518

Liu, B. F., Austin, L., & Jin, Y. (2011). How publics respond to crisis communication strategies: The interplay of information form and source. *Public Relations Review, 37*(4), 345–353. doi:10.1016/j.pubrev.2011.08.004

Liu, B. F., Fraustino, J. D., & Jin, Y. (2015). How disaster information form, source, type, and prior disaster exposure affect public outcomes: Jumping on the social media bandwagon? *Journal of Applied Communication Research, 43*(1), 44–65. doi:10.1080/00909882.2014.982685

Liu, B. F., & Mehta, A. M. (2021). From the periphery and toward a centralized model for trust in government risk and disaster communication. *Journal of Risk Research, 24*(7), 853–869. doi:10.1080/13669877.2020.1773516

Liu, B. F., Xu, S., Lim, J. R., & Egnoto, M. (2019). How publics' active and passive communicative behaviors affect their tornado responses: An integration of STOPS and SMCC. *Public Relations Review, 45*(4), 101831. doi:10.1016/j.pubrev.2019.101831

Liu, P. L. (2020). COVID-19 information seeking on digital media and preventive behaviors: The mediation role of worry. *Cyberpsychology, Behavior, and Social Networking, 23*(10), 677–682. doi:10.1089/cyber.2020.0250 PMID:32498549

Lund, B., & Ma, J. (2022). Exploring information seeking of rural older adults during the COVID-19 pandemic. *Aslib Journal of Information Management, 74*(1), 54–77. doi:10.1108/AJIM-04-2021-0118

Maduz, L., Prior, T., Roth, F., & Käser, M. (2019). *Individual disaster preparedness: Explaining disaster-related information seeking and preparedness behavior in Switzerland*. ETH Zurich.

Malla, S. B., Dahal, R. K., & Hasegawa, S. (2020). Analyzing the disaster response competency of the local government official and the elected representative in Nepal. *Geoenvironmental Disasters, 7*(1), 1–13. doi:10.118640677-020-00153-z

Marchionini, G. (1995). *Information seeking in electronic environments (No. 9)*. Cambridge University Press. doi:10.1017/CBO9780511626388

Matthes, J. (2006). The need for orientation towards news media: Revising and validating a classic concept. *International Journal of Public Opinion Research, 18*(4), 422–444. doi:10.1093/ijpor/edh118

Maykrantz, S. A., Gong, T., Petrolino, A. V., Nobiling, B. D., & Houghton, J. D. (2021). How Trust in information sources influences preventative measures compliance during the COVID-19 pandemic. *International Journal of Environmental Research and Public Health, 18*(11), 5867. doi:10.3390/ijerph18115867 PMID:34070713

McDermid, P., Craig, A., Sheel, M., Blazek, K., Talty, S., & Seale, H. (2023). Information seeking behaviors of individuals impacted by COVID-19 international travel restrictions: An analysis of two international cross-sectional studies. *Frontiers in Communication, 8*, 1101548. doi:10.3389/fcomm.2023.1101548

Milliyet. (2020). *İşte Kovid-19 savaşçısı bilim insanları*. Access at https://www.milliyet.com.tr/gundem/iste-kovid-19-savascisi-bilim-insanlari-6154577

Munir, K., Ergene, T., Tunaligil, V., & Erol, N. (2004). A Window of Opportunity for the Transformation of National Mental Health Policy in Turkey Following Two Major Earthquakes. *Harvard Review of Psychiatry, 12*(4), 238–251. doi:10.1080/10673220490509615 PMID:15371066

Murzintcev, N., & Cheng, C. (2017). Disaster hashtags in social media. *ISPRS International Journal of Geo-Information, 6*(7), 204. doi:10.3390/ijgi6070204

Muturi, N. (2022). The influence of information source on COVID-19 vaccine efficacy and motivation for self-protective behavior. *Journal of Health Communication*, *27*(4), 241–249. doi:10.1080/10810730.2022.2096729 PMID:35793310

Neuwirth, K. (1995). *The Influence of Severity, Vulnerabilty, and Response Efficacy on Information Seeking and Behavioral Intention*. Paper presented at the Annual Meeting of the Association for Education in Journalism and Mass Communication, Washington, DC.

Neuwirth, K., Dunwoody, S., & Griffin, R. J. (2000). Protection motivation and risk communication. *Risk Analysis*, *20*(5), 721–734. doi:10.1111/0272-4332.205065 PMID:11110218

Pan, S. L., Cui, M., & Qian, J. (2020). Information resource orchestration during the COVID-19 pandemic: A study of community lockdowns in China. *International Journal of Information Management*, *54*, 102143. doi:10.1016/j.ijinfomgt.2020.102143 PMID:32394997

Peters, C., Schrøder, K. C., Lehaff, J., & Vulpius, J. (2022). News as they know it: Young adults' information repertoires in the digital media landscape. *Digital Journalism (Abingdon, England)*, *10*(1), 62–86. doi:10.1080/21670811.2021.1885986

Prasetyo, Y. T., Castillo, A. M., Salonga, L. J., Sia, J. A., & Seneta, J. A. (2020). Factors affecting perceived effectiveness of COVID-19 prevention measures among Filipinos during enhanced community quarantine in Luzon, Philippines: Integrating Protection Motivation Theory and extended Theory of Planned Behavior. *International Journal of Infectious Diseases*, *99*, 312–323. doi:10.1016/j.ijid.2020.07.074 PMID:32768695

Prentice-Dunn, S., & Rogers, R. W. (1986). Protection motivation theory and preventive health: Beyond the health belief model. *Health Education Research*, *1*(3), 153–161. doi:10.1093/her/1.3.153

Rad, R. E., Mohseni, S., Kamalzadeh Takhti, H., Hassani Azad, M., Shahabi, N., Aghamolaei, T., & Norozian, F. (2021). Application of the protection motivation theory for predicting COVID-19 preventive behaviors in Hormozgan, Iran: A cross-sectional study. *BMC Public Health*, *21*(1), 1–11. PMID:33388037

Rahmi, R., Joho, H., & Shirai, T. (2019). An analysis of natural disaster-related information-seeking behavior using temporal stages. *Journal of the Association for Information Science and Technology*, *70*(7), 715–728. doi:10.1002/asi.24155

Reagan, J. (1996). The "repertoire"; of information sources. *Journal of Broadcasting & Electronic Media*, *40*(1), 112–121. doi:10.1080/08838159609364336

Reynolds, B., & Seeger, M. (2005). Crisis and emergency risk communication as an integrative model. *Journal of Health Communication*, *10*(1), 43–55. doi:10.1080/10810730590904571 PMID:15764443

Rogers, R. W. (1985). Attitude change and information integration in fear appeals. *Psychological Reports*, *56*(1), 179–182. doi:10.2466/pr0.1985.56.1.179

Ryan, B. (2018). A model to explain information seeking behaviour by individuals in the response phase of a disaster. *Library & Information Science Research*, *40*(2), 73–85. doi:10.1016/j.lisr.2018.05.001

Sagun, A., Bouchlaghem, D., & Anumba, C. J. (2009). A scenario-based study on information flow and collaboration patterns in disaster management. *Disasters, 33*(2), 214–238. doi:10.1111/j.1467-7717.2008.01071.x PMID:18699856

Sheldon, P., Rauschnabel, P. A., Antony, M. G., & Car, S. (2017). A cross-cultural comparison of Croatian and American social network sites: Exploring cultural differences in motives for Instagram use. *Computers in Human Behavior, 75*, 643–651. doi:10.1016/j.chb.2017.06.009

Shen, Z., Zhong, Z., Xie, J., Zhang, Q., & Li, S. (2022). The effects of information-seeking behaviors on risk perception during the COVID-19 pandemic: A cross-sectional correlational survey. *Psychology Research and Behavior Management, 15*, 1707–1719. doi:10.2147/PRBM.S368537 PMID:35844830

Skarpa, P. E., & Garoufallou, E. (2021). Information seeking behavior and COVID-19 pandemic: A snapshot of young, middle aged and senior individuals in Greece. *International Journal of Medical Informatics, 150*, 104465. doi:10.1016/j.ijmedinf.2021.104465 PMID:33887589

Smith, R. A., Ferrara, M., & Witte, K. (2007). Social sides of health risks: Stigma and collective efficacy. *Health Communication, 21*(1), 55–64. doi:10.1080/10410230701283389 PMID:17461752

Sommerfeldt, E. J. (2015). Disasters and information source repertoires: Information seeking and information sufficiency in postearthquake Haiti. *Journal of Applied Communication Research, 43*(1), 1–22. doi:10.1080/00909882.2014.982682

Soroya, S. H., Farooq, A., Mahmood, K., Isoaho, J., & Zara, S. (2021). From information seeking to information avoidance: Understanding the health information behavior during a global health crisis. *Information Processing &Amp. Management, 58*(2), 102440. PMID:33281273

Spialek, M. L., & Houston, J. B. (2018). The development and initial validation of the Citizen Disaster Communication Assessment. *Communication Research, 45*(6), 934–955. doi:10.1177/0093650217697521

Steinberg, A., Wukich, C., & Wu, H.-C. (2016). Central social media actors in disaster information networks. *International Journal of Mass Emergencies and Disasters, 34*(1), 47–74. doi:10.1177/028072701603400103

Sultana, T., Dhillon, G., & Oliveira, T. (2023). The effect of fear and situational motivation on online information avoidance: The case of COVID-19. *International Journal of Information Management, 69*, 102596. doi:10.1016/j.ijinfomgt.2022.102596 PMID:36415624

Sun, Y., Hu, Q., Grossman, S., Basnyat, I., & Wang, P. (2021). Comparison of COVID-19 information seeking, trust of information sources, and protective behaviors in China and the US. *Journal of Health Communication, 26*(9), 657–666. doi:10.1080/10810730.2021.1987590 PMID:34702136

Szostek, J. (2018). News media repertoires and strategic narrative reception: A paradox of dis/belief in authoritarian Russia. *New Media & Society, 20*(1), 68–87. doi:10.1177/1461444816656638

Tabachnick, B. G., & Fidell, L. S. (1996). *Using multivariate statistics*. Harper Collins.

Thomson, R., Ito, N., Suda, H., Lin, F., Liu, Y., Hayasaka, R., . . . Wang, Z. (2012). Trusting tweets: The Fukushima disaster and information source credibility on Twitter. *Iscram. Proceedings of the 9th International ISCRAM Conference*.

Thorson, K., & Wells, C. (2016). Curated flows: A framework for mapping media exposure in the digital age. *Communication Theory*, *26*(3), 309–328. doi:10.1111/comt.12087

Van Asselt, M. B. A., Langendonck, R., Van Asten, F., Van der Giessen, A., Janssen, P. H. M., Heuberger, P. S. C., & Geuskens, I. (2001). *Uncertainty&RIVM's Environmental Outlooks.* RIVM Report.

Wahl, S., & Grimm, M. (2016). How to Find an Alternative: A Typology of Cancer Patients' Information Behavior with Regard to Complementary and Alternative Medicine. *International Journal of Communication and Health*, 10.

Wang, P., Ahorsu, D. K., Lin, C., Chen, I., Yen, C., Kuo, Y., Griffiths, M. D., & Pakpour, A. H. (2021). Motivation to have covid-19 vaccination explained using an extended protection motivation theory among university students in china: The role of information sources. *Vaccines*, *9*(4), 380. doi:10.3390/vaccines9040380 PMID:33924604

Ward, J. W., & Hansen, K. A. (1993). *Search strategies in mass communication.* Longman Publishing Group.

Westcott, R., Ronan, K., Bambrick, H., & Taylor, M. (2017). Expanding protection motivation theory: Investigating an application to animal owners and emergency responders in bushfire emergencies. *BMC Psychology*, *5*(1), 1–14. doi:10.118640359-017-0182-3 PMID:28446229

WHO. (2020, March). *WHO Director-General's opening remarks at the media briefing on COVID-19* [Media Brief]. Access at https://www.who.int/director-general/speeches/detail/who-director-general-s-opening-remarks-at-the-media-briefing-on-covid-19---11-march-2020

Williams, E. J., & Joinson, A. N. (2020). Developing a measure of information seeking about phishing. *Journal of Cybersecurity*, *6*(1), tyaa001. doi:10.1093/cybsec/tyaa001

Wukich, C. (2016). Government social media messages across disaster phases. *Journal of Contingencies and Crisis Management*, *24*(4), 230–243. doi:10.1111/1468-5973.12119

Yates, C., & Partridge, H. (2015). Citizens and social media in times of natural disaster: Exploring information experience. *Information Research*, *20*(1).

Yavetz, G., Aharony, N., & Sofer, Y. Y. (2022). Information needs and seeking behaviors of Israeli citizens during the COVID-19 outbreak. *Aslib Journal of Information Management.*

Zaremohzzabieh, Z., Samah, A. A., Roslan, S., Shaffril, H. A. M., D'Silva, J. L., Kamarudin, S., & Ahrari, S. (2021). Household preparedness for future earthquake disaster risk using an extended theory of planned behavior. *International Journal of Disaster Risk Reduction*, *65*, 102533. doi:10.1016/j.ijdrr.2021.102533

Zhang, Q. (2021). Is It a "Window of Opportunity" to Develop a New Normal of Government-Society Cooperation in Emergency Management? *The China Nonprofit Review*, *12*(2), 257–263. doi:10.1163/18765149-12341379

Zhao, X., Ma, Z., Xu, S., & Austin, L. L. (2022). How information repertoire affects vaccine hesitancy: Processes of information verification and cognitive elaboration. *Health Communication*, 1–11. doi:10.1080/10410236.2022.2154017 PMID:36510367

Chapter 15
Digital Literacy and Health Workers:
A Study of Kashmir

Mir Kouser Gulzar
Islamic University of Science and Technology, Awantipora, India

Maryam Jameel Naik
Department of Journalism and Mass Communication, Islamic University of Science and Technology Awantipora Kashmir, India

ABSTRACT

This chapter is an effort to provide a detailed examination of digital literacy among healthcare professionals in the region of Kashmir, which is located in the north of India. In the contemporary era, technology acts as the backbone of the healthcare in current landscape. The chapter examines the current status of digital literacy among health workers emphasizing the challenges they face and opportunities available for improving their digital skills. It offers strategic insights and recommendations to bridge the digital divide and empower healthcare workers with the necessary possible competencies. The chapter aims to stimulate a future where healthcare professionals in Kashmir are fluent at harnessing digital tools to increase healthcare efficiency.

INTRODUCTION

Humans from birth to death learn basic and foundational skills like reading, writing, language, and other social skills but as technology grows and changes, the learning demands change as well. We see schools getting updated with their curriculum, we update our homes by introducing technological gadgets for daily work, and long distances and impossible-to-reach areas become possible with the introduction of communication technologies. To use all these technologies, gadgets, and services we need to learn the skills to operate and use them and for that, the term used is *Digital literacy*. According to the American Library Association, digital literacy is the ability to use information and communication technologies to

DOI: 10.4018/979-8-3693-0896-7.ch015

find, evaluate, create, and communicate information, requiring both cognitive and technical skills (Digital Literacy, 2023). We have come to believe in the promise of technology and its potential to improve our lives in new and exciting ways, to enhance our capabilities, and to enable us to achieve all our dreams and aspirations (Begley, 2017). The technologies today are deeply integrated in all aspects of life and digital literacy helps to navigate the complexities created by the rise of information and communication technologies. While numeracy and basic literacy are still fundamental to learning, digital literacy has emerged as another critical life skill and is now, per the World Economic Forum, part of the 21st-century toolkit (Leal, 2022). Sustainable Development Goal 4 is about ensuring inclusive and equitable quality education and promoting lifelong learning opportunities for all, and target 4 of it talks about the relevant skills for decent work which includes digital and other technological skills. Digital literacy is seen as an international concern and in this regard, a lot of steps have been taken by organizations globally to tackle the need. For instance, the Digital Literacy Guidelines of UNESCO are to be utilized by world bodies when pursuing digital literacy projects, and the Digital Literacy Framework of 2019 by UNICEF in collaboration with other bodies to research and publish on digital literacy across the globe (Leal, 2022). The vision of the global strategy is to improve health for everyone, everywhere by accelerating the development and adoption of appropriate, accessible, affordable, scalable, and sustainable person-centric digital health solutions to prevent, detect, and respond to epidemics and pandemics, developing infrastructure and applications that enable countries to use health data to promote health and well-being, and to achieve the health-related sustainable development goals and the triple billion targets of WHO's Thirteen General Programme of Work, 2019-2023 (WHO, 2021)

DIGITAL HEALTH AND HEALTHCARE SYSTEMS WORLDWIDE

Digital health refers to the use of digital technologies for providing healthcare. In its earlier avatar, it was called eHealth with the use of communication technologies, and then mHealth with the usage of mobile technologies (Bakshi, 2021). Digitalization is the forthcoming term for the integration of technology in existing processes to foster their efficacy, efficiency, and effectivity after IoT, Smart Devices, Big Data, and co (Meister, 2016). Digital literacy worldwide is marked by a systematic shift in the way the globe functions, communicates and accesses information. Stephanie Allen, Global Public Health and Social Service Leader says, "COVID-19 has accelerated numerous existing and/or emerging healthcare trends, particularly around health equity, and environmental and sustainability. Additionally, shifting consumer preferences and behaviors, the integration of life sciences and the healthcare sector, rapidly evolving digital health technologies, new talent and care delivery models, and clinical innovation continue to be top of mind for healthcare executives globally. How they respond to these challenges while continuing to address the pandemic will be critically important in 2022" (Deloitte, 2022). However, just as we see AI Artificial Intelligence evolving and integrating into our lives, from virtual assistants to personalized recommendations, the healthcare industry is on the verge of this paradigm shift. These technologies are expected to bring about a positive change in patient care and health treatment deliveries. It is also understood that technological innovations alone are not sufficient to address the global challenges worldwide. The innovations need funds, human resources, raw materials, and much more which jointly can provide us a sustainable environment. There is an example of such collaboration for change, also called "*Sormas Foundations open-source mobile eHealth platform.*" This was a collaboration between the Nigeria Centre for Disease Control and the Ghana Health Service to manage the risk of the COVID-19 pandemic

(World_Economic_forum, 2023). It was a surveillance eHealthcare platform of Nigeria and Ghana to implement disease control and management platforms including surveillance and early detection of outbreaks. The collaboration discussed above and like this can be more helpful if digital solution providers including both public and private sectors and governments have a hand-to-hand relationship. Another example of such collaboration would be *Turn.io's Chatbot application.* It allowed more than eleven million symptom checks in South Africa (McKinsey, 2021). These examples help us to get to know the present scenario of different countries. People consider COVID-19 the biggest catalyst for the acceleration of innovative modes. Reports say that up to 40% of United States are receiving telehealth services including a 75% reduction in waiting times through emergency rooms (Kearney, 2023). The paper also provides examples of Middle East countries like Saudi Arabia, and the United Arab Emirates (UAE) which have already begun introducing regulations around the use of AI in medical devices. Countries across the globe are recognizing the potential of digital health to revolutionize the way healthcare is accessed and delivered. The focus is on facilitating the exchange of health information, ensuring interoperability between systems, and enhancing patient care through digital tools. However, (Louise_et_al, 2022) suggests that in underdeveloped countries the need of the hour while implementing digital technology in the health sector is to take into consideration the marginalized groups of society and people of different age groups and demographic regions. We see educated people and mostly youth face not much friction while using smart technologies while people of more age and those living in rural areas with limited access to technologies, the internet, electricity, and other necessities face a lot of issues. As the world collectively invests in digital health infrastructure, the outcomes of this race are expected to redefine the future of healthcare, making it more proactive, personalized, and globally interconnected.

DIGITAL LITERACY AND HEALTHCARE IN INDIA

Though the term digital literacy now encompasses the technical and financial ability to utilize available technology along with access or lack of access to the internet, the gap it refers to is constantly shifting with the development of technology (Zhou, 2022). Despite some improvement in recent years, a third of the world's population resides within the range of mobile broadband networks. Despite that, limited device availability, combined with a lack of digital know-how and skills, impedes efforts to get more people online, particularly in rural areas. only 53% of the world's population has access to high-speed broadband and about 2.9 billion people suffer from the digital divide globally (Davos, 2022). Oxfam India which is a non-government organization released a data about the digital divide in India and found a significant digital divide between rural and urban India. Besides the digital growth of 13% in a year, only 31% of the rural population uses the internet compared to 67% of the urban population. (IAS, 2022). The report further demonstrates Muslims are the last internet-using community compared to Sikh Christians and Hindus in India. Women are 15% less likely to own a mobile phone and 33% less likely to use mobile internet services than men. They constitute only one-third of internet users in India (IAS, 2022). The digital health system in India has seen significant growth in recent years which has revolutionized the healthcare landscape. Telemedicine has emerged as a critical component, especially in the wake of the COVID-19 Pandemic, providing a platform for individuals to consult healthcare professionals remotely. This proves to be a boon, especially for those residing in remote areas enhancing health accessibility as it is clear from the official records that more than half of the Indian population (65%) live in rural areas (PR, 2021). The Government of India 2017 laid the importance of digitalization in the healthcare system in its National Health Policy (NHP) of 2017 using the National Digital Health Mission (NDHM) as a platform that can act as the foundation on which the national digital health ecosystem can be built. It aims to build a strong, holistic, integrated, and comprehensive public digital infrastructure (Kapoor, 2022). Furthermore, the advent of health applications and online health portals has empowered individuals to access a plethora of health-related information, schedule appointments, order medications and even monitor their health conditions. Electronic Health Records (EHRs) have streamlined record keeping and information sharing among healthcare providers, ultimately improving the overall efficiency and quality of healthcare services.

DIGITAL HEALTH AT COMMUNITY LEVEL IN INDIA

Under the uniform National Digital Health Mission (NDHM), the Government of India intends to introduce a uniform system of Electronic Medical Records (EMR) also called Electronic Health Records (EHR) for faster and more effective surveillance. Ayushman Bharat Scheme is a provision of teleconsultation in subcentres. Under this provision, opinions can be taken from the consultant doctors and regular routine medications at the subcentre itself. National Teleconsultation Service (NTS) of the Ministry of Health and Family Welfare is the first of its kind online Outpatient Department (OPD) service offered by a country's government to its citizens (Kapoor, 2022). Below are some of the existing systems of digital health in India:

Despite these advancements, challenges persist, hindering the seamless adoption and integration of digital literacy and technology in healthcare.

Kashmir: A Brief History and Digital Health

Kashmir, also called paradise on Earth is located in northern India and northeast Pakistan, and has been entangled in a protracted conflict for several decades. The conflict primarily revolves around the territorial dispute between India and Pakistan over the region. The roots of the conflict are traced back to the partition of British India in 1947 and the subsequent independence of both India and Pakistan. The

Table 1. Existing system of digital health in India

User	Technology
AWW (Anganwadi Worker)	ICDS-CAS (Integrated Child Development Services- Common Application Software)
ASHA (Accredited Social Health Activist)	ASHA-Nidhi
ANM (Auxiliary Nurse Midwife)	ANMOL application (ANM Online)
Individual	e-Health Record Card, Helplines, Adherence, Life-related digital applications,
Pregnant Women	Kilkari application
Patient-Doctor	e-Sanjeevani, Telemedicine/national teleconsultation
Some other important healthcare platforms	RCH (Reproductive and Child Health) Portal

Source: D Y Patil Journal of Health Sciences 2022

two sides are divided by a "line of control" (LOC) agreed to in 1972, although neither country recognizes it as an international boundary (Britannica, 2023). Article 370 was included into the constitution of India on 17 October 1949 that exempted the state from Indian constitution except from Article 1 and Article 370 and allows the state to frame its own constitution (Agarwal, 2022). On August 5, the Indian government announced it was scrapping Article 370 of the constitution, which effectively abrogated the autonomy of the Kashmir region. The government shouldered the move considering it an opportunity to make a move and secure Kashmir's complete integration into the Indian Union (Mukhopadhyay, 2019). High-speed internet was cut down in the region on 5th August 2019 onwards for 18 months in the meantime COVID-19 happened across the globe and on 30 January 2020, India reported its first positive case of Novel Coronavirus from Kerala with a student, who was studying in Wuhan University and had travelled to India (Perappadan, 2020). The virus hit India severely and on March 18, 2020, Kashmir Valley reported its first positive case for COVID-19 in Srinagar. (The-Print, 2020). Soon after Indian Government announced the lockdown on 25 March 2020 and there have been four lockdowns of various phases in India which demanded everything online. The twin crises in Kashmir have choked off access to healthcare. Treatment under the Ayushman Bharat Scheme (a government health assurance scheme for low-income groups) had already run into trouble because of the internet ban in Kashmir since August 2019. The stakeholders are unable to get the accurate print copy of the Ayushman Bharat Golden cards because of the low internet speed which sets their treatment cancelled in the hospitals (Scroll, 2020). The social institutions in Kashmir suffered the most because of the double lockdown COVID-19 lockdown and banned high-speed internet) during the COVID-19 crises. Iqbal Saleem, a professor of surgery, wrote, "This is so frustrating. Trying to download the guidelines for intensive care management…24 MBs and one hour, still not able to do so." The low-speed 2G internet stops health workers in the region from accessing current information, public health guidelines, and research on the coronavirus, as well as accurate updates on transmission in the region (Radhakrishn, 2020). Generally, the internet speed required to perform day-to-day office work includes video calls with screen sharing, ending emails with attachments, and viewing videos; the internet speed on average should be between 15-20 Mbps. The internet speed is at 250kbps in Kashmir which is 50 times less than the minimum desired speed (SLFC, 2020). However, after COVID-19 dedicated efforts have been made by the administration to create an enabling environment for digital literacy to bridge the gap between government programs and citizen requirements in which 209 government services have been integrated with Rapid Assessment System (RAS) for real-time feedback of citizens (Rising-Kashmir, 2022). In February 2013, Government of Jammu and Kashmir introduced the Artificial Intelligence (AI) in healthcare sector for clinical documentation, revenue management, medical records etc. the key categories of the applications of AI includes diagnosis and treatment recommendations, patient engagement and adherence, and administrative activities. Although there are many instances in which AI can perform healthcare tasks as well or better than humans, implementation factors will prevent large scale automation of healthcare professional jobs for a considerable period (Kashmir, 2023).

In the sphere of digital technology, Kashmir has been on a transformative journey, encountering both progress and hurdles. The integration of digital tools and platforms into healthcare has been a promising step towards improving medical services. However, the availability and accessibility of digital infrastructure remain uneven, particularly in remote areas of Kashmir, highlighting the need for equitable technological advancements. The healthcare workers of Kashmir, especially the ASHA's have demonstrated remarkable dedication and resilience amidst these technological disparities. ASHA's, often the first point of contact for healthcare in rural and remote regions, have played a pivotal role in raising awareness about preventive measures, maternal healthcare, and immunization programs. The introduction of Asha has been an evident development in the health of rural people. Their activities support their upliftment which in turn improves the nation as it is rightly said *the soul of a nation lies in the village* (Eruthickal, 2016). Nurses in Kashmir have also showcased exemplary commitment to providing healthcare services, especially during times of crisis. With all this, it is imperative to address the digital divide and provide comprehensive training and resources to healthcare workers. By conducting this study on digital literacy among ASHA workers and nurses, we aim to shed light on the digital competencies within the healthcare workforce of Kashmir. empowering ASHAs and nurses with proper digital skills will contribute to a more resilient and efficient healthcare system, ensuring that the promise of accessible and quality healthcare in Kashmir is fulfilled in the digital age.

REVIEW OF LITERATURE

Machado-et-al (2021) studied the impact of Covid-19 on the hesitancy of vaccines. The paper revealed that the acceptance of the COVID-19 vaccine decreased from more than 70 to 50 percent in 8 months from January 2020. The main reason behind the decrease was the influence of misinformation on social media. We see social media become one of the main carriers of misinformation. Content creators and online platforms start influencing people by highlighting conspiracy theories and audiences without the knowledge of factual and reliable sources fell prey to this web and it is never never-ending process. Thus, digital literacy is one of the necessary tools one should have especially during the times of crises. Kuek (2019) talks about the digital literacy among the health care staff in Australia and found that majority of the staff has high digital literacy however, a group of staff members showed negative response. This group reported anxiety using information technology tools in healthcare. The main reason behind is seen the lack of proper computer skills, infrastructure and poor attitude towards the new digital tools. The study helps us to conclude that the role of workplaces in implementing technological tools and educating the working staff is undeniable. Since the present chapter focuses on the digital literacy among healthcare workers in Kashmir some studies have been done so far on different themes, for instance Shoib and Arafat (2020) studied the telepsychiatry in Kashmir. they tried to explore the scenario of Kashmir during the pandemic when the Indian Psychiatric Society released a position statement on 30 March 2020, advocating the use of available technology to reach the marginalized section of society through online platforms but in Kashmir, the scenario was much challenging because of low-speed internet which put challenges in the online consultation. The paper also advocates the absence of a functioning community mental health team and the lack of proper funding for effective and culturally specific strategies for a place like Kashmir. Garratt et al. (2020) wrote an article about an online learning platform called Aqoon. The platform provides online courses and education and during the crises of COVID-19 Aqoon seems to have helped a lot of students throughout Kashmir. The article mentions some of the learner reflections from different regions who have been linked with the platform to gain a deep understanding of health as well as cross-cultural mental health scenarios. The book chapter by Scott et al. (2020) in a book chapter talks about the progressively improving condition of ASHA workers in the health sector as they contribute much to healthcare and are one of the front workers of the department. It mentions that ASHA workers receive 28 days of training including eight days of induction and 20 days of skill-based training on reproductive, maternal, neonatal, and child health, and five days of training on Non-Communicable Diseases (NCDs). The study further focuses on the challenges generally related to insufficient training and supervision. In a lot of parts of India are where there is no awareness of ASHA workers or their role in communities. ASHA workers also face some notable challenges including remuneration, lack of supplies, transport and other resources. Sachs et al. (2009) on page 102 highlights the health literacy of ASHA workers in Azamgarh and Uttar Pradesh of India where a group of ASHA workers were seen having varying levels of Knowledge about their job. They had little knowledge about the forms they needed to fill out. The book chapter highlights that no part of training deals with the logistics of ASHA's duties which creates more work for other hospital staff. Although the research is a decade old but it gives us an insight to understand the developmental progress throughout the years. We tried to study the recent condition of ASHA workers in parallel to the above book chapters and found that ASHA workers today in 2023 are still one of the marginalized stakeholders of healthcare system. Bandyopadhyay (2023) highlights that besides huge workload, ASHA workers are considered to be volunteers, rather than employees, and instead of wages are generally paid on an incentive basis. For example, ASHA's are paid for ensuring a woman gives birth in hospital or ensuring a child receives a full programme of immunization against vaccine- preventable diseases. Article mentions that during the pandemic, ASHA workers were placed on the frontline of the government's pandemic response. They had to go door to door to screen people for COVID-19 infection and also had to arrange for formal testing of those suspected to be infected. They were at the forefront of taking infected people to the quarantine centres. In response in May 2022, India's one million-plus group of ASHAS were honoured with a World Health Organization Global Health Leaders Award. This award is not enough to fill the cost of bread and butter for the families of ASHA workers as most of them are the only breadwinners of their families.

The Literature review highlights the ups and downs and also the increased progress of healthcare workers in India and Kashmir. However, an overlooked and understudied area within this context is the level of digital literacy among these professionals. As we move forward, it is imperative to recognize and address this gap in research, focusing on understanding and enhancing the digital literacy of health workers.

ANALYSIS

The study weighed on a comprehensive exploration of digital health in the region of Kashmir. Recognizing the importance of diverse perspectives, we conducted a series of interviews involving thirteen individuals including five ASHA (Accredited Social Health Activists) and eight Nurses. In-depth interviews were conducted with the participants including telephonic and face-to-face interviews. The participants were selected to represent a cross-section of the population offer a vivid view of how individuals from different backgrounds engage with and perceive digital health technologies. The age diversity within the sample pool ranging from 20 to 45 age group, allowed to uncover the generational nuance in the adoption and acceptance of digital health tools. Younger participants provided perspectives shaped by digital native experiences, while older participants offered insights into the growing dynamics and barriers associated with integrating digital health into traditional healthcare practices.

Geographical considerations and gender diversity also played a vital role in this research, acknowledging the diverse healthcare landscape in Kashmir. Interviewing participants from both rural and urban areas, we aimed to understand how digital technologies are accessed and experienced across different areas and different genders (male and female). Emphasizing the importance of digital literacy, the researchers explore how it significantly impacts healthcare delivery, making it more efficient and accessible. The chapter identifies the barriers that health workers face in achieving adequate digital literacy, ranging from infrastructure challenges to training gaps. Furthermore, the chapter proposes strategic solutions, including targeted training institutes and policy advocacy, to bridge these gaps and propel healthcare in Kashmir into a digitally empowered future.

The questionnaire consisted of 22 questions which were divided into different themes. The first theme was a statistical theme including name, age, occupation, residence, experience, and access to digital technology. The next theme included questions about the utilization of digital technologies both personally and in workplaces. This was followed by the section including challenges in using digital technology and integration into the healthcare system followed by questions about training, resources, educational programs, policies, and other governmental support, recommendations, etc.

The findings are divided into potential themes. Let's try to delve into each of the themes to get a full insight into digital literacy among healthcare workers in Kashmir.

LIMITATIONS OF THE STUDY

One significant limitation of the book chapter this chapter is the limited size plan as the researchers focused on a restricted number of participants. The geographical scope is also confined with primary emphasis on Kashmir. India is a vast and diverse country with numerous states, varied demographics and cultural distinctions. Due to resource constrains and time limitations researchers are unable to include more extensive range of participants and regions. The conclusions drawn may not be universally applicable. Every research problem starts with a specific purpose and in this chapter the main objective is to explore the dimension of digital literacy among healthcare workers inn Kashmir. the study's scope is intentionally narrowed to provides foundational understanding of this specific context. This study represents a starting point rather than a conclusive endpoint. Purpose is to lay down the groundwork and identify initial patterns in the given context. There has been no systematic research done on the present given theme in Kashmir and this study serves as a critical baseline for the subsequent research. Moving forward the researchers recognize the importance of contextualizing the research within a broader perspective and are committed to enhancing these sections to provide a more comprehensive foundation for the study. This will involve incorporating relevant secondary data and expanding the background to establish a clearer link between the research objectives and the broader academic perspective.

The theme access and knowledge about digital literacy sheds light on the disparities in familiarity and proficiency with digital technologies among healthcare workers in Kashmir. the findings highlight a significant divide in digital literacy based on age and occupation, particularly in the context of smartphone usage. Interviews reveal that all healthcare workers in the study irrespective of age or role have got smart phones. This gives a foundational level of access to digital technology, which could be potential avenue for improving digital literacy across the board. The research reveals a noticeable age-related gap in technical capacity that younger nurses exhibit a good level of familiarity and comfort with digital technologies while older nurses and ASHA workers are much less exposed to digital advancements.

Digital Literacy Challenges

The theme of Challenges in digital literacy brings multifaced barriers that healthcare workers in Kashmir face. Participants especially Nurses (from age group 35 to 45) and all ASHA workers continuously

Figure 1. Access and knowledge about digital literacy

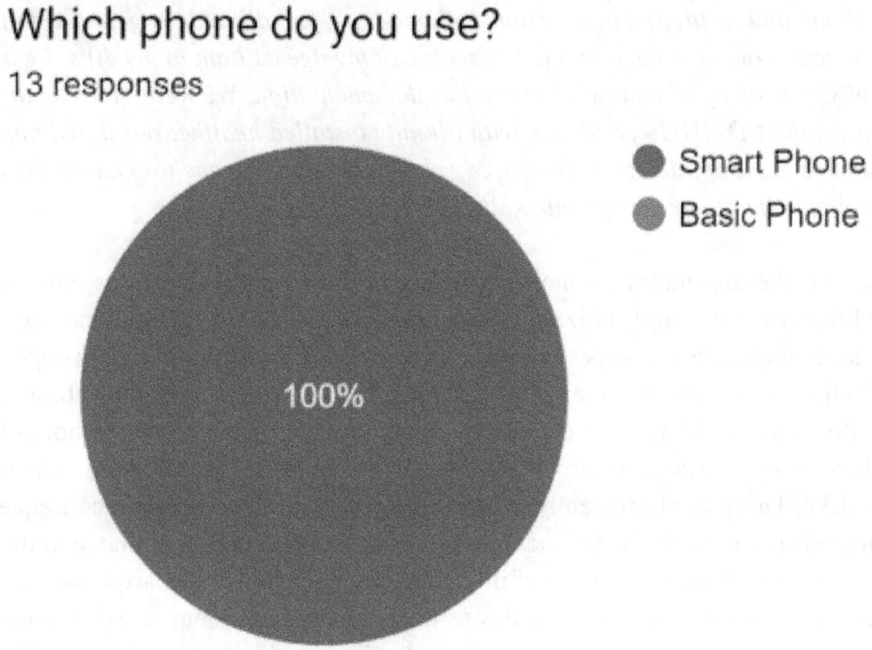

highlighted the fundamental challenge as a lack of basic digital knowledge. They expressed a need for tailored training programs focusing on special needs. Internet connectivity issues have also been one of the dominating challenges of digital literacy in Kashmir as expressed by the participants, especially during the time of COVID-19. The internet service was suspended by the Government in Kashmir on August 5 2019 after the abrogation of Article 370 of the Indian constitution which gave a special status to Kashmir. After the abrogation of Article 370, all the communication channels including internet was suspended in Kashmir. while postpaid mobile services were restored after some time but internet remained blocked. In January 2020, 2G internet access was allowed while highspeed internet remained shut in Kashmir for 18 months.

We in this region of the world had to deal with double pressure during COVID-19, one was of the pandemic and another lack of internet connectivity. The state announced in-front of the world that 2G internet has been restored in Kashmir but we were neither able to conduct online meetings where training programs were held nor were able to watch any YouTube videos freely. A single 2-minute video took 5 minutes to open and used to buffer in the middle so many times. (Shakir Nabi, face-to-face interview, 05 September 2023)

The respondents also highlighted Cultural and language barriers as culture and language play an important role in shaping attitudes toward digital literacy. Female nurses and ASHA workers mentioned cultural conservatism as one of the leading factors in the adoption of digital skills.

I am a mother of 5 children and I feel so hesitant to spend time on the mobile phone. Although my children teach me to send messages on WhatsApp and they have also downloaded some other applications like Facebook and Instagram in my mobile phone but I feel difficult to get used to the interface. The language is tough and it is not suitable for people of my age as I am in my 40's. I ask my children to fill the Excel sheets of my official work and other documentation. We were given smartphones from authorities during the COVID-19 pandemic with already installed healthcare-related applications but I am hesitant to use those applications as well. My children again help me to read all the notifications. (Hafeeza, Telephonic interview, 7 September, 2023)

This narration makes us understand the significance of user-friendly interfaces. We see the absence of this feature hinders the seamless utilization of digital health tools. The cultural barrier is particularly related to gender-related roles and expectations in a society like Kashmir. interview depicted that there is a dominant belief that women, especially those in rural areas of Kashmir are not habitual to use smartphones especially those of elderly women. despite being provided with the smartphones by the health department, these women hesitate to use the devices due to concerns regarding unintended actions and other security risks. This fear of accidently triggering functions to lead stressful consequences including calling someone unintentionally, uploading pictures of self and family online, and threat of access to bank details are some of the perceptions of insecurities associated with smartphones. However, male health workers are away from these insecurities as they are very confident in using smart phones and the internet. Another important finding that needs to be discussed is that rural women health workers of elderly age consequently rely on male family members for information that reaches to them mixed with the perceptions and expectations of male members. Other than this they only reach to What's App groups for further and other information. Young female nurses in rural areas have good exposure to digital technology compared to their aged counterparts.

Utilization of Digital Health Tools

The participants under this theme highlighted some of the same issues discussed above related to accessibility, usability, cultural acceptance and knowledge gaps. One of the interesting findings under this heading is lack of knowledge regarding the sources to follow and trust upon for credible information. The participants when asked which platforms do they use for credible and reliable information mentioned about the What's App news groups, Face book and YouTube. Three out of thirteen participants were able to name some of the reliable online sources like WHO [1]Mayo Clinic[2], Dr. Eric Berg DC[3]. We found that place like Kashmir requires a multidimensional approach and tailoring solutions to bridge the gaps so that people related to healthcare can harness the full potential of digital health tools for improved healthcare delivery.

Training and Educational Programs

This theme sheds light on the efforts and platforms provided by the authorities to enhance the digital literacy among healthcare workers in Kashmir. The respondents gave both positive and negative responses highlighting the critical role of internet connectivity and pattern of training programmes. Participants acknowledged the availability of training programs during the crises of COVID-19 and after. This depicts the recognition of the importance of digital literacy in healthcare in Kashmir. The concerns raised by the participants were of the lack of reliable and consistent internet connectivity during the times of COVID-19. Four out of thirteen participants showed satisfaction with the training programs which helped them to get used to the documentation especially physical data shifting to excel sheets and other documentation. There is another interesting finding related to training and educational programmes Nurses who are working in the private sector in the Kashmir division reported a lack of structured training programs and other educational workshops within their respective healthcare facilities.

I have been working in the private sector as a nurse since 2017. Since then, we have never attended any workshop or other formal training program from the institution. However, during COVID-19 when everything went online, those of us who are Tec savvy were given the responsibility to do online formalities and conduct online meetings to share the required information with the working staff. We also had some staff already working on the hospital computers who used to do all the online formalities thus, we nurses were never integrated into roles that make use of online formalities. One thing that changed for us is earlier we used to deliver the test reports to the patients physically but now they could download them on mobile phones and for that those of us working in hospital labs were required to share the documents online (sometimes personally otherwise through the default link to given phone numbers). (Anonymous, face to face interview, 05 September 2023)

Government Policies and Support

While participants acknowledged the policies, they emphasized the need for more effective implementation and practical application at the grassroots level. They stressed that mere formulation of policies is not enough, and talked about the importance of translating these policies into tangible actions and outcomes that directly benefit healthcare workers. One interesting finding under this theme is when the participants were asked about the most national program on digital literacy called National Digital Literacy Mission NDLM, only a single participant could answer it directly who had little knowledge about the program. The remaining twelve participants were hesitant to this question and tried to avoid it at first and when asked again, almost all of them asked for the full form of NDLM and tried to guess from the name as a digital literacy mission programme. Very few of the participants were able to name some other health care programmes initiated by Government. None of the private sector participants knew about any of these health-related programs.

ASHA Workers and Nurses Counterpart Each Other

We thought of making this theme at last because some of the major and interesting findings can be summed up under this theme. Research came up with the results that ASHA workers, who are incredibly vital to the healthcare system, seem having a considerable gap in education and digital literacy compared to their counterparts, such as nurses. All the ASHA workers in the study were less qualified, they could hardly read and write the text in English. They act as care providers at community levels and along with duties like access to healthcare, medicine, and sanitization they are also responsible for the awareness of health issues among pregnant women and other marginalized sections of the community. Keeping in mind the role of these workers, they must be highly efficient in the given areas and also in digital health but they were seen as the most subdued group among healthcare workers in Kashmir.

CONCLUSION

The challenges and opportunities surrounding digital literacy among healthcare workers in Kashmir paint a vivid picture of the need for comprehensive strategies to harness the potential of technology. Digital literacy can empower healthcare professionals, enhance patient care, and transform healthcare delivery. However, there are barriers to overcome, particularly in the context of rural healthcare workers, especially women, and their varying levels of digital literacy.

One prominent challenge lies in the disparity of digital literacy between different groups of healthcare workers. Nurses, due to their formal training and potential exposure to digital tools, may possess a certain level of familiarity with technology compared to Accredited Social Health Activists (ASHA) workers, who often come from less privileged backgrounds with limited educational opportunities. Addressing this disparity is crucial to ensure equal access to digital literacy benefits across the healthcare sector.

To bridge this gap, targeted digital literacy programs need to be designed and implemented, catering specifically to the educational backgrounds and comfort levels of different healthcare worker groups. These programs should start with the foundational digital literacy training, teaching basic skills and gradually progressing to more advanced applications in healthcare. The training should be hands-on, interactive and accessible, allowing healthcare workers to learn and practice in a supportive environment.

The unique context of Kashmir, being a conflict zone with different culture nuances adds layers of complexity to the digital literacy area. The influence of the conservative societal outlook, especially towards women's use of technology and the linguistic diversity of the region further complicates the promotion of digital literacy. However, there are encouraging aspects including the acknowledgment and appreciation of government initiatives aimed at promoting digital literacy is a positive sign. Government policies and other programs if effectively implemented can significantly bridge the digital divide and empower healthcare workers with the necessary digital skills.

Collaboration among stakeholders, including government bodies, healthcare institutions, educational organizations, and technology providers is critical for creating a comprehensive ecosystem that supports digital literacy and integration. Through a positive and holistic approach, healthcare workers in Kashmir can harness the transformative potential of digital literacy, ultimately leading to improved healthcare delivery and better health outcomes for the community.

REFERENCES

Agarwal, N. (2022). Article 370 of Indian constitution. *ipleaders*.

Bakshi, N. a. (2021). *History and future of digital health*. Itihasa Research and Digital.

Bandyopadhyay, O. (2023). *Health without wealth: the plight of India's ASHA workers*. British Safety Council.

Begley, S. (2017). *Digital Literacy: realizing the promise of technology*. Academic Press.

Britannica. (2023). *Kashmir, geography and travel.* Author.

Davos. (2022). *This is how to counter the global digital divide.* World Economic Forum.

Deloitte. (2022). Are we finally seeing the long promised transformation. In *Global Health Care outlook*. Author.

Digital Literacy. (2023, june 6). Retrieved from Ed Teach Review: https://www.edtechreview.in/trends-insights/insights/what-is-digital-literacy-its-importance-and-challenges/

Eruthickal. (2016). *Role of ASHA workers in rural development with reference to Kottayam Distritct*. Baselius College.

Garratt. (2020). Telemedical education during national emergencies: Learning from Kashmir. *The Clinical Teacher*. PMID:32602614

IAS. (2022). *India inequality report 2022 digital divide*. Next IAS.

Kapoor, S. (2022). *Digital Health Ecosystem in India: present ststus, challanges and way forward*. Research Gate.

Kashmir, G. (2023). *To revolutionise healthcare, J&K government to intriduce AI in health sector*. Greater Kashmir.

Kearney. (2023). *The digital revolution could reshape healthcare in the Middle East*. CNBC Arabia.

Kuek, H. (2019). Healthcare staff digital literacy levels and their attitudes towards information systems. *Health Informatics Journal*. PMID:30983476

Leal, B. a. (2022). *The Digital Literacy Imperative*. CSIS.

Machado. (2021). The relationship between the Covid-19 Pandemic and Vaccine Hesitancy A scoping review of literature until August 2021. *PubMed Central*.

McKinsey. (2021). *Unlocking digital healthcare in lower and middle income countries*. MicKinsey and Company.

Meister, D. a. (2016). *Digital Health and Digital biomakers enabling value chains on health data*. Gruyter.

Mukhopadhyay, N. (2019). *The abrogation of Kashmir's special status: why now*. Al Jzaeera.

Patil. (2022). Existing system of digital health in India. *D Y Patil Journal of Health Sciences*.

Perappadan, B. (2020). *India's first coronavirus infection confirmed in Kerala*. The Hind.

PR. (2021). *Economic survey highlights thrust on rural development*. Press Information Bureau.

Radhakrishn, A. (2020). COVID-19 restricted internet impacts on health in Kashmir. *Health and Human Rights Journal*.

Rising-Kashmir. (2022). *J&K setting benchmark in imolementing PM's Digital Indian Compaign*. Rising Kashmir.

Sachs. (2009). *Improving access, service delivery and efficiency of public health system in rural India*. Author.

Scott. (2020). India's Auxiliary Nurse-Midwife, Anganwadi Workers, and Accredited Social Health Acttivist Programs. In H. B. Perry (Ed.), Health for people: National Community Health Worker Programs from Afghanistan to Zimbabwe. Academic Press.

Scroll. (2020). *Lockdown after lockdown: How access to non Covid healthcare has been chocked off in Kashmir.* Scroll.

Shoib & Arafat. (2020). *Potentialities and challanges of digital health in psychiatry in Kashmir.* Sage Publications.

SLFC. (2020). *Using 2G to fight a Pandemic in a digital world.* Software Freedom Law Center India.

The-Print. (2020). *Kashmir Valley records its first case of Coronavirus in Srinagar.* The Print.

WHO. (2021). *Global Strategy on Digital Health 2020-2025. World Health Organization.*

Zhou, J. (2022). *The digital divide, what it is and what is being done to close it.* Investopia.

ENDNOTES

1. World Health Organization, the United Nations agency working to promote health, keep the world safe and serve the vulnerable.
2. Mayo Clinic is a non-profit American Academic medical centre and a top ranked hospital with campus in Arizona, Florida etc. it focuses on integrated healthcare, education, and research.
3. Dr. Eric Berg is a chiropractor who specializes in weight loss through nutritional and natural methods and also provides all health-related information, explanation on diseases on his top-rated YouTube channel.

Chapter 16
Family Communication and COVID-19:
Communication Dynamics During the Stay-at-Home Period

Cihan Çakır
https://orcid.org/0000-0002-4100-365X
Avrasya University, Turkey

ABSTRACT

The COVID-19 pandemic has affected people's lifestyles as well as communication processes and family communication in very different ways. Some of these are social isolation and physical distance during the pandemic period. This situation has led to family members having less face-to-face contact with each other, reduced visits to relatives due to travel restrictions, and limiting non-family relationships. This situation affected the communication dynamics within the family and strained the emotional bonds between family members. During the pandemic period, dependence on and use of communication technologies has increased. Families continued their communication through virtual platforms and used tools such as video calling, messaging, and social media more. In this regard, the aim of this chapter is to address the communication difficulties faced by families during the COVID-19 pandemic and to offer solutions to develop healthy communication dynamics during the stay-at-home period.

INTRODUCTION

The COVID-19 epidemic has also affected family communication on a global scale. During the pandemic, governments have decided to impose a lockdown of cities, regions and countries. This situation also pushed the families living in these places to rearrange their communication structure. Although strict lockdown rules were eased after the effects of the pandemic subsided, families tried to adapt to the changes. This situation has increased the importance of family communication. Because during the closure process, through intra-family communication, some families were positively affected by the

DOI: 10.4018/979-8-3693-0896-7.ch016

closure and managed to communicate effectively with each other, while others were unable to establish this communication and were negatively affected (Mikucki-Enyart & Maguire, 2021, p.145).

The COVID-19 epidemic has redesigned the patterns of daily life (Fuchs, 2020, p.376). This change in daily life has also affected family communication and the relationships of family members. Family members who had to stay at home with the pandemic found themselves interacting with each other more. This situation has allowed family members to get closer to each other and get to know each other more closely, and has generally increased their face-to-face communication rather than technology-mediated communication (Sharma, 2021, p.430). However, increasing communication does not always mean that positive or healthy communication will increase. In other words, the epidemic may have brought family members closer to each other, but this does not necessarily indicate that the family members communicate well with each other. In such cases, the decrease in communication within the family may lead to family members falling apart and increasing the relational distance even if the physical distance is close. In this sense, the quality of the content of the communication becomes important. As a result of poor communication, some family members may face exclusion (Dorrance Hall et al., 2022, p.57). Considering this, it is a concept that directs and determines behaviors such as communication, social support and coping. How the epidemic affects the way individuals within the family communicate and how constructive and supportive conversations along with positive communication affect family communication, as well as what effects negative conversations and unhealthy communication have on family communication (Maguire, 2012, p.23).

In this regard, the aim of this section is to address the communication difficulties faced by families during the COVID-19 epidemic and to offer solutions to develop healthy communication dynamics during the stay-at-home period. The epidemic may cause changes and increased stress in family relationships. The department aims to guide families in strengthening their communication skills and make the stay-at-home process healthier and more supportive. This book chapter will help understand the impact of the COVID-19 pandemic on communication dynamics between family members by focusing on family communication in the field of communication studies. It will help families strengthen their communication skills and create a healthy communication environment by providing analysis and solution suggestions for communication difficulties that arise during the stay-at-home period. Additionally, this chapter will provide a resource that can be used to guide families throughout the community by addressing common issues families face during the pandemic. In the light of this information, the planned study aims to offer some solution suggestions to the field. These; Developing active listening and empathy skills within the family, encouraging open and honest communication between family members, learning and applying conflict management strategies, using positive language and tone in communication, learning stress management techniques and applying them within the family, sharing and supporting families' concerns about the epidemic. It includes keeping communication channels open for It is believed that these solution suggestions will help family members develop a better understanding of communication both with each other and with people in other segments of society, help families create a healthier and more supportive communication environment during the epidemic, and make it easier for family members to support each other (Maguire, 2012, p.23).

FAMILY COMMUNICATION DURING THE COVID-19 PANDEMIC

Family communication is a process that includes many elements. First, family communication is the mechanism of most early socialization experiences. Most people learn to communicate, and perhaps more importantly, to think about communication, by observing and interacting with family members (Bruner, 1990, p.36). These early interactions later form the basis for habitual communication behaviors. They also serve as a model for future interactions (Nagy et al., 2021, p.1). Second, family communication is the means by which family members establish, maintain, and terminate close relationships. People form their families through social interaction. People flirt to form a family. Individuals who date move toward marriage based in part on their evaluations of interaction styles (Ogolsky & Monk, 2019, p.430). After families are formed, members continue to relate to each other through communication. Spouses use communication strategies to maintain their marriage (Stafford, 2020, p.2347). Children's relationships with their parents are influenced by both the amount and type of interaction that occurs in these relationships (Hesse et al., 2018, p.458). Adolescents' relationships with family members mature in part because the communication patterns that characterize their relationships change. In addition, ending relationships is also possible through family communication. Divorce is associated with certain communication patterns (Baudat et al., 2020, p.428). Along with these elements, there are many theories about family communication.

The theory of family communication patterns is used to understand family communication during the epidemic. Family communication patterns theory also explains the ways in which individuals in the family communicate with each other and how both parties establish a common communication with the orientation of speaking and complying in parent-child communication. Conversational orientation indicates how open members of the family are to talking to each other. In other words, the opinions of people in the family and their willingness to communicate are seen in families with a high conversational orientation. Conformity orientation describes the compliance of family members with each other's views and ideas, especially children's compliance with their parents' ideas. In families with high harmony orientation, there is a sense of unity and a set of family rules (Koerner & Fitzpatrick, 2002, p.72, Lillie, 2023, p.3).

The uncertainties in social life that have changed with the pandemic have led to negative emotions such as stress, anger and sadness in people. This situation guided the emotional and cognitive behaviors of family members. In other words, while communicating within the family, people were able to behave negatively due to the effects of the pandemic. Because people were suddenly stuck at home in an unusual way and had to get involved in each other's routines. This situation may cause deterioration in family relationships (Solomon et al., 2016, p.510). Many people, in order to cope with this unfamiliar situation and when they could not get along with other members of the family, resorted to technological devices such as smartphones, computers or televisions, and tried to fill the physical gap caused by social distance with these devices. However, rather than filling this gap, technological devices increased people's feelings of loneliness (Curran & Seiter, 2021, p.2).

The use of electronic devices does not always have negative effects on family communication during the pandemic. When considered from the perspective of older people, these communication technologies have been useful in keeping them in touch with their relatives and reducing the risk of leaving their homes and contracting the pandemic (Skalacka & Pajestka, 2021, p.277). The use of digital communication technologies, especially social media, helps reduce the level of loneliness for older people (Fumagalli et al. 2021, p.4). With the help of video calling applications, elderly people can communicate with their distant family members or close friends and thus meet their social support needs from their homes.

However, some studies show that face-to-face communication is important for elderly people in reducing their depression and stress levels, and that the use of digital technology by elderly people who are away from face-to-face communication during the pandemic does not have a positive effect on them, and these positive effects only increase as a result of face-to-face interactions. It appears that there is no difference, especially between elderly people living alone and those living with other family members, as long as there is no face-to-face communication (Fingerman et al., 2021 p.117). In this sense, when considered from the perspective of older people, digital communication cannot replace face-to-face communication.

Again, in many countries, relatives and family communications have been tried to be carried out with the help of digital technological devices due to the pandemic. For this reason, technological devices have been used very frequently to continue daily tasks and relationships such as work, education, and communication (Carroll et al., 2020, p.1). This increase in the use of technological devices during the pandemic has also had some effects on family communication. Children are among those most affected by this, and parent-child relationships can be disrupted through technological devices (Drouin et al., 2020, p.729). Studies say that too much technological device use can disrupt parent-child interaction, family activities and parenting behaviors within the family. This situation describes the interruption of family communication due to the use of technological devices, and this situation is called technoference. Technoference is of great importance in family communication because it interrupts face-to-face communication within the family and affects people's perceptions and behaviors (McDaniel & Coyne, 2016, p.87). Because parents' technoference experiences can negatively affect their interactions with their children and reduce their interest and sensitivity towards their children. In addition, parents who spend too much time with technological devices are less able to focus on their children and cannot be aware of their needs and demands and cannot show appropriate parental behavior. At the same time, children may face very harsh reactions when they try to cut off their ties with technological devices in order to find the attention they expect from their parents (McDaniel, 2019, p.73). This situation is especially seen especially during the pandemic period, as people who are forced to stay at home cause them to do both work, family and parenting duties at home at the same time (Montag & Elhai, 2020, p.2). As a result, young children, especially in their developmental age, may develop a sense of distrust towards their parents and feel that they are not taken into account and cared for, and they have the potential to behave this way to other people by exhibiting these behaviors they inherited from their parents in their future relationships and interactions. This may lead children to believe that excessive use of technological devices is normal and correct, and may lead them to establish their communicative processes in their future social lives through technological devices. Thus, it can lead to consequences such as inattention, disregard for the needs of others, and failure in interpersonal communication in children (McDaniel, 2019, p.75). In this sense, it seems important for the developmental processes of children that families, especially parents, prefer face-to-face communication with their children during the pandemic period and respond to their wishes and needs (Weaver, 2021, p.137).

Most studies focusing on the parent-child relationship during the pandemic focus on the relationship between young children and their parents. However, adolescents were affected by the pandemic process (Liu et al., 2021, p.2). Especially children studying at university, while away from home, had to return to their families' home with the closure and had to stay away from university life, face-to-face classes and friends (Fegert et al., 2020). In this sense, the pandemic has also had negative effects on adolescents in university and high school. Considering that adolescents are now moving away from their families, spending more time with their friends in social life and trying to be independent, the pandemic process and measures removing adolescents from these environments has had negative consequences for both their parents and themselves (Janssen et al., 2020).

When the effects seen during the pandemic process are considered within the scope of family communication, the other affected group is seen as romantic partners. As a result of the pandemic, romantic partners and families have had to develop new routines and communication strategies under increased stress and psychological pressures during this period (Jones, et al., 2021, p.152). The stress caused by the pandemic not only harms individual family members, but also harms marriages. During the epidemic, people have to adapt to a life that is both emotionally and mentally challenging, such as adapting to change, locking themselves at home, and adapting their work and working life to working remotely (Carbone, 2020, p.163; Martin et al., 2022, p). .one). This process can be more exhausting for married couples who have to deal with such stress. This situation may affect the tolerance and constructive communication levels of couples towards each other. As a result, the level of welfare in marriage may decrease (Prime et al., 2020, p.633). The social isolation brought about by the pandemic process has increased the time people spend with their family members. The stress brought by both the pandemic process and daily life, combined with constantly seeing one's romantic partner and family, increases the tension between family members by causing relational and communication difficulties (Luetke et al., 2020, p.748). As a result, couples who are confined to their homes within the family have engaged in many anxiety behaviors, such as ending their relationships due to concerns such as fear of job loss and health fear that come with the pandemic, to divorce and engaging in behaviors that lead to domestic violence (Kofman & Garfin, 2020, p.200; Usher et al., 2020, p.550). However, the effects of the pandemic have been positive for some families and couples. The necessity of establishing close relationships brought about by the pandemic allowed these couples and families to meet the need for social support, bringing family members closer together and allowing couple relations to improve and reach an even better point. Although these couples had the same concerns during the pandemic process, they showed coping behavior and chose to communicate with each other with the intention of solving these problems in a positive way. This situation increased the stability and continuity of marriages. This determination to solve problems has made marriages and family relationships more resilient against major problems (Afifi et al., 2006, p.380).

COPING STRATEGIES

When we look at the studies conducted in the field, the primary strategies of families and couples to cope with these problems are to think about good things, to think less about the negatives brought by the pandemic, to constantly deal with something and keep themselves busy and to stay away from thinking about these negatives, to pray to God through religion, to be open and open with the people around them. It has been revealed that they can overcome these negative effects by sharing their feelings clearly. In other words, developing coping strategies rather than avoiding the problem is seen as a more effective method to overcome the problem. For romantic partners, listening to each other and paying attention to partner sensitivity remains an important condition (Kar et al., 2021, p.2).

What is important in coping with the negative effects during the pandemic is the social support of family members to each other. These supports can be seen as informational, emotional, instrumental and evaluation supports. Information support is seen as advice and information sharing, and during periods of uncertainty such as pandemics, this information can reduce people's increasing levels of stress and anxiety. Emotional support can occur through family members showing love and care to each other in difficult situations, and it involves helping each other emotionally by trying to understand each other. In this way, people have a stronger emotional structure, know that other family members are always with them, and can stand stronger against the stress of the pandemic (Kindness et al, 2017, p.3). Instrumental support can be understood as the physical support that family members provide to each other. Particularly during the pandemic, supports such as sharing the increased housework load can bring family members closer to each other and enable healthy communication to be established. Finally, evaluation support encourages social comparison and increases self-esteem (Malecki and Demaray, 2003, p.233). As a result, these types of social support have an important place in families' strategies to cope with stress and anxiety during the pandemic.

Another coping strategy is seen as entertainment media. Entertainment media such as video games are tools that facilitate coping behaviors with the effects of the pandemic (Wolfers & Schneider, 2020, p.2). People can resort to video games and entertaining content to get rid of the stressful situations of the pandemic (Cahill, 2021, p.3). Video games differ from other media and can develop coping strategies. The main difference here comes from interaction. The player can overcome the feeling of loneliness and pressure by interacting with other players playing the game. This helps to correct the negative mood and turns into an action that gives pleasure to the person. Since these games require more attention and attention, they reduce the feeling of stress by making you forget. People who focus on the game forget the stress during the pandemic process (Bowman, 2021, p.650). Video games allow people to escape from reality, relax, be happy and cope with stress. It is basically seen as a tool to escape from anxiety and stress during the pandemic process. In this sense, it is said that this escape emerged as a strategy to cope with the epidemic based on media and video games (Barr & Copelanda-Stewart, 2021, p.2). People also realize their emotional regulation by playing video games, and this shows that more durable and healthy families emerge in family communication. This is true not only for children and adolescents but also for adults. Video games help with emotional regulation for every member of the family (Caro & Popovac, 2021, p.615). Playing games as a form of entertainment allows family members to spend time together, spend their free time together, and thus cope with the negative effects of the pandemic. In this sense, it can be said that there is a connection between gaming and family engagement (Balmford & Davies, 2020, p.5).

Coping strategies that occur during stressful times are of great importance in family communication. These strategies affect the strength and quality of family members' communications and relationships (Maguire, 2012, p. 76). Since family communication is different from other relationships that people establish in social life, good family communication is an important factor in maintaining family harmony, overcoming problems together, social support and coping with problems such as stress and anxiety. In this way, family members can get closer to each other and contribute positively to family communication. Especially in times of peak stress and anxiety, such as the pandemic, it makes it easier for people in the family to help each other when they can talk about themselves and their concerns with each other. On the contrary, in families where communication and interaction within the family is unhealthy and negative, problems grow and progress. In this sense, the value of positive family communication increases during crisis periods such as pandemics (Hado & Feinberg, 2020, p.411). In summary, when studies in the literature on the positive and negative effects of the COVID-19 epidemic on family communication are evaluated, it is generally seen that the pandemic has negative effects on families and individuals (Marks et al, 2023, p.123). However, family members can also have the chance to strengthen their bonds by turning these negative effects of the pandemic into positive ones through communication among themselves.

CONCLUSION AND DISCUSSION

As can be seen from the discussed situations, the COVID-19 pandemic has affected family communication in various ways. Factors such as social isolation, use of communication technologies, increased stress level, communication difficulties and solidarity during the stay at home period have shaped communication within the family. During this period, it is important to improve communication skills, establish empathy, provide open and understanding communication, and create a supportive environment within the family. In light of these ideas, this book chapter focuses on the communication difficulties faced by families during the COVID-19 epidemic and the changes in communication within the family during this period. The epidemic period causes changes and increased stress in family relationships. In this section, these changes have been tried to be revealed and communication strategies that will help families cope with these difficulties have been presented, and solution suggestions have been tried to be given to make the process of staying at home healthier and more supportive. In this regard, within the scope of the chapter, the changing dynamics and difficulties in family communication were discussed and an attempt was made to examine how family communication was affected during the COVID-19 epidemic and the new dynamics that emerged. In this sense, the fact that the study touches on elements such as Contributing to Social Problems, Understanding Psychosocial Effects, Strengthening Family Relations, Applied Guidance and Examining Various Perspectives and Experiences are the factors that emphasize the importance and original value of the study. This study aims to create positive impacts at the societal and individual level by providing families with healthy communication skills and helping them better understand the challenges of staying at home.

The study offers solution suggestions on the subject. First of all, family members need to show empathy and understanding to each other for healthy communication. Empathy is an ability based on understanding other people's emotional states and understanding their perspective. The stay-at-home process that occurs with COVID-19 can cause family members to experience emotional difficulties. Empathy can help family members better focus on each other's emotional states and support each other during this difficult time. In this sense, family members can organize regular family meetings to ensure healthier communication and ensure that each family member shares their emotional state. In these meetings, everyone can express themselves by giving everyone the opportunity to speak in turn and for others to listen. In addition, rapprochement can be established between family members by doing empathy development exercises and helping family members better understand each other's feelings. Additionally, family members will be able to improve family communication during crisis periods such as pandemics by encouraging each other to support each other on emotional issues and taking care not to exclude anyone emotionally.

Second, family members can strengthen family ties by communicating openly and honestly with each other. Open and honest communication enables family members to accurately express their inner thoughts and feelings. Uncertainties and concerns that arise during the COVID-19 period can be resolved through open communication, and family members can help understand and provide support to each other by sharing these concerns with each other. In this regard, it is important to provide a safe environment for family members to express their emotional states and concerns. In addition, making time for open communication and organizing regular meetings as a family to discuss certain issues plays a critical role during the pandemic. Additionally, it is valuable to encourage emotional conversations and create an environment that allows everyone to express their opinions openly.

Thirdly, people listening to each other effectively can make the process go more smoothly. Effective listening is important to increase mutual understanding. Family members should listen carefully to each other, sincerely try to understand each other and show mutual respect. Effective listening provides the opportunity to understand the feelings, thoughts and perspectives of other family members. Effective listening allows you to correctly understand the speaker's messages and confirm these messages. Effective listening creates a deeper emotional bond between family members. The interest and empathy shown during listening can make other family members feel emotionally close. Effective listening can prevent or reduce possible conflicts within the family. Listening carefully to the thoughts and concerns of other family members can prevent disagreements caused by misunderstandings or misunderstandings. Effective listening increases trust and respect among family members. Family members who feel listened to and understood have more trust in each other and create a more respectful communication environment. Effective listening allows problems within the family to be solved more easily. Listening helps understand all perspectives and allows for more comprehensive and constructive solutions to problems. Effective listening encourages family members to seek emotional support and support each other. This support enables them to overcome difficulties and difficult periods within the family more easily. When listening effectively, family members should focus fully on the person speaking and try to understand their feelings, needs and thoughts, without allowing interruptions while listening. In addition, while listening, one should try to understand the emotional state of the speaker by watching the body language of others, using empathetic expressions and asking questions.

Another solution suggestion is conflict management. Effective conflict management helps family members better understand each other's perspectives and emotional states. This increases empathy and understanding. Healthy managed conflicts increase trust within the family and strengthen relationships. Openly discussing and resolving problems strengthens the bonds between family members. Conflict management enables family members to better understand their emotional reactions and effects, and this awareness increases emotional control and promotes a healthier communication style within the family. Managing family conflicts effectively provides a positive model for family members. By observing these healthy conflict resolution methods within the family, children will be able to apply them in their own future relationships. Conflict management enables more effective and sustainable solutions to problems within the family, which helps family members live happier and more satisfying lives. Poor management of conflicts can lead to further harm within the family. Physical and emotional harm can result from long-term conflicts. Therefore, conflict management plays a critical role in preventing such harm. Conflict management is a process that requires the participation and cooperation of everyone in the family. It is important for family members to use their emotional intelligence to create a positive communication environment and resolve conflicts in a positive way. Managing family conflicts effectively increases family happiness and ensures the continuation of healthy relationships. In this sense, during the pandemic, family members should allow everyone to share their feelings and opinions in order to handle conflicts constructively, encourage compromise and understanding to find a fair solution between the parties, and determine steps to solve problems together, using a non-binding tone.

Finally, family members must balance technology use. The importance of balancing the use of technology in family communication is increasing today, because technology can significantly affect the interaction of families with each other. Technology can help family members communicate with each other more quickly and easily, access information and entertainment; However, excessive use and misuse can have negative effects on communication and relationships within the family. In this regard, balancing technology use allows family members to spend quality time with each other. Limiting the use of technology in family communication allows family members to focus on each other, which strengthens family ties and contributes to the development of healthy relationships. Communicating face to face, rather than through technology tools, can increase emotional connection. Emotional cues such as facial expressions, body language and tone of voice can make communication deeper and more meaningful. Excessive use of technology can cause family members to become distant and isolated from each other. To prevent this situation, it is important to limit the use of technology in a balanced way. Conscious and balanced use of technology within the family is considered important in providing children with an exemplary model of correct and healthy technology use. This can help children manage technology correctly and establish healthy relationships. Establishing periodic digital detox periods to balance technology use can offer family members the opportunity to take a break from technology, connect more with each other, and focus on other activities. As a result, balancing the use of technology in family communication allows for healthier and more meaningful relationships, and direct interaction and face-to-face communication between family members is balanced with technology, so that healthy family ties can be maintained and strengthened. In this sense, family members should encourage quality time between family members by limiting the use of technology in certain periods of time, organize activities that will strengthen family ties by using technology as a tool in family activities, make agreements within the family to reduce technology use, and comply with these agreements. They should encourage each other.

In addition, the process of staying at home may affect the communication between parents and children. Children may have difficulty understanding routine changes and being away from the outside world. It is important for parents to support and understand their children during this period. Parents should talk to their children openly and understandingly so that they understand the process and what is happening, give children the opportunity to express their feelings, and listen to their concerns. Additionally, children should be encouraged to learn and have fun through educational activities, games and creative activities. Apart from this, the process of staying at home can create different dynamics for married couples. While being together for a long time can cause conflict and tension, it can also provide the opportunity to better understand and support each other. In this sense, it becomes important to balance time within the family and respect individual spaces. It is important to take time to improve communication skills and understand each other better. Expressing emotions is important to increase mutual understanding, and making an effort to resolve potential conflicts constructively is critical for married couples. When considered from the perspective of older people, older individuals may experience physical isolation and lack of social connection while staying at home. This can lead to emotional difficulties and feelings of loneliness. In this regard, it is important to provide emotional support by frequently communicating face to face with elderly individuals. It is possible to reduce the social isolation of older individuals by establishing digital connections using technological tools. Elderly individuals should be encouraged to maintain their daily routines and engage in physical activities. It is believed that these suggestions can help families strengthen their communication skills and create a healthy communication environment. At the same time, it will be able to support families in managing this process more effectively by providing analysis and solution suggestions for communication difficulties that arise during the stay at home process.

Within the scope of these discussions, future studies can examine in more depth the effects of technology use on family communication during pandemic periods. Research can be conducted on which technology tools provide more effective communication between families and how the correct use of these tools can be encouraged. In addition, it can examine how empathy and understanding can be increased in family communication, how these elements strengthen the connection within the family, and how these skills can be improved during pandemic processes. It can also focus on the emotional health and well-being of families during the stay-at-home period. During these processes, research can be conducted on how to better respond to the psychological needs of family members and how to strengthen psychological support systems. Additionally, it can put the communication between children and teens and parents under the spotlight during the stay-at-home period. In this process, research can be conducted on the emotional needs of children and young people, communication barriers and effective communication strategies for these age groups. It can examine the communication dynamics and harmony of married couples during the stay-at-home period and strategies to strengthen their relationships during this period. Research can be conducted to develop communication guides suitable for the needs of married couples. Can address communication dynamics within the family from a gender perspective. Research can be conducted on how family communication is shaped in the context of gender roles and expectations and how these dynamics are affected during the pandemic process. It can examine the communication dynamics of families from different cultures during their stay at home. Research can be conducted on how cultural diversity affects communication within the family and how cultural sensitivity can be increased in this process. Communication training and awareness programs can be developed to strengthen families' communication skills and enable them to manage the stay-at-home process more effectively. Research can be conducted on the impact and applications of such programs. It can examine how families communicate through virtual communities and online support groups during the pandemic period and the effects of these platforms on family dynamics. It can examine what kind of adaptation process families' experiences and communication strategies gained from this process led to in the post-pandemic period. It can examine the effects of increased stress during the pandemic on family communication and strategies for coping with stress. More research can be done in this area to understand the positive effects of coping with stress on family communication. Can examine how to effectively resolve family conflicts during the pandemic and mediation methods. Research can be conducted to develop effective strategies for resolving family conflict. It can examine how domestic violence increased during the pandemic and the effects of this situation on family communication. Researching effective strategies to prevent and intervene in domestic violence can contribute to studies in this field. It can examine the effects of education and guidance services provided to families during the pandemic on intra-family communication dynamics. More research can be done to understand the role of such services in strengthening families' communication skills. Finally, future studies can examine families' creative communication strategies during the pandemic and the effects of these strategies on family connection. More research can be done on how creative approaches such as art, music and games can shape family communication.

As a result, this study tries to explain, within its limitations, the changing family communication dynamics during the pandemic process. It is expected that the study will serve as a resource for future studies. It is thought that the studies and practices that have been done and will be carried out in these areas are of critical importance for the more effective presentation and understanding of future family communication studies.

REFERENCES

Afifi, T. D., Hutchinson, S., & Krouse, S. (2006). Toward a theoretical model of communal coping in postdivorce families and other naturally occurring groups. *Communication Theory*, *16*(3), 378–409. doi:10.1111/j.1468-2885.2006.00275.x

Balmford, W., & Davies, H. (2020). Mobile Minecraft: Negotiated space and perceptions of play in Australian families. *Mobile Media & Communication, 8*(1), 3–21. doi:10.1177/2050157918819614

Barr, M., & Copeland-Stewart, A. (2021). Playing video games during the COVID-19 pandemic and effects on players' well-being. *Games and Culture, 17*(1), 1–18. doi:10.1177/15554120211017036

Baudat, S., Van Petegem, S., Antonietti, J. P., & Zimmermann, G. (2020). Parental solicitation and adolescents' information management: The moderating role of autonomy-supportive parenting. *Journal of Child and Family Studies, 29*(2), 426–441. doi:10.100710826-019-01687-z

Bowman, N. D. (2021). Interactivity as demand: Implications for interactive media entertainment. In P. Vorderer & C. Klimmt (Eds.), *The Oxford handbook of entertainment theory* (pp. 646–670). Oxford University Press.

Bruner, J. (1990). *Acts of meaning*. Harvard University Press.

Cahill, T. (2021). *Gaming as coping in response to COVID-19 pandemic-induced stress: results From a U.S. national survey*. International Communication Association.

Carbone, S. R. (2020). Flattening the mental ill-health curve: The importance of primary prevention in managing the mental health impacts of COVID19. *Mental Health & Prevention, 19*, 161–181. doi:10.1016/j.mhp.2020.200185 PMID:32566473

Caro, C., & Popovac, M. (2021). Gaming when things get tough? Examining how emotion regulation and coping self-efficacy influence gaming during difficult life situations. *Games and Culture, 16*(5), 611–631. doi:10.1177/1555412020944622

Carroll, N., Sadowski, A., Laila, A., Hruska, V., Nixon, M., Ma, D. W., & Haines, J. (2020). The impact of COVID-19 on health behavior, stress, financial and food security among middle to high income Canadian families with young children. *Nutrients, 12*(8), 1–14. doi:10.3390/nu12082352 PMID:32784530

Curran, T., & Seiter, J. S. (2021). The role of relational worry due to COVID-19 in the links between video chat apprehension, loneliness, and adhering to CDC guidelines. *Journal of Social and Personal Relationships, 38*(6), 1869–1876. Advance online publication. doi:10.1177/0265407520985264

Dorrance Hall, E., Earle, K., Silverstone, J., Immel, M., Carlisle, M., & Campbell, N. (2022). Changes in family communication during the COVID-19 pandemic: The role of family communication patterns and relational distance. *Communication Research Reports, 39*(1), 56–67. doi:10.1080/08824096.2021.2025045

Drouin, M., McDaniel, B. T., Pater, J., & Toscos, T. (2020). How parents and their children used social media and technology at the beginning of the COVID-19 pandemic and associations with anxiety. *Cyberpsychology, Behavior, and Social Networking, 23*(11), 727–736. doi:10.1089/cyber.2020.0284 PMID:32726144

Fegert, J. M., Vitiello, B., Plener, P. L., & Clemens, V. (2020). Challenges and burden of the Coronavirus 2019 (COVID-19) pandemic for child and adolescent mental health: A narrative review to highlight clinical and research needs in the acute phase and the long return to normality. *Child and Adolescent Psychiatry and Mental Health, 14*(1), 20. doi:10.118613034-020-00329-3 PMID:32419840

Fingerman, K. L., Ng, Y. T., Zhang, S., Britt, K., Colera, G., Birditt, K. S., & Charles, S. T. (2021). Living alone during COVID-19: Social contact and emotional well-being among older adults. *The Journals of Gerontology. Series B, Psychological Sciences and Social Sciences*, *76*(3), 116–121. doi:10.1093/geronb/gbaa200 PMID:33196815

Fuchs, C. (2020). Everyday life and everyday communication in coronavirus capitalism. *Communication. TripleC*, *18*(1), 375–399. doi:10.31269/triplec.v18i1.1167

Fumagalli, E., Dolmatzian, M. B., & Shrum, L. J. (2021). Centennials, FOMO, and loneliness: An investigation of the impact of social networking and messaging/VoIP apps usage during the initial stage of the Coronavirus pandemic. *Frontiers in Psychology*, *9*(12), 620739. doi:10.3389/fpsyg.2021.620739 PMID:33633646

Hado, E., & Feinberg, L. (2020). Amid the COVID-19 pandemic, meaningful communication between family caregivers and residents of long-term care facilities is imperative. *Journal of Aging & Social Policy*, *32*(4–5), 410–415. doi:10.1080/08959420.2020.1765684 PMID:32441209

Hesse, C., Mikkelson, A. C., & Saracco, S. (2018). Parent – child affection and helicopter parenting: Exploring the concept of excessive affection. *Western Journal of Communication*, *82*(4), 457–474. doi:10.1080/10570314.2017.1362705

Janssen, L. H. C., Kullberg, M. J., Verkuil, B., Van Zwieten, N., Wever, M. C. M., Van Houtum, L. A. E. M., Wentholt, W. G. M., & Elzinga, B. M. (2020). Does the COVID-19 pandemic impact parents' and adolescents' well-being? An EMA-study on daily affect and parenting. *PLoS One*, *5*(10), e0240962. doi:10.1371/journal.pone.0240962 PMID:33064778

Jones, H. E., Yoon, D. B., Theiss, J. A., Austin, J. T., & Lee, L. A. (2021). Assessing the effects of covıd-19 on romantic relationships and the coping strategies partners use to manage the stress of a pandemic. *Journal of Family Communication*, *21*(3), 152–166. doi:10.1080/15267431.2021.1927040

Kar, N., Kar, B., & Kar, S. (2021). Stress and coping during COVID-19 pandemic: Result of an online survey. *Psychiatry Research*, *295*, 1–5. doi:10.1016/j.psychres.2020.113598 PMID:33264677

Kindness, P., Masthoff, J., & Mellish, C. (2017). Designing emotional support messages tailored to stressors. *International Journal of Human-Computer Studies*, *97*, 1–22. doi:10.1016/j.ijhcs.2016.07.010

Koerner, A. F., & Fitzpatrick, M. A. (2002). Toward a theory of family communication. *Communication Theory*, *12*(1), 70–91. doi:10.1111/j.1468-2885.2002.tb00260.x

Kofman, Y. B., & Garfin, D. R. (2020). Home is not always a haven: The domestic violence crisis amid the COVID-19 pandemic. *Psychological Trauma: Theory, Research, Practice, and Policy*, *12*(1), 199–201. doi:10.1037/tra0000866 PMID:32478558

Lillie, H. M., Venetis, M. K., & Chernichky-Karcher, S. (2023). Resilience communication mitigates the negative relational effects of topic avoidance: Evidence from parental caregiving and COVID-19 pandemic contexts. *Personal Relationships*, 1–22. doi:10.1111/pere.12508

Liu, K., Yang, Y., Li, M., Li, S., Sun, K., & Zhao, Y. (2021). Parents' and adolescents' perceptions of parental involvement and their relationships with depression among Chinese middle school students during the COVID-19 pandemic. *Children and Youth Services Review, 129*, 106190. doi:10.1016/j.childyouth.2021.106190 PMID:34511675

Luetke, M., Hensel, D., Herbenick, D., & Rosenberg, M. (2020). Romantic relationship conflict due to the COVID-19 pandemic and changes in intimate and sexual behaviors in a nationally representative sample of American adults. *Journal of Sex & Marital Therapy, 46*(8), 747–762. doi:10.1080/0092623X.2020.1810185 PMID:32878584

Maguire, K. (2012). *Stress and coping in families*. Polity Press.

Malecki, C. K., & Demaray, M. K. (2003). What type of support do they need? Investigating student adjustment as related to emotional, informational, appraisal, and instrumental support. *School Psychology Quarterly, 18*(3), 231–252. doi:10.1521cpq.18.3.231.22576

Marks, L. D., Dollahite, D. C., Kelley, H. H., Kimball, E. R., & James, S. (2023). Exploring influences of the COVID-19 pandemic on family communication: Negative, positive, or both? *Marriage & Family Review, 59*(2), 121–142. doi:10.1080/01494929.2023.2170014

Martin, L. N., Giff, S. T., Ribeiro, S., Fyffe, S., & Renshaw, K. D. (2022). Changes in relationship quality in the COVID-19 pandemic: Associations with pandemic stressors and couple communication. *The American Journal of Family Therapy*, 1–17. doi:10.1080/01926187.2022.2073293

McDaniel, B. T. (2019). Parent distraction with phones, reasons for use, and impacts on parenting and child outcomes: A review of the emerging research. *Human Behavior and Emerging Technologies, 1*(2), 72–80. doi:10.1002/hbe2.139

McDaniel, B. T., & Coyne, S. M. (2016). "Technoference": The interference of technology in couple relationships and implications for women's personal and relational well-being. *Psychology of Popular Media Culture, 5*(1), 85–98. doi:10.1037/ppm0000065

Mikucki-Enyart, S. L., & Maguire, K. C. (2021). Introduction to the special ıssue on family communication in the Covıd-19 pandemic. *Journal of Family Communication, 21*(3), 145–151. doi:10.1080/15267431.2021.1933038

Montag, C., & Elhai, J. D. (2020). Discussing digital technology overuse in children and adolescents during the COVID-19 pandemic and beyond: On the importance of considering Affective Neuroscience Theory. *Addictive Behaviors Reports, 12*, 100313. doi:10.1016/j.abrep.2020.100313 PMID:33364321

Nagy, E., Thompson, P., Mayor, L., & Doughty, H. (2021). Do foetuses communicate? Foetal responses to interactive versus non-interactive maternal voice and touch: An exploratory analysis. *Infant Behavior and Development, 63*, 101562. doi:10.1016/j.infbeh.2021.101562 PMID:33831801

Ogolsky, B. G., & Monk, J. K. (2019). Dating and couple formation. In B. H. Fiese, M. Celano, K. Deater-Deckard, E. N. Jouriles, & M. A. Whisman (Eds.), APA handbook of contemporary family psychology: Vol. 1. Foundations, methods, and contemporary issues across the lifespan (pp. 427–443). American Psychological Association. doi:10.1037/0000099-024

Prime, H., Wade, M., & Browne, D. T. (2020). Risk and resilience in family well-being during the COVID-19 pandemic. *The American Psychologist, 75*(5), 631–643. doi:10.1037/amp0000660 PMID:32437181

Sharma, A. (2021). Positive impacts of COVID-19 pandemic on various aspects. *Psychology (Savannah, Ga.), 58*(2), 430–436. doi:10.17762/pae.v58i2.1868

Skalacka, K., & Pajestka, G. (2021). Digital or In-Person: The relationship between mode of interpersonal communication during the COVID-19 pandemic and mental health in older adults from 27 countries. *Journal of Family Nursing, 27*(4), 275–284. doi:10.1177/10748407211031980 PMID:34286604

Solomon, D. H., Knobloch, L. K., Theiss, J. A., & McLaren, R. M. (2016). Relational turbulence theory: Explaining variation and subjective experiences and communication within romantic relationships. *Human Communication Research, 42*(4), 507–532. doi:10.1111/hcre.12091

Stafford, L. (2020). Communal strength, exchange orientation, equity, and relational maintenance. *Journal of Social and Personal Relationships, 37*(8–9), 2345–2365. doi:10.1177/0265407520923741

Usher, K., Bhullar, N., Durkin, J., Gyamfi, N., & Jackson, D. (2020). Family violence and COVID-19: Increased vulnerability and reduced options for support. *International Journal of Mental Health Nursing, 29*(4), 549–552. doi:10.1111/inm.12735 PMID:32314526

Weaver, J. L., & Swank, J. M. (2021). Parents' lived experiences with the COVID-19 pandemic. *The Family Journal (Alexandria, Va.), 29*(2), 136–142. doi:10.1177/1066480720969194

Wolfers, L. N., & Schneider, F. M. (2020). Using media for coping: A scoping review. *Communication Research*, 1–25. doi:10.1177/0093650220939778

Chapter 17
Verification Platforms in Combating Disinformation on COVID-19 Vaccine News "Dogrula"

Aygül Atay
Independent Researcher, Turkey

ABSTRACT

This chapter examines the fact-checking content focusing on misinformation and fake news about COVID-19 vaccines, especially in the media, through the example of Doğrula (doğrula.org), an international fact-checking organization (ICFN) approved fact-checking platform. The data were obtained from the website of the relevant platform (www.dogrula.org). Based on the problem that many distortions, fake news, and claims about COVID-19 vaccines are shared through digital media, the study examines Doğrula's evaluations of the posts about COVID-19 vaccines circulated in digital media channels. The descriptive analysis method, one of the qualitative research types, was used in the study. Data were obtained through the document analysis technique. Due to a large amount of data to be analyzed within the scope of the study, it covers a one-year period from 25.02.2021 to 25.02.2022, the date when Doğrula first published content.

"Because it is difficult to tell the truth, there is only one truth, but this truth is alive, and therefore its face is constantly changing like that of a living creature"

Franz Kafka

DOI: 10.4018/979-8-3693-0896-7.ch017

SUMMARY

In the digital media environment, disinformation content called "misinformation" or "fake news" spreads rapidly and reaches the masses. For example, during the Covid-19 pandemic, much fake news was produced about vaccines, which are seen as one of the effective methods of preventing or preventing the disease. All this constituted one of the prominent examples of the phenomenon defined as "infodemic". Verification platforms, which aim to provide individuals with accurate information, have a severe role in combating the "infodemic" in terms of detecting and verifying false information and fake news. In the post-truth era, we are in, many changes have occurred with the development of communication technologies. With the increase in digitalization, individuals have become producers-consumers by creating and disseminating news on social media. As a result, Digital channels have surpassed traditional media in terms of access to news. According to the Reuters Institute 2021 Digital News Report, social media has overtaken television as Turkey's most used news source (2022).

With the spread of digitalization and new media channels, the number of information and news sources is increasing daily. This has made news production no longer an area of specialization, and individuals have shifted from being consumers to producers. Thus, the problem of misinformation and fake news has become increasingly widespread. With the speed of dissemination in the digital environment, this misinformation and fake news can reach large masses within minutes. WHO conceptualized this situation as "misinformation epidemic", in other words, "infodemic". Verification platforms, which emerged as a response to the spread of misinformation and fake news, play a functional role in confirming the accuracy of the news or information shared. Through verification platforms, confusion is eliminated, and the source of information is questioned. Although the need for news verification dates back to ancient times, the possibilities of new media have paved the way for the emergence of digital verification platforms (Kavaklı, 2009). Digital verification platforms enable "...the evaluation of verifiable claims in public statements through the investigation of primary and secondary sources" (Brandtzaeg and Folstad, 2017: 65).

Verification platforms, which emerged in the US in the 2000s, spread all over the world in a short period. The increase in the number of fact-checking platforms worldwide has created the need to create standardization by bringing these platforms together. In 2015, the International Fact-Checking Network (IFCN) was established within the Poynter Institute for Media Studies in Florida, USA. The IFCN has set some principles for news verification platforms and named this Code of Principles. Fact-checking platforms that undertake to create content following these principles become IFCN signatories as members of the network. The membership control of the signatory platforms is reviewed every year, and the memberships of the platforms that meet the conditions are renewed. Three verification platforms from Turkey are members of this network and are IFCN signatories. The first one is Doğruluk Payı, the second one is Teyit, and the third one is Doğrula. These verification platforms have played an active role in verifying health issues, related claims, misinformation, and fake news that emerged during the Covid-19 pandemic.

In this context, this study examines the fact-checking content focusing on misinformation and fake news about Covid-19 vaccines, especially in the media, through the example of Doğrula (doğrula.org), an International Fact-Checking Organization (ICFN) approved fact-checking platform. The data was obtained from the website of the relevant platform (www.dogrula.org). Based on the problem that many distortions, fake news, and claims about Covid-19 vaccines are shared through digital media, the study examines Doğrula's evaluations of the posts about Covid-19 vaccines circulated in digital media channels. The descriptive analysis method, one of the qualitative research types, was used in the study. Data were obtained through the document analysis technique. Due to a large amount of data to be analyzed within the scope of the study, it covers a one-year period from 25.02.2021 to 25.02.2022, the date when Doğrula first published content.

INTRODUCTION

After the 2016 US Presidential elections, the concept of "fake news" has become a focal point for journalism. Although 2019 is the year the concept gained momentum, this is not a new phenomenon. The concept of "disinformation" during the World Wars and "freak journalism" or "yellow journalism" during the Spanish Wars dates back to 1896 (Campbell, 2001; Crain, 2017'den akt. Molina, Sundar, Le ve Lee, 2019: 4). Fake news is news without verifiable facts, where the core of the story is a fabrication. Sometimes this is deliberately designed to mislead readers, sometimes it is clickbait. Recently, it is observed that the number of such news has increased, especially due to its easy and fast dissemination online. Along with fake news, digital tools make it easier for a large number of actors to produce and quickly disseminate various types of content text, images, bots, etc. (McGonagle, 2017: 206). In the digital age, the spread of misinformation is a major problem. The public is misinformed and misled by news containing false information. According to Molina, Sundar, Le, and Lee (2019), fake news or fabricated information that is false has become a major phenomenon in the context of digital media (ss. 1). In the post-truth era, it can be said that the impact of false news has increased not only in the media but also in many different fields. It is possible to see the effects of this situation especially during political election periods. On the one hand, this effect can be observed in major events that affect society. The spread of misinformation and fake news increases in situations such as pandemics, conflicts and natural disasters. In 2019, all measures, treatments and precautions taken to protect against the coronavirus outbreak that has affected the world are of course very important. However, access to accurate information and protection from disinformation caused by false news is just as important in this process. Accuracy and impartiality are among the principles of journalism. Especially in news on health, these principles should be emphasized more in terms of their impact on society. Hundreds of misinformation and fake news about the Covid-19 pandemic and vaccines have been circulated digitally. In this process, just as the coronavirus turned into a pandemic, misinformation and fake news turned into an infodemic called "misinformation epidemic" (World Health Organization [WHO], nd).

Basic journalistic principles such as source verification, fact-checking and accountability can easily be bypassed or ignored by individuals or organizations sharing content on Twitter, Facebook or other social networks. The impact of this is often described in terms such as "trolls", "fake news", "fake media" and "alternative facts". The neglect of the ethical dimension of journalism in social media negatively affects the credibility of news. The involvement of users in news production and sharing leads to the emergence of concepts such as fake and misleading news. Given the proliferation and rapid spread of fake news and misinformation in digital environments, individuals alone are no longer sufficient to access accurate information. This has created the need for verification platforms where users can check suspicious information. Meeting this requirement is especially useful in eliminating information confusion on issues where there are conflicting views. Although the need for news verification dates back to ancient times, the possibilities of the new media environment have led to the emergence of verification platforms in digital media. Digital verification platforms enable "...the assessment of verifiable claims in public statements through the investigation of primary and secondary sources" (Brandtzaeg ve Folstad, 2017: 65). Initially emerging in the US in the 2000s, the history of verification platforms has extended to Turkey. The International Fact-Checking Network, founded in 2015 by the Poynter Institute, aims to bring together fact-checking platforms from around the world. These are the core principles of the IFCN guidelines: commitment to impartiality, commitment to transparency of sources, commitment to transparency of financial resources and organizational structure, commitment to transparency of methods and procedures, and commitment to open and honest verification. These principles provide a common ground for verification platforms. Although there are dozens of fact-checking organizations in Turkey, the verification platforms that are recognized as compliant with IFCN principles and have the IFCN badge are Doğruluk Payı, Teyit and Doğrula. These verification platforms have played an active role in verifying health issues, related claims, misinformation and fake news that have emerged during the Covid-19 pandemic.

The study examined verification content focusing on misinformation and fake news about Covid-19 vaccines, especially in the media, through the sample of Doğrula (doğrula.org), an International Fact-Checking Organization (ICFN) approved verification platform. Data was obtained from the website of the relevant platform (www.dogrula.org). Based on the problematic of sharing many distortions, fake news and allegations about Covid-19 vaccines through digital media, Doğrula's evaluations of the posts circulated in digital media channels about Covid-19 vaccines are discussed. Descriptive analysis method, one of the qualitative research types, was used in the study. Data were obtained through document analysis technique. Due to the large amount of data to be analyzed within the scope of the study, the sample covers the one-year period from 25.02.2021 to 25.02.2022, the date when Doğrula first published content. The study is limited to the claims, information and news about Covid-19 vaccines covered by the "Doğrula" platform in 2021 and 2022. Verify was chosen because it is an IFCN signatory (member) and a platform that frequently raises Covid-19 allegations.

In this study, firstly, the concept of post-truth and the dissemination of false news in digital media in the "post-truth" era we are in are explained. In the second part, the new media order in the post-truth era is mentioned and disinformation on social media in the post-truth era is addressed. At the same time, the concepts of misinformation and fake news and the "infodemic" that came to the agenda with the pandemic were discussed. The third part of the article provides general information about verification platforms and the functioning of the "Dogrula.org" platform in the sample. The fourth section presents the findings and the evaluation of these findings within the framework of the examination of news and information on Covid-19 vaccines and the vaccination process by Doğrula.

AN OVERVIEW OF THE CONCEPT OF POST-TRUTH

The concept of post-truth was first coined in 1992 by the American It is mentioned in the article "Government of Lies" by Steve Tesich in The Nation magazine. Tesich states in his article that a large part of the American public accepts without question the political propaganda of the Bush administration as fact (Özkaya, 2020). Tesich argues that events such as the Watergate Scandal, the Iran-Contra Scandal and the Gulf War have affected the US public's connection with reality. Tesich argued that these experiences lead individuals to equate the truth with bad news and push them to avoid the truth (Toktay, 2019: 44). In a sense, Tesich criticizes the fact that people no longer seek the truth but rather accept the information they encounter without questioning it. Later, the concept of post-truth was elaborated by American academic Ralph Keyes in his 2004 book "The Post-Truth Era: Dishonesty and Deception in Contemporary Life" published by American academic Ralph Keyes in 2004. In the book, Keyes argues that the lies told by authorities have numbed society, making lying easy and commonplace. Like Tesich, Keyes also noted that these have the effect of desensitizing society to the lies that are exposed (Schackmuth, 2018: 13; Doruk Şahin, 2018: 152; Toktay, 2019: 44). The author explains that in the post-truth age, lying is done using softer sounding words. Keyes depicts the concept of the after-truth as an unethical twilight zone that allows us to conceal the truth without thinking we are liars (Keyes, 2004: 22'den akt. Çöllüoğu,: 100). Keyes describes this period as "the product of an era in which honesty has become nothing" (Keyes, 2004'den akt. Köse, 2020:201).

Since it was chosen as the word of the year in 2016, the concept of "post-truth" has become highly visible and has been frequently discussed in the context of news ethics. The Oxford Dictionary defines post-truth as "a state in which objective facts are less influential in forming public opinion than emotions and personal beliefs" (Oxford Dictionaries, 2021). The concept is explained in relation to Trump's winning the presidency of the United States of America and the widespread discourse that the resources belonging to the British health system were transferred to the European Union during the Brexit process. The foundations of the concept of post-truth are discussed under different headings according to researchers. Yalın Alpay explained the foundations of this period as postmodernism, new media, declining trust in democracy and populism. Although researchers approach the concept from different perspectives, the impact of postmodernism and the proliferation of new media environments constitute a common denominator in terms of studies. While postmodern thinkers characterize the concept of post-truth as a meaning, they argue that meaning is a construction and think that there cannot be a single meaning, meaning can change subjectively and therefore cannot be an objective truth. In this postmodern age where truth has become insignificant, different truths created by individuals according to their ideology are created and circulated in the digital media environment.

POST-TRUTH NEW MEDIA

With the technology that Castells conceptualized as "web 2.0", users have become active in the internet environment from a passive state and have become not only consumers of media content but also producers of this content (Castells, 2013). While the activation of users is a positive development in terms of freedom of expression, it has negative consequences for the spread of misinformation. Although it is seen that social media creates an environment of freedom for individuals and allows them to present different opinions, it highlights that individuals are constantly exposed to similar ideas through concepts such as "echo chambers" and "filter bubbles" and are exposed to posts around certain topics.

Alçiçek (2021) states that new media channels are places of distorting memory and that new media channels are the application area of the beyond the truth (ss. 195). In the post-truth era, it has become impossible to distinguish what is true and what is false in the digital media environment. This situation has raised "the problem of the dissemination of produced content before it has matured and its accuracy has been verified" (Bayraktutan ve Binark, 2013: 70). According to Al-Rawi (2019), social media has increased the spread of fake news due to its integrated shareability and connectivity features (ss. 688). While the digital world has transformed the way news content is presented, disseminated and consumed, it has also created different options in news production. It is no longer only the manipulation of the news text, but also the modification of content such as photographs and videos with digital tools and the dissemination of misinformation. This situation has brought along the possibility that a certain part of the news may be wrong rather than the whole news. Kavaklı (2019) states that certain journalistic practices play an important role in the proliferation of the production of false or fake news. Kavaklı (2019), in his study titled "Combating Fake News and Internet Verification Platforms", explains that reasons such as the commercial concerns of digital media, users becoming producers-consumers and the difficulty of control mechanisms in social media can cause the spread of fake news on social media (ss. 677-678). One of the biggest problems in the post-truth era is the production of fake news and its rapid dissemination. Aydın (2020) characterizes the biases that make social media vulnerable to misinformation as three types: cognitive, social and algorithm-related biases. Cognitive bias refers to the use of the brain in processing information. The brain, bombarded with information, uses shortcuts to process information. Social bias refers to bias arising from the social plane. It is explained in terms of having an idea about a user by looking at other users they follow. Algorithm-driven bias is the type of bias structured by search engines or social media that reinforces social prejudices and makes users vulnerable (Kocabay Şener, 2018: 360-361). Algorithms bring up areas that users interact with. In this way, in the context of post-truth, it creates an obstacle to accessing accurate information. Thus, in a world of manipulation, users continue to spread fake news, oblivious to everything. Social media channels have taken various steps to combat disinformation. Facebook and Instagram have started working with IFCN member verification platforms, and TikTok has also partnered with verification organizations. Twitter, with its new name X, aims to prevent misinformation with its Birdwatch feature. The Birdwatch feature tests the process by which posts containing false information are flagged by specific people. Allows people to identify information in Tweets they feel is misleading and write notes that provide informative context (Coleman, 2021). WhatsApp has restricted forwarded messages. Although these steps taken by digital platforms may seem like small efforts, they are very important steps in the fight against disinformation. Studies show that false news on social networks spreads faster, farther and deeper than real news (Törnberg, 2018: 2). The increase in disinformation and users' belief in misinformation or fake news has brought the debate on combating disinformation to the agenda. In 2019, fake news and misinformation about the coronavirus outbreak and vaccines that affected the world revealed the importance of combating disinformation. The number of verification platforms that play an important role in this struggle is increasing both in Turkey and around the World. In this respect, verification platforms that examine the allegations raised on social media, check the information and share it with the public have come to the fore. In 2015, the International Fact-Checking Newtwork (IFCN) organization was established to bring together fact-checking platforms around the world to operate in line with certain principles. IFCN supports verification platforms and the fight against misinformation through its trainings and the projects it supports. The current IFCN member verification platforms in Turkey are Doğruluk Payı, Teyit and Doğrula.

FACT CHECKING AND VERIFICATION PLATFORMS

In the post-truth era, in digital environments, individuals spread misinformation to increase their visibility, to be liked and for many other reasons. It can be said that the spread of disinformation increases especially in posts made during social events such as fires, epidemics and natural disasters. In emergencies, digital media has become an information overload. As a solution to the problem of disinformation in the digital environment, tools, technologies and techniques aimed at informing about verification have emerged in many countries (Silverman, 2015: 9). Verification platforms, which have the task of combating disinformation and informing the public accurately, have adopted certain principles in the verification process. The details of these principles may vary between platforms, but in general, verification platforms are based on objectivity, transparency, reliability and openness. Fact-checking organizations examine and evaluate claims, news, information or discourse against a set of standards. Platforms should publish their principles and guidelines on their websites and make them accessible to users. In 2015, the Poynter Institute launched the International Fact-Checking Network, which aims to bring together fact-checking platforms from around the world. The IFCN has set out the basic principles that verification platforms should adhere to and created a guideline. These principles are: commitment to the principle of impartiality, commitment to the principle of transparency of sources, commitment to the principle of transparency of financial resources and organizational structure, commitment to transparency of methods and procedures, and commitment to open and honest verification. These principles provide a common denominator for verification platforms in general. Verification platforms aiming to become IFCN signatories can apply regardless of country, provided that they fulfill the necessary conditions. If deemed appropriate as a result of IFCN assessments, the platform becomes an IFCN signatory for one year, i.e. it carries the IFCN badge. IFCN is not a membership-only organization, but is open to participation by any organization that adopts IFCN's principles and is certified by independent auditors who adhere to those principles (Uzunoğlu & Uyar, 2021: 8).

The history of news verification dates back to the emergence of journalism. With the "new journalism" practices that developed after the 1890s, verification became an integral part of the workflow (EDAM, 2020: 2). Snopes, the world's first independent fact-checking platform, was founded in 1994. Spinsanity4, founded in the same years, is also among the first examples. Founded in 2003, FactCheck.org, PolitiFact and MediaMatters in 2004, and NewsBusters in 2005, the fact-checking platform has spread rapidly around the World (EDAM, 2020: 2). On the other hand, First Draft Network (firstdraftnews.com) was established in 2015 to combat fake news. Various media organizations, agencies and platforms have become members. In 2017, Google launched a fact-checking service to verify news and articles (Eroğlu ve Çakmak, 2020: 312).

The fight against disinformation in Turkey, as in the rest of the world, started with the impact of digitalization. In the information age, which is also called the information age, fact-checking mechanisms need to keep pace with these technological developments. This is where the concept of independence comes to the fore. Verification bodies are divided into two in terms of their structure. The first is the fact-checking mechanisms within the corporate media structure, and the second is the fact-checking centers established by civic initiatives (Uzunoğlu & Uyar, 2021: 9). There is no fact-checking center within the corporate media in Turkey, although there is a need for institutions of two different structures to coexist (Şener, 2018'den akt. Uzunoğlu & Uyar, 2021: 10).

"DOGRULA.ORG" AS A DIGITAL VERIFICATION PLATFORM

The website dogrula.org was launched in 2017 with the aim of verifying suspicious information and news circulating on the internet. Doğrula, which started publishing in 2017-2019 with a different structure and editorial staff, was taken over by the Digital Society Research Association as of February 2021. Since then, the entire structure and staff of Doğrula has changed (dijitaltoplumarastirmalari.org). The Digital Society Research Association aims to facilitate and improve the quality of learning through digital channels with the motto "conscious digital society". In this framework, it aims to produce projects that will increase the fight against information pollution and spread awareness of digital media literacy" and one of these projects is the website named doğrula.org (dijitaltoplumarastirmalari.org/hakkimizda). Doğrula states that he acts with the awareness that verifications without a basis will affect the sector over time and emphasizes that they make their verifications impartially by basing them on a foundation. At the top of the website of the verification platform dogrula.org are the categories about us, verifications, from the team and contact us. The Validations category is divided into validations, election 2023 and Covid-19 (https://www.dogrula.org). In the Verifications category, the accuracy of claims that are especially on the agenda, frequently circulated by users and highly interactive are verified. Validations are currently scored as true and false, and some claims are accompanied by details of how they are false. When the content of the verification is entered, the name and photo of the author who evaluated the claim are displayed in the upper right corner. Below this are the platforms and names of the platforms where the news was disseminated, and just below this are the sources. In the conclusion section, the assessment of the accuracy of the news is stated. Below the evaluation, the claim is given as it is in circulation. The evidence section includes information on which sources or data the author used during the evaluation. Doğrula is eligible to become an IFCN signatory on September 8, 2022.

ALLEGATIONS ABOUT COVID-19 VACCINES IN DOĞRULA

Table 1. COVID-19 vaccine in relation to claims (table, dogrula.org on the site that was created to be compiled from analysis)

Analysis Date On	News/Share The Title Of The	Know to Share/Claim For	the result of the verification
2021 April 14,	Turkey's domestic coronavirus vaccine Phase 3 phase emergency use Approval could receive the idea that	'Turkey's first indigenous vaccine, Phase-3 phase you can get approved for emergency use'	Right
15 April 2021	19 million in Turkey vaccination in the front row in the world with the claim that	"Turkey vaccination numeral 19 million ranks first in the world" rhetoric	-is misleading
April 19, 2021	from ear to ear: how vaccines 'trash' happened?	"Never in the trash vaccine to the appointment of the person who's not coming he's gone"	Wrong
April 30, 2021	delaying the second dose of the vaccine reduces the rate of protection against the virus of claim	BioNTech vaccine 2. the dose of the vaccine will lessen the impact to be made 6-8 weeks	-
June 18, 2021	Covid-19 vaccine to people magnet feature doesn't get	Covid-19 vaccine after vaccination with vaccine shot that sees the function of the body where the metal and pulled magnet	False
, June 18, 2021	that could go to Germany and those who are not Vaccinated	"two doses of the travelers from Turkey, Germany Biontech vaccine requirement brought the"	Wrong
June 25, 2021	of vaccines for the Covid-19 variants of the Delta is ineffective against the claim that	'vaccinesineffective', 'NewWavesounds'	Wrong
25 June 2021	in the UK, USA and Covid-19 vaccine payment of the claim that	President Recep Tayyip Erdogan's AK Party provincial advisory June 25, 2021 Hatay Expanded in his speech at the meeting of Europe and in the US both in the most advanced parts in Covid-19 vaccine expressed that they are paid.	Wrong

Table 1. Continued

Analysis Date On	News/Share The Title Of The	Know to Share/Claim For	the result of the verification
June 29, 2021	Biontech rebels 'inflammation of the heart' very rare side effects	Pfizer-BioNTech vaccine in young men of heart inflammationin the lead.	-
June 30, 2021	second dose is different Covid-19 vaccine to be 'better protection' claim that	scientists 1. dose 2. the dose Covid-19 vaccine they claim that the implementation of more effective	-
June 30, 2021	12-year-old racket and the cause of death was Covid-19 vaccine not	Giavazzi of the first Covid-19 vaccine his life after he was shot kaybettigI claim	False,
July 2, 2021	Pfizer-BioNTech vaccine, 99% of graphene oxide contains a claim	Pfizer-BioNTech vaccine, 99% of graphene oxide included. Moreover, this graphene oxide can affect the human body with the claim that the	False
9 July 2021	BioNTech emergency vaccine approved for use in Turkey are there?	"Dr. Ümit Aktaş" share your account with BioNTech emergency vaccine approved for use in Turkey and was not completed Phase 3 studies of this vaccine is not getting claimed.	-
July 19, 2021	in Canada Covid-19 vaccine pilots can fly with the	pilots in Canada is prohibited to fly when all infused	Wrong
2021 July 19,	Mike Tyson T-shirt anti-vaccine message does not contain	Mike Tyson "in God I trust vaccines not to" T-shirt with anti-vaccine message to give to pose for photos and alleged that Tyson anti-vaccine claim that is	False
2021 July 19	Covid-19 vaccine to the people who receive the claim that the blood can't give	blood for the Red Cross refused to give the claim that people who have been vaccinated,	False
2021 July 28	anti-vaccine doctor Eleonora Brigliadori an Italian actress by the name of	#Aldanmaasiolmaturkiyetagon Twitter was among the titles agenda. "Italian doctor after 18 months after vaccination, people will begin to fall like flies, warned that" the claim that	False
2021 July 29,	The Simpsons scene anti-vaccine message responding	to The Simpsons in the effect of the vaccine information regarding the claim with	False
10 August 2021	BioNTech of the founders and Uğur şahin Özlem turec Covid-19 vaccine had	BioNTech of the founders and Ugur Sahin Özlem turec 's Covid-19 claim that a vaccine is not	False,
2021 August 16,	Bill Gates and Melinda French Gates Covid-19 vaccine rejected	the claim that it does not and Ugur Sahin Özlem turec	False,
August 17, 2021	Delta depends on the variant in the UK, only 64% of deaths, is composed of vaccinated individuals	in the UK Covid-19-related deaths%64% from the hangingconsists of the claim that	False
25 August 2021	Sean Brooks not Medicine Residency Training	Sena Brooks Covid-19 mRNA vaccine against the rebels in a video for some of the claims you make, and that person is that of a doctorate, from Oxford is at 23% is the publication of book 48, 21 years of expertise in the field of Physiology in medicine to say that it is	Wrong
2021 August 27,	minister of Australia Dominello his claim that the vaccine had facial palsy after	the minister's covid-19 vaccine that had facial palsy after the claim	False
, August 31, 2021	implanted in the body for the chip is detected with the claim that a QR reader,	QR (Datamatrix) you open the program the next arm closer to read the chip 's claim that	False

Table 1. Continued

Analysis Date On	News/Share The Title Of The	Know to Share/Claim For	the result of the verification
2021 September 6,	Uğur şahin end of the year until 1 trillion dose not 3 billion doses of vaccine will be produced has announced that	BioNTech offounder Ugur Sahin, BioNTech and Pfizer Partnership a trillion dose of the vaccine that it will producethe description of the claim	False,
September 8, 2021	demonstrators in Brazil rebel were gathering to protest	in Brazil on September 7,demonstrations, referring to thisglobal protest on a scale of a rebel is the claim that	False
2021 September 8	'universal vaccination the U.S. Supreme Court has canceled' the claim that	the U.S. Supreme Court's Covid-Found harmful for the canceled claim 19 universal vaccination vaccines	False,
September 9, 2021	251 times more carrying the virus is hitting on the claim that	the Delta variant in fully vaccinated individuals viral load 251 times more claim that is	False,
September 13, 2021	get rid of Romania and killing people are stopped on the grounds that the claim that	by the government of Romania of coronavirus could not be stopped and isolated vaccination vaccines, citing that took people to die, in other countries they are marketing their hands remaining in the claim that the vaccines	False
2021 14 September,	the Reuters News title 'the new rule about testing and vaccination in The' Associated	Reuters in Maltepe anti-vaccine rally "thousands of people protested the new Turkish vaccine and test rules," header to the service claim	True
14 September 2021	mRNA claim that vaccines cause blood to clot	mRNA vaccines that cause the blood to clot claim	False
15 September 2021	Fatih Erbakan mRNA vaccines claim that it alters the DNA of	Erbakan mRNA with no change future generations of human DNA vaccines and non-resembling a human being to be born, they claimed.	Wrong
23 September 2021	Fatih Erbakan's showed that the modified DNA was alleged that babies	Erbakan,a press conferenceat tailed, three-armed, one-eyed by showing pictures of babies are covered with hair and his whole body mRNA vaccines claimed that caused this situation.	Wrong
2021 September 24	of that claim is not a medical doctor and tureci Uğur şahin Özlem	Özlem Uğur şahin is not a medical doctor and of the claim that turecito pair with it and produced a covid-19 vaccine doubts about the reliability of	Wrong
27 September 2021	babies Ozdag Hope Covid-19 vaccine claim is made to the	new born babies Covid-19 vaccine to the claim that there is	False
2021 September 28	photo of human blood showing that unvaccinated hanging and come in different colors	and hanging on the images of blood was taken from the claim that unvaccinated people	False
3 October 2021	in Gibraltar, 100%after vaccination was not brought under curfew	in Gibraltar vaccination despite the completion of covid-19 cases are on the rise for this reason, when the application starts quarantine for 14 days, the claim that	False
2021 October 6	Video in Romania, the anti-vaccine protest doesn't show	a video that's In Romania Covid-19 vaccine to the claim that the actions of	False
2021 12 October	Coronavirus vaccine, due to the claim that the baby was born completely black eyes with	Coronavirus vaccine because it is completely black and the claim that a newborn baby's eyes experienced various health problems tolerances	False
, October 13, 2021	Pfizer COVID-19 vaccine Comirnaty received FDA approval in the name	of Pfizer COVID-19 vaccine by the U.S. Food and Drug Administration (FDA) approval is not the claim that	False

Table 1. Continued

Analysis Date On	News/Share The Title Of The	Know to Share/Claim For	the result of the verification
19 October 2021	Gates vaccines to reduce the population didn't want to use	the gates in the video, he said he would never use, the claim that the population is decreasing	False,
October 20, 2021	dead or official evidence that the pilot made an emergency landing there	, American Airlines, Delta Airlines pilot 2.COVID-19 vaccine to claim that died during the flight after	Wrong
20 October 2021	interference in the image 'Pzifer' didn't make the vaccine	interference in the video Pzifer the claim that the vaccine is the cause of	False
2021 October 20,	vaccine research and production in fetal cell lines used in	COVID-19 vaccine in the fetus that are included in the claim	False
22 October 2021	four legs and sleeves Baby was born to pregnant women, the reason mRNA vaccine for	the reason why the baby was born four legs and sleevesof the pregnant women mRNA vaccine claim that is	False,
October 26, 2021	Hijama therapy Covid-Claim to rid the body 19 vaccine	be vaccinated but didn't want to do it anyway, just in case survival for the rest of you from the effects of this vaccine for purposes ofleechesmethods should be used, such as the claim that	False
2021 October 27	fainted from the excitement of talking to Prince Charles, died from the vaccine	vaccine center, was taken on a visit to Charles, and Charles gone down while talking with the person that hangsiclaims	False
2021 October 28,	the Ministry of Health in Ireland vaccine-related sudden death, and there was a poster that contains a warning	poster at the entrance to the rebel headquarters in Ireland, a warning of sudden death the claim that contained	False
2021 November 5,	stop the infusion of Japan and ivermectin treatment, the occurrence of the claim	is discarded and vaccines in Japan Ivermectin treatment that is passed to the claim	False
11 November 2021	Red Cross, Covid-19 accept blood donations from those who rebel	"people who have been vaccinated can't give blood, the claim of	False
2021 November 17	common side effect of the vaccine the government of Australia to pay compensation to people	on Twitter wouldbe a sharing, and some news sites, accordingIn Australiatens of thousands of people Covid-19vaccines and the sideeffects are due to the Australian government to sue led.	-
18 November 2021	Australia's Hospital of occupancy Covid-19 vaccine has nothing to do with	Australia's Hospital of occupancy Covid-19 vaccineoriginated from the claim that	False
2021 November 19	vaccine research, it's not cause climate change show	Users heart defects are actually COVID-19 vaccines can cause side effects, but this is shown the reasons of climate change in order to cover up the claim of	False
2021 November 25,	claimed to be due to Vaccine really love priest,	the priest in the video, Covid-19 vaccine is due to the claim that	False
2021 November 29,	Dr. Thomas, who committed suicide Jendges he didn't leave behind any notes	Dr. jendges to in his suicide note, "now Covid-19 vaccine that occurred in the face of Genocide you didn't want to be a part of a part" he wrote that the claim	is false
2 December 2021	vaccination Swedish passport under the skin micro chip implants application is not passed to	Sweden Covid-19 rebel passport for a microchip under the skin when you start the application specifies that the claim	is false
2021 December 8,	Uğur şahin video is old, dated, Dr. Hawk had two doses of	"Pfizer CEO Dr. Ugur Sahin, produced by the company Pfizer, BioNTech it wasn't the vaccine.the claim of " the	False

Table 1. Continued

Analysis Date On	News/Share The Title Of The	Know to Share/Claim For	the result of the verification
9 December 2021	died from congestion of the children not being vaccinated in the video,	the video of the kids in Covid-19 vaccine is due to the claim that	False
2021 15 December	the German farmers 'protest pandemic has nothing to do with	the German farmers' protestof the claim that the vaccine is related to	False
24 December 2021	the World Health Organization has distorted the words of the president of the	DSO of the head of "some countries are using vaccines to kill children," said the claim was	False,
January 11, 2022	Rebel was Health Minister. Images of being replaced, the injector vaccine	dose reminder while Fahrettin Big TURKOVAC the nurse of the vial and the syringe filled inside take the medication injector replace it with anotherdFDA's claim	False
2022 January 19,	the World Health Organization's Covid-19 vaccine, of which 2.5 million is a side effect that he admits the claim that	the World Health Organization's Covid-19 vaccine, of which 2.5 million is a side effect that he admits the claim that	False
20 January 2022	World Health Organization, the reminder dose meaningless' has made a public statement	'Who dose reminder meaningless' description in the form of his claim	False
24 January 2022	Vaccine Center in England it is not required by law has been closed due to safety concerns	in the UK the Vaccine Centeris closed in accordance with the law of the claim that	False
26 January 2022	Athlete Dalila Jakupovic to having a stroke about Covid-19 not	Dalila Jakupovic to you about having a stroke, the cause of Covid-19 vaccine is the claim that	False
26 January 2022	in France Covid-19 vaccine is an obstacle to the claim that life insurance	and the insurance company stated that the vaccine is sourced from the death of experimental drugs and treatments that are not covered by insurance refused to pay the family of the person asserting the claim that	False
2 February 2022	rebel against the idea that the protest made konvoyl truckers Italian passport	Italian passport rebel against truckers convoy protest his claim	False
2022 February 4	Bill Gates "Vaccination with 15% of the population can be reduced by," said the claim,	"Microsoft founder Bill Gates, in a TED Talk in 2010, vaccination of the world's population with about 10-15% that could reduce up to be announced." the claim is	False,
February 7, 2022	Pope Francis, "to enter heaven covid-19 vaccine required" there's no evidence that says	Pope Francis, "to enter heaven covid-19 vaccine required" that says the claim is	False
February 18, 2022	Australia the images in the anti-vaccine protesters claim that showing	the images in Australia, the anti-vaccine Protesters showthe claim Digi	False

DISCUSSION AND CONCLUSION

The Covid-19 pandemic has not only been a health problem, but has also brought along a situation that has led to the spread of misinformation and fake news called infodemic. The fact that misinformation and fake news about vaccines, which is the most effective method in combating the pandemic, constitutes the infodemic once again emphasizes how critical it is to access accurate information. In this process, the widespread use of digital media platforms and the rapid increase in the number of users on these channels cause misinformation and fake news to reach large masses more easily. It is known that verification platforms, which have emerged with the aim of enlightening the society with accurate information, preventing the spread of misinformation and fake news, and verifying misinformation and fake news in the media, have shown a significant increase with the widespread use of digital media. This situation shows that it has become imperative to deliver "true" information and control false information against rapidly spreading "fake" news, because while "lies" spread rapidly around the world, "true" information may lag behind or arrive late in this process. In the post-truth era, it is possible to speak of the hegemony of lies and manipulated information. Especially due to the structure and characteristics of digital media platforms, a lot of information and news that is lively, distorted or decontextualized is rapidly disseminated. As stated in the conceptual background of the research, digital media tools are an integral component of the post-truth era. In the Covid-19 pandemic, which has affected the whole world, it is seen that there is intense disinformation in the new media. The tag, mention and repost features of digital media tools pave the way for the rapid spread of fake news and misinformation. Therefore, it has become as important to protect against disinformation in this process as it is to protect against the Covid-19 pandemic. Increasing information pollution and disinformation in new media has led to the emergence of fact-checking platforms around the world. During the Covid-19 pandemic, verification platforms have also tried to combat disinformation. In the study sample, the fact-checking platform Verify examined 70 claims about Covid-19 vaccines on February 25, 2021 and February 25, 2022. Of these, 2 claims are true and 6 claims are uncertain. It is seen that 62 of the total 70 claims are false. In this case, the rate of false claims can be stated as 88-89%. Based on the data, it has been determined that most of the information contained in the allegations does not reflect the truth or is not completely accurate. In general, allegations often involve the creation of false names and hypotheses of uncertain veracity. It was found that the allegations were recirculated with features of digital media such as liking and re-sharing. It is also observed that a certain claim is circulated through different digital media channels. It was observed that accounts with a high number of followers were instrumental in spreading disinformation to large masses by sharing the allegations in question. It can be said that most of the content produced on Covid-19 vaccines has qualities such as lies, disinformation, distortion and decontextualization. These contents have a function in line with the nature of the post-truth era. In order to mitigate the impact of the post-truth concept and combat disinformation, it is very important for users to confirm the content they encounter in digital media through various verification platforms and not to share content that they are not sure of its accuracy.

REFERENCES

Alçiçek, M. (2021). Bir Belleği Çarpıtma Dinamiği Olarak Post – Truth ve Yeni Medya. *Doğu Batı Düşünce Dergisi.*, *97*, 195–208.

Alpay, Y. (2020). *Yalanın Siyaseti*. Destek Yayınları.

Binark, M., & Bayraktutan, G. (2013). *Ayın Karanlık Yüzü: Yeni Medya ve Etik*. Kalkedon.

Brandtzaeg, P., & Følstad, A. (2017). Trust and Distrust in Online Fact-Checking Services. *Communications of the ACM*, *60*(9), 65–71. doi:10.1145/3122803

Castells, M. (2013). Enformasyon Çağı: Ekonomi, Toplum ve Kültür. İstanbul Bilgi Üniversitesi Yayınları, 3.Baskı.

Coleman, K. (2021). *Introducing Birdwatch, a community-based approach to misinformation.* https://blog.twitter.com/en_us/topics/ product/2021/introducing-birdwatch-a-community-based-approach-to-misinformation

Çöllüoğlu, M. (2023). Hakikat Ötesi Çağda Sosyal Medya Haberleri: Doğrulama Platformları Üzerinden Bir İncelenme. *Simetrik İletişim Araştırmaları Dergisi, 3*(2), 97–122.

Dictionaries, O. (2021). *Definition of post-truth adjective.* https://www.oxfordlearnersdictionaries.com/definition/english/posttruth?q=post+truth

Dijital Toplum Araştırmaları Derneği. (n.d.). *Hakkımızda.* www.dijitaltoplumarastirmalari.org/hakkimizda

Dijital Toplum Araştırmaları Derneği. (n.d.). https://www.dogrula.org/

Doğrula. (n.d.). https://www.dogrula.org/

Eroğlu, Ş., & Çakmak, T. (2020). Post-Truth Dönemini Anlamak: Hacettepe Üniversitesi Bilgi ve Belge Yönetimi Bölümü Öğrencilerinin Yeni Medya Araçları Kapsamında Bilgi Bozuklukları ve Doğrulama Algılarının Değerlendirilmesi. *Pamukkale Üniversitesi Sosyal Bilimler Enstitüsü Dergisi, 39*, 307–325.

Fake news, lies and propaganda: how to sort fact from fiction. (2020). https://guides.lib.umich.edu/fakenews

Kavaklı, N. (2019). Yalan Haberle Mücadele ve İnternet Teyit/Doğrulama Platformları. *Erciyes İletişim Dergisi, 6*(1), 663–682. doi:10.17680/erciyesiletisim.453398

Kocabay Şener, N. (2018). "Doğruluk Kontrol Merkezi" ve "Yalan Haber" Kavramlarına İlişkin İçeriklerin Medyada Yansımasının Araştırılması. *Akdeniz Üniversitesi İletişim Fakültesi Dergisi, (AKİL) Kasım,* (30), 355–373.

Köse, H. (2020). Dijimodern Çağda Hakikat, Sonrası ve Kamu Yararı. In H. S. Siyaset & M. U. İ. Felsefe (Eds.), *Bülent Özçelik* (pp. 201–231). Nika Yayınevi.

McGonagle, T. (2017). "Fake news" false fears or real concerns? *Netherlands Quarterly of Human Rights, 35*(4), 203–209. doi:10.1177/0924051917738685

Molina, M. D., Sundar, S. S., Le, T., & Lee, D. (2019). "Fake news" is not simply false information: A concept explication and taxonomy of online content. *The American Behavioral Scientist.*

Özkaya, A. (2020). *Post Truth (Gerçeklik Ötesi): Yalanların Gerçekmiş Gibi Sunulduğu Bir Dünyada, Hakikatin Anlamı Nedir?* evrimagaci.org

Silverman, C. (2018). *Doğrulama El Kitabı: Kriz Anlarında Dijital Verilerin Doğrulanması İçin Rehber.* European Journalism Centre. http://verificationhandbook.com/book_tr/

Toktay, Y. (2019). *Sosyal Medyada Dezenformasyon, Manipülasyon ve Propaganda Etkisi: Zeytin Dalı Harekatı Örneği, Yayımlanmamış Yüksek Lisans Tezi.* Marmara Üniversitesi Sosyal Bilimler Enstitüsü.

Törnberg, P. (2018). Echo chambers and viral misinformation: Modeling fake news as complex contagion. *PLoS One, 13*(9), 1–21. doi:10.1371/journal.pone.0203958 PMID:30235239

Uzunoğlu, S., & Uyar, V. (2021). Türkiye'de Doğru Bilgiyi Aramak: Çöldeki Vahanın Peşinde. *Newslab Turkey.* https://www.newslabturkey.org/ wp-content/uploads/2021/04/rh-2.pdf

World Health Organization (WHO). (2020). *Novel Coronavirus (2019-nCoV) situation report–13.* https:// www.who.int/docs/defaultsource/coronaviruse/situationreports/ 20200202-sitrep-13-ncov-v3.pdf

Chapter 18
An Investigation of the Visitor's Spatial Experience in Virtual Exhibitions

Rana Öztürk
İstinye University, Turkey

Simge Esin Orhun
Marmara University, Turkey

ABSTRACT

Along with the technological advancements in the digitalisation of physical objects and spaces, the COVID-19 pandemic has created an urgent necessity for cultural institutions to display exhibition content online. Exhibition making is a process of knowledge production through an order of display that is integrated into the spatial and architectural context of an exhibition space. The authors believe that virtual tours that are developed by simply creating a replica of the physical exhibition and the virtual display of individual artifacts offer limited spatial experience. They believe that virtual exhibitions as alternatives to physical experience of exhibitions still require a critical reflection in terms of their spatial context, effectiveness, benefits, and limitations. By examining the results of a three-week workshop with communication design students, the chapter discusses the current use of staging and navigation possibilities for displaying digital content. It further highlights the spatial relationality as a key concern for the translation of physical exhibitions into virtual space.

INTRODUCTION

The Covid 19 pandemic has created an urgent necessity to operate in the online world for institutions and professionals working across all sectors, including arts and culture. The pandemic and the enforced lockdowns have radically changed how people interact with their physical environments and dramatically effected the economic, social and cultural operations of societies across the globe. The closing down of public spaces and services also brought to a halt the regular activities of cultural spaces. Social distance

DOI: 10.4018/979-8-3693-0896-7.ch018

Figure 1. Shows the difference in increase in online activity just in two weeks
(Nemo, 2020, p.12)

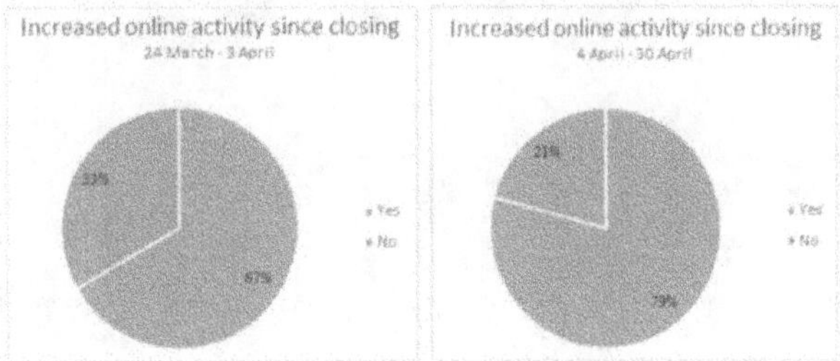

and isolation enforcements effected the functioning of museums and galleries that host exhibitions. Many exhibitions have been closed or postponed interrupting cultural activities and the access of audiences to cultural heritage and art. This has caused devastating financial consequences for the museums, forcing them to find other ways of accessing audiences using the Internet and digital technologies. Museums started to take immediate steps to provide their services using digital technologies to overcome this loss, which seemed to be going to last for an unknown period. There was a sudden increase in the production of digital content offered on the Internet, from small-scale cultural events, talks, screenings, etc. to larger scale festivals, performances, exhibitions, and even international art biennials. Many museums also directed their audience to virtual tours of their exhibitions, even though most were already available through Google Art and Culture.

According to a survey by the Network of European Museums Association in May 2020, three weeks after the closure, more than 80 per cent of the museums have increased their online services and the visibility of their cultural displays on online platforms. (figure 1). Between 10 to 150 per cent increase was observed in virtual visits to 2 out of every 5 museum. Work tasks of 30 per cent of museum staff have been reconfigured to support online services. Museums and galleries initially increased their use of social media, which was later followed by the increasing of their virtual and online exhibitions to reach their audiences. (figure 2) As a result, digital technologies became central for museums' adaptation to this new global situation. The report also says that these digital services helped museums to reach their audiences in social isolation. They also provided participation possibilities for the audience, enabling them share their own stories and items online. At the same time, the museums also offered their educational materials online and acted as informal education institutions, instilling a sense of safety within the society (NEMO, 2020).

While virtual tours were promoted as substitutes for actual museum visits and a good way to spend time during closure, the potential of virtual exhibitions as alternatives to physical experience of exhibitions still requires a critical reflection in terms of their effectiveness, benefits and limitations.

In this chapter, we will focus on virtual exhibition as one of the major online tools to provide artistic and cultural works to distant audiences and discuss how effectively they translate the actual experience of the museum visit to an online one. After a close look at some examples of virtual versions of physical exhibitions held by national and international institutions, we recognized that in the virtual tours, the architectural space and the artifacts in the exhibition were simply copied and installed in 3D format in parallel with the capabilities of the technology, whereas no concern was given to the possibility that a virtual exhibition would not be able to provide same spatial experience like the experience in the physical world (Nack and Waern, 2012). However, physical bodily movements are restricted to hands

Figure 2. The change in the number of museums that has reverted to online services
(Nemo, 2020, p.12)

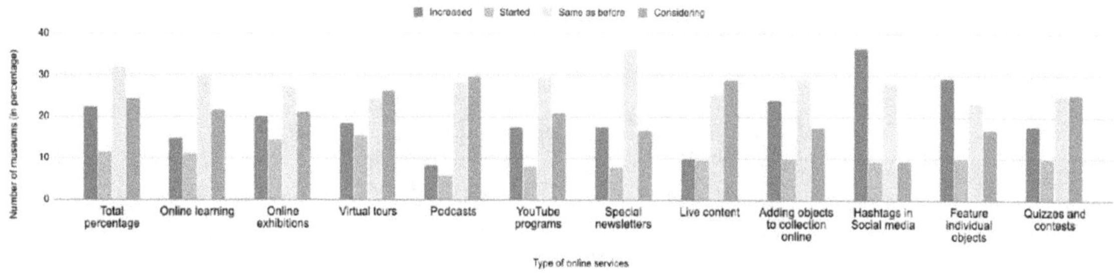

and eyes directed by a technological device. Besides, touring the exhibition by feet that took some time had also been replaced with teleportation or dragging the pegman figure, which is much quicker and prompt locomotion methods. So, due to the incomparable loss in the experience of the visitor, we think that virtual exhibitions should provide a better spatial experience to the visitor in order to meet the aims and intentions of the exhibition.

As a matter of fact, exhibition making is a process of knowledge production through an order of display that is very much integrated into the spatial and architectural context of an exhibition space. In a physical exhibition, curatorial decisions regarding the site, space, wall divisions, grouping and juxtaposition of objects, and other display strategies create this order through which the audience encounters the objects as part of a spatial experience. The "staging" of objects creates a "flow" and possible routes of "navigation" inside an exhibition that construct relational narratives amongst the objects in that specific spatial layout.

While place and space have been inseparable in our experience of the real world until now, when we experience the Web spatially, as a place, we assume that it must also have the usual attributes of spatiality, like moving, getting closer, getting lost, etc. Web-based space allows 'free' and interactive real-time navigation in a 3D space that reproduces more or less realistically the museum galleries in a virtual world. They are usually reproduced as realistically as possible to provide the experience of an actual visit, with the added value of the multimedia information, navigation through hypertext and spatial movement, and the possibility to manipulate the visuality of objects by zooming in and rotation (Sylaiou S. et al, 2014).

This chapter examines the spatial experience offered by virtual exhibitions by sharing the results of a workshop that examined how visitors using VR can connect with the spatial essence of exhibitions and to what extent the flow provided by navigation tools that are offered in VR satisfies the audience. We intend to share the results of a 3-week workshop that was held with Communication Design students of Özyegin University in Istanbul, Turkey in March 2021 and 2022. The students were assigned a list of virtual exhibitions offered by major art and culture institutions across the world. Each student navigated through and examined two different exhibitions and they answered a series of questions regarding their Satisfaction from the Visit, the Orientation and Narrative Recognition provided by the VR exhibitions and their experience of Navigation and Route Monitoring in VR visits. Their answers and experiences provided the ground for us to analyse the spatial experience in these virtual exhibitions through the navigation and wayfinding possibilities and visitor experience offered by their respective institution. Our analysis intended to explore the strengths and weaknesses of visitor experience in virtual exhibitions and discuss if the spatial context that create a relational narrative among the exhibited items in a physical exhibition space could be created as effectively in their virtual copies, so that the audience can interpret and appreciate the items within such a spatial context. Overall, through our findings we hope to contribute to the discussion on to what extend and in what ways VR technologies can contribute to exhibition making and exhibition cultures.

The following two sections are based on the literature regarding exhibitions and VR technologies. The first part introduces exhibitions as spatially integrative knowledge systems and discusses how the staging of an exhibition is crucial for the creation of narratives across an exhibition space. The second part examines applications of VR technologies in the field of exhibition. In the objectives and methodology section, we defined four stages of wayfinding, upon which we developed the survey questions that were described in the methodology part. Lastly, in the final section we shared the results of our study by analysing the written answers of the students.

EXHIBITIONS AS SPATIALLY INTEGRATIVE KNOWLEDGE SYSTEMS

Exhibitions: Narratives of Cultural Displays Within Space

For an understanding of the virtual experience of an exhibition, we need to first understand how an actual exhibition functions in physical terms and the ways in which it creates an environment of experience for the audience. Basically, an exhibition is the public display of objects, artefacts or art works to be seen and experienced by an audience. Very often this happens in a physical space of a gallery, museum or cultural institutions, and in some cases other alternative public spaces. Hence, an exhibition involves an act of deliberately presenting certain objects at a certain place so that other people can see them. By being exhibited the items on display gain significance for their audience. Chad Dawkins describes "exhibition as a visual presentation" and highlights that considering an exhibition as such "requires that we see the connection of the event-thing of an exhibition to a place in time and space" (Dawkins, 2021, 2-3). Accordingly, exhibition is a presentation that is offered to a group of people "to be seen in a distinct space and time" (Dawkins, 2021, 3). It is only within this distinct space and time the objects on display gain meanings and associations that is beyond their mere existence as objects. "The 'context' established by the exhibition confers upon objects a meaning that is above and beyond any significance they may already possess, whether as cultural artefacts or artworks" (Dziekan, 2012, p.31). Hence, the main constituent elements of an exhibition are the exhibited items, the exhibition space they are presented in, and the audience that is expected to see this within this space. Exhibitions are then meaning making mechanisms, and create a context for the items they are presenting through which the audience interprets and appreciates the items. The exhibition functions as a medium of communication that creates interactions between ideas, objects and people.

This study mainly focuses on the audience experience within space and our concern here is to understand how that experience is shaped by the various processes of contextualization in the making of an exhibition. Contextualization occurs through a curatorial process that involves various steps starting from the development of the idea of an exhibition. In a museum, this can arise from the museum's collection, which needs then to be turned into an ordered display. A collection itself does not represent a value to the audience without such curatorial presentation. Each exhibition involves various curatorial decisions, starting with the selection of items to be exhibited, the display strategies that determine how and in what order these items will be encountered by the audience, and potential meanings and associations that will occur through the togetherness of these items, both as a selected group of objects and the juxtapositions within the exhibition. An exhibition narrative emerges as a result of these decisions and each item starts to also function within the context generated through the exhibition. An exhibition is not simply about display of individual items, but it is a narrative that is established in the togetherness and order of the objects on display. As also highlighted by Dizekan in reference to Vergo (1989, p.46), objects become "elements of a narrative, forming part of a thread of discourse which is itself one element in a more complex web of meanings", gaining expanded roles and meanings beyond their functions as cultural or historical items when they are exhibited as part of an exhibition[1] (Dziekan, 2012, p.31). Speidal's definition of the exhibition includes this added dimension that takes into account complex relationships formed within time and space: "the public display of objects and performances of actions in a spatio-temporal constellation that is intended to be meaningful with an overarching narrative or discourse" (Speidal, 2001). In such a constellation, exhibitions function as "spatially integrative knowledge systems" as they organise non-spatial information to generate new knowledge within space, based on a narrative designed by the curator.

As Boris Groys highlights "Every exhibition tells a story, by directing the viewer through the exhibition in a particular order; the exhibition space is always a narrative space" (Groys, 2008, p.43). Hence the narrative of an exhibition is tightly connected to how the exhibition is laid out in the exhibition space. The layout and the space of the exhibition provide the additional context for the visitors to experience the exhibited items as part of a narrative. This narrative unfolds for the visitors as they wander within the exhibition. Blazwick and Wilson claims that visiting an exhibition is not only a visual experience for the visitor but also an embodied experience through which they perceive the art works while also encountering other visitors. "Works of art are rarely encountered in isolation. They are experienced in relation to each other and articulated by the architectonics of a building and the unconscious choreography of other people. Museums are activated by wandering groups and individuals who are busy looking at art and each other" (Blazwick & Wilson 2000, p. 31). For an audience visiting an exhibition is a temporal experience, and it is through walking through the exhibition that the narrative unfolds, and is experienced spatially. Exhibition creates a meaning making sequentiality. According to Mieke Bal, "Putting one thing next to another, in other words, produces a time-bound relationship, a linear progression between the two elements." Narrative in this sense comes quite close to syntax. What happens to a single sentence in language, or sequence in film, is bound to rules that make meaning-production possible, and it is plausible to consider an exhibition's juxtapositions and combinations, lightning and distance as similarly rule-bound in order to be meaningful" (Bal, 2009, p.13). Each walk is unique to the visitor but could be guided through the design and layout of the exhibition. Possible paths and potential moves of the visitor can be foreseen while planning the layout, which could also change the reading of the works and the unfolding of the narrative or create multiple narratives.

The task of curation then is more than deciding what to exhibit, but it requires the articulation of the "exhibition space" through the display of objects. This is not simply about engaging with the architectural space of a museum or a gallery. Rather, it involves a dynamic spatial and perceptual network constituted by architecture, display items and the audience who will navigate within these. Exhibition making is a process of creating an order of display that is integrated into the spatial and architectural context of an exhibition space and this space is activated by the visitor's navigation within it. "Each exhibition must demand and generate a different exhibition space" (Wu Huang, 2008).

Staging the Exhibition in Space

We call this order of display created through a curatorial perspective in an exhibition space "staging", which shapes how objects in an exhibition are perceived in relation to each other as part of a certain narrative. A relational narrative occurs within the exhibition through the layout and staging of an exhibition. Space functions as the main integrative element of an exhibition and the visitor experiences the whole order of the exhibition as part of the architectural layout while walking. The "staging" determines possible routes of "navigation" inside an exhibition and creates a "flow" for the visitors through which they perceive potential relational narratives that occur amongst the objects in that specific relational layout. Just as any spatial experience within an architectural building, the exhibition is experienced in perceptual fragments that are built up to create a whole through the process of physical movement. This movement is guided and informed by the curator's plan for how the artworks are placed.

Mieke Bal likens the work of a curator to exhibit a number of works under best possible conditions to developing a *sceneography* (Bal, 2009, p.16). Just like in a theatre play where the stage functions as the fictional set for the fictional activities of actors, the exhibition space also creates a fictional setting for the viewer to see the presented works suspended from their everyday life. "But the gallery space also isolates the viewer from the art. This turns the gallery space into a stage separated from the spectator. To make a convincing exhibition, the curator arranges the objects like still personages, as in a *tableau vivant.*" In an exhibition both the objects on display and the visitors become actors and "it is the interaction between them that constitutes the play." "In its mobility, and in the change over time that it entails, mise-en-scéne fits nicely as a metaphor for the experience of an exhibition because it creates an affective relationship with the spectators on the basis of, among other things, spatial arrangements" (Bal, 2009, p. 17).

Documenta 11 exhibition designer Wilfried Kuehn highlights the significance of the visitor's movement in relation to the exhibited work in determining how that work is perceived and interpreted. While he speaks specifically of the exhibition of time-based installations in contemporary art exhibitions, according to him, this subjective move of the visitor needs to be taken into consideration in the staging of an exhibition as if one is creating a landscape or an environment to be temporally experienced through movement. "If we use the exhibition as a way of installing diverse media freely and beyond typological restrictions of white or black cubes, we can think of the contemporary museum as a place that is organized like a city and a garden where situations and spatial constellations are to be conquered by the visitor" (Kuehn, 2020).

> *We see that the visitor as a subject may claim a space that is defined by their proper understanding and positioning, and it may change during time following subjective movement. . . . Moving through a landscape garden like Stowe, you are driven by a vital relation between your gaze and your body movement, which makes you change your physical position in relation to architectural presences like pavilions: buildings you see while you move, buildings that act as viewpoints which make you move, buildings that are related to one another in such a way that your body is moving in-between them. Spaces are here organized according to time, the garden being a viewing machine that presupposes a moving subject. (Kuehn & Nash, 2020)*

This movement within space is the necessary condition for a real engagement with the exhibition, and this viewing never results in a fixed meaning. Dzieken highlights how the architectural structures and the exhibition design have been increasingly more intertwined through a greater concern to "create a continuum across external architecture, interior architecture and exhibition design" and as a result of the use of dramatic display and presentation strategies the artwork exhibited is experienced as "an outcome of a performed process (both in the sense of simulated, read 'staged', and lived, read 'experienced'), rather than as a fixed, consolidated artefact" (Dzieken, 2012, p. 34). The "flow" within an exhibition then needs to be understood as "fluidity" in the meaning making process, which emerges through navigation and spatial experience for each visitor. And it is only at the very end of the visit the viewer can finally make sense of the full picture presented in the exhibition, in Nash's words, "following the parcours set out by the exhibition organizer or curator, which you may vary depending on your particular interests, focusing attention on particular works as opposed to others and so on. Then at the end you make some judgments or observations which you couldn't do until your visit was finished: "This section was too crowded, that period of work was not so interesting, that juxtaposition was key to the whole presentation and so on" (Kuehn & Nash, 2020).

Architect, artist and art historian Frederick Kiesler's idea of living space views exhibition as a galaxy in which all elements are equally important and intercorrelated. In this galaxy, no artefact is distinct from its environment. "The traditional art object, be it a painting, a sculpture or a piece of architecture, is no longer seen as an isolated entity but must be considered within the context of this expanding environment. The environment becomes equally important as the object, if not more so, because the object breathes into its surroundings but also inhales the realities of the environment, no matter what the space" (Kiesler, 2004, p. 42).

In modern museological practice, exhibition space as a "white cube" that presents a neutral background for the art works is very common. The exhibition space with white walls, no windows and even artificial lightning across the gallery, intends to exhibit the art works for pure aesthetic experience, detaching them from any social, political, everyday life contexts. However, this kind of spatial presentation has also created its own conventions and values and elevated the work to the status of a sacred object detached from the outside world and creates a constructed context based on the ideology of the modern museum and gallery system (O'Doherty, 1999). Similarly, Tony Bennet's *exhibitionary complex* highlights the role of exhibitions and display practices in museums in the construction of knowledge and how such institutions are mechanisms for exercising power by shaping cultural and historical narratives (Bennett, 1995). Hence, any artefact or art work presented in an exhibition is not only perceived within the architectural and spatial context of its exhibition space, its meaning and appreciation is also shaped by the institutional structure it is placed in. In a museum the visitor navigates and engages in a meaning making process within such a loaded institutional and cultural framework.

Some curators critically engage with the institutional or cultural framework of an exhibition space through site-specific investigations, producing, installing or exhibiting work in a way specifically designed for that space. This creates and added layer for the audience while navigating through the exhibition and requires further perception and awareness of the specific history, context and purpose and atmosphere of that specific place, which is even further difficult to grasp through a virtual experience.

Apart from the institutional structures behind an exhibition, techniques of display create a rhetorical power that creates the desired affect on the viewer (Bann, 1995). The desired spatial experience and possible routes and navigation options are offered to the visitor through a layout, which is planned based on many factors including not only the relationship between the exhibited items, but also the overarching exhibition theme, the specific qualities of the architectural building, security, safety and lightning conditions demanded by regulations and exhibited items. Depending on the content presented, wall divisions, vitrines, and plinths can be needed and special wall colours and lightning can be used to create an atmosphere. And additional visual material such as labels, maps, signs, and informative text can be also used to guide the audience within the exhibition. Hence, in this study we ask what kind of change occurs in this spatial frame when an exhibition is experienced in VR? Can that space hold the spatial qualities and potential informative and navigation possibilities for the viewer?

EXHIBITIONS AND VIRTUAL REALITY SPACE

In the previous section, we indicated that the exhibiting space is one of the main contexts that creates a meaning-making frame for artefacts in an exhibition. Because of this reason we are interested in the user experience of a virtual exhibition space as it creates a boundless universe in which the perception of the visitor may be enhanced or distorted. In this section we will introduce the VR technologies and common navigation techniques used in online exhibitions.

VR has been defined as "a computer-generated, simulated experience that allows users to interact with an immersive, three-dimensional environment by way of pose tracking and near-eye displays" (Becher, 2023). While virtual reality is included under the terminology of extended reality (XR), the features of the advanced interface of VR maintains navigation and interaction in 3D virtual environments (Goode, 2019). Applications for integrating this immersive sensory experience that digitally simulates a virtual environment have developed for a range of fields including gaming, architecture, medical, real estate, training, therapy, education, military, etc.

In virtual environments users can realize three separate activities: i. moving around (exploring), ii. interacting with visual objects (manipulating/ interacting) and constructing new structures (contributing) (Parés & Parés, 2001). As a matter of fact, these separate activities rely on one experience of the user, which is navigation. Locomotion is a term that covers all these features in VR environment, which basically refers to moving from one place to another. The user moves around without the necessity of walking by foot, while it becomes his main interaction within the space. Moreover, the objects in the virtual environment can be held and moved by the user by using special gloves and joysticks. So, as a whole, the virtual environment can construct new structures when all of the pieces is perceived as a whole in which the objects and space are both interacted offers an alternative to construct new structures (Yong Min Kim et al, 2021).

Maintaining Navigation in VR has been an important area both for application and for research as active navigation requires moving around without the physical restrictions. Mainly, two locomotion methods have been used with VR technologies: first one is, dragging the with the pegman icon with joystick which is similar to changing place in time. Second one is the teleportation method which involves clicking with pointing devices to travel from point to point. The user's intuitive knowledge of the real world is transferred to manipulate the virtual environment through the use of headmounted displays, gloves, etc. (Shahbaz & De Amicis, 2023; Negrón et al., 2020).

Teleportation is widely known with the application of Google street view that was featured in Google Maps and Google Earth. Google Street View displays interactively panoramas of combining multiple photographic images with overlapping fields of view to produce a segmented panorama or high-resolution image (Mann & Picard, 1994). Within the Smart Navigation system, the primary user interface element used by Google to connect Maps to Street View is Pegman, which the user can drag and drop or double click their cursor on any place or object he wants to explore (Ionescu, 2009).

Figure 3. The National Gallery, Exhibition view through Google Street View (https://www.nationalgallery.org.uk/visiting/virtual-tours/google-virtual-tour)

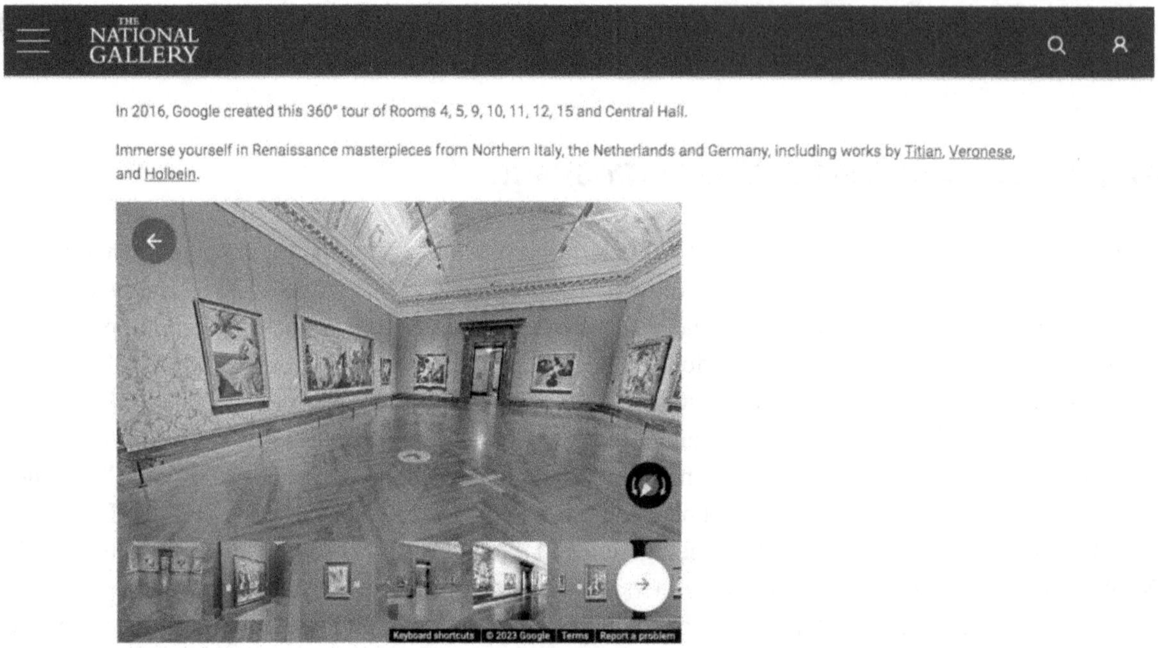

A more improved version of this technology has been the viewing and navigation system of different technologies that provide 3D space as dollhouse. Dollhouse is a VR system that allows experts in architecture and interior design to design houses alternating top-down and internal views of the virtual spaces (Barricelli et al, 2016). So, with this technology, the user can make use of 2 different viewpoints: a small-scale view of the interior space and a full-scale top-down view of the entire space (Ibayashi et al., 2015).

These teleportation methods can be applied by using 2 different hardware (Vilar & Rebelo, 2008):

i. Non immerse VR: A conventional screen displays the scenes and the user can travel in the environment using both locomotion methods either by keystrokes or by the use of a mouse, joystick or similar pointing devices. In order to make the experience more realistic, speakers or headsets can give out sound. The user looks at the screen and uses his imagination to be in the environment rather than being in that virtual three-dimensional environment. Because of this reason, while non immersive VR is safer than real world and is the simpler and cheaper way to interact with VR, it is considered as being not the best way to promote the sense of presence and fails to turn the user experience as real as possible.
ii. Immersive VR systems: The user's teleporting experience is supported by some equipment such as Head Motions Displays (HDM) and gloves among others. A typical HMD has two miniature display screens and an optical system that channels the images from the screens to the eyes, thereby, presenting a stereo view of a virtual world. The position and orientation of the users' head is continuously measured by a motion tracker and it allows the image generating computer to adjust the

Figure 4. The National Gallery, Sainsbury Wing, Doll House projection by Matterport

scene representation to the current view. As a result, the viewer can look around and walk through the surrounding virtual environment. The main advantage of this system is the high sense of realism and presence that participants experiment.

To explore both locomotion methods, regardless of hardware, a study was conducted to 21 participants that involved navigation in a virtual urban settlement. According to the results, the study identified that teleportation approach time saving, fun and quick way for navigation and boosts users' sense of achievement. However, as teleportation is composed of rapid and prompt movements, but users couldn't overcome immediate problems. So, for efficient navigation, teleportation has to demand longer time for the user to perceive the instant changes in the scene (Kim et al, 2021; Bozgeyikli et al, 2019; Coomer et al, 2018; Vlahović et al., 2018).

Most of the VR exhibitions that we came across involved explorative tasks. Since in VR environments it is not possible to have an embodied experience of space, we believe that locomotion becomes a significant aspect to be considered and carefully designed, in order for the visitors to make sense of the exhibition as a spatially integrative knowledge system, rather than just concentrating on the artefacts. Maintaining the accuracy of cognitive representation of real world spatial information becomes the

Figure 5. The National Gallery, Sainsbury Wing, View of Interior Space by Matterport

utmost important in virtual exhibitions in order for the visitors to grasp the relational narrative that is constructed through displays within space.

OBJECTIVES AND METHODOLOGY

Objectives

For any design, ergonomics play an important role that refers to the safety and usability of the product as well as comfort and efficiency. From the architectural point of view, maintaining the navigation in the building is an important aspect to satisfy the user need in the frame of the functionality of a building. The efficiency of the interaction between the user and the building is related to the studies of wayfinding.

Wayfinding studies basically aim to understand the effect of verbal and visual abilities of users in their communication for directions to find the way from one place to another (Raubal, 2001). In unfamiliar environments, people make use of external information to complement their orientation. In that sense, human mind is able to cope with the environments that they have never seen (Norman, 1989).

In the frame of this study, we focused on the wayfinding qualities of virtual environments. In order to explore the problem, we worked on virtual exhibitions in order to provide a constructed set of information that is staged in a well-defined space. We believe that if we can examine and investigate the navigation and orientation of users in the virtual environment, we will be able to identify key aspects in their process of travelling and how they deal with the information that is embedded in the exhibition. We claim that, the transferring of physical exhibitions to their digital versions needs new strategies to be sought for proper use experience.

In parallel with the objectives of this study, wayfinding stages are introduced as key tools of the users' perception of space and reception of art through locomotion in a virtual space. Having control over these stages show if the people are able to position themselves in space (Lidwell et al 2010; Wodtke &Govella, 2009). This study focuses on below stages of wayfinding:

1. Orientation: Refers to defining one's location in relation with close objects and the intended place. Landmarks provide strong orientation cues, and provide locations with memorable identities. Signage is one of the easiest ways to tell a person where they are and where they can go.
2. Route Decision: Refers to selecting a path to get to the intended place. Simple routes can be followed most efficiently with the use of clear narrative directions or signs. Maps provide more robust mental representations of the space, and are superior to other strategies when the space is very large, complex, or poorly designed.
3. Route Monitoring: Refers "to observing and checking the chosen path that it is leading to the intended place". For better route monitoring, locations should be connected with paths that have clear beginnings, middles, and ends. The paths should enable a person to gauge their progress along their lengths using clear lines of sight to the next location, or signage indicating relative location.
4. Destination Recognition: Refers to spotting the intended place. Hence destinations should have clear and consistent identities.

Upon these stages, this study intends to explore how the visitors who hasn't visited any virtual exhibition, move in the environment and orient themselves in a spatially integrated system.

Method

This comprehensive study intends to identify the needs, perceptions and reactions of users while exploring an unfamiliar exhibition environment in a virtual space. As the end-users are an integral part of exhibitions, we used survey as our research method with the aim to obtain cues that will guide future studies on the development and realization of virtual exhibitions and VR environments. A questionnaire with open-ended questions was designed as the tool for data collection, since we wanted to get a deeper insight into the student experience through detailed answers, which would provide thorough and descriptive information about their VR museum visit experience (Mathers, Fox & Hunn, 2007).

In the first stage of the research, virtual tours and exhibitions were examined to understand the possible advantages and disadvantages of the technology combined with hardware. Secondly, a survey that includes a questionnaire with open-ended questions was designed in parallel with the detected flaws of VR exhibitions. In the third stage, a 3-week workshop was designed to explore the visitors' wayfinding experiences in virtual exhibitions. Their navigation in the environment was examined based on the questionnaire that aimed to find out their feelings, experiences and reactions during navigation, how they engaged with the exhibition content and their satisfaction with a purposeful movement within the virtual space. 11 national and 11 international exhibitions[2] were selected and each student were randomly given one national and one international exhibition to examine. We made sure different VR technologies were used in the selected exhibition. They were either constructed by the Google Streetview technology or the Dollhouse approach, so that we could see the benefits and limitations of each technology. The students were asked to use the teleportation approach as locomotion method on desktop VR and afterwards they were directed to answer the questionary for both exhibitions. Desktop VR navigation was preferred in this study, since in an immersive VR environment, the visitor cannot perceive the space around equally and not knowing what is in the back may add to user stress, together with motion sickness (Hunt & Waller, 1999). Finally, based on an analysis of each answer, we identified general spatial tendencies in VR exhibitions and possible strategies for the development of the design of virtual exhibitions for better visitor experience.

This aforementioned workshop was realized in spring 2021, with the students of Communication Design of Özyegin University. 25 student participants were given specific instructions to visit and analyse these virtual exhibitions. They were guided to tour the exhibitions based on what they learned about virtual exhibition space and navigation during the workshop. They were asked to complete a questionary directly after their navigation within the virtual exhibitions. The evaluation presented here is based on their assessment of the virtual visit through their answers to the questionnaire. The evaluation involved only one participant at a time. User errors while navigating as well as the time needed to complete the tasks were not recorded, because it was not our intention to test the users' performance, but the efficiency of wayfinding features of virtual exhibitions. The evaluation used cued testing, which involves explaining to the users the purpose of the project and asking them to perform specific tasks and to answer questions. This process involves three specific steps:

i. **Goal setting:** Users are given general information on VR technologies, VR exhibitions and navigational objectives.
ii. **Exploration**: Users explore the interface and discover useful/ satisfactory/unsatisfactory navigation possibilities in the selected virtual exhibitions.
iii. **Investigation:** By answering the questions in the questionnaire, users interpret the VR systems' responses to their navigation decisions and assess its functionality through the spatial movement. The questions are as follows:
    1. General question: Are you interested in exhibitions? Why? If this was not an assignment would you go out the physical space of the exhibition and/or visit VR museum?
    2. Do you like the VR exhibitions you visited? Why/Why not?
    3. What was the most interesting aspect (theme, displaying of Works, navigation, interface, etc.)
    4. What kind of interactions took place in the VR exhibitions you visited? To what extend you were able to do something in the VR?
    5. For your exhibition, how was the content organised? (historical sequence, geographical, alphabet, subject wise… et?)
    6. Regarding Orientation: Did you recognize the start of the exhibition area? Were there any landmarks that you can detect? What kind of a signage system was there?
    7. Regarding Route Decision: Were you given choices for your instant route or you have to go with one decided flow?

8. Regarding Route Monitoring: Were you able "not to get lost"? (Because you are on the visit, we are not necessarily looking for a specific destination.) Were you able to get back and find the same point at the end? How?
9. Regarding Destination Recognition: Although we were just touring around, was there any specific guides to indicate what exhibitions rooms/hall were on your way or around you? Were you given information about a specific room that you wanted to go but that is not on your route?
10. After finishing your visit, what was your feeling? If you were able, would you like to go and visit the physical museum itself?

iv. **Evaluation:** Based on the participants' answers to the questionnaire, key issues and limitations in the experience of spatiality through navigation and interface are examined.

FINDINGS

The answers we got from the students show that there are shared concerns regarding certain aspects of virtual museum experience. We specifically wanted the students to test the navigational and way finding capacities of virtual museums and how these affected their orientation in space and interactions with the display items. These also determined how much they could grasp the display order and their abilities to structure the narrative content that could be attained through their visit. Finally, this experience also affected the student's motivation to continue the online visit and their general sense of satisfaction from the visit, overall reflecting the effectiveness of virtual exhibitions.

Satisfaction From the Visit: 75% of the students preferred to visit museums on physical site. The students expressed their concerns and frustration about not being able to experience the exhibition fully using other senses of the body. Students mostly stated that if they had the chance or if this were not an assignment, they would prefer to visit the actual museum rather than the VR. %25 of the students found virtual visits practical and satisfactory as they could access museological artefacts via online museums even if it was not possible to physically go to many museums due to geographic distance and other limitations.

The students also expressed their concerns and frustrations about not having an actual spatial experience and lack of an embodied experience of the exhibition using other senses beyond the visual. For example one student who examined the Jean Paul Getty Museum expressed this as follows: "I was happy to discover new art but experience-vise I was not satisfied. I think the VR experience will never replace being in that environment. In the visiting experience, I can set my pace, I can change the angles that I am looking at and I can feel the art rather than see it." Another student who visited Rijks Museum highlighted that a virtual visit to the museum is highly insufficient, because an actual visit to Rijks is a totally different experience as an activity that takes a whole day. Accordingly, "The showing is nice, detailed, and informative, but this is not Rijks all about." The student also highlighted the importance of the actual architectural structure of the museum and its location and relationship to the rest of the city as important factors in the experience, and in the absence of such spatial experience the VR museum is separated form its urban context and architectural essence.

Another student who examined the Chora Museum highlighted the limitation of movement as a factor that led to the superficiality of the experience, since a full spatial experience involves body movement and the act of looking at the same time: "I did not like the VR exhibition because I was not able to move and I felt stuck. It felt like a superficial experience. I just saw the museum in parts so I could not really visit the museum. I just explored the parts of it. So I was not satisfied with the experience." The student highlighted that in VR experience you only use your sense of seeing and it is necessary to experience the museum with other senses too.

One positive aspect highlighted by some of the students is that in VR exhibitions the visual quality of images are so great that the viewer has the chance to have close-up views of art works and see every minute detail. However, despite the ease of access to artefacts and information, visiting a VR museum lacks the spatial experience and "instead, it felt like I was browsing through normal museum photos on the Internet," as one student highlights. So the visual presentation of items requires more than just the photographic representation, either via photographs or scanned imagery of the exhibition space, for a more enhanced museum experience. In order for a VR exhibition to function as something more than that, it needs to provide a sense of the spatial context within which a relational narrative unfolds for the viewer.

Orientation and Narrative Recognition: Our study showed that the students who had greater satisfaction in VR exhibitions could more easily orient themselves within space in relation to different sections of the exhibition. As a result they could also grasp the spatial context of the exhibition more clearly. Such sense of orientation is also very much dependent on how the virtual experience was designed. Virtual museums that are rendered through the Google Street View technology seems to offer less efficient orientation experience than those made using Matterport technology. This is partly because in Google Street View you can loose the sense of location within an architectural space while wandering through rooms and it becomes impossible to position yourself in relation to a specific point.

Students had relatively easier navigation experience in smaller size exhibitions. Very often these exhibitions were temporary exhibitions organized by art and culture institutions, such as Yapı Kredi Kültür Sanat, an art centre in Istanbul, rather than large museums. We think that in smaller temporary exhibitions it was possible to develop VR exhibitions with greater interactive and informative tools, unlike large-scale museums that hold big collections. Among these, the doll-house view option seems to be a useful mode for users since it gives an overview of the whole architectural structure and its divisions and how the exhibition is laid out within that structure. A student who visited the Turhan Selçuk Exhibition at Yapıkredi Art and Cultural Centre wrote, "Thanks to the 'dollhouse view' mode and the easy to use floor navigator I was able to recognize every part of the exhibition. It took me less than 10 minutes to create a 'mental map' of the exhibition entirely." The same student also highlighted: "I never got lost in the exhibit and was able to find my way around with ease. The 'dollhouse view' function and the small size and simple shape of the exhibition allowed to me navigate clearly, I never felt like I was getting lost or 'thrown around' by the VR navigation controls."

However, another student who explored the Rijks Museum expressed his/her frustration about orientation and wayfinding in the absence of such a guiding structure. "First of all, I can't perceive the place in the Rijks Museum, I can't figure out where I should go. The reason for this is that it does not show us the plan of the place; only buttons are placed to pass to certain floors. However, the works exhibited on this floor are not specified." The same student also highlighted that this virtual museum was not necessarily designed for appropriate VR qualities, and that prevented the visitor to make connections between artefacts and make it a greater experience than simply seeing images of art works, "because I think that the exhibition should make some connections and leave memories. Visiting an exhibition or a museum isn't just about that moment, it's a journey for me."

A student visiting the Museo Galileo also wrote that she got lost at every possible direction change she wanted to make. "Because there wasn't anything that told me where I was, I wandered around not knowing where I was. I couldn't find the same point but I could transport to any room I wanted at the end by clicking on the map on the right side of the website, but I think it would be better if I could see where I was in the first place, on the map." This also shows the necessity of identification of reference points in order to keep oriented within the exhibition. In this case, the virtual exhibition is not supporting the cognitive faculties of the visitor and the mental map of the environment is difficult to grasp if the user's locomotion is based on merely clicking certain arrows or sections, rather than an embodied moving around that allows perception of the surrounding.

However, even in smaller exhibitions offering easy orientation there was difficulty in following the display order and understanding the exhibition narrative through the spatial layout. Regarding his experience of MASP (Museu de Arte Sao Paulo), one student wrote, "To be clear, I did not become disoriented because the exhibition is small, but it is unclear which photographs are displayed first and which photographs are displayed last. So, because you can't follow a flow, I went through all of the works at random. I was able to avoid getting lost thanks to the compass in the lower right corner." Even though the student could find a way of orienting himself, the randomness of display distorted the curatorial contextualization and potential relational meanings between photographs.

On the other hand, when the students that identified structured information within the exhibition, such as episodic, chronological or thematic grouping and continuation between rooms, they expressed that following the overall content of the exhibition became easier. "When there is a historic sequence, it becomes easy to follow the artefacts in the frame of the content and student afterwards can remember the content." said one after a visit to the Louvre. In a different museum, the organization of information was based on an annual chronology, which made it easier to follow a narrative.

Navigation and the Ability to Monitor the Route: The response by students showed that for a more enhanced spatial experience and experience of artefacts relationally, other navigational tools are required. It is through spatial navigation that a visitor can understand the exhibition narrative. According to student reports, when the students struggled with navigation tools, they got overwhelmed by the VR visit and they hardly remembered the exhibition content afterwards. In some exhibitions they found it easy to navigate, in others controlling the teleportation while looking for directions created a loss of orientation and dizziness; as one students says: "I also got bored trying the get used to the website's system just because the controls were not easy to control for me." According to another student, the navigation options in Chora Museum "was very limited. There weren't any moving options; you could only stand in the middle of the place. In the bottom, there were parts to click to move around the museum. So I was able to go from part to part. With the buttons I could change my view up and down and right to left."

Regarding the route decision, there were also problems about the potential paths to be determined by the limited navigation options. "Definitely given options about the route, I can easily choose which room to enter. But of course there were times when I had to stick to one flow" said one of the students. In relation to VR visit to Anne Frank's House, a student also expressed the difficulty of following a certain route: "I was able to go back and get to the point where I could start, but that was because I could go to the entrance with a single click (pressing 0th floor). It doesn't have a complex structure, but there are obviously some design flaws. I changed floors while trying to get into the next room."

The flaws in navigation design also limited the visits, since it was easy not to see some artifacts at all. After visiting Çorum Boğazköy Museum a student commented that "navigational arrows has to be defined and designed: it became more comfortable to go where I want to go with the mouse. Because when I went by pressing the arrows, I did not have the opportunity to examine some of the works."

Overall, the difficulties encountered through the VR exhibition visit were decreasing the student's motivation to continue the visit. A majority of the students were frustrated by the navigational controls and constantly having to try to find the arrows to click. The limitations of the interactive tools almost shadowed the content of the exhibitions.

All students highlighted that the main interaction with the exhibited items was based on navigational tools. Due to weaknesses in the design of navigation, the exploration of the space and examining the artefacts within that space became the foremost challenge in the visits. One student mentioned an online game at VR Rijksmuseum, in which the visitor looks for and finds keys in artworks based on hints. To find the keys the player needs to walk through the museum and check every painting several times, and a secret word opens after all the keys are found. Despite the limitations of spatial experience, the student has mentioned that by playing this game you can learn a lot about the art works and artists. Hence, gamification can be a tool for greater visitor satisfaction for virtual museums.

CONCLUSION

Taking exhibitions as essentially spatial ordering of artefacts, this study aimed to understand the effectiveness of VR exhibitions in terms of the spatial experience they offered to the visitor and the ways in which navigation tools in a VR exhibition could enhance or limit the visitor's engagement with the spatial context of the exhibition. In parallel with this aim, this research embraced VR as a powerful technology to enhance the experience of exhibition content in various ways, but not sufficiently integrated to sustain the spatial experience provided by the physical space. Using methods and ideas in the fields of exhibition making, wayfinding studies and VR practices, we designed this research to explore the Visitor Satisfaction in VR exhibitions, the Orientation and Narrative Recognition tools provided, and the visitor's experience of Navigation and Route Monitoring in VR exhibitions.

The study was based on a 3-week workshop with Communication Design students of Özyeğin University, in which they examined a list of VR exhibitions designed by museums or smaller culture and art institutions. The students were asked to take part in a survey that was based on a series of open-ended questions regarding the effectiveness of their virtual visit, the user interface design and navigation tools they had to use, how these tools shaped their orientation and wayfinding experience within the exhibition space and their engagement with the spatially ordered exhibition items and the overall narrative.

Based on the student response we can conclude that insufficient interface, wayfinding and navigation options results in a limited visitor experience with two potential results. The exhibition design either presents an artefact-focused experience for the visitor, meaning the viewer can engage with individual items as images, but cannot grasp the overall narrative of the exhibition since the relationality between objects is lost. In most cases, spatial coordination was not provided and the visitor had difficulty in knowing where they are located in the exhibition spatially. In other cases where there was insufficient interface, some art works were not experienced in detail since navigation did not allow a clear flow and interaction with art works fully. While high resolution images and zooming option were impressive and provide a very detailed view of art works, this was often not supported by sufficient information about the works.

The student answers showed that for keeping the visitors on track and in connection with the exhibited content, an exhibition needs to satisfy the following:

- provide a sense of location and orientation for the visitor at any stage of the visit
- give users navigation controls that allow them to have different direction options
- provide a relational context that gives a sense of how the works are juxtaposed and related within a narrative
- provide sufficient information about the individual artefacts
- create an easy understanding of possible routes and flows within the exhibition

Based on these conclusions, while we do not intend to claim that VR is an unsuitable medium for exhibitions, we think that current VR tools do not do justice to the actual content and contextualization of exhibitions. A VR tour lacks many qualities of a physical exhibition visit in the absence of a spatial relational context. Hence, we do believe that virtual exhibitions need a unique language in order to be efficient in terms of providing a sense of relationality between artefacts. Kristof and Satran (1995) indicate "People expect familiar paradigms of media to guide them through uncharted territories of information. Each medium brings with it a unique language of orientation." Hence the VR tools for exhibitions still require development of their unique language in order to translate the staging of an exhibition in a virtual situation. In a physical exhibition, curatorial decisions regarding the site, space, wall divisions, grouping and juxtaposition of objects, and other display strategies create an order through which the audience encounters the objects as part of a spatial experience. In VR exhibition, this requires other tools that could benefit from the unique qualities of the interactivity of digital tools. VR exhibitions should not be simply about virtual presentation of artefacts, nor try to represent physically installed exhibitions. Instead, it is necessary to explore what other strategies can be developed in order to present a relational context for artefacts within exhibitions.

One strategy is to consider the virtual environment as a context for "networked knowledge". Beaulieu and De Rijcke discuss museum collections as part of networked digital image databases and talk about the potential of digital images as interactive interfaces that lead to other networked images through the metadata attached to them (Beaulieu & De Rijcke, 2016). This points at the possible shift from a spatial relationality to a networked experience through images of artefacts.

Martijn Stevens (2016) also points at the loss of essential properties of exhibited items: "Removed from galleries in brick-and-mortar institutions and stripped of their physical or tangible qualities, artworks appear on the Internet as virtual, hyperlinked objects with the fundamental properties or "crucial bits of art" essentially lost in the process" (pp. 17-18). As a result they start to function as part of an online database, which is not about being "present in a particular time and space"; and "because artworks are no longer necessarily material things that exist in three-dimensional space, the question is not simply to establish *that* they exist but rather *how* they exist or how they function within a given context." Accordingly, "the power of an online database consists in the possibility of establishing multiple connections between items that are historically and geographically far removed" (Stevens, 2016, p. 18). In this context, art works can be part of a relational context through "the experience of proximity in terms of affinity, connectivity, and attraction, which is not necessarily dependent on the material presence of an object", nor the spatial relationality (p. 21).

In a similar vain Heiko Schmid also highlighted the need to develop online exhibition formats "as phenomena building on their own technological means and rules, if we wish to allow them to gain relevance." In a world of post-Internet condition, "in which digital technologies impact all aspects of everyday life, we need to critically, or, in more specific terms, adversarially, readapt the way we structure online art reception" (Schmid, 2021, p. 62).

Parallel to these views, we have also come across quite effective online examples that use VR as a storytelling technique. In those, the strategy to use VR technology aimed to support the visitor experience by providing alternative ways to better comprehend the exhibited collection. Such practices show that technology can create varying perspectives, help visitors feel a connection with the artist and enhance the whole experience of the exhibition (Richardson, 2023). However, these examples were often inspired by the collection of an exhibition and had a semi-independent character as they did not directly combine with the forces of gravity and the spatial experience. Besides, some of these tools are located in the physical exhibition area and cannot be used by the visitors that connect online.

We believe there is still a lot of space for improvement in this field. With the integration of virtual and augmented reality technologies into online services of museums, it became easier for the audience to connect with the content of the modern museum even from afar. These technologies support people who lack mobility or who are unable to do in-person visits due to various reasons, to see art from their homes. As Nills Pokel (2017) highlights, the distinctive feature of these technologies are their "ability to create a true first-person perspective" (mentioned by Richardson, 2023). Once they are used together with other physical and online tools, they have the potential to enhance and multiply our experiences of cultural artifacts.

REFERENCES

Arash, S.B., & Raffaele, D. A. (2023). An empirical evaluation of enhanced teleportation for navigating large urban immersive virtual environments. *Frontiers in Virtual Reality, 3*. doi:10.3389/frvir.2022.1075811

Bal, M. (2009). Exhibition as the Syntax of the Face. *Grammar of the Exhibition. MJ. Manifesta Journal*, (7), 13–21.

Bann, S. (1995). Shrines, Curiosities and the Rhetoric of Display. In L. Cooke & P. Wollen (Eds.), Visual Display: Culture Beyond Appearances. Bay Press.

Barricelli, B. R., Gadia, D., Rizzi, A., & Marini, D. L. R. (2016). Semiotics of virtual reality as a communication process. *Behaviour & Information Technology, 35*(11), 879–896. doi:10.1080/0144929X.2016.1212092

Beaulieu, A., & de Rijcke, S. (2016). Networked Knowledge and Epistemic Authority in the Development of Virtual Museums. In Museums in a Digital Culture: How Art and Heritage Become Meaningful. Amsterdam University Press.

Becher, B. (2023). What is Virtual Reality? *Built In*. https://builtin.com/media-gaming/-what-is-virtual-reality

Bennett, T. (1995). The Exhibitionary Complex. In *The Birth of the Museum: History, Theory, Politics*. Routledge.

Blazwick, I., & Wilson, S. (2000). *Tate Modern: the handbook*. Tate Publishing.

Boletsis, C. (2017). The new era of virtual reality locomotion: A systematic literature review of techniques and a proposed typology. *Multimodal Technol. Interact., 1*(4), 24. doi:10.3390/mti1040024

Bozgeyikli, E., Raij, A., Katkoori, S., & Dubey, R. (2019). Locomotion in virtual reality for room scale tracked areas. *International Journal of Human-Computer Studies, 122*, 38-49. doi:10.1016/j.ijhcs.2018.08.002

Coomer, N., Bullard, S., Clinton, W., & Williams-Sanders, B. (2018). Evaluating the effects of four VR locomotion methods: joystick, arm-cycling, point-tugging, and teleporting. In *Proceedings of the 15th ACM Symposium on Applied Perception*. Association for Computing Machinery. 10.1145/3225153.3225175

Dawkins, C. (2021). The Definition of Exhibition in Art Historical Inquiry. *Academia Letters*. Advance online publication. doi:10.20935/AL3779

Goode, L. (2019). Get Ready to Hear a Lot More About 'XR'. *Wired*.

Hunt, E., & Waller, D. (1999). *Orientation and Wayfinding: A Review*. University of Washington.

Ibayashi, H., Sugiura, Y., Sakamoto, D., & Miyata, N. (2015). Dollhouse VR: a multi view, multi-user collaborative design workspace with VR technology. *SIGGRAPH Asia 2015 Posters*. doi:10.1145/2820926.2820948

Ionescu, D. (2009). Google Street View Gets Smart Navigation. *PC World*. https://www.pcworld.com/article/529530/google-98.html

Kiesler, F. (1942). Note on Designing the Gallery and Press Release Pertaining to the Architectural Aspects of the Gallery. In Peggy Guggenheim & Frederick Kiesler: The Story of Art of this Century. Guggenheim Museum Publications.

Kim, Y. M., Lee, Y., Rhiu, I., & Yun, M. H. (2021). Evaluation of locomotion methods in virtual reality navigation environments: An involuntary position shift and task performance. *International Journal of Human-Computer Studies, 1071*, 5819. doi:10.1016/j.ijhcs.2021.102691

Kristof, R., & Satran, A. (1995). *Interactivity by design: creating & communicating with new media*. Adobe Press.

Lidwell, W., Holden, K., & Butler, J. (2010). *Universal Principles of Design*. Rockport Publishers.

Mann, S., & Picard, R. W. (1994). Virtual bellows: constructing high-quality stills from video. In *Proceedings of the IEEE First International Conference on Image Processing*. IEEE. 10.1109/ICIP.1994.413336

Mathers, N., Fox, N. & Hunn, A. (2007). *Surveys and Questionnaires*. The NIHR RDS for the East Midlands/Yorkshire & the Humber.

Nack, F., & Wærn, A. (2012). Mobile digital interactive storytelling—A winding path. *New Review of Hypermedia and Multimedia, 18*(1-2), 3–9. doi:10.1080/13614568.2011.641418

Nash, M., & Kuehn, W. (2020). *Exhibition Staging: Notes and Queries*. Platform 6 Talks. Available at https://www.documenta-platform6.de/exhibition-staging-notes-and-queries/

Negrón, A. P. P., López, G. L., & Aguirre, H. R. O. (Eds.). (2020). *Virtual Reality Designs* (1st ed.). CRC Press. doi:10.1201/9781003019589

NEMO. (2020). *Survey on the impact of the COVID-19 situation on museums in Europe Final Report.* Network of European Museum Organizations. https://www.ne-mo.org/fileadmin/Dateien/public/NEMO_documents/NEMO_COVID19_Report_12.05.2020.pdf

Norman, D. A. (1989). *The Design of Everyday Things.* DoubleDay.

Parés, N., & Parés, R. (2001). Interaction-Driven Virtual Reality Application Design (A Particular Case: El Ball del Fanalet or Lightpools). Presence: Teleoperators and Virtual Environments, 10(2), 236-245. doi:10.1162/105474601750216830

Raubal, M. (2001). *Agent- Based Simulation of Human Wayfinding: a perceptual model for familiar buildings* [Unpublished Dissertation]. Viena University of Technology.

Schmid, H. (2021). Adversarial Interfaces. In Art Museums and Digital Cultures: Rethinking Change. Universidade NOVA de Lisboa.

Speidal, K. (2021). *What is an exhibition? Cultures, concepts, cognition & curation.* Seminar at Institute of Fine Arts and Media Art. https://base.uni-ak.ac.at/courses/2021W/S04063/

Stevens, M. (2016). Touched from a Distance: The Practice of Affective Browsing. In Museums in a Digital Culture: How Art and heritage Become Meaningful. Amsterdam University Press.

Sylaiou, S., Killintzis, V., Paliokas, I., Mania, K., & Patias, P. (2014). Usability Evaluation of Virtual Museums' Interfaces Visualization Technologies. In VAMR 2014, Part II, LNCS 8526 (pp. 124–133). Springer International Publishing.

Vergo, P. (1994). The Rhetoric of Display. In R. Miles & L. Zavala (Eds.), *Towards the museum of the future: new European perspectives.* Routledge.

Vilar, E., & Rebelo, F. (2008). Virtual reality in wayfinding studies. In *Proceedings of the 2008 AHFE International Conference (2nd International Conference on Applied Human Factors and Ergonomics jointly with 12th International Conference on Human Aspects of Advanced Manufacturing - HAAMAHA).* USA Publishing.

Vlahović, S., Suznjevic, M., & Kapov, L. S. (2018). Subjective Assessment of Different Locomotion Techniques in Virtual Reality Environments. *2018 Tenth International Conference on Quality of Multimedia Experience (QoMEX),* 1-3. 10.1109/QoMEX.2018.8463433

Wodtke, C., & Govella, A. (2009). *Information Architecture: Blueprints for the Web* (2nd ed.). New Riders.

ENDNOTES

1 According to Peter Vergo (1989), "Every acquisition (and indeed disposal), every juxtaposition or arrangement of an object or work of art, together with other objects or works of art, within the context of a temporary exhibition or museum display means placing a certain construction upon history, be it the history of the distant or more recent past, of our own culture or someone else's, of mankind in general or a particular aspect of human endeavour" (pp. 2–3).

2 International Museums: Museo Galileo, Natural History Museum- United Kingdom, Thyssen-Bornemisza Museo Nacional, Vincent Van Gogh Museum, Dali Theatre Museum, The Louvre Museum, Anne Frank House, Museo Frida Kahlo, Rijksmuseum- Amsterdam, Jean Paul Getty Museum, MASP - Museu de Arte de São Paulo Assis Chateaubriand. National Museums: Ankara Etnografic Museum, Çanakkale Troy Museum, Eskişehir Odunpazarı Modern Museum, Gaziantep Zeugma Mosaic Museum, Istanbul Topkapi Museum, Yapi Kredi Culture and Arts Center "Karagözlüm İki Gözüm Exhibition", Yapi Kredi Culture and Arts Center "Hagop Ayvaz: A Chronicle of Theatre Exhibition", Yapı Kredi Culture and Arts Center "Turhan Selcuk Retrospective", Chora Museum- Istanbul, Çorum Boğazköy Museum, İstanbul Modern "In Pursuit of the Present Exhibition."

Chapter 19
Rethinking the Shift in Communication Dynamics Post Pandemic

Arzu Kizbaz
Istinye University, Turkey

ABSTRACT

German philosopher Goethe expressed, "Emotions unite people, while ideas separate them," emphasizing the essential role of emotions in effective communication. The era of the pandemic, which mandated social isolation, underscored the inherent human need for face-to-face interaction. The surge in social media usage post-pandemic and the rapid integration into the digital age have resulted in a decline in face-to-face communication, leading to reduced interaction among individuals. This study seeks to investigate the evolving dynamics of communication in Generation Y, characterized by an increasing social media usage rate, and Generation Z, which is distancing itself from heavy social media usage post-pandemic. Through in-depth interviews, the research will scrutinize how these generations have adjusted their communication patterns within the realm of interpersonal communication giving particular attention to aspects such as listening, empathy, feedback, effective speaking, and appreciation.

"Words are only painted fire; a look is the fire itself". Mark Twain

INTRODUCTION

The phrase "Actions speak louder than words," coined by Dale Carnegie, actually emphasizes the role of body language and interpersonal communication in the communication process and how body language takes precedence over words.

DOI: 10.4018/979-8-3693-0896-7.ch019

During the pandemic, the inability to fully perceive body language makes communication more challenging because the masks necessary to combat the pandemic conceal the facial expressions we use without thinking, especially those micro expressions that convey and perceive sincerity, trustworthiness, and good intentions (York, 2020).

Communication involves not only body language but also emphasizes the importance of the communication environment. Doğan Cüceloğlu expresses the significance of the communication environment with the following words (Cüceloğlu, 2018:76): "The totality of people, objects, and events within the communication situation, which have qualities that can affect the communication process, is called the communication environment. Every human relationship takes place within an environment. Therefore, before saying something important, a person looks around at their surroundings and wants to see who is present. The communication environment also has a sociocultural aspect. When looking at the sociocultural aspect of the communication environment, it focuses on how individuals establish relationships within a framework based on values that are important in societal life".

In the pandemic era, the absence of a communication environment has given rise to misunderstandings and disrupted communication processes. When individuals gather for communication, the use of masks has posed challenges, and even when they are not physically together due to being in different settings, they still encounter communication issues. Pre-existing communication challenges have become more prominent post-pandemic, exacerbated by the habits developed during this period or the distancing from traditional communication settings. Extended periods spent in the digital realm also contribute significantly to this problem.

Digitalization and digital adaptation have accelerated even more with the pandemic, and people's adaptation processes have shortened because there has been a mandatory need for adjustment. Digital communication, particularly through social media and online platforms, has played an increasingly crucial role during the pandemic in sustaining and strengthening communication. The shift to flexible working arrangements has made digital environments, including spending more time on social media platforms, shopping, and meeting daily communication needs, a mandatory aspect of life. However, individuals experiencing recurring digital fatigue and a need for socialization have expressed a longing for human-centered communication.

Sinan Canan expresses the triggering of dependency by solitude with the following words (Canan, 2020:88): 'It is known that some individuals are more prone to addiction, while others are more resilient. One of the factors that most influences a person's potential for addiction is known to be social isolation and loneliness.'

The sense of social isolation and loneliness during the pandemic has led to an increase in social media addiction. The acceleration of digital transformation, the sudden shift of every transaction to digital platforms, and the restrictions imposed by the pandemic have disrupted relationships by affecting people's moods. The inability to engage in long-term face-to-face communication, which also contributed to individuals becoming more intolerant, has even reached the point of not greeting each other and has been normalized. The new habits gained through digital life have continued even after the end of the pandemic. Generation Z has now added the goal of hybrid working to their career plans and has chosen to adapt to this arrangement.

According to the We Are Social 2022 report, internet users are seen to spend an average of 7 hours online daily, and this time has decreased to 6 hours and 37 minutes according to the latest research. This data alone is an indicator of the importance given to in-person communication after the pandemic (We are Social, 2022).

When examining the articles published on communication processes during the pandemic period, it is observed that many of them focus on similar outcomes. The perspective of these studies on the pandemic and the changing habits in this context can be summarized as follows:

In the information society, the internet and social media have increased their impact and usage areas. Especially during the pandemic period, an increase in internet and social media usage rates has been revealed. The forefronting of individual lifestyles, stay-at-home campaigns, and precautionary measures have directly influenced the use of the internet and social media. While the internet and social media have positive aspects, they also have negative features. In this period of increased internet and social media usage, it is essential to promote proper new media literacy, pay attention to disinformation on the internet, and avoid spending all leisure time solely through technology (Yıldırım O, İpek İ, 2020:90).

Post-pandemic social media usage has increased the level of addiction, and the use of social media has become even more ingrained with the pandemic. Post-pandemic social life has given way to social media and a new world of life. It has been observed that communication has undergone a digital transformation during the pandemic. While the pandemic weakened and superficialized face-to-face communication, it strengthened the communication in the new world of social media. As body language communication was restricted, digital body language became a universal language. It has been revealed that emojis, which display digital body languages, lead to the visual representation and perception of many emotions and thoughts. The pandemic has led young people, like all age groups, to feel health concerns and maintain distance. The COVID-19 pandemic has affected face-to-face communication directly, leading to a more superficial approach to relationships, downplaying emotions, and, in short, initiating the roboticization of communication and relationships parallel to the development of the technology world (Terkan R, 2022:46).

Research conducted on communication and relationships during the pandemic has revealed findings indicating a change. Examining the intergenerational formation and effects of this existing change will also allow for an important observation in this field.

This research aims to shed light on the changing communication dynamics of Generation Y and Generation Z, defined as digital natives, during and after the pandemic. The points where Generation Y and Generation Z converge and diverge are also significant outcomes of the study.

This research will focus on Generation Y, where the social media usage rate is 90.8%, and Generation Z, where the social media usage rate is 64.8%, according to Commencis's 2020 Social Media Report. The study aims to address the changing habits of these generations before and after the pandemic based on their social media usage patterns.

Distinguishing Between Communication and Interpersonal Communication

In a general sense, communication can be defined as the transmission of information, emotions, and thoughts through written, spoken, visual, and auditory means. The most significant difference between communication and interpersonal communication is that interpersonal communication is a specific type of communication that occurs between individuals, involving an interactive process. Face-to-face communication is the most effective example of interpersonal communication. During the pandemic, the lack of this interaction has negatively impacted communication processes.

Berger (2013:293-295) outlines five significant changes that emerge when contrasting communication on the internet with face-to-face communication:

Written Format: Internet communication, in contrast to verbal interaction, is inherently written. Unlike synchronous verbal communication, written communication occurs asynchronously, affording individuals more time for contemplation before expressing their thoughts.

Unstructured Format: Non-internet communication typically follows a more straightforward structure. Individuals can directly call a specific person or engage in face-to-face conversations, whereas online communication allows individuals to express their thoughts or requests without specifying a particular recipient, waiting to see who responds.

Anonymity: In face-to-face communication, participants' identities are evident, allowing connections between the communicator and the individuals involved. However, online communication enables individuals to mask their identities, making anonymous comments and shares.

Broad Audience Reach: Online communication often entails broadcasting or sharing content with a considerably larger audience. While individuals naturally focus on themselves, broadcasting, akin to many offline conversations, encourages a shift towards others, prompting less self-disclosure and more content sharing. Nonetheless, broadcasting does little to alter people's inherent self-focus, thereby promoting self-presentation.

Diminished Social Interaction: In face-to-face communication, the audience is physically present and conspicuous. This encourages communicators to be more self-aware, noticing even subtle changes in body language. This aspect is notably reduced in the online environment.

In direct communication, the instantaneous nature of communication within a specific setting, the option to call the desired person for a meeting, the visibility of communicators' identities, the mutual focus of individuals in communication, the ability to engage in physical social interaction, and the effective utilization of body language represent the pivotal outcomes of face-to-face communication. The conjunction of body language with expressive power paves the way for effective communication, characterizing this effectiveness as a mutually satisfying and joyful process for both parties.

Communication dynamics function uniquely in digital natives, a generation that, despite being conscious of time lost, has been unable to reduce the time spent on social media platforms, adding new habits during and after the pandemic.

The Concept of Generation Y and Generation Z

The concept of generation, as examined in the Turkish Language Association Dictionary, refers to a group of individuals who were born in the same years, embraced the conditions of the same era, and consequently experienced similar difficulties and shared destinies. The Turkish Language Association Glossary of Social Science Terms categorizes individuals forming age clusters of approximately twenty-five to thirty years as a generation. In the Turkish Language Association's Philosophy of History and Cultural History, it defines a generation as a community of individuals who share a sense of new life and are separated by newly drawn lines from the predetermined ones (TDK, 2023).

To better highlight the difference between the Y and Z generations in ongoing communication processes, it is necessary to take a closer look at the characteristics of the Y and Z generations.

The Y generation, characterized by being the first generation to grow up with the allure of digital media, two-thirds of its members were introduced to computers before the age of five. Despite being more adversely affected by the global economic crisis compared to other generations, these individuals, who can access friends, families, information, and entertainment at any moment of the day, have maintained their optimism. Accustomed to being the center of attention and holding high expectations, generation Y members also clearly define their goals (Zemke et al., 2013; 120-125).

The Z generation is a generation born between 2000 and 2020, in a period of rapid technological development. The most prominent feature of this era has been digitization and technological advancements. Children exposed to various forms of access and transportation at an early age are growing up intertwined with technology. The Z generation prefers playing with tablets and similar devices rather than simple and primitive toys during their childhood. The place of technology in their daily life practices is steadily growing. Being in constant visual and auditory communication through digital means, this generation can exhibit antisocial behaviors in face-to-face communication. Individualism and independence are prominent for the Z generation, which partly brings along loneliness. Due to developing a virtual socialization network through social media, they spend less time outdoors. Computers and smartphones are vital and indispensable for many of them. They have high information access capacity and can adapt quickly to changes in time. In line with these developments, they are aware of the need to constantly update themselves to survive in society (Alpak & Düzenli, 2019). Generation Y and Generation Z share similar characteristics as digital natives, and in this context, it is necessary to examine the habits of digital natives.

Communication Approaches of Digital Natives

Digital natives are individuals born into the digital age, characterized by advanced digital skills. They have a structure that can move faster, perform multiple tasks simultaneously, be active in online communities, and prioritize privacy.

According to Prensky (2001: 3), there was difficulty in finding a suitable term to express the current generation, referring to the children growing up in the network environment. However, later, as an expert who delved into this subject, he stated that the most appropriate designation, considering the native use of the digital language by this generation, is "digital native." Prensky's term "digital native" for this generation growing up with new technologies has become widely accepted to describe this generation.

Digital natives are inherently in harmony with the virtual environment from birth, and these connections are considered natural. Therefore, the distinction between digital natives and digital immigrants is based on the perception of using the internet/digital world.

The inherent closeness of digital natives to technology and social networks is a significant characteristic that sets them apart from other generations. However, within this natural flow, it is also possible to observe digital fatigue in them after the pandemic. As all conditions changed with the pandemic, even digital natives found themselves unable to prefer being in front of screens at this intensity. Issues related to time management have arisen and continue to arise among young people who receive information without filtering and spend time on social media. Even digital natives who prefer to exist on social media during the pandemic have prioritized face-to-face communication after the pandemic and described the time spent on social media as wasted time.

Evolving Dynamics Amidst the Pandemic

In the pandemic period, with the absence of face-to-face communication, individuals turned to social media to establish connections. The greatest harm of the pandemic has been the inability of already susceptible individuals to detach from social media. The prolonged screen times and the execution of almost every activity through screens, coupled with the scarcity of face-to-face communication, eventually led people to refrain from turning on their cameras even in online meetings and educational settings. The pandemic intensified existing dependencies and weakened people's ability for face-to-face communication.

Çakır (2014:200) summarizes this situation as follows: "Screens covering the roads, streets, public transportation, ferries, waiting rooms, meeting spaces, educational institutions, government agencies, and every imaginable place, prevent individuals from being alone with themselves, listening to themselves, and engage them. It complicates interaction with other people. Spectatorship turns into a general role, a way of life. Image addiction is the superior product of all these processes. An individual tired of constantly watching someone else now wants to be seen on screens. They crave for it. Because being on the screen seems satisfying, thinking that everyone is watching. Being on the screen promises happiness. It is perceived as gaining attention, being valued, and understood. These are significant humane needs that have been taken away from the individual in modern life. The satisfaction that cannot be achieved in social life is sought to be substituted through screens, through being seen. New media has made this possible but has also brought along numerous problems."

The impact of new media and the communication era on all generations is the preference for remote communication and interpersonal communication processes to decrease, as individuals can be faster independent of time and place. The shift to hybrid job searches by Generation Z is also a result of these habits. Another factor triggering these habits is a society that rapidly adapted to the digital during the pandemic, going beyond the digital age. The speed of adaptation to the digital has distanced society from interactive interpersonal relationships and face-to-face communication. Humans, being social beings, have prioritized socializing and face-to-face communication as soon as the pandemic ended.

THE PURPOSE OF THE RESEARCH

By nature, humans are social beings. They are inclined to communicate and understand the unspoken through body language. Even social distances are determined by the proximity one feels to the person they are communicating with. Especially during the pandemic, the concept of 'social distance' has entered our lives, significantly impacting interpersonal communication. This research will inquire into how human-centered communication, which was lost during the pandemic, is being restructured in the post-pandemic era, particularly among Generation Y and Generation Z. It will question what this communication and relationship are built upon as they undergo restructuring.

THE UNIVERSE AND THE SCOPE OF THE RESEARCH

The research focuses on the Y and Z generations, identified as digital natives.

Prensky argues that "digital natives" refer to the generation born after 1980, emphasizing their differences from the preceding generation, digital immigrants. He notes that they use a distinct digital language and have a different thought structure compared to digital immigrants (Prensky, 2001). According to Prensky (2001), digital natives are characterized as follows:

- They speak the digital language, which is the language of computers and the internet, as their native language.

- They are constantly connected to the network; their mobile phones or computers are always on.
- They possess the ability to multitask, such as listening to music while reading and comprehending something else simultaneously.
- When seeking information, they turn to the internet before printed sources because quick access to information is highly important for this generation.
- Rather than reading lengthy texts, they prefer learning through graphics and opt for "gamified" learning over a serious environment.

Their attention can quickly shift to something else, and they may choose not to pay attention to things that do not interest them.

In the context of qualitative research, face-to-face interviews were conducted with each digital native using the in-depth interview method, and structured questions were posed.

THE METHODOLOGY OF THE RESEARCH

The research will make use of the qualitative research approach through in-depth interviews. In this specific investigation, the in-depth interview technique was employed with a structured set of questions.

A distinctive characteristic of a structured conversation is the systematic and predetermined arrangement of questions directed towards participants. In structured interviews, responses may adhere to established categories or involve rigidly formulated questions. Consequently, structured interviews are perceived as the data collection method most closely aligned with quantitative approaches (Punch, 2005). The inquiries directed at generations Y and Z are outlined below.

1. Did the frequency of your use of digital communication tools increase during the pandemic? If yes, which platform did you use the most?
2. When reflecting on your experiences during the pandemic, what was the most challenging aspect in interpersonal communication processes?
3. In your opinion, what were the facilitating and hindering aspects of the pandemic?
4. Can you express the emotional impact of the pandemic on you in one word?
5. Can you describe in one word the emotion you felt when the pandemic ended?
6. In your view, what underlying issues contribute to intergenerational conflicts during the pandemic?
7. Did the pandemic change your perspective on life, career, people, sector, or work methods? If yes, how?
8. How did your routines and habits change during the pandemic?
9. Have you made any changes to your life and routines after the pandemic?
10. Can you mention one positive and one negative habit that the pandemic has influenced in you?
11. Did your use of social media change in terms of filtering and usage time after the pandemic?
12. What do you think about the significance of appreciation as the most crucial feedback in interpersonal communication and development? Can you express its share in face-to-face communication and personal growth in one word?
13. Can you say that your sense of empathy has become more effective after the pandemic?
14. Has there been any change in your feedback-giving habits before and after the pandemic?

15. Do you consider yourself an active listener? Is there any change in this trait before and after the pandemic?
16. Do you believe you lost your face-to-face communication and effective speaking habits after the pandemic? If yes, why?
17. How does the idea of distancing yourself from social media usage and embracing digital minimalism make you feel?
18. Do you consider the time you spend on social media to be a loss?
19. Has the importance you place on face-to-face communication increased after the pandemic?
20. In your opinion, is it necessary to frame interpersonal communication, including body language, spatial unity, gestures, facial expressions, and words, in order to be understood?

In the context of these questions, the changes in the communication dynamics of Generation Y and Generation Z during and after the pandemic will be traced.

Qualitative research is a form of knowledge generation in which individuals strive to understand their own potential, unravel mysteries, and explore the depths of social structures and systems constructed through their efforts. In qualitatively designed research, there is an effort to achieve a profound understanding of the event or phenomenon under investigation (Morgan, 1996).

FINDINGS AND DISCUSSIONS

Communication is a two-way process. This statement indicates that communication is an interaction between a sender and a receiver. The interaction between two parties, which involves the exchange of information and sharing of meaning, expresses mutual communication. Two-way communication describes a form of interaction where both the transmission of information and feedback are integrated with each other.

Even when people communicate face-to-face, they are still at risk of misunderstanding due to the incorrect use of body language. The pandemic period, with individuals staying at home and avoiding socialization, has further exacerbated this handicap. People who haven't been able to gather for an extended period have lost some of the essential skills for effective communication, and their eloquence has suffered. An example of this can be seen in online meetings, especially in educational settings, where participants may choose not to turn on their cameras. Individuals who veer away from their daily routines and experience discomfort at home have impeded their visibility and attentiveness.

Before the pandemic, the transition from face-to-face communication and interaction to remote work, due to the changes in all conditions after the pandemic, has led to significant changes in communication and interaction processes for those who were previously engaged in face-to-face communication. This process, which affects not only Generation Y and Z but also all individuals, has left different traces in each generation. This research aims to thoroughly examine the impact of this phenomenon by asking questions. In this research, Commencis's 2020 Social Media Report is examined, focusing on Generation Y, where social media usage is at 90.8%, and Generation Z, where social media usage is at 64.8%. This study will address the habits and changes created by social media in Generation Y and Generation Z before and after the pandemic.

Table 1. Responses and analysis of Generation Y on a conceptual basis

Answers	Generation Y
1	Platform: Online Meeting, Phone
2	Lack of face-to-face communication, invisible gestures
3	Facilitating Aspect: Working from home, returning to nature Hindering Aspect: Inability to make contact, Fear of death
4	Helplessness, anxiety
5	Relaxation, loneliness
6	Viewpoint, intervention
7	Turning to nature
8	Hygienic habits
9	Spending time in nature, wearing a mask in winter
10	Positive habit: Reduce plastic consumption, reduce carbon footprint, Paying attention to hygiene Negative habit: Gaining weight
11	Social media usage time increased
12	Importance, Necessity
13	Yes. I'm more empathetic
14	More feedback
15	I was always an active listener
16	No
17	Loneliness, relaxation
18	Sometimes
19	Absolutely
20	Absolutely

Furthermore, another focal point of this research is to explore the intersections and divergences in terms of communication dynamics within Generation Y and Z, identifying the areas where they overlap and differ.

The data presented in the table above reveals a significant increase in online meetings and phone usage within Generation Y during the pandemic. The findings were derived through inquiries pertaining to the evolving communication dynamics during and post the pandemic period addressed to Generation Y.

According to Generation Y, the absence of face-to-face communication and the inability to perceive facial expressions during the pandemic are identified as factors negatively influencing communication. While Generation Y characterizes the positive impact of the pandemic as a reconnection with nature and the adoption of remote work practices, they define the negative impact as the hindrance to engaging in face-to-face communication and the prevailing fear of mortality.

Generation Y signifies a shift in their perspectives, indicating that the pandemic triggered feelings of anxiety, followed by a sense of relief in the post-pandemic era. Additionally, Generation Y acknowledges a heightened awareness of hygiene practices and a revised outlook on sustainability, manifesting in a conscious reduction in plastic consumption to mitigate their carbon footprint.

Identifying weight gain as a negative consequence, Generation Y demonstrates an increased awareness of sustainability concerns, coupled with a commitment to reduce plastic consumption for environmental conservation. Notably, they report an uptick in social media usage, underscoring the significance of acknowledgment and recognition during this period.

Generation Y asserts their constant role as active listeners, maintaining that the pandemic did not adversely impact their capacity for both listening and providing feedback. Contemplating a decrease in social media usage, they articulate anticipated emotions of relief and loneliness, highlighting a nuanced emotional spectrum.

While elucidating the absence of and the importance attributed to face-to-face communication, Generation Y accentuates the imperative of effective communication for forging robust connections. In their evaluation, Generation Y acknowledges the necessity of effective communication in cultivating strong bonds, noting the continuity of their communication styles before and after the pandemic, coupled with an inclination towards nature.

Throughout the pandemic and its aftermath, Generation Y displays an awareness of their responsibilities towards sustainable living, further emphasizing their commitment to environmental conservation through reduced plastic consumption.

Upon posing identical questions to Generation Z, the ensuing results were derived.

The findings derived from the examination of Generation Z can be succinctly outlined as follows:

During the pandemic, Generation Z exhibited a pronounced inclination towards Instagram and YouTube. Positive consequences for Generation Z materialized in enhanced time management skills and an increased reliance on online education platforms. However, Generation Z grappled with the absence of face-to-face communication. Experiencing negative emotions such as unhappiness and anxiety during the pandemic, Generation Z reported a subsequent shift towards emotions characterized by happiness, well-being, and relief as the pandemic abated.

Digital natives, asserting that intergenerational conflicts primarily arise from a deficit in empathy, communicated a positive shift in their perspectives towards the hybrid work model. Simultaneously, they observed a deterioration in people's moods. Generation Z indicated that the pandemic induced changes in nutritional patterns, sleep routines, and digital habits, fostering adaptation to hygiene practices, social distancing, early waking, and engagement in hybrid work.

While acknowledging positive effects such as enhanced intra-family communication and solitary time, Generation Z also recognized negative impacts, including pessimism, heightened cleanliness obsession, and alterations in sleep patterns. The pandemic led to an increase in the time spent on social media by Generation Z. Utilizing descriptors such as "success, strength, courage, self-confidence, necessity, and satisfaction" to articulate the sense of appreciation, Generation Z highlighted their ability to cultivate empathy, provide attentive feedback, and consistently act as active listeners.

Although Generation Z acknowledged challenges in effective communication post-pandemic, they found the notion of distancing from social media to be daunting and challenging. Simultaneously, they perceived the time spent on social media as a loss. Underscoring the significance of interpersonal communication, Generation Z emphasized the pivotal role of body language, spatial unity, and facial expressions in facilitating effective communication.

In this investigation, the amalgamation of key aspects shared between Generation Y and Generation Z is systematically compiled into a comprehensive table. The primary commonalities encompass the dearth of face-to-face communication, the obscured visibility of facial expressions, the challenges in socializing, and the prevalence of a post-pandemic sense of relief superseding anxiety. Noteworthy

Table 2. Responstes and analysis of Generation Z on a conceptual basis

Answers	Generation Z
1	Platform: Instagram, YouTube
2	Lack of face-to-face communication, invisible gestures
3	Facilitating Aspect: Accessible educational platforms, managing time Hindering Aspect: Inability to socialize
4	Confusion, helplessness, unhappiness, anxiety
5	Happiness, health, relaxation, longing
6	Miscommunication, Lack of empathy
7	Hybrid work, deterioration of people's mood
8	Sleep, Nutrition and Digital Habits
9	Spending time in nature, getting up early, paying attention to hygiene, maintaining social distance, Working with hybrid system
10	Positive habit: Intra-family communication, not procrastinating, being with yourself, hygiene. Negative habit: Pessimism, introversion, anxiety, shyness, obsession with cleanliness, inactivity, changing sleep habits
11	Social media usage time increased
12	Success, Strength, Courage, Self-confidence, Necessity, Satisfaction
13	Yes. I'm more empathetic
14	More feedback
15	I was always an active listener
16	Yes
17	Difficult, restrictive, scary
18	Yes
19	Yes
20	Yes

shared experiences include the establishment of a routine involving spending time in nature or outdoor settings following the pandemic, the identification of weight gain and physical inactivity as adverse outcomes of the pandemic, the articulation of appreciation as an intrinsic need, the accentuation of empathetic development, the propensity for increased feedback provision, the consistent adherence to active listening practices, and the expressed inclination toward distancing from social media with connotations of loneliness and trepidation. Furthermore, both Generation Y and Generation Z uniformly prioritize interpersonal communication in the aftermath of the pandemic, underscoring the paramount importance of face-to-face interactions.

In the research examining changes and habits during and after the pandemic, the divergent aspects of Generation Y and Generation Z have been identified based on their responses to the posed questions. While Generation Y inclined toward online meetings and phone usage, Generation Z turned their focus to Instagram and YouTube. Generation Y prioritized working from home and embracing nature, whereas Generation Z gave precedence to accessing educational platforms and managing time more efficiently. Conflicts were attributed to perspectives by Generation Y, whereas Generation Z characterized them as a lack of empathy and communication. Generation Y emphasized the pandemic's positive role in reconnecting with nature, while Generation Z highlighted the significance of hybrid work and the decline in

Table 3. Resemblances of the responses of Generation Y and Generation Z

Answers	Resemblances of the Responses Generation Y and Z
2	Lack of face-to-face communication, invisible gestures
3	Y: Hindering Aspect: Inability to make contact Z: Hindering Aspect: Inability to socialize
4	Helplessness, anxiety
5	Relaxation
9	Spending time in nature
10	Negative habit: Inactivity, gaining weight
11	Social media usage time increased
12	Necessity
13	Yes. I'm more empathetic
14	More feedback
15	I was always an active listener
17	Y: Loneliness Z: Scary
19	Y: Absolutely Z: Yes
20	Y: Absolutely Z: Yes

people's moods. The pandemic altered hygiene habits in Generation Y and impacted sleep, nutrition, and digital habits in Generation Z. The pandemic instilled a positive habit of tracking the carbon footprint in Generation Y, while such awareness was not evident in Generation Z. While Generation Y asserts the preservation of effective speaking habits post-pandemic, Generation Z indicates a decline in these habits. Despite Generation Z viewing time spent on social media as a loss, occasional agreement from Generation Y indicates a discrepancy in the responses of this shared digital-native generation.

Table 4. Disresemblances of the responses of Generation Y and Generation Z

Answers	Disresemblances of the Responses Generation Y and Z
1	Platform: Y: Online Meeting, Phone / Z: Instagram, YouTube
3	Y: Facilitating Aspect: Working from home, returning to natüre Z: Facilitating Aspect: Accessible educational platforms, managing time
6	Y: Viewpoint, intervention Z: Miscommunication, Lack of empathy
7	Y: Turning to natüre Z: Hybrid work, deterioration of people's mood
8	Y: Hygienic Habits Z: Sleep, Nutrition and Digital Habits
10	Positive habit: Y: Reduce carbon footprint. Positive habit Z: -
16	Y: No / Z: Yes
18	Y: Sometimes Z: Yes

CONCLUSION

In the words of Mark Twain, "Kindness is the language which the deaf can hear and blind can see". This statement actually refers to face-to-face communication in interpersonal communication. A person's politeness can be understood not only through words but also through their actions and body language. After the pandemic period, there have been days when people longed for and had the opportunity to go out, meet, and socialize, and the longing for this has become apparent. Regarding the definition of interpersonal communication, Fiske states the following (Fiske, 1996:45):

Interpersonal communication is the most commonly used form of communication throughout a person's life. The fundamental definition of interpersonal communication is the process of exchanging information between two or more individuals.

According to Gerbner (1967:43), communication is viewed as a social interaction involving mutual message exchange.

In social interaction, the impact of social media cannot be denied in this digital age.

Social media plays a significant role in creating new communication and relationships among young people (Rachel, 2016).

According to the We Are Social report for the 4th Quarter of 2022, 4 out of 5 people use smartphones, and the time spent on the internet is decreasing. Podcasts are on the rise. According to the February 2023 report for Turkey, the time spent on the internet has decreased by 4.8%, with Instagram being identified as the platform where the most time is spent.

In the 2020 Commencis Social Media report, social media usage was determined to be 90.8% in the Y generation and 64.4% in the Z generation. This percentage aligns with the data obtained from the Z generation interviewed within the scope of this research, where they describe spending time on social media as wasted time.

In the scope of this research, an increase in social media dependency during the pandemic has been observed among Generation Y and Generation Z. Findings indicate a high level of uncertainty and anxiety felt by both generations during the pandemic. The lack of face-to-face communication has caused discomfort for both Generation Y and Generation Z. Effects such as weight gain and discomfort due to inactivity have been observed in both generations, along with an increase in time spent on social media. As the pandemic came to an end, a sense of relief was felt by both Generation Y and Generation Z, and they expressed habits such as providing more feedback, emphasizing the necessity of appreciation, and consistently being active listeners. The idea of distancing from social media was expressed as loneliness for Generation Y and as frightening for Generation Z. The end of the pandemic and the importance of face-to-face communication were equally emphasized for both Generation Y and Generation Z.

The points of divergence between Generation Y and Generation Z are evident in their online behaviors, with Generation Y displaying a preference for online meetings, while Generation Z intensifies its usage of Instagram. Generation Y views a return to nature as a positive impact, whereas Generation Z emphasizes the positive effect of time management. Generation Y attributes conflicts during the pandemic to differing perspectives, while Generation Z identifies a lack of empathy as the root cause. Generation Y emphasizes increased hygiene and a concern for carbon footprint, while Generation Z does not specify any habits. Generation Y asserts that it has not lost its face-to-face communication habits, whereas Generation Z claims to have lost them. The most significant contrast lies in Generation Z perceiving time spent on social media as a loss, whereas Generation Y occasionally considers it only as a minor loss.

This study indicates that Generation Y, labeled as digital natives, occasionally categorizes social media as a time-wasting activity, whereas Generation Z characterizes the time spent on social media as a loss. Despite its potential benefits, the utilization of social media is deemed a time-wasting endeavor when not employed conscientiously. The habit of staying at home during the pandemic has resulted in prolonged screen time, fostering a new habit in this regard.

After the pandemic, the transformation of digital habits has led to the dulling of certain qualities. Personal attributes such as curiosity, patience, and self-awareness may decline with digitization and technology usage. During the pandemic, most young people became unhappy and hopeless. The source of unhappiness is often described by Goleman as follows: The cause of mental clutter is often the reason for unhappiness (Goleman, 2020:53). The starting point is the ability to focus.

The pandemic has shown the same effects for everyone experiencing that process. Along with hopelessness, negative effects such as spending time on social media, subsequent loss of time management skills, focus issues, and changes in sleep and eating patterns have disrupted individuals' routines. The most valuable trait during this period is to exhibit resilience against all these negative factors. Kahneman associates this situation with optimism and says: The main benefit of optimism is resilience in the face of adversity (Kahneman, 2011: 305). Being resilient against negativity is actually a trait we need to develop, and especially during the pandemic, it has been possible to test this ability.

Nevzat Tarhan emphasized that, during the pandemic, communicators bear the primary responsibility, stating (Tarhan, N., 2020): "Social isolation ideally involves physical isolation. However, when the situation transforms into psychological isolation, it leads to an increase in physical distance."

To overcome the negative effects of the pandemic, individuals can engage in conscious use of digital platforms, evoke curiosity by spending time in nature, and embark on a self-discovery process. Creating awareness through the self-discovery process, developing new skills, strengthening social relationships, slowing down, and enhancing the sense of patience can be beneficial activities. Establishing a digital balance in their lives, prioritizing face-to-face communication, increasing awareness of social media usage, using social media with a focus on benefits, dedicating time to themselves, implementing digital detox practices, and enhancing digital literacy are crucial steps for effective communication and overcoming the negative effects of the pandemic, as Jim Rohn stated, "Effective communication is 20% what you know and 80% how you feel about what you know."

REFERENCES

Berger, J. (2013). Beyond Viral: Interpersonal Communication in the Internet Age. *Psychological Inquiry*, *24*(4), 293–296. doi:10.1080/1047840X.2013.842203

Çakır, M. (2014). *Görsel Kültür ve Küresel Kitle Kültürü*. Ütopya Yayınevi.

Canan, S. (2020). *İFA, İlişkiler ve Stres*. TutiKitap.

Cüceloğlu, D. (2018). *Yeniden İnsan İnsana*. Remzi Kitabevi.

Fiske, J. (1996). *Kitle İletişim Çalışmalarına Giriş*. Ark Yayınları.

Gerbner, G. (1967). *Mass Media and Human Communication Theory*. Holt, Rinehart And Winston.

Goleman, D. (2020). *Odak, Çev. Filiz Nayır Deniztekin*. Varlık Yayınları.

Kahneman, D. (2011). *Hızlı ve Yavaş Düşünme, Çev. Osman Çetin – Filiz Nayır Deniztekin*. Varlık Yayınları.

Morgan, D. L. (1996). *Focus groups as qualitative research (C. 16)*. Sage Publications.

Prensky, M. (2001). Digital Natives, Digital Immigrants. *On the Horizon, 9*(5).

Punch, K. F. (2005). *Introduction to Social Research–Quantitative & Qualitative Approaches*. Sage.

Rachel, E. (2016). *Experts say kids are growing up with more anxiety and less selfesteem*. Retrieved from https://childmind.org/article/howusing-social-media-affects-teenagers

Tarhan, N. (2020). *Pandemi döneminde iletişimin önemi.* Retrieved from https://uskudar.edu.tr/tr/icerik/5809/prof-dr-nevzat-tarhan-pandemi-doneminde-iletisimin-onemi-ortaya-cikti

Taş, F. (2020). Covid-19 Pandemi Sürecinde Yetişkinler Arasında Yüz Maskesi Kullanma Pratiği ve Tekniği Üzerine Değerlendirme ve Öneriler. *Halk Sağlığı Hemşireliği Dergisi, 2*(2), 52–56.

TDK. (2023). https://sozluk.gov.tr/

Terkan, R. (2022). Pandemi Sürecinin İletişime Etkileri: İlişkilere Yansıması. *Scientific Journal of Innovation and Social Sciences Research, 2*(1), 45–56.

Yıldırım, O., & İpek, İ. (2020). Yeni Koronavirüs Salgını Dolayısıyla Gündeme Gelen Sosyal İzolasyon ve Gönüllü Karantina Döneminde İnternet ve Sosyal Medya Kullanımı. *İletişim Kuram ve Araştırma Dergisi, 52*.

York, D. (2020). How to build Rapport? *Harward Business Review.* Retrieved from https://hbr.org/2020/09/how-to-build-rapport-while-wearing-a-mask?autocomplete=true

Zempke, R., Raines, C., & Filipczak, B. (2013). Generations at Work: Managing the Clash of Boomers, Gen Xers, and Gen Yers in the Workplace (2nd ed.). Amacom.

KEY TERMS AND DEFINITIONS

Communication Dynamics: Communication dynamics is a complex concept that encompasses various factors defining communication processes and interactions among people.

Digital Age: "Digital age" describes the current period marked by the extensive utilization and incorporation of digital technologies.

Digital Natives: Generation, who is growing up with new technologies.

Interpersonal Communication: Interpersonal communication refers to the exchange of information, thoughts, feelings, and meaning between two or more people.

Post Pandemic: The period or conditions that come after a pandemic.

Compilation of References

Abarca, A., Alpízar, F., Sibaja, G., & Rojas, C. (2013). *Técnicas cualitativas de investigación*. UCR.

Abdalla, J. (2020). *US universities switch to online courses due to coronavirus*. https://www.aljazeera.com/news/2020/03/universities-switch-online-courses-due-coronavirus200310202804023.html

Abonizio, H. Q., Barbon, A. P. A. C., Rodrigues, R., Santos, M., Martínez-Vizcaíno, V., Mesas, A. E., & Junior, S. B. (2023). How people interact with a chatbot against disinformation and fake news in Covid-19 in Brazil: The CoronaAI case. *International Journal of Medical Informatics, 177*, 105134. Advance online publication. doi:10.1016/j.ijmedinf.2023.105134 PMID:37369153

Adaklı, G. (2006). *Türkiye'de Medya Endüstrisi*. Ütopya Yayınları.

Adisa, T. A., Gbadamosi, G., & Osabutey, E. L. (2017). What happened to the border? The role of mobile information technology devices on employees' work-life balance. *Personnel Review, 46*(8), 1651–1671. doi:10.1108/PR-08-2016-0222

Afifi, T. D., Hutchinson, S., & Krouse, S. (2006). Toward a theoretical model of communal coping in postdivorce families and other naturally occurring groups. *Communication Theory, 16*(3), 378–409. doi:10.1111/j.1468-2885.2006.00275.x

Agamben, G. (2020, February 27). Covid-19: Gerekçesiz Bir Acil Durumun Yarattığı İstisna Hali. Terrabayt. https://terrabayt.com/dusunce/covid-19-gerekcesiz-bir-acil-durumun-yarattigi-istisna-hali/

Agarwal, N. (2022). Article 370 of Indian constitution. *ipleaders*.

Agostino, D., Arnaboldi, M., & Diz-Lema, M. (2021). New development: COVİD-19 as an accelerator of digital transformation in public service delivery. *Public Money & Management, 41*(1), 69–72. doi:10.1080/09540962.2020.1764206

Ahad, A. D., & Lim, S. M. A. (2014). Convenience or nuisance? The 'WhatsApp' dilemma. *Procedia: Social and Behavioral Sciences, 155*, 189–196. doi:10.1016/j.sbspro.2014.10.278

Ahmed, S. J., & Navle, V. (2021). Text and Sentimental Analysis on Big Data. *International Journal of Scientific Research in Computer Science, Engineering and Information Technology, 7*(2), 324-334. doi:10.32628/CSEIT217269

Ahmed, S. T. (2020). Managing news overload (MNO): The COVID-19infodemic. *Information (Basel), 11*(8), 375. doi:10.3390/info11080375

Akintola, M., Bello, M. B., & Daramola, D. S. (2016). Usage of WhatsApp as a social media platform among undergraduates in Kwara State. *Nigerian Journal of Educational Technology, 1*(1), 1–14.

Alajmi, B. M., & Khalil, O. (2022). The extent of and motivation for disaster information seeking behavior via social networking sites. *Journal of Electronic Resources Librarianship, 34*(3), 219–244. doi:10.1080/1941126X.2022.2099026

Albertazzi, D., & Bonansinga, D. (2023). Beyond anger: The populist radical right on TikTok. *Journal of Contemporary European Studies*, 1–17. doi:10.1080/14782804.2022.2163380

Alçiçek, M. (2021). Bir Belleği Çarpıtma Dinamiği Olarak Post – Truth ve Yeni Medya. *Doğu Batı Düşünce Dergisi.*, *97*, 195–208.

Al-Dmour, H., Masa'deh, R., Salman, A., Abuhashesh, M., & Al-Dmour, R. (2020). Influence of social media platforms on public health protection against the COVID-19 pandemic via the mediating effects of public health awareness and behavioral changes: Integrated model. *Journal of Medical Internet Research*, *22*(8), e19996. doi:10.2196/19996 PMID:32750004

Alhemimah, A. (2023). How COVID-19 impacts travel-health information seeking and tourists' travel intentions: A protection motivation theory-based model. *Journal of Destination Marketing & Management*, *27*, 100757. doi:10.1016/j.jdmm.2022.100757

Aliperti, G., & Cruz, A. M. (2019). Investigating tourists' risk information processing. *Annals of Tourism Research*, *79*, 102803. doi:10.1016/j.annals.2019.102803

Almanza, J. de J. (2003). La comunicación de las malas noticias en la práctica médica. *Neurologia, Neurocirugia, Psiquiatria*, *36*(4), 165–176. https://bit.ly/3ynZdhL

Alon, T., Doepke, M., Olmstead-Rumsey, J., & Tertilt, M. (2020). *The Impact of Covid-19 on Gender Equality*. National Bureau of Economic Research. doi:10.3386/w26947

Alpay, Y. (2020). *Yalanın Siyaseti*. Destek Yayınları.

Alpert, L. I., & Hagey, K. (2020). Coronavirus Is Giving Readers Plenty of News. But Local Outlets Are Still Teetering. *Wall Street Journal*. Retrieved from https://www.wsj.com/articles/news-outlets-win-audiences-yet-lose-revenue-during-coronavirus-crisis-11584708390?mod=searchresults&ns=prod/accounts-wsj

Al-Rasheed, M. (2020). Protective behavior against COVID-19 among the public in Kuwait: An examination of the protection motivation theory, trust in government, and sociodemographic factors. *Social Work in Public Health*, *35*(7), 546–556. doi:10.1080/19371918.2020.1806171 PMID:32970542

Aluç, E., Serttaş, A., Gürkan, H., Sarıkaya, T., & Kalkan Aluç, Y. (2022). Ukrayna-Rusya Savaşı Sırasında Ülkelerin Kullandıkları Deepfake Videoların İncelenmesi. *Uluslararası Medya ve Toplum Sempozyumu Tam Metinler Kitabı*, 1-13.

Álvarez Aparicio, A. I. (2020). Comunicación de malas noticias en el ámbito sanitario en tiempos de COVID-19. La comunicación telefónica. *Revista de Comunicación y Salud*, *10*(2), 211–248. doi:10.35669/rcys.2020.10(2).211-248

Alves, A. E. (2003, May-June). ¿Cómo comunicar malas noticias a nuestros pacientes y no morir en el intento? *Revista Argentina de Cardiología*, *71*(3). https://bit.ly/3f3bDEj

Andersen, K. N., Medaglia, R., & Henriksen, H. Z. (2012). Social media in public health care: Impact domain propositions. *Government Information Quarterly*, *29*(4), 462–469. doi:10.1016/j.giq.2012.07.004

Andrejevic, M. (2013). *Infoglut: How too much information is changing the way we think and know*. Routledge. doi:10.4324/9780203075319

Angoletto, R., & Queiroz, V. C. (2020). COVID-19 and the challenges in education. *The Centro de Estudos Sociedade e Tecnologia*, *5*, 2.

An, S., Schulz, P. J., & Kang, H. (2023). Perceived COVID-19 susceptibility and preventive behaviors: Moderating effects of social support in Italy and South Korea. *BMC Public Health*, *23*(1), 1–11. PMID:36624437

Antena 3. (2017). *España es el país con más bares del mundo con más de 250.000 establecimientos.* https://www.antena3.com/noticias/economia/espana-es-el-pais-con-mas-bares-del-mundo_2017102359ee45720cf2fc58bffee31a.html

Antheunis, M. L., Tates, K., & Nieboer, T. E. (2013). Patients' and health professionals' use of social media in health care: Motives, barriers, and expectations. *Patient Education and Counseling*, *92*(3), 426–431. doi:10.1016/j.pec.2013.06.020 PMID:23899831

Apostolakis, I., Koulierakis, G., Berler, A., Chryssanthou, A., & Varlamis, I. (2012). Use of social media by healthcare professionals in Greece: An exploratory study. *International Journal of Electronic Healthcare*, *7*(2), 105–124. doi:10.1504/IJEH.2012.049873 PMID:23079026

Appelgren, E. (2004). *Convergence and divergence in media: different perspectives.* ICCC 8th International Conference on Electronic Publishing, Brasilia, Brazil.

Aqili, V. D., & Nejad, V. M. (2016). A study on news anchors' meta-language and non-verbal factors and their impact on audiences. *The International Journal of Social Sciences (Islamabad)*, *6*(1), 1–9.

Aranda, C. I., Cedillo, R., del Campo, M. G., Omelas, R. O., & Góngora, J. (2014, September-October). Factores que influyen y dificultan la comunicación de malas noticias en el personal de salud. *Acta Universitaria*, *24*(5), 20–26. doi:10.15174.au.2014.600

Arash, S.B., & Raffaele, D. A. (2023). An empirical evaluation of enhanced teleportation for navigating large urban immersive virtual environments. *Frontiers in Virtual Reality*, *3*. doi:10.3389/frvir.2022.1075811

Arık, E. (2018). *Dijital Mahremiyet*. Literatürk Yayınları.

Armstrong, C. L., Cain, J. A., & Hou, J. (2021). Ready for disaster: Information seeking, media influence, and disaster preparation for severe weather outbreaks. *Atlantic Journal of Communication*, *29*(3), 121–135. doi:10.1080/15456870.2020.1731512

Arnaud, A., & Schminke, M. (2012). The ethical climate and context of organizations: A comprehensive model. *Organization Science*, *23*(6), 1767–1780. doi:10.1287/orsc.1110.0698

Arriaga, M., Francisco, R., Nogueira, P., Oliveira, J., Silva, C., Câmara, G., Sørensen, K., Dietscher, C., & Costa, A. (2022). Health Literacy in Portugal: Results of the Health Literacy Population Survey Project 2019-2021. *International Journal of Environmental Research and Public Health*, *19*(4225), 4225. Advance online publication. doi:10.3390/ijerph19074225 PMID:35409905

Ataguba, J. E. (2020). COVID-19 Pandemic, a war to be won: Understanding its economic implications for Africa. *Applied Health Economics and Health Policy*, *18*(3), 325–328. doi:10.100740258-020-00580-x PMID:32249362

Augenbraun, E. (2011). Occupy Wall Street and the limits of spontaneous street protest. *The Guardian.* Retrieved from: https://www.theguardian.com/commentisfree/cifamerica/2011/sep/29/occupy-wall-street-protest

Auken, I. (2016, November 10). Welcome To 2030: I Own Nothing, Have No Privacy And Life Has Never Been Better. *Forbes*. https://www.forbes.com/sites/worldeconomicforum/2016/11/10/shopping-i-cant-really-remember-what-that-is-or-how-differently-well-live-in-2030/

Aupers, S., & Houtman, D. (2010). Religions of Modernity: Relocating the Sacred to the Self and the Digital. In S. Aupers & D. Houtman (Eds.), *Religions of modernity: Relocating the sacred to the self and the digital* (pp. 1–30). Brill. doi:10.1163/ej.9789004184510.i-273

Austin, L., Liu Fisher, B., & Jin, Y. (2012). How audiences seek out crisis information: Exploring the social-mediated crisis communication model. *Journal of Applied Communication Research, 40*(2), 188–207. doi:10.1080/00909882.2012.654498

Ayarra, M., & Lizarraga, S. (2001). Malas noticias y apoyo emocional. *Anales del Sistema Sanitario de Navarra, 24*(Suplemento 2), 55–63.

Azap, A. (2019). *Aşı Karşıtlarının İddiaları ve Bilimin Yanıtları*. Türk Tabipleri Birliği (Turkish Medical Association). https://www.ttb.org.tr/userfiles/files/As%CC%A7%C4%B1%20kars%CC%A7%C4%B1tlar%C4%B1n%C4%B1n%20iddialar%C4%B1%20ve%20gerc%CC%A7ekler.pdf

Azmi, R., Tibben, W., & Win, K. T. (2016). Motives behind Cyber Security Strategy Development: A Literature Review of National Cyber Security Strategy. *Australasian Conference on Information Systems.*

Back, A. L., Arnold, R. M., Tulsky, J. A., Baile, W. F., & Edwards, K. (2010, June). Could I add something? Teaching communication by intervening in real time during a clinical encounter. *Academic Medicine, 85*(6), 1048–1051. doi:10.1097/ACM.0b013e3181dbac6f PMID:20505408

Bahagia, B., Wibowo, R., Muniroh, L., Al Wahid, A., Rizkal, R., Noor, Z. M., & Karim, A. (2022). The drawbacks and advantages of TikTok in student amid pandemic COVID-19. *Jurnal Basicedu, 6*(3), 5302–5310. doi:10.31004/basicedu.v6i3.2459

Baile, W. F., Buckman, R., Lenzi, R., Glober, G., Beale, E. A., & Kudelka, A. P. (2000). SPIKES—a six-step protocol for delivering bad news: Application to the patient with cancer. *The Oncologist, 5*(4), 302–311. doi:10.1634/theoncologist.5-4-302 PMID:10964998

Bakshi, N. a. (2021). *History and future of digital health.* Itihasa Research and Digital.

Balcı, A. (2020). The Effects of Pandemics on Education, with a Focus on COVID-19. *International Journal of Leadership Studies. Theory into Practice, 3*(3), 75–85.

Ball-Rokeach, S. J., Kim, Y. C., & Matei, S. (2001). Storytelling neighborhood: Paths to belonging in diverse urban environments. *Communication Research, 28*(4), 392–428. doi:10.1177/009365001028004003

Bal, M. (2009). Exhibition as the Syntax of the Face. *Grammar of the Exhibition. MJ. Manifesta Journal,* (7), 13–21.

Balmford, W., & Davies, H. (2020). Mobile Minecraft: Negotiated space and perceptions of play in Australian families. *Mobile Media & Communication, 8*(1), 3–21. doi:10.1177/2050157918819614

Banco, E. (2021). *Anuncio - Hipoteca Inteligente EVO Banco.* https://www.youtube.com/watch?v=Sxzdg5pD7ec

Bandura, A. (2000). Exercise of human agency through collective efficacy. *Current Directions in Psychological Science, 9*(3), 75–78. doi:10.1111/1467-8721.00064

Bandyopadhyay, O. (2023). *Health without wealth: the plight of India's ASHA workers.* British Safety Council.

Bann, S. (1995). Shrines, Curiosities and the Rhetoric of Display. In L. Cooke & P. Wollen (Eds.), Visual Display: Culture Beyond Appearances. Bay Press.

Barricelli, B. R., Gadia, D., Rizzi, A., & Marini, D. L. R. (2016). Semiotics of virtual reality as a communication process. *Behaviour & Information Technology, 35*(11), 879–896. doi:10.1080/0144929X.2016.1212092

Barr, M., & Copeland-Stewart, A. (2021). Playing video games during the COVID-19 pandemic and effects on players' well-being. *Games and Culture, 17*(1), 1–18. doi:10.1177/15554120211017036

Bartel, F. (2022). *The Triumph of Broken Promises: The End of the Cold War and the Rise of Neoliberalism*. Harvard University Press.

Başar, M., Arslan, S., Günsel, E., & Akpınar, M. (2019). Öğretmen adaylarının uzaktan eğitim algısı. *Journal of Multidisciplinary Studies in Education, 3*(2), 14–22.

Basch, C. H., Hillyer, G. C., & Jaime, C. (2020). COVID-19 on TikTok: Harnessing an emerging social media platform to convey important public health messages. *International Journal of Adolescent Medicine and Health, 34*(5), 367–369. doi:10.1515/ijamh-2020-0111 PMID:32776899

Bascuñán, M.L. (2013). Comunicación de "malas noticias" en salud. *Revista Médica Clínica Las Condes, 24*(4), 685-693. doi:10.1016/S0716-8640(13)70208-6

Bascuñán, M. L., Roizblatt, A., & Roizblatt, D. (2007). Comunicación de malas noticias en medicina: Un estudio exploratorio. *Revista de Medicina de la Universidad de Navarra, 52*(2), 28–31. https://bit.ly/3f8vvpD PMID:17886712

Bashirian, S., Jenabi, E., Khazaei, S., Barati, M., Karimi-Shahanjarini, A., Zareian, S., Rezapur-Shahkolai, F., & Moeini, B. (2020). Factors associated with preventive behaviours of covid-19 among hospital staff in iran in 2020: An application of the protection motivation theory. *The Journal of Hospital Infection, 105*(3), 430–433. doi:10.1016/j.jhin.2020.04.035 PMID:32360337

Batey, M. (2013). El significado de la marca. Cómo y porqué ponemos sentido a productos y servicios. Granica.

Baudat, S., Van Petegem, S., Antonietti, J. P., & Zimmermann, G. (2020). Parental solicitation and adolescents' information management: The moderating role of autonomy-supportive parenting. *Journal of Child and Family Studies, 29*(2), 426–441. doi:10.100710826-019-01687-z

Bauman, Z. (2007). *Vida de consumo*. Fondo de Cultura Económica.

Beaulieu, A., & de Rijcke, S. (2016). Networked Knowledge and Epistemic Authority in the Development of Virtual Museums. In Museums in a Digital Culture: How Art and Heritage Become Meaningful. Amsterdam University Press.

Becher, B. (2023). What is Virtual Reality? *Built In*. https://builtin.com/media-gaming/-what-is-virtual-reality

Beck, G., & Haskins, J. (2022). *The great reset: Joe Biden and the rise of 21st century fascism*. Forefront Books; Mercury Ink.

Beer, T. (2021, January 26). Report: American Billionaires Have Added More Than $1 Trillion In Wealth During Pandemic. *Forbes*. https://www.forbes.com/sites/tommybeer/2021/01/26/report-american-billionaires-have-added-more-than-1-trillion-in-wealth-during-pandemic/

Begley, S. (2017). *Digital Literacy: realizing the promise of technology*. Academic Press.

Bek, M. G. (2023). Disseminating and resisting online hate speech in Turkey. In B. Di Fátima (Ed.), *Hate speech on social media: A global approach* (pp. 121–141). LabCom Books.

Belli, L. F. (2020). Recomendaciones para la comunicación de malas noticias por teléfono durante la pandemia por SARS-CoV-2. *Revista Panamericana de Salud Pública, 44*, 1–6. Advance online publication. doi:10.26633/RPSP.2020.69 PMID:32523607

Benesch, K. (2021). Hakikat ve Hakikat Sonrası İlişkisi Modernizm ve Postmodernizm İlişkisi Midir? *Cógito, 104*, 49–66.

Bennett, M., & Alison, D. (1996). Discussing the diagnosis and prognosis with cancer patients. *Postgraduate Medical Journal, 72*(843), 25–29. doi:10.1136/pgmj.72.843.25 PMID:8746281

Bennett, T. (1995). The Exhibitionary Complex. In *The Birth of the Museum: History, Theory, Politics*. Routledge.

Bennett, W. L., & Segerberg, A. (2012). The logic of connective action: Digital media and the personalization of contentious politics. *Information Communication and Society*, *15*(5), 1–240. doi:10.1080/1369118X.2012.670661

Berger, J. (2013). Beyond Viral: Interpersonal Communication in the Internet Age. *Psychological Inquiry*, *24*(4), 293–296. doi:10.1080/1047840X.2013.842203

Bergman, M. M. (2010). Hermeneutic Content Analysis: Textual and Audiovisual Analyses within a Mixed Methods Framework. In A. Tashakkori & C. Teddlie (Eds.), *SAGE Handbook of Mixed Methods in Social & Behavioral Research* (pp. 379–396). SAGE Publications. doi:10.4135/9781506335193.n16

Bergström, J., Uhr, C., & Frykmer, T. (2016). A complexity framework for studying disaster response management. *Journal of Contingencies and Crisis Management*, *24*(3), 124–135. doi:10.1111/1468-5973.12113

Bernardo, Y., & Brunet, N. (2010). Comunicación de malas noticias. *Cuadernos de crisis y emergencias, 9*(2), 48-58. https://bit.ly/3f9YTeO

Betton, V., Borschmann, R., Docherty, M., Coleman, S., Brown, M., & Henderson, C. (2015). The role of social media in reducing stigma and discrimination. *The British Journal of Psychiatry*, *206*(6), 443–444. doi:10.1192/bjp.bp.114.152835 PMID:26034176

Bhatt, M. A., & Arshad, M. (2016). Impact of WhatsApp on youth: A sociological study. *Social Sciences*, *4*(2), 2016.

Binark, M., & Bayraktutan, G. (2013). *Ayın Karanlık Yüzü: Yeni Medya ve Etik*. Kalkedon.

BİP. (2022a). *Information Security Policy*. Retrieved from: https://bip.com/en/information-security-policy/

BİP. (2022b). *Privacy Policy*. Retrieved from: https://bip.com/en/privacy-policy/

BİP. (2022c). *Safety*. Retrieved from: https://bip.com/en/safety/

BİP. (2022d). *Corporate Communication Platform*. Retrieved from: https://bip.com/en/corporate-communication-platform/

BİP. (2022e). *End to End Encryption*. Retrieved from: https://bip.com/en/end-to-end-encryption-bip/

BİP. (2022f). *Help Center*. Retrieved from: https://bip.com/en/help-center/

Bıyıklı, C., & Özgür, A. O. (2021). Teachers solution suggestions for the problems experienced in the synchronous distance education process during the Covid – 19 pandemic. *Journal of Open Education Applications and Research*, *7*(1), 110–147.

Blanco-Herrero, D., Gallardo-Camacho, J., & Arcila-Calderón, C. (2021). Health Advertising during the Lockdown: A Comparative Analysis of Commercial TV in Spain. *Int. J. Environ. Res. Public Health, 18*, 1054. doi:10.3390/ijerph18031054

Blanco-Herrero, D., Arcila-Calderón, C., & Gallardo-Camacho, J. (2022). Efectos del confinamiento y la pandemia en los anuncios emitidos en las dos principales cadenas de televisión privadas en España. *Palabra Clave (La Plata)*, *25*(1), e2512.

Blasco, M. M., Castellà, C. O., & Raso, M. L. (2020). Impact of the Covid-19 pandemic on media consumption in Spain. *Revista Latina de Comunicación Social*, (78), 155–167. doi:10.4185/RLCS-2020-1472

Blazwick, I., & Wilson, S. (2000). *Tate Modern: the handbook*. Tate Publishing.

Bode, L., & Vraga, E. K. (2018). See something, say something: Correction of global health misinformation on social media. *Health Communication*, *33*(9), 1131–1140. doi:10.1080/10410236.2017.1331312 PMID:28622038

Boix, C. J. (2017). Fundamentos del Branding. Claves para construir una marca poderosa. Barcelona: Editorial Profit.

Boletsis, C. (2017). The new era of virtual reality locomotion: A systematic literature review of techniques and a proposed typology. *Multimodal Technol. Interact., 1*(4), 24. doi:10.3390/mti1040024

Bonilla, Y., & Rosa, J. (2015). #Ferguson: Digital protest, hashtag ethnography, and the racial politics of social media in the United States. *American Ethnologist, 1*(42), 4–17. doi:10.1111/amet.12112

Borges do Nascimento, I. J., Pizarro, A. B., Almeida, J. M., Azzopardi-Muscat, N., Gonçalves, M. A., Björklund, M., & Novillo-Ortiz, D. (2022). Infodemics and health misinformation: A systematic review of reviews. *Bulletin of the World Health Organization, 100*(9), 544–561. doi:10.2471/BLT.21.287654 PMID:36062247

Bouhnik, D., Deshen, M., & Gan, R. (2014). WhatsApp goes to school: Mobile instant messaging between teachers and students. *Journal of Information Technology Education, 13*(1), 217–231. doi:10.28945/2051

Bowles, J., Larreguy, H., & Liu, S. (2020). Countering misinformation via WhatsApp: Preliminary evidence from the COVID-19 pandemic in Zimbabwe. *PLoS One, 15*(10), e0240005. Advance online publication. doi:10.1371/journal.pone.0240005 PMID:33052967

Bowman, N. D. (2021). Interactivity as demand: Implications for interactive media entertainment. In P. Vorderer & C. Klimmt (Eds.), *The Oxford handbook of entertainment theory* (pp. 646–670). Oxford University Press.

Boyce, C. N. P. (2006). *Conducting In-Depth Interviews: A Guide for Designing and Conducting In-Depth-Interviews for Evaluation Input.* Watertown: Pathfinder International.

Boyce, C., & Neale, P. (2006). *Conducting In-Depth Interviews: A Guide for Designing and Conducting In-Depth-Interviews for Evaluation Input.* Watertown: Pathfinder International.

Boyer, D. (2013). *The Life Informatic: Newsmaking in the Digital Era.* Cornell University Press.

Bozgeyikli, E., Raij, A., Katkoori, S., & Dubey, R. (2019). Locomotion in virtual reality for room scale tracked areas. *International Journal of Human-Computer Studies, 122*, 38-49. doi:10.1016/j.ijhcs.2018.08.002

Bozkurt, A. (2020). Koronavirüs (Covid-19) Pandemi süreci ve pandemi sonrası dünyada eğitime yönelik değerlendirmeler: Yeni normal ve yeni eğitim paradigması. *Açıköğretim Uygulamaları ve Araştırmaları Dergisi, 6*(3), 112–142.

Bozkurt, A., & Sharma, R. C. (2020). Emergency remote teaching in a time of global crisis due to CoronaVirus pandemic. *Asian Journal of Distance Education, 15*(1), i–vi. doi:10.5281/zenodo.3778083

Brandtzaeg, P., & Følstad, A. (2017). Trust and Distrust in Online Fact-Checking Services. *Communications of the ACM, 60*(9), 65–71. doi:10.1145/3122803

Brennan, H. (2021). A qualitative case study on TikTok: The silver lining for brands during the coronavirus pandemic. *Elon Journal of Undergraduate Research in Communications, 12*(2), 5–12.

Brill, M., Holman, C., Morris, C., Raichoudhary, R., & Yosif, N. (2017). Understanding the Labor Productivity and Compensation Gap. *U.S. Bureau of Labor Statistics, 6*(6). https://ecommons.cornell.edu/handle/1813/77533

Britannica. (2023). *Kashmir, geography and travel.* Author.

Bronner, S. E. (2003). *A Rumor about the Jews: Antisemitism, Conspiracy, and the Protocols of Zion.* Oxford University Press.

Brown, D. (2003). *The Da Vinci code*. Doubleday.

Bruner, J. (1990). *Acts of meaning*. Harvard University Press.

Bruns, A., & Burgess, J. E. (2011). The use of Twitter hashtags in the formation of ad hoc publics. *Proceedings of the 6th European Consortium for Political Research (ECPR) General Conference.*

Bruns, A., Harrington, S., & Hurcombe, E. (2020). 'Corona? 5G? or both?': The dynamics of COVID-19/5G conspiracy theories on Facebook. *Media International Australia, Incorporating Culture & Policy, 177*(1), 12–29. doi:10.1177/1329878X20946113

Buckman, R. (1984). Breaking bad news: why is it still so difficult? British Medical Journal, 288(6430), 1597-1599. doi:10.1136/bmj.288.6430.1597

Buckman, R. (1992). How to break bad news. A guide for health care professionals (J. Hopkins, Ed.). Academic Press.

Buckman, R. A. (2005). Breaking bad news: The SPIKES strategy. *Community Oncology, 2*(2), 138–142. doi:10.1016/S1548-5315(11)70867-1

Bull, S. S., Levine, D., Schmiege, S., & Santelli, J. (2013). Recruitment and retention of youth for research using social media: Experiences from the Just/Us study. *Vulnerable Children and Youth Studies, 8*(2), 171–181. doi:10.1080/17450128.2012.748238

Burbach, R. (2001). *Globalization and Postmodern Politics: From Zapatistas to Hightech Robber Barons.* Pluto Press.

Büyükbaykal, G. N. (2012). Türkiye'de yerel basının işlevi ve önemi. *İstanbul Üniversitesi İletişim Fakültesi Dergisi, 0*(23), 83-88.

Çağlar, G. (2021). COVİD-19 pandemisinde bilgi edinme kaynakları, medya kullanım alışkanlıkları ve aşıya yönelik tutumlar. *Akdeniz Üniversitesi İletişim Fakültesi Dergisi,* (36), 178–202.

Cahill, T. (2021). *Gaming as coping in response to COVID-19 pandemic-induced stress: results From a U.S. national survey.* International Communication Association.

Cai, Q., Okada, A., Jeong, B. G., & Kim, S-J. (2021). Civil Society Responses to the COVID-19 Pandemic. *China Review, 21*(1), 107–138.

Çakır, M. (2014). *Görsel Kültür ve Küresel Kitle Kültürü.* Ütopya Yayınevi.

Campbell, D. T., & Stanley, J. C. (1963). *Experimental and Quasi-Experimental Designs for Research.* Houghton Mifflin.

Canan, S. (2020). *İFA, İlişkiler ve Stres.* TutiKitap.

Can, E. (2020). Korona virüs (Covid-19) pandemisi ve pedagojik yansımaları: Türkiye'de açık ve uzaktan eğitim uygulamaları. *Journal of Open Education Applications and Research, 6*(2), 11–53.

Carbone, S. R. (2020). Flattening the mental ill-health curve: The importance of primary prevention in managing the mental health impacts of COVID19. *Mental Health & Prevention, 19,* 161–181. doi:10.1016/j.mhp.2020.200185 PMID:32566473

Caro, C., & Popovac, M. (2021). Gaming when things get tough? Examining how emotion regulation and coping self-efficacy influence gaming during difficult life situations. *Games and Culture, 16*(5), 611–631. doi:10.1177/1555412020944622

Carr, M. (2016, January). Public–private partnerships in national cyber-security strategies. *International Affairs, 92*(1), 43–62. doi:10.1111/1468-2346.12504

Carroll, N., Sadowski, A., Laila, A., Hruska, V., Nixon, M., Ma, D. W., & Haines, J. (2020). The impact of COVID-19 on health behavior, stress, financial and food security among middle to high income Canadian families with young children. *Nutrients, 12*(8), 1–14. doi:10.3390/nu12082352 PMID:32784530

Carter, C. (Director). (1993, September 10). *The X Files* [Crime, Drama, Mystery]. Ten Thirteen Productions, 20th Century Fox Television.

Case, D. O. (2005). Principle of least effort. In K. E. Fisher, S. Erdelez, & L. E. F. McKenchnie (Eds.), *Theories of Information Behavior* (pp. 289–292). American Society for Information Science and Technology by Information Today.

Casero-Ripollés, A. (2020). Impact of Covid-19 on the media system. Communicative and democratic consequences of news consumption during the outbreak. *El Profesional de la Información, 29*(2), 1–11. doi:10.3145/epi.2020.mar.23

Castells, M. (2013). Enformasyon Çağı: Ekonomi, Toplum ve Kültür. İstanbul Bilgi Üniversitesi Yayınları, 3.Baskı.

Castells, M. (2008). *Enformasyon Çağı: Ekonomi, Toplum ve Kültür: Ağ toplumunun Yükselişi, Kılıç, E. (Çev.), 2. Baskı.* İstanbul Bilgi Üniversitesi Yayınları.

Castells, M. (2012). *İsyan ve Umut Ağları: İnternet Çağında Toplumsal Hareketler, Kılıç, E. (Çev).* Koç Üniversitesi Yayınları.

Cati, A. (2021). Piccole finestre sul nonumano — Immagini per l'educazione ambientale nell'era della pandemia. In T. Lancioni & F. Villa (Eds.), *Visual Cultural Studies 2* (pp. 77–96). Mimesis Edizioni.

CBA. (Ed.). (2019). *Recomendaciones para la comunicación de malas noticias*. Documento CBA nº 16. Comité Bioética Asistencial (CBA), Generalitat Valenciana y Departamento de Salud de Castelló. https://bit.ly/3oze2cX

Ceron, A. (2015). Internet, news, and political trust: The difference between social media and online media outlets. *Journal of Computer-Mediated Communication, 20*(5), 487–503. doi:10.1111/jcc4.12129

Cervi, L., Tejedor, S., & Marín-Lladó, C. (2021). TikTok and the new language of political communication. *Cultura, Lenguaje y Representación*, 267-287.

Chakrabarty, D. (2020). An Era of Pandemics? What is Global and What is Planetary About COVID-19. *Critical Inquiry*. https://critinq.wordpress.com/2020/10/16/an-era-of-pandemics-what-is-global-and-what-is-planetary-about-covid-19/

Chan, A. K. M., Nickson, C. P., Rudolph, J. W., Lee, A., & Joynt, G. M. (2020). Social media for rapid knowledge dissemination: Early experience from the COVID-19 pandemic. *Anaesthesia, 75*(12), 1579–1582. doi:10.1111/anae.15057 PMID:32227594

Charles, W., & Magtanong, R. (2022). Ethical Benefits and Drawbacks of Digitally Informed Consent. Applied Ethics in a Digital World, 101-123

Chayko, M. (2018). *Süper Bağlantılı* (B. Bayındır, D. Yengin, & T. Bayrak, Trans.). Der Yayınları.

Cheng, C., & Espanha, R. (2021). Revisão Crítica: Uma Abordagem aos Estudos Sobre o Uso dos Media Sociais Durante a Pandemia Covid-19. *Comunicação & Sociedade, 40*, 149–167. doi:10.17231/comsoc.40(2021).3174

Chen, H., Chiang, R. H., & Storey, V. C. (2012). Business Intelligence and Analytics: From Big Data to Big Impact. *Management Information Systems Quarterly, 36*(4), 1165–1188. doi:10.2307/41703503

Chen, J., & Wang, Y. (2021). Social Media Use for Health Purposes: Systematic Review. *Journal of Medical Internet Research, 23*(5), 1–16. doi:10.2196/17917 PMID:33978589

Chen, Q., Min, C., Zhang, W., Ma, X., & Evans, R. (2021). Factors driving citizen engagement with government TikTok accounts during the COVID-19 pandemic: Model development and analysis. *Journal of Medical Internet Research, 23*(2), 1–13. doi:10.2196/21463 PMID:33481756

Chen, Q., Min, C., Zhang, W., Wang, G., Ma, X., & Evans, R. (2020). Unpacking the black box: How to promote citizen engagement through government social media during the COVID-19 crisis. *Computers in Human Behavior, 10*, 106380. doi:10.1016/j.chb.2020.106380 PMID:32292239

Che, S., & Kim, J. H. (2023). Sentiment impact of public health agency communication strategies on TikTok under COVID-19 normalization: Deep learning exploration. *Journal of Public Health (Berlin)*, 1–12. doi:10.100710389-023-01921-5 PMID:37361279

Che, S., Zhang, S., & Kim, J. H. (2022). How public health agencies communicate with the public on TikTok under the normalization of COVID-19: A case of 2022 Shanghai's outbreak. *Frontiers in Public Health, 10*, 1039405. doi:10.3389/fpubh.2022.1039405 PMID:36505000

Chesser, A., Ham, A. D., & Woods, N. K. (2020). Assessment of Covid-19 Knowledge Among University Students: Implications for Future Risk Communication Strategies. *Health Education & Behavior, 47*(4), 540–543. doi:10.1177/1090198120931420 PMID:32460566

Chew, C., & Eysenbach, G. (2010). Pandemics in the age of Twitter: Content analysis of Tweets during the 2009 H1N1 Outbreak. *PLoS One, 5*(11), 271–275. doi:10.1371/journal.pone.0014118 PMID:21124761

Chisty, M. A., Islam, M. A., Munia, A. T., Rahman, M. M., Rahman, N. N., & Mohima, M. (2021). Risk perception and information-seeking behavior during emergency: An exploratory study on COVID-19 pandemic in Bangladesh. *International Journal of Disaster Risk Reduction, 65*, 102580. doi:10.1016/j.ijdrr.2021.102580 PMID:34540577

Cho, J., Lee, H. E., & Kim, H. (2019). Effects of communication-oriented overload in mobile instant messaging on role stressors, burnout, and turnover intention in the workplace. *International Journal of Communication, 13*, 21.

Choukou, M., Sanchez-Ramirez, D., Pol, M., Uddin, M., Monnin, C., & Syed-Abdul, S. (2022). Covid-19 infodemic and digital health literacy in vulnerable populations: A scoping review. *Digital Health, 8*, 1–13. doi:10.1177/20552076221076927 PMID:35223076

Chow, M., & Stanford, K. (2021). *Cuatro tendencias de la era COVID-19 que tendrán un impacto duradero en los productos y las experiencias de consumo*. Available at: https://www.thinkwithgoogle.com/intl/es-es/futuro-del-marketing/transformacion-digital/covid-19-tendencias-1-ano/

Christensen, H. S. (2011). Political activities on the Internet: Slacktivism or political participation by other means? *First Monday*. Advance online publication. doi:10.5210/fm.v16i2.3336

Chu, D. (2017). #CautionBusinesses: Using Competitors' Hashtags Could Possibly Lead to Trademark Infringement, Catholic University. *The Journal of Law and Technology, 25*(2), 387–413. https://scholarship.law.edu/jlt/vol25/iss2/8

Church, K., & De Oliveira, R. (2013, August). What is up with WhatsApp? Comparing mobile instant messaging behaviors with traditional SMS. In *Proceedings of the 15th International Conference on Human-Computer Interaction with Mobile Devices and Services* (pp. 352-361). 10.1145/2493190.2493225

Çiçeklioğlu, A. Ş., & Ünal, R. (2021). Haber üretimi ve dağıtımı bağlamında TikTok uygulaması ne vaat ediyor. *İlef Dergisi,* 69-98.

Çiftçi, M. E., Ayhan, B. (2023). 'The first to report wins': The McDonaldization of digital journalism in Turkey. *Journal of Applied Journalism & Media Studies*. doi:10.1386/ajms_00100_1

CIS. (2020). *Índice de confianza del consumidor. Mes de diciembre evolución de resultados Estudio nº 3304 Diciembre 2020*. https://www.cis.es/cis/export/sites/default/-Archivos/ICC/2020/ICC_12-20_3304.pdf

CIS. (2021). *Índice de confianza del consumidor. Mes de diciembre evolución de resultados Estudio nº 3345 Diciembre 2021*. https://www.cis.es/cis/export/sites/default/-Archivos/ICC/2021/ICC_12-21_3345.pdf

CIS. (2022). *Índice de confianza del consumidor. Mes de abril evolución de resultados Estudio nº 3361 Abril 2022*. https://www.cis.es/cis/export/sites/default/-Archivos/ICC/2022/ICC_04-22_3361.pdf

Clark, C., Davila, A., Regis, M., & Kraus, S. (2020). Predictors of COVID-19 voluntary compliance behaviors: An international investigation. *Global Transitions*, *2*, 76–82. doi:10.1016/j.glt.2020.06.003 PMID:32835202

Clark, R. (2016). "Hope in a hashtag": The discursive activism of# WhyIStayed. *Feminist Media Studies*, *16*(5), 788–804. doi:10.1080/14680777.2016.1138235

Cobb, N. K., Graham, A. L., & Abrams, D. B. (2010). Social network structure of a large online community for smoking cessation. *American Journal of Public Health*, *100*(7), 1282–1289. doi:10.2105/AJPH.2009.165449 PMID:20466971

Coleman, K. (2021). *Introducing Birdwatch, a community-based approach to misinformation*. https://blog.twitter.com/en_us/topics/ product/2021/introducing-birdwatch-a-community-based-approach-to-misinformation

Çöllüoğlu, M. (2023). Hakikat Ötesi Çağda Sosyal Medya Haberleri: Doğrulama Platformları Üzerinden Bir İncelenme. *Simetrik İletişim Araştırmaları Dergisi*, *3*(2), 97–122.

Colman, E., Wanat, M., Goossens, H., Tonkin-Crine, S., & Anthierens, S. (2021). Following the science? Views from scientists on government advisory boards during the COVID-19 pandemic: A qualitative interview study in five European countries. *BMJ Global Health*, *6*(9), e006928. doi:10.1136/bmjgh-2021-006928 PMID:34580072

Coombs, T. (2015). *Ongoing Crisis Communication: Planning, Managing, and Responding*. Sage publications.

Coomer, N., Bullard, S., Clinton, W., & Williams-Sanders, B. (2018). Evaluating the effects of four VR locomotion methods: joystick, arm-cycling, point-tugging, and teleporting. In *Proceedings of the 15th ACM Symposium on Applied Perception*. Association for Computing Machinery. 10.1145/3225153.3225175

Corrigan, P. (2010). *The Sociology of Consumption*. SAGE Publication.

Costa-Sánchez, C., & López-García, X. (2020). Comunicación y crisis del coronavirus en España. Primeras lecciones. *El Profesional de la Información*, *29*(3). Advance online publication. doi:10.3145/epi.2020.may.04

Couts, A. (2015, January 18). The new era of hashtag activism. *The Kernel*. Retrieved from https://kernelmag. dailydot.com/issue-sections/features-issue-sections/11390/hashtag-activism-real/

Cüceloğlu, D. (2018). *Yeniden İnsan İnsana*. Remzi Kitabevi.

Cummings, C. L., Rosenthal, S., & Kong, W. Y. (2021). Secondary risk theory: Validation of a novel model of protection motivation. *Risk Analysis*, *41*(1), 204–220. doi:10.1111/risa.13573 PMID:32790201

Cummins, R. (2021a). Exploiting Fear to Lock Down Freedom. In J. Mercola & R. Cummins (Eds.), *The Truth About COVID-19: Exposing The Great Reset, Lockdowns, Vaccine Passports, and the New Normal*. Chalsea Green Publishing.

Cummins, R. (2021b). How the Pandemic Plans Unfolded. In J. Mercola & R. Cummins (Eds.), *The Truth About COVID-19: Exposing The Great Reset, Lockdowns, Vaccine Passports, and the New Normal*. Chalsea Green Publishing.

Cummins, R. (2021c). Take Back Control. In J. Mercola & R. Cummins (Eds.), *The Truth About COVID-19: Exposing The Great Reset, Lockdowns, Vaccine Passports, and the New Normal*. Chalsea Green Publishing.

Curran, T., & Seiter, J. S. (2021). The role of relational worry due to COVID-19 in the links between video chat apprehension, loneliness, and adhering to CDC guidelines. *Journal of Social and Personal Relationships*, *38*(6), 1869–1876. Advance online publication. doi:10.1177/0265407520985264

Curşeu, P. L., Coman, A. D., Panchenko, A., Fodor, O. C., & Raţiu, L. (2021). Death anxiety, death reflection, and interpersonal communication as predictors of social distance towards people infected with COVID. *Current Psychology (New Brunswick, N.J.)*, 1–14. PMID:33686325

Da Silva Pereira, A. A., & Hitotuzi, N. (2023). Enhancing speaking skills and vocabulary in the eal classroom through TikTok: A literature review. *International Journal of English Linguistics*, *13*(5), 22–33. doi:10.5539/ijel.v13n5p22

Daud, I., Listiana, E., & Fauzan, R. (2023). Social media marketing activities (SMMAs) as stimulus on purchase intention with customer engagement as mediator on@ avoskinbeauty TikTok's account. Asian *Journal of Economics. Business and Accounting*, *23*(4), 35–45.

Davos. (2022). *This is how to counter the global digital divide.* World Economic Forum.

Dawkins, C. (2021). The Definition of Exhibition in Art Historical Inquiry. *Academia Letters*. Advance online publication. doi:10.20935/AL3779

de Castro Pérez, I. (2021). *Impacto del covid-19 en la industria publicitaria española.* https://repositorio.comillas.edu/xmlui/bitstream/handle/11531/46556/TFG%20-%20De%20Castro%20Perez%2C%20Irene.pdf?sequence=3

de Paepe, L., Zhu, C., & DePryck, K. (2018). Drop-out, retention, satisfaction and attainment of online learners of Dutch in adult education. *International Journal on E-Learning*, *17*(3), 303–323.

de Wilde, P., Koopmans, R., Merkel, W., Strijbis, O., & Zürn, M. (Eds.). (2019). *The Struggle Over Borders: Cosmopolitanism and Communitarianism.* Cambridge University Press. doi:10.1017/9781108652698

De Wolf, R., Heyman, R., & Pierson, J. (2013). Privacy by Design through social requirements analysis of social network sites from a user perspective. In European Data Protection: Coming of Age. Springer Science+Business Media.

Dedi. (2022). *Anasayfa.* Retrieved from: https://dedi.com.tr/

Deloitte. (2022). Are we finally seeing the long promised transformation. In *Global Health Care outlook.* Author.

Demiray, U., & Ve İşman, A. (2003). *History of distance education. Online Distance Book.* Tojet.

Demirbilek, Y., Pehlivantürk, G., Özgüler, Z. Ö., & Meşe, E. A. (2020). COVID-19 outbreak control, example of Ministry of Health of Turkey. *Turkish Journal of Medical Sciences*, *50*(9), 489–494. doi:10.3906ag-2004-187 PMID:32304192

Deneen, P. J. (2018). *Why liberalism failed.* Yale University Press. doi:10.12987/yale/9780300223446.001.0001

Denning, D. E. (1982). *Cryptography and Data Security.* Addison-Wesley Publishing Company.

DePaula, N., Hagen, L., Roytman, S., & Alnahass, D. (2022). Platform Effects on Public Health Communication: A Comparative and National Study of Message Design and Audience Engagement Across Twitter and Facebook. *JMIR Infodemiology*, *2*(2), 1–18. doi:10.2196/40198 PMID:36575712

Desilver, D. (2018, August 7). *For most U.S. workers, real wages have barely budged in decades.* Pew Research Center. https://www.pewresearch.org/short-reads/2018/08/07/for-most-us-workers-real-wages-have-barely-budged-for-decades/

Deuze, M. (2005). What is journalism? Professional identity and ideology of journalists reconsidered. *Journalism*, *6*(4), 442–464. doi:10.1177/1464884905056815

Deuze, M. (2008). Understanding journalism as newswork: How it changes and how it remains the same. *Westminster Papers in Communication and Culture*, *5*(2), 4–23. doi:10.16997/wpcc.61

Devi, T. S., & Rivera, S. (2014). Use of Social Networking Site in the University of Swaziland by the Health Science Student: A Case Study. *Journal of International Management*, *1*(1), 17–24.

Diao, Z., Wang, Q., Naizheng, S., & Yuhan, Z. (2017). Study on Data Security Policy Based On Cloud Storage. *IEEE 3rd International Conference on Big Data Security on Cloud.* https://ieeexplore.ieee.org/document/7980332

Dictionaries, O. (2021). *Definition of post-truth adjective.* https://www.oxfordlearnersdictionaries.com/definition/english/posttruth?q=post+truth

Dictionary, C. (2022). *Security.* Retrieved from: https://dictionary.cambridge.org/dictionary/english/security

Diers-Lawson, A., Johnson, S., Clayton, T., Kimoto, R., Tran, B. X., Nguyen, L. H., & Park, K. (2021). Pandemic communication: Information seeking, evaluation, and self-protective behaviors in Vietnam and the Republic of Korea. *Frontiers in Communication*, *6*, 731979. doi:10.3389/fcomm.2021.731979

Digital Literacy. (2023, june 6). Retrieved from Ed Teach Review: https://www.edtechreview.in/trends-insights/insights/what-is-digital-literacy-its-importance-and-challenges/

Digital Transformation Office of The Presidency of Türkiye. (2022). *About Us.* https://cbddo.gov.tr/hakkimizda/

Dijital Toplum Araştırmaları Derneği. (n.d.). *Hakkımızda.* www.dijitaltoplumarastirmalari.org/hakkimizda

Dijital Toplum Araştırmaları Derneği. (n.d.). https://www.dogrula.org/

Doğan, A., & Paydar, S. (2019). Öğretmen adaylarının açık ve uzaktan öğrenme ortamlarına yönelik görüşleri. *Educational Technology*, *1*(2), 154–162.

Doğrula. (n.d.). https://www.dogrula.org/

Domínguez, M., & Sapiña, L. (2017). "Others Like Me". An Approach to the Use of the Internet and Social Networks in Adolescents and Young Adults Diagnosed with Cancer. *Journal of Cancer Education*, *32*(4), 885–891. doi:10.100713187-016-1055-9 PMID:27251633

Dorrance Hall, E., Earle, K., Silverstone, J., Immel, M., Carlisle, M., & Campbell, N. (2022). Changes in family communication during the COVID-19 pandemic: The role of family communication patterns and relational distance. *Communication Research Reports*, *39*(1), 56–67. doi:10.1080/08824096.2021.2025045

Drouin, M., McDaniel, B. T., Pater, J., & Toscos, T. (2020). How parents and their children used social media and technology at the beginning of the COVID-19 pandemic and associations with anxiety. *Cyberpsychology, Behavior, and Social Networking*, *23*(11), 727–736. doi:10.1089/cyber.2020.0284 PMID:32726144

Dugguh, S. I., & Dennis, A. (2014). Job satisfaction theories: Traceability to employee performance in organizations. *IOSR Journal of Business and Management*, *16*(5), 11–18. doi:10.9790/487X-16511118

Duman, S. N. (2020). Salgın döneminde gerçekleştirilen uzatktan eğitim sürecinin değerlendirimesi. *Milli Eğitim C.*, *49*(1), 95–112. doi:10.37669/milliegitim.768887

Dunwoody, S., & Griffin, R. J. (2015). Risk information seeking and processing model. In H. Cho, T. Reimer, & K. A. McComas (Eds.), *SAGE Handbook of Risk Communication* (pp. 102–116). Sage Publications. doi:10.4135/9781483387918.n14

Durmuş, Y., & Göztaş, A. (2023). *Deepfake: Post-Truth Çağı İnsanlarında Fırsat ve Tehditlere Yönelik Algılar. In Medya ve Kültür Odağında İletişim.* Akademisyen Kitabevi.

Dursun, Ç. (2004). Haber, Hakikat ve İktidar İlişkisi. Elips kitap.

Dylko, I., & McCluskey, M. (2012). Media Effects in an Era of Rapid Technological Transformation: A Case of User-Generated Content and Political Participation. *Communication Theory, 22*(3), 250–278. doi:10.1111/j.1468-2885.2012.01409.x

Ebn Ahmady, A., Seyedzadeh Sabounchi, S., Mirmohammadsadeghi, H., & Rezaei, A. (2014). A suitable model for breaking bad news: Review of recommendations. *The Journal of Medical Research*, 1–15. doi:10.5171/2014.776618

Ebrahim, A. H., Saif, Z. Q., Buheji, M., AlBasri, N., Al-Husaini, F. A., & Jahrami, H. (2020). COVID-19 information-seeking behavior and anxiety symptoms among parents. *OSP Journal of Health Care and Medicine, 1*(1), 1–9.

Eguizábal, R. (2011). Teoría de la Publicidad (3rd ed.). Cátedra.

Eken, Ö., Tosun, N., & Eken, D. T. (2020). Urgent and compulsory move to distance education upon covid-19: A general evaluation. *The Journal of National Education, 49*(1), 113–128.

Ellwart, T., Happ, C., Gurtner, A., & Rack, O. (2015). Managing information overload in virtual teams: Effects of a structured online team adaptation on cognition and performance. *European Journal of Work and Organizational Psychology, 24*(5), 812–826. doi:10.1080/1359432X.2014.1000873

Elsner, J. N., Sadler, T. D., Zangori, L., Friedrichsen, P. J., & Ke, L. (2022). Student interest, concerns, and information-seeking behaviors related to COVID-19. *Disciplinary and Interdisciplinary Science Education Research, 4*(1), 1–11. doi:10.118643031-022-00053-2 PMID:37520636

Enroth, H. (2023). Crisis of Authority: The Truth of Post-Truth. *International Journal of Politics Culture and Society, 36*(2), 179–195. [REMOVED HYPERLINK FIELD] doi:10.100710767-021-09415-6 PMID:34703077

Erfidan, A. (2019). *Derslerin uzaktan eğitim yoluyla verilmesiyle ilgili öğretim elemanı ve öğrenci görüşleri: Balıkesir Üniversitesi örneği.* Balıkesir Üniversitesi, Fen Bilimleri Enstitüsü.

Eroğlu, Ş., & Çakmak, T. (2020). Post-Truth Dönemini Anlamak: Hacettepe Üniversitesi Bilgi ve Belge Yönetimi Bölümü Öğrencilerinin Yeni Medya Araçları Kapsamında Bilgi Bozuklukları ve Doğrulama Algılarının Değerlendirilmesi. *Pamukkale Üniversitesi Sosyal Bilimler Enstitüsü Dergisi, 39*, 307–325.

Eruthickal. (2016). *Role of ASHA workers in rural development with reference to Kottayam Distritct.* Baselius College.

España, S. (2021). *Schweppes: Imperfectamente perfecta.* https://www.youtube.com/watch?v=xPUB5zdr1Xw

Espanha, R. (2020a). A Literacia em Saúde e a Comunicação de Risco em Saúde. *Comunicação Pública, 15*(29), 1–13. doi:10.4000/cp.11303

Espanha, R. (2020b). O valor da comunicação em gestão pública um exemplo aplicado à área da saúde pública. In J. Toledo (Ed.), *Comunicação estratégica e orientada: a visão de 21 renomados autores em 5 países* (pp. 337–363). Rede Integrada.

Espinosa-Mirabet, S., & Puntí-Brun, M. (2021). Revisión de la formación en habilidades comunicativas en los planes de estudio de Medicina de Cataluña. In *Cuestiones transversales en la innovación de la docencia y la investigación de las ciencias sociales y jurídicas: especial referencia al impacto del covid-19, las nuevas tecnologías y metodologías, las perspectivas de género y la diversidad* (pp. 487–509). Dykinson.

European Commission. (2021). *Factsheet on key consumer data 2020.* Accessed online 20 March 2023 at: https://commission.europa.eu/system/files/2021-03/120321_key_consumer_data_factsheet_en.pdf

Eysenbach, G. (2011). Infodemiology and infoveillance tracking online health information and cyberbehavior for public health. *American Journal of Preventive Medicine*, *40*(5, Suppl 2), 154–S158. doi:10.1016/j.amepre.2011.02.006 PMID:21521589

Fadhli, R., Ibrahim, C., Igiriza, M., & Ilmi, B. (2023). How libraries in Indonesia use TikTok: A content analysis of library accounts on the platform. *Artículo de investigación, 36*(96), 27-44.

Fake news, lies and propaganda: how to sort fact from fiction. (2020). https://guides.lib.umich.edu/fakenews

Fan, X., Luo, J., & Wang, X. (2023). Understanding TikTok usage: Communication strategy of ByteDance based on the background of new media. In *2022 4th International Conference on Literature, Art and Human Development (ICLAHD 2022)* (pp. 226-236). Atlantis Press.

Fan, L., Yu, H., & Gilliland, A. J. (2023). Aggravated anti-Asian hate since Covid-19 and the #stopasianhate movement: Connection, disjointness, and challenges. In B. Di Fátima (Ed.), *Hate speech on social media: A global approach* (pp. 35–74). LabCom Books.

Fegert, J. M., Vitiello, B., Plener, P. L., & Clemens, V. (2020). Challenges and burden of the Coronavirus 2019 (COVID-19) pandemic for child and adolescent mental health: A narrative review to highlight clinical and research needs in the acute phase and the long return to normality. *Child and Adolescent Psychiatry and Mental Health, 14*(1), 20. doi:10.118613034-020-00329-3 PMID:32419840

Fell, L. (2020). Trust and COVID-19: Implications for Interpersonal, Workplace, Institutional, and Information-Based Trust. *Digit. Gov.: Res. Pract.*, *2*(1), 1–5.

Feng, S., Berndt, A., & Ots, M. (2023). Residents' videographic practices on TikTok (Douyin): Enacting and communicating social sustainability during a COVID-19 lockdown. *Journal of Media Business Studies*, 1–22. doi:10.1080/16522354.2023.2207160

Ferreira, G., Fernández-Antón, T., Baleriola, J., & Aleida, R. (2015). Competencia en comunicación en el currículo del estudiante de Medicina de España (1990-2014): De la Atención Primaria al Plan Bolonia. Un estudio descriptivo. *Atencion Primaria, 47*(7), 399–410. doi:10.1016/j.aprim.2014.09.007 PMID:25435473

Fingerman, K. L., Ng, Y. T., Zhang, S., Britt, K., Colera, G., Birditt, K. S., & Charles, S. T. (2021). Living alone during COVID-19: Social contact and emotional well-being among older adults. *The Journals of Gerontology. Series B, Psychological Sciences and Social Sciences*, *76*(3), 116–121. doi:10.1093/geronb/gbaa200 PMID:33196815

Finkelstein, M. A. (2010). Individualism/collectivism: Implications for the volunteer process. *Social Behavior and Personality, 38*(4), 445–452. doi:10.2224bp.2010.38.4.445

Fink, S. (1986). *Crisis Management: Planning for the Inevitable.* American Management Association.

Firmansyah, M. R., & Junaedi, F. (2022). Production management model and distribution of TikTok content as a football information media in@ footballfandom_id account. *Symposium of Literature, Culture, and Communication (SYLECTION), 1*(1), 169-175. 10.12928ylection.v1i1.11327

Fiske, J. (1996). *Kitle İletişim Çalışmalarına Giriş.* Ark Yayınları.

Flores-Funes, D., Aguilar-Jiménez, J., Lirón-Ruiz, R. J., & Aguayo-Albasini, J. L. (2020). ¿Comunicamos correctamente las malas noticias en medicina? Resultados de un taller de formación basado en videos y debriefing. *Educación Médica, 21*(2), 118–122. doi:10.1016/j.edumed.2018.07.005

Fuchs, C. (2017). Social Media: A Critical Introduction. *Sage (Atlanta, Ga.).*

Fuchs, C. (2020). Everyday life and everyday communication in coronavirus capitalism. *Communication. TripleC, 18*(1), 375–399. doi:10.31269/triplec.v18i1.1167

Fuchs, C. (2021). *Communicating COVID-19: Everyday Life, Digital Capitalism, and Conspiracy Theories in Pandemic Times*. Emerald Publishing Limited. doi:10.1108/9781801177207

Fujimori, M., Shirai, Y., Asai, M., Kubota, K., Katsumata, N., & Uchitomi, Y. (2014). Effect of communication skills training program for oncologists based on patient preferences for communication when receiving bad news: A randomized controlled trial. *Journal of Clinical Oncology, 32*(20), 2166–2172. doi:10.1200/JCO.2013.51.2756 PMID:24912901

Fuller, G. W., Johnston, A., & Regan, A. (2020). Housing prices and wealth inequality in Western Europe. *West European Politics, 43*(2), 297–320. doi:10.1080/01402382.2018.1561054

Fumagalli, E., Dolmatzian, M. B., & Shrum, L. J. (2021). Centennials, FOMO, and loneliness: An investigation of the impact of social networking and messaging/VoIP apps usage during the initial stage of the Coronavirus pandemic. *Frontiers in Psychology, 9*(12), 620739. doi:10.3389/fpsyg.2021.620739 PMID:33633646

Fusaro, D. (2022). *Odio la resilienza: Contro la mistica della sopportazione*. Rizzoli.

Gaenssle, S., & Budzinski, O. (2021). Stars in social media: New light through old windows? *Journal of Media Business Studies, 18*(2), 79–105. doi:10.1080/16522354.2020.1738694

Gaile, S. M. (2013). The role and functions of social media in modern society. Is social media worthwile for local media? *Journalısm Research, Science Journal Communication Information, 0*(6), 43–62.

García-Díaz, D. (2006). Comunicando malas noticias en Medicina: Recomendaciones para hacer de la necesitad virtud. *Medicina Intensiva, 30*(9), 452–459. doi:10.1016/S0210-5691(06)74569-7 PMID:17194403

Garratt. (2020). Telemedical education during national emergencies: Learning from Kashmir. *The Clinical Teacher*. PMID:32602614

Gavilan, D., Martinez-Navarro, G., & Fernández-Lores, S. (2017). Universitarios y redes sociales informativas: Escépticos totales, moderadores duales o pro-digitales. *Comunicar. Revista Científica de Educomunicación, 25*(53), 61–70. doi:10.3916/C53-2017-06

Geçer, E., Yıldırım, M., & Akgül, Ö. (2022). Sources of information in times of health crisis: Evidence from Turkey during COVID-19. *Journal of Public Health (Berlin), 30*(5), 1113–1119. doi:10.100710389-020-01393-x PMID:33072495

Geetha Rani, E., & Chetana, D. T. (2023). A Survey of Recent Cloud Computing Data Security and Privacy Disputes and Defending Strategies. In J. C. Bansal, H. Sharma, & A. Chakravorty (Eds.), *Congress on Smart Computing Technologies. CSCT 2022. Smart Innovation, Systems and Technologies* (Vol. 351). Springer. doi:10.1007/978-981-99-2468-4_31

Gentile, L., Bertuccio, P., Ancona, A., Cucchi, A., Dallagiacoma, G., Godoy, M. A., Signorelli, C., & Odone, A. (2023). Can YouTube be trusted as a source of quality and reliable information on Covid-19 vaccination in Italy? *Acta Biomedica*. Advance online publication. doi:10.23750/abm.v94is3.14558 PMID:37695176

Gentzkow, M. (2018). *Media and Artificial Intelligence*. Standford University. Accessed Date: 20.09.2023: http://web.stanford.edu/~gentzkow/research/ai_and_media.pdf

Gerbner, G. (1967). *Mass Media and Human Communication Theory*. Holt, Rinehart And Winston.

Gewin, V. (2020). COVID-19 bekletilirken öğretimi çevrimiçi taşımak için beş ipucu. *Doga, 580*, 295–296.

Gezmen, B., & Gürkan, H. (2016). *Haber Uygulamaları*. Artes Yayınları.

Gibson, A. N. (2016). Building a progressive-situational model of post-diagnosis information seeking for parents of individuals with down syndrome. *Global Qualitative Nursing Research, 3*. doi:10.1177/2333393616680967 PMID:28462351

Gieryn, T. F. (1999). *Cultural boundaries of science: Credibility on the line*. University of Chicago Press.

GIZ. (2020). *Guía técnica orientadora para el acompañamiento psicosocial remoto. Deutsche Gesellschaft für, Internationale Zusammenarbeit (GIZ)* GmbH.

Gladwell, M. (2010, October 4). Small change: Why the revolution will not be tweeted. *The New Yorker*. Retrieved from https://www.newyorker.com/magazine/2010/10/04/small-change-malcolm-gladwell

Glass, G. V., & Hopkins, K. D. (1984). *Statistical Methods in Education and Psychology*. Prentice Hall.

Glenn, C. L. (2015). Activism or 'slacktivism?': Digital media and organizing for social change. *Communication Teacher, 29*(2), 81–85. doi:10.1080/17404622.2014.1003310

Glik, D. C. (2007). Risk communication for public health emergencies. *Annual Review of Public Health, 28*(1), 33–54. doi:10.1146/annurev.publhealth.28.021406.144123 PMID:17222081

Gobierno de España. (2022). *Crisis sanitaria COVID-19: Normativa e información útil*. Available at: https://administracion.gob.es/pag_Home/atencionCiudadana/Crisis-sanitaria-COVID-19.html

Goel, S. (2020). National Cyber Security Strategy and the Emergence of Strong Digital Borders. *Connections: The Quarterly Journal, 19*(1), 73-86.

Golding, W. (1954). *Lord of the flies*. Faber and Faber.

Goleman, D. (2020). *Odak, Çev. Filiz Nayır Deniztekin*. Varlık Yayınları.

Gómez-Sancho, M. (2016). Cómo dar las malas noticias en medicina (3a ed.). Plataforma Editorial.

Gonçalves, G., Piñeiro-Naval, V., & Toniolo, B. P. (2021). Who Do the Portuguese Trust? Government Communication Management in the Covid-19 Pandemic. Comunicação e sociedade, 40, 169-187. doi:10.17231/comsoc.40(2021).3251

González-Castro, J. L., Ubillos-Landa, S., Puente-Martínez, A., & Gracia-Leiva, M. (2021). Perceived vulnerability and severity predict adherence to COVID-19 protection measures: The mediating role of instrumental coping. *Frontiers in Psychology, 12*, 674032. doi:10.3389/fpsyg.2021.674032 PMID:34295285

González-Padilla, D. A., & Tortolero-Blanco, L. (2020). Social media influence in the COVID-19 Pandemic. *International Braz J Urol, 46*(suppl.1), 120–124. doi:10.15901677-5538.ibju.2020.s121 PMID:32550706

Goode, L. (2019). Get Ready to Hear a Lot More About 'XR'. *Wired*.

Gordillo Navas, G. C., Trujillo Martínez, J. D., & Filizzola Bermúdez, J. D. (2020). Estrategia de simulación para aplicar el protocolo SPIKES en la comunicación de malas noticias. *Universitas Medica, 61*(3). Advance online publication. doi:10.11144/Javeriana.umed61-3.spik

Gowan, M. E., Kirk, R. C., & Sloan, J. A. (2014). Building resiliency: A cross-sectional study examining relationships among health-related quality of life, well-being, and disaster preparedness. *Health and Quality of Life Outcomes, 12*(1), 85. doi:10.1186/1477-7525-12-85 PMID:24909780

Gran, A., Booth, P., & Bucher, T. (2021). To be or not to be algorithm aware: A question of a new digital divide? *Information Communication and Society, 24*(12), 1779–1796. doi:10.1080/1369118X.2020.1736124

Grasso, V., & Crisci, A. (2016). Codified hashtags for weather warning on Twitter: An Italian case study. *PLoS Currents*, 8. doi:10.1371/currents.dis.967e71514ecb92402eca3bdc9b789529 PMID:27500010

Grau-Rebollo, J. (2021). Confinement narratives: TV advertising during the coronavirus outbreak in Spain. *Perifèria, revista de recerca i formació en antropologia, 26*(1), 7-28. doi:10.5565/rev/periferia.822

Greenberg, L. W., Ochsenschlager, D., O'Donnell, R., Mastruserio, J., & Cohen, G. J. (1999, June). Communication bad news: A pedriatric department's evalua-tion of a simulated intervention. *Pediatrics, 103*(6), 1210–1217. doi:10.1542/peds.103.6.1210 PMID:10353931

Guillén-López, O. B., & Olascoaga-Mesía, S. C. (2017). Habilidad de los médicos residentes para comunicar malas noticias. *Revista de la Sociedad Peruana de Medicina Interna, 30*(2), 77–81. doi:10.36393pmi.v30i2.65

Guilluy, C. (2019). *Twilight of the elites: Prosperity, the periphery, and the future of France* (M. DeBevoise, Trans.). Yale University Press.

Gül Ünlü, D., Kuş, O., & Göksu, O. (2020). Videolarda gerçek hayattaki gibi değilim, rol yapmaktayım: TikTok kullanıcılarının benlik performansları üzerine bir inceleme. *Intermedia International E-journal, 7*(12), 115–128. doi:10.21645/intermedia.2020.70

Gülpınar Demirci, V., & Buluz Kömeçoğlu, B. (2022). Sosyal Ağlarda Veri Gizliliği: Türkiye'de Whatsapp Gizlilik Sözleşmesine Gösterilen Tepkilerinin Duygu Analizi. *Kafkas Üniversitesi İktisadi ve İdari Bilimler Fakültesi Kaüiibfd, 13*(26).

Güngör, M. (2015). *Ulusal Bilgi Güvenliği: Strateji ve Kurumsal Yapılanma*. Bilgi Toplumu Dairesi Başkanlığı.

Guo, M. (2020). Second screening: Measuring second screen user behavior in a social television viewing environment. *International Journal on Media Management, 22*(2), 97–116. doi:10.1080/14241277.2020.1803326

Gurak, J. L. (2014). Trust and Internet Activism: From Email to Social Networks. In Cyberactivism on The Participatory Web. Routledge.

Gürkan, H., Serttaş, A., & Sarıkaya, T. (2023). The virtual mask: The dark underbelly of digital anonymity and gender identity construction in Turkey. *Journal of Arab and Muslim Media Research*. doi:10.1386/jammr_00068_1

Gürkan, H. (2019). The Experiences of Women Professionals in the Film Industry in Turkey: A Gender Based Study. *Acta Universitatis Sapientia-Film and Media Studies Journal, 16*(1), 205–219. doi:10.2478/ausfm-2019-0011

Gürkan, H. (2019). The Experiences of Women Professionals in the Film Industry in Turkey: A Gender-Based Study. *Acta Univ. Sapientiae. Film and Media Studies, 16*, 205–219.

Gutiérrez, A., & Tyner, K. (2012). Educación para los medios, alfabetización mediática y competencia digital. *Comunicar. Revista Científica de Educomunicación, XIX*(38), 31–39. doi:10.3916/C38-2012-02-03

Guttman, N. (2000). Public health communication interventions. *Sage (Atlanta, Ga.)*.

Güvenli Haberleşme Uygulaması Dedi. (2022). *Dedi.* Retrieved from: https://btider.org.tr/dedi

Hado, E., & Feinberg, L. (2020). Amid the COVID-19 pandemic, meaningful communication between family caregivers and residents of long-term care facilities is imperative. *Journal of Aging & Social Policy, 32*(4–5), 410–415. doi:10.1080/08959420.2020.1765684 PMID:32441209

Hall, R. H. (1987). *Organizations: Structures, Processes & Outcomes*. Prentice-Hall International Inc.

Halupka, M. (2014). Clicktivism: A systematic heuristic. *Policy and Internet, 6*(2), 115–132. doi:10.1002/1944-2866.POI355

Han, B.-C. (2020, May 24). *Byung-Chul Han: COVID-19 has reduced us to a 'society of survival'*. EURACTIV: https://www.euractiv.com/section/asia-pacific/interview/byung-chul-han-covid-19-has-reduced-us-to-a-society-of-survival/

Han, B.-C. (2020). *Psikopolitika: Neoliberalizm ve Yeni İktidar Teknikleri*. Metis Yayınları.

Hanson, C. L., West, J., Thackeray, R., Barnes, M. D., & Downey, J. (2014). Understanding and predicting social media use among community health center patients: A cross-sectional survey. *Journal of Medical Internet Research, 16*(11), 1–11. doi:10.2196/jmir.3373 PMID:25427823

Hardt, M. (1999). Affective Labor. *Boundary 2, 26*(2), 89–100.

Hawn, C. (2009). Take Two Aspirin And Tweet Me In The Morning: How Twitter, Facebook, And Other Social Media Are Reshaping Health Care. *Health Affairs, 28*(2), 361–368. doi:10.1377/hlthaff.28.2.361 PMID:19275991

Hemminger, B. M., Lu, D., Vaughan, K. T. L., & Adams, S. J. (2007). Information seeking behavior of academic scientists. *Journal of the American Society for Information Science and Technology, 58*(14), 2205–2225. doi:10.1002/asi.20686

Henley, J. (2020, March 2). Support for Eurosceptic parties doubles in two decades across EU. *The Guardian*. https://www.theguardian.com/world/2020/mar/02/support-for-eurosceptic-parties-doubles-two-decades-across-eu

Herman, E. S., & Chomsky, N. (2012). *Rızanın İmalatı: Kitle Medyasının Ekonomi Politiği*: bgst Yayınları.

Hesse, C., Mikkelson, A. C., & Saracco, S. (2018). Parent – child affection and helicopter parenting: Exploring the concept of excessive affection. *Western Journal of Communication, 82*(4), 457–474. doi:10.1080/10570314.2017.1362705

Hess, K., & Waller, L. (2020). Charting the media innovations landscape for rural and regional newspapers. *Australian Journalism Review, 42*(1), 59–74. doi:10.1386/ajr_00019_1

Hester, J. B., & Gibson, R. (2007). The agenda-setting function of national versus local media: A time-series analysis for the issue of same-sex marriage. *Mass Communication & Society, 10*(3), 299–317. doi:10.1080/15205430701407272

Hisamitsu, A. (2005). Intellectual Property Strategy in Japan. *International Journal of Intellectual Property — Law, Economy, and Management, 1*, 5–12. https://ipaj.org/english_journal/pdf/Intellectual_Property_Strategy.pdf

Hochuli, A., Hoare, G., & Cunliffe, P. (2021). *The End of the End of History: Politics in the Twenty-First Century*. Zero Books.

Hofstede, G. (2001). *Culture's consequences: Comparing values, behaviors, institutions and organizations across nations*. Sage Publishing.

Hofstede, G. (2011). Dimensionalizing cultures: The Hofstede model in context. *Online Readings in Psychology and Culture, 2*(1), 8. doi:10.9707/2307-0919.1014

Horspool, A., & Lange, C. (2012). Applying the scholarship of teaching and learning: Student perceptions, behaviours and success online and face-to-face. *Assessment & Evaluation in Higher Education, 37*(1), 73–88. doi:10.1080/02602938.2010.496532

Horwitz, R. B. (2021). Trump and the "deep state.". *Policy Studies, 42*(5–6), 473–490. doi:10.1080/01442872.2021.1953460

Hospital 12 de Octubre. (2020). *Protocolo para la comunicación telefónica de malas noticias a familiares de pacientes con coronavirus en situación de últimos días*. Equipo de soporte a cuidados paliativos del H.U. 12 de octubre. https://tinyurl.com/ys52785c

Hospital Sant Joan de Déu. (2016). *La primera noticia. Claves para el profesional*. https://bit.ly/2QIAKCU

HouZ.DuF.JiangH.ZhouX.LinL. (2020). Assessment of public attention, risk perception, emotional and behavioural responses to the COVID-19 outbreak: social media surveillance in China. medRxiv 2020.03.14.20035956.

Hovendan, D., & Bartlett, C. (2013). The Digital Government. *Strategy+Business.* Retrieved from: https://digitaledition.strategy-business.com/publication/?i=145911&article_id=1308784&view=articleBrowser&ver=html5

Hung, L. T. (2022). TikTok content in communication strategy: Politics of the 15th general election in Malaysia. *Higher Education and Oriental. Studies, 2*(6).

Hunt, E., & Waller, D. (1999). *Orientation and Wayfinding: A Review.* University of Washington.

Hürriyet. (2020). *Koronaya karşı 26 dev savaşçı.* Access at https://www.hurriyet.com.tr/gundem/koronaya-karsi-26-dev-savasci-41478997

Hurwitz, J., Nugent, A., Halper, F., & Kaufman, M. (2013). *Big Data for Dummies. John Wiley & Sons.*

Hussain, A., Ali, S., Ahmed, M., & Hussain, S. (2018, July 3). The Anti-vaccination Movement: A Regression in Modern Medicine. *Cureus, 10*(7). Advance online publication. [REMOVED HYPERLINK FIELD] doi:10.7759/cureus.2919 PMID:30186724

Huurne, E. T., & Gutteling, J. (2008). Information needs and risk perception as predictors of risk information seeking. *Journal of Risk Research, 11*(7), 847–862. doi:10.1080/13669870701875750

Huxley, A. (1932). *Brave New World.* Chatto & Windus.

IAS. (2022). *India inequality report 2022 digital divide.* Next IAS.

Ibayashi, H., Sugiura, Y., Sakamoto, D., & Miyata, N. (2015). Dollhouse VR: a multi view, multi-user collaborative design workspace with VR technology. *SIGGRAPH Asia 2015 Posters.* doi:10.1145/2820926.2820948

Icke, D. (2020a, March 18). *The truth behind the coronavirus pandemic, COVID-19 lockdown & the economic crash* (B. Rose, Interviewer) [London Real]. https://freedomplatform.tv/the-truth-behind-the-coronavirus-pandemic-covid-19-lockdown-the-economic-crash-david-icke/

Icke, D. (2020b, April 6). *The coronavirus conspiracy: How COVID-19 will seize your rights & destroy our economy* (B. Rose, Interviewer) [London Real]. https://freedomplatform.tv/the-coronavirus-conspiracy-how-covid-19-will-seize-your-rights-destroy-our-economy-david-icke/

Icke, D. (2020c, November 15). *David Icke Exposes The Great Reset* (A. Jones, Interviewer) [InfoWars]. https://banned.video/watch?id=5fbe601dc77bbc4fc3cbfcd6

Icke, D. (2021a, February 2). *The Awakening World Truth Summit with David Icke* (S. Smith, Interviewer) [TCN.VIdeo]. https://tcn.video/david-icke-the-awakening-world-truth-summit

Icke, D. (2021b, March 6). *The Awakening Part 2 with David Icke* (S. Smith, Interviewer) [TCN.VIdeo]. https://tcn.video/david-icke-the-awakening-part-2

İleti, H. (2022). *Havelsan İleti.* Retrieved from: https://www.havelsan.com.tr/en/sectors/information-and-communication/products/security/havelsan-ileti

Imran, M., Elbassuoni, S., Castillo, C., Diaz, F., & Meier, P. (2013). Extracting information nuggets from disaster-Related messages in social media. *Iscram, 201*(3), 791–801.

Indira, A. (2023). Utilization and rationalization of TikTok application for hospital health promotion during COVID-19 pandemic. *International Journal of Environmental, Sustainability, and Social Science*, *4*(1), 115–124. doi:10.38142/ijesss.v4i1.466

International Advertising Bureau. (2020b). *Monthly Flash de Inversión y Audiencia en Medios Digitales IAB-PwC. Seguimiento mensual Febrero – Marzo*. International Advertising Bureau - Spain. Available at: https://iabspain.es/estudio/flash-mensual-de-inversion-y-audiencias-en-medios-digitales-febrero-marzo-2020/

Ionescu, D. (2009). Google Street View Gets Smart Navigation. *PC World*. https://www.pcworld.com/article/529530/google-98.html

Izzo, N. (2023). Valerio, "Pandemic, humanities and the legal imagination of the disaster". In C. F. Stychin (Ed.), *Law, Humanities and the COVID Crisis*. University of London Press.

Jameson, F. (1988). Cognitive Mapping. In C. Nelson & L. Grossberg (Eds.), Marxism and the interpretation of culture (pp. 347–360). Macmillan Education.

Janssen, L. H. C., Kullberg, M. J., Verkuil, B., Van Zwieten, N., Wever, M. C. M., Van Houtum, L. A. E. M., Wentholt, W. G. M., & Elzinga, B. M. (2020). Does the COVID-19 pandemic impact parents' and adolescents' well-being? An EMA-study on daily affect and parenting. *PLoS One*, *5*(10), e0240962. doi:10.1371/journal.pone.0240962 PMID:33064778

Jin, X., & Spence, P. R. (2021). Understanding crisis communication on social media with CERC: Topic model analysis of tweets about Hurricane Maria. *Journal of Risk Research*, *24*(10), 1266–1287. doi:10.1080/13669877.2020.1848901

Jin, Y., Liu, B. F., & Austin, L. L. (2014). Examining the role of social media in effective crisis management: The effects of crisis origin, information form, and source on publics' crisis responses. *Communication Research*, *41*(1), 74–94. doi:10.1177/0093650211423918

Jones, A. (2022). *The great reset: And the war for the world*. Skyhorse Publishing.

Jones, H. E., Yoon, D. B., Theiss, J. A., Austin, J. T., & Lee, L. A. (2021). Assessing the effects of covıd-19 on romantic relationships and the coping strategies partners use to manage the stress of a pandemic. *Journal of Family Communication*, *21*(3), 152–166. doi:10.1080/15267431.2021.1927040

Jones, J. H., & Salathé, M. (2009). Early assessment of anxiety and behavioral response to novel swine-origin influenza A (H1N1). *PLoS One*, *4*(12), e8032. doi:10.1371/journal.pone.0008032 PMID:19997505

Junta de Castilla y León & Sacyl. (2020). Protocolo para profesionales sanitarios para la comunicación telefónica de malas noticias a familiares de pacientes con coronavirus en situación de cuidados de últimos días. In *Protocolo integral de actuación ante situaciones específicas de gravedad, últimos días y fallecimiento en la crisis COVID-19*. DG de Planificación y Asistencia Sanitaria y la DG de Sistemas, calidad y Prestación farmacéutica de la GRS. https://tinyurl.com/2cpj534h

Juran Institute. (1994). *Gestión de la Calidad. Mejora de la calidad en los servicios*. AENOR.

Juzefovičs, J., & Vihalemm, T. (2020). Keeping channels open or screening out? The digital practices of Baltic Russian-speakers during the Russia-Ukraine conflict. *Russian Journal of Communication*, *12*(3), 262–283. doi:10.1080/19409419.2020.1851454

Kahlor, L. (2010). PRISM: A planned risk information seeking model. *Health Communication*, *25*(4), 345–356. doi:10.1080/10410231003775172 PMID:20512716

Kahneman, D. (2011). *Hızlı ve Yavaş Düşünme, Çev. Osman Çetin – Filiz Nayır Deniztekin*. Varlık Yayınları.

Kahraman, M., E., (2020). COVID-19 Salgınının Uygulamalı Derslere Etkisi ve Bu Derslerin Uzaktan Eğitimle Yürütülmesi: Temel Tasarım Dersi Örneği. *İMÜ Sanat Tasarım ve Mimarlık Fakültesi Dergisi, 6*(1), 44-56.

Kalaylıoğlu, Y., Öztürk, A. M., & Eker, G. B. (2020). *The economic and social impact of COVİD-19 on women and men: Rapid gender assessment of COVİD-19 implications in Turkey. United Nations Entity for Gender Equality and the Empowerment of Women.* UN Women.

Kampp. (2022). *Hakkında.* https://www.kamapp.com/hakkinda/

Kapoor, S. (2022). *Digital Health Ecosystem in India: present ststus, challanges and way forward.* Research Gate.

Karadağ, F., Aslan, S., Budakoglu, I., Kucukkarapinar, M., Yay, A., & Ucar, O. (2020). *Turkey COVID-19 Snapshot Monitoring (COSMO Turkey): Monitoring knowledge, risk perceptions, preventive behaviours, and public trust in the current coronavirus outbreak in Turkey.* PsychArchives.

Kar, N., Kar, B., & Kar, S. (2021). Stress and coping during COVID-19 pandemic: Result of an online survey. *Psychiatry Research, 295*, 1–5. doi:10.1016/j.psychres.2020.113598 PMID:33264677

Kashmir, G. (2023). *To revolutionise healthcare, J&K government to intriduce AI in health sector.* Greater Kashmir.

Kassim, N. H., Mohamed Noor, N., Ali, J. K., Saleh, J., Dealwis, C., & Nurhisham, M. A. (2020). Sustaining job performance through technology acceptance with the usage of WhatsApp mobile application. *International Journal of Service Management and Sustainability, 5*(1), 1–26.

Kavada, A. (2010). Activism Transforms Digital: The Social Movement Perspective. In Digital Activism Decoded: The New Mechanics of Change. IDebate Press.

Kavaklı, N. (2019). Yalan Haberle Mücadele ve İnternet Teyit/Doğrulama Platformları. *Erciyes İletişim Dergisi, 6*(1), 663–682. doi:10.17680/erciyesiletisim.453398

Kaye, P. (2023). *Breaking Bad News: a ten step approach.* Scion Publishing Ltd.

Kearney. (2023). *The digital revolution could reshape healthcare in the Middle East.* CNBC Arabia.

Kemp, S. (2020, April 24). *Report: Most important data on digital audiences during coronavirus.* Growth Quarters—The Next Web. https://thenextweb.com/growth-quarters/2020/04/24/reportmost-important-data-on-digital-audiences-during-coronavirus/

Khatri, C., Chapman, S. J., Glasbey, J., Kelly, M., Nepogodiev, D., Bhangu, A., & Fitzgerald, E.STARSurg Committee. (2015). Social media and internet driven study recruitment: Evaluating a new model for promoting collaborator engagement and participation. *PLoS One, 10*(3), 1–11. doi:10.1371/journal.pone.0118899 PMID:25775005

Kholisoh, N., & Sulastri, R. (2017). New Media Technology in Developing Effective Organizational Internal Communication. *Humaniora, 8*(1), 21–29. doi:10.21512/humaniora.v8i1.3693

Kiesler, F. (1942). Note on Designing the Gallery and Press Release Pertaining to the Architectural Aspects of the Gallery. In Peggy Guggenheim & Frederick Kiesler: The Story of Art of this Century. Guggenheim Museum Publications.

Kim, H. K., Ahn, J., Atkinson, L., & Kahlor, L. A. (2020). Effects of COVID-19 misinformation on information seeking, avoidance, and processing: A Multicountry comparative study. *Science Communication, 42*(5), 586–615. doi:10.1177/1075547020959670

Kim, J., Livingstone, M. A., Jin, B., Watts, M., & Hwang, J. (2023). Fundamentals of Digital Health Literacy: A Scoping Review of Identifying Core Competencies to Use in Practice. *Adult Learning, 0*(0). Advance online publication. doi:10.1177/10451595231178298

Kim, J., Merrill, K. Jr, Collins, C., & Yang, H. (2021). Social TV viewing during the COVID-19 lockdown: The mediating role of social presence. *Technology in Society*, *67*, 97–116. doi:10.1016/j.techsoc.2021.101733 PMID:34538985

Kim, S. J. (2016). A repertoire approach to cross-platform media use behavior. *New Media & Society*, *18*(3), 353–372. doi:10.1177/1461444814543162

Kim, S., Austin, L., Liu, B. F., & Jin, Y. (2022). Exploring differences in crisis literacy and efficacy on behavioral responses during infectious disease outbreaks. *Public Relations Review*, *48*(3), 1–13. doi:10.1016/j.pubrev.2022.102204

Kim, Y. C., & Ball-Rokeach, S. J. (2006). Civic engagement from a communication infrastructure perspective. *Communication Theory*, *16*(2), 173–197. doi:10.1111/j.1468-2885.2006.00267.x

Kim, Y. M., Lee, Y., Rhiu, I., & Yun, M. H. (2021). Evaluation of locomotion methods in virtual reality navigation environments: An involuntary position shift and task performance. *International Journal of Human-Computer Studies*, *1071*, 5819. doi:10.1016/j.ijhcs.2021.102691

Kindness, P., Masthoff, J., & Mellish, C. (2017). Designing emotional support messages tailored to stressors. *International Journal of Human-Computer Studies*, *97*, 1–22. doi:10.1016/j.ijhcs.2016.07.010

Kırık, M. A. (2014). Uzaktan eğitimin tarihsel gelişimi ve Türkiye'deki durumu. *Marmara University Journal of Communication*, (21), 84.

Kızılkaya, Z. Z. (2022). Gençlerin TikTok kullanım ve doyumu üzerine nitel bir araştırma. *Anemon Muş Alparslan Üniversitesi Sosyal Bilimler Dergisi*, *10*(1), 231–247. doi:10.18506/anemon.962352

Knight, P. (2000). *Conspiracy culture: From the Kennedy assassination to The X-files*. Routledge.

Kobak, K. (2022). # TikTokkapansın hareketi: Twitter'da sosyal ağ analizi. *MANAS Sosyal Araştırmalar Dergisi*, *11*(1), 309–319. doi:10.33206/mjss.935068

Kocabay Şener, N. (2018). "Doğruluk Kontrol Merkezi" ve "Yalan Haber" Kavramlarına İlişkin İçeriklerin Medyada Yansımasının Araştırılması. *Akdeniz Üniversitesi İletişim Fakültesi Dergisi, (AKİL) Kasım*, (30), 355–373.

Koçer, B. Y. (2021). Dijital etnografi perspektifinden TikTok'ta müziğin kullanımı ve performans pratikleri. *Motif Akademi Halkbilimi Dergisi*, *14*(36), 1317–1332.

Koerner, A. F., & Fitzpatrick, M. A. (2002). Toward a theory of family communication. *Communication Theory*, *12*(1), 70–91. doi:10.1111/j.1468-2885.2002.tb00260.x

Kofman, Y. B., & Garfin, D. R. (2020). Home is not always a haven: The domestic violence crisis amid the COVID-19 pandemic. *Psychological Trauma: Theory, Research, Practice, and Policy*, *12*(1), 199–201. doi:10.1037/tra0000866 PMID:32478558

Kopecka-Piech, K. (2011). Media convergence concepts. *Mediaeval Studies*, *46*(3), 1–19.

Koranyi, B. (2023, March 10). Analysis: Wage catch-up to prolong Europe's inflation battle. *Reuters*. https://www.reuters.com/markets/europe/wage-catch-up-prolong-europes-inflation-battle-2023-03-10/

Köse, H. (2020). Dijimodern Çağda Hakikat, Sonrası ve Kamu Yararı. In H. S. Siyaset & M. U. İ. Felsefe (Eds.), *Bülent Özçelik* (pp. 201–231). Nika Yayınevi.

Köseoğlu, A. (2023). TikTok'ta mahremiyet algısının dönüşümü. *İNİF E- Dergi*, *8*(1), 172-188.

Kostagiolas, P. A., Kourouthanassis, P. E., Martzoukou, K., Korfiatis, N., & Niakas, D. (2018). Information seeking behavioural paths of physicians for diabetes mellitus care: A qualitative comparative analysis of information needs, sources, and barriers. *Health Systems (Basingstoke, England)*, *7*(1), 13–28. doi:10.1080/20476965.2017.1390050 PMID:31214336

Krämer, N. C., Winter, S., Benninghoff, B., & Gallus, C. (2015). How "social" is Social TV? The influence of social motives and expected outcomes on the usage of Social TV applications. *Computers in Human Behavior*, *51*, 255–262. doi:10.1016/j.chb.2015.05.005

Kreps, G. L. (2009). Applying Weick's model of organizing to health care and health promotion: Highlighting the central role of health communication. *Patient Education and Counseling*, *74*(3), 347–355. doi:10.1016/j.pec.2008.12.002 PMID:19150591

Kreuter, M. W., & McClure, S. M. (2004). The Role of Culture in Health Communication. *Annual Review of Public Health*, *25*(1), 439–455. doi:10.1146/annurev.publhealth.25.101802.123000 PMID:15015929

Krippendorff, K. (2018). *Content analysis: An introduction to its methodology*. Sage publications.

Krippendorf, K. (1980). *Content Analysis: An Introduction to its Methodology*. Sage Publication.

Kristof, R., & Satran, A. (1995). *Interactivity by design: creating & communicating with new media*. Adobe Press.

Kubrick, S. (Director). (1964, January 29). *Dr. Strangelove or: How I Learned to Stop Worrying and Love the Bomb*. Stanley Kubrick Productions.

Kuek, H. (2019). Healthcare staff digital literacy levels and their attitudes towards information systems. *Health Informatics Journal*. PMID:30983476

Kunova, M. (2020). *Digital News Report 2020: Covid-19 accelerates digital shifts in the media industry*. https://www.journalism.co.uk/news/digital-news-report-2020-Covid-19-has-accelerated-digital-shifts-in-the-media-industry/s2/a757201/

Kunova, M. (2020). *Digital News Report 2020: COVID-19 accelerates digital shifts in the media industry*. https://www.journalism.co.uk/news/digital-news-report-2020-covid-19-has-accelerated-digital-shifts-in-the-media-industry/s2/a757201/

Lachlan, K. A., Hutter, E., Gilbert, C., & Spence, P. R. (2021). From what I've heard, this is bad: An examination of Americans' source preferences and information seeking during the COVID-19 pandemic. *Progress in Disaster Science*, *9*, 100145. doi:10.1016/j.pdisas.2021.100145

Lachlan, K. A., Spence, P. R., Lin, X., Najarian, K., & Del Greco, M. (2016). Social media and crisis management: CERC, search strategies, and Twitter content. *Computers in Human Behavior*, *54*, 647–652. doi:10.1016/j.chb.2015.05.027

Laclau, E. (2005). *On Populist Reason*. Versus.

Lai, C. H., & Tang, T. (2015). Understanding local news consumption and community participation via the lens of information repertoires and media multiplexity. *Mass Communication & Society*, *18*(3), 325–349. doi:10.1080/15205436.2014.995768

Lai, C. H., & Tang, T. (2018). From information behaviors to disaster preparedness: Navigating individuals' general and disaster curation in US, China, and Australia. *Computers in Human Behavior*, *88*, 37–46. doi:10.1016/j.chb.2018.06.023

Lai, C., & Tang, T. (2021). Disaster communication behaviors in the U.S. and China: Which channels do you use and with whom? *Journal of Applied Communication Research*, *49*(2), 207–227. doi:10.1080/00909882.2021.1900588

Lalazaryan, A., & Zare-Farashbandi, F. (2014). A review of models and theories of health information seeking behavior. *International Journal of Health System and Disaster Management*, *2*(4), 193. doi:10.4103/2347-9019.144371

Lasch, C. (1979). *The culture of narcissism: American life in an age of diminishing expectations.* Norton.

Lasch, C. (1991). *The true and only heaven: Progress and its critics.* W.W. Norton & Company.

Lasswell, H. D. (1927, August). The Theory of Political Propaganda. *The American Political Science Review, 21*(3), 627–631. doi:10.2307/1945515

Latzer, M. (2013). Media convergence. Handbook on the digital creative economy, SSRN *Electronic Journal.* 123-133.

Lau, J., Yang, B., & Dasgupta, R. (2020). Will the coronavirus make online education go viral. *Times Higher Education.* https://www.timeshighereducation.com/features/will-coronavirus-make-online-educationgo-viral

Lawless, M., Augoustinos, M., & LeCouteur, A. (2018). Dementia on Facebook: Requesting information and advice about dementia risk-prevention on social media. *Discourse, Context & Media, 25,* 44–51. doi:10.1016/j.dcm.2018.01.011

Lay's, E. S. P. (2020). *El aperitivo estuvo y estará. Campaña verano 2020.* Available at: https://www.youtube.com/watch?v=q0pICV_9bHo

Lazebnik, T., Bunimovich-Mendrazitsky, S., Ashkenazi, S., Levner, E., & Benis, A. (2022). Early detection and control of the next epidemic wave using health communications: Development of an artificial intelligence-based tool and its validation on COVID-19 data from the US. *International Journal of Environmental Research and Public Health, 19*(23), 1–17. doi:10.3390/ijerph192316023 PMID:36498096

Leal, B. a. (2022). *The Digital Literacy Imperative.* CSIS.

Lee, C. (2015). The double-edged sword: The effects of journalists^ social media activities on audience perceptions of journalists and their news products. *Journal of Computer-Mediated Communication, 20*(3), 312–329. doi:10.1111/jcc4.12113

Lee, C. S., Ker, E. S., Ng, C. H., Ye, J., & Watson-Manheim, M. B. (2020). Effects of mobile instant messaging applications in the workplace. *Proceedings of the Association for Information Science and Technology, 57*(1), e354. doi:10.1002/pra2.354

Lee, S. K., Lindsey, N. J., & Kim, K. S. (2017). The effects of news consumption via social media and news information overload on perceptions of journalistic norms and practices. *Computers in Human Behavior, 75,* C. doi:10.1016/j.chb.2017.05.007

Lee, Y. H., & Hsieh, G. (2013). Does slacktivism hurt activism? the effects of moral balancing and consistency in online activism. *Proceedings of the SIGCHI Conference on Human Factors in Computing Systems,* 811-820. 10.1145/2470654.2470770

Le, H. T., Nguyen, D. N., Beydoun, A. S., Le, X. T. T., Nguyen, T. T., Pham, Q. T., Ta, N. T. K., Nguyen, Q. T., Nguyen, A. N., Hoang, M. T., Vu, L. G., Tran, B. X., Latkin, C. A., Ho, C. S. H., & Ho, R. C. M. (2020). Demand for health information on COVID-19 among Vietnamese. *International Journal of Environmental Research and Public Health, 17*(12), 4377–4389. doi:10.3390/ijerph17124377 PMID:32570819

Lei, S. A., & Gupta, R. K. (2010). College Distance Education Courses: Evaluating Benefits and Costs from Institutional. *Faculty and Students' Perspectives. Education, 130*(4), 616-631.

Lenin, V. İ. (1992). *Ne Yapmalı? Hareketimizin Canalıcı Sorunları, Erdost, M. (Çev.), 4. Baskı.* Sol Yayınları.

León-Amenero, D., & Huarcaya-Victoria, J. (2019). El duelo y cómo dar malas noticias en medicina. *Anales de la Facultad de Medicina. Universidad Nacional Mayor de San Marcos, 80*(1), 80–91. doi:10.15381/anales.v80i1.15471

Lid Rosenholm, I. (2022). *Health communication on TikTok: A qualitative study of credibility on a humorous platform.* https://www.diva-portal.org/smash/get/diva2:1667733/FULLTEXT01.pdf

Lidwell, W., Holden, K., & Butler, J. (2010). *Universal Principles of Design*. Rockport Publishers.

Lievrouw, L., & Livingstone, S. (2002). *Handbook of new media: Social shaping and consequences of ICTs*. Sage.

Li, J., Qin, P., Quan, Y., & Tan-Soo, J. S. (2023). Using Protection Motivation Theory to examine information-seeking behaviors on climate change. *Global Environmental Change*, *81*, 102698. doi:10.1016/j.gloenvcha.2023.102698

Li, J., & Zheng, H. (2022). Online information seeking and disease prevention intent during COVID-19 outbreak. *Journalism & Mass Communication Quarterly*, *99*(1), 69–88. doi:10.1177/1077699020961518

Lillie, H. M., Venetis, M. K., & Chernichky-Karcher, S. (2023). Resilience communication mitigates the negative relational effects of topic avoidance: Evidence from parental caregiving and COVID-19 pandemic contexts. *Personal Relationships*, 1–22. doi:10.1111/pere.12508

Lim, M. (2017). Freedom to hate: Social media, algorithmic enclaves, and the rise of tribal nationalism in Indonesia. *Critical Asian Studies*, *49*(3), 411–427. doi:10.1080/14672715.2017.1341188

Li, N., Yan, J., & Wu, F. (2021). Research on the current situation and development strategy of health communication in a short TikTok Video: The "Dingxiang Doctor". *Scientific and Social Research*, *3*(3), 144–149. doi:10.36922sr.v3i3.1170

Liu, B. F., Austin, L., & Jin, Y. (2011). How publics respond to crisis communication strategies: The interplay of information form and source. *Public Relations Review*, *37*(4), 345–353. doi:10.1016/j.pubrev.2011.08.004

Liu, B. F., Fraustino, J. D., & Jin, Y. (2015). How disaster information form, source, type, and prior disaster exposure affect public outcomes: Jumping on the social media bandwagon? *Journal of Applied Communication Research*, *43*(1), 44–65. doi:10.1080/00909882.2014.982685

Liu, B. F., & Mehta, A. M. (2021). From the periphery and toward a centralized model for trust in government risk and disaster communication. *Journal of Risk Research*, *24*(7), 853–869. doi:10.1080/13669877.2020.1773516

Liu, B. F., Xu, S., Lim, J. R., & Egnoto, M. (2019). How publics' active and passive communicative behaviors affect their tornado responses: An integration of STOPS and SMCC. *Public Relations Review*, *45*(4), 101831. doi:10.1016/j.pubrev.2019.101831

Liu, K., Yang, Y., Li, M., Li, S., Sun, K., & Zhao, Y. (2021). Parents' and adolescents' perceptions of parental involvement and their relationships with depression among Chinese middle school students during the COVID-19 pandemic. *Children and Youth Services Review*, *129*, 106190. doi:10.1016/j.childyouth.2021.106190 PMID:34511675

Liu, P. L. (2020). COVID-19 information seeking on digital media and preventive behaviors: The mediation role of worry. *Cyberpsychology, Behavior, and Social Networking*, *23*(10), 677–682. doi:10.1089/cyber.2020.0250 PMID:32498549

Liu, W., Xu, W., & John, B. (2021). Organizational disaster communication ecology: Examining interagency coordination on social media during the onset of the COVID-19 pandemic. *The American Behavioral Scientist*, *65*(7), 914–933. doi:10.1177/0002764221992823

Li, Y., Guan, M., Hammond, P., & Berrey, L. E. (2021). Communicating COVID-19 information on TikTok: A content analysis of TikTok videos from official accounts featured in the COVID-19 information hub. *Health Education Research*, *36*(3), 261–271. doi:10.1093/her/cyab010 PMID:33667311

Lopes, F., Araújo, R., & Magalhães, O. (2021). Covid-19: A Pandemic Managed by Official Sources Through Political Communication. *Comunicação e Sociedade*, *40*, 17–32. doi:10.17231/comsoc.40(2021).3520

Lovejoy, K., & Saxton, G. D. (2012). Information, community, and action: How nonprofit organizations use social media. *Journal of Computer-Mediated Communication*, *17*(3), 337–353. doi:10.1111/j.1083-6101.2012.01576.x

Lowry, L. (1993). *The giver*. Listening Library/Random House.

Luetke, M., Hensel, D., Herbenick, D., & Rosenberg, M. (2020). Romantic relationship conflict due to the COVID-19 pandemic and changes in intimate and sexual behaviors in a nationally representative sample of American adults. *Journal of Sex & Marital Therapy*, *46*(8), 747–762. doi:10.1080/0092623X.2020.1810185 PMID:32878584

Luiijf, E., Besseling, K., & Graaf, P. D. (2013). Nineteen national cyber security strategies. *Int. J. Critical Infrastructures*, *9*(1/2), 3–31. doi:10.1504/IJCIS.2013.051608

Lund, B., & Ma, J. (2022). Exploring information seeking of rural older adults during the COVID-19 pandemic. *Aslib Journal of Information Management*, *74*(1), 54–77. doi:10.1108/AJIM-04-2021-0118

Lupton, D. (2014). The commodification of patient opinion: The digital patient experience economy in the age of big data. *Sociology of Health & Illness*, *36*(6), 856–869. doi:10.1111/1467-9566.12109 PMID:24443847

Machado. (2021). The relationship between the Covid-19 Pandemic and Vaccine Hesitancy A scoping review of literature until August 2021. *PubMed Central*.

Madden, M., Cortesi, S., Gasser, U., Lenhart, A., & Duggan, M. (2012). *Parents, Teens and Online Privacy*. Pew Research Center. Retrieved from: https://www.pewresearch.org/internet/2012/11/20/parents-teens-and-online-privacy/

Madrileña, M. (2020). *Anuncio 1 Grupo Mutua Madrileña Navidad 2020 (06/12/2020)*. Available at: https://www.youtube.com/watch?v=18PbhF8K9Sg

Maduz, L., Prior, T., Roth, F., & Käser, M. (2019). *Individual disaster preparedness: Explaining disaster-related information seeking and preparedness behavior in Switzerland*. ETH Zurich.

Maguire, K. (2012). *Stress and coping in families*. Polity Press.

Mahou, T. V. (2020). *Ahora más que nunca, Juntos para Siempre | Mahou*. Available at: https://www.youtube.com/watch?v=o3DjRl1fBYY

Mair, P. (2006). Ruling the Void. *New Left Review*, *42*, 25–51.

Makarova, E. L., & Makarova, E. A. (2019). The functional model of using visualization and digitalization for media literacy development in media education process. *Slovak Republic Media Education.*, *59*(4), 547–556.

Malecki, C. K., & Demaray, M. K. (2003). What type of support do they need? Investigating student adjustment as related to emotional, informational, appraisal, and instrumental support. *School Psychology Quarterly*, *18*(3), 231–252. doi:10.1521cpq.18.3.231.22576

Malecki, K. M. C., Keating, J. A., & Safdar, N. (2021). Crisis Communication and Public Perception of COVID-19 Risk in the Era of Social Media. *Clinical Infectious Diseases*, *72*(4), 697–702. doi:10.1093/cid/ciaa758 PMID:32544242

Malla, S. B., Dahal, R. K., & Hasegawa, S. (2020). Analyzing the disaster response competency of the local government official and the elected representative in Nepal. *Geoenvironmental Disasters*, *7*(1), 1–13. doi:10.118640677-020-00153-z

Mamuli, L., Mutsotso, S., & Namasaka, D. (2013). The influence of communication channels on management practices in Kenyan public universities. *International Journal of Academic Research in Progressive Education and Development*, *2*(1), 257–267.

Manganello, J., Bleakley, A., & Schumacher, P. (2020). Pandemics and PSAs: Rapidly Changing Information in a New Media Landscape. *Health Communication*, *35*(14), 1711–1714. doi:10.1080/10410236.2020.1839192 PMID:33106041

Mann, S., & Picard, R. W. (1994). Virtual bellows: constructing high-quality stills from video. In *Proceedings of the IEEE First International Conference on Image Processing*. IEEE. 10.1109/ICIP.1994.413336

Marchionini, G. (1995). *Information seeking in electronic environments (No. 9)*. Cambridge University Press. doi:10.1017/CBO9780511626388

Marks, L. D., Dollahite, D. C., Kelley, H. H., Kimball, E. R., & James, S. (2023). Exploring influences of the COVID-19 pandemic on family communication: Negative, positive, or both? *Marriage & Family Review*, *59*(2), 121–142. doi:10.1080/01494929.2023.2170014

Martínez-Sanz, R., Buitrago, Á., & Martín-García, A. (2023). Communication for health through TikTok. Study of influencers in the pharmaceutical field and connection with their audience. *Revista Mediterránea de Comunicación/Mediterranean Journal of Communication*, *14*(1), 83–98.

Martin, L. N., Giff, S. T., Ribeiro, S., Fyffe, S., & Renshaw, K. D. (2022). Changes in relationship quality in the COVID-19 pandemic: Associations with pandemic stressors and couple communication. *The American Journal of Family Therapy*, 1–17. doi:10.1080/01926187.2022.2073293

Mathers, N., Fox, N. & Hunn, A. (2007). *Surveys and Questionnaires*. The NIHR RDS for the East Midlands/Yorkshire & the Humber.

Matthes, J. (2006). The need for orientation towards news media: Revising and validating a classic concept. *International Journal of Public Opinion Research*, *18*(4), 422–444. doi:10.1093/ijpor/edh118

Maykrantz, S. A., Gong, T., Petrolino, A. V., Nobiling, B. D., & Houghton, J. D. (2021). How Trust in information sources influences preventative measures compliance during the COVID-19 pandemic. *International Journal of Environmental Research and Public Health*, *18*(11), 5867. doi:10.3390/ijerph18115867 PMID:34070713

McCracken, G. (2005). *Culture and consumption II. Markets, meaning, and Brand Management*. Indiana University Press.

McDaniel, B. T. (2019). Parent distraction with phones, reasons for use, and impacts on parenting and child outcomes: A review of the emerging research. *Human Behavior and Emerging Technologies*, *1*(2), 72–80. doi:10.1002/hbe2.139

McDaniel, B. T., & Coyne, S. M. (2016). "Technoference": The interference of technology in couple relationships and implications for women's personal and relational well-being. *Psychology of Popular Media Culture*, *5*(1), 85–98. doi:10.1037/ppm0000065

McDermid, P., Craig, A., Sheel, M., Blazek, K., Talty, S., & Seale, H. (2023). Information seeking behaviors of individuals impacted by COVID-19 international travel restrictions: An analysis of two international cross-sectional studies. *Frontiers in Communication*, *8*, 1101548. doi:10.3389/fcomm.2023.1101548

McDonald's. (2020). *"Es hora de volver a encontrarnos", la nueva campaña de #McDonald's.* Available at: https://www.youtube.com/watch?v=mAxAlwv0PmA

McGonagle, T. (2017). "Fake news" false fears or real concerns? *Netherlands Quarterly of Human Rights*, *35*(4), 203–209. doi:10.1177/0924051917738685

McGraw, T. (2020). *Spending 2020 Together on Twitter*. Available at: https://blog.twitter.com/en_us/topics/insights/2020/spending-2020-together-on-twitter

McIntyre, L. (2018). *Post-Truth*. MIT Press. doi:10.7551/mitpress/11483.001.0001

McKinsey. (2021). *Unlocking digital healthcare in lower and middle income countries*. MicKinsey and Company.

Mcluhan, M. (1962). *Gutenberg Galaxy: The making of typographic man.* Retrieved December 2, 2021, from http://www.ocopy.net/wp-content/uploads/2017/10/mcluhan-marshall_the-gutenberg-galaxy-the-making-of-typographic-man.pdf

Mcluhan, M. (1967). *The medium is the massage: An inventory of effects.* Retrieved December 5, 2021, from https://designopendata.files.wordpress.com/2014/05/themediumisthe massage_marsh allmcluhan_quentinfiore.pdf

McLuhan, M. (1994). *Understanding media: The extensions of man.* MIT press.

Meade, A. (2020). *More than 150 Australian newsrooms shut since January 2019 as Covid-19 deepens media crisis.* Available at: https://www.theguardian.com/media/2020/may/18/more-than-150-australian-news-rooms-shut-since-january-2019-as-Covid-19-deepens-media-crisis

Medialdea, S. (2020). *La mitad de los sanitarios sufren estrés postraumático y un 40% están emocionalmente agotados.* ABC. 19 mayo 2020. https://bit.ly/3u5BUWu

Meese, J., & Hurcombe, E. (2021). Facebook, news media and platform dependency: The institutional impacts of news distribution on social platforms. *New Media & Society, 23*(8), 2367–2384. doi:10.1177/1461444820926472

Meister, D. a. (2016). *Digital Health and Digital biomakers enabling value chains on health data.* Gruyter.

Memmi, D. (2014). Information overload and virtual institutions. *AI & Society, 29*(1), 75–83. doi:10.100700146-012-0428-9

Merco. (2022). *Monitor de Reputación Sanitaria – Hospitales.* https://tinyurl.com/ytnnhwbw

Mercola, J. (2021a). Event 201 and the Great Reset. In J. Mercola & R. Cummins (Eds.), *The Truth About COVID-19: Exposing The Great Reset, Lockdowns, Vaccine Passports, and the New Normal.* Chalsea Green Publishing.

Mercola, J. (2021b). Successful Protocols Suppressed. In J. Mercola & R. Cummins (Eds.), *The Truth About COVID-19: Exposing The Great Reset, Lockdowns, Vaccine Passports, and the New Normal.* Chalsea Green Publishing.

Mercola, J., & Cummins, R. (2021). *The Truth About COVID-19: Exposing The Great Reset, Lockdowns, Vaccine Passports, and the New Normal.* Chalsea Green Publishing.

Meriç, E., Çakıcı, Z., & Başer, B. (2022). Health communication and health information seeking on social media: A study on COVID-19 online support groups on Facebook. In Covid Communication II (pp. 137-160). Klaipeda: SRA Academic Publishing.

Mheidly, N., & Fares, J. (2020). Leveraging media and health communication strategies to overcome the COVID-19 infodemic. *Journal of Public Health Policy, 41*(4), 410–420. doi:10.105741271-020-00247-w PMID:32826935

Mihelj, S., & Jmenez-Martinez, C. (2020). Digital nationalism: Understanding the role of digital media in the rise of 'new' nationalism. *Nations and Nationalism, 27*(2), 331–346. doi:10.1111/nana.12685

Mikucki-Enyart, S. L., & Maguire, K. C. (2021). Introduction to the special ıssue on family communication in the Covıd-19 pandemic. *Journal of Family Communication, 21*(3), 145–151. doi:10.1080/15267431.2021.1933038

Miles, M. B., & Huberman, A. M. (1994). Qualitative data analysis: An expanded sourcebook. *Sage (Atlanta, Ga.).*

Milley, K. M., Chima, S. A., Cummings, K. L., & Emery, J. D. (2021). Look who's talking now: Cancer in primary care on Twitter. An observational study. *BJGP Open, 5*(1), 1–10. doi:10.3399/bjgpopen20X101134 PMID:33199305

Milliyet. (2020). *İşte Kovid-19 savaşçısı bilim insanları.* Access at https://www.milliyet.com.tr/gundem/iste-kovid-19-savascisi-bilim-insanlari-6154577

Milton, M. (2010). *Networks and States.* The MIT Press.

Ministerio de Sanidad. (2021). *Cuidados paliativos. Guía para Atención Primaria.* Instituto Nacional de Gestión Sanitaria, Ministerio de Sanidad. https://tinyurl.com/twkaywkd

Misconceptions About Vaccines: History of Anti-Vaccination Movements. (2022, April 20). History of Vaccines: https://historyofvaccines.org/vaccines-101/misconceptions-about-vaccines/history-anti-vaccination-movements

Molina, M. D., Sundar, S. S., Le, T., & Lee, D. (2019). "Fake news" is not simply false information: A concept explication and taxonomy of online content. *The American Behavioral Scientist.*

Mols, A., & Pridmore, J. (2020). Always available via WhatsApp: Mapping everyday boundary work practices and privacy negotiations. *Mobile Media & Communication.*

Monika, P. (2013). *Communication in Employees' Motivation and Remuneration System.* Academic Press.

Montag, C., & Elhai, J. D. (2020). Discussing digital technology overuse in children and adolescents during the COVID-19 pandemic and beyond: On the importance of considering Affective Neuroscience Theory. *Addictive Behaviors Reports, 12*, 100313. doi:10.1016/j.abrep.2020.100313 PMID:33364321

Montaña Blasco, M., Ollé Castellà, C., & Lavilla Raso, M. (2020). Impacto de la pandemia de Covid-19 en el consumo de medios en España. *Revista Latina de Comunicación Social, 78*, 155-167. https://www.doi.org/10.4185/RLCS-2020-14

Moore, P., Gómez, G., & Kurt, S. (2012). Comunicación médico-paciente: Una de las competencias básicas pero diferente. *Atencion Primaria, 44*(6), 358–365. doi:10.1016/j.aprim.2011.07.008 PMID:22079197

Moorhead, S. A., Hazlett, D. E., Harrison, L., Carroll, J. K., Irwin, A., & Hoving, C. (2013, April 23). A new dimension of health care: Systematic review of the uses, benefits, and limitations of social media for health communication. *Journal of Medical Internet Research, 15*(4), 1–17. doi:10.2196/jmir.1933 PMID:23615206

Mora-Rodríguez, A., & Melero-López, I. (2021). Seguimiento informativo y percepción del riesgo ante la Covid-19 en España. *Comunicar, Revista Cien-tífica de Educomunicación, 29*(66), 71–81. doi:10.3916/C66-2021-06

Morgan, D. L. (1996). *Focus groups as qualitative research (C. 16).* Sage Publications.

Morozov, E. (2009). The Brave New World of Slacktivism. *Foreign Policy.* https://foreignpolicy.com/2009/05/19/the-brave-new-world-of-slacktivism/

Morozov, E. (2011). *The Net Delusion: The Dark Side of Internet Freedom.* Perseus Books Public Affaires.

Mukhopadhyay, N. (2019). *The abrogation of Kashmir's special status: why now.* Al Jzaeera.

Mukhtar, S. (2020). Psychological health during the coronavirus disease 2019 pandemic outbreak. *The International Journal of Social Psychiatry, 66*(5), 512–516. doi:10.1177/0020764020925835 PMID:32434402

Mundo, E. (2020). *España, el país con más bares y restaurantes del mundo, pide convertirlos en Patrimonio de la Humanidad.* Accessed 20 March 2023: https://www.elmundo.es/viajes/espana/2020/06/19/5eeb49defdddffe66b8b4587.html

Munir, K., Ergene, T., Tunaligil, V., & Erol, N. (2004). A Window of Opportunity for the Transformation of National Mental Health Policy in Turkey Following Two Major Earthquakes. *Harvard Review of Psychiatry, 12*(4), 238–251. doi:10.1080/10673220490509615 PMID:15371066

Murzintcev, N., & Cheng, C. (2017). Disaster hashtags in social media. *ISPRS International Journal of Geo-Information, 6*(7), 204. doi:10.3390/ijgi6070204

Muturi, N. (2022). The influence of information source on COVID-19 vaccine efficacy and motivation for self-protective behavior. *Journal of Health Communication, 27*(4), 241–249. doi:10.1080/10810730.2022.2096729 PMID:35793310

Myers, J. (2021, December 10). These charts show the growing gap between the world's richest and poorest. *World Economic Forum.* https://www.weforum.org/agenda/2021/12/global-income-inequality-gap-report-rich-poor/

Nack, F., & Wærn, A. (2012). Mobile digital interactive storytelling—A winding path. *New Review of Hypermedia and Multimedia, 18*(1-2), 3–9. doi:10.1080/13614568.2011.641418

Naeem, S. B., & Bhatti, R. (2020). The Covid-19 'infodemic': A new front for information professionals. *Health Information &amp. Library Journal, 37*(3), 233–239. doi:10.1111/hir.12311 PMID:32533803

Nagy, E., Thompson, P., Mayor, L., & Doughty, H. (2021). Do foetuses communicate? Foetal responses to interactive versus non-interactive maternal voice and touch: An exploratory analysis. *Infant Behavior and Development, 63*, 101562. doi:10.1016/j.infbeh.2021.101562 PMID:33831801

Nash, M., & Kuehn, W. (2020). *Exhibition Staging: Notes and Queries*. Platform 6 Talks. Available at https://www.documenta-platform6.de/exhibition-staging-notes-and-queries/

Neate, R. (2020, March 11). Super-rich jet off to disaster bunkers amid coronavirus outbreak. *The Guardian.* https://www.theguardian.com/world/2020/mar/11/disease-dodging-worried-wealthy-jet-off-to-disaster-bunkers

Nechushtai, E. (2018). Could digital platforms capture the media through infrastructure? *Journalism, 19*(8), 1043–1058. doi:10.1177/1464884917725163

Negrón, A. P. P., López, G. L., & Aguirre, H. R. O. (Eds.). (2020). *Virtual Reality Designs* (1st ed.). CRC Press. doi:10.1201/9781003019589

Nemes, M. Z. (2023). Going Viral. *Hungarian Journal of English and American Studies, 29*(1), 121–142.

NEMO. (2020). *Survey on the impact of the COVID-19 situation on museums in Europe Final Report.* Network of European Museum Organizations. https://www.ne-mo.org/fileadmin/Dateien/public/NEMO_documents/NEMO_COVID19_Report_12.05.2020.pdf

Neuwirth, K. (1995). *The Influence of Severity, Vulnerabilty, and Response Efficacy on Information Seeking and Behavioral Intention.* Paper presented at the Annual Meeting of the Association for Education in Journalism and Mass Communication, Washington, DC.

Neuwirth, K., Dunwoody, S., & Griffin, R. J. (2000). Protection motivation and risk communication. *Risk Analysis, 20*(5), 721–734. doi:10.1111/0272-4332.205065 PMID:11110218

Nguyen, M. H., Gruber, J., Fuchs, J., Marler, W., Hunsaker, A., & Hargittai, E. (2020). Changes in Digital Communication During the COVID-19 Global Pandemic: Implications for Digital Inequality and Future Research. *Social Media + Society, 6*(3). Advance online publication. doi:10.1177/2056305120948255 PMID:34192039

Nielsen, R. K., Kalogeropoulos, A., & Fletcher, R. (2020). *Most in the UK Say News Media have Helped them Respond to COVİD-19, But a Third Say News Coverage has Made the Crisis Worse.* Reuters Institute for the Study of Journalism.

Nielson, R. K., A. Cornia, A. Kalogeropoulos. (2016). *Challenges and opportunities for news media and journalism in an increasingly digital, mobile, and social media environment.* Council of Europe report DGI: 18.

Nielson, R. K. (2012). *Ten Years that Shook the Media World Big Questions and Big Trends in International Media Developments.* The Reuters Institute for the Study of Journalism.

Nikiforova, A. (2023). Data Security as a Top Priority in the Digital World: Preserve Data Value by Being Proactive and Thinking Security First. In A. Visvizi, O. Troisi, & M. Grimaldi (Eds.), *Research and Innovation Forum 2022. RIIFORUM 2022. Springer Proceedings in Complexity.* Springer. doi:10.1007/978-3-031-19560-0_1

Norman, D. A. (1989). *The Design of Everyday Things.* DoubleDay.

Novielli, M. R. (2022). *Storia del cinema giapponese nel nuovo millennio.* Marsilio.

Núñez, S., Marco, T., Burillo-Putze, G., & Ojeda, J. (2006). Procedimientos y habilidades para la comunicación de las malas noticias en urgencias. *Medicina Clínica, 127*(15), 580–583. doi:10.1157/13094002 PMID:17145016

Nutbeam, D. (2021). From health education to digital health literacy – building on the past to shape the future. *Global Health Promotion, 28*(4), 51–55. doi:10.1177/17579759211044079 PMID:34719292

O'Connor, S. (2021, April 25). 'We are drowning in insecurity': Young people and life after the pandemic. *Financial Times.* https://www.ft.com/content/77d586cc-4f3f-4701-a104-d09136c93d44

O'Hara, K. P., Massimi, M., Harper, R., Rubens, S., & Morris, J. (2014, February). Everyday dwelling with WhatsApp. In *Proceedings of the 17th ACM Conference on Computer Supported Cooperative Work & Social Computing* (pp. 1131–1143). ACM.

O'Sullivan, J., & Fortunati, L. (2018). Situating the social sustainability of print media in a world of digital alternatives. *Telematics and Informatics*, 37.

OberCom. (2023). *Retrato digital de Portugal: caracterização e tendências de utilização das redes sociais - 2015 a 2023.* OberCom – Observatório da Comunicação. https://obercom.pt/retrato-digital-de-portugal-caracterizacao-e-tendencias-de-utilizacao-das-redes-sociais-2015-a-2023/

Oficial, C. U. P. R. A. (2021). *CUPRA x Ansu Fati. Our wish for 2021.* Available at: https://www.youtube.com/watch?v=jtjj_3Yo8Qs

Ofori-Parku, S., & Moscato, D. (2018). Hashtag Activism as a Form of Political Action: A Qualitative Analysis of the #BringBackOurGirls Campaign in Nigerian, UK, and U.S. Press. *International Journal of Communication, 12*, 23. https://ijoc.org/index.php/ijoc/article/view/8068

Ogolsky, B. G., & Monk, J. K. (2019). Dating and couple formation. In B. H. Fiese, M. Celano, K. Deater-Deckard, E. N. Jouriles, & M. A. Whisman (Eds.), APA handbook of contemporary family psychology: Vol. 1. Foundations, methods, and contemporary issues across the lifespan (pp. 427–443). American Psychological Association. doi:10.1037/0000099-024

Okay, A., Ašanin Gole, P., & Okay, A. (2021). Turkish and Slovenian health ministries' use of Twitter: A comparative analysis. *Corporate Communications, 26*(1), 176–191. doi:10.1108/CCIJ-01-2020-0019

Ollé, R., & Riu, D. (2009). El nuevo Brand Management. Cómo plantar marcas para hacer crecer negocios. *Gestion.*

Orwell, G. (1949). *Nineteen Eighty-Four.* Secker & Warburg.

Oteyza, A. M., Balmoria, B. E., & Sabularse, M. (2018). Effectiveness of Oral and Written Communication of University Employees. *Asia Pacific Journal of Multidisciplinary Research, 6*(1), 88–95.

Özdemir Çakır, H. Ö. (2023). Influencer pazarlamasının satın alma davranışına etkisi: TikTok örneği. *Anasay, 0*(24), 165–183. doi:10.33404/anasay.1249855

Özdemir, K. & Nacar, R. (2020). Yerli ve Milli Sosyal Medyayı Tercih Etme Nedenleri. *Journal of Süleyman Demirel University Institute of Social Sciences, 3*(38), 42-69.

Özdoğan, A. Ç., & Berkant, H. G. (2020). Covıd-19 pandemi dönemindeki uzaktan eğitime ilişkin paydaş görüşlerinin incelenmesi. *Milli Eğitim Dergisi, 49*(1), 13–43. doi:10.37669/milliegitim.788118

Özdoyran, G. (2020). Post-Truth Çağı, Kuram-Yüklü Gözlem Sorunu ve Yeni Medya: Facebook "Düz Dünya Türkiye" Grubu Örneği. *Egemia Ege Üniversitesi İletişim Fakültesi Medya Ve İletişim Araştırmaları Hakemli E-Dergisi*, (7), 139–169.

Özgül, B. A., & Veneti, A. (2022). The Different Organizational Structures of Alternative Media: Through the Perspective of Alternative Media Journalists in Turkey and Greece. *Digital Journalism (Abingdon, England)*, *10*(8), 1302–1321. doi:10.1080/21670811.2021.1943482

Özkaya, A. (2020). *Post Truth (Gerçeklik Ötesi): Yalanların Gerçekmiş Gibi Sunulduğu Bir Dünyada, Hakikatin Anlamı Nedir?* evrimagaci.org

Öztürk, A., Erkan, C., & Erkuş, U. (2021). Türkiye'deki Sosyal Medya Kullanıcılarının Zorlayıcı Politikalar Sonrasındaki Sosyal Medya Kullanımında Alternatif Arayışlar ve Değişimler. *Mediterranean Summit 5th International Social Sciences Congress Book of Full Text*, 60-75.

Palupi, N. D., Meifilina, A., & Harumike, Y. D. N. (2020). The effect of using TikTok applications on self-confidence levels. *JOSAR*, *5*(2), 66–74.

Pan, S. L., Cui, M., & Qian, J. (2020). Information resource orchestration during the COVID-19 pandemic: A study of community lockdowns in China. *International Journal of Information Management*, *54*, 102143. doi:10.1016/j.ijinfomgt.2020.102143 PMID:32394997

Parés, N., & Parés, R. (2001). Interaction-Driven Virtual Reality Application Design (A Particular Case: El Ball del Fanalet or Lightpools). Presence: Teleoperators and Virtual Environments, 10(2), 236-245. doi:10.1162/105474601750216830

Park, A., Bowling, J., Shaw, G. Jr, Li, C., & Chen, S. (2019). Adopting Social Media for Improving Health: Opportunities and Challenges. *North Carolina Medical Journal*, *80*(4), 240–243. doi:10.18043/ncm.80.4.240 PMID:31278188

Park, H., Reber, B. H., & Chon, M. G. (2016). Tweeting as health communication: Health organizations' use of Twitter for health promotion and public engagement. *Journal of Health Communication*, *21*(2), 188–198. doi:10.1080/10810730.2015.1058435 PMID:26716546

Park, H., Rodgers, S., & Stemmle, J. (2011). Health organizations' use of Facebook for health advertising and promotion. *Journal of Interactive Advertising*, *12*(1), 62–77. doi:10.1080/15252019.2011.10722191

Parrott, S., Billings, A. C., Hakim, S. D., & Gentile, P. (2020). From# endthestigma to# realman: Stigma-challenging social media responses to NBA players' mental health disclosures. *Communication Reports*, *33*(3), 148–160. doi:10.1080/08934215.2020.1811365

Patil. (2022). Existing system of digital health in India. *D Y Patil Journal of Health Sciences.*

Perappadan, B. (2020). *India's first coronavirus infection confirmed in Kerala.* The Hind.

Perceptions, A. (2020). *Coronavirus Effect on Advertising Report.* Available at: https://www.advertiserperceptions.com/wp-content/uploads/2020/03/03.25.2020-Coronavirus-Effect-on-Advertising-WEBINAR-PDF-1.pdf

Pérez, P., & Lobato, M. (2021). *Un nuevo año, ¿un nuevo comienzo?* Google. Available at: https://www.thinkwithgoogle.com/intl/es-es/insights/descubriendo-al-nuevo-consumidor-nuevo-comienzo/

Perez-Escoda, A., & Jimenes-Narros, C. (2020). Social Networks' Engagement During the COVİD-19 Pandemic in Spain: Health Media vs. Healthcare Professionals. *International Journal of Environmental Research and Public Health*, *17*(14), 5261. doi:10.3390/ijerph17145261 PMID:32708231

Periódico, E. (2020). *Cultura de cuarentena: Begoña Alberdi, la soprano que cada noche regala ópera a sus vecinos.* Accessed 20 March 2023 at: https://www.elperiodico.com/es/ocio-y-cultura/20200317/cultura-cuarentena-begona-alberdi-soprano-regala-opera-vecinos-sant-antoni-7892439

Peters, C., Schrøder, K. C., Lehaff, J., & Vulpius, J. (2022). News as they know it: Young adults' information repertoires in the digital media landscape. *Digital Journalism (Abingdon, England)*, *10*(1), 62–86. doi:10.1080/21670811.2021.1885986

Pianese, T., & Belfiore, P. (2021). Exploring the Social Networks' Use in the Health-Care Industry: A Multi-Level Analysis. *International Journal of Environmental Research and Public Health*, *18*(14), 1–14. doi:10.3390/ijerph18147295 PMID:34299746

Picard, R. G. (2010). The Future of the News Industry. In J. Curran (Ed.), *Media and Society* (pp. 365–379). Bloomsbury Academic.

Pickle, K., Quinn, S. C., & Brown, J. D. (2002). HIV/AIDS coverage in black newspapers, 1991-1996: Implications for health communication and health education. *Journal of Health Communication*, *7*(5), 427–444. doi:10.1080/10810730290001792 PMID:12455762

Pierson, J., (2012). Online Privacy in Social Media: A Conceptual Exploration of Empowerment and Vulnerability. *Digiworld Economic Journal*, *88*, 99-120.

Pınarbaşı, G. (2023). TikTok'ta bir alt kültür örneği olarak cadılık kültürü ve büyü uygulamaları: WitchTok örneği. *Medya ve Kültür*, *3*(1), 90–128.

Plate, S. B. (2020). Cinema: The Georeligious Aesthetic. *CrossCurrents, 70*(3), 203–205.

Porat, T., Nyrup, R., Calvo, R. A., Paudyal, P., & Ford, E. (2020). Public Health and Risk Communication During COVID-19—Enhancing Psychological Needs to Promote Sustainable Behavior Change. *Frontiers in Public Health*, *8*(573397), 1–15. doi:10.3389/fpubh.2020.573397 PMID:33194973

Postman, N. (1985). *Amusing Ourselves to Death: Public Discourse in the Age of Show Business.* Viking Penguin.

Poulton, M. C. (2023). Realism, the Real, and Mediated Reality: Hirata Oriza and Beyond. In J. Nakamura & K. Saltzman-Li (Eds.), *Realisms in East Asian Performance* (pp. 160–174). University of Michigan Press.

PR. (2021). *Economic survey highlights thrust on rural development.* Press Information Bureau.

Prasetyo, Y. T., Castillo, A. M., Salonga, L. J., Sia, J. A., & Seneta, J. A. (2020). Factors affecting perceived effectiveness of COVID-19 prevention measures among Filipinos during enhanced community quarantine in Luzon, Philippines: Integrating Protection Motivation Theory and extended Theory of Planned Behavior. *International Journal of Infectious Diseases*, *99*, 312–323. doi:10.1016/j.ijid.2020.07.074 PMID:32768695

Prensky, M. (2001). Digital Natives, Digital Immigrants. *On the Horizon, 9*(5).

Prentice-Dunn, S., & Rogers, R. W. (1986). Protection motivation theory and preventive health: Beyond the health belief model. *Health Education Research*, *1*(3), 153–161. doi:10.1093/her/1.3.153

Presidency of the Republic of Türkiye Digital Transformation Office. (2020). *Information and Communication Security Guide.* https://cbddo.gov.tr/SharedFolderServer/Genel/File/BG_REHBER.pdf

Presuel, R., & Sierra, J. (2019). Algorithms and the News: Social Media Platforms as News Publishers and Distributors. *Revista De Comunicación*, *18*(2), 261–285. doi:10.26441/RC18.2-2019-A13

Prime, H., Wade, M., & Browne, D. T. (2020). Risk and resilience in family well-being during the COVID-19 pandemic. *The American Psychologist*, *75*(5), 631–643. doi:10.1037/amp0000660 PMID:32437181

Puig, N. (2011). *Emocions i publicitat. El lligam emocional entre l'emissor i el receptor de la publicitat*. Tesi doctoral. Accessed 20 March 2023 at: https://www.tesisenred.net/handle/10803/31846

Pulido, C. M., Villarejo-Carballido, B., Redondo-Sama, G., & Gómez, A. (2020). COVID-19 infodemic: More retweets for science-based information on coronavirus than for false information. *International Sociology*, *35*(4), 377–392. doi:10.1177/0268580920914755

Punch, K. F. (2005). *Introduction to Social Research–Quantitative & Qualitative Approaches*. Sage.

Rabow, M., & Mcphee, S. J. (1999). Beyond breaking bad news: How to help patients who suffer. *The Western Journal of Medicine*, *171*(4), 260–263. https://bit.ly/3yo06qB PMID:10578682

Rachel, E. (2016). *Experts say kids are growing up with more anxiety and less selfesteem*. Retrieved from https://childmind.org/article/howusing-social-media-affects-teenagers

Radhakrishn, A. (2020). COVID-19 restricted internet impacts on health in Kashmir. *Health and Human Rights Journal*.

Rad, R. E., Mohseni, S., Kamalzadeh Takhti, H., Hassani Azad, M., Shahabi, N., Aghamolaei, T., & Norozian, F. (2021). Application of the protection motivation theory for predicting COVID-19 preventive behaviors in Hormozgan, Iran: A cross-sectional study. *BMC Public Health*, *21*(1), 1–11. PMID:33388037

Rahmi, R., Joho, H., & Shirai, T. (2019). An analysis of natural disaster-related information-seeking behavior using temporal stages. *Journal of the Association for Information Science and Technology*, *70*(7), 715–728. doi:10.1002/asi.24155

Rajendran, J. A., Baharin, H., & Kamal, F. M. (2019, November). I understand Instant Messaging in the Workplace. In *International Visual Informatics Conference* (pp. 640-652). Springer.

Rajhans, K. (2012). Effective organizational communication: A key to employee motivation and performance. *Interscience Management Review*, *2*(2), 81–85.

Ramadanty, S., & Martinus, H. (2016). Organizational communication: Communication and motivation in the workplace. *Humaniora*, *7*(1), 77–86. doi:10.21512/humaniora.v7i1.3490

Rando-Cueto, D., de las Heras-Pedrosa, C., & Paniagua-Rojano, F. J. (2023). Health communication strategies via TikTok for the prevention of eating disorders. *Systems*, *11*(6), 274. doi:10.3390ystems11060274

Rastegar-Mojarad, M., Ye, Z., Wall, D., Murali, N., & Lin, S. (2015). Collecting and Analyzing Patient Experiences of Health Care From Social Media. *JMIR Research Protocols*, *4*(3), 1–14. doi:10.2196/resprot.3433 PMID:26137885

Raubal, M. (2001). *Agent- Based Simulation of Human Wayfinding: a perceptual model for familiar buildings* [Unpublished Dissertation]. Viena University of Technology.

Reagan, J. (1996). The "repertoire"; of information sources. *Journal of Broadcasting & Electronic Media*, *40*(1), 112–121. doi:10.1080/08838159609364336

Rebello, C., Marchetti, M. A., Lemonica, L., & Moreira, G. A. (2017). The P-A-C-I-E-N-T-E Protocol: An instrument for breaking bad news adapted to the Brazilian medical Reality. *Revista da Associação Médica Brasileira*, *63*(1), 43–49. doi:10.1590/1806-9282.63.01.43 PMID:28225878

Republic of Türkiye Ministry of Transport and Infrastructure. (2022). *National Cyber Security Strategy and Action Plan*. Retrieved from: https://hgm.uab.gov.tr/uploads/pages/strateji-eylem-planlari/ulusal-siber-guvenlik-stratejisi-ve-eylem-plani-2020-2023.pdf

Reynolds, B., & Seeger, M. (2005). Crisis and emergency risk communication as an integrative model. *Journal of Health Communication*, *10*(1), 43–55. doi:10.1080/10810730590904571 PMID:15764443

Richards, I. (2014). Differences over difference: Journalism beyond the metropolis. *Australian Journalism Review, 36*(1), 5–14. doi:10.1386/ajr.41.1.5_1

Riquelme, A., Martín, M., & Ortigosa, J. M. (2011). ¿Cómo dar malas noticias? Adaptación de La comunicación con el enfermo y el manejo de información. In *Manual de atención psicosocial.* Instituto Monsa de Ediciones. https://bit.ly/2QxBQRI

Rising-Kashmir. (2022). *J&K setting benchmark in imolementing PM's Digital Indian Compaign.* Rising Kashmir.

Rivadossi, S. (2023). Estetica del vuoto in Mori Mariko — Un uso strategico del discorso sullo Zen. In L'estetica del vuoto — Suoni, silenzi, vuoti, pieni, presenze, assenze. Edizioni Ca' Foscari. doi:10.30687/978-88-6969-701-2/010

Rivas, C. (2020). *La Inversión Publicitaria cae un -22,2% en los nueve primeros meses de 2020. Infoadex.* Available at: https://www.infoadex.es/home/inversion-publicitaria-cae-22-septiembre-2020/

Rodríguez-Salvador, J. J. (2010). *Comunicación clínica: cómo dar malas noticias.* https://bit.ly/3f8xWrS

Rodríguez-Sanz, J., Kurtz, C., & Álvarez-Ude, F. (2011). Aspectos clave de la comunicación no verbal en la consulta. *FMC: Formación Médica Continua-da en Atención Primaria, 18*(7), 401-409. https://bit.ly/2SZ8b4M

Rogers, E. M. (1995). *Diffusion of Innovations (4th ed.).* The Free Press.

Rogers, R. W. (1985). Attitude change and information integration in fear appeals. *Psychological Reports, 56*(1), 179–182. doi:10.2466/pr0.1985.56.1.179

Romero, A. (2022). La capacitat de comunicar males notícies. Com ensenyen les universitats d'Andalusia a comunicar males notícies als estudiants de Medicina. Unpublished Final Degree Project of Advertising and Public Relations, University of Girona.

Ross, G. (Director). (2012, March 23). *The Hunger Games* [Action, Adventure, Sci-Fi]. Lionsgate, Color Force.

Rossi, R., Socci, V., Talevi, D., Mensi, S., Niolu, C., Pacitti, F., Di Marco, A., Rossi, A., Siracusano, A., & Di Lorenzo, G. (2020). COVID-19 Pandemic and Lockdown Measures Impact on Mental Health Among the General Population in Italy. *Frontiers in Psychiatry, 11*, 790. doi:10.3389/fpsyt.2020.00790 PMID:32848952

Roth, R., Ajithkumar, P., Natarajan, G., Achuthan, K., Moon, P., Zinzow, H., & Madathil, K. C. (2021). A study of adolescents and young adults' TikTok challenge participation in South India. *Human Factors in Healthcare, 1*, 100005. doi:10.1016/j.hfh.2022.100005

Rotman, D. (2011) From Slacktivism To Activism: Participatory Culture In The Age Of Social Media. In *ACM CHI 2011: Conference on Human Factors In Computing Systems.* ACM Press. 10.1145/1979742.1979543

Rufai, S. R., & Bunce, C. (2020). World leaders' usage of Twitter in response to the COVID-19 pandemic: A content analysis. *Journal of Public Health (Oxford, England), 42*(3), 510–516. doi:10.1093/pubmed/fdaa049 PMID:32309854

Ruiz-Cabrera, S., & Gürkan, H. (2023). Effects of Turkish cultural products on its foreign policy toward Africa: Turkish TV series as an example of soft power in Kenya, Mozambique, and Senegal. *El Profesional de la Información, 32*(2), 1–16. doi:10.3145/epi.2023.mar.26

Ryan, B. (2018). A model to explain information seeking behaviour by individuals in the response phase of a disaster. *Library & Information Science Research, 40*(2), 73–85. doi:10.1016/j.lisr.2018.05.001

Sabillon, R., Cavaller, V., & Cano, J. (2016). National Cyber Security Strategies: Global Trends in Cyberspace. *International Journal of Computer Science and Software Engineering, 5*(5), 67-81. www.IJCSSE.org

Sachs. (2009). *Improving access, service delivery and efficiency of public health system in rural India.* Author.

Sagun, A., Bouchlaghem, D., & Anumba, C. J. (2009). A scenario-based study on information flow and collaboration patterns in disaster management. *Disasters, 33*(2), 214–238. doi:10.1111/j.1467-7717.2008.01071.x PMID:18699856

Şahin, G. (2015). *Soğuk Savaş Sonrası Değişen Güvenlik Anlayışı Bağlamında Nato* [Phd Thesis]. Trakya Üniversitesi Sosyal Bilimler Enstitüsü, Edirne.

Sahu, P. (2020). Closure of universities due to coronavirus disease 2019 (COVID-19): Impact on education and mental health of students and academic staff. *Cureus, 2019*(4), 4–9. doi:10.7759/cureus.7541 PMID:32377489

Salazar, E. (2017). Hashtags 2.0 - An Annotated History of the Hashtag and a Window to its Future. *Icono 14, 15*(2), 16-54. 10.7195/ri14

Sampogna, G., Bakolis, I., Evans-Lacko, S., Robinson, E., Thornicroft, G., & Henderson, C. (2017). The impact of social marketing campaigns on reducing mental health stigma: Results from the 2009–2014 Time to Change programme. *European Psychiatry, 40*, 116–122. doi:10.1016/j.eurpsy.2016.08.008 PMID:27997875

Schiavo, R. (2013). *Health communication: From theory to practice*. John Wiley & Sons.

Schmid, H. (2021). Adversarial Interfaces. In Art Museums and Digital Cultures: Rethinking Change. Universidade NOVA de Lisboa.

Scholz, T. (2010). Infrastructure: Its Transformations and Effect on Digital Activism. In Digital Activism Decoded: The New Mechanics of Change. IDebate Press.

Schub, T., Swan-Potras, L., & Rabin, K. (2022). Big Shots: A Social Media Campaign to Honor Local Heroes who Promote Covid-19 Vaccine Literacy and Increase Vaccine Acceptance. *The American Behavioral Scientist, 0*(0), 1–8. doi:10.1177/00027642221138272

Schwab, K., & Malleret, T. (2020). *The Great Reset*. Forum Publishing.

Scott. (2020). India's Auxiliary Nurse-Midwife, Anganwadi Workers, and Accredited Social Health Acttivist Programs. In H. B. Perry (Ed.), Health for people: National Community Health Worker Programs from Afghanistan to Zimbabwe. Academic Press.

Scroll. (2020). *Lockdown after lockdown: How access to non Covid healthcare has been chocked off in Kashmir.* Scroll.

Segarra, T. (2020). *Ahora mismo hay que hacer lo más posible y decir lo menos possible.* Accessed 23 March: https://www.modaes.com/back-stage/toni-segarra-ahora-mismo-hay-que-hacer-lo-mas-posible-y-decir-lo-menos-posible

Sekeris, P. G. (2017). Counter-Elite. In F. M. Moghaddam (Ed.), *The SAGE Encyclopedia of Political Behavior* (Vol. 1–2, pp. 152–153). SAGE Publications. doi:10.4135/9781483391144

Sepulveda, R., & Espanha, R. (2022). Online social media and public health institutions: An analysis of the Portuguese National Health Service on Instagram. *Cadernos de Saúde Societal, 3*, 63–73.

Ser, C. (2020). *El Confinamiento Lleva a Récord Histórico el Consumo de Televisión: 5 Horas al Día por Persona.* Available at: https://bit.ly/3VfU6dZ

Shafqat, N., & Masood, A. (2016). Comparative Analysis of Various National Cyber Security Strategies. *International Journal of Computer Science and Information Security, 14*(1), 129–136.

Shannon, C. E., & Weaver, W. (1949). *The Mathematical Theory of Communication.* University of Illinois Press.

Sharf, S. (2013, Novembre 7). The Secret Behind Twitter's IPO: How The Hashtag Became A Worldwide Phenomenon. *Forbes*. Retrieved from: https://www.forbes.com/sites/samanthasharf/2013/11/07/the-secret-behind-twitters-ipo-how-the-hashtag-became-a-worldwide-phenomenon/?sh=7a5813a4fd4d

Sharlet, J. (2011, November 10). Inside Occupy Wall Street – Rolling Stone. *Rolling Stone*. https://www.rollingstone.com/politics/politics-news/inside-occupy-wall-street-236993/

Sharma, A. (2021). Positive impacts of COVID-19 pandemic on various aspects. *Psychology (Savannah, Ga.)*, *58*(2), 430–436. doi:10.17762/pae.v58i2.1868

Shearer, E. (2020). *Local news is playing an important role for Americans during COVİD-19 outbreak*. https://www.pewresearch.org/fact-tank/2020/07/02/local-news-is-playing-an-important-role-for-americans-during-Covid-19-outbreak/

Sheldon, P., Rauschnabel, P. A., Antony, M. G., & Car, S. (2017). A cross-cultural comparison of Croatian and American social network sites: Exploring cultural differences in motives for Instagram use. *Computers in Human Behavior*, *75*, 643–651. doi:10.1016/j.chb.2017.06.009

Shengjie, J. (2021). TikTok analysis. *Journal of Frontiers of Society. Science and Technology*, *1*(1), 8–12.

Shen, Z., Zhong, Z., Xie, J., Zhang, Q., & Li, S. (2022). The effects of information-seeking behaviors on risk perception during the COVID-19 pandemic: A cross-sectional correlational survey. *Psychology Research and Behavior Management*, *15*, 1707–1719. doi:10.2147/PRBM.S368537 PMID:35844830

Shirky, C. (2011). The political power of social media: Technology, the public sphere, and political change. *Foreign Affairs*, *90*(1), 28–41.

Shoib & Arafat. (2020). *Potentialities and challanges of digital health in psychiatry in Kashmir*. Sage Publications.

Silva, M., Machete, A., Gonçalves, A., Teixeira, A., Alves, B., & Silva, C. (2022). Estratégias Comunicacionais da Direção-Geral da Saúde – estudo das Publicações no Twitter Sobre a COVID-19. *Revista Comunicando*, *11*(1), 2–19.

Silverman, C. (2018). *Doğrulama El Kitabı: Kriz Anlarında Dijital Verilerin Doğrulanması İçin Rehber*. European Journalism Centre. http://verificationhandbook.com/book_tr/

Simón, S. J. (2021). *Disseny d'un model d'anàlisi per a la qualitat percebuda: productes, destinacions i serveis*. Doctoral Thesis. Accessed 20 March 2023 at: https://www.tdx.cat/handle/10803/673754#page=1

Singer, J. B. (2010). Quality control: Perceived effects of user-generated content on newsroom norms, values, and routines. *Journalism Practice*, *4*(2), 127–142. doi:10.1080/17512780903391979

Skalacka, K., & Pajestka, G. (2021). Digital or In-Person: The relationship between mode of ınterpersonal communication during the COVID-19 pandemic and mental health in older adults from 27 countries. *Journal of Family Nursing*, *27*(4), 275–284. doi:10.1177/10748407211031980 PMID:34286604

Skarpa, P. E., & Garoufallou, E. (2021). Information seeking behavior and COVID-19 pandemic: A snapshot of young, middle aged and senior individuals in Greece. *International Journal of Medical Informatics*, *150*, 104465. doi:10.1016/j.ijmedinf.2021.104465 PMID:33887589

SLFC. (2020). *Using 2G to fight a Pandemic in a digital world*. Software Freedom Law Center India.

Smailhodzic, E., Hooijsma, W., Boonstra, A., & Langley, D. J. (2016). Social media use in healthcare: A systematic review of effects on patients and on their relationship with healthcare professionals. *BMC Health Services Research*, *16*(1), 1–14. doi:10.118612913-016-1691-0 PMID:27562728

Smith, R. A., Ferrara, M., & Witte, K. (2007). Social sides of health risks: Stigma and collective efficacy. *Health Communication, 21*(1), 55–64. doi:10.1080/10410230701283389 PMID:17461752

Sobczak, K. (2022). The "CONNECT" Protocol: Delivering bad news by phone or video call. *International Journal of General Medicine, 15*, 3567–3572. doi:10.2147/IJGM.S358723 PMID:35392027

Solana López, I., Juez Martel, I., Martínez Moreno, E., de Zea Luque, C., Martín Fernández de Soignie, A. M., Sánchez Baños, N., & Guerra Martínez, J. A. (2022). Humanización en la comunicación de malas noticias en el paciente oncológico y paliativo. *Oncología (Ecuador), 32*(3), 266–272. Advance online publication. doi:10.33821/639

Soliman, D. A., & Salem, M. S. (2014). Investigating intention to use mobile instant messenger: The influence of sociability, self-expressiveness, and enjoyment. *The Journal of American Academy of Business, Cambridge, 19*(2), 286–293.

Solomon, D. H., Knobloch, L. K., Theiss, J. A., & McLaren, R. M. (2016). Relational turbulence theory: Explaining variation and subjective experiences and communication within romantic relationships. *Human Communication Research, 42*(4), 507–532. doi:10.1111/hcre.12091

Sommerfeldt, E. J. (2015). Disasters and information source repertoires: Information seeking and information sufficiency in postearthquake Haiti. *Journal of Applied Communication Research, 43*(1), 1–22. doi:10.1080/00909882.2014.982682

Sørensen, K., Levin-Zamir, D., Duong, T. V., Okan, O., Brasil, V. V., & Nutbeam, D. (2021). Building health literacy system capacity: A framework for health literate systems. *Health Promotion International, 36*(S1), 13–23. doi:10.1093/heapro/daab153 PMID:34897445

Soriano, M. R. T. (2013). Internet as a Driver of Political Change: Cyber-pessimists and Cyber-optimists. *Revista del Instituto Español de Estudios Estratégicos, 1*, 332–352.

Soroya, S. H., Farooq, A., Mahmood, K., Isoaho, J., & Zara, S. (2021). From information seeking to information avoidance: Understanding the health information behavior during a global health crisis. *Information Processing &Amp. Management, 58*(2), 102440. PMID:33281273

Söyler, M., & Tekindal, M. A. (2021). Covid-19 Pandemisi, Siyasi Rejimler ve Liberal Demokrasi. *OPUS International Journal of Society Researches*, 3832-3868. doi:10.26466/opus.885216

Spaho, K. (2012). Organizational communication process. *Ekonomski Vjesnik, 25*, 318–318.

Speidal, K. (2021). *What is an exhibition? Cultures, concepts, cognition & curation.* Seminar at Institute of Fine Arts and Media Art. https://base.uni-ak.ac.at/courses/2021W/S04063/

Spialek, M. L., & Houston, J. B. (2018). The development and initial validation of the Citizen Disaster Communication Assessment. *Communication Research, 45*(6), 934–955. doi:10.1177/0093650217697521

Spiezia, V., & Vivarelli, M. (2002). Innovation and Employment: A Critical Survey. In N. Greenan, Y. L'Horty, & J. Mairesse (Eds.), *Productivity, Inequality, and the Digital Economy* (pp. 101–125). The MIT Press. doi:10.7551/mitpress/5609.003.0009

Srnicek, N. (2017). *Platform Capitalism.* Polity Press.

Stafford, L. (2020). Communal strength, exchange orientation, equity, and relational maintenance. *Journal of Social and Personal Relationships, 37*(8–9), 2345–2365. doi:10.1177/0265407520923741

Steinberg, A., Wukich, C., & Wu, H.-C. (2016). Central social media actors in disaster information networks. *International Journal of Mass Emergencies and Disasters, 34*(1), 47–74. doi:10.1177/028072701603400103

Stephens, E. (2018). #Creator The man behind the hashtag. *Brunswick Review, 15*, 44-46. Available at: https://www.brunswickgroup.com/media/4309/br15_44-46_hashtag_v10_cw.pdf

Stevens, M. (2016). Touched from a Distance: The Practice of Affective Browsing. In Museums in a Digital Culture: How Art and heritage Become Meaningful. Amsterdam University Press.

Storsul, T., & Dagny, S. (2007). *Ambivalence Towards Convergence: Digitalization and Media Change*. Nordicom, University of Gothenburg.

Strijbis, O., Teney, C., & Helbling, M. (2019). Why Are Elites More Cosmopolitan than Masses? In M. Zürn, O. Strijbis, P. de Wilde, R. Koopmans, & W. Merkel (Eds.), The Struggle Over Borders: Cosmopolitanism and Communitarianism (pp. 37–64). Cambridge University Press. doi:10.1017/9781108652698.002

Suarez-Lledo, V., & Alvarez-Galvez, J. (2021). Prevalence of Health Misinformation on Social Media: Systematic Review. *Journal of Medical Internet Research, 23*(1), 1–17. doi:10.2196/17187 PMID:33470931

Sultana, T., Dhillon, G., & Oliveira, T. (2023). The effect of fear and situational motivation on online information avoidance: The case of COVID-19. *International Journal of Information Management, 69*, 102596. doi:10.1016/j.ijinfomgt.2022.102596 PMID:36415624

Sun, S., Liu, Z., Zhai, Y., & Wang, F. (2022). COVID-19 vaccines on TikTok: A big-data analysis of entangled discourses. *International Journal of Environmental Research and Public Health, 19*(20), 13287. doi:10.3390/ijerph192013287 PMID:36293868

Sun, Y., Hu, Q., Grossman, S., Basnyat, I., & Wang, P. (2021). Comparison of COVID-19 information seeking, trust of information sources, and protective behaviors in China and the US. *Journal of Health Communication, 26*(9), 657–666. doi:10.1080/10810730.2021.1987590 PMID:34702136

Sutton, J., Renshaw, S. L., & Butts, C. T. (2020). The First 60 Days: American Public Health Agencies' Social Media Strategies in the Emerging COVID-19 Pandemic. *Health Security, 18*(6), 454–460. doi:10.1089/hs.2020.0105 PMID:33047982

Sylaiou, S., Killintzis, V., Paliokas, I., Mania, K., & Patias, P. (2014). Usability Evaluation of Virtual Museums' Interfaces Visualization Technologies. In VAMR 2014, Part II, LNCS 8526 (pp. 124–133). Springer International Publishing.

Szostek, J. (2018). News media repertoires and strategic narrative reception: A paradox of dis/belief in authoritarian Russia. *New Media & Society, 20*(1), 68–87. doi:10.1177/1461444816656638

Szyld, D., F Arriaga, A., & León-Castelao, E. (2021). El debriefing clínico, retos y oportunidades en el ámbito asistencial; aprendizaje en la reflexión colectiva para mejorar los sistemas sanitarios y la colaboración interprofesional. *Simulación Clínica, 3*(2), 69–73. doi:10.35366/101430

Tabachnick, B. G., & Fidell, L. S. (1996). *Using multivariate statistics*. Harper Collins.

Taleb, N. N. (2007). *1960-The Black Swan: The Impact of the Highly Improbable*. Random House Trade Paperbacks.

Tam, M. S. (2022). Türk TikTokerların içerik paylaşım pratikleri üzerine nicel bir araştırma. *Trt Akademi, 7*(14), 182–211.

Tang, W., Ren, J., & Zhang, Y. (2018). Enabling trusted and privacy-preserving healthcare services in social media health networks. *IEEE Transactions on Multimedia, 21*(3), 579–590. doi:10.1109/TMM.2018.2889934

Tarhan, N. (2020). *Pandemi döneminde iletişimin önemi.* Retrieved from https://uskudar.edu.tr/tr/icerik/5809/prof-dr-nevzat-tarhan-pandemi-doneminde-iletisimin-onemi-ortaya-cikti

Tarradellas, C. (2020). *Sigamos haciendo las cosas buenas que hemos aprendido - Espetec Casa Tarradellas.* https://www.youtube.com/watch?v=9CGAObU1lZY

Taş, F. (2020). Covid-19 Pandemi Sürecinde Yetişkinler Arasında Yüz Maskesi Kullanma Pratiği ve Tekniği Üzerine Değerlendirme ve Öneriler. *Halk Sağlığı Hemşireliği Dergisi*, *2*(2), 52–56.

Taylor, E. (2007). How best to communicate bad news over the telephone. *End of Life Care, 1*(1), 30-37. https://tinyurl.com/tmc4fb55

TDK. (2023). https://sozluk.gov.tr/

Teoh, C. S., & Mahmood, A.K. (2017). National Cyber Security Strategies for Digital Economy. *International Conference on Research and Innovation in Information Systems (ICRIIS)*. 10.1109/ICRIIS.2017.8002519

Terkan, R. (2022). Pandemi Sürecinin İletişime Etkileri: İlişkilere Yansıması. *Scientific Journal of Innovation and Social Sciences Research*, *2*(1), 45–56.

Tesich, S. (2021). Yalanlar Rejimi. *Cogito*, *104*, 23–28.

Thackeray, R., Neiger, B. L., Burton, S. H., & Thackeray, C. R. (2013). Analysis of the purpose of state health departments' tweets: Information sharing, engagement, and action. *Journal of Medical Internet Research*, *15*(11), 1–10. doi:10.2196/jmir.3002 PMID:24217361

The-Print. (2020). *Kashmir Valley records its first case of Coronavirus in Srinagar*. The Print.

Thomson, R., Ito, N., Suda, H., Lin, F., Liu, Y., Hayasaka, R., . . . Wang, Z. (2012). Trusting tweets: The Fukushima disaster and information source credibility on Twitter. *Iscram. Proceedings of the 9th International ISCRAM Conference*.

Thorson, K., & Wells, C. (2016). Curated flows: A framework for mapping media exposure in the digital age. *Communication Theory*, *26*(3), 309–328. doi:10.1111/comt.12087

Thurston, I. (2018). *Everything is Permitted, Restrictions Still Apply: A Psychoanalytic Perspective on Social Dislocation, Narcissism, and Post Truth*. Routledge. doi:10.4324/9780429432101

Toktay, Y. (2019). *Sosyal Medyada Dezenformasyon, Manipülasyon ve Propaganda Etkisi: Zeytin Dalı Harekatı Örneği, Yayımlanmamış Yüksek Lisans Tezi*. Marmara Üniversitesi Sosyal Bilimler Enstitüsü.

Tombleson, B., & Wolf, K. (2017). Rethinking the circuit of culture: How participatory culture has transformed cross-cultural communication. *Public Relations Review, 43*(1), 14-25. doi:10.1016/j.pubrev.2016.10.017

Topor, S. (2023). Values for the Cyber Security Strategy for a National Critical Infrastructure. *Romanian Cyber Security Journal, 5*(1), 97-106. doi:10.54851/v5i1y202309

Törnberg, P. (2018). Echo chambers and viral misinformation: Modeling fake news as complex contagion. *PLoS One*, *13*(9), 1–21. doi:10.1371/journal.pone.0203958 PMID:30235239

Treat, J. W. (1995). *Writing Ground Zero: Japanese Literature and the Atomic Bomb*. The University of Chicago Press.

Tsao, S. F., Chen, H., Tisseverasinghe, T., Yang, Y., Li, L., & Butt, Z. A. (2021). What social media told us in the time of COVID-19: A scoping review. *The Lancet. Digital Health*, *3*(3), 175–194. doi:10.1016/S2589-7500(20)30315-0 PMID:33518503

Tufekci, Z. (2017). *Twitter and tear gas: The power and fragility of networked protest*. Yale University Press.

Túñez-López, M., Vaz-Álvarez, M., & Fieiras-Ceide, C. (2020). Covid-19 and public service media: Impact of the pandemic on public television in Europe. *Professional de la Infarmacion.*, *29*(5), 1–16.

Turkle, S. (1995). *Life on the screen: Identity in the age of the Internet*. Simon & Schuster.

Uçkan, Ö. (2012). "Dijital Aktivizm" mi, "Aktivizm" mi? *Yeşil Gazete*. https://yesilgazete.org/blog/2012/06/01/dijital-aktivizm-mi-aktivizm-mi-ozgur-uckan/

Uğurhan, Y. Z. C., & Yaşar, İ. H. (2021). TikTok'taki reklam ve sponsorlu içeriklerin satın alma niyeti üzerindeki rolü: Sosyo-demografik değişkenler özelinde bir inceleme. *Abant Sosyal Bilimler Dergisi*, *21*(2), 243–269.

Usher, K., Bhullar, N., Durkin, J., Gyamfi, N., & Jackson, D. (2020). Family violence and COVID-19: Increased vulnerability and reduced options for support. *International Journal of Mental Health Nursing*, *29*(4), 549–552. doi:10.1111/inm.12735 PMID:32314526

Uzunoğlu, S., & Uyar, V. (2021). Türkiye'de Doğru Bilgiyi Aramak: Çöldeki Vahanın Peşinde. *Newslab Turkey*. https://www.newslabturkey.org/ wp-content/uploads/2021/04/rh-2.pdf

Valentine, D. (2002). Distance learning: Promise, problems, and possibilities. *Online Journal of Distance Learning Administration*, *5*(3).

Van Asselt, M. B. A., Langendonck, R., Van Asten, F., Van der Giessen, A., Janssen, P. H. M., Heuberger, P. S. C., & Geuskens, I. (2001). *Uncertainty&RIVM's Environmental Outlooks*. RIVM Report.

Van Dijk, J. (2016). *Ağ Toplumu* (Ö. Sakin, Trans.). Epsilon Yayıncılık.

Van Kampen, K., Laski, J., Herman, G., & Chan, T. M. (2022). Investigating COVID-19 vaccine communication and misinformation on TikTok: Cross-sectional study. *JMIR Infodemiology*, *2*(2), 1–9. doi:10.2196/38316 PMID:36338548

van Zoonen, L. (2012). I-Pistemology: Changing truth claims in popular and political culture. *European Journal of Communication*, *27*(1), 56–67. doi:10.1177/0267323112438808

Varguillas, C., & Ribot de Flores, S. (2007). Implicaciones conceptuales y metodológicas en la aplicación de la entrevista en profundidad. *Laurus: revista de educación*, *13*(23), 249-262. https://bit.ly/3oQt7Hj

Venter, K. (2003). Coping with isolation: The role of culture in adult distance learners' use of surrogates. *Open Learning*, *18*(3), 271–287. doi:10.1080/0268051032000131035

Ventola C. L. (2014). Social media and health care professionals: benefits, risks, and best practices. *P & T: A Peer-Reviewed Journal for Formulary Management, 39*(7), 491–520.

Vergo, P. (1994). The Rhetoric of Display. In R. Miles & L. Zavala (Eds.), *Towards the museum of the future: new European perspectives*. Routledge.

Vicente, L. (2020). *La comunicación de males notícies en l'àmbit de la salut. Investigació sobre la comunicación de les males notícies en medicina, la seva evolució i l'adaptació a les necessitats especials en situación de COVID-19*. https://bit.ly/3oyL1hs

Vilar, E., & Rebelo, F. (2008). Virtual reality in wayfinding studies. In *Proceedings of the 2008 AHFE International Conference (2nd International Conference on Applied Human Factors and Ergonomics jointly with 12th International Conference on Human Aspects of Advanced Manufacturing - HAAMAHA)*. USA Publishing.

Villa, B. (2007). Recomendaciones sobre cómo comunicar malas noticias. *Nure investigación*, (31). https://bit.ly/33Z6erh

Villagran, M., Goldsmith, B., Witenberg-Liles, E., & Baldwin, P. (2010). Creating COMFORT: A Communication-based model for Breaking Bad News. Communication Education. Issue 3. *Communication Education*, *59*(3), 220–234. doi:10.1080/03634521003624031

Vlahović, S., Suznjevic, M., & Kapov, L. S. (2018). Subjective Assessment of Different Locomotion Techniques in Virtual Reality Environments. *2018 Tenth International Conference on Quality of Multimedia Experience (QoMEX)*, 1-3. 10.1109/QoMEX.2018.8463433

Wachowski, L., & Wachowski, L. (Directors). (1999, June 23). *The Matrix*. Warner Bros., Village Roadshow Pictures, Groucho Film Partnership.

Wade, M., & Shan, J. (2020). New development: COVİD-19 as an accelerator of digital transformation in public service delivery. *MIS Quarterly Executive*, *19*(3), 213–220. doi:10.17705/2msqe.00034

Wahl, S., & Grimm, M. (2016). How to Find an Alternative: A Typology of Cancer Patients' Information Behavior with Regard to Complementary and Alternative Medicine. *International Journal of Communication and Health*, 10.

Wang, C. C., Yang, Y. Y. H., & Tseng, C. Y. (2016, June). Always on Duty? The Positive and Negative Effects of Using Mobile Social Networking Tools for Work. *PACIS*, 270.

Wang, C., Cheng, Z., Yue, X.-G., & McAleer, M. (2020). Risk Management of COVID-19 by universities in China. *Journal of Risk and Financial Management*, *13*(2), 36. doi:10.3390/jrfm13020036

Wang, P., Ahorsu, D. K., Lin, C., Chen, I., Yen, C., Kuo, Y., Griffiths, M. D., & Pakpour, A. H. (2021). Motivation to have covid-19 vaccination explained using an extended protection motivation theory among university students in china: The role of information sources. *Vaccines*, *9*(4), 380. doi:10.3390/vaccines9040380 PMID:33924604

Wang, W., & Liu, Y. (2015). Communication message cues and opinions about people with depression: An investigation of discussion on Weibo. *Asian Journal of Communication*, *25*(1), 33–47. doi:10.1080/01292986.2014.989238

Wang, Y., Hao, H., & Platt, L. S. (2021). Examining risk and crisis communications of government agencies and stakeholders during early-stages of COVID-19 on Twitter. *Computers in Human Behavior*, *114*(106568), 1–13. doi:10.1016/j.chb.2020.106568 PMID:32982038

Ward, J. W., & Hansen, K. A. (1993). *Search strategies in mass communication*. Longman Publishing Group.

We Are Social & Meltwater. (2023). *Digital 2023 global overview report*. https://datareportal.com/reports/digital-2023-global-overview-report

We are Social and Houtsuite. (2023). *The Changing World of Digital in 2023*. https://wearesocial.com/uk/blog/2023/01/the-changing-world-of-digital-in-2023/

Weaver, J. L., & Swank, J. M. (2021). Parents' lived experiences with the COVID-19 pandemic. *The Family Journal (Alexandria, Va.)*, *29*(2), 136–142. doi:10.1177/1066480720969194

Webb, G. (2014). *Dark alliance: The CIA, the Contras, and the crack cocaine explosion*. Seven Stories Press.

Weinstein, A. (2011, October 7). "We Are the 99 Percent" Creators Revealed. *Mother Jones*. https://www.motherjones.com/politics/2011/10/we-are-the-99-percent-creators/

Westcott, R., Ronan, K., Bambrick, H., & Taylor, M. (2017). Expanding protection motivation theory: Investigating an application to animal owners and emergency responders in bushfire emergencies. *BMC Psychology*, *5*(1), 1–14. doi:10.118640359-017-0182-3 PMID:28446229

West, R., Raw, M., McNeill, A., Stead, L., Aveyard, P., Bitton, J., Stapleton, J., McRobbie, H., Pokhrel, S., Lester-George, A., & Borland, R. (2015). Health-care interventions to promote and assist tobacco cessation: A review of efficacy, effectiveness and affordability for use in national guideline development. *Addiction (Abingdon, England)*, *110*(9), 1388–1403. doi:10.1111/add.12998 PMID:26031929

Whatsapp. (2022). *Privacy Policy.* Retrieved from: https://www.whatsapp.com/legal/privacy-policy

White, M. C. (2020, December 30). Wall Street minted 56 new billionaires since the pandemic began—But many families are left behind. *NBC News.* https://www.nbcnews.com/business/business-news/wall-street-s-best-year-ever-why-pandemic-has-been-n1252512

WHO. (2020, March). *WHO Director-General's opening remarks at the media briefing on COVID-19* [Media Brief]. Access at https://www.who.int/director-general/speeches/detail/who-director-general-s-opening-remarks-at-the-media-briefing-on-covid-19---11-march-2020

WHO. (2021). *Global Strategy on Digital Health 2020-2025. World Health Organization.*

WHO. (n.d.). *Infodemic*. WHO (World Healty Organizastion): https://www.who.int/health-topics/infodemic#tab=tab_1

Widodo, J., Qur'ani, H. B., & Putra, C. R. W. (2023). Abbreviations in the comment column of the Tribunnews account on TikTok. *Journal of Wood Science*, *2*(7), 946–956.

Williams, A. M. (2013). Who shot JFK? Here are 6 conspiracy theories. *USA Today*. https://www.usatoday.com/story/news/nation-now/2013/11/21/john-kennedy-conspiracy-theories-assasination/3661891/

Williams, E. J., & Joinson, A. N. (2020). Developing a measure of information seeking about phishing. *Journal of Cybersecurity*, *6*(1), tyaa001. doi:10.1093/cybsec/tyaa001

Wilson, C. (2012). Alfabetización mediática e informacional: Proyecciones didácticas. *Comunicar. Revista Científica de Educomunicación*, *20*(39), 15–24. doi:10.3916/C39-2012-02-01

Witt, M. M., & Jankowska, K. A. (2018). Breaking bad news in genetic counseling—Problems and communication tools. *Journal of Applied Genetics*, *59*(4), 449–452. doi:10.100713353-018-0469-y PMID:30255485

Wodtke, C., & Govella, A. (2009). *Information Architecture: Blueprints for the Web* (2nd ed.). New Riders.

Wolcott, H. F. (1994). Transforming Qualitative Data: Description, Analysis, and Interpretation. *Sage (Atlanta, Ga.).*

Wolfers, L. N., & Schneider, F. M. (2020). Using media for coping: A scoping review. *Communication Research*, 1–25. doi:10.1177/0093650220939778

World Economic Forum (Director). (2020a, March 6). *The Great Reset | Launch session 3 June 2020* [YouTube]. https://www.youtube.com/watch?v=pfVdMWzKwjc

World Economic Forum (Director). (2020b, July 14). *COVID-19: The Great Reset* [YouTube]. https://www.youtube.com/watch?v=VHRkkeecg7c&t=2133s

World Economic Forum. (2020). *This is how COVID-19 is affecting the advertising industry.* Available at: https://www.weforum.org/agenda/2020/06/coronavirus-advertising-marketing-covid19-pandemic-business/

World Federation of Advertisers. (2020). *Eighty Percent of Multinationals Deferring Campaigns But the Same Number Are Creating New Content in Response to the COVID-19 Crisis.* World Federation of Advertisers - WFA. Available at: https://wfanet.org/knowledge/item/2020/04/07/Eighty-percent-of-multinationals-deferring-campaigns-but-the-same-number-are-creating-new-content-in-response-to-the-Covid19-crisis

World Health Organization (WHO). (2020). *Novel Coronavirus (2019-nCoV) situation report–13.* https://www.who.int/docs/defaultsource/coronaviruse/situationreports/ 20200202-sitrep-13-ncov-v3.pdf

World Health Organization. (2017). *WHO strategic communications framework for effective communication.* https://www.who.int/docs/default-source/documents/communicating-for-health/communication-framework.pdf

World Health Organization. (2020). *Coronavirus disease (COVID-19) advice for the public.* https://www.who.int/emergencies/ diseases/novel-coronavirus-2019/advice-for-public

World Health Organization. (2022). *Coronavirus disease (COVID19) advice for the public.* Available at: https://www.who.int/emergencies/diseases/novel-coronavirus-2019/advice-for-public

Wukich, C. (2016). Government social media messages across disaster phases. *Journal of Contingencies and Crisis Management, 24*(4), 230–243. doi:10.1111/1468-5973.12119

Wu, T., He, Z., & Zhang, D. (2020). Impact of Communicating With Doctors Via Social Media on Consumers' E-Health Literacy and Healthy Behaviors in China. *The Journal of Health Care Organization. Inquiry, 57*, 1–7. doi:10.1177/0046958020971188 PMID:33238788

Xin, M., Luo, S., Wang, S., Zhao, J., Zhang, G., Li, L., Li, L., & Lau, J. T. (2022). The Roles of Information Valence, Media Literacy and Perceived Information Quality on the Association Between Frequent Social Media Exposure and COVID-19 Vaccination Intention. *American Journal of Health Promotion, 37*(2), 189–199. doi:10.1177/08901171221121292 PMID:35972385

Xue, H., & Taylor, L. (2022). When do people believe, check, and share health rumors on social media? Effects of evidence type, health literacy, and health knowledge. *Journal of Health Psychology, 28*(7), 607–619. doi:10.1177/13591053221125992 PMID:36168751

Yang, G. (2016). Narrative agency in hashtag activism: The case of #BlackLivesMatter. *Media and Communication, 4*(4), 13–17. doi:10.17645/mac.v4i4.692

Yao, H. (2020). The more exposure to media information about COVİD-19, the more distressed you will feel. *Brain, Behavior, and Immunity, 87*, 167–169. doi:10.1016/j.bbi.2020.05.031 PMID:32413557

Yates, C., & Partridge, H. (2015). Citizens and social media in times of natural disaster: Exploring information experience. *Information Research, 20*(1).

Yavetz, G., Aharony, N., & Sofer, Y. Y. (2022). Information needs and seeking behaviors of Israeli citizens during the COVID-19 outbreak. *Aslib Journal of Information Management.*

Yeboah, J., & Ewur, G. D. (2014). The impact of WhatsApp messenger usage on students' performance in Tertiary Institutions in Ghana. *Journal of Education and Practice, 5*(6), 157–164.

Yenal, A. Ç. (2009). *Uzaktan Eğitim.* Yayınlanmış Yüksek Lisans Tezi, Yeditepe Üniversitesi Sosyal Bilimler Enstitüsü.

Yeo, T. E. D., & Chu, T. H. (2017). Sharing "sex secrets" on Facebook: A content analysis of youth peer communication and advice exchange on social media about sexual health and intimate relations. *Journal of Health Communication, 22*(9), 753–762. doi:10.1080/10810730.2017.1347217 PMID:28796578

Yıldırım, O., & İpek, İ. (2020). Yeni Koronavirüs Salgını Dolayısıyla Gündeme Gelen Sosyal İzolasyon ve Gönüllü Karantina Döneminde İnternet ve Sosyal Medya Kullanımı. *İletişim Kuram ve Araştırma Dergisi, 52.*

Yoneyama, S. (2020). Rethinking Human-Nature Relationships in the Time of Coronavirus: Postmodern Animism in Films by Miyazaki Hayao & Shinkai Makoto. *The Asia-Pacific Journal, 18*(16). https://apjjf.org/2020/16/Yoneyama.html

York, D. (2020). How to build Rapport? *Harward Business Review.* Retrieved from https://hbr.org/2020/09/how-to-build-rapport-while-wearing-a-mask?autocomplete=true

Zaremohzzabieh, Z., Samah, A. A., Roslan, S., Shaffril, H. A. M., D'Silva, J. L., Kamarudin, S., & Ahrari, S. (2021). Household preparedness for future earthquake disaster risk using an extended theory of planned behavior. *International Journal of Disaster Risk Reduction, 65*, 102533. doi:10.1016/j.ijdrr.2021.102533

Zelizer, B. (2015). Terms of choice: Uncertainty, journalism, and crisis. *Journal of Communication, 65*(5), 888–908. doi:10.1111/jcom.12157

Zelizer, B. (2019). Why journalism is about more than digital technology. *Digital Journalism (Abingdon, England), 7*(3), 343–350. doi:10.1080/21670811.2019.1571932

Zempke, R., Raines, C., & Filipczak, B. (2013). Generations at Work: Managing the Clash of Boomers, Gen Xers, and Gen Yers in the Workplace (2nd ed.). Amacom.

Zhang, Q. (2021). Is It a "Window of Opportunity" to Develop a New Normal of Government-Society Cooperation in Emergency Management? *The China Nonprofit Review, 12*(2), 257–263. doi:10.1163/18765149-12341379

Zhang, W., Mei, J., Song, W., Evans, R., & Xiang, Y. (2021). Why do citizens engage with the TikTok accounts of public hospitals in China? *SAGE Open, 11*(4), 1–11. doi:10.1177/21582440211061568

Zhao, X., Ma, Z., Xu, S., & Austin, L. L. (2022). How information repertoire affects vaccine hesitancy: Processes of information verification and cognitive elaboration. *Health Communication*, 1–11. doi:10.1080/10410236.2022.2154017 PMID:36510367

Zhong, R. (2020). *The Coronavirus exposes education's digital divide*. https://www.nytimes.com/2020/03/17/technology/china-schools-coronavirus.html

Zhou, P., You, J., & Wu, W. (2021). Research on health communication strategies of short video on popular medical science. In *2021 3rd International Conference on Economic Management and Cultural Industry (ICEMCI 2021)* (pp. 1060-1063). Atlantis Press. 10.2991/assehr.k.211209.172

Zhou, Q., & Jung, H. (2019). Learning and sharing creative skills with short videos: A case study of user behavior in TikTok and Bilibili. In *Int. Assoc. Soc. Des. Res. Conf* (No. 10, pp. 25-50). Academic Press.

Zhou, J. (2022). *The digital divide, what it is and what is being done to close it*. Investopia.

Zhu, C., Xu, X., Zhang, W., Chen, J., & Evans, R. (2020). How health communication via TikTok makes a difference: A content analysis of TikTok accounts run by Chinese provincial health committees. *International Journal of Environmental Research and Public Health, 17*(1), 192. doi:10.3390/ijerph17010192 PMID:31892122

Žižek, S. (2012, April 24). Occupy Wall Street: What is to be done next? *The Guardian*. https://www.theguardian.com/commentisfree/cifamerica/2012/apr/24/occupy-wall-street-what-is-to-be-done-next

Zizek, S. (2020, March 18). *Gözetlemek Ve Cezalandırmak Mı? Evet, Lütfen!* terrabayt: https://terrabayt.com/dusunce/gozetlemek-ve-cezalandirmak-mi-evet-lutfen/

Žižek, S. (1996). "I Hear You with My Eyes"; or, The Invisible Master. In R. Salecl & S. Žižek (Eds.), *Gaze and voice as love objects* (pp. 90–128). Duke University Press. doi:10.1215/9780822379447-005

Zuboff, S. (2019). *The age of surveillance capitalism: The fight for a human future at the new frontier of power*. Profile Books.

Zuhairi, A., Wahyono, E., & Suratinah, S. (2006). The historical context, current development, and future challenges of distance education in Indonesia. *Quarterly Review of Distance Education, 7*(1), 95–101.

Zulli, D. (2020). Evaluating hashtag activism: Examining the theoretical challenges and opportunities of# BlackLivesMatter. *Participations, 17*(1), 197–215.

About the Contributors

Enes Aluç is a 2021 graduate of Işık University's MA program in Cinema TV. He is working on the representation of Religious Figures in Turkish Cinema. He is an Instructor at İstinye University.

Aygül Atay. In 2019, she graduated from Istanbul Arel University, Department of Media and Communication Systems. Then, in the Department of Media and Cultural Studies, she studied "The Construction of Masculinity in Media: Zuhal Topal'la Sofrada Program" and completed master's degree. She has worked in the fields of gender, cinema theories and digital media. "Gender in Fairy Tales in the Context of Feminist Theory", "Discussing Lanthimos Films in the Context of Gender: The Lobster, The Killing of a Sacred Deer and The Favourite", "Literary Adaptations in Cinema: The Case of Dvoynik and The Double". In 2021, at Üsküdar University 8th International Communication Days/Crisis Communication in the Digital Age Symposium, she presented his academic studies titled "Reproduction of Risk in the Covid-19 Pandemic: The Case of Public Service Announcements" at Üsküdar University 8th International Communication Days/Crisis Communication in the Digital Age Symposium. In 2022, she presented his paper titled "Examination of Graduate Theses on Digital Violence" at Üsküdar University 9th International Communication Days / Communication Studies in the Digital Age Symposium. His articles in the field of cinema were published in various journals. She worked as an editor at digital publishing organizations and news verification platforms in the media sector. She currently works as a freelance writer and editor for organizations such as Harvard Business Review Turkey, Milliyet Molatik, NewsLab Turkey. She is the Founding Editor of Inequality Awareness Network. She is currently studying for second master's degree in Visual Communication and Digital Media at Marmara University.

Daniel Brandão holds a PhD in digital media, in the domain of audiovisual and interactive content creation, at the University of Porto (2014), where he developed the project Museum of Ransom (), a participatory website that collects videos made by citizens about the city's daily life, aiming at legitimizing their cultural heritage vocation. He also co-coordinated the project Citadocs: creation of collaborative mini-documentaries, born in Future Places Medialab for Citizenship. He holds a degree in communication design (2004) and a master's degree in multimedia art (2008), both at the Faculty of Fine Arts of the University of Porto. He is assistant professor at the Department of Communication Sciences at Institute of Social Science, University of Minho, and integrated researcher at the Communication and Society Research Centre. He is co-principle investigator of the project bYou: Study on Children and Young People's Experiences and Expressions of the Media (PTDC/COM-OUT/3004/2020), and integrates the teams of the research projects ECHO: Echoing the Communal Self (EXPL/ART-DAQ/0037/2021) and HERIC 2D: Health Risk Communication (2022.06008.PTDC), all of them funded by Portuguese

Foundation for Science and Technology. He is co-chair of DIGICOM (International Conference on Design and Digital Communication), has co-edited several books on design and has participated in several scientific committees of international conferences and journals. With vast teaching experience in public and private universities in the areas of communication design, audiovisual and multimedia, he has worked in Polytechnic Institute of Cávado and Ave, Escola Superior Artística do Porto, College of Art and Design — Matosinhos, Universidade Católica Portuguesa — Braga. He has worked with several institutions in the area of culture, with particular emphasis on the Serralves Foundation, and its Museum of Contemporary Art, with which he collaborated for six years.

Zindan Çakıcı graduated as the top-ranking student from Kadir Has University, Faculty of Communication in 2018. He completed his master's degree in the Department of Strategic Communication Management at Galatasaray University in 2020. In the same year, Çakıcı initiated his doctoral studies in the Media and Communication Studies Program at Galatasaray University, where he is currently enrolled. Throughout his academic journey, Çakıcı has been honored with nine awards from notable institutions and organizations, including KalDer, Tühid, TRT, and KKB. These awards recognize his outstanding projects in the fields of communication and social responsibility. Çakıcı's research interests encompass migration and refugee studies, public diplomacy, and new media. Currently, Çakıcı continues to contribute to the academic community through his research activities and scholarly pursuits.

Cihan Çakır graduated from Selcuk University, Faculty of Communication, Department of Journalism in 2012. He completed his master's degree in Selcuk University, Institute of Social Sciences, Department of Journalism in 2015 with his thesis titled "Sports Media as a Field where Hegemonic Masculinity is Reproduced: An Analysis on Masculinity Discourses in Sports News". He completed his doctorate in 2023 with his thesis titled "The Social Capital Creation Potential of Virtual Spaces: An Analysis on Social Media" at the same university. Currently, he continues his studies in the fields of social media, media and psychology, virtual spaces, computers and technology in human behavior, gender, masculinity, mobile media, family communication, and digital journalism.

Özlem Çetin Öztürk received her Master's degree in Radio, Television, and Cinema from Lyon Lumière II University in France after graduating from Galatasaray University Faculty of Communication in 2008. She completed her Ph.D. at the Institute of Social Sciences of Marmara University, specializing in Communication Sciences. Her dissertation focuses on hacktivism in the context of social movements. She is actively pursuing her academic endeavors on social media and digital activism at Istanbul Gelisim University within the Department of New Media and Communication.

Branco Di Fátima is a non-fiction writer with a PhD in Communication Sciences from the University Institute of Lisbon (ISCTE). He is the author of the reportage book Dias de Tormenta (Geração Editorial, 2019) and editor of the collections Hate Speech on Social Media (LabCom | EdiPUCE, 2023), Internet - Comunicação em Rede (IGOV, 2013) and Outros Olhares: Debates Contemporâneos (Leiditathi, 2008). He has published more than 80 scientific works and has been part of the teams of 10 research projects funded by national and international organizations. His current research interests include the study of the pathologies and dysfunctions of democracy, journalistic genres, digital methods, and social media analysis. He is currently a contract researcher at LabCom - University of Beira Interior (UBI), in Portugal.

Övünç Ege obtained her first B.A. from Hacettepe University, Department of Archaeology in 2014, her second B.Sc. from Istanbul Arel University, Department of Media and Communication Systems in 2019, M.A. in Media and Cultural Studies from Istanbul Arel University in 2021. She is currently pursuing her Ph.D. in Communication Sciences at Istinye University. Ege is a research assistant at Özyeğin University, Faculty of Architecture and Design, Department of Communication Design. She draws on gender, mythology, cinema, and media in her academic work with an interdisciplinary approach.

Simge Esin Orhun, born in 1974 in Ankara, Turkey, obtained her Bachelor Degree in 1995 in Architecture. Further continuing her education, she obtained her Master's Degree in Architecture in 1995 and PhD in 2007. Between the years 1996-2003, she worked in a variety of architectural companies as a project architect and took part in the design and implementation projects of large scale projects like airports, shopping centers and mixed developments. She started teaching on Communication Design since 2003 in different universities. She took part in national and international workshops as co-partner. Her main areas of teaching are spatial communication, interactive exhibiting, ergonomics and scenography. Her research interests focus on interactive applications in physical space, interactive media design education, spatial organizations of public spaces and design-driven innovation. She obtained her full Professorship in Design from Marmara University in 2023, where she is currently teaching and researching on different areas of design.

Sílvia Espinosa-Mirabet holds a PhD in Audiovisual Communication and Advertising from the University Autonomous of Barcelona (UAB) and is currently Vice Dean of the Faculty of Tourism & Communication at the University of Girona (UdG). Her long academic and professional career related to the world of radio, has not prevented her work from moving between communication, health or tourism, presenting a marked interdisciplinary character. Her extensive experience in the media has allowed her to direct and produce research related to the history of women in radio. Member of the research team Targetslab-GREP(UdG), her research is reflected in several International conferences, International research stays, more than 25 scientific articles in indexed journals, and 25 books and book chapters .

Aslı Güngör Eral works as Ass. Prof. Dr. at Balıkesir University. She holds her Ph.D. from İstanbul University Department of Radio, Television and Cinema. She focuses on new media, media literacy, media and communication studies.

Ebru Güzeloğlu has been a faculty member at Ege University, Faculty of Communication, Department of Public Relations and Publicity since 2017. She conducts academic studies and provides theoretical and practical training in the field of effective communication, particularly in civil initiatives and youth work. She has publications on social awareness, perception, and strategic communication in the disciplines of marketing communication and public relations. She has also served as a coordinator, researcher, and trainer in national and international projects involving various groups from civil society.

Nuno Martins is PhD in Digital Media (2013) from the University of Porto, having been a doctoral fellow of the UT Austin-Portugal Program of the Foundation for Science and Technology; Master in Multimedia Art (2007) and a degree in Communication Design (2003) from the Faculty of Fine Arts of the University of Porto. In 2002, during his undergraduate degree, he was a fellow of the Socrates / Erasmus Program, having studied at the Willem de Kooning Academy - Hogeschool Rotterdam, in the

Netherlands. Associate Professor at the School of Design (ESD) of the Polytechnic Institute of Cávado and Ave (IPCA); Director of the master's degree in Digital Design; and Coordinator of the Disciplinary Area of Communication Design. Since 2008, he lectures at IPCA in the degree courses in Graphic Design and in the Master in Digital Design. ID+ Integrated Researcher (Institute for Research in Media Design and Culture), regularly attending conferences and international scientific publications in the field of Communication Design; and Founder and Chairman by DIGICOM - International Conference on Design & Digital Communication.

Emre Meriç graduated from Kadir Has University, Faculty of Communication, with degrees from the Department of Public Relations and Information, as well as the Department of New Media in 2018. He completed his master's degree in Corporate Communication and Public Relations Management at Kadir Has University in 2020. In the same year, Meriç commenced his doctoral studies in the Public Relations and Publicity Program at Istanbul University, where he is currently enrolled. Throughout his academic journey, Meriç has been honored with awards from notable institutions and organizations, including Tühid, TRT, and KKB. These awards recognize his outstanding projects in the fields of communication and social responsibility. His research interests encompass public relations, health communication, and digital games.

Nemanja Milošević is a researcher in the field of Communication at the University of Deusto (Bilbao, Spain). He has previous education experiences in Cultural Anthropology and European Studies. Now, his main research focuses on audio-visual media at the intersection of culture and politics, with specific emphasis on the legitimacy crisis in politics and the culture of liberalism. His Ph.D. dissertation included the research of narratives that expressed dissent online by including accusations of conspiracy and anti-politics claims.

Asuman Özgür Keysan held a Ph.D. in School of Government and Public Policy from the University of Strathclyde, UK. Her Ph.D. thesis analysed how and in what ways voices of women activists from ten different women's organisations in Turkey contribute to the meaning of civil society and/or produce alternative understandings to the dominant views of civil society in Turkey. She previously completed two master's programmes in European Studies at the Middle East Technical University (METU), Turkey and in Political Research at the University of Strathclyde, UK. She is an author of book titled Activism and Women's NGOs in Turkey: Civil Society, Feminism and Politics (2018). Her main fields of interest are gender politics, civil society theories and practices, Turkish politics, gender and migration and qualitative research methods. She is a faculty member of Political Science and Public Administration Department at Atılım University, Turkey.

Rana Öztürk has completed her Ph.D. with her thesis Narratives of Global Modernity: International Contemporary Art Exhibitions as Places for Mapping Relational Geographies at the National College of Art and Design, Dublin in 2015. She has also been a research scholar at the Graduate School of Creative Arts and Media (GradCAM) throughout her doctoral studies. Besides her academic work, until now she has also worked as a curator, coordinator, editor, and translator for various organizations and art events. Her most recent curatorial work Sinopale's Relational Atlas took place as a series of online events and artistic work as part of Sinopale 8, International Sinop Biennial in Turkey (January-June 2022). Previously, she curated Tempo Incognito: On Flows, Rhythm, and Movements, at Depo İstanbul in 2021, she co-curated with Sinem Dişli Repetition & Cycle Talks and Performance Series I & II at SALT Galata, Istanbul (October 2017 & March 2018) and curated Carpe Noctem, a solo photography exhibition by Aslı Narin at Milli Reasürans Art Gallery in İstanbul (2018), We All Live on the Same Sea at Sirius Art Centre, Ireland (2014), Temporarily Shelved as part of the 3rd International Sinop Biennial in Turkey (2010) (co-curated with Vaari Claffey), and Slow Space Fast Pace as part of Cork Art Trail, Ireland (2007). Since 2018, she has been working as an Assistant Professor in the Department of New Media and Communication at İstinye University in Istanbul.

Mònica Puntí-Brun holds a PhD in Human Sciences and Culture from the University of Girona (UdG) about journalism and proximity digital media. Professor of UdG and Universitat Oberta de Ccatalunya (UOC), her main lines of research are scientific and health communication, corporate communication, digital communication, digital or cyber media and proximity media. These are the topics of her academic publications and with which she participates in international conferences.

Ceren Saran holds her Ph.D. from Galatasaray University, Media and Communication Studies. She completed her MA at Galatasaray University and her BA in Journalism from Istanbul University. Her Ph.D. thesis focuses on algorithms, audience monitoring and its integration into editorial processes in online newsrooms regarding the critical political economy of digital media. Her research interests are political economy of media and communication, critical digital media, journalism, and Internet studies. She is an assistant professor at Uskudar University Faculty of Communication.

Tugay Sarıkaya completed his undergraduate studies at Kadir Has University, majoring in the Radio, Cinema, and Television Department in 2012. Subsequently, he pursued his Master of Arts in New Media at the same institution, focusing his thesis on the limited impacts of social media and the relevance of the opinion leader theory during the Arab Spring, specifically analyzing the cases of Tunisia and Egypt. In 2019, he secured admission to the Ph.D. program in Media and Communication Studies at Istanbul Commerce University. He earned his Ph.D. from the Institute of Communication Sciences and Internet at Istanbul Commerce University, with a dissertation titled "The Effect of Interaction in Virtual Communities on Social Media: Shaping and Reproduction of Cultural Memory, Neighborhood Identity, and Culture." Presently, Tugay Sarıkaya holds a Ph.D. degree and serves as a research assistant at Istinye University in the Department of Radio, Television, and Cinema. He has contributed numerous articles to both national and international journals.

Burcu Şentürk received her PhD in Politics from University of York in 2014. She currently works as an Associate Professor in Ege University, Department of Business Administration. She has published books and articles on gender inequalities, sociology of work, migration, organizational studies.

Jordi Serra Simón is Adjunct Lecturer at the University of Girona. His research fields are related to the study of perceived quality, destination management, tourism, advertising and branding. He is co-author of articles about public relations, education and digitalization. Contact: Department of Philology and Communication, University of Girona, Building Sant Domènec II, Pl. Ferrater i Mora, 1, Campus Barri Vell, Girona, Spain.

Elif Üstündağlı Erten is an academic researcher with a diverse research portfolio spanning marketing, consumer behavior, and societal trends. She has contributed to various scholarly journals and publications, delving into topics such as activism, consumer identity, online shopping, and sustainability. Her work reflects a keen interest in understanding consumer perspectives, and offers insights into contemporary marketing and societal dynamics.

Ali Erhan Zalluhoğlu graduated from Ege University FEAS and continued his master education in Ege University Social Sciences Institute. He finished his PHD in Ege University Social Sciences Institute in 2016. He is focusing on marketing and supply chain management but also conducts research on strategic management, smart digitalization and entrepreneurship. He still serves as the vice president of the department and vice dean in the faculty.

Index

H

I

J

L

M

N

O

P

R

S

T

V

W

Y